Race in 21st Century America

Race in 21st Century America

~:~

Curtis Stokes
Theresa Meléndez
Genice Rhodes-Reed

EDITORS

Michigan State University Press
East Lansing

Michigan State University Press
East Lansing, Michigan 48823–5202
Printed and bound in the United States of America.
07 06 05 04 03 02 01   1 2 3 4 5 6 7 8 9 10

LIBRARY OF CONGRESS CATALOGING-IN-PUBLICATION DATA
Race in 21st century America / edited by Curtis Stokes, Theresa Meléndez, Genice Rhodes-Reed.
p. cm.
Includes bibliographical references.
ISBN 0-87013-574-0 (alk. paper)
1. United States—Race relations. 2. Racism—United States. I. Title: Race in twenty-first
century America. II. Stokes, Curtis. III. Meléndez, Theresa. IV. Rhodes-Reed, Genice.
E184.A1 R29 2001
305.8'00973—dc21
2001000313

Cover design by Heidi Dailey
Book design by Sharp Des!gns, Lansing, MI

Visit Michigan State University Press on the World Wide Web at:
www.msupress.msu.edu

To the "wretched of the earth" and all
who struggle for a racial democracy.

CURTIS STOKES

Para el porvenir de neustra gente.

THERESA MELÉNDEZ

In memory of my mother, Ruby L. Rhodes,
who taught me to love.

GENICE RHODES-REED

Contents

PART II. THE SOCIAL AND CULTURAL BOUNDARIES OF RACE

Contents

PART III. RACE AND PUBLIC POLICY

Acknowledgments

The genesis of this book was an academic conference, "Race in 21st Century America: A National Conference," that occurred at Michigan State University (MSU) on 7-10 April 1999; the idea for the conference originated with one of the editors while he was assistant director of African American studies at Columbia University; it was subsequently developed through discussions within the Black History Committee at MSU. The outcome of those discussions was that a small group of black MSU faculty and staff eventually reached out to other communities of color on campus, notably Latinos, Asian Pacifics, and American Indians, and together individuals from those communities organized a national conference that was genuinely and deeply inclusive, racially, ethnically, and ideologically. This was based upon our strong consensus that any meaningful conversation about the contentious and emotionally difficult topic of "race" in twenty-first-century America must embrace an open tent approach, rather than uncritically adhering to the typically restrictive liberal, black-white model of racial discourse; that is, it must be reflective of the complex demographic and ideological dimensions of the United States as we make the transition toward the third millennium. Thus, some 1,500 people from around the country preregistered for a four-day conference that included nearly 150 speakers and panelists. This book is principally a selection of the papers presented at the race conference.

We note that our efforts were made a lot easier by the valuable contributions of other members of the thirteen-person, university-wide race conference planning committee: Aaron Brenner (James Madison College); George Cornell (Native American Institute); Murray Edwards (Office of Minority Student Affairs); Darlene Clark Hine (Department of History); Jorge Chapa (Julian Samora Research Institute); Mimi Sayed (Lyman Briggs School); Gloria Smith (College of Education); Geneva Smitherman (Department of English); Steven Weiland (Jewish Studies Program); and Margaret Chen-Hernandez (Multicultural Center). The conference was jointly sponsored by the Black History Committee and James Madison College. Among the members of the Black History Committee were Freddie B. Watson (Student Life Department); Murray Edwards (Office of Minority Student Affairs); and Rodney Patterson (Office of Minority Student Affairs). Danny Layne, Julian Samora Research Institute, with some valuable assistance from Aaron Brenner and Murray Edwards, provided a wonderful service by largely organizing and managing our race conference web site. The conference was effectively run out of James Madison College and thus we owe a special debt to that academic unit, most importantly to its Faculty Affairs Committee, former deans William B. Allen and Norman Graham, staff members Debra Mills (who tirelessly handled our budget and much else), Kim Allan, Deanna Edwards, Donna Hofmeister, Connie Hunt, Carolyn Koenigsknecht, Lucy Ramsey, Ragan Royal, Jeff Judge, Grant Littke, and Jackie Stewart. Several James Madison College faculty members were also quite helpful; these were Katherine See, Aaron Brenner, Okey Iheduru, Allison Berg, Louise Jezierski, Simei Qing, Swarna Rajagopalan, Colleen Tremonte, and Jonas Zoninsein. There were many James Madison College students who assisted with the conference, most notably those in the W. E. B. Du Bois Society and Robert Gray, a professorial assistant; additionally, Robert's technological strengths made him an extraordinary asset in the construction of the book project.

Other influential roles were played by Dr. Lee N. June, vice president for student affairs and services, Dr. Dorothy Harper Jones, consultant to the provost, and Dr. Robert F. Banks, assistant provost; while their considerable financial assistance was valued, it was above all their insights into how to translate a large and multidimensional conference into something that would engage the entire MSU community, especially its large student population, that proved most beneficial.

Importantly, Dr. Lou Anna K. Simon, provost, never wavered in her generous support of the race conference.

Many local groups and university units cosponsored the race conference: the College of Social Science; the City of East Lansing; the City of Lansing; Lansing Community College; the Urban Affairs Programs; the International Studies and Programs; the Office of the Vice Provost for Computing and Technology; the Office of the President; the Office of the Provost; the College of Agriculture and Natural Resources; the Vice President for Finance and Operation and Treasurer; the Office of the Vice President for Governmental Affairs; the Detroit College of Law at Michigan State University; Career Services and Placement; Educational Support Services; the David Walker Research Institute; the National Council of African-American Men; the Black Faculty, Staff and Administrators Association; the College of Arts and Letters; the College of Communication Arts and Sciences; the College of Veterinary Medicine; the Pre-College Programs, College of Human Medicine; the College of Natural Science; the College of Engineering; the College of Human Ecology; the College of Osteopathic Medicine; the College of Nursing; the Eli Broad College of Business; the Athletic Department; the Office of Minority Student Affairs; the Office of the Registrar; the Julian Samora Research Institute; Automotive Services; and Media Communications.

We also offer a special word of thanks to Evelyn Hu-DeHart, chairperson of the Department of Ethnic Studies (University of Colorado at Boulder), James Jennings, professor of political science and senior fellow in the William Monroe Trotter Institute (University of Massachusetts-Boston), Frederick R. Lynch, Department of Government (Claremont McKenna College), and Robert Weissberg, Department of Political Science (University of Illinois at Urbana-Champaign) for their helpful comments on the design of the conference.

Finally, we would be remiss if we did not acknowledge the contributions that folks at MSU Press made, especially Fred Bohm, Director, Julie L. Loehr, Editor in Chief, and Martha Bates, Acquisitions Editor; their patience, encouragement, and attention to detail was much appreciated. In the end, however, we accept all responsibility for whatever limitations the book contains.

Foreword

DARLENE CLARK HINE

The Race in 21st Century America conference held at Michigan State University in April 1999 was a historic gathering of approximately one hundred and fifty of the most insightful and accomplished scholars in America, all determined to illuminate the conundrum of race. The illuminating, original, and accessibly written papers selected for this anthology reflect the depth and breadth of investigation and thought of a contemporary generation of anthropologists, historians, linguists, sociologists, philosophers, economists, political scientists, social activists, and others about what is arguably the most troubling problem in American life.

When W. E. B. DuBois prophesied in 1903 that the critical dilemma of the twentieth century would be the problem of the color line, few could have anticipated the terrible accuracy of his words or the enormous devastation of adherence to racial dogma, ideologies of white supremacy, and notions of black and colored peoples' inferiority would wreak upon our society and the world. As we stand poised on the cusp of a new era, a new millennium, it behooves Americans of every hue, ethnicity, class, sexual orientation, and gender to reflect deeply on how far we have come on our journey toward recognition of basic humanity. Yet, while some of us enthusiastically embrace our differences as well as our similarities, it is well to assess the distance, collectively, we must travel to resolve the continuing scourge of racism, discrimination, and inequality of opportunity that smothers the desires and dreams of too many Americans.

The conference atmosphere was charged with palpable excitement as a spirited urgency pulsated through the sessions, in the corridors, and on the buses that transported participants to different venues across Michigan State University's beautiful campus. Scholars, students, administrators, public policy activists, and others crossed boundaries of traditional disciplines and probed myriad facets of our constructed identities, giving sustained consideration to geographical region, cultural practices, gender roles and representation, social-economic status, and ideology. Graduate students exuded an eagerness to make contact with authors of important works, to connect faces to the ideas and theories with which they, and we, daily grapple in our courses, lectures, writings, and lives. This volume captures the essence of the conference and provides academic and public audiences with important analyses certain to propel us into a useful understanding of the profound complexity of race and racism as well as the actions needed to chart a new course for a much needed transformation of American race relations. We know that the old dichotomy of black versus white is no longer accurate or useful.

I was privileged to have shared in the conceptualization and planning of this conference. The program committee reflected a cross section of academicians and administrators, all mobilized and inspired by the committed leadership of Curtis Stokes of James Madison College. For over two years, Stokes worked on and thought about this conference. And when he was not contacting scholars to invite them to participate, he was busily engaged in the essential work of fund raising. He deserves our gratitude, respect, and admiration, as do all members of the planning committee.

The Race in 21st Century America conference is part of a larger context of forces set in motion by Executive Order No. 13050, which President William Jefferson Clinton issued in 1997 to create the Initiative on Race and authorize the appointment of an advisory board under the leadership of the distinguished historian John Hope Franklin. Charged with the task of advising the president on issues of race and racism, the board launched a fifteen-month series of conversations and forums with private citizens and corporate, religious, and local leaders. The board's hearings and meetings concentrated on deciphering the role race plays in a wide array of institutions and cultural practices, as well as in public policy, including civil rights enforcement, education, poverty, employment, housing, and stereotyping; the board also examined the role of race in the administration of justice, health care, and immigration laws. In the end, the board advocated the continued use of dialogue as a tool for finding common ground.

One of the greatest strengths of the board's 1998 published report, *One America in the 21st Century: Forging a New Future*, and one that is shared by this anthology, is the detailed discussion of the changing nature of "race" in America. As its many authors attest, for too long the terms of "race analyses" have been much too narrow. In *One America* and in this anthology, race is complicated. There are at least five categories for race in contemporary America: American Indian or Alaska Native; black or African American; Native Hawaiian or other Pacific Islander; white or non-Hispanic white; Hispanic or Latino. But there is yet another complication in our racially heterogeneous society. Today, the growing use of the term "biracial," referring to the offspring of racial crossings, or children of mixed race marriages and parentage, signals an important lexical intervention with profound political and economic ramifications. Most important, biracial Americans illuminate the anachronistic nature of existing racial categories and constructions. They underscore the nuanced complexity of racial taxonomy to a degree unique in the history of race relations in the United States. Michigan State University sociologist Ruben G. Rumbaut points to "our chimerical, and calumnious, conceptions of 'race'—pigments, as always, of our imagination—. . . [as] a bitter legacy." It is this bitter legacy that President Clinton's Initiative on Race and the race conferences movement of the 1990s, including the National Conference on Racial and Ethnic Diversity, "What's Next? American Pluralism and the Civic Culture," held at Smith College in 1999, and the Race Symposium at Stanford University, sought to obliterate, to purge, so that Americans in the twenty-first century will at last recognize the humanity of us all.

America now stands as the world's preeminent postindustrial superpower. Still, its myriad minorities and immigrant populations continue to press for greater participation in a rational economy and for equal access to the social and educational systems. These diverse groups, make, and rightly so, incessant demands for a more equitable share of political power. The authors of the articles in this anthology facilitate our collective determination to extricate this country from the difficulties and disparities of race, conjoined with class, sexuality, and gender. It bears reiteration that racial discrimination does violence to human dignity and personality and devalues the culture and lifestyles of those described as "other."

The Advisory Board of the Initiative on Race cautioned in *One America*: "We wish to make it clear that this Report is not a definitive analysis of the state of race relations in America today. That task should be undertaken by the many scholars and experts on race relations, only a few of whom we had the opportunity to meet during the course of the past year" (10). The Michigan State Conference was a continuation and elaboration of the conversations that the Initiative launched. The conference participants agreed that within the context of race in America, one of the most pressing challenges before us is to identify the forces, to make visible the underlying systemic factors, and mount a concerted movement to traverse and eradicate the economic barriers that divide us. Furthermore, they concur that collectively, scholars and community groups, must inculcate in the next generation a deep appreciation for those moments and times when differences are irrelevant and even retrograde. We must underscore the importance for all Americans to make real our ideals of justice, dignity, respect, and equality of opportunity. We are indeed one America. But we have some distance to go before this union is made perfect. This volume illuminates our path.

Race in 21st Century America: An Overview

CURTIS STOKES AND THERESA MELÉNDEZ

I. LOOKING BACKWARD TO OUR RACIAL FUTURE

Curtis Stokes

America's "color-line," as W. E. B. Du Bois famously put it at the beginning of the twentieth century, is its most defining characteristic. Similarly, President Bill Clinton was essentially correct when, calling for a year-long "national conversation" on race in June 1997, he said that "of all the questions of discrimination and prejudice that still exist in our society, the most perplexing one is the oldest, and in some ways today the newest: the problem of race."[1] As we begin a new century, American public policy, political culture, and everyday racial interaction continue to be fundamentally shaped by "white privilege" and its consequent social, economic, and political subordination of black, brown, and red Americans. But are the racial problems of the past and present those of the future? Is not the "color-line" being so radically transformed by immigration, intermarriage, and the gains of the Civil Rights Movement that the very idea of "race" is no longer a useful category or explanatory model for examining continuing inequalities between whites and "communities of color?" To the contrary, our contention is that though the contours of "race" are indeed changing, race remains the starting point for examining the condition of black, brown, and red Americans.

The American republic, whatever the demographic facts on the ground in 1787, was founded as a self-consciously "white" nation. To be sure, both poor whites and white women were ambiguously included in the new nation; yet, even if ambiguously, they were considered members of the white family, though "whiteness" (like race itself), at bottom a political idea and practice, was still in the process of being constructed. There was, however, no uncertainty concerning the status of Indians and blacks, especially the latter. While James Madison, principal architect of the Constitution, favored a measure of controlled political diversity within the new nation to counter feared popular risings by poor whites against the propertied classes, he and other leading founders agreed on the requirements of a culturally and racially homogenous republic for developing and maintaining a civilized and good society. John Jay, co-author of the *Federalist Papers*, suggests as much in 1787: "Providence has been pleased to give this one connected country to one united people—a people descended from the same ancestors, speaking the same language, [and] professing the same religion. . . ."[2] Similarly the first Naturalization Act, adopted by the U.S. Congress on 1 March 1790, declared that "any alien, being a free white person . . . may be admitted to become a citizen" of the United States.[3] Others need not apply. Regarding American Indians, Thomas Jefferson, arguably the most progressive of the leading founders, occasionally and half-heartedly encouraged them to give up their traditional way of life and join the American Republic as equals with whites (which, in effect, likely would have meant political and cultural suicide for American Indian nations). But more typically, he wrote that "if ever we are constrained to lift the hatchet against any [Indian] tribe . . . we will never lay it down till that tribe is exterminated, or is driven beyond the Mississippi. . . . In war, they will kill some of us; we shall destroy all of them." Later, in 1812 he wrote that the American government had no choice but "to pursue [the Indians] to extermination, or drive them beyond our reach." Jefferson's stricture that Indians must be "extirpated from the earth" or remove themselves from the paths of white settlers summarizes the views of many leading founders on American Indians.[4] One would have to look hard to find a twentieth-century racial demagogue who said such things with more clarity than Jefferson.

The status of Africans as slaves in the United States was institutionalized by the original Constitution of 1787 and philosophically shaped by the growing belief

in African inferiority. Even if blacks were to be emancipated, so the typical argument went, they must be removed from the United States less they physically and
morally contaminate the white race. For example, Jefferson, who philosophically
supported gradual abolition, insisted that blacks, once freed, must "be removed
beyond the reach of mixture" to avoid "staining the blood" of the white race. Later,
Abraham Lincoln, claiming the white racial ideal of the founding generation and
speaking in the 1850s, said that "there is a physical difference between the two
[blacks and whites], which, in my judgment, will probably forever forbid their living together upon the footing of perfect equality; and inasmuch as it becomes a
necessity that there must be a difference, I . . . am in favor of the race to which I
belong having a superior position." Despite the claims of Lincoln apologists that
there was a change of heart a few months before his assassination, there is
absolutely nothing in the public record to indicate that Abraham Lincoln ever
explicitly disavowed the foregoing (and similar) remarks.[5] It is this white racial
ideal, crafted and embraced by white America from Jefferson to Lincoln, that represents a still unacknowledged intellectual cornerstone of the American Founding.

By the beginning of the Civil War, the original 400,000 African slaves, perhaps the most indigenous population group in the country (excluding American
Indians, most of whom did not seek to be part of the nation), had become more
than 4 million people. Along with the expropriation of American Indian lands,
their labor played the crucial role in the early development of nineteenth-century
American capitalism. Despite this indelibly crucial impact upon American society
by African people, throughout the late nineteenth and early twentieth centuries,
as some 20 million European immigrants sought opportunities in the United
States, the meaning of race was constructed by defining African people in America
as the "other" through which all groups in the nation would increasingly measure
their "whiteness" and thus find their place within the evolving racial hierarchy.[6]

Toward the end of the twentieth century a new effort began to reconfigure the
place of blacks in the United States; this too would occur against the backdrop of
immigration patterns that increasingly brought blacks into contact with the new
arrivals. Additionally, growing intermarriage rates between these new arrivals and
whites might, as in earlier centuries, contribute to deepening the historical isolation of blacks in the United States.[7] U.S. Census Bureau projections indicate that
people of color will constitute nearly 50 percent of the U.S. population by 2050
and that Latinos will replace blacks as the largest minority group by 2010, if not
sooner. Furthermore, nearly 70 percent of people of Mexican descent in the United
States (who constitute two-thirds of all Latinos in this country) are either first or

second-generation residents, though most of them are U.S. citizens; also, some 61 percent of Asians in the United States are foreign born.[8] Is it possible that this time around perhaps the principal participants in the continuing drama of an evolving racial hierarchy in which blacks are identified as the "other" (the group to distance oneself from) could be people of color? The nineteenth century witnessed the Irish and increasingly the Jews, for instance, being constructed as "white," thereby making it difficult to forge any meaningful political alliance among the oppressed and consequently contributing to the further isolation of blacks in the United States; the twenty-first century might inaugurate a racial arrangement in which a segment of the Latino and Asian Pacific population (if not much of it) could be accorded a status similar to that of some nineteenth- and early twentieth-century European ethnic groups. Recall Thomas Jefferson's eighteenth-century invitation to American Indians to join the American republic as equals with whites; as noted previously this disingenuous offer was rejected by most Indian nations.

It is against this backdrop of the continuance of an evolving racial hierarchy of power and privilege in the twenty-first century, the national retreat in the last two decades of the twentieth century from the limited gains of the Civil Rights Movement, and on-going tensions among communities of color, that the increasing call for a "new" paradigm of race, originating principally from some prominent intellectuals and activists in the Latino and Asian Pacific communities (and elsewhere outside the African American community), must be understood. This new paradigm of race is to challenge the "old" paradigm which supposedly saw America essentially through the prism of black-white relations.[9] It is certainly the case that African Americans must come to terms with the demographic, political, and intellectual realities of twenty-first–century America; racial and political discourse in the United States, which was largely shaped during several centuries of historical interaction between blacks and whites, needs to be reexamined. Moreover there is much historical overlap among the experiences of people of color in the United States; therefore these need to be better understood. Blacks, far less than Latinos, Asian Pacifics, and American Indians, have not adequately appreciated this. Yet it remains vitally important that other communities of color, Asian Pacifics and Latinos in particular, recognize that what Alexis de Tocqueville, visiting the United States in 1831, called the problem of the "three races" (the red, the black, and the white) has not yet come close to being addressed; indeed it cannot so long as the nation and its leaders fail to take seriously the continuing centrality of race in American life and political culture, which was bequeathed to us by founders of the Republic.[10]

Thus, calls for a "new" paradigm of race, without fully valuing the historical persistence of the "otherness" quality of blackness in the United States, could easily drift and be sidetracked into the construction of an American version of the former Apartheid system in South Africa; as such, blackness would remain the real face of "race" in America.

NOTES

1. President Bill Clinton's "Remarks at the University of California at San Diego, June 14, 1997" *The Black World Today* (internet posting 23 June 1997).

2. Alexander Hamilton, James Madison, and John Jay, *The Federalist Papers* (New York: New American Library, 1961), 38.

3. As referenced in Juanita Tamayo Lott, *Asian Americans: From Racial Category to Multiple Identities* (Walnut Creek, Cali.: Altamira Press, 1998), 69–70. Also, see the internet site of the U.S. Immigration and Naturalization Service.

4. Richard Drinnon, *Facing West: The Metaphysics of Indian-Hating and Empire-Building.* (Norman: University of Oklahoma Press, 1997), 78–116. Also, see Joyce Appleby and Terence Ball, eds. *Thomas Jefferson: Political Writings* (Cambridge: Cambridge University Press, 1999), 500–39.

5. Emmanuel Chukwudi Eze, ed. *Race and the Enlightenment: A Reader* (Cambridge, Mass.: Blackwell Publishers, 1997), 97–103, and Philip Van Doren Stern, ed., *The Life and Writings of Abraham Lincoln* (New York: The Modern Library, 1940), 463. Also, see the important new work by historian Lerone Bennett, Jr., *Forced into Glory: Abraham Lincoln's White Dream* (Chicago: Johnson Publishing Company, 2000).

6. See, for example, the following works that explore the phenomenon of "whiteness" as it applies, respectively, to Irish and Jews in the United States: Noel Ignatiev, *How the Irish Became White* (New York: Routledge, 1995), and Karen Brodkin, *How Jews Became White folks & What That Says About Race in America* (New Brunswick, N.J.: Rutgers University Press, 2000).

7. Roderick J. Harrison and Claudette E. Bennett, "Racial and Ethnic Diversity" in *State of the Union in the 1990s, Volume Two: Social Trends,* ed. Reynolds Farley (New York: Russell Sage Foundation, 1995), 141–210. While such intergroup/interracial marriages are increasing among all groups in the United States, they still occur less frequently between blacks and whites, or between blacks and other racial/ethnic groups: "Marriage outside of one's racial or ethnic group is an extremely rare event in the United States: More than 95 percent of all couples in 1990 were married to someone of the same race or ethnicity. Blacks and whites are the least likely of any racial-ethnic group to intermarry. American Indians have the highest

rate of intermarriage (about 74 percent), and African Americans have the lowest rate (about 6 percent)"—Spain, Daphne. "America's Diversity: On the Edge of Two Centuries," (Washington, D.C.: Population Reference Bureau, May 1999), 8. These figures are likely to change with the release of 2000 Census Bureau data on this topic.

8. Jorge Del Pinal and Audrey Singer, "Generations of Diversity: Latinos in the United States" (Washington, D.C.: Population Reference Bureau, 1997), 6; Frank D. Bean and Marta Tienda, *The Hispanic Population of the United States* (New York: Russell Sage Foundation, 1990), 17–22 and 56–75; Pyong Gap Min, *Asian Americans: Contemporary Trends and Issues* (Thousand Oaks, Calif.: Sage Publications, 1995), 10–37.

9. See, for example, the valuable collection of essays in Paul M. Ong, ed., *The State of Asian Pacific America: Transforming Race Relations* (Los Angeles: UCLA Asian American Studies Center and Asian Pacific Public Policy Institute, 2000); Michael A. Olivas, "The Chronicles, My Grandfather's Stories, and Immigration Law: The Slave Traders Chronicle as Racial History" in *Critical Race Theory: The Cutting Edge*, ed. Richard Delgado (Philadelphia: Temple University Press, 1995), 9–20; Richard Delgado, *When Equality Ends: Stories about Race and Resistance* (Boulder, Colo.: Westview Press, 1999).

10. Tocqueville wrote that "I do not think that the white and black races will ever be brought anywhere to live on a footing of equality . . . But I think that the matter will be still harder in the United States than anywhere else;" Alexis de Tocqueville, *Democracy in America* (New York: Anchor Books, 1969), 356.

II. RACE DIALOGUES FOR THE NEW MILLENNIUM

Theresa Meléndez

The dialogue on race, as the new millennium dawns, reveals a continuum of political positions on the analysis of race relations and on the forging of new paths toward the kind of society we envision for the future. Recognizing that dialogue requires equalizing the ground for discussion, we believe that our national conference in April 1999, "Race in 21st Century America," achieved that goal (or as closely as possible) by bringing together thinkers and scholars from all aspects of U.S. intellectual society as well as from differing political viewpoints. We wanted the discussants to reflect on the impact of race on our nation, past and present, constructing a base of knowledge to help move toward a more equitable society. The conference consisted of some 25 panels, about 150 panelists and keynote speakers, and some 1,500 registered participants. This volume reflects only a small portion of those discussions and abstracts them into four categories: (1) "The Concept of Race," (11) "The Social and Cultural Boundaries of Race," (111) "Race and Public Policy," and (1v) "Strategies for Racial and Social Justice." By necessity, we have limited the range achieved in the conference; and subsequently, not all issues are covered nor all points of view represented. However, through these selections we have attempted to exemplify the spirit of the conference. Notwithstanding this limit, from this collection emerges themes we find essential to the dialogue on race relations: (1) the racialization of certain groups in the United States; (2) along with the concept and impact of 'othering'; (3) tied historically and culturally to the first two, the implications of the rhetoric employed in contemporary U.S. racial discourse; and (4) the critical need to create a new multi-racial, multi-issue social movement. These themes, of course, are intricately linked in the social formation of U.S. society, both civic and state (as well as in the essays), and are differentiated by the particular interest or focus from which each scholar writes. It is important to underline the specificity of the various positions in this volume along with whatever similarities one finds.

As we review the studies, we recognize an overriding theoretical purview, reminiscent of the Gramscian war of position: competing ideologies in a constant flux of seeking and achieving political power and influence.[1] The scholars themselves often indicate this concern through a constant use of bellicose terms and phrases: "mobilization, battleground fatalities, gaining terrain, waging war, tactical attacks," etc. These terms, however, are more than metaphor or trope of discourse, for they imply the immediacy of the racial crisis in our nation, the hostilities and antagonisms that fracture us, and the debilitating effects of our confrontations. (It brings to mind Lorna Dee Cervantes' lines, in "Poem for the Young White Man Who Asked Me How I, an Intelligent, Well-read Person Could Believe in the War between Races": "I know you don't believe this./You think this is nothing but faddish exaggeration. But they/are not shooting at you."[2]) Using the war of position as a lens from which to analyze these essays allows us to identify the complexity of the ideological terrain of struggle, its many sites or centers of contention, and the understanding that social relations, hegemonic or not, are in "unstable balance," and hence, inherently have the capacity for transformation.

Gramsci reminds us that enduring crises, such as race relations, reveal "incurable structural contradictions," which the political forces struggle to "cure" or "overcome" in maintaining power; these efforts form what he calls the "terrain of the conjunctural" where opposition takes place. He believes it imperative to differentiate the occasional from the "organic" movements, an arduous but necessary task, before proceeding with political strategizing. That is, one must decide whether the power relations forming the crisis are incidental or integral to the maintenance of the hegemonic system. What is at stake is understanding the requisite historical forces necessary to make changes in the society.[3]

The jockeying for positions in the national debates over race is not new; certainly this theme has been prevalent before in our history. However, this new war of position at the end of the century differs from others that have taken place in earlier times, up to the Civil Rights era, for a number of reasons. First, the nature of the players has increased so that a broader, more inclusive number of voices is recognized, due in part to the changing demographics of the United States. Second, there is the recognition that intersecting gender, sexuality, and class, with race and ethnicity profitably complicate the issues and offer new perspectives on the subject. And finally, the rapid growth of communication technology and a looser trade market have globalized the effects of race relations everywhere. These dynamics form part of the social conditions we must analyze in understanding the historical moment of 'race' in the U.S.; and significantly, they also create the political and ideological fronts from which we can strategize. What this indicates for civil society is the need to articulate the various positions clearly, to understand the interests from which they derive, to decide which serve the nation most responsibly, and then to act upon those decisions.

In their influential work, *Racial Formations in the United States*, Michael Omi and Howard Winant discuss the changes that have occurred in framing the discourse on race as paradigm shifts, new or different grounds from which to perceive the concept of race. They remind us that this is contested terrain and that "the very meaning of racial equality is at stake."[4] The term race itself is also problematic.

Although the term 'race' has been used for centuries, it was deployed generally to mean nations or peoples and did not become a term of distinction or approbation for the varieties of human beings until an alignment of economic and political forces occurred that created its necessity, sometime after the encounter between Europe and the Americas. That is, the usage of the term to signify hierarchical distinctions arises as a consequence of the need to legitimate the separation of groups of people for the purpose of formulating and maintaining the nation's socio-economic system. This racialization of certain groups in the United States was a frontal assault (Gramsci's war of movement or war of maneuver) on particularly vulnerable communities (native political enemies, slaves, indentured servants, immigrants) that ensured property rights for the few and a life of labor and limited citizenship for the many.

As the ideology of racialization is taken up by the general public, the concept of race becomes reified and naturalized. In this form as "common knowledge," the social sciences are able to utilize it to explain the consequences of social and economic inequities over hundreds of years: the lack of achievement of people of color. Just who is part of what race, how race is defined, how many races there are, and what their level on the social continuum may be, become a matter of opinion. What remains clear is who is at the top. Bio-genetic research, however, reveals the falsity of race as a physical fact. As Alan Goodman states: "Race is very real; but it is not biology" (p. 44).

In recent times, racialization has been based on "culture" or "difference." Social theorists or public intellectuals now cite cultural or behavioral characteristics of groups of people to explain lack of success and/or to justify exclusion, in what has been labeled the "new racism," "new nativism," or "color-blind" policies. And the concept of "difference" when applied to race or ethnicity can imply not variation as such, but departure from the norm. At the same time, what complicates the use of the term race is its appropriation by communities of color as a flag of identity to mark the history of struggles and to rally a sense of belonging and shared consciousness.

It appears to some of our scholars that the end of racialization and race as taxonomy may emerge as the heterogeneity of the U.S. population increases, through either immigration, interracial marriage, or assimilation, or even as a result of a more effective education. It is important to remember that these positions do not imply a consensus, and in fact, represent ideologies that may be at odds with one another. Indeed, in the larger literature on questions of racialization there are dramatic differences in approach between, for example, William Julius Wilson, who argues for "the declining significance of race," and Angelo N. Ancheta, who claims: "the recognition of basic racial differences has to be the starting point of any vision for a multi-racial and multi-ethnic society, especially one that is being transformed by global migration."[5] A further complication and theoretical intensification would examine whether U.S. society is necessarily, contractually exclusionary, and therefore whether concepts of citizenship and rights might *ever* overcome problems of racialization. In this regard, Charles Mills' *The Racial Contract* charts a middle ground between the contractarian pessimism of Carole Pateman and a liberal endorsement of the values of the Constitution (as K. Anthony Appiah recently has signaled).[6]

We might take Evelyn Hu-DeHart's essay, "Black and White and Beyond," to discuss the war of position in the arena of contention most central to her interests: the university campus. When she outlines the recent consequences of racism and discrimination in urban centers, such as the 1992 Los Angeles riot (due among other reasons, to "an active and deliberate disinvestment" [see p. 85] in these communities), she is here clearly describing a war of maneuver, with the participants engaged in war-like assaults and confrontations, not only between the police and the citizens, but between people of color as well. The war of position in institutions of higher education takes place over the contours and conditions of multiculturalism. On the one side, there is "corporate . . . or liberal multiculturalism" in which difference or diversity is marked as natural without explaining that "most differences carry real and differential meanings of power and privilege" [p. 88]. Diversity may be celebrated as a practice of civility, but the actual epistemological foundations of the university remain the same; entrenched educational practices that maintain the status quo have not been challenged. One of the most significant terrains from which to understand these power plays is the history of ethnic studies, as Hu-DeHart formulates it. It is here that the university hegemony exerts its force by seemingly promoting ethnic studies through their establishment, while at the same time, undermining the potential transformational power ethnic studies might engender. This is accomplished through various strategies that will make the new programs ineffective: underfunding, hiring weak program directors and/or insufficient numbers of personnel, denying faculty control of research programs, duplicating curriculum offerings in other disciplines, etc. On the other side, there is the force of ethnic studies itself, what Hu-DeHart calls its "primary responsibility": "the interrogation of received wisdoms and truths" and "the demonstration of alternative ways of constructing knowledge" [p. 90]—in other words, ethnic studies serves to question and to revitalize the bases of old epistemologies. Another tactic employed by this opposition is the formation of a new "rainbow coalition of students" who understand that ethnic studies is not only for minorities and who are willing to struggle together to enforce their beliefs [p. 91]. An extension of entrenched interests on this cultural front in the public arena can be seen in the "resurgence of American nativism" in which the war of position can be followed through the employment of a "situational racial identity," especially as it applies to Asian Americans [p. 92ff.]. Here, says Hu-DeHart, racialization of a certain group, in this case, its marking as a "model minority," takes place to create divisions among people of color when convenient to the perpetuation of a social hierarchy or to demean that group when other needs, such as immigrant-bashing, are more important. The similarity in both campus and public arenas is the manipulation of racial identities in a seemingly benign fashion—celebrating diversity or inscripted favorable characteristics—yet the project is one of hegemonic forces furthering their own interests.

On the other hand, Nathan Glazer offers us a different site of contention [...] of Race in the United States": assimilation through [...] himself on the biological front [...] he discusses both. To focus on [...] believe that race is biologically [...] lient and portentous (as he calls [...] population, whose numbers, [...] since the early history of the [...] ted for increases. These may be [...] ination on census forms is self-ancestry" [p. 74]. That is to say, [...] an be an arbitrary choice. This [...] belief that people of color oper- [...] to choose how one lives. [...] pts and/or statistics: racial pop- [...] d ethnic groups, and intermar- [...] inning with a nation that could [...] he Census of 1790, and marking [...] in Americans, Caribbeans, and [...] have to talk about the future of [...] tegy in including other groups [...] sides the white against which to [...] the multi-racial nature of our

society. He states that "the nonwhite races differ enormously in their capacity to enter the mainstream," and thus, we should speak of "two kinds of races in the United States," those who rise economically and assimilate "to some American norm" and "those that do not" [p. 75]. Of the various races, the African American, for a number of historical and social reasons, he says, are in the group that "do not." Here Glazer indicates that race in fact does have an economic and social base as he creates the race of the successful and the race of the failed, the race of the American and the race of the non-American American.

He then reports that African Americans are also the least likely of all racial and ethnic groups to intermarry and the most likely to denominate a child with one black parent as black. Other racially mixed couples, with the nonwhite parent Indian or Asian, are more likely to call their children white. In this category, by not explaining the reasons groups may choose to do so, Glazer implies the playing ground is level for all groups. He concludes by stating that he believes the significance of race in the future will decline first for the nonwhite races, "leaving aside the black," and that given the intermarriage figures, the census then may note two races, as in the Census of 1790. The future of race, he says, is "assimilation" or "amalgamation"—the mixing of peoples until finally "even longer in the future," there will be only one race [p. 77]. He fails to mention, however, the color of this "race."

Another definitive concept in race studies is the process known as 'othering': a dynamic that defines the self in terms of the other, through a distinction of class, religion, ethnicity, gender, sexuality, etc. Some psychoanalytic theories propose this process as a basic universal mode of defining the self, but when created in response to "specific socio-political demands" (see Ibish), the *other* becomes dangerous, debased, and essentialized. Edward Said, in *Orientalism* (1978), the landmark text in this regard, links such dangerous othering to the material base of colonialism, and a large literature has appeared in response to Said's concepts and prescriptions. Specifically, the most important question which Said's work has raised concerns his totalization of a regime or discourse of othering, and therefore the terms and conditions for the possibility of not othering the other. Two important respondents to Said are Homi Bhabha and Gayatri Spivak: briefly, the former attempts to demonstrate that colonial discourse is fissured or "ambivalent" at its core, and therefore endlessly producing "hybrids" which counter any attempt to discipline and fix colonial subjectivities; while the latter, running closer to Said, seeks a method of "strategic essentialism" by which the colonized might, in a highly mobile manner, short-circuit colonialism's racial fixities.[7]

In the formulation of a national identity, the historical bases of shared language, culture, and territory converge in relation to who or what is conceptualized as not belonging to those bases—the foreign, the outcast, the exotic, the marginal—even when those so designated are an integral part of that nation. The boundaries are drawn ideologically by power relations that maintain control and define collective values of benefit to the empowered, through force or persuasion, that is, through warfare or propaganda. This process allows those forces in control of political and educational institutions, business, and mass media, to conjure an illusory *other*, sometimes blatantly, often through subtle and insidious means.

Othering is a form of representation that imposes particular characteristics on a group and one that can be manipulated for any means. How groups are viewed, the nature of their collectivity as seen from the outside, strongly influences identity formation of individuals within the group, and concomitantly, how they will be treated. Mass media and film, for example, or written history can convey effective messages through stereotypes that can represent whole communities in the U.S. as criminal or alien, or just as powerfully through omission, obliterate the presence of a people. Some scholars maintain, in fact, that the highest form of racism may be the invisibility produced in this way. In this volume, the scholars chart the way social and political exigencies—national wars, tight labor markets, increased immigration, business public relations, legal policies—affect the way certain communities are and have been demarcated throughout U.S. history. They stress how the violence of past racial and ethnic relations continues to define the relationships into the present. In fact, an underlying current in these essays is the assertion that old forms of bigotry are consistently "re-charged, re-imagined, and re-vitalized" (see Madrid). And we are reminded that because othering is not founded on reality but rather on political arbitrariness, no group is immune.

The power dynamics of othering can be changed, according to our writers, through a variety of ways: by reclaiming the ideal of tolerance, by vigilant examination of representation and the ways of defining groups, and by offering counter examples and alternative histories. While some caution us that the very act of denying stereotypes repeats the image and thus may reinforce the association, it is also believed that "fundamental political change in a democracy almost always comes from the boundaries of society" (see Marable). Those most likely to promote change, in other words, would be those most affected, most marginalized by othering.

Arturo Madrid, in "Aliens, Misfits, and Interlopers," argues that othering is always the "sub-text" embedded in the questioning of anyone who does not appear to be what is conventionally thought of as "American." In this war of position, the ideological ground derives historically from the exclusionary founding principles of the U.S. and from the political expediencies of the past. Here, the conjunctions may seem to be both organic and occasional to the development of the United States as a nation, except for the fact that both movements are integral in creating a very particular "imagined community." What is at stake in this terrain is the control of the power of naming: who defines what we are, an act of definition that determines who belongs. Madrid traces this struggle first to the economic, religious, and political rivalries attending European nations since the fifteenth century in their competitive colonization of the Americas, each insisting on its own brand of identity politics. This earlier ideological war of position (and maneuver) culminates in the formation of the thirteen colonies, characterized, he says, "more by exclusion than inclusion" and complicated by the introduction of racialized subjects [p. 104]. As the U.S. moves from becoming a continental, then hemispheric, and finally, global power, the national and foreign policies of imperial expansion result in a "human mix . . . even more complex and therefore more problematical for members of U.S. society" [p. 105].

The contemporary war of position in othering, reinforced by the past, is fought over three ideological points, invoked behind a screen of patriotism and distorted "American" values: the importance of a homogeneous population; the belief in the primacy of the individual; and the success of the American dream (work hard and you will succeed). Madrid contends that the narrative of othering, seen through these lens, engenders antagonisms, negates histories, exploits difficult economic and social issues, and places the burden of proof on the backs of people of color: that the "socio-economic problems U.S. society is experiencing have a cultural foundation . . . [and that] xenophobia and racism are not the problem" [pp. 113-14]. He reminds us that "bigotry does not disappear, [it merely] takes on other forms" [p. 114].

Most scholars would agree that public discourse[8] on race relations has changed since the end of the Civil Rights Movement, that period of concerted efforts by communities and by the government to push for social and economic reforms needed to correct the inequities of racial discrimination. The Civil Rights Act of 1964 and other similar legislation did confer a measure of legal grounds from which to contest discriminatory actions; also, the social movements of those times argued for the power of the people to speak and to act for self-determination and for freedom from oppressive policies. Racial tolerance seemed to be in vogue, along with an expansive growth of social programs. But as the health of the national economy weakened in the last quarter of the century, so did the rhetoric on racial equality: *achieving* equity or parity gave way to *celebrating* diversity and difference. *Poor* became *lazy; immigrant* became *alien; affirmative action* became *reverse discrimination; race* became *the race card; assimilation* became *overcoming difference*. A definite nostalgia for "the good ole days" of the pre–Civil Rights era—pictured falsely as a time free from racial strife—has now become prevalent. Some scholars believe that the racist rhetoric has always been constant, however, and that the new idiomatic configurations serve to further obscure the racial biases underlying them. The terms achieve a different meaning when placed in the context of the structural inequalities in our society. The influence of this discourse is such that it affects the way we view immigration, educational opportunity, the judicial system, the labor market, and most significantly, that it informs the "paradigms of dominant knowledge" (see Valdés).

Manning Marable, in his essay "On Race and History," places his position squarely on the issue of social morality in "that uneven and often interrupted dialogue and debate" on the "common political project called democracy" [p. 257]. He begins his battle by analyzing the grounds for dialogue, questioning for example, who took part in President Clinton's "conversation on race." In order for dialogue to have meaning and potential for influence, Marable understands that one must examine the relation of that discourse to its subject and its articulation with social realities. In this case, because he believes that the current criminal justice system— a prime example of institutional racism—has become the new form of lynching for black and Latino young men, the conversation could have profitably begun with prison inmates discussing their experiences. In a broader instance, he explains how national debates on public policy have been influenced by conservative foundations that invest funds in research biased toward their views and fostering a "climate of hostility" among the U.S. population. "Race," he says, "is used to mystify and obscure social reality, to preserve the underlying hierarchy of class power and privilege" and to undermine struggles for social justice by "appeals to racial division" [p. 261]. The way to combat this rhetoric is to first listen to those most affected by the issues, and then to "be true to your values," whether the majority agrees or not. His moral position is derived from the recognition that not only do the "ideologues of the Far Right" understand the importance of expounding their values, that is to say, of staking out their terrain, but also that the successes of the Black Freedom Movement stem from a long history of "link[ing] politics with morality." Marable sets the "intellectual and moral bankruptcy" of his opposing forces against the "good conscience" and "historical responsibility" of those who battle evil [p. 264].

This volume underscores the idea that to converse in the race dialogue is to acknowledge the power of discourse, to challenge the bases of rhetorical constructions, and to take a public stand for the possibility of racial unity. William Julius Wilson calls for a "new public dialogue" that highlights commonalities instead of differences and that demonstrates how social and economic reforms benefit *all* facets of society.

The authors in this collection vary not only in their political positions but also in their assessments of the limits of dialogue and of the progress that can be made in attaining social justice. Still, the majority agree that to achieve "real equality," not simply formal or legal equality, the nation must broaden the field beyond identity politics, "beyond black and white," beyond race and ethnicity, beyond the old paradigms that no longer obtain. That the multi-racial or multi-cultural society in the U.S. is becoming more so is readily evident, and its changing complexion has long been forecast demographically. The spectrum of the multi-cultural, however, is refracted by differences of class, political stance, gender, and sexuality, as within each denominated group, by divergences in history, language, religion, and racial identity. Yet numbers and complexities of race alone cannot suffice—witness the example of South Africa before the recent changes in power. How we view race, how communities are treated, is commensurate with national and international policies and ensuing economic difficulties and anxieties; and how these broader forces determine our experiences is the basis for understanding U.S. social relations. Race as a transnational phenomenon is an issue as apparent as the daily newspaper or nightly television news; it is no longer the domain of any one group or nation.

Indeed, there is a large literature today surrounding questions of modernization and globalization, and the impact of capitalism's monoculture on the hopes for a more plural world.

Immanuel Wallerstein is perhaps the most famous explicator of a world that went global centuries ago, and Armand Mattelart is the dean of similar researches with respect to the particularites of communications technologies.[9] The debate over the impact of such globalization runs from the sunny to the gloomy, as exemplified by recent works by Arjun Appadurai and Fredric Jameson. Briefly, Wallerstein is "neither optimistic nor pessimistic" about a coming world "better or worse" than the present; Appadurai imagines that the impact of new media provides new opportunities for subaltern agency and self-representation; and Jameson forecasts mostly the destructive power of the coming monoculture.[10]

Urvashi Vaid in "What's Sexuality Got to Do with It?" reminds us of the importance of broadening our view of social justice to take in not only the global perspective but also the differences within our communities. She outlines the position of identity politics for racial and ethnic groups as well as for the queer movement: its strengths for empowering groups and community building, and its weakness as a transformative vehicle aimed at institutionalized injustices. Inclusion into society seems to be its main value. Mainstream society responds to identity politics, gay or racial/ethnic, by tenuous accommodation and by creating "zones of freedom," but leaves unchanged the structural barriers to full equality. The main dilemma for strengthening these social justice movements and hindering the political unity necessary to develop more influence, she says, is the very basis of identity politics, its organizing around a singular issue or identity, instead of formulating an overriding ideological basis for transforming society. The position of what she calls the "conservative right" has no such problem and indeed, is waging a powerful "mobilization" to "restore the very values and hierarchies that social justice movements have struggled to transform" [p. 429]. To engage in a successful battle against these forces, Vaid says, we can learn from the "queer context." Because this movement radically challenges established structures, such as family and religion, it necessarily must move beyond the identity issue to accomplish its goals. The gay and lesbian movement clearly intersects with every other progressive movement for social justice that seeks to end discrimination, but only by supplementing identity politics with a definition of "the kind of society we want to live in" can a "strong and motivated base" be achieved. This can be accomplished by a "systematic and creative grassroots community organizing" to create the constituency support needed for social justice, to expand the defense of social policies necessary for change, and to be more successful both nationally and locally. In this way, Vaid lays out her position and sets up its battle-plan: "We can and we must have the courage of our values to take the risk of joint action and new cooperation" [p. 430].

The players in the war of position in the race dialogues recognize the commonalities of goals and the conjunction of strategies, and in fact, often overlap in their inquiries and conclusions, and by and large, are not at odds with one another in the broadest sense of seeking to achieve social justice. Gramsci believed that to create a hegemonic opposition, strategic alliances, not necessarily the unity of all positions, were essential. This is not pluralism under a new name, but a perception that what is pluralistic is the means used to stratify the population. As scholars and intellectuals, we acknowledge, of course, that theory cannot be separated from either political practices or social realities, recognizing in this way that each historical and specific impetus will create numerous results, and thus our fronts are many. Hegemonic forces can be responded to from a variety of points of resistance, neither necessarily competitive nor adversarial, when the power relations are clearly understood.

To redress past and present inequities and to contextualize our situation within a global framework, the scholars in this volume outline a number of strategies. The histories of exclusion must first be brought to the forefront so that we can proceed from an informed position. We must rebuild a "constituency for social justice" (see Vaid) through coalitions and alliances, with leaders who articulate a vision of strength from unity, but we must remember at the same time to attend to the voices of the marginalized and disempowered. Social justice cannot be established without ensuring an economic democracy and a redistribution of political power. Above all, the scholars maintain we must replace complacency with challenge, the status quo with hazardous change, and doubt with faith in ourselves that indeed, we shall overcome.

NOTES

1. See Stuart Hall's work on Gramsci for a reading of the significance of the concept of the war of position for purposes of racial politics: "Gramsci's Relevance for the Study of Race and Ethnicity," *Journal of Communications Inquiry* 10, no. 2 (1986): 5–27.
2. *Emplumada* (Pittsburgh: University of Pittsburgh Press, 1981), 35.
3. Antonio Gramsci, *Selections from the Prison Notebooks*, ed. Quintin Hoare and Geoffrey Nowell Smith (New York: International Publishers, 1981), 179–81.
4. *Racial Formation in the United States: From the 1960s to the 1980s* (London: Routledge, 1989), 138.
5. Wilson, *The Declining Significance of Race: Blacks and Changing American Institutions*, 2d ed. (Chicago: University of Chicago Press, 1980); and Ancheta, *Race, Rights, and the Asian American Experience* (New Brunswick: Rutgers University Press, 1998), 171.
6. Mills, *The Racial Contract* (Ithaca: Cornell University Press, 1997), 6–7; and K. Anthony Appiah and Amy Gutman, *Color Consciousness: the Political Morality of Race* (Princeton: Princeton University Press, 1996), 182.
7. Robert J.C. Young's two books nicely outline the debate taking place among these figures. See *White Mythologies: Writing History and the West* (New York: Routledge, 1990), especially chapters 7, 8, and 9; and *Colonial Desire: Hybridity in Theory, Culture and Race*, especially chapter 7.
8. We use the term "discourse" advisedly. There is a large literature from the last twenty years, mostly in the wake of texts by Michel Foucault, that attempt to theorize discourse as a closed epistemological formation. In this Foucauldian sense—one which, by the way, Said endorses—discourses strictly are impermeable to counter-discourses. We do not believe this to be the case, either historically or theoretically. But a succinct version of Foucault's position is Paul A. Bové, "Discourse," in *Critical Terms for Literary Study*, 2d ed., ed. Frank Lentricchia and Thomas McLaughlin (Chicago: University of Chicago Press, 1995), 50–65.
9. For a brief self-survey of Wallerstein's views, see *Utopistics: Or, Historical Choices of the Twenty-*

First Century (New York: New Press, 1998); and, for Mattelart, see *The Invention of Communication* (Minneapolis: University of Minnesota Press, 1996).

10. Wallerstein, 90. And see Appadurai, *Modernity at Large: Cultural Dimensions of Globalization* (Minneapolis: University of Minnesota Press, 1996), and Jameson and Masao Miyoshi, eds., *The Cultures of Globalization* (Durham: Duke University Press, 1998).

PART I

The Concept of Race

~:~

Social Origins of the Idea of Race

AUDREY SMEDLEY

In the mid-seventeenth century, some planters wrote to one of the trading companies that supplied laborers to the British island colonies. They pleaded that the company not send any more Irishmen. "Send us some Africans, for the Africans are civilized and the Irish are not" (Liggio 1976, 30-31). Letters and requests of this sort were frequent, as the demand for labor by the end of the seventeenth century had grown enormously. Early colonists knew that they could not survive without Africans as laborers, and they said so time and time again, as nearly all historians today acknowledge.[1] Two centuries later, this image of Africans was totally inverted, and Africa itself became a land of wild animals and savages incapable of civilization. What happened in this time period to so transform the image of African peoples? The shortest, most accurate, and most succinct answer is the invention of the idea of "race."

Scholars today have largely accepted the view that "race" is a cultural invention.[2] It represents attitudes and beliefs about human differences that began to evolve in the late seventeenth century in North America and the plantations of the Caribbean Isles and continued to develop throughout the nineteenth century (Smedley [1993] 1999). The most salient aspect of the developing race ideology was a subtle but profound shift in European thought about peoples who originated in

Africa. Although other peoples, like Amerindians, were also accorded inferior race status, it was the changing status of Africans in North America that was most critical for the development of European-American ideas of "race."[3]

THE HISTORICAL BACKGROUND

During the Middle Ages, when Europeans first ventured out to explore the coasts of Africa, its peoples were seen by those who had interests in overseas adventure as just another kind of human beings. Mediterranean peoples, in particular, had long had contact with East Africans and peoples south of the Sahara. The Islamic world, which dominated the Mediterranean lands as well as those of the Near and Middle East, had incorporated an even wider variety of peoples than the Roman world, and both empires had experiences with peoples from inner Africa. Dark-skinned Africans were well known, from Spain and Portugal to Italy and the Balkans, and as far away as Turkey and Iran.[4] Some of the Africans in Europe were slaves or servants, while others were not. Some individuals of African ancestry were clearly people of high status, like Lorenzo di Medici, the first Duke of Florence, and St. Maurice, the patron saint of Magdeburg (Germany), an African hero who led the Children's Crusade.

When Portuguese sailors began to venture into the Atlantic in the 1440s and encountered peoples on the coasts of Africa, they were received with hospitality, and were able to establish trading relationships with these peoples. By the 1480s they were trading with the kings of the Kongo. Letters back and forth between political leaders, merchants, and traders indicate that, despite the differences in cultures, the first Europeans showed respect for the peoples and states that they visited, and engaged in relationships of mutual trust (Connah 1987). On Columbus's voyages across the Atlantic, his ships stopped at Ceuta, on the West African coast, and sailors were able to load provisions and water, supplied by local African peoples. Most significantly, Columbus employed African sailors, whose knowledge of the coasts, the trade winds, and navigation on the Atlantic were of immeasurable importance to his ventures. Africans accompanied most of the conquistadors in their conquests of the New World (see Franklin and Moss 1988, 30-32). In general, the peoples of southern Europe at the beginning of the Age of Exploration had no reason to look upon Africans as inferior forms of human beings.

The peoples of northern Europe had much less contact with human physical diversity. From the British Isles through the Scandinavian lands, throughout the

Middle Ages, geographic isolation prevented interaction with the Mediterranean world, until the Age of Discovery, when great advances in the technology of sailing vessels prompted more people to travel. The vast majority of peoples in northern Europe at this time therefore probably never saw another human being who differed physically very much from themselves. Yet a few people of African or Asian origin had lived in England from earliest times. Peter Fryer (1984, 1) notes that there were "African soldiers in the Roman imperial army that occupied the southern part of (the) island for three and a half centuries." Evidence of individual Africans has been discovered throughout the next thousand years. In the sixteenth century, a small group of Africans were attached to the court of King James IV of Scotland, and at least one African musician was employed by Henry VII and later Henry VIII. According to Fryer, African slaves were brought to England from the 1570s onward as servants for the fashionably wealthy, as prostitutes, and as court entertainers. Presumably they learned English and some served as interpreters on voyages back to Africa, as many had done for the Portuguese and Spanish.

In the eighteenth century, there were an estimated ten to twenty thousand Africans in Britain (Fryer 1984, 67-72), most of whom worked as servants. Many were children attached to aristocratic families, who seem initially to have treated them as exotic pets and who often grew attached to them, as did Catherine the Great of Russia, who adored the little boy from the Congo who had been given to her. She named him Hannibal, after the general who had conquered Rome. He grew up as part of the Russia aristocracy and became a general in the Russian army. His grandson, Alexander Pushkin, became Russia's greatest poet. Although few in number, blacks held a wide variety of statuses in European societies.[5] Until the seventeenth century, there was little indication that they were widely perceived as inferior. They were just some of the varieties of peoples from around the world who were occasionally seen in the port cities of Europe. They learned the languages and cultures of the peoples among whom they lived and participated fully in those sectors of the European cultures that had accepted them.

It is, nevertheless, true that demeaning statements about Africans made by individual writers can be found in the literature, particularly following the Middle Ages. Negative portrayals of Africans by travelers and ordinary writers increased during the seventeenth and eighteenth centuries, mirroring the stereotypes that were becoming part of popular imagery. This was true both in most of the western European countries and in their colonial outposts. By the end of the eighteenth century, blackness itself had taken on a number of negative features associated specifically with Africans.

Yet, negative characterizations of any people, regardless of how strongly they are held, do not in themselves constitute the full reality of "race" and racism. They merely reflect the kind of extreme ethnocentrism that has arisen in history from time to time, which can and does diminish when social and political circumstances change.[6]

The appearance of the ideology of race is best understood when we look at the history of the English in North America and the Caribbean. Historians have been able to document the processes by which England's colonial populations were first "racialized," and how such ideas exacerbated and magnified human differences. It was in the English colonies where the earliest elements of race ideology were manufactured and clearly expressed. Some of the roots of race ideology, however, lie in English cultural history, especially in English conflicts with the peoples they called the "wild Irish."

After the English invasion of the twelfth century, the English establishment (or Anglo-Normans) desperately wanted to extend their control westward into Irish territory. For the next five centuries, intermittent hostilities with the Irish ensued as various English armies attempted to conquer these lands. From time to time these armies (mostly private militia) would penetrate into Irish territory and gain some ground. Yet Irish resistance led to frustrations and retreats. Even the less aggressive strategies used by the English to incorporate or assimilate the pastoral Irish groups resulted in failures, or at best only partial victories.

By the sixteenth and seventeenth centuries, the English had placed a standing army in Ireland and were prepared for new military onslaughts. English motivations for their repeated attempts to conquer the Irish were primarily to take over and settle on the land and grow crops to feed the growing towns of England and for the overseas trade in grains and other foodstuffs. English businessmen had learned about new techniques for the production of sugar from Italian, Spanish, and Portuguese entrepreneurs in the eastern Mediterranean. These latter had established plantations, using slave labor from surrounding regions and imported slaves. The success of these plantations became a model for many of the English adventurers, whose ambitions were primarily the acquisition of wealth and control of international trade.

The Irish refused to surrender to the English, however, letting it be known that they would rather die than be enslaved on their own lands. The partial failure of the English to conquer Ireland by the end of the sixteenth century led many English adventurers to turn their attention to the New World, where the Spanish had already successfully conquered large territories and were accumulating enormous wealth. Some of the adventurers and would-be colonists in Virginia and other areas returned in the mid-seventeenth century to participate in conquests in Ireland. The circumstances faced by English colonists in the New World and the cultural values that they brought with them are essential background for any understanding of the process of transforming various peoples into "races."

The Invention of the "Savage"

What is of interest to us are the attitudes that the English developed toward the Irish during those long centuries of conflict. Documents from the thirteenth to the seventeenth centuries reveal a long-standing hatred and demonization of the Irish which reached its zenith during the reign of Elizabeth I (1559-1603). Frequently called "the Wild Irish," they were described as "rude, beastly, ignorant, cruel and unruly infidels" (Liggio 1976, 8), as "cannibals, heathens, superstitious, idolatrous, unclean and loathsome, wicked, barbarous and uncivil."[7] Sets of laws, like the Statutes of Kilkenny in 1366-67, attempted to segregate the mostly young male English settlers in Ireland from the "wild Irish" and prevent the assimilation of Irish cultural features in the English settlements. The English thus outlawed inter-marriage with Irish women, the wearing of Irish dress, the use of Irish language, and other forms of social interaction. These were perhaps the first apartheid laws of the Western world.[8]

By the sixteenth century, the Irish had become the quintessential "savages" in the popular imagery of the English. Like most western Europeans, following the explorations of the fifteenth through the seventeenth centuries the English had divided their known world into the "civilized" and the "uncivilized," and savagery represented the most extreme form of the uncivilized human condition. Savages were heathens, having no knowledge of proper government or religion; they were nomadic in their habits, naked, rude, irrational, violent, evil, superstitious, and given to treachery, stealing, and other forms of immoral behavior. In the sixteenth century came the first explicit statements that savages were incapable of civilization, and these were applied to the Irish. Despite the fact that the Irish had long been converted to Catholic Christianity, and, indeed, in part because of their loyalty to the Roman Church, such images induced widespread public hatred of the Irish on the part of Protestant England. Most importantly, this image of savagery became part of the cultural knowledge and values of the English and governed the mind-set of seventeenth-century Englishmen in their encounters with other peoples. It was a mind-set that they brought to the New World, and it formed a precedent for how they were to treat indigenous Americans and, later, Africans.

Descriptions by sixteenth-century Spanish conquistadors and priests of the native peoples of the New World led many Englishmen to see similarities between the Irish and the Indians even before they established their first colony at Jamestown in 1607. They saw in both indigenous peoples the same barbarous and uncivilized qualities, and both came to be perceived as impediments to the progress of civilization. For many English leaders, the only solution was to remove native peoples from their lands, or control them and put them to work as slave laborers. Thus, when the English set out to settle the New World, their leaders already had a vision of the world they wanted to create, one of large plantations whose English owners would be made wealthy by the use of slave or forced labor. This was what they had tried, but failed, to establish in Ireland.

Several points should be noted. First, slavery had long been accepted as proper and legal throughout most of the Old World. This was especially true in the Mediterranean world, where slavery had continued uninterrupted since Greco-Roman times. In these regions, the vast majority of slaves were themselves either Europeans or from surrounding North African and Near Eastern areas, although slaves from East and West Africa were increasingly being imported.[9] Second, the Spanish had already conquered and were busily exploiting the resources of a large part of the New World. It was understood that their success in this was due to the use of slave labor, increasingly brought from Africa. Third, although the English themselves were evolving a political philosophy of individual freedom and equality, and slavery had long been eliminated from English society, the English elite were not opposed to forced labor or slavery. In fact, several proposals had been made in Parliament to legally impose slavery on the English poor in the sixteenth century.[10] Furthermore, many had long advocated or supported the use of servile labor in Ireland.

It was within this context that some English settlers in the New World attempted to enslave the native peoples. Within a short time after the beginning of colonization, hostilities with Indians erupted. Often deliberately instigated by the English, warfare became an increasingly dominant feature of relations between Indians and Europeans.[11] The perception of Indians as savages was the foundation for policies that constantly separated and excluded even converted Indians from participation in the life of the colonies. Early on, the colonists envisioned external reserve areas for those Indians who were friendly or with whom they had concluded treaties. Even the few Indians who voluntarily worked for the colonists were never really trusted. In time, all Indians were conflated into a common imagery of a weak population that must succumb to the advances of European civ-ilization. Although most historical instances of conquest prior to this time had led to the conquering peoples incorporating and assimilating their victims into a com-mon society, the English had determined that savages could not be assimilated into civilized society; hence their fairly uniform and widespread attitude that savages must be kept apart.

The new society created by the early colonists, especially in Virginia, was one in which competition among European colonists was powerful and pervasive. The majority of settlers were men on a quest for wealth; they were not concerned with the niceties of proper society. Many were from the laboring class or were small-scale gentry, torn from their moorings in kinship and church-based communities. Others were taken from the poorhouses and jails of England, Ireland, and Scot-land. They recognized few loyalties and were a hardened, brash, and brawling lot. They came to this furthermost outpost of the world to make their fortunes and had few scruples about how this was to be done. They were aggressive and often violent men who began to exploit one another as soon as they arrived in the New World, and turned to violence against the Indians when they could not force them to easily surrender their crops and lands (Morgan 1975).

THE PROBLEM OF LABOR

The new colonies of Virginia, and later Maryland and South Carolina, struggled to survive, to build a viable society, and to create wealth for themselves. Yet they faced a major problem, and that was a shortage of labor. During the first few years, Virginia settlers survived on the hospitality of Indians, or on what they could steal or extort from them. A decade later there were several hundred more settlers, and tobacco had been discovered. Processing tobacco is labor-intensive, and, for a while, it brought tremendous wealth to a few men with large landholdings. Yet there was never enough labor either for food crops or for tobacco. From the begin-ning too many Englishmen were unwilling or unable to provide for themselves. Their main objectives in the New World were acquiring land, establishing farms and plantations, and getting others to work for them. The demand for laborers was uppermost in the minds of colony leaders, who tended to be the first and largest landowners, especially after the establishment of tobacco cultivation. The only way to become wealthy or increase one's wealth was to own land and sufficient labor-ers to grow and process tobacco at low cost.

In an economy based on the philosophy of free labor, most ordinary servants and laborers were paid a wage. But when the price of tobacco fell, wage labor became too expensive. The periodic rise and fall of tobacco prices became a powerful theme in the history of the Virginia colony. Within two decades, the colonists had turned to a form of labor that had made its first appearance in England but in the colonies was to become the most common form of labor for the next six decades. This was indentured servitude, a type of labor based on a contract of indebtedness, during which a person was bound to work, receiving only food, clothing, and housing, for a period of four to seven years, to pay off the costs of transport to the New World and lodging once there. In the hands of those colonists driven by greed, indentured servitude became a system of chattel ownership, with servants bought and sold, forced to live with the minimum of food and clothing, brutally punished for minor violations, and housed in miserable conditions. Under this system, prisoners, the homeless, the poor of England, Irishmen, and Scots captured in war, were forced to provide labor in the tobacco fields and farms of the new colonies. In the mid–seventeenth century, large numbers of Irishmen were brought to the English islands of Jamaica and Barbados to work as slaves. In the beginning they outnumbered both native labor and African slaves purchased from the Spanish.

This system of labor was the immediate precursor to the institutionalization of racial slavery. Many historians have noted that this form of exploitation of labor was already tantamount to slavery, even before slave laws were passed (Morgan 1975). The Virginia colonists' treatment of their servants and the freed poor was sufficiently scandalous that from time to time the English king or his representatives, the governors and lords, attempted to pass laws against the colony leaders' "inhumane severity to servants" (Morgan 1975, 282). Yet the colonial leaders, vying with one another for power and fortune, jealous and angry over taxes and the lowering price of tobacco, showed only indifference to the plight of the poor.

Africans had been brought to the mainland colonies in a small trickle since 1619. Historians have long debated whether Africans were slaves from their first entry into Jamestown, or whether they were initially treated like other servants. It seems that many or most were already assimilated to Spanish or English culture, but the record is incomplete. Some experts have observed that their status was ambiguous. The evidence shows that their positions in colonial society were clearly flexible, reflecting not only the lack of uniformity in attitudes toward them, but also a fluid social system with widely diverse statuses.

Many historians have now concluded that most Africans were not differentiated from other servants. Nearly all lived under miserable conditions, and many protested and ran away together. Whites and blacks shared similar conditions; they lived, worked, ate, drank, and played together, and they also intermarried. They served their time of indenture and some became free. Some freed blacks themselves became property owners, owning both land and slaves. They had the same rights as freed white men; they contracted business, engaged in commerce and financial dealings, participated and voted in the assembly, and exercised all other rights in the body politic.[12] Some behaved with the brashness and aggressiveness that characterized white men, reflecting conformity to a common culture.

During the early decades of the new colonies, few servants survived long enough to gain their freedom. This changed, however, in the latter half of the seventeenth century, as increasing numbers of servants survived their period of servitude and sought to establish themselves as householders owning land, animals, tools, and houses. Yet they came up against a system that denied them the bounties of their freedom. By midcentury virtually all protected and usable land had been confiscated from the Indians by a few very wealthy men. The only lands available to newly freed men were marginal lands or lands belonging to Indian tribes. Although all freedmen were supposed to be provided with a piece of land and a household for themselves, along with tools and some domestic animals, this soon became virtually impossible. Many were forced into a situation in which they had to either work for some other (large) landowner or try to rent land from a landholder, most of whom charged exorbitant fees. Others became rootless, homeless "beggars," living on the margins of colonial settlements, often stealing from other settlers or the Indians, and given to violence against those whom they saw as weak.

All of the poor—blacks, whites, mulattoes, and Indians, servants and freedmen—were exploited, often very harshly. Unable to acquire land and better themselves, they began protesting against the government and aristocracy. They demanded that the government allow them to attack local Indian areas and confiscate more lands. They also wanted freedom from the servitude that oppressed them, and an end to government corruption and patronage. Their dissatisfaction was registered by mid-century. Resentment toward colonial leaders came to a head in 1676 with Bacon's Rebellion, when thousands of whites, Africans, and "mixed" peoples rose up in opposition to the policies and practices of the colonial regime. *Some historians argue today that this uprising against the wealthy and powerful elite, involving such diverse people joined in a common cause, is clear evidence that race and racism did not yet exist.*[13] The poor of all colors found themselves in a common dilemma. Government documents and letters show that colonial leaders feared the solidarity exhibited among the poor. The evidence suggests that the white poor perceived their circumstances and those of other nonwhite servants as being essentially the same.

INVENTING SLAVERY . . . AND "RACE"

The rebellion failed, but it was a turning point. In the aftermath, colonial leaders deliberately and consciously sought ways of establishing better social control over those elements of society that threatened their authority. What was needed, in their eyes, was a docile, totally controllable labor force, at the least possible expense, and some social mechanism for preventing rebellions in the future. One solution was to create an intermediate, or buffer, category of people, between the small elite cadre and the large masses of working people. Such a class of people would be provided access to some forms of wealth and status, would identify their interests with the large planters, and would be expected to defend established government against the poor (Allen 1997).

Colony leaders took the first, critical, society-wide steps toward creating the idea and ideology of race by consciously separating out the European poor from blacks and Indians, using a divide-and-conquer philosophy. They began providing privileges and material goods to freed Europeans, while retaining in extended slavery those newly arrived from Africa. As we have seen, the English had a precedent for this in the first apartheid laws enforcing the separation of English settlers in Ireland from the Irish natives. Now they had other mechanisms for dividing the poor, including the use of visible physical characteristics and ancestry.

Numerous circumstances foreshadowed and made possible, perhaps even inevitable, these decisions. First, the Indians did not make good slaves. They were perceived as weak because they died of Old World diseases to which they had no immunity. They also were not present in large numbers. They were on their own territory and often ran away, finding supporters among other Indians, and could rarely be recaptured. Second, the Irish were ineffective as slaves, as experiences in the English West Indian islands and later in South Carolina demonstrated. They were perceived as aggressive and violent, refusing to work in the hot sun, often prone to drink, and they tended to run away and join their fellow Catholics (the Spanish and French) in conspiracies against the English. Most importantly, they had no previous experience or knowledge of tropical agriculture. Third, ordinary

English people at home became critical of the abusive treatment of their fellow citizens in the colonies, and opposed their use as slaves. Consequently, the supply of English servants began to dwindle as increasing numbers refused to venture out to the colonies, and as the poor found more employment at home.

Africans, on the other hand, were different in a way that had nothing initially to do with their color. They were heathens and were not English, and could claim no rights to English laws of protection, a reality that more and more plantation owners came to realize. Moreover, there was no international body or nation-state that would or could protest their treatment, making them vulnerable to permanent enslavement. Some property owners, having recognized this vulnerability early on, had started to retain Africans in servitude longer than the normal seven years, with impunity. (At the same time, many other Africans had sued for their freedom and had obtained it under English laws and customs, showing the absence of uniform policies and practices with regard to Africans.) Furthermore, Africans had immunities to Old World diseases that Europe and Africa had shared for thousands of years. They were also tropical people who could labor long hours in the hot sun, to which they had long been acclimated. Their reputations for strength and durability began to precede them. Many writers of the time described Africans as "strong," in contrast to Indians, who were perceived as weak. Most of all, Africans had skills that were desperately needed in the New World, as had been demonstrated in the Spanish colonies, where large numbers of hispanized and newly immigrant Africans were producing great wealth. It is these realities that many historians have failed to recognize and include in their analyses of the causes of African slavery.

Africans of the fifteenth and sixteenth centuries had numerous skills. Some had experience smelting iron ore and manufacturing tools and implements; there were blacksmiths, goldsmiths and tinsmiths. There were rope makers, basket makers, brick makers, house builders, thatchers, potters, carpenters, and other woodworkers. Some were cattle keepers and breeders. Some were weavers of cloth, caulkers, tanners and other leather workers, calabash carvers, and boatbuilders. Most of all, they were all farmers, and, given their knowledge, could be put to work within days after landing on American shores. This was particularly true in the rice fields of South Carolina, where Africans reproduced a rice culture that was endemic to many parts of West Africa (Morgan 1998). In other words, to many early English colonists, Africans were indeed civilized.

No wonder the planters of the late seventeenth and eighteenth centuries preferred Africans as slaves. They commonly exchanged captive Indians for Africans, and sometimes refused to accept Irish prisoners. Most importantly, they recognized their increasing dependence on African labor. The fate of the Georgia colony, which started as a nonslave settlement using freed convicts and other poor as laborers in the 1730s, represents a prime example of this dependence. Within a few years colony leaders made it clear that they could not survive without Africans; their many petitions to the trustees of the colony, pleading for African slaves, eventually led to the full legal acceptance of slavery. By 1750 Georgia was well on its way to success and wealth, like its neighbor South Carolina, with black slavery as the foundation of the economy.

The establishment of slavery and its institutionalization throughout the New World colonies was not the result of a single, dramatic, or sudden decision, but of numerous decisions and agreements among Europeans who were motivated by self-centered interests. Edmund Morgan (1975, 297) has argued that Englishmen in the colonies converted to slavery simply by buying slaves instead of servants. Yet it must also be clear that laws regarding the use and control of slaves and governing the relationships between free people and slaves had to be promulgated to give legitimacy to the institution. The advantages of having slaves for life were obvious, he notes, since the Spanish, the Dutch, and other Europeans were already successfully engaged in the use of African slaves. The only people who could be retained in such positions were either Indians, by virtue of conquests, or Africans; but as we saw previously, Indians did not make good slaves. The ease with which Africans could be purchased, from the Dutch or Spanish, or from the English islands of Barbados or Jamaica, increased toward the end of the century, and was greatly facilitated when some English entrepreneurs became themselves involved in shipping slaves direct from the continent.

Over the years 1690-1725, Africans, Indians, African Americans, and their descendants were separated out by a long series of discriminatory laws that made slavery permanent and reduced them to the status of property. By 1723, even free blacks in Virginia were prohibited by law from exercising their right to vote. They were denied the ownership of certain types of property, and both Indians and blacks were forbidden to intermarry with whites.

Historian Philip Morgan observed: "In general the distance between plain white folk and black slaves grew progressively wider throughout the course of the eighteenth century. In the middle to late seventeenth century, black slaves and the poor sections of the white community associated closely and openly. By the turn of the eighteenth century, however, cooperation and alliances between white servants and black slaves began to dissolve, in part because of the actions taken by the planter class, in part because servant numbers declined, and in part because the black population became more numerous and alien" (1998, 300). Virginia historian Edmund Morgan claims that by a series of acts the Virginia Assembly did what it could to foster the contempt of whites for blacks and Indians (1975, 331). Gradually, folk attitudes were developed that made it very clear that more than just slavery separated Africans and their descendants from European settlers.

Peter Fryer, in analyzing the rise of racism in Britain, places its origin in the same circumstances that gave rise to race and racism in the southern states of North America. "Racism," he says, "emerged in the oral tradition in Barbados (a British island) in the seventeenth century, and crystallized in print in Britain in the eighteenth, as the ideology of the plantocracy, the class of sugar-planters and slave-merchants that dominated England's Caribbean colonies. It emerged, above all, as a largely defensive ideology—the weapon of a class whose wealth, way of life, and power were under mounting attack" (1984, 184).

All whites, rich and poor, were homogenized into a common category of free people, while blacks, mulattoes, and Indians were reduced to the status of slave property or outcasts. However, opposition to slavery was mounting, as many English people decried the establishment of such an institution in English territory and with the assumed protection of English law. Under such attacks, the leaders of the colonies found it necessary to rationalize these policies. At first the justification for all actions leading to permanent slavery was predicated on the fact that Africans now being brought directly to the colonies were heathens and aliens to European society. They were already slaves in Africa, it was argued, and under the Christian English, enslavement in the New World would save their souls and train them in the arts of civilization.

However, slavery transforms people into property. For several centuries English culture had glorified property rights, which were perceived as the basis of English freedom. Thus, the defense of slavery soon became equated with the defense of white property rights, now conceived as inviolable and inalienable. In the slave systems of North America property rights took precedence over the human rights of slaves. Pro-slavery arguments, which continued from the latter half of the eighteenth century through the nineteenth century, required planters to ignore and diminish the human rights of slaves.

Myths began to emerge in popular discourse that magnified the differences between Africans, Indians, and Europeans. The idea that Africans were a separate and distinct kind of humans began to appear in some of the rationalizations for slavery. The conditions of slavery greatly increased both the status and the behavioral differences between blacks and whites, and contributed to an enhanced notion of a large and unbridgeable gulf between these peoples. The people being shipped to the colonies direct from Africa did not have the knowledge of European cultures and experiences that earlier Africans had. They appeared alien to both Europeans and older African Americans. They were perceived to have barbarous and "uncivilized" characteristics, including heathenism and resistance to authority. Thus Africans became the new "savages" in the minds of European Americans. The idea of savagery as a condition of all Africans was extended even to those whose ancestors had been in the Americas for generations, regardless of whether they had ever been, or were still, slaves.

During the Revolutionary era, abolitionists became increasingly active, and European critics accused colonists of hypocrisy in advocating freedom for themselves from British "tyranny" while keeping hundreds of thousands of people in slavery. American society reacted by emphasizing a new argument for African slavery in the form of a belief that became widespread in popular culture. Increasingly focusing on physical differences, pro-slavery forces advanced what they thought was an unassailable argument for preserving African slavery: Africans, because of their biological differences, were naturally inferior and thus best suited for the role of slaves. The physical characteristics of Africans had become markers of their inferior social status.

Institutionalizing the Racial Worldview

The argument of African inferiority took firm hold of the American and British consciousness and became imbedded as a culturally created mindset and a major facet of the racial worldview. Both ordinary people and intellectuals, on both sides of the Atlantic, found a useful paradigm to justify the inequality of Africans, Indians, and whites in the "Great Chain of Being," a natural hierarchy of all living beings ranging from the lowliest insects to reptiles, mammals, apes, humans, the angels, and finally to God. Human varieties formed a natural hierarchy, with Europeans on top and Africans on the bottom, and with all other "races" located in between. Africans, it was argued, were closest to the apes in their position on the great chain, while Europeans were the norm for superior humanity.

From the end of the eighteenth century, scientists and scholars published numerous works explaining, and fabricating, the ways in which Africans were inferior to Europeans. The term "race" was now widely used. It reflected the different ranks on the Great Chain of Being, and diverse physical traits had become symbols of this natural inequality. Grotesque descriptions of Africans became part of the popular myths. The manufacture of such myths was necessary in part because, after the Great Awakening of the mid–eighteenth century, most slaves had become Christians. The problem for the pro-slavery forces now became how to enslave fellow Christians. Winthrop Jordan states the solution to the dilemma very clearly: "slavery could survive only if the Negro were a man set apart; he simply had to be different if slavery was to exist at all" (1968, 184).

Finally, a proposal was introduced at the end of the eighteenth century by some of the leading scientists that Africans were a separate and inferior species of human. More than two hundred years after Africans had been brought into the colonies, scholars debated the taxonomic position of Africans and ultimately projected them as a distinct and inferior species. As a way of defending slavery and keeping all blacks distinct from whites, this idea was widely accepted by the American public in the nineteenth century, whether or not they owned slaves. Those who opposed the notion, on religious grounds, that Africans were a species created separately from normal humans turned to another argument: that Africans had been reduced to a subnormal species status as a result of degeneration. Whatever the views of those public intellectuals who were attempting to explain "the Negro's" place in the natural scheme of things, all called upon the growing fields of science to validate popular conceptions of human differences and thus to strengthen and confirm the racial worldview.[14]

After the Civil War official slavery ended, but race statuses and the ideology that had been fabricated about them remained deeply entrenched in the culture and the public consciousness. Powerful economic, political, and social forces were generated to keep the racial ranking in place, and these forces have been successful for well over a hundred years. Public segregation, social separation, and the allocation of low-status, dirty, and demeaning jobs only to blacks has been the widespread reflection of the racial worldview.[15]

There was an ironic development in the nineteenth century that had an unanticipated and powerful effect beyond the colonial situation. Some Europeans at home saw "race" as a useful way of dividing their own societies, with the purpose of structuring and justifying permanent inequality. It was not until Europeans began to impose racial ranking on one another, when race reached its peak of development with the Nazi Holocaust of this century, that Western societies began to perceive what a terrible idea race is.[16]

In summary, "race," reflecting a growing ideology about human differences, originated as a social fact of life in colonial America and in England's island plantations long before science began to try to explain it in naturalistic or biological terms. "Race" did not originate as a neutral taxonomic term in science. It was a folk idea created to reflect and to rationalize separate, distinct, and exclusive divisions in an already inegalitarian society. It was designed to make social, political, and economic inequality a God-given part of nature. It was also a fabrication of a new form of human social identity intended to be natural, rigid, and as unalterable as are innate biological features.[17]

Some of the key qualities of the idea of "race" are its flexibility and usefulness. In the nineteenth century the racial worldview became virtually a universal way of looking at human differences, promulgated by all of the expanding European powers as a way of justifying their dominance over peoples who were, for the most part, physically as well as culturally different from themselves. But, as in the case of the internal construction of racial categories in Europe itself, neither physical nor cultural differences were crucial for structuring racial ideology to benefit a particular political agenda. From their inception, racial categories have been arbitrary and subjective, and racial ideology itself is capable of being molded to fit the exigencies of any social or political situation.

In the United States we have been conditioned to believe in race and the notion that it has something to do with our biological selves. Yet modern scientists, since the middle of the twentieth century, have learned that no amount of investigation into the physical or genetic variations of human populations will tell us anything about "race." The actual genetic diversity in the human species defies all categorization into exclusive or distinct entities. The reality of human physical diversity does not correspond to conventional racial classifications.[18] With biologists, geneticists, and others denying that such categories are valid, or claiming that "race" has no meaning in biology, we are being forced to confront the real meaning of the term—that is, its socio-historical meaning as a product of Western colonizing and exploitative cultures.

"Race" became a way of looking at the world's peoples, dividing them into separate, discrete, and exclusive populations, arbitrarily linking each with distinct physical and behavioral (and moral and intellectual) features conceived as inherited and unalterable, and socially ranking each grouping so that they have unequal access to society's resources and rewards. Race was, and still is, in North America, a matter of power, prestige, wealth, and privilege. It is about how some Europeans used physical differences among the populations they conquered or enslaved to socially stratify society. That it has had unintended or unanticipated consequences that have had ramifications throughout the world and has brought horror and destruction to millions of people in the twentieth century could not have been foreseen by the originators of the idea and ideology of "race" in the eighteenth century.

The question is, where do we go with this new knowledge and understanding in the twenty-first century? What are the implications of the new scientific knowledge of human differences which indicate that there are greater genetic or innate differences *within* "races" than between them? What does this new perspective mean for people who have had to structure their institutions around the idea of "race" and "racial differences," in our home lives and neighborhoods, in newspapers, journals, and magazines, in churches and other social forms, in various forms of recreation, music preferences, food habits, body decorations, reading habits, educational interests, and all the other aspects of our cultural selves? Does this mean that the idea of race will gradually disappear from our consciousness and our perceptions of the world? Will we begin to see human physical variations as just a normal aspect of our variable species, having no social significance? Or will we continue to use skin color, hair texture, eye shape, and other features of physiognomy as symbols of racial social identities, ignoring ambiguities and contradictions? Will we continue to act upon assumptions of racial ranking and inferiority?

All of the evidence of human history suggests that change is inevitable. Even as we are focusing on and discussing "race" and "racism" in contemporary forums, the ideology of race is already undergoing change. American society and many other societies in the Western world are becoming more and more complex and heterogeneous with the vast immigrations of Third World peoples. Indeed, the mobility of the human species is greater today than it has ever been, leading not only to greater contacts among people who are different from one another physically and culturally, but also to greater levels of intermating, a fact that has always characterized human group interaction. From this mixing of peoples new physical variations are being created that do not fit existing paradigms or categories of "race" in any of those nations where racial identity has been important.

At the same time, Americans have become better educated in general about the meaning of race and race differences. Despite the continued intermittent appearance of so-called scientific publications, like the infamous *The Bell Curve*, authored by Richard Herrnstein and Charles Murray in 1994, that purport to document "race" differences in intelligence and other forms of behavior, studies indicate that attitudes have changed and are continuing to change as society itself is being transformed by legislation, social policies, education, and the personal experiences of individuals in the workplace and in wider social interactions.[19] The significance of "race" may well be declining, but if so it is in ways we are yet unable to predict.

NOTES

1. See Philip D. Morgan (1998); Edmund S. Morgan (1975); and David Brion Davis (1966).

2. Ashley Montagu ([1964] 1971) was the first prominent anthropologist in the twentieth century to disavow the idea of race as a biological or scientific concept and to argue that it was a myth.

3. Works that deal with the history of the idea of race are appearing much more frequently today. One of the earliest was that of Thomas Gossett (1965). In recent years, several more studies of the history of the idea of race have been published. See Audrey Smedley ([1993] 1999); Theodore Allen (1994, 1997); and Ivan Hannaford (1996).

4. Frank Snowden (1970, 1983) was one of the first of several modern scholars to demonstrate the presence of black Africans in the European historical context.

5. During the Middle Ages, most of the great artists, painters, and sculptors of Europe included black subjects in some of their works, children often beautifully dressed, stately gentlemen and women attired in the best clothing, indicating their status and the esteem with which Europeans held them. Africans were not homogenized into a "racial type"; the portraits are those of individuals, each unique. This suggests that racial stereotypes did not play a role in European thinking about Africans until well into the seventeenth century, and sometimes later. See, for example, Allison Blakely (1993) and Peter Fryer (1984).

6. The processes of state formation and the crystallization of power taking place at this time that ultimately led to the structuring of the contemporary nation-states in Europe gave rise to extreme ethnocentrism as Europeans fought over and negotiated their modern identities. Warfare always generates extreme hatred and denigration of the "enemies" and depends upon strong feelings of patriotism or nationalism. From an anthropological perspective, virtually all peoples have some degree of ethnocentrism—that is, the feeling that one's own culture or way of life is best, and that other societies and cultures are not quite as good. The physical features of some Africans, for example, were seen as ugly or remarkable in some way. These were subjective judgments on the part of individual writers, not widespread social stereotypes.

7. See Canny (1973); Allen (1997); Quinn (1966); and Myers (1983).

8. The British were at the threshold of the ideology of race in their growing demonization of

the Irish during the sixteenth century. Clearly their attitudes and beliefs had nothing to do with color or any other physical dissimilarities.

9. The term "slave" was taken from the Slavic peoples, who were preferred slaves during ancient times and especially during the Middle Ages.

10. Protestant capitalist ideology held that the poor were responsible for their own condition. Therefore, some leaders thought that all of the poor should be forced to work. That is why proposals to transform the poor into slaves were fairly widely supported among the English elite during the sixteenth and seventeenth centuries.

11. For descriptions of the relationships between English settlers and Indians, and the consequences of extreme English ethnocentrism in the New World, see Robert Berkhofer Jr. (1978); Gary B. Nash (1992); and Roy Harvey Pearce (1988), among many others.

12. See Edmund S. Morgan (1975); Theodore W. Allen (1997); and Winthrop D. Jordan (1968).

13. See Theodore W. Allen (1997). Historian Lerone Bennett Jr. (1984) has pointed out the same phenomenon. Europeans did not know they were white, and were not conscious of a "racial" identity until the notion was created in their heads. The evidence that poor whites saw themselves as first as a class of impoverished people who were being thwarted in their desire to better themselves is manifest in most of the documentation of primary sources. It is extraordinary how much of this evidence was overlooked by historians of the late nineteenth and early twentieth centuries.

14. For a history of the role of science in the development, elaboration, documentation, and confirmation of "race" and popular race ideology, see Smedley ([1993] 1999) and Stepan (1982).

15. George Fredrickson's ([1971] 1987) study of nineteenth-century white attitudes toward blacks is still the best and most comprehensive work on this topic.

16. See Smedley ([1993] 1999) for a discussion of the evolution of racial ideology in Europe and during the rest of the nineteenth century.

17. For a provocative philosophical exploration of "race" as identity in the United States, see Webster (1992).

18. See Bodmer and Cavalli-Sforza (1976); Lewontin (1995); Livingstone (1969); Marks (1995), and especially Littlefield, Lieberman, and Reynolds (1982).

19. There have been numerous scholarly reactions to the Herrnstein and Murray theses. Among the many good ones is Fraser (1995).

REFERENCES

Allen, Theodore W. 1994. *The invention of the white race.* Vol. 1. London and New York: Verso Publishers.

———. 1997. *The invention of the white race*. Vol. 2. London and New York: Verso Publishers.

Banton, Michael. 1977. *The idea of race*. London: Tavistock.

Banton, M., and J. Harwood. 1975. *The race concept*. New York: Praeger.

Bennett, Lerone, Jr. 1984. *Before the Mayflower: A history of the Negro in America, 1619–1964*. Chicago: Johnson Publishers.

Berger, P. L., and T. Luckman. 1966. *The social construction of reality*. New York: Doubleday.

Berkhofer, Robert F., Jr. 1978. *The white man's Indians*. New York: Alfred A. Knopf.

Blakely, Allison. 1993. *Blacks in the Dutch world: The evolution of racial imagery in a modern society*. Bloomington: Indiana University Press.

Bodmer, W. E., and L. L. Cavalli-Sforza. 1976. *Genetics, evolution and man*. San Francisco: W. H. Freeman.

Canny, Nocholas P. 1973. The ideology of English colonialization: From Ireland to America. *William and Mary Quarterly*, 3d ser., 30:575–98.

Connah, Graham. 1987. *African civilizations*. New York: Cambridge University Press.

Davis, David Brion. 1966. *The problem of slavery in Western culture*. Middlesex, England: Penguin Books.

Franklin, John Hope, and Alfred A. Moss Jr. 1988. *From slavery to freedom*. 6th ed. New York: Alfred A. Knopf.

Fraser, Steven. 1995. *The bell curve wars: Race, intelligence, and the future of America*. New York: Basic Books.

Fredrickson, George M. 1977. White images of black slaves in the southern United States. *Annals of the New York Academy of Sciences* 292:368–75.

———. 1988. *The arrogance of race*. Middletown, Conn.: Wesleyan University Press.

———. [1971] 1987. *The black image in the white mind*. Middletown, Conn.: Wesleyan University Press.

Fryer, Peter. 1984. *Staying power: The history of black people in Britain*. London and Boulder, Colo.: Pluto Press.

Gossett, Thomas F. [1965] 1997. *Race: The history of an idea in America*. New ed. New York and Oxford: Oxford University Press.

Hannaford, Ivan. 1996. *Race: The history of an idea in the West*. Washington, D.C.: Woodrow Wilson Center Press; Baltimore: Johns Hopkins University Press.

Jordan, Winthrop D. 1968. *White over black: American attitudes toward the Negro, 1550–1812*. Baltimore: Penguin.

Lewontin, Richard. 1995. *Human diversity*. New York: Scientific American Library, a division of HPHLP.

Lieberman, Leonard. 1968. The debate over race: A study in the sociology of knowledge. *Phylon* 29:127–41.

Liggio, Leonard. 1976. English origins of early American racism. *Radical History Review* 3, no. 1:1–36.

Littlefield, Alice, Leonard Lieberman, and Larry Reynolds. 1982. Redefining race: The potential demise of a concept in physical anthropology. *Current Anthropology* 23(6): 641–56.

Livingstone, Frank B. 1969. On the non-existence of human races. In *The concept of race*, edited by A. Montagu. New York: Free Press.

Marks, Jonathan. 1995. *Human biodiversity: Genes, race, and history.* New York: Aldine de Gruyter.

Montagu, Ashley. [1964] 1971. *Man's most dangerous myth: The fallacy of race.* New York: World Publishing.

Morgan, Edmund S. 1975. *American slavery, American freedom.* New York: W. W. Norton.

Morgan, Philip D. 1998. *Slave counterpoint: Black culture in the eighteenth-century Chesapeake and Lowcountry.* Chapel Hill and London: University of North Carolina Press.

Myers, James P., ed. 1983. *Elizabethan Ireland.* Hamden, Conn.: Archon Books.

Nash, Gary B. 1992. *Red, white, and black: The peoples of early America.* 3d ed. Englewood Cliffs, N.J.: Prentice Hall.

Pearce, Roy H. [1953] 1988. *Savagism and civilization.* Berkeley: University of California Press.

Puzzo, Dante. 1964. Racism and the Western tradition. *Journal of the History of Ideas* 25(4): 579–86.

Quinn, David B. 1966. *Elizabethans and the Irish.* Ithaca, N.Y.: Cornell University Press.

Sanders, Ronald. 1978. *Lost tribes and promised lands: The origins of American racism.* Boston: Little, Brown and Co.

Smedley, Audrey. [1993] 1999. *Race in North America: Origin and evolution of a worldview.* Boulder, Colo.: Westview Press.

Snowden, F. M., Jr. 1970. *Blacks in antiquity: Ethiopians in the Greco-Roman experience.* Cambridge, Mass.: Harvard University Press.

———. 1983. *Before color prejudice.* Rev. ed. Cambridge, Mass.: Harvard University Press.

Stepan, Nancy. 1982. *The idea of race in science: Great Britain 1800–1960.* London: Macmillan.

Webster, Yehudi. O. 1992. *The racialization of America.* New York: St. Martin's Press.

2

Six Wrongs of Racial Science

ALAN H. GOODMAN

INTRODUCTION: AN UPSET STOMACH

A friend recently convinced me to buy a bottle of thirty-six TUMS® Ultras in assorted fruit flavors, a product of SmithKline Beecham, containing 800 mg of calcium per tablet. I also purchased less-expensive bottles of Drug Guild's "Calcium Antacid Tablets" and "Equate extra strength antacid tablets." The former contains 150 peppermint-flavor tablets, containing 400 mg of calcium per tablet. The latter, manufactured by Perrigo Company, contains 96 tropical-flavor tablets, each with 600 mg of calcium.

On all the bottles the first sentence under the heading IMPORTANT INFORMATION ON OSTEOPOROSIS is exactly the same: "*Regular exercise and a healthy diet with enough calcium helps teen and young adult white and Asian women maintain good bone health and may reduce their risk of osteoporosis later in life.*" The producers of antacids and calcium supplements apparently have agreed that the scientific research is unambiguous on the fact that regular exercise, a healthy diet, and enough calcium may help young women of some race/ethnic groups. Conversely, the benefits are either not proven or not to be had for members of other race/ethnic groups.

Assuming for a moment that the osteoporosis information is based on solid research, problems quickly arise in moving from groups in research studies to real individuals. Who is white or Asian, and who, exactly, is not? Will the TUMS® benefit a teenager with an Asian mother and an African American father? Should a Latina regularly exercise to help prevent osteoporosis if she thinks of herself as white, but not if she thinks of herself as black? Whose opinion counts when she thinks of herself as black but her physician considers her to be white? Will the TUMS® benefit a dark-skinned white, but not a light-skinned black? Are Native Americans considered Asians, as they are in most racial typologies, or another race, as they are in the U.S. Census? If they are Asians, does that mean they can benefit from taking TUMS®? Conversely, if their race is Native American will they not benefit? Below the fluidities of group membership, deeper problems may exist. Is the generalization a valid one? Is racial science good science?

My research focuses on the everyday uses of race in science. The osteoporosis information is an example of medical advice and treatment that is based on an individual's purported race. Under the medical advice is "everyday racial science," in which individuals, their bones, bodies, and minds, are unproblematically divided into racial groups. Rather than focus on the more obvious racial science at work in studies of minds, behavior, and intelligence,[1] I wish to show that subtle uses of race, exemplified by the TUMS® label, may cause even more harm. The bottom line is that wherever race is used as shorthand for human biological variation, the results will be badly flawed. People who believe or act upon the results may cause harm to others and themselves.

This chapter is organized around six reasons why racial science is bad science, both wrong and harmful. The first has to do with the ideological and theoretical incompatibility of race with evolutionary theory. The second, third, and fourth reasons highlight the fundamental incompatibility of race with the structure or "facts" of human variation. The last two reasons focus on the incompatibility of a changing and ill-defined concept with the scientific necessities of replicability. No one reason shows certainly that race is a myth or a totally useless scientific concept. However, the combined consequences lead to the conclusion that biological race should be placed on the scrap heap of outdated scientific ideas.

SIX REASONS WHY RACE IS WRONG AND HARMFUL

Race is a Pre-Darwinian and Prescientific Concept
that is Incompatible with Evolutionary Theory.

The idea of biological race embodies two central beliefs (Hannaford 1996; Smedley 1999):

• Humans are divisible into a small and discrete number of types.
• Types are old, primordial, fixed, and unchanging.

In addition, biological race takes on power and meaning in the common implications that

• Types have defining characteristics and are hierarchically arranged.
• The type explains the individual: an individual's biology and behavior are in large part explicable by the type/race of which the individual is a member.

The idea of racial types emerged from the Platonic notion of ideal types and the Christian idea of a great chain of being. The Platonic notion of ideal types holds that the physical and material world is a reflection of a world of pure ideals. The real world of ideals is explicitly stable; change exists only in the potential for devolution or poor copy from the ideal. This method of science and philosophy is neither experimental nor empirical; rather, it is based on discovery through thinking about or imagining ideal types. An inanimate object, such as a chair, although a human construction, is evaluated as to how closely it conforms to the ideal type chair. But is there an ideal chair? What are its dimensions, materials, and characteristics? Who gets to imagine it?

In a similar way, ideal types of animals and plants were imagined. Existing fauna and flora may be evaluated as to how closely they resemble the ideal type of each animal and plant. Plato imagined ideal male and female types, and ideal solders, servants, and aristocrats. Individuals could be evaluated in relationship to how well they exemplified these ideal types.

Platonic idealism, of course, is flawed, because it rests on the assumption that there are ideal types "out there." It is thoroughly incapable of seeing how types are socially constructed. This lack of reflexivity is all the more obvious in the ranking of races embedded in the great chain of being. While Platonic idealism set up the notion of ideal types, it is the idea of a "great chain of being" that provides an explicit ranking and worth.

The early Christian idea of a great chain of being arranges "all God's creatures" on rungs or stairs (Lovejoy 1936). The higher the rung one occupied, the closer one was to God, and the lower the rung, the further one was from God. As is made clear in drawing, Christian Europeans, the constructors of the great chain, occupied the top rungs, while other humans were further down the chain, typically placed between Europeans and the primate species.[2] Each type or species and each race had a fixed and unchanging place relative to God.

The preceding not withstanding, there was little officially sanctioned and scientific concern over differences in humans before 1492. This changed when Europeans began to develop trade routes and expand markets (Hannaford 1996), along with the development of North American slavery (Smedley 1999). After 1492, the idea of race became useful as a means of justifying European capitalist expansion.

The goal of the now developing science of human variation was to name and describe types and to then demonstrate the unique behavioral and biological characteristics of each type. The agreed upon start of this natural science, which was later to become anthropology, includes Buffon's *Histoire Naturelle* (1749) and Linnaeus's racial classification in the tenth edition of *Systema Naturae* (1758). For Linnaeus, race explained, or at least correlated with, systems of government and psychological characteristics. In addition to classifying a "monstrosus" species of homo with various subspecies types, and a wild man (Ferus) type of *Homo sapiens*, Linnaeus recognized four racial types: Americanus, Europaeus, Asiaticus, and Afer. According to Linnaeus (1758), Americanus is regulated by custom and paints himself with fine red lines; Asiaticus is haughty and covetous and governed by opinion; Afer is indolent, anoints himself with grease, and is governed by caprice; and Europaeus is gentile, acute, inventive, and governed by law. Unsurprisingly, Linnaeus was a European.

Following Buffon and Linneaus, other French, German, British, and American natural historians continued to tinker with racial classifications and to consider why variation existed. After the middle of the eighteenth century, race became a worldview and a paradigm for both scientists and politicians. It became a popularly recognized concept, so much so that race was often taken to be natural and real. It filtered into languages and etched itself on the minds of eighteenth- to twentieth-century Europeans (Hannaford 1996; Smedley 1999; Stepan 1982; Todorov 1993). The process by which a folk idea such as race becomes a scientific one and is then made to seem real is surely variable. However, it is clear that ideas that are useful to the ruling class (with control of legislation, access to and control over information, and so on) tend over time to be accepted as certain, natural, and real (Fields 1990; Mills 1997).

There is disagreement over whether race is any less typological today than it was centuries ago. In a 1985 survey, half of all physical anthropologists agreed with the statement, "there are biological races within the species *Homo sapiens*" (Lieberman, Stevenson, and Reynolds 1989). Unlike in Buffon's time, typology has now fallen out of vogue. In fact, "typologist" is one of the worst epithets one can hurl at a physical anthropologist. Physical anthropologists who believe race is biologically real, therefore, claim that they are not typologists. George Gill, a forensic anthropologist, defends this position by arguing:

Confusion and ambiguity surrounding the controversial four letter word "race" was alleviated greatly by the early 1950s following the classic work of Coon, Garn and Birdsell (1950).... The underlying basis for the race concept (and racial taxonomy) has shifted entirely in recent decades from a typological to a population one. (Gill 1994, 163)

To the contrary, Coon, Garn, and Birdsell (1950) did not and could not transform race. They tried to graft race into a population framework, but the graft failed to take. Populations are dynamic and respond to evolutionary pressures at local levels. Races, on the other hand, are poorly defined and unchanging groupings. If races become populations, they no longer are races. In a review of Coon's *The Living Races of Man* (1965), a book in which Coon expands upon the prior study (Coon, Garn, and Birdsell 1950), Buettner-Janusch summarizes: "Typology, typology, typology, nothing but typology" (1966, 187).

The concept of race remains a typological and nonevolutionary concept. As well as race fit an idealist and typological worldview, it misfit Darwinian theory, in which variations accumulate and humans change over time and place. No matter how race is recast, it cannot shake its typological core and accommodate the fluidity of human variation. To paraphrase the paleontologist G. G. Simpson, all ideas about humanity before 1859—not least, type and race—are invalid.

Surprisingly, then, many continue to use race despite the fact that the notion of fixed, ideal types should logically have been replaced well over a hundred years ago with the advent of Darwinism and the ascension of evolutionary theory in biology and anthropology. I suggest that the concept survives where it does not fit either fact or theory, because: (1) it became reified by constant use, (2) it became conflated with human variation, and (3) it was and is politically useful.

Most Traits Are Continuous, Varying, and Clinally Distributed.

Human variation tends to be gradual, with only subtle differences between nearby groups. The more distant two groups are from each other, the greater the difference will be between them. In contrast, the idea of race implies that variation is discontinuous and sharp between racial groups, and inconsequential within a race. Human variation, however, is not like that.

A biological variable or trait is a measurable quality or quantity. It can be most anything one might think of, such as the color of one's eyes, the blood group one belongs to, or the rate at which one loses hair with age. In addition to traits possessed by individuals, traits can also define and characterize groups. On average, females are shorter than are males and African Americans have darker skin than do whites. The frequency of the Duffy Fy^a allele is 9.5 in Guyana and 7.8 among the Bantu of the Republic of South Africa (Molnar 1992). The rate of low birth weight in Illinois in the 1990s was 13.2 percent among infants born to African American women and 4.3 percent among infants born to white women (David and Collins 1997).

A potential problem with moving from individual-level traits to group-level traits may occur when the group's statistics (average, frequencies, etc.) are used to characterize individuals. In the preceding examples, knowing that the Duffy Fy^a allele is more common in Guyana than among the Bantu does not ascertain whether a specific individual actually has the allele. Each person needs to be tested individually. Similarly, females are shorter than males, but this does not mean that every female is short or that every male is tall.

Furthermore, if groups are defined on the basis of biological trait frequencies, then there are typically no clear borders where one group begins and another ends. Say, for example, we decide to use height to define groups. If we determined that there were to be two groups, where would we make the division between tall and short people? The "cutoff" point is arbitrary and often chosen for convenience. Those near the cutoff are more like each other than they are like others in their group.

Similarly, it is impossible to fix boundaries between races. There are no natural gaps. The division point is arbitrary and up to the whim of the classifier. The continent from which one originates, no less than one's race, is meaningless.

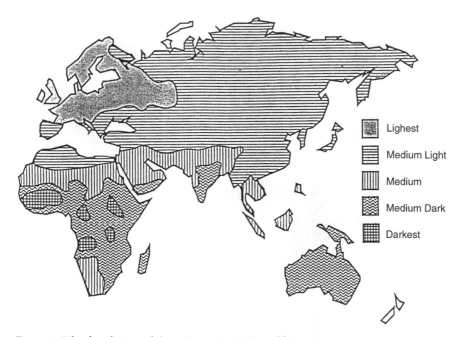

Figure 1. The distribution of skin color in the "old world" circa 1492. Note that variation is mostly on a north-to-south gradient.

The classification of a continuous trait such as skin color into discrete units diminishes the complexity of human variation, and, as a result, how well we can understand that variation. With continuous variation central tendencies become nearly meaningless; types are nonpredictive. Individuals near the race/type borders are more like individuals just over the border, though classified differently, than they are like most individuals in their race/type. This form of continuous variation is called clinal variation.

The geographic distribution of skin color varies clinally mainly on a north-south gradient (Figure 1). Africa and Asia are home to both light- and dark-skinned people. Taking into account the pattern of variation is the first step to understanding the cause of skin color variation. Might it be related to the protection dark skin affords against skin cancer or the greater ability of light-colored skin to facilitate the synthesis of vitamin D? These are the types of questions that can be asked when variation is not reduced to race.

The frequency of the sickle cell gene peaks in West Africa and gradually decreases as one moves away from West Africa (Angola) or another epicenter such as Northeast Arabia (figure 2).

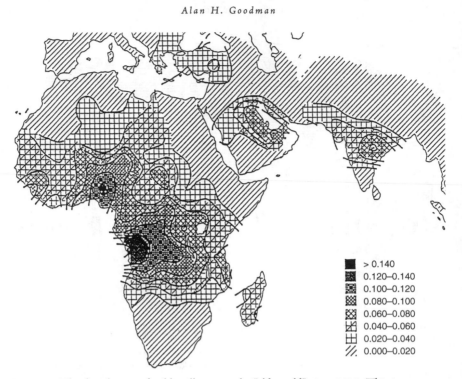

Figure 2. The distribution of sickle cell trait in the "old world" circa 1492. This is an example of clinal variation.

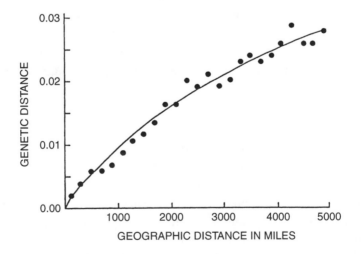

Figure 3. A plot of the relationship between genetic distance and geographic distance (from Templeton 1998).

Clinal variation, or variation that accumulates with distance, is the rule. Templeton (1998) has recently redrawn a graph of human genetic distance versus geographic distance (figure 3). Geographic distance almost totally explains genetic distance. In 1962 Frank Livingstone pointed out that "there are no races, only clines." Moreover, as will be reinforced in the following, thinking racially prevents one from understanding how variation evolved and why it might be significant.

Most Trait Pairs Are Nonconcordant.

The racial approach to human variation rests on the assumption that two or more traits tend to vary together in a consistent way. The importance of this, if it were true, is that one trait could explain or predict another. The truth, however, is exactly the opposite.

A few traits, the exceptions, are concordant. Height is concordant with leg length, and slightly less strongly with weight. In a similar way, skin color is concordant with hair and eye color, and less so with hair texture. However, knowing skin color provides no insight into height or any other anthropometric attribute. There is no reason it should. This is one reason why it might be said, "race is skin deep."

To get a feel for nonconcordance, imagine a layer cake in which each layer is a trait (figure 4). The top layer is skin color and the third layer is ear length. Also imagine that geographical groups from around the world occupy each place in the layer. Placing a pin through them would link up the values for a specific group for each trait as the pin passes through the layer. Alternatively, one could imagine that individuals are represented, and passing the pin through a specific spot would provide the individual's values for each trait. If the layer cake exemplifies human variation, then the color of the top layer will not give any insight into the color (or trait distribution) in the deeper layers. Knowing skin color tells us nothing of deeper traits.

Within-Group Variation Is Much Greater than Among-Group Variation.

There is no agreed upon test for whether humans are in any reasonable way groupable into subspecies or races. However, the clearest test is by statistical apportionment of variation within races versus among races. This test assesses the proportion of variation that is statistically explained by race. Humans fail the test.

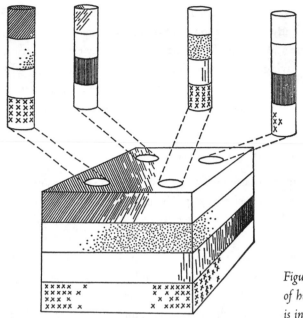

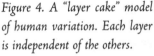

Figure 4. A "layer cake" model of human variation. Each layer is independent of the others.

The notion of subspecies has been under intellectual attack in zoology since the 1950s (Wilson and Brown 1953). At this time it was realized that many local varieties simply had *not* been reproductively isolated for long enough to have evolved and differentiated to a consequential degree. If they did not separately evolve, then most of the variation within the species would be distributed rather uniformly over the species, so that small groups of individuals would contain most of the species variation. If, on the other hand, they had been isolated for some time, then some of the variation would concentrate in the groups. The same small group of individuals would explain a smaller proportion of the species variation.

In thinking about humanity's past, we are faced with the realization that we are a relatively young species. In addition, we have a long generation time, and we seem to have encountered few major barriers that would cause reproductive isolation. It would therefore seem that there should not be very much variation among groups or so-called races. Although this model of small variation among races is not a common perception, it turns out to be true.

To think about the distribution of human variation, imagine a simple scenario: a trait that takes on two values—short or tall, type O blood or not type O blood. Green marbles represent one value and red marbles represent the other.

There are three races represented by three clear jars. On a species level there are 50 percent green and 50 percent red marbles. Thinking about human variation, should the green and red marbles go into each race jar in the 50 percent proportion, or in some very different proportion, perhaps as much as 100 percent green marbles in one race jar and 100 percent red marbles in another? The former might be called a state of extreme "racelessness" and the latter a state of extreme "raceness." Interestingly, most students think of human variation as more like the latter. Yet, in reality, human variation is more like the former.

In a classic article published in 1972, Richard Lewontin estimated the proportion of human variation that could be statistically explained by races. Lewontin took data on blood group polymorphisms (those who have two or more alleles in high frequency, such as blood types A, B, AB, and O) and tested how the blood groups were distributed and how much variation was explained at three levels:

+ by local group
+ within a race but among local groups
+ among races

The first level of variation is equivalent to the small group of individuals discussed previously. The second level is the additional variation that is found within races, which is equivalent to several small chunks combining to form one large chunk. Finally, the last level is what is actually explained by race. Lewontin found that on average 85.4 percent of variation was explained at the first level, while only 6.3 percent of variation was explained by purported race (Lewontin 1972). In other words, the green and red marbles are nearly equally distributed. On average, two individuals of the same purported race are only marginally more genetically alike than any two individuals chosen at random.

Because of nonconcordance and within-group variation, race has little explanatory power. If we know a person's race, we know little more about that person. Race tells us little about the processes governing human variation, and its predictive value for individual traits is trivial. Finally, the roughly 6 percent of biological variation that is statistically explained by race is better explained by geographic proximity or clines (figure 3). Because genetic variation simply increases with geographic distance, race is not even necessary to explain this small fraction of variation. Race is totally replaceable.

Although there is no single test for subspecies or racial structure, the one most often agreed upon builds off of Lewontin's analysis of the apportionment of variation. If the relative degree of variation among races is great compared to the variation within a single race, then one might suggest that subspecies or races are meaningful in at least an evolutionary perspective. On the other hand, if the relative degree of variation among races is small compared to the variation within a single race, then races are less meaningful. The F_{st} of Wright (1969) is essentially the proportion of variation explained between races versus the proportion explained within race.

In the nonhuman literature the standard quantitative threshold used to determine if there is a potential subspecies structure is an F_{st} of 0.25 to 0.30 or greater (Smith, Chiszar, and Montanucci 1997). From a larger set of data than Lewontin's, the human F_{st} has recently been calculated to be 0.156 (Barbujani et al. 1997). Humans thus fail the test for biological races.

To summarize to this point, human variation tends to be continuous and nonconcordant. The fact of continuous variation makes problematical any efforts to think an individual is like the average of his or her group. It also makes the dividing lines between races rather arbitrary. The fact of nonconcordant variation calls into question any effort to do more than explain a single trait based on that trait. We end up with circularities: skin color explains race and race explains skin color, but neither explains much else. In some senses, these two problems parallel and forecast the two practical ways that race is used: as an identification method, and as a predictor.

The fact that almost all variation is statistically found within local groups seems counterintuitive. We are socialized into keying on physical features that do vary and have come to signify different groups. Yet, below the skin we are much the same. As previously noted, we have not had time to differentiate and we are not reproductively isolated.

The Classification Is Not Stable across Space and Time.

The practice of classification of objects into groups is something we do regularly. Classification helps us to order and make sense of our world. Even when classification systems are imperfect, even when they skip complexities, they may still be useful. Hat size does not account for the shape of the head, but it is a useful place to start looking for a good fit. Without much thought we divide the entire variation in human morphology into a few sizes: small, medium, large, and sometimes extra small and extra large. With this great reduction of human morphological variability, almost everyone can find a sweater that fits well enough. The idea of social class is an abstraction; one might even say it is socially constructed. It is defined in different ways by different people, and it is certainly dynamic and unstable.

So why not think of races as a useful first effort at classification? Unfortunately, because of instabilities in racial classification, combined with the conflation of biology and culture, this analogy fails with terrible consequences when it is applied to human variation. With racial classification, division points are arbitrary and up to the whim of the classifier. Thus, an individual who is classified as "European" or "white" at one time and place may be classified as "mixed," "Hindu," "quadroon," "octoroon," "colored," "mulatto," "mestizo," or "black" at another time and place (Lee 1993). Jews were considered to be a separate race (or even many racial types) before World War II, but they came to be classified as white after World War II (Sacks 1998). Similar "whitening" happened for the Irish and Southern Europeans (Jacobson 1998). Fish (1995) describes how the race of his wife and daughter changes when they fly from the United States to Brazil. Their biologies do not change, but the cultural classification system does.

Changing racial classification is fine if one has a good sense of how it is changing. If one manufacturer's size small is too tight, you try a size medium. However, because sciences such as medicine are based on repeatability, changing classifications are often disastrous. Would you want your physician to base a critical decision about your treatment on his understanding of a racial group in Brazil or based on races from the late 1800s? As I will detail in the following, the TUMS® label is exactly this type of mistake.

Research into the identification of an individual's race based on his or her skull shape provides an example of the difficulties inherent in any system of racial classification.. A common problem in forensic science is identification of homicide victims, so much research has gone into the effort to enable scientists to determine race based on measurements taken from skulls. Imagine a large group of skulls from individuals who have been socially defined as white, black, and Native American. Giles and Elliot (1962) showed that one could separate about 85 percent of the skulls into the appropriate racial groups by applying a statistical procedure called discriminant function to a series of skull measurements. In this case, all the skulls were from the previous century or older.

However, for this procedure of "racing skulls" to have some utility it would seem that a high percentage of correct classification would also be necessary when this procedure is applied to skulls today. When the method of Giles and Elliot was applied to contemporary skulls of known race—that is, when it was re-tested—

the percentage of skulls that were correctly classified was reduced to around one in three. The procedure is therefore no better than random. The reasons for this seem obvious enough: (1) there is great variation within race and little variation among races, and (2) the race groups that Giles and Elliot's skulls came from no longer exist (Goodman 1997).

If you do not believe that races change—not just by social definition, but in their biology, too—then consider the following. Steve Ousley reports in the introduction to a computer program (FORDISC-2) that a discriminant function formula can separate the skulls of U.S. white males born between 1840 and 1890 from those born between 1930 and 1980 with 88-96 percent accuracy.

The point is that racial classification and the perceptions of racial boundaries are thoroughly fluid. Because of this fluidity one can never be certain how well a racial generalization will apply.

The Conflation of Biology and Lived Experience.

When pronouncements are made about racial variation in health or some other trait, there is typically little discussion of the underlying source of the variation. Is a racial difference in hypertension due to genetic differences among races, or does such a difference have a more transient association with race, perhaps being due to differences in living conditions? If the former is true, then it will lead to research and practice in one direction. If the latter is true, it will lead in an entirely different direction. Leaving race as a proxy variable for either lived experience or genetics makes extremely problematical any effort to confidently act on the data.

The conflation of biology and lived experience is a double leap of scientific faith (Goodman 1997; 2000). The first leap of faith is in assuming that a difference between two groups is genetic without controlling for environmental factors and lived experience. The second leap is in assuming that a genetic difference falls along racial lines. The first leap might be called geneticization (Lippman 1991). We live in an age in which many things are thought to be genetic in their origins, but this is often an underexamined theory. The second leap might be called the geneticization of race. Even if there are race differences, and even if an outcome is genetically determined, there is still no reason to leap to the conclusion that race is a proxy for genetics or that the genes break along socially constructed and fluid racial lines.

If a disease turns out to be genetic, then we are still faced with the assumption that races are genetically distinct. However, the preceding discussion on the apportionment of variation has made it clear that this is not so. If a disease is in large part nongenetic, then this implies that race is only a transitional covariate of a nonracial cause. As the conditions of life, such as access to medical care, diet, and exposure to lead in childhood change, the strength of the racial generalizations change.

A recent example of this type of double leap of scientific faith comes from a recent article on race and birth weight (David and Collins 1997). It is widely believed that a large portion of the variation in mean birth weight between black and white babies in the United States is genetic. Thus, the relationship of *in utero* conditions to low birth weight in blacks has been largely neglected in the research. In addition to presenting and comparing the birth weights of babies born to U.S.–born white and black women in Illinois between 1980 and 1995, David and Collins (1997) also presented the birth weights of babies born to African-born women during that timespan. If differences in birth weight between the races are due to genetics, then birth weights of babies born to African-born women should be near the birth weights of babies born to U.S.–born black women. If one invokes an additive model of human variation, then the birth weights of babies born to African American women would be expected to be between the African and U.S. white means, and approximately 25 percent of the way from the African mean and 75 percent from the white mean.[3]

The results of the study, however, are nothing like this. The mean birth weight of the babies born to U.S. white women was 3,446 grams, and that of the babies born to African women was 3,333 grams. Babies born to U.S.–born black women had an average birth weight of only 3,089 grams, much lower than either of the other groups. The explanation for this distribution of birth weights is, therefore, certainly not genetics. Seemingly, the place to look is in diet, health care, and other socioeconomic conditions that are known to affect *in utero* conditions. Such an example clearly shows how erroneous it can be to make scientific generalizations based on racial classifications.

To summarize, these six points show that human biological variation is real, but that racial classification is not a useful way to think about it. Race and racism are real, and so is human variation. However, taking race to be a determinant of human biological variation simply does not fit the facts. Such an assumption holds back scientific work, and may even cause harm.

Race and Osteoporosis:
An Everyday Misuse of Race

In the nineteenth and early twentieth centuries, the idea was pervasive that certain races got certain diseases. Whites, for example, got cancer, a disease of civilization.[4] This paradigm of racially distinct diseases has slowly been updated in epidemiological discourse by the idea that race is a disease risk factor. Work on osteoporosis and bone loss provides an example. Osteoporosis is an age-related disorder characterized by decreased bone mass and increased susceptibility to fractures. By 1980 it was estimated that osteoporosis affected fifteen to twenty million people in the United States and that it was the underlying cause of about 1.3 million fractures per year (Wasserman and Barzel 1987). Osteoporosis is a serious health problem, and better understanding of its etiology is obviously critical for improved screening, treatment, and prevention.

Since at least the nineteenth-century, white scientists have thought that blacks have thicker bones than whites. In his "Introduction to Anthropology" Dr. Theodor Waitz wrote:"The skeleton of the Negro is heavier, the bones thicker. . . . This is especially the case with regard to the skull, which is hard and unusually thick, so that in fighting, Negroes, men and women, butt each other like rams without exhibiting much sensibility" (1863, 93).

Over a century later, a review of the etiology of osteoporosis listed race as the third risk factor, after age and sex and before heredity, physical activity, and dietary factors (Wasserman and Barzel 1987). The section on race begins with the declarative sentence:"It is a well-known fact that blacks do not suffer from osteoporosis" (1987, 285). That"fact" is backed up by reference to one and only one study: a seminal paper by Mildred Trotter, G. E. Bowman, and R. R. Paterson (1960) on bone density changes by age, sex, and race. Given that physicians routinely vary osteoporosis treatment decisions based on their perceptions of the race of their patients, and now given that TUMS® excludes black women from its label, it is worth ensuring that the study of Trotter and colleagues (1960) proves the point that"blacks do not suffer from osteoporosis."

Deconstructing the Trotter Study

Trotter, Bowman, and Paterson (1960) measured the bones of eighty cadavers from Washington University, selected to provide twenty black males, twenty black females, twenty white males, and twenty white females. Individuals' ages at death ranged from twenty-five to one hundred years, and the mean group ages at death varied from 59.6 in black males to 67.2 in white females. The authors do not provide a description of the method of selecting cadavers or matching their race-sex samples for causes of death, socioeconomic status, diet, or other known risk factors. The dried bones were weighed and their volumes estimated by displacement of millet seed. Ten different bones were studied on each cadaver.

The authors conclude that cervical, thoracic, and lumbar vertebra, sacra, humeri, and ulnae are heavier in blacks than in whites. They did not find a significant racial difference for radii, tibiae, ribs, and femora. The latter bone is particularly noteworthy because femoral neck fractures are one of the most serious effects of osteoporosis. Finally, Trotter and colleagues note that the decline in bone density with age, *"occurred at approximately the same rate"* in each *sex-race group* (57, emphasis added). Race or sex differences, where they did occur, were due to the fact that one group started with greater mean density. For example, bone density of black males at seventy years may be equal to or less than that of white males at sixty years of age. The clinical significance, in my opinion, is that different sex-race groups cross a threshold of bone density at different mean ages. On average, blacks start with more bone, but they suffer bone loss at much the same rate as do whites.

Remember for a moment that races do not get diseases; individuals do. It is of more than theoretical importance to know if a proclamation of group protection pertains to individuals. Related to this, in a follow-up study, Trotter and Hixon (1973) provide scatterplots of the original data of Trotter, Bowman, and Paterson (1960) on individual bone densities by age, sex, and race. The scatterplots are instructive because they provide a visual sense of the degree of variation within race-sex groups, and of how well individuals conform to the central tendency of the group. Figure 5 is a copy of the scatterplot of bone densities for the radius. White males are represented by open circles, white females by open squares, black males by black dots, and black females by black squares. This scatterplot clearly illustrates an overall trend of declining bone densities with age. Far less clear is a racial difference in the rate of decline in density with age. In fact, of the six lowest bone density points, one represents a black female and the remaining five represent black males.

What, then, is the basis for the "well-known fact that blacks do not suffer from osteoporosis" (Wasserman and Barzel 1987, 285)? What seems to have occurred was a double leap of faith. First, a condition (cysts, osteoporosis) was determined to be genetic (although environment was not adequately examined).

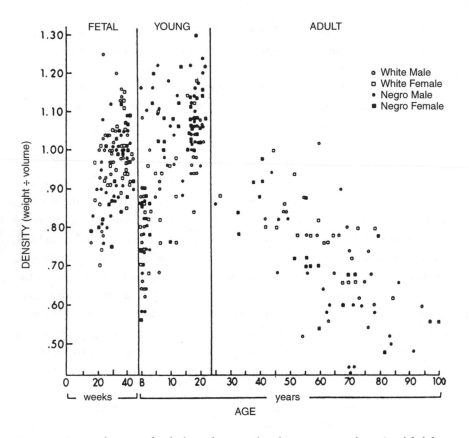

Figure 5. Scatter diagram of radii bone density values by race, sex, and age (modified from Trotter and Hixon 1973, 12, fig. 2).

Could the differences in bone density of the subjects have been due to diet or other known risk factors, such as exposure to sunlight and activity patterns? In the absence of such data there was an assumption of genetic etiology. Then, it was assumed that anything that was genetic was panracial, a characteristic of all members of the racial-type.

Although Wasserman and Barzel (1987) do not cite them, other studies have also found "racial differences" in bone density and fracture rates. However, even if there were a million studies showing such a difference, it would still not follow from this that blacks are immune to osteoporosis, that they should not be given advice and treatment to help prevent or slow bone loss, or that they should not be encouraged to take TUMS®. Blacks do suffer from age-related bone loss, they do suffer from bone breaks due to bone loss, and they do suffer the consequences of medical neglect.

Conclusions

In a *Newsweek* cover story, Sharon Begley recently declared that when it comes to a critique of race, "scientists got there first" (1995, 67). Ashley Montagu (1942) made clear over a half century ago that race is not a reality; it is not a thing. Rather, it is the phlogiston of our time. We tend to think of it as a reality because constant use and lack of questioning of its underlying reality have reified it. Race is a way of constructing and thinking about human variability, but it is a poor and outdated construct.

Definitions of race are varied and protean. For example, some classifications are based on geographic origin (with some assumed biological concordance), others are based on clusters of traits, and others still are based on bureaucratic and social definitions (again, with an assumption of a biological basis). There is no agreed upon definition (Brace 1982). Furthermore, all efforts at a scientific (widely accepted, reliable) definition have failed. Brace captures the assumptive and protean nature of race when he comments on racialist research:

> The connection between the biology discussed and the races named at the end is never clearly spelled out, and in fact the attentive reader cannot discover, from the information presented, just how the racial classification was constructed— other than the fact that this just seems to be the way anthropologists have always done things. (Brace 1982, 21)

With so many differences in definition it is not surprising that there is also no agreement on the names and numbers of races. The inability to define race, to agree on how many there are, or to agree upon what biological criteria make a race, shows that this concept is slippery at best, making for problematic politics and biology.

Despite efforts to reinvent it, race remains a typological concept that has little use as an explanatory variable. Race and adaptation do not fit well together. Adaptations occur on the scale of individuals and local groups, responding to specific, local environmental conditions, and the responses are mostly nongenetic. Human variation is far more complex and intricately varietal than race allows for, and certainly does not obey racial boundaries. Race in epidemiological studies should be considered scientific malpractice. It is a form of ideological iatrogenesis.

Unfortunately, the same flawed logic that is inherent to racial studies of intelligence and behavior also applies to racial studies of less politicized traits, such as susceptibility to osteoporosis. If one considers the countless, everyday places where race is used inappropriately, then one can get a sense of the hidden harms of thinking race and human variation are one and the same. Thus, I do not call for an end to race. Race is very real, but it is not biology. Realizing this makes clear some research challenges: studies of human variation free of a racial model, studies of social differences in racial thinking and racial formation, and studies of the consequences of racism on health and other outcomes.

ACKNOWLEDGMENTS

Thanks to Debra Martin (Hampshire College) for bringing to our attention the racial assumption in writing on osteoporosis, and to Michelle Murrain (Hampshire College), who alerted me to the TUMS® label. Special thanks to Curtis Stokes for providing the best of forums in which to share ideas about the significance of race. Parts of this paper are a revision of Goodman (1997).

NOTES

1. My focus here is not on the clearly racist science that all too often continues. For example, J. Philippe Rushton, the contemporary devotee of esoteric racial measurements, claims that black males produce more testosterone and have larger genitalia than do whites (1994). Rushton uses this fact to explain a diversity of phenomena, from the AIDS epidemic to purported intelligence differences among races. In Rushton's pop evolution, races put their energies into either sexuality or intelligence—that is, big brains or big penises. Pseudoscientific works such as this need to be challenged, and many have done so. Fewer have focused on the more subtle uses of race.

2. Although the great chain of being is no longer a common motif, the idea of a ranking of progress or evolution remains. In nearly all trees of racial evolution published to this date, "Caucasians" are placed on the highest branches, most separated from apes, while non-Caucasians are placed closer to the apes and sometimes on lower branches (see discussion in Wolpoff and Caspari 1997)

3. That Europeans contributed to the gene pool of African Americans (perhaps contributing as much as 25 percent of the African American gene pool) is widely acknowledged in the genetics literature (Kittles and Royal 1999). The recent finding that Thomas Jefferson fathered a child of a slave, Sally Hemming, is one example of the permeability of racial borders (Foster et al. 1998).

4. This same essentialist thinking is what provided the ideological basis for the infamous Tuskegee syphilis study of 1932. The belief was that the course of syphilis would be different in blacks than in whites, that syphilis might transfer to whites via sexual relations, and that an epidemic of syphilis in blacks might further show their inability to cope with civilization (Brandt 1978).

REFERENCES

Barbujani, G., A. Magagni, E. Minch, and L. L. Cavalli-Sforza. 1997. An apportionment of human DNA diversity. *Proceedings of the National Academy of Science* 94:4516–19.

Begley, Sharon. 1995. Three is not enough. *Newsweek*, 13 February, 67–69.

Brace, C. L. 1982. The roots of the race concept in American physical anthropology. In *A history of American physical anthropology, 1930–1980*, edited by F. Spenser. New York: Academic Press, 11–29.

Brandt, Allan M. 1978. Racism and research: The case of the Tuskegee syphilis study. *Hastings Center Reports* 8(6):21–29.

Buettner-Janush, J. 1966. Review of *The living races of man*, by Carleton Coon. *American Journal of Physical Anthropology* 25:182–88.

Buffon, Counte de. 1749. Varieties of the human species. In *Natural history, general and particular*, translated by William Smellie. London: T. Cadell and W. Davies.

Coon, Carleton S., Stanley Garn, and Joseph Birdsell. 1950. *Races: A study in the problem of race formation in man*. Springfield, Ill.: Charles C. Thomas.

Coon, Carleton (with Edward E. Hunt). 1965. *The living races of man*. New York: Alfred A. Knopf.

David, R. J., and J. W. Collins. 1997. Differing birth weight among infants of U.S.–born blacks, African-born blacks, and U.S.–born whites. *New England Journal of Medicine* 337:1209–14.

Fields, Barbara J. 1990. Slavery, race, and ideology in the United States of America. *New Left Review*, 95–118.

Fish, Jefferson. 1995. Mixed blood. *Psychology Today* (Nov./Dec.): 61, 76, 80.

Foster, E. A., M. Jobling, P. Taylor, P. Donnelly, P. de Kniff, R. Mieremet, T. Zerjal, and C. Tyler-Smith. 1998. Jefferson fathered slave's last child. *Nature* 396:27–28.

Giles, E., and O. Elliot. 1962. Race identification from cranial measurements. *Journal of Forensic Sciences* 7:247–57.

Gill, George W. 1994. A forensic anthropologist's view of the race concept. Abstract, American Academy of Forensic Sciences, 46th Annual Meetings, pp. 163.

Goodman, Alan. 1997. Bred in the bone? *The Sciences* (March/April): 20–25.

———. 2000. Why genes don't count (for racial differences in health). *American Journal of Public Health* 90(11):1699–1702.

Hannaford, I. 1996. *Race: The history of an idea in the West.* Washington, D.C.: Woodrow Wilson Center Press.

Jacobson, Mathew. 1998. *Whiteness of a different color.* Cambridge: Harvard University Press.

Kittles, R., and C. Royal. 1999. Genetic variation and affinities of African Americans: Implications for disease gene mapping. Paper presented at Wenner Gren International Symposium no. 124, 11–19 June, Teresopolis, Brazil.

Lee, S. M. 1993. Racial classifications in the U.S. census: 1890–1990. *Ethnicity and Racial Studies* 16(1): 75–94.

Lewontin, R. C. 1972. The apportionment of human diversity. *Evolutionalry Biology* 6:381–98.

Lieberman, Leonard, B. W. Stevenson, and Larry T. Reynolds. 1989. Race and anthropology: A core concept without consensus. *Anthropology and Education Quarterly* 20:67–73.

Linnaeus, C. 1758. *Systema naturae.* 10th ed. Stockholm: Laurentii Salvii.

Lippman, A. 1991. Prenatal genetic testing and screening: Constructing needs and reinforcing inequalities. *American Journal of Law and Medicine* 17(1–2):15–50.

Lovejoy, A. O. 1936. *The great chain of being.* Cambridge: Harvard University Press.

Mills, C. 1997. *The racial contract.* Ithaca, N.Y.: Cornell University Press.

Molnar, S. 1992. *Human variation: Races, types, and ethnic groups.* 3d ed. Englewood Cliffs, N.J.: Prentice Hall.

Montagu, Ashley. 1942. *Man's most dangerous myth: The fallacy of race.* New York: Columbia University Press.

Rushton, J. Phillipe. 1994. *Race, evolution and behavior.* New Brunswick, N.J.: Transactions.

Sacks, Karen. 1998. *How Jews became white folks.* New Brunswick, N.J.: Rutgers University Press.

Smedley, Audrey. 1999. *Race in North America.* 2d ed. Boulder, Colo.: Westview Press.

Smith, H. M., D. Chiszar, and R. R. Montanucci. 1997. Subspecies and classification. *Herpetological Review* 28:13–16.

Stepan, N. 1982. *The idea of race in science: Great Britain 1800–1960.* London: Macmillan.

Templeton, A. R. 1998. Human races: A genetic and evolutionary perspective. *American Anthropologist* 100(3):632–50.

Todorov, T. 1993. *On human diversity.* Cambridge: Harvard University Press.

Trotter, Mildred, G. E. Bowman, and R. R. Paterson. 1960. Densities of bones of white and Negro skeletons. *Journal of Bone and Joint Surgery* 42:50–58.

Trotter, Mildred, and Barbara B. Hixon. 1973. Sequential changes in weight, density, and percent ash weight of human skeletons from an early fetal period through old age. *Anatomical Record* 179:1–18.

Waitz, Theodor. 1863. *Introduction to anthropology*. London: Longman, Green, Longman and Roberts.

Wasserman, S. H. S., and U. S. Barzel. 1987. Osteoporosis: The state of the art in 1987: A review. *Seminars in Nuclear Medicine* 4:283–92.

Wilson, E. O., and W. L. Brown. 1953. The subspecies concept and its taxonomic applications. *Systematic Zoology* 2:97–111.

Wolpoff, M., and R. Caspari. 1997. *Race and human evolution*. New York: Simon and Schuster.

Wright, S. 1969. *Evolution and the genetics of populations, volume 2. The theory of gene frequencies*. Chicago: University of Chicago Press.

3

Different Forms of Mixed Race: Microdiversity and Destabilization

Naomi Zack

Introduction

I am going to focus on two claims about mixed race in this essay: First, that the existence of individuals of mixed race is an important practical problem for the folk idea of race; and second, that mixed-race identities ought to be recognized. Before developing these claims, it may be useful to recall how race itself is biologically unreal.

The folk idea of race, which still prevails in our culture, is accepted as a foundation for both racism and remedies against racism. This is the idea that race is a biological reality of human difference that can be studied by scientists. Everyone is presumed to belong to one—and only one—of three or four races, except for small numbers of people who may be "mixed." While racial mixture no longer represents the egregious social taboo it once did, it still connotes deviance in conventional terms, and inauthenticity in traditions of liberation.

However, race itself is unreal as a physical substratum of difference. There is no reliable genetic basis for any racial group. All observable traits associated with physical race, such as skin color, hair texture, and bone structure, are inherited, but they are not all uniformly inherited by every member of any one racial group.

There is greater variation within each racial group for such traits than between any two groups (Appiah 1996, 1997). Recent DNA analyses have failed to confirm sufficient statistical differences in human hereditary material to correspond to social racial difference: When variations in mitochondrial DNA (inherited from mothers), genetic material from Y chromosomes (inherited from fathers), and nuclear DNA (inherited from both parents) are correlated with the main racial groups recognized in society, the result is that only 6 percent of the variations can be attributed to socially designated racial differences. This is less than the percentage necessary to posit the existence of races in other species, and it is 6 percent of the 0.2 percent of human genetic material that varies within the species. The plausible conclusion in terms of human biology is that all humans are part of the same evolutionary lineage, that there is but one human race (Angier 2000; American Anthropological Association, 1998).

As general characteristics, blackness, whiteness, Asianess, and Indianess are no more than ideas that were projected onto groups, based on the presumed geographical origins of their ancestors, or on selected differences in physical appearance. Geographical origins of ancestors do not in themselves explain racial differences in descendants. Most human groups have interbred with other groups, so that isolated breeding populations are the exception rather than the rule. There are few, if any, groups today whose members are all descendants of inhabitants living in the same location during a prehistoric time period.

Caste systems, enforced breeding segregation based on ideas of racial difference, and other breeding taboos have confined selected hereditary traits of appearance to some groups. Yet the traits thus selected have been arbitrary, and are therefore only contingently, and often metaphorically, associated with designated racial identities. So-called skin-color difference, for instance, is actually variation in shade, which is rarely measured objectively. Height, by contrast, would be a far more exact measure of physical difference—and one clearly just as arbitrary.

What, then, is the basis for racial identification? In the modern period, race has been an invention of Europeans (and Americans), imposed on the inhabitants of colonized areas in ways that have economically benefited the group that identified itself as white. The histories of black chattel slavery, indigenous land appropriation, indigenous genocide, Jewish genocide, and the European and American appropriation of human labor and natural resources in non-European parts of the world provide the records of racialization in this socially constructed sense.

The Practical Problem of Mixed Race

Besides the contingent nature of racial typing that has been based on ancestral geography and physical appearance, the criteria for racial categorization have also been arbitrary. This is strikingly obvious in the American case of black and white difference. In the eighteenth and nineteenth centuries, a black person was defined as someone with black ancestors, in variable percentages. In some states it was one-fourth, others one-eighth or one-sixteenth. By 1900, the one-drop rule, which referred to the fiction of one drop of "black blood," became the law of the land. By the 1920 census, a black person was defined as someone with a black ancestor anywhere in their family history, and a white person as someone with no black ancestors (Davis 1991; Williamson 1980; Zack 1993). The existence of this definition attested to the extensive amount of white-black mixture that had begun in colonial days and accelerated during slavery. In 1900, about 20 percent of the black population was visibly mixed. Mid–twentieth century sociologists and anthropologists estimated that between 70 and 90 percent of the black population had some white ancestry and that 5 percent of the white population had some black ancestry (Piper 1992; Blackburn 2000).

With the one-drop rule, the definitions of black and white were set up as logical contradictories. Black equaled at least one black ancestor; white equaled no black ancestors. Two logical contradictions cannot both be true and they cannot both be false. Thus, according to the American definitions for black and white, a person had to be either black or white, but could not be both black and white, or neither. However, mixed black and white people are both black and white, and Asians and Indians are neither black nor white. Indeed, the one-drop rule, with its focus on fantasies of white purity, has supported a false perception that American racial difference and racial problems concern only the white and black groups. Therefore, something is radically wrong with this one-drop rule, even as a stipulative definition.

The problems with black and white racial definitions are not merely theoretical. In practice, these definitions fail to allow for the existence of people who have known ancestry from more than one racial group. (As already noted, there has always been a visible mixed-race population, as well as nonapparent racial mixture, in the United States.) Interracial marriage was illegal throughout most of American history, particularly in the former slave-holding states. In 1967, the Supreme Court struck down all remaining antimiscegenation legislation. Between 1970 and 1990, the number of children in mixed-race families increased from five hundred thousand to two million (Spickard 1989; "White House adopts new racial categories" 1997).

Furthermore, since the 1970s an American mixed-race movement has gained voice and political momentum. Members of AMEA (American Multi-Ethnic Association) and Project RACE (Reclassify All Children Equally) have lobbied for mixed-race recognition on local and national levels. A recent accomplishment was the decision by the federal Office of Management and Budget (OMB) that beginning with the 2000 census, people will be allowed to check as many boxes for racial membership as apply to them, instead of just one box, as has been the case since 1920. ("White House adopts new racial categories" 1997). (As of this writing, it has been determined that the one-drop rule will continue to be used to determine the official racial identity of those who check both 'black' and something else on the 2000 census forms [Holmes 2000].) While the OMB ruling does not directly recognize the existence of mixed race, it does begin to recognize the racial identities of those who do not fit into the old system.

It bears emphasis, however, that mainstream recognition of mixed-race identities can amount to no more than a social parity for mixed-race individuals. Such parity merely allows those who are of mixed race to affirm distinctive racial identities, in the same ways that members of the old recognized groups have had the freedom to affirm their identities as white, black, Asian, or Native American. If there were such a thing as race, biologically, the histories of human migration and group interbreeding would entail that the majority of human beings were mixed race. The groups that are presently demanding recognition as mixed race tend to be minorities within nonwhite minorities, who are directly aware of the close ancestry of more than one main racial group. In the final analysis, however, insofar as there is no biological foundation for the three or four acknowledged races, neither is there a biological foundation for mixed-race groups. That is, if race is biologically unreal, than so is mixed race.

What is it exactly that needs to be recognized, in terms of the existence of mixed race? First, there is the following moral claim: People with parents of more than one race ought to be allowed to claim as much of their heredity as they want, and they should make this choice themselves rather than have it imposed on them (Root 1992, 1996; Zack, 1993, 1998b). The American cultural and legal tradition has supported and reinforced conventional social mores in matters of race. Situations and incidents of extreme cruelty and injustice have been corrected only after long periods of debate, civil disobedience, or violent objection. It is therefore difficult to construct either legal or moral grounds for mixed-race recognition, solely within the American context. The one exception within this context is the state of Hawaii, where mixed-race has traditionally been accepted (Davis 1995).

The Universal Declaration of Human Rights, issued by the United Nations, asserts that all individuals have rights to free association and that all have rights not to be treated differently because of racial difference. When mixed-race individuals are compelled to identify themselves in a way that obliterates part of the grounds on which they would identify—because others who are not mixed identify on such grounds—their rights to freedom of association are violated. Furthermore, when mixed-race individuals are denied racial identities of their choice, while those who are not mixed race are not so denied, mixed-race individuals are being discriminated against on the basis of race. There would be no violation of rights if racial identity had a factual biological foundation. Without such a foundation, all racial identity can be viewed as an issue of choice that ought to be relegated to the individuals whose identity is at stake.

One pragmatic objection to freedom for mixed-race identity affirmation is that the results might be complicated. Starting with just four main racial groups of black, white, Asian, and Indian, there are fifteen possibilities for mixed-race identity: black, white, Asian, and Indian—that is four; plus, all four combined, which equals five. Then, by twos: black/white, black/Asian, Asian/white, black/Indian, Indian/white and Indian/Asian, which brings the total to eleven; there are, in addition, black/white/Asian, black/white/Indian, Asian/white/Indian, and Asian/black/Indian. These identities can further vary depending on when in family history the mixture occurred and where the person lived (Jaimes 1995; Piper 1992; Root 1992, 1996; Wilson 1992; Zack 1998a). It should also be noted that some who identify as mixed might nonetheless reaffirm the one-drop rule (Azoulay 1997; Piper 1992).

Anyone who believes that such complexity in racial identities is a bad thing needs to justify that evaluation based on fundamental principles of freedom and equality that are taken for granted in contemporary pluralistic democracies. The fact that the American tradition does not embrace such racial complexity can provide no more than an argument of the form: This is how things have been done here, therefore, this is how things should be done here.

The objection to complexity in racial identities cannot be based on biological facts, because the science of biology does not support the folk racial divisions that the traditionalist might want to defend. Beyond this point, I think that there are two objections to the recognition of mixed-race identity that do have merit. The first objection usually comes from nonwhites who want to preserve traditional nonwhite identities on the grounds of established liberatory traditions. For instance, most African Americans have always been aware of a wide range of racial mixture in their own families and communities, but they have nonetheless created unified racial identities as a basis for liberation (Williamson 1980). Now that some progress has been made in the form of the civil rights legislation of the 1960s, voting redistricting, and affirmative action, some African Americans are concerned that a recognized mixed black-and-white group might make claims as a minority that would compete with black entitlements. There is no simple answer to this anxiety, except to point out that even if recognized as mixed, mixed-race people would still not have the same advantages as whites in American society. Competing claims of nonwhite groups could be addressed through coalitions in political contexts, and they could be negotiated in open fora in discursive contexts.

The second objection I'll consider is that traditional racial identities have consoled generations under conditions of injustice by providing a sense of belonging based on shared identity and historical oppression. In contrast to this kind of grounding, demands for complex mixed-race identity recognition sound brittle, alienating, and superficial. The answer to this objection requires a sharper examination of the structures of traditional racial identities. I think it can be shown that the normality of the devils we know is not as uniform or socially intelligible as one might think.

The rules for how one becomes a member of any of the four recognized racial groups in this country are all different: White identity is based on a family genealogy of absence of nonwhite ancestors. Black identity is based on the presence of black ancestors, presumably ultimately from Africa, and strictly speaking, only one is required. Asian identity derives from a number of ethnicities and foreign nationalities of kin, all of which sources are now subsumed under a category stipulated as Asian. Native American identity is based on the geographical location of ancestors and/or adherence to traditional Native American cultural practices.

Actually, Native American identity, as constructed by Native Americans, is not what EuroAmericans would recognize as racial at all. Consider the recent controversy over the remains of Kennewick man. "Kennewick Man" is the name given to a skeleton that was found in 1996 as a result of flooding of the Columbia River in Kennewick, Washington. Preliminary studies of the bones indicated a well-preserved middle-aged man who lived in that area more than nine thousand years ago. Of particular anthropological interest were measurements indicating that the skull had "caucasoid" characteristics. These characteristics are not the same as "caucasian" characteristics, which most anthropologists (correctly) now consider to be a modern, culturally determined racial construction. Nonetheless, anthropologists interpreted the caucasoid characteristics of Kennewick Man to mean that he had more in common with modern Europeans and some south Asians, such as the Ainu of Japan, than with Native Americans. There are a few other caucasoid skeletons of the same period as Kennewick Man, and thus far such finds have been used to support new speculations about early American history, for instance, that the ancestors of Native Americans were not present on this continent before Europeans were. Therefore, a number of academic anthropologists eagerly anticipated further tests of the Kennewick remains.

However, the Native American Graves Protection and Repatriation Act of 1990 and the Archeological Resources Protection Act of 1979 require that the government determine whether human remains found on federal land are Native American. If so, they must be returned to the Indian tribe that has a basis for claiming them. The Umatilla Indians, consisting of tribes from the Kennewick area in Oregon, Washington, and Idaho, claimed the Kennewick remains for reburial. (So did the Asatru Folk Assembly, who are practitioners of an Old Norse religion in California, but that is another subject.) The Army Corp of Engineers placed Kennewick Man in a secure vault pending a court decision. One of the parties in the case is a group of anthropologists acting independently of their academic institutions, who want to pursue hypotheses about caucasoids in early human migrations (Preston 1997; *Runestone* 1997, Minthorn 1997; Slayman 1997). However, the Umatillas have claimed that they already know all they need to know about Kennewick Man. This was how Armand Minthorn, speaking for the Umatillas, put it:

> If this individual is truly over 9,000 years old, that only substantiates our belief that he is Native American. From our oral histories, we know that our people have been part of this land since the beginning of time. We do not believe that our people migrated here from another continent, as the scientists do. We also do not agree with the notion that this individual is Caucasian. Scientists say that because the individual's head measurements do not match ours, he is not Native American. We believe that humans and animals change over time to adapt to their environment. And our elders have told us that Indian people did not always look the way we look today. (Minthorn 1997)

The EuroAmerican anthropologists assume that Native American identity must be based on empirical physical measurements. If the physical measurements conform to those of an abstract human biological type, or to a "race," then that settles the matter of identity. That is, the measurements in themselves would be inconclusive without a mediating idea of race. Race, in this sense, is an example of what the eighteenth-century philosopher George Berkeley criticized as *abstract general ideas*. (Berkeley 1982) An abstract general idea is assumed to refer to all members of a certain group, as entire entities. Man, for example is an abstract general idea, as might be your idea of a *Bic pen*. But, while Bic pens are referents of the abstract general idea of a Bic pen, because they are all the same, human beings are not referents of the abstract general idea "man," because they are not all the same in any quality to which the word "man" is supposed to refer. By contrast, the Indian idea of what EuroAmericans would call racial identity is not an abstract general idea at all, but a concrete historical one. According to the EuroAmerican anthropologists, it is a contingent fact exactly where on earth a person of a given race or racial type happens to be at any time in history. Thus, a caucasoid individual could have been in North America more than nine thousand years ago. But, according to Minthorn, speaking for the Umatillas, anyone who was in North America more than nine thousand years ago would have had to be a Native American, and if he were in the Columbia River area, he would have had to be a member of one of the tribes whose ancestral land that area is. Thus, it would seem that being a Native American is not something that can be abstracted from geography—or from history, for that matter.

The variations in the ways in which traditional, acknowledged racial identities are constructed suggest that racial membership in general is not a universal human form of connection. The notion that racial belonging is uniform is thus an illusion, like biological race. Perhaps the greatest resistance to the recognition of mixed race identity is based on a sense of the threat it poses to the old paradigm of biological race itself. Complex mixed-race identities, once allowed—whatever "allowed" can decently mean in the realm of race—will without question continue to proliferate. Some mixed-race individuals will not be sure about which aspects of their heredity they want to affirm; others will change their minds, probably more than once (Root 1996); and still others may opt out of racial identification altogether (Lawrence 1995). Such vacillation, in conjunction with growing awareness of the biological flimsiness of all racial categories, cannot but undermine the taxonomy of race as we know it. Given the human havoc and misery caused by that false taxonomy, I cannot believe that would be a bad thing.

REFERENCES

American Anthropological Association. 1998. AAA statement on race. *Anthropology Newsletter* 39(3):3.

Angier, Natalie. 2000. Do races differ? *New York Times*, 22 August, D1 and D6.

Appiah, K. Anthony. 1996. Race, culture, identity. In *Color conscious: The political morality of race*, edited by Naomi Zack and Amy Gutman. Princeton, N.J.: Princeton University Press.

———. 1997. 'But would that still be me?': Notes on gender, 'race' ethnicity as sources of identity. In *RACE/SEX: Their sameness, difference and interplay*, edited by Naomi Zack. New York: Routledge.

Azoulay, Karya Gibel. 1997. *Black, Jewish, and interracial*. Durham, N.C.: Duke University Press.

Berkeley, George. 1982. *A treatise concerning the principles of human knowledge*, edited by Kenneth Winkler. Indianapolis: Hackett Publishing Company.

Blackburn, Daniel G. 2000. Why race is not a biological concept. In *Race and racism in theory and practice*, edited by Berel Lang. Lanham, Md.: Rowman and Littlefield.

Davis, F. James. 1991. *Who is black?* University Park: Pennsylvania State University Press.

———. 1995. The Hawaiian alternative to the one-drop rule. In *American Mixed Race: The culture of microdiversity*, edited by Naomi Zack. Lanham, Md.: Roman and Littlefield.

Hannaford, I. 1996. *Race: The history of an idea in the West*. Baltimore: Johns Hopkins University Press.

Holmes, Steven A. 2000. New policy on census says those listed as white and minority well be counted as minority. *New York Times*, 11 March, A-9

Jaimes, M. Annette. 1995. Some kind of Indian. In *American mixed race: The culture of microdiversity*, edited by Naomi Zack. Lanham, Md.: Roman and Littlefield.

Lawrence, Cecile Ann. 1995. Racelessness. In *American mixed race: The culture of microdiversity*, edited by Naomi Zack. Lanham, Md.: Roman and Littlefield.

Minthorn, Armand. 1997. Human remains should be reburied. Position paper. Posted in its entirety at *http://www.ucinet.com/~umatribe/kennman.htm* and partially quoted in Preston (1997).

Piper, Adrian. 1992. Passing for white, passing for black. *Transitions* 58:4–58.

Preston, Douglas. 1997. The lost man. *The New Yorker* 16 June, 70–81.

Root, Maria P. P., ed. 1992. *Racially mixed people in America*. Newbury Park, Calif.: Sage Publications.

———. 1996. *The multiracial experience*. Newbury Park, Calif.: Sage Publications.

The Runestone. 1997. Summer issue, web posting: *http://www.runestone.org/km.html*.

Slayman, Andrew L. 1997. A battle over bones. *Archaeology* 50(1): *www.he.net/~archaeol/970/etc/specialreport.html*.

Spickard, Paul. 1989. *Mixed blood: Intermarriage and ethnic identity in twentieth-century America*. Madison: University of Wisconsin Press.

White house adopts new racial categories. 1997. *New York Times*, 29 October, A-1.

Williamson, Joel. 1980. *New people*. New York: Free Press.

Wilson, Terry. 1992. Blood quantum. In *Racially mixed people in America*, edited by Maria P. P. Root. Newbury Park, Calif.: Sage Publications.

Zack, Naomi. 1993. *Race and mixed race*. Philadelphia: Temple University Press.

———. 1996. Race and philosophic meaning. In *RACE/SEX: Their sameness, difference and interplay*, edited by Naomi Zack. New York, Routledge.

———. 1997. *RACE/SEX: Their sameness, difference and interplay*. New York: Routledge.

———. 1998a. *Thinking about race*. Belmont, Calif.: Wadsworth.

———. 1998b. Mixed black and white race and public policy. In *Race, class, gender and sexuality: The big questions*, edited by Naomi Zack, Laurie Shrage, and Crispin Sartwell. Malden, Mass.: Blackwell Publishers.

———, ed. 1995. *American mixed race: The culture of microdiversity*. Lanham, Md.: Roman and Littlefield.

4

Beyond Race? Ideological Color Blindness in the United States, Brazil, and South Africa

GEORGE M. FREDRICKSON

As we enter the twenty-first century, three nations with long histories of racial differentiation and color consciousness—the United States, Brazil, and South Africa—would appear to share a commitment to going beyond race and achieving an egalitarian society in which skin color no longer matters. In South Africa, the African National Congress has come to power under the banner of "nonracialism"; Brazil prides itself on its "racial democracy"; and in the United States the tide seems to have turned against race-based compensatory policies and toward "color-blind" constitutionalism. Superficially these ideologies of race transcendence are similar, and the abstract proposition that phenotype and ancestry should not affect rights or status in an egalitarian society is unchallengeable. Yet the relation to reality and the programmatic adequacy of each of these conceptions is debatable. There is good reason to pay critical attention to the role played by ideological color blindness in these societies, given their long histories of white advantage and black disadvantage. The denial of race may be a denial of those histories.

Comparative study of South Africa, the United States, and Brazil has noted major differences in historic patterns of race relations, but has also detected a recent convergence.[1] The end of legalized segregation in the American South and of apartheid in South Africa has brought these nations into line with Brazil as places where racial inequality is no longer sustained by law in an explicit way. The powerful and respectable in all these societies now claim to be opposed to racism and affirm that the policies they advocate are the best way to eliminate it (if, in fact, they concede that it still exists). Open espousals of white supremacy are limited to fringe groups like the Ku Klux Klan in the United States and the Afrikaner Resistance Movement in South Africa.

But what is "racism," and how can we be so sure that it has been eliminated or contained? Critics of the dominant or emerging theories of what constitutes racial equality are challenging the assumption that racism is present only when its proponents affirm the existence of innate biological differences among physically distinguishable population groups. Those who have uncovered a "new racism" also deny that state sanction and legal inequality are necessary to the maintenance of white supremacy. A broadened conception of racism draws attention to the ways that culture can serve as a surrogate for biology. According to the British sociologist and cultural critic Paul Gilroy, "where culture or subculture is defined as a fixed and impermeable quality of human life," the shift from genetics to culture is "a difference of degree rather than any fundamental divergence."[2] Racism based on reified and essentialized views of culture, often in the form of stereotypes about "national" or ethnic character, predated the scientific racism of the nineteenth century and the first half of the twentieth, and has survived its decline in cogency and respectability.[3] Even if group culture is regarded as changeable, the belief that some cultures are superior to others can offer outgroups a Hobson's choice between assimilation and subordination that denies their right to cultural self-determination. It is from this perspective that the antidote to racism is seen as some form of multiculturalism, rather than assimilation, amalgamation, or integration.[4]

Critics of the adequacy of official color blindness also point to the persistence of relatively subtle and illusive patterns of discrimination by individuals, organizations, and institutions that require race-conscious remedies. The recognition that unfairness may result from customary behaviors and procedures, even in the absence of conscious prejudice or bigotry, is central to the case for affirmative action—various forms of extra effort and special consideration that conflict with the notion that racial equality requires absolute color blindness in law and public policy. Debates about the meaning of racism and antiracism have occurred in all three countries with which we are concerned, but they have played out differently in each. The United States, Brazil, and South Africa have differing histories, cultural patterns, and racial and ethnic demographies. Hence the convergences, while undeniable and significant, should not be overstated. Similar ideologies and policies may have varying, even contrasting, meanings depending on the context. Looking at the meaning of race and racism in each case will reveal critical differences as well as similarities.

In his famous dissent in *Plessy v. Ferguson* (1896), the Supreme Court decision that gave legal sanction to racial segregation in the United States, Justice John Harlan affirmed that "Our constitution is color blind and neither knows nor tolerates classes among citizens," meaning that it does not permit the kind of invidious distinctions between whites and blacks that he believed were implicit in the Jim Crow laws being passed at that time in the southern states. In his view, these laws were "conceived in hostility to, and enacted for the purpose of humiliating, citizens of a particular race," and as such were "inconsistent not only with the equality of rights that pertains to citizenship but with the personal liberty enjoyed by every one within the United States."[5] The black struggle for equality that led to the Civil Rights Acts of 1964 and 1965 was viewed by many of its supporters as a campaign for the total separation of law and race. Equal access to public facilities and the ballot box meant that race should not be used, either overtly, as in the case of the Jim Crow laws, or implicitly, as in the case of suffrage restrictions, to prevent a class of citizens from exercising their constitutional rights.

Nevertheless, Martin Luther King Jr., the most prominent black civil rights leader, and Lyndon B. Johnson, the president who was responsible for getting the Civil Rights Acts of 1964 and 1965 through Congress, both understood that substantive equality required more than outlawing official racism. King's book *Why We Can't Wait*, published in 1964, and Johnson's 1965 speech at Howard University both argued that it is not yet a fair race when some of the contestants come to the starting line with injuries and disabilities resulting from centuries of slavery and state-enforced racial discrimination.[6] Out of a sense of the burdens imposed by a history of oppression on African Americans came the affirmative action programs requiring categorization by race and the setting of goals and timetables for the greater inclusion of blacks among those endowed with opportunities for social and economic mobility. "In order to get beyond racism," argued Supreme Court Justice Harry Blackmun in 1978, "we must first take account of race. There is no other way. And in order to treat some persons equally, we must treat them differently. We cannot—we dare not—let the Equal Protection Clause perpetuate racial supremacy."[7]

Recognizing race for the purpose of combating the legacy and persistence of racism has always been controversial, but affirmative action did not encounter substantial popular opposition until the 1990s. The Republican Party, which had previously supported most affirmative action policies and had even initiated some of them during the Nixon administration, was the principal fount of the assault. The decision of Republicans like Governor Pete Wilson of California to use "racial preferences" as a wedge issue against the Democrats has helped turn public opinion against affirmative action.

While this political opposition was emerging, the Supreme Court and other federal courts persisted in a trend that began in the late 1970s to limit the application of affirmative action and other race-conscious policies to circumstances that were defined more and more narrowly. First the Bakke decision of 1978 outlawed numerical quotas for admissions to higher education, but permitted race to be taken into account if the aim was a diverse student body rather than the rectification of past injustices. Then a series of decisions limited affirmative action or federal intervention in state and local election arrangements to cases where past discrimination could be clearly demonstrated. Finally, in the *Hopwood v. Texas* decision of 1996, a circuit court overruled Bakke and forbade the use of race as one criterion among many for university admission. If the Supreme Court sustains this principle, affirmative action in public higher education will be a thing of the past, and it may not even survive in private institutions.[8] More generally, any government action that makes explicit use of race, even as a means of overcoming disadvantage, is currently under the gun. The assault on affirmative action, which has achieved victory by popular referenda in California and Washington, is justified in one of two ways: either affirmative action has served its purposes and is no longer needed (because blacks no longer suffer from racial discrimination) or it was never justified in the first place because it violated the nonracial or color-blind character of America's law or basic principles.[9]

Both propositions are dubious. Innumerable books and studies, ranging from careful journalism to quantitative social science, document beyond the shadow of a doubt that African Americans are still disadvantaged when they seek opportunities or amenities comparable to those routinely enjoyed by whites. Racism, defined here simply as unfair treatment resulting from a perception of physical difference, is alive and well, and true equality of opportunity remains an elusive goal.[10]

It is also misleading to say that the Constitution is inherently a nonracial or color-blind document. Before the Reconstruction era, the Constitution sanctioned racial slavery and official discrimination against those defined as nonwhite. The Thirteenth, Fourteenth, and Fifteenth Amendments respectively outlawed slavery, extended citizenship to anyone born in the United States, and made it unlawful to deny the vote to anyone because of "race, color, or previous condition of servitude." Although the Thirteenth and Fourteenth Amendments, unlike the Fifteenth, made no mention of race, their primary purpose was to free blacks from racial slavery and provide them with the substantive rights of American citizenship. The specificity of the Fourteenth amendment was revealed in its exclusion from citizenship of Indians born in the United States but not taxed. The Fifteenth Amendment was explicitly targeted at blacks in ways that had unfortunate consequences; for the vote was later denied to blacks through the discriminatory application of seemingly nonracial qualifications. Yet the implicit or explicit focus on the citizenship rights of blacks in particular in the Reconstruction amendments— and, more importantly, the enforcement clauses that went with them—gave to Congress the power to pass legislation that goes beyond enunciating a general egalitarianism and addresses specific and practical obstacles to the attainment of equal rights for African Americans. In contrast to the Civil Rights Act of 1964, which extended its umbrella beyond African Americans to women and other minorities, the Voting Rights Act of 1965 and its reinforcement by subsequent legislation were more group-specific, and clearly sanctioned the recognition of racial demography and the history of black exclusion from the suffrage in determining whether the voting arrangements of states and localities gave substantive political equality to African Americans.[11]

Affirmative action, like careful scrutiny of electoral districts and procedures, is a way of taking account of race in order to combat racial discrimination and disadvantage. Two leading civil rights enforcers of the Kennedy-Johnson era, Attorney General Nicholas Katzenbach and Assistant Attorney General Burke Marshall, argued eloquently in *The New York Times Magazine* in February 1998 that affirmative action is well within the bounds of the Constitution. Here is their response to the argument that special consideration based on race violates the Fourteenth Amendment by discriminating against whites: "For racial bias to be a problem, it must be accompanied by power. Affirmative action programs are race-based not to show preference of one race over another but to resolve that problem."[12] In other words, one does not discriminate against an empowered majority when one gives a leg up to members of minority groups who have long been denied access to a fair share of power and opportunity. It is difficult to resist the conclusion that the current epidemic of constitutional color blindness in the United States provides camouflage for an insidious new racism that, if unchecked, will thwart further progress toward racial equality.

Unlike the United States and South Africa, Brazil does not have a history of segregation laws or officially mandated discriminatory practices. It is also evident that color lines have been less rigid, as reflected in a more tolerant attitude toward miscegenation and a greater fluidity of racial identity. Mulattos have been viewed as part white, rather than as simply black, and there has been the possibility of changing one's color classification and rising in the chromatic hierarchy—as crudely reflected in the claim that "money whitens." Hence wealth and education have turned some blacks (*pretos*) into browns (*pardos*) and some light browns (*morenos*) into whites (*brancos*).[13]

Yet there is another side to the Afro-Brazilian story that brings out the positive aspects of what happened to African Americans after emancipation. The abolition of slavery in Brazil in 1888 left the mass of ex-slaves without the kind of constitutional rights and protections authorized (if not made immune from judicial nullification) by the Reconstruction amendments in the United States. There was no legalized segregation, but there was also no Freedmen's Bureau and no effort to secure access to suffrage. A simple literacy requirement prevented most Afro-Brazilians from voting for several generations after emancipation. Recent studies show clearly that black and brown Brazilians have been, and remain to this day, severely disadvantaged relative to their white fellow citizens—in income, living conditions, educational attainment, access to employment, and political power.[14]

One especially telling indication of the denial of equal opportunity is the incredible disparity between the proportion of the total population that is of acknowledged African descent—about 45 percent—and their minuscule representation among university students—only 1 percent at the University of São Paulo, for example. Brazilian sociologists have calculated that whites have an 8.5 times better chance than blacks of ever becoming university students, and a 5 times better chance than browns. This compares with the 1.4 times advantage of Euro-Americans over African Americans.[15] One reason Brazil may seem less racially stratified than the United States or South Africa is that poverty is more obviously multiracial. According to the 1980 census, 91.6 percent of Afro-Brazilians were at or below the poverty line, but no less than 41 percent of those deemed poor on the basis of their earnings were classified as white.[16] Economic inequality and race do correlate strongly, but in Brazil it is more difficult than in South Africa or the United States to distinguish the effects of deliberate racial discrimination and oppression from the disparities produced by a dominant class's normal inclination to neglect the welfare of the poor and disfranchised, whatever color they happen to be.

The history of racial ideologies in Brazil is more variable and complicated than most observers have realized. As Thomas Skidmore has shown, scientific racism had a vogue in Brazil in the late nineteenth and early twentieth centuries that was reflected in immigration policies designed to attract Europeans and thus "whiten" the country.[17] The recently emancipated Afro-Brazilians were regarded as a superfluous and expendable population. Limitation of suffrage to the literate and a lack of provision for the education of the freed people made Afro-Brazilians as politically voiceless (and thus as weakly positioned to influence the distribution of public resources) as blacks in South Africa before 1994 or southern African Americans before 1965. The eugenics movement, with its advocacy of public policies aimed at "race improvement," spread to Brazil, but the sheer size of the black and brown population there encouraged deviation from the Anglo-American preference for "pure" races. Most Brazilian eugenists eventually concluded that a mixed race was more adaptable to the climate and conditions of their country than was a purely white one.[18]

Brazilian conceptions of race relations changed in the period between the 1920s and the 1940s, as European immigration declined and Afro-Brazilians received symbolic recognition as contributors to a distinctive Brazilian culture that synthesized Portuguese and West African ingredients. In the fertile imaginations of intellectuals like Gilberto Freyre, Brazil contrasted sharply with the United States because of its encouragement of the cultural cross-fertilization and even biological mixing of Europeans and Africans. Thus was born the myth of Brazil as a "racial democracy" free of North American-style prejudice and discrimination. Yet the literary and artistic celebration of black and brown Brazil did not lead to political and economic empowerment. For the most part, Brazilians of distinguishable African ancestry remained impoverished, illiterate, and powerless.[19]

The post–World War II period brought these inequalities to the surface and exposed them to the light of day. Yet the sociological research of Florestan Fernandes and others in the 1950s and 1960s blamed Afro-Brazilian disadvantage almost exclusively on the legacy of slavery and the normal tendency of capitalism to grind down the poor. The possibility that the racial prejudices and discriminatory practices of contemporary white Brazilians played a substantial role was not seriously entertained.[20] It was not until the 1980s and 1990s that the myth of Brazil as a "racial democracy"—in spirit and intention, if not in results—was seriously challenged. Social scientists and historians demonstrated that racial prejudice was alive and well in Brazil and was directed as much, or almost as much, at mulattos (pardos) as at blacks (pretos). They also found that patterns of economic and social discrimination were pervasive and effective, although they differed in character and intensity by region, with São Paulo showing more resemblance to North America's hierarchical biracialism than did Salvador, for example. The weight of the evidence makes its clear that the characterization of Brazil as a "racial democracy" is a myth that obscures the fact that substantial inequalities correlated with race persist and that Afro-Brazilians remain second-class citizens, from the perspective of economic, social, and political power, if not in the eyes of the law.[21] That Brazil has a race problem has been difficult for elites to acknowledge, but they have done so to the extent of enacting antidiscrimination legislation. Enforcement has been feeble, however, and affirmative action remains unthinkable because of the entrenched belief that North American or South African style white supremacy, the legacies of which may justify policies, has never existed—and could never exist—in Brazil.

In the United States the claim that prejudice and discrimination are no longer a serious obstacle to African American opportunity and equality is called by its critics "the new racism," or "color-blind racism." In Brazil the continued affirmation that Brazil has a deeply rooted "racial democracy" might be described as the same old racism that has long obscured the realities of racial privilege and subordination. What *is* new is a growing realization, at least among social scientists and intellectuals, that such terms as "racism" and "white supremacy" might be applicable after all.

What is called "nonracialism" in South Africa is abstractly similar to America's color-blind constitutionalism and Brazil's ideal of racial democracy. Yet there is a critical difference in the origins and function of the African National Congress's conception of a nonracist state and the conceptual analogues in the United States and Brazil. Whites in South Africa never claimed, as it would have been patently absurd to do so, that the constitution that was in effect between 1910 and 1993 was color-blind. This constitution specifically denied non-Europeans the right to sit in parliament and countenanced their exclusion from the voting rolls in three of the four provinces of the Union. The doctrine of apartheid, as elaborated after the coming of the Afrikaner Nationalists to power in 1948, ruled out any prospect of interracial democracy by closing loopholes allowing a relatively small fraction of the nonwhite population to take part in the political process. The relegation of black politics to the dependent Homelands or Bantustans reflected a belief that representative government could succeed only in polities that were ethnically and racially homogeneous. If there is a sense in which South Africa before the 1990s was a democracy, it was, like the American South under slavery and segregation, a "Herrenvolk democracy"—a form of government in which one racial or ethnic group endows its own members with full citizenship and the right to political participation while denying these to the subordinated "Others," whether conquered indigenes or former slaves, who are treated like rightless aliens in the land of their birth.[22]

"Nonracialism" in South Africa was a revolutionary slogan of the oppressed. It was asserted by blacks in their long struggle against a blatantly discriminatory form of minority rule that presented itself as opening the way to ethnic or national self-fulfillment for all segments of the South African population. It is important to recognize that apartheid was more often rationalized in terms of cultural essentialism (*volkgeists*) than in the idiom of biological determinism or genetics. The biblical literalism of Afrikaner Calvinism limited the impact of eugenics and the kind of racialized Darwinism that served white supremacists well in the United States and even, for a time, in Brazil. An adherence to its own conception of cultural diversity and group self-determination was central to the propaganda of apartheid, which helps to explain why American multiculturalism has not traveled very well to South Africa.[23]

In South Africa, therefore, nonracialism became the banner of the oppressed rather than a myth to conceal the persistence of inequality, as it has long been in Brazil and has recently become in the United States. The belief affirmed in the ANC's Freedom Charter of 1955 that "South Africa belongs to all who live in it, white and black" has been controversial. After all, South Africa might well be considered a land that the whites have stolen from the blacks. Nonracialism, which meant that equal rights and full recognition of South African national identity should be accorded to all the groups separated under apartheid—Africans, "Coloreds," Indians, and whites—was challenged by Africanists in the 1950s on the grounds that an ANC-sponsored alliance of group-specific antiapartheid organizations gave disproportionate influence to whites and Indians.[24]

The rival Pan Africanist Congress, formed in 1959, demanded priority for black African culture, identity, and claims to the soil, but the PAC's black nationalist definition of the cause did not prevail. In the 1970s, the Black Consciousness Movement mounted a similar but somewhat more inclusive challenge to the ANC's nonracialist ideology. Indians and Coloreds were invited to affirm their "blackness" and join the struggle, but whites, even the most radical and antiracist among them, were excluded. Nevertheless, when resistance culminated in the domestic upheavals and international pressures of the 1980s, it was the United Democratic Front, which endorsed the Freedom Charter and served as the domestic surrogate for the banned ANC, that stood in the forefront, relegating Black Consciousness groups like the Azanian People's Organization (AZAPO) and the National Forum to the margins of the struggle.[25] When Nelson Mandela emerged from twenty-seven years of captivity in 1990 to lead South Africa to liberation, he did so with an undiminished commitment to the nonracialism that he had espoused in the 1950s and early 1960s. As he told the United States Congress a few months after his release from prison, his aim was to transform "this complex South African society, which has known nothing but racism for three centuries ... into an oasis of good race relations, where the black shall to the white be sister and brother, a fellow South African, an equal human being—both citizens of the world."[26]

The durability and success of the ideology of nonracialism was due to a number of factors. One was the direct antithesis it offered to the philosophy of apartheid and the appeal that it had for believers in universalist ideals of human rights and human solidarity, both within South Africa and throughout the world. Christianity and Marxism, the most influential belief systems of the educated African elite that led the struggle against apartheid, both affirmed a nonracialist ideal. Furthermore, significant ethnic divisions among Africans, as well as between Africans and the Colored and Indian minorities, made identity politics among the oppressed a luxury that the movement could ill afford, even if it failed to weaken the oppressors by garnering significant white support. Yet imported Western ideologies and the strategic requirements of the struggle may not be the whole story behind the triumph of nonracialism. Historian Shula Marks has called attention to the probable influence of indigenous African cultures, with their tendency to favor exogamy over endogamy and their openness to the assimilation of ethnic strangers into their tribal communities. Such cultural traditions, she argues, may have predisposed Africans to accept what she calls "non-racism."[27]

What is the future of nonracialism in South Africa? Will it go down in history as an effective slogan for the overthrow of apartheid that proved unworkable in a more pluralistic and democratic setting? Nonracialism has proved difficult to implement consistently for two quite distinct reasons. First and most obvious is the sheer fact of ethnic and racial diversity in a country that has as great a variety of colors and cultures as any in the world. Cultural diversity is well reflected in the fact that South Africa now has eleven official languages. Denying the existence of multiculturalism in the name of a common South African identity will not make ethnic particularism or ethnic politics go away. The ANC-dominated government elected in 1994 and reelected in 1999 has had to make some pragmatic concessions to the subnationalism of Zulus and Afrikaners. A growing emphasis on distinctive Indian and Colored identities and interests, as might well have been expected from insecure minorities that are unlikely to disappear in the foreseeable future, may also require some accommodation on the part of the African majority. The

Constitution and Bill of Rights protect individuals in their adherence to particular cultural traditions and practices. Will this be enough, or will rights have to be accorded to groups as well as individuals? In fact, Kwazulu still represents a kind of nation within the nation, the quasi-autonomous preserve of Gatsha Buthelezi and the Inkatha Party. Formal group representation under some form of ethnic federalism is out of the question because of the resemblance any such policy would have to efforts made by the white minority government in the 1980s to reform apartheid without abolishing it. The politicization of ethnicity is obviously a great potential threat to the unity of the new South Africa, but what North American multiculturalists call a "politics of recognition" is unavoidable, and the question of how to make it compatible with national cohesion and domestic tranquility is one of the greatest challenges that South Africa faces.

A second problematic aspect of nonracialism stems from an interpretation of it that inhibits efforts to challenge the economic and social position of the relatively affluent and well-situated white minority. The transition from white minority rule to black majority power in the early 1990s was accomplished relatively peacefully because the whites understood nonracialism to mean that they would not be divested of their property, economic leverage, or social amenities. Even the predominantly white civil service was granted tenure. As a result, no real revolution has occurred except in the realm of racial or ethnic status. South Africans of European origin still hold the lion's share of the country's wealth, natural resources, educational advantages, and career opportunities, while the mass of Africans remain impoverished and lacking in opportunities that most whites take for granted. Rectifying the legacy of apartheid would seem to call for a substantial redistribution of wealth and privilege, or at the very least some kind of affirmative action program. After years of seeking to influence corporate hiring policies by informal pressure (especially by favoring in the awarding of contracts firms that were black-owned or that practiced affirmative action) the government enacted an Employment Equities Act in 1998, prescribing American-style affirmative action for all firms with fifty or more employees. Quite predictably, many whites have protested that the government has violated its own professed principle of "nonracialism." Leading the charge are the white liberals in the Democratic Party, which, because of its successes in the recent election, has become the official opposition. White anger against affirmative action inspires antiwhite feeling among blacks, who are likely to feel that whites have gotten off much too easily as it is.[28]

Nonracialism, if interpreted as the denial of special consideration under the law or in public policy for any racially defined group, renders impossible the redistribution of wealth and opportunity that justice for black South Africans would seem to require. The problem with a literal-minded application of nonracialism, as with color-blind constitutionalism and the myth of racial democracy, is (in the words of Justice Blackmun) that it is likely to "perpetuate racial supremacy." It precludes official discrimination in the present but does not compensate adequately for the toll that three centuries or more of race-based oppression has taken on its surviving victims.

In my opinion, substantive racial equality in the United States, Brazil, and South Africa can be achieved only if a combination of strong affirmative action policies and antipoverty measures creates a much more equitable distribution of wealth and opportunity. South Africa and Brazil lead the world in the maldistribution of wealth, while the United States outranks other Western industrial nations in its degree of economic inequality. While affirmative action is necessary to make the dominant institutions and enterprises of these societies reflect the diversity of their populations, social democratic or class-based reforms are needed to reduce significantly the gaps between the "haves," who are predominantly white, and the "have nots," who are disproportionately black and brown. Yet, whether such a tilt to the left in individual nations is possible in today's world economy—dominated as it is by the multinational corporations and their agents in the World Bank and the International Monetary Fund—is a sobering question. Hope is always more efficacious than despair, but optimism would be unwarranted. It is consoling to remember, however, that past struggles for racial justice have achieved much against great odds. Martin Luther King Jr. and Nelson Mandela never succumbed to discouragement, even in the face of what others thought were insuperable obstacles. We should follow their example.

NOTES

1. Anthony W. Marx, *Making Race and Nation: A Comparison of the United States, South Africa and Brazil* (Cambridge: Cambridge University Press, 1998), 269–74; Thomas E. Skidmore, "Bi-racial U.S.A. vs. Multi-racial Brazil: Is the Contrast Still Valid?" *Journal of Latin American Studies* 25 (1993): 373–86; George M. Fredrickson, *Black Liberation: A Comparative Study of Black Ideologies in the United States and South Africa* (New York: Oxford University Press, 1995), 319–23.

2. Paul Gilroy, *"There Ain't No Black in the Union Jack": The Cultural Politics of State and Nation* (Chicago: University of Chicago Press, 1988), 110.

3. See David Theo Goldberg, *Racist Culture: Philosophy and the Politics of Meaning* (Cambridge, Mass.: Blackwell, 1993), 70–80 and passim, for an incisive analysis of "cultural race."

4. See Charles Taylor, *Multiculturalism: Examining the Politics of Recognition*, ed. and intro. Amy Gutman (Princeton, N.J.: Princeton University Press, 1994).

5. Quoted in Stephan Thernstrom and Abigail Thernstrom, *America in Black and White: One Nation, Indivisible* (New York: Simon and Schuster, 1997), 33.

6. Martin Luther King Jr., *Why We Can't Wait* (New York: Signet Books, 1964), 134. Johnson's speech is quoted in George M. Fredrickson, *The Comparative Imagination: On the History of Racism, Nationalism, and Social Movements* (Berkeley: University of California Press, 1997), 171.

7. Quoted in Thernstrom and Thernstrom, *America in Black and White*, 414.

8. Ibid., 412–20, summarizes these cases.

9. Ibid. Thernstrom and Thernstrom argue strongly for the latter position.

10. See, for example, Andrew Hacker, *Two Nations: Black and White, Separate, Hostile, and Unequal* (New York: Scribners, 1992); Douglas S. Massey and Nancy A. Denton, *American Apartheid: Segregation and the Making of the Underclass* (Cambridge, Mass.; Harvard University Press, 1993); and David K. Shipler, *A Country of Strangers: Blacks and Whites in America* (New York: Alfred A. Knopf, 1997).

11. See J. Morgan Kousser, *Colorblind Injustice: Minority Voting Rights and the Undoing of the Second Reconstruction* (Chapel Hill: University of North Carolina Press, 1999).

12. Nicholas deB. Katzenbach and Burke Marshall, "Not Color Blind Just Blind," *New York Times Magazine*, 22 February 1998, 42–45. This essay argues convincingly, in my opinion, for the constitutionality of race-based policies.

13. The classical historical account and analysis of the contrast between Brazil's fluid three-category system of race relations and the rigid black-white dichotomy found in the United States is Carl N. Degler, *Neither Black nor White: Slavery and Race Relations in Brazil and the United States* (New York: Macmillan, 1971).

14. Evidence of these disadvantages can be found in a number of recent works. See especially France Winddance Twine, *Racism in a Racial Democracy: The Maintenance of White Supremacy in Brazil* (New Brunswick, N.J.: Rutgers University Press, 1998); George Reid Andrews, *Blacks and Whites in Sao Paulo, Brazil, 1888–1988* (Madison: University of Wisconsin Press, 1991); and Pierre Michel Fontaine, ed., *Race, Class, and Power in Brazil* (Los Angeles: University of California Press, 1985).

15. Twine, *Racism in a Racial Democracy*, 1, 60.

16. I. K. Sundiata, "Late Twentieth Century Patterns of Race Relations in Brazil and the United States," *Phylon* 68, no. 1 (1987): 70, 74.

17. Thomas E. Skidmore, *Black into White: Race and Nationality in Brazilian Thought* (New York: Oxford University Press, 1974).

18. See Nancy Stepan, *"The Hour of Eugenics": Race, Gender, and Nation in Latin America* (Ithaca, N.Y.: Cornell University Press, 1991), 153–69.

19. Skidmore, *Black into White*, 173–205; Twine, *Racism in a Racial Democracy*, 6–9, 112–13.

20. Skidmore, "Bi-racial U.S.A. vs. Multi-racial Brazil," 375–76; Florestan Fernandes, *The Negro in Brazilian Society*, trans. Jacqueline D. Skiles, A. Brunel, and Arthur Rothwell (New York: Atheneum, 1971).

21. See note 14 above. For evidence of the lack of a strong mulatto advantage over blacks, see appendix B of Andrews, *Blacks and Whites*, 249–58. Several of the essays in Fontaine, ed., *Race, Class and Power*, offer data that contradicts the racial democracy myth, as does Twine, *Racism in a Racial Democracy*. On regional differences, see Kim D. Butler, *Freedoms Given, Freedoms Won: Afro-Brazilians in Post-Abolition Sao Paulo and Salvador* (New Brunswick, N.J.: Rutgers University Press, 1998).

22. See Pierre L. van den Berghe's pioneering *Race and Racism: A Comparative Perspective* (New York: John Wiley, 1967), which compares the United States and South Africa with Brazil and Mexico; and George M. Fredrickson, *White Supremacy: A Comparative Study in American and South African History* (New York: Oxford University Press, 1981).

23. See Saul DuBow, *Scientific Racism in Modern South Africa* (Cambridge: Cambridge University Press, 1995), 246–83.

24. These developments are described and analyzed in Fredrickson, *Black Liberation*, 237–52 and 277–86.

25. Ibid., 297–313.

26. Quoted in ibid., 312.

27. Shula Marks, *The Tradition of Non-Racism in South Africa*, Eleanor Rathbone Memorial Lecture, Somerville College, Oxford, 1994 (Liverpool: Liverpool University Press, 1995).

28. An incisive analysis of the South African situation at the time of the election of 2 June 1999 is Mark Gevisser, "Seeking South Africa's Dream," *The Nation* 268 (7 June 1999): 19–22. See also Suzanne Daley, "South Africa: The Voters Realign the Opposition," *New York Times*, 6 June 1999, 14.

5

The Future of Race in the United States

NATHAN GLAZER

The title, "The Future of Race in the United States," leads us to think first of all of the two races that at the beginning made up the United States—the white and the black, the peoples of the British Isles, with a sprinkling from France, Germany, the Netherlands, and other European countries, and the peoples of Africa, brought here as slaves. Yet today we have to think of more races, such that our title might well have been "The Future of Races in America."

There were, of course, even at the beginning more than the two races: There were the American Indians, who we now call the Native Americans. We do not know what their numbers were. They were probably substantial, but in time, in the course of our history, American Indians were reduced to a mere fragment, the smallest of the groups we consider minorities today. Thirty years ago there were less than a million American Indians in the United States. Today there are more than two million who declare themselves to the census to be Indians (which is the only way the census has to count race: One selects one's race from a list, and there is no one who can contradict one's choice). Many persons who have only a trace of Indian origin in their ancestry may call themselves Indian, regardless of tribal affiliation; but whatever the recent remarkable growth percentage-wise in the number who call themselves Indians, they make up less than 1 percent of the population, and few are of unmixed Indian ancestry. Is this a portent of what we may expect of the future races in America?

But to return to the beginning: There were in 1790 only two races recorded in the census, the white and the black. Blacks then numbered 20 percent of the population. In time that percentage dropped, to about the 12 percent it is today. It dropped not because blacks did not reproduce as fast as whites, or survive as well as whites, but because the huge influx of immigrants in the nineteenth and early twentieth centuries was European, and thus numbers of immigrants were added to the natural growth of the native white population.

Until 1965 one could say, yes, there were only two races to contend with in thinking of the future of race in the United States, the white and the black. Since 1965 the situation has been transformed. Our nation, still almost three-quarters European in origin, now grows by a million immigrants a year, and these immigrants are overwhelmingly not European, but Asian (of many origins), Latin American, Caribbean, and African. "Hispanics" or "Latinos" is not a racial category for the census: as the census makes clear, a person who considers himself Hispanic—and the census includes a special question that gives each person an opportunity to indicate whether he or she is Hispanic, and to specify what kind of Hispanic he is—may be of any race. But a very large percentage of Hispanics are indeed of another race, primarily of the race of the original settlers of this hemisphere, and we generally think of them as a category parallel to that of the African Americans. Thus, when we are informed of the racial or ethnic composition of a school or a city, it is generally broken down into the categories white, black, Hispanic, and, if there are enough of them, Asian.

I go into all this to make it clear, though I think it is generally understood, that when we speak of race in America today we cannot speak of only the two great races whose interaction has determined so much of our history, or only of the fate of one of those races, which was held in subjection as slaves, and is still marked by its history as a lower caste in American society. There are now other races to add to the mix. Asians of all kinds may constitute only 3 or 4 percent of the population, and Hispanics only 10 percent, but those percentages are growing rapidly, owing to the impact of immigration. In California, our largest state, both Asians and Hispanics already outnumber African Americans. In New York City, where it was once possible to ignore Asians in discussing the ethnic makeup of the city, because there were so few of them, it is no longer possible to be that cavalier—Asians make up more than 7 percent of the population of the city, and that percentage is rising rapidly.

We therefore have to talk about the future of races in the United States, not the future of race. The first fact to be aware of in considering this question is that the nonwhite races differ enormously in their capacity to enter the mainstream in terms of education, income, and occupation. They do not all suffer in comparison with the generally superior economic and social position of whites. Some of the Asian groups have a higher income than do white Americans. More of them have gone to college, and more of them are in professional occupations. That is not a sign of a deprived group, though by one statistic or another one may be able to argue there persists a degree of discrimination that may be reducing their opportunities and achievement. At least one group of Hispanics, the Cubans, is economically and politically dominant in South Florida, and exercises a national political power that would be the envy of any ethnic group.

So we have to talk about two kinds of races in the United States: those who show the pattern that was characteristic of many European groups—that is, a pattern of economic rise through the generations and of assimilation to some American norm—and those that do not. The reality is that the racial group that has struggled and continues to struggle hardest to raise its economic and social position and its political power is the oldest, the African American. Despite the fact that it has been here the longest, that it is the most American, that it has English as its native tongue, other, newer groups in American society, immigrant and speaking a foreign language, have steadily surpassed the African American group in income, occupation, and wealth. First there were the various European immigrant groups. Now we see the same process among the Asian groups and some of the Hispanic groups.

Every group, of course, has its problems. There are many poor people even among the most prosperous Asian groups—we speak of averages when we describe a group, and many can fall well below the average. Yet it is clear that the group with the greatest problems is our oldest race, the African American. Those problems are familiar to everyone: We do not know and would probably disagree on how to sort out the causes of these problems, how much to attribute to the heritage of slavery, how much to the existence of severe prejudice and discrimination, how much to the existence of prejudice and discrimination today, how much to internally generated problems and failures. Our best social scientists have not been able to come to a consensus on how to distribute responsibility for these problems across the array of causes. Yet this group's handicaps in the effort to move upward are clear. The African American race is more separated from the white and from the other races than any other racial or ethnic group, even those made up of relatively recent immigrants. We see this separation in many key areas of life—in residence, where blacks are the most concentrated in inner cities; in schools, where they are again the most concentrated; in income, where blacks on average do no better than the Hispanic groups; in employment, where their unemployment rate is regularly twice that of other groups in the society. I will not continue this litany.

Is the future of race in this country, then, one in which all the races but the black continue to progress and to assimilate into the majority race? That, after all, was the course taken by the immigrant groups of the nineteenth and early twentieth centuries, the Irish, the Italians, the Jews, the Poles, and others, many of whom were considered, at the time of their immigration and for decades afterward, to be so different from the original English settlers as to be considered unassimilable. A recent book is titled *How the Irish Became White;* other recent books describe how the immigrant groups from Eastern and southern Europe, who were once considered racially different, in time, so to speak, "became white"—that is, were accepted as part of the majority and considered to be people with no important characteristics that significantly differentiated them from the old white majority.

Is this what will happen in time to African Americans? Is this what will happen in time to the various Asian groups, the various Hispanic groups? In time, yes. But how much time? I have recently been looking at some very interesting statistics which suggest to us at what rate these newer nonwhite groups will become part of the majority, the way the Irish, the Jews, and the Italians have "become white." I would like to report two sets of statistics: the rates of intermarriage among the various groups, and how the races of the children of the intermarried are reported by their parents to the census. From 1970 census data: 33 percent of Indian men had white wives, and 35 percent of Indian women had white husbands. In Los Angeles in 1979, 41 percent of Chinese, 61 percent of Japanese, and 28 percent of Koreans married outside the group. If one excludes marriages to other Asians, these rates are still high, as 30 percent of Chinese, 50 percent of Japanese, and 19 percent of Koreans married non-Asians. In New York City, 56 percent of Central Americans, 63 percent of Cubans, and 38 percent of Dominicans married outside their group (1975 figures). Only Puerto Ricans had a low outmarrying rate, at 30 percent.[1] Yet even this rate far surpasses the rising rate for African Americans. In 1970, the intermarriage rate for blacks was a minuscule 1 or 2 percent. In 1980 it was estimated at 1.2 percent for black women and 3.6 percent for black men. The rate varies greatly by sex and by region, and is increasing rapidly, but from a very small base. In 1980, the highest rate was 16.5 percent for black men in the western states. Note how much smaller this is than the rates I have reported for Asians and Hispanics.[2] Equally striking are the figures, compiled by Mary Waters, of what race parents in intermarried couples assign to their children. Whether the mother or the father is black, the majority of children of an intermarried couple are reported to the census as black. In contrast, the majority of the children of intermarried couples in which the non-white parent is Indian or Asian are reported to be white. The new groups are thus not only becoming white in terms of social status; considering their high intermarriage rates, and the way they report the race of their children, they are becoming white in census terms.

We thus have two racial scenarios operating today: the nonwhite races, if they are not African American, are becoming white, through intermarriage and the racial identity of their children. One can see this process operating among blacks, too, but at a much slower rate. What is the future of race in America? For the non-white races, leaving aside the black, the significance of race, the salience of race, will continue to decline. I believe that this will be true for blacks, too, but the rate of decline will be much slower. I do believe, following the expectation of an early American sociologist of race, Robert E. Park, a man who learned much about race while working for Booker T. Washington, and helped him write one of his books, that the future of races in contact is assimilation—or, to take the stronger term, amalgamation. But this is in the long run, and it may be in the very long run. As the Gauls and the Franks became French, the Celts, the Anglo-Saxons, and the Normans became English, I believe that the black and white races in the United States will eventually become one. But for many decades to come, one race will continue to be sharply marked out in America, because of its history and its distinctive problems and because of the ingrained attitudes of whites, built up over centuries and transmitted to newcomers.

The time may well come when, owing to the inroads of intermarriage, the census will be back, as it was in 1790, to only two races, the white and the black. Then, even further in the future, we will become just one race, the race that is being created by the mixing of peoples in the United States.

NOTES

1. Mary C. Waters, "Multiple Ethnic Identity Choices," in *Beyond Pluralism*, ed. Wendy F. Katkin, Ned Landsman, and Andre Tyree (Urbana and Chicago: University of Illinois Press, 1998).

2. Ibid.

6

21st-Century America: Black and White and Beyond*

E V E L Y N   H U - D E H A R T

When thinking of race relations in America at the end of the century and the millennium, we can recall the words of Charles Dickens, writing about the French Revolution: "These are the best of times, and the worst of times." We seem to be moving into a strange new world, in which race relations appear simultaneously to be getting better and growing worse, more clarified, yet also more confusing. After the Civil Rights movement led by Dr. Martin Luther King, with legal apartheid dismantled, most Americans have learned a new, race-sensitive etiquette, and many have learned to reject the language and rhetoric of demagogues like David Duke (even if, unfortunately, some may still resonate with his sentiments). Government, corporations, and campuses celebrate diversity and discuss difficult issues that arise out of the commitment to multiculturalism.

To assess properly where we are heading, it is necessary to set the stage by providing a brief historical overview of diversity in the past three decades. The loosening of immigration and citizenship provisions, coupled with the social turmoil provoked in various Third World societies by U.S. political and military

---

*This was a keynote address given at the "Race in 21st Century America" conference.

intervention, produced a new wave of immigration to the United States, beginning in the mid-1960s and continuing to the present. In just thirty years, the demographic changes in this nation have been dramatically accelerated in the direction of further diversity. Today, the population of the United States is approximately 275 million. Of this, about 30 percent are ethnic minorities or "peoples of color"— that is, not belonging to the dominant group of whites or European-descended Americans whose culture and image this nation has historically reflected. According to the 1990 census, which is the most complete data available to date (and which will be updated when the 2000 census is taken and analyzed in a few years):

- There are 30 million African Americans, an increase of 13.2 percent since 1980. They are concentrated in Washington, D.C., and the southern states of Mississippi, Louisiana, South Carolina, and Georgia. States in the Northeast and Midwest, and Alaska, have experienced the greatest growth in this population. There has been no growth in the West or Southwest; in fact, these regions have seen declines in this population.

- There are 7.3 million Asian and Pacific Islanders, up 108 percent from 1980, making this the fastest growing group. By the end of the century, this figure is expected to top 10 million. This very dramatic increase is due largely to immigration, accounting for the fact that some 80 percent of this population is foreign-born, and many speak English as a second language or not at all. Asian/Pacific Americans are concentrated in California, where they constitute almost 10 percent of the total population, in Hawaii, where they make up more than 60 percent of the population, and in New York at 4 percent. Highest growth rates in this population, however, have been experienced in midwestern, northeastern, and southern states, such as Minnesota, Massachusetts, and Georgia.

- At 22.5 million strong and the second-fastest growing group, next to Asian Americans, Latinas/os or Hispanics are expected to surpass African Americans in number by the end of the century. Their almost 60 percent growth since 1980 can also be attributed primarily to immigration. Not surprisingly, they are concentrated in the Western and Southwestern states, including California, where they comprise almost 26 percent of the population; in Texas, New Mexico, Arizona, and Colorado. Florida and New York are other states with significant Latina/o populations. States not usually identified with Latinas/os, such as Nevada and Virginia, have experienced recent influxes.

- Finally, the Native American population has grown by almost 38 percent since 1980, up to two million in 1990, a phenomenon that certainly, in this case, cannot be attributed to immigration. Birth rates would have to be impossibly high to account for this growth. The most plausible explanation is the resurgence of Native American pride and hence greater willingness on the part of many Americans to claim this particular identity as their primary one on the census forms.
- White Americans—what the census classifies as "non-Hispanic whites"—comprise about 70 percent of the population, but have experienced by far the slowest growth rate, at only 6 percent, the combination of low immigration and birth rates. Northern New England and the Upper Midwest remain the whitest areas of the country.

The upshot of these new immigration patterns is that the American population is fast becoming more "colored" and more diverse—by race, ethnicity, religion, language, food, music, arts, literature, and so on. In fact, with over half of its population already that diverse by 1993, California gives us a glimpse of the national future, which is projected to become by the year 2050 "majority minority." Projecting into the year 2000, demographers tell us that white Americans will hold steady at around 71 percent of the U.S. population, while African Americans and American Indians will also hold fairly steady at 13 percent and 1 percent, respectively. By contrast, Asian/Pacific Americans will grow to 4 percent or more of the U.S. population, while Latinas/os will account for 11 percent. Both percentages are expected to continue to grow.

Besides statistics and geographic distribution patterns, there are some other important features about each group that need to be noted in order to understand where this nation is heading in race and race relations. Within each of these broadly defined categories, there is tremendous diversity and complexity. This is especially true for Latinas and Latinos and Asian/Pacific Americans.

The "Hispanic" or "Latina/o" category theoretically includes all those peoples in the United States who trace their origins to a region in the Americas originally colonized by Spain. There is, therefore, though remote in some cases, at least some connection to a common history, and there is, for the most part, a linguistic commonality in Spanish. Most also identify with the Catholic religion, a legacy of

Spanish colonialism. Other than these unifying features, however, there are as many aspects, if not more, that divide and distinguish these peoples. The terms "Hispanic" or "Latina/o" are represented by a variety of ethnicities and national origins, which are, in turn, fragmented by race, class, and legal status.

The major Latina/o identities are Mexican Americans or Chicanas/os, Puerto Ricans, and Cuban Americans. Increasing numbers of new arrivals from this category are coming from Central America and such South American countries as Colombia and Peru.

Racially, these peoples can be black, as are many of the Puerto Ricans, who also tend to be of working- or lower-class origins; mestizo, as in the case of the majority of Mexican Americans because of their roots in the Greater Southwest; or white, as are most of the Cuban Americans, who came from the middle and upper classes of Cuba after the socialist revolution of Fidel Castro in 1959 made life inconvenient for them. One can even be Asian—Chinese or Japanese—and also Latina/o.

They represent different generations and legal statuses, from fifth- and sixth-generation Mexican Americans, to Puerto Ricans who are born in the United States, to—increasingly so—recent immigrants, both documented and "illegal."

These many divisions—race, generation, legal status—also reflect class differences. In other words, while for the most part Latinas/os still struggle to achieve the American dream, they are by no means all poor or working class, and it would be a mistake to identify them too closely with an urban underclass.

Another group with extreme internal diversity—even more so than Latinas/os—are the Asian/Pacific Americans. More than twenty ethnic groups, with as many different languages and almost as many religions, characterize this category. The major Asian/Pacific ethnicities are, in order of numerical size in the United States: Chinese, Filipino, Japanese, Asian Indian, Korean, Hawaiian, Samoan, Guamanian, Cambodian, Laotian, Hmong, Thai, and other Melanesian and Micronesian groups. Here there is no common history, however remote, and no linguistic or religious unity, in any real sense. The only thing that binds this large assortment of ethnicities together is their national origin in an enormous part of the world designated by the West as "the Orient." While some Pacific Islanders are "native born" to the region now incorporated into the United States (i.e., Hawaii, American Samoa, Guam), all others in the United States are immigrants. As such, these immigrants span a timeline of at least one hundred and fifty years, from the Chinese who came during the California Gold Rush days of the mid-nineteenth century to the new Asian immigrants of today. Well over 50 percent of Asian/Pacific Americans are foreign born, and many still speak primarily in their native, non–English tongue.

Native Americans are, of course, also extremely diverse. While genocide and forced assimilation from 1492 on have resulted in the elimination or near decimation of hundreds of indigenous nations and tribes, hundreds of tribes and two million self-identified Native Americans exist today, with many increasingly aggressive in pursuing treaty rights to land, water, and natural resources, as well as in asserting constitutional rights as U.S. citizens to religious freedom. Some native peoples are also transnational in identity, such as the Papagos and Yaquis of Arizona, who, as Native peoples, can be found on both sides of the U.S.-Mexican border, or the Mohawk and Chippewa of the northern United States, who share a common identity and history with others living in Canada.

In contrast, African Americans have the greatest internal unity, although they, too, have been diversified by recent immigrants from Africa and the Caribbean. After all, think of the most recent black victims of police brutality in New York City: the unarmed Abner Louima, beaten and sodomized by white policemen, was a Haitian immigrant, while Amadou Diallo, shot forty-one times by white policemen while standing unarmed in the doorway of his apartment, was a West African immigrant. Still, the vast majority of African Americans can, and do, trace their origins to the slave trade and the shared experience of over four centuries of slavery and Jim Crow, to the American South, to plantations, and to rural origins. For African Americans, being defined racially as "black" means that race is clearly understood in the context of white supremacy, and acts as a unifying force.

Historically in the United States, therefore, race and race relations have been conceived of in binary, or bi-polar, black and white terms; historically, one is either black or white. For this reason, nonwhites in the nineteenth century, including native peoples and the Chinese immigrants, were usually subsumed under the "black" category in laws regulating race relations. This hegemonic paradigm has dominated our thinking and our practices to the present day.

Yet, if we put all of what I have enumerated together, the most immediate and logical conclusion at the closing of the twentieth century, one would think, is that "*America is not just black and white.*" Race is not just a black-white affair, and racial conflicts will take on increasingly unfamiliar forms, involving new players or pitting as antagonists parties previously not known to have had much contact with each other. Increasingly, overt racial conflicts, or frontline confrontations, will not be *only* or *always* between black and white Americans. Racialization and racial formations will take on new shapes, and racial discourse will assume new sounds and echoes. Other racialized groups have arrived on the stage, and their presence cannot be denied. They are active participants, not mere passive bystanders.

Yet, unlike some colleagues and observers of the American racial scene who have declared rather categorically that America is "not black and white," I take the stance that America is not *just* black and white. Race is, indeed, still very much black and white, but it is also more than that: race now goes *beyond* black and white. In other words, the primary paradigm of black and white has been destabilized because of "postality"—a term coined by Epifanio San Juan Jr., meaning post–Civil Rights, post–Cold War, postcolonial, postmodern, and now, in the wake of anti–immigrant Proposition 187, anti–affirmative action Proposition 209, and anti-bilingual education Proposition 229, post-multicultural as well.

First, let us explore briefly what it means to say that race still means "black" and race relations are still "black and white." Think of the recent brutal killing in Jaspar, Texas, of a totally innocent black man by a couple of uneducated white skinheads, whose crime was so heinous that just about everybody in Jaspar and across Texas (a state not often known for progressive race thinking and race relations) rejected their crude, white supremacist ideology and utterly deplorable action. Dragged to his death, the black victim's lynching by truck is eerily reminiscent of the days of Jim Crow. Equally evocative of black history, this time the heyday of the Civil Rights movement, has been the current mobilization of antiracism activists, from former Mayor Dinkins to actor Susan Sarandon, and thousands of known and lesser-known New Yorkers and Americans of all colors in between, to protest the Diallo shooting. With Major Giuliani seemingly reincarnated as Sheriff Bull Connor, these protestors amassed in the thousands at New York police headquarters, willingly submitting to arrest for acts of civil disobedience, thus bringing forth from all of us powerful memories of the civil rights struggle aimed at freeing black Americans from the white supremacist society propped up by a complicit state.

Nevertheless, we need also to perceive that in "postality" race has advanced beyond black and white. To illustrate this point, we can look to the Los Angeles uprising of 1992 in the aftermath of the Rodney King trial to provide a vivid demonstration—a site where African Americans, Latinas/os, and new Asian immigrants were the key players in a most public racial drama, while whites hid offstage.

In urban environments outside the South, such as south-central Los Angeles, whites have moved out, physically and economically, since the late 1960s. They have uprooted their families, closed their factories (in many cases sending the jobs overseas), and sold or abandoned their shops and businesses. Along with this desertion went not only good jobs in basic industries such as steel, auto, and rubber, that paid good union wages of $10 to $15 per hour and benefits, but taxes and commitments to local institutions, such as public schools. In short, what happened was nothing less than an active and deliberate disinvestment in previously vital communities.

Into the vacuum created by this white withdrawal came entrepreneurial new immigrants and eager workers from Mexico, Central America, the Caribbean, and Asia. Unlike the African Americans and older Mexican Americans in the communities the whites left behind, these new Americans have not, for the most part, been scarred by generations of racial subordination and discrimination. Moreover, some, notably Korean immigrants, have come with education and modest capital, as well as an entrepreneurial orientation, willing to open up any kind of business anywhere, because they have understood that a small, family business can be an effective entry point to integration into American society. In this respect, they have done what immigrants in America have always done—found an unoccupied economic or labor niche, then swiftly moved in. Thus, at one time in Kansas City, Korean immigrants became hot dog street vendors; in New York City they are still green grocers; and in Los Angeles before the riot they owned liquor stores and gun shops. To these people, it mattered not what product or service they sold, as long as there was a demand.

For their part, the new Central and Latin American immigrants took the low-paying jobs that the few new industries brought into this community—jobs in garment and furniture making, hotels, and other services that paid $5 an hour with little or no benefits. According to Los Angeles community activist Eric Mann: "Today, some 500,000 Angelenos, almost all of them immigrants, labor year-round for less than $10,000 full-time in a de facto sweatshop sector of the economy—one that by its nature simultaneously fails to attract and virtually excludes African Americans."[1] No wonder the longtime black residents of this old community flared up and let loose their pent-up frustration and anger at those closest by, namely the immigrant Korean shopkeepers and their Central American neighbors. Reginald Denny notwithstanding, whites were basically nowhere in sight, certainly not the suddenly unavailable Los Angeles Police Department (LAPD).

Black hopelessness and Latino poverty exploded, in the 1992 riot, seemingly in the face of the relatively more prosperous Korean immigrant business owners. In some sense, the latter filled the physical space and assumed the role of surrogates for the missing whites, those who were largely responsible for disinvesting in this community and who continued to hold the purse strings and make vital political and economic decisions for Los Angeles. Despite being presided over by a black mayor (Bradley) at the time, white corporate America, boosted by international finance, had continued to make investment and development decisions that largely bypassed south-central L.A. and its black residents. The family businesses of the Koreans, numerous and ubiquitous though they may be, could not begin to meet the demand for good paying jobs, and could not be held accountable for finding the solutions.

The Los Angeles riot of 1992 was the nation's first multicultural riot. Most of the people arrested were not African American or Korean, but Latinos, mainly recent, Spanish-speaking immigrants. In this setting, "what" and "who" is "white," and conversely, what and who is "black," is changeable and confusing. Putting it another way, we may have to look through brown and yellow and red to see white and black, in that white and black are sometimes filtered through the other colors, so that black and white are also brown and yellow. As Gary Okihiro put the question so bluntly and provocatively, "Is yellow black or white?"[2]

Aside from the inner cities, where else can we find multiculturalism and its discontents flaring up? Where else do we see the rigid black-white racial paradigm challenged and problematized? One premier site is the institutions of higher education across the country. At the end of the millennium we are not likely to see "white supremacy" delivered the old-fashioned way, by Klansmen and state agents against hapless black students, as it was in the days of the Civil Rights movement at Ol' Miss and other southern campuses. Rather, we see respectable citizens and institutional leaders taking up positions against an array of vulnerable targets representing the multicultural threat, all done, deceptively, in the name of "managing diversity," "valuing diversity," or "celebrating diversity." Again, let me briefly set the stage.

In the name of diversity and multiculturalism, our colleges and universities have strived to recruit African American, Latina/o, Native American, and Asian American students, as well as international students and in some cases women students, to complement the existing core of white male and often middle-class students. Additionally, we have tried to diversify the faculties of these institutions by adding women teachers and teachers of color. Finally, the last tier of this tripartite approach has been an attempt to introduce new courses to the curriculum that speak to the experiences and contributions of women and Americans of non–Western heritage to the formation of American society and culture. Additional bonuses at these institutions may be conferences and freshmen orientation workshops on tolerance, cultural diversity, and racism, and other kinds of so-called sensitivity training for all sectors of our campus community. Also attempted, with varying degrees of success, have been policies and speech codes designed to curb sexual and racial harassment, both verbal and physical. Recently, in the name of diversity and tolerance, these institutions have also begun to move on the front of providing safer environments for gay, lesbian, bisexual, and transgendered students, faculty, and staff.

The good news is that most campuses during the past quarter century have made progress on the diversity front, in the name of multiculturalism. In states such as California, the dramatically changed demographics in society have altered the nature of student bodies, with or without adequate policies in place; Berkeley is now "majority-minority," meaning that the combined students of color outnumber white students, who comprise no more than a third of the student body. Even private universities such as Stanford are inching toward half white, half minority student bodies. The bad news is that the faculty and the curriculum have maintained to a surprisingly large degree the status quo ante: that is, not much has changed, at least where faculty of color and where curricular innovations that seriously challenge the Eurocentric paradigms, perspectives, and epistemologies are concerned. (Progress for white women has been significantly more measurable.) The problem lies, simply and bluntly, in the kind of multiculturalism campuses practice, what I call "corporate multiculturalism," or "liberal multiculturalism." Let me use my own campus's diversity plan to illustrate my critique.

The Boulder campus diversity plan, issued in 1994, contains a definition of "diversity" that begins: "We are committed to making the University of Colorado at Boulder a community in which diversity is a fundamental value. *People are different and the differences among them are what we call diversity (italics added).*" Thus, diversity is reduced to a simple matter of "differences," whatever those differences may be, and with no differentiation among them. These differences include, but are "not necessarily limited to ethnicity, race, gender, age, class, sexual orientation, religion, and physical abilities." Moreover, as the next sentence in this definition makes clear, the differences are "natural," implying they are normal and fixed: "Diversity is a natural and enriching hallmark of life." Finally, all of us who are different must create a "climate of healthy diversity," in which "people value individual and group differences, respect the perspectives of others, and communicate openly"—in other words, we must practice civility, another key component of campus and corporate multiculturalism. Nowhere in this definition is it stated or even hinted or implied that differences are socially and historically constructed and hierarchically arranged, and that most differences carry real and differential meanings of power and privilege. Totally ahistorical, this definition is thus devoid of social context and significance. In the worst sense, it is purely ideological propaganda.

What the designers of this corporate multicultural model did not realize is that some faculty and most students are not stupid. Enough of us have figured out the contradictions of this project to expose it for what it is. Furthermore, there are concrete signs that corporate multiculturalism has sown the seeds of its own destruction, and is now reaping the fruits of what it has planted.

Indeed, one of the most egregious errors of campus diversity projects is that university leadership (administrators, regents, elected faculty and student leaders, alumni, etc.), like the media, politicians and legislators, policy makers, pundits, and others in the society at large, have not broken out of a rigid black-white paradigm in understanding race and race relations. In fact, they may be among the most guilty in perpetuating this kind of outdated thinking. This can be explained, if not entirely excused, by habit and tradition. It must be acknowledged that African Americans led the Civil Rights movement which broke down legal apartheid in this country, and black students led the struggle to extend civil rights into our institutions of higher education, most notably in the form of black students occupying administrative buildings, sometimes with guns in their hands, as in the case of Cornell University in 1968, demanding the opening up of educational opportunities and the curriculum to previously excluded groups. To placate these students and buy peace, colleges and universities acceded to their list of demands, usually headed by creation of the first Black Studies programs; these in turn initiated the ethnic studies curricular movement.

Chicana/o, Puerto Rican, Native American/American Indian, and Asian/ Pacific American studies soon followed suit, their student supporters, respectively and sometimes as coalitions, occupying buildings and making similar demands. However, colleges and universities have been much slower and more hesitant to respond to the needs of these students, and this has become especially problematic in the case of Asian Americans and Latinas/os, the fastest growing nonwhite student groups on our campuses. Witness the situation on the Michigan State University campus, where recently (early spring 1999) Latina/o students checked out five thousand library books, loaded them on a truck, and carted them away: the point of this publicity-seeking *movido*, of course, was to call attention to the sorry fact that, despite its establishment of the Julian Samora Center some years ago in the name of one of the founders and most esteemed scholars of Chicano studies, this university has yet to offer a credible Latina/o studies major to its undergraduates. The students also wanted to protest the deplorably low numbers of tenure-track Latino/o professors at this institution. With this well-publicized act, MSU Latina/o students and their allies have added their university's name to an already long list of campuses whose students have demonstrated for more ethnic studies in multiple and creative ways, including undertaking drastic measures such as hunger strikes. Yet this university, like mine and most of the large and prominent, public and private universities, would loudly proclaim its commitment to diversity and even tout its successes with audacity despite the absence of a well-designed, staffed, and funded comprehensive ethnic studies curriculum.

So, from a national perspective, how does ethnic studies fare at the *fin de siècle*? As chair of the second-largest ethnic studies department (next to UC Berkeley), let me offer a view from the trenches. This report on the state of ethnic studies is offered in the context of my critique of corporate or liberal culturalism. Thirty years after its founding, the field of ethnic studies finds itself in a paradoxical situation, boasting some long-established programs and departments, yet intellectually marginalized, its necessity in the academy touted, yet its scholarly merits almost universally ignored. Born out of student activism in the late 1960s, ethnic studies programs were created by administrators as "fire insurance" to placate and appease militant students they did not know how to handle. In the mid-1990s, a new generation of students are once again demonstrating for either the creation or the enhancement of ethnic studies programs on their campuses. In the intervening years, campus administrators have embraced "multiculturalism" and set out determinedly to diversify student bodies, staffs, faculties, and curriculums. However, at the end of the decade and the century, the field of ethnic studies is meant to be seen but not heard, its scholars sometimes treated like unemancipated children or colonial subjects without full citizenship rights.

In other words, the success of ethnic studies appears to have brought about a backlash, not only in the highly visible and contested arena of cultural politics waged by the likes of the National Association of Scholars, but coming from institutional forces that seek to weaken the very ethnic studies programs they have engendered in the first place. Why is ethnic studies beleaguered even as it continues to spread on U.S. campuses? Why is it both promoted and undermined?

On most campuses, administrators have denied ethnic studies the one academic currency that it most needs: recognition and respect as a legitimate scholarly field that constructs, disseminates, and imparts knowledge in a distinctive way. This is accomplished primarily by withholding due respect for ethnic studies faculty, whose work these administrators have largely failed to appreciate and whose approach to scholarship they may, indeed, have difficulty fully comprehending. Ethnic studies scholars perceive as their primary responsibility the interrogation of received wisdom and truths—particularly those that are presented as universal truths without regard to the context and perspectives of those generating such knowledge. Equally important is the demonstration of alternative ways of constructing knowledge, so as to redefine the nature of knowledge and how it is used to understand both our physical world and the human condition.

Most campus administrators understand that they need ethnic studies, yet they fear the field. They need it because an ethnic studies program is the surest way to demonstrate commitment to diversity: It immediately puts color into the curriculum, and its largely nonwhite faculty promotes faculty diversity more rapidly than hiring in other disciplines. At the extreme, elite universities with better resources believe that they can achieve instantaneous multicultural credibility by hiring an academic star or two to launch—with appropriate fanfare—a high-profile department, center, or institute.

Yet administrators also appear to distrust ethnic studies. Once an ethnic studies program has been established and administrators have taken public relations credit for doing so, they often refuse to build it up. They appear to be afraid of strengthening a force that they never really wanted to create—a critical mass of free-thinking, independent-minded faculty of color with an intellectual base of their own in ethnic studies. With academic roots in traditional disciplines, most deans and provosts have never bothered to become familiar with the scholarship produced by ethnic studies scholars.

The undermining of ethnic studies has taken shape with alarming consistency across the country. Common practices include installing weak and pliable program directors and department chairs, sometimes after rejecting strong scholars selected by the faculty, and refusing to hire more than a handful of full-time faculty members in an ethnic studies department, then swelling its ranks with part–time or non–ethnic studies oriented personnel, who may then be given voting rights to dilute the strength of the legitimate, full-time, ethnic studies faculty. Sometimes the research component is separated from the teaching faculty, for example, by setting up distinct units for research and instruction, and by denying ethnic studies faculty control over an ethnic studies research center. These administrative decisions can be especially fatal to the legitimacy of ethnic studies in research universities.

Administrators sometimes employ divide-and-conquer tactics to destroy solidarity and marginalize individuals, who may then be driven to leave ethnic studies and join another department. Administrators also have allowed other departments to set up course offerings that duplicate those in ethnic studies, and they have counted minority hires in mainstream departments against promised positions in ethnic studies, whether or not those faculty members define their work around minority communities and ethnic studies concerns. Administrators have delayed approval of degree programs in ethnic studies even when many students have indicated they want to major in the field, or have delayed granting departmental status to a program even when it has a comprehensive curriculum and faculty in place. Such practices suggest an underlying disrespect for ethnic studies faculty and their work. While other faculties on a campus may experience some of the same heavy-handed practices, the number visited on ethnic studies faculties may be unique and can be devastating.

All of this brings us back to the students. During the past five years, we have seen organized demonstrations on behalf of ethnic studies by a rainbow coalition of students on campuses across the country. In a few notable cases, such as protests at UCLA, the University of Colorado at Boulder, and Northwestern University, students staged hunger strikes. At Princeton and Stanford Universities, Asian American students—typically stereotyped as docile and apolitical—occupied the president's office and disrupted faculty senate meetings to press their demands for Asian American and ethnic studies programs. Asian American and Chicana/o students, because of their rapidly rising numbers on campuses, have been the most visible leaders and participants in the recent wave of protests.

When students of color organize politically and press for ethnic studies, they typically are not doing so at the behest of faculty members in ethnic studies; indeed, such faculty members are almost nonexistent on some of the campuses that have witnessed demonstrations. Instead, the students often see themselves as engaged in a form of antiracist and anticolonial struggle, not unlike the massive protests against South African apartheid that American students engaged in a generation ago. For similar reasons, progressive white students often are involved with the struggle to help ethnic studies gain space and legitimacy at their institutions. All these students understand what most administrators, white faculty, and the news media have failed to grasp—that ethnic studies is not a minority program for minorities only, and it is no longer confined to Black Studies.

Who are these noisy students who have been so aggressively pushing for their interests? Ironically, they come from the ranks of those formerly excluded students of color now admitted to our colleges and universities in the name of diversity. Once they have been admitted, however, the campus diversity plan provides no blueprint for how to deal with them or address their needs and interests, other than to exhort them to tolerate differences and practice civility. By abandoning the "civility" mode of operation so fervently urged by administrators, student activists have served notice that they do not buy into the corporate model of diversity, and they reject token gestures in the curriculum that do not critically challenge the entrenched Eurocentric model or broaden the traditional black-white racial formations.

What is the problem with corporate or liberal multiculturalism, as practiced on our campuses? Simply put, it does not address the question of power and structural inequality. Differences are not differentiated; the sources and causes of these differences are never examined, discussed, interrogated or articulated, thus leaving the impression that they are just "out there." They materialize somehow, somewhere, without any attempt at contextualization—that is, without specification of historically and socially constructed categories of inequality and systems of hierarchy, of racism and institutional discrimination. In short, corporate and liberal multiculturalism consigns the Other to recognizable standards of difference but fails to question the power relations that define for the Other *how* and *why* they are different; liberal multiculturalism does not seriously question the status quo. In this way, "ethnic" peoples remain peripheral, and only those at the center of privilege are powerful enough to elude the stamp and odor of multiculturalism (those at the center are not part of the "differences" that need to be managed). This myopia has blinded institutional leaders to the changing nature and dynamics of American diversity, reducing all "others" to the same difference. Thus, the diversity project as we know it on our campuses is complicit in the perpetuation of the racial order as historically constructed.

A phenomenon to watch in the matter of race and race relations in the twenty-first century is the resurgence of American nativism, embodied by Proposition 187 of California, with imitations spreading across the country. In a nutshell, Proposition 187 represents the racialization of immigrants, particularly Mexican immigrants as "illegal aliens," and Asian immigrants as "perpetual aliens." This new nativism both criminalizes problematic immigrants and renders them forever outsiders, never to belong in American society.

From the enactment of the Immigration Reform and Control Act (IRCA) in 1988 into the late 1990s, the social construction of the illegal alien as an unsavory and most undesirable, racialized social element has continued to take shape. According to this social construction, an illegal alien is not merely someone who enters the country without proper documents; rather, he is the dark-skinned

Arab/Muslim religious fundamentalist and terrorist who blows up the World Trade Center in New York City or (as initially thought) the federal building in Oklahoma City; he is the black Caribbean sociopath who shoots innocent white passengers on the Long Island commuter train; she is the pregnant Mexican welfare cheat who crosses the border in San Diego to have babies who then become U.S. citizens and in turn enable the mother to claim welfare benefits. They are the unassimilable Southeast Asian war refugees too eager to take any job at any wage, thus depressing the wage scale and robbing the livelihood of bona fide, longtime Americans; they are the Mexican and Asian youth gangs contributing disproportionately to our urban crime problem; they are the single Latino men loitering around suburban street corners, urinating in the streets, sleeping under the bushes of residential homes; they are the children crowding into our urban public schools, demanding bilingual education and other costly special services; and they are the families without insurance who jam our public hospital emergency rooms. Television and the print media provide numerous other lurid and colorful examples of this "nativist paranoia." The image and rhetoric of "invasion," reminiscent of the "yellow peril" invasion a century ago, has effectively produced the desired hysteria among a broad spectrum of the American public.

In short, illegal aliens are terrorists, criminals, welfare cheats, and freeloaders, a social burden who exacerbate our urban crime problem and severely strain the public resources that our taxes support. Gone is the idea that immigrants have built this country and exemplify prized American virtues of family and hard work. In fact, when some immigrants work hard these days, that, too, is turned against them, because their work ethic depresses wages and deprives Americans of jobs. A common refrain is heard: "Asians are unfair because they work too hard."[3]

Local, state, and national politicians have seized on the illegal alien problem for political gain. They figure it is a no-loss proposition for them, since illegal aliens cannot vote and have no voice. In contrast, by getting tough with illegal aliens, they have everything to gain with those who do vote, by providing them with a convenient scapegoat on which to vent their frustrations.

A subset of the illegal alien construction is the "perpetual alien" designation increasingly applied to Asian immigrants. The current Chinese "spy" scandal, coupled with the earlier campaign finance scandal involving sleazy Asian fund-raisers for President Clinton, have revived a concept that sent well over one hundred thousand Japanese Americans to concentration camps during World War II. This is the idea that, unlike European immigrants, who quickly assimilate as Americans, Asians can never be trusted to become loyal to their newly adopted country.

Eternally subject to questions of "dual loyalty," Asian immigrants as "perpetual immigrants" must therefore be put under constant surveillance, their integration into mainstream American institutions monitored and, if necessary, curtailed. Consider Kissinger, Brzynski, Albright—three European immigrants who have risen to the exalted position of American secretary of state, entrusted with negotiating the national security interests of the United States with their countries of birth. Where is even remotely an Asian American counterpart?

Yet, and here is the interesting twist about the construction of Asian Americans at the end of the twentieth century: while they are maligned over and over again as potentially disloyal and untrustworthy immigrants—a burden imposed on them since the nineteenth century, when they first arrived on these shores, and carried to its most extreme expression in the concentration camps of WWII—they are also frequently praised as a "model minority," even paraded before other, "less successful," minorities as paragons of American virtue to be closely emulated.

There is an irony to the construction of race for white and black Americans on the one hand, and the other racialized groups on the other. Despite deep-seated and widely distributed hostility against them, only the most virulent and crudest white supremacist would deny that blacks are American, or that Americans can be black, as they are most assuredly white. The same cannot be said about Latinos/as or Asians in America, regardless of how many generations they have been here.

If we really want to follow where postmodern race and race relations are heading, I suggest we follow the twists and turns of the Asian American trajectory. Asian Americans are, first of all, constructed as aliens not to be trusted, as foreigners perpetually strange, and at the same time, as model minorities, meaning they are good immigrants and eminently assimilable. Thus depicted, they signal to the dominant, white Americans that they can be used as allies as their own numbers steadily dwindle proportionately. In this regard, Asian Americans have been characterized as "honorary whites," "probationary whites," "near whites," "almost whites," and "whites-in-waiting." In short, the racial identity being imposed on Asian Americans is situational: at times they are lumped with other bad immigrants, illegal and not to be trusted and hence not to be integrated; at other times they are seen as pliable immigrants, susceptible to subtle political manipulation, such as voting the right way in order to preserve white privilege.

A good example of the latter kind of racial construction for Asian Americans is the appeal made by proponents of California's Proposition 209 to Asian Americans for their support, by convincing them that they would immediately benefit when race-preferential practices were cut off for African Americans and Latinos/as. As is the case for whites, according to this argument, affirmative action has constituted "reverse discrimination" for deserving Asian Americans. This same sentiment motivated five Chinese American families in San Francisco to sue the school district's admissions policies to the academically rigorous and highly selective Lowell high school when their children were denied places. Chinese Americans already make up 45 percent of Lowell's school population, the maximum allowed under a desegregation plan devised by a coalition of civil rights groups led by the NAACP sixteen years ago to ensure that the school would not be reserved just for Chinese Americans, but would reflect the city's diverse population. By lending credence to the "model minority" construct, these Asian Americans are *being positioned*, and indeed are *positioning themselves*, to be white by behavior, values, and disposition.

Whether viewed as immutably foreign or highly assimilable, Asian Americans have been "racially triangulated" vis-à-vis blacks and whites, according to a provocative thesis advanced by political scientist Claire Jean Kim to explain the apparently fluctuating and situational racial identification of Asian Americans. In other words, Asian Americans have been situated not so much in a fixed position between black and white as shunted back and forth between the two poles, alternately reinforcing one or the other, but always for the purpose of "reproducing patterns of white power and privilege."[4] Thus, at all times, dominant whites call the shots and determine with which pole (black or white) Asian Americans should be identified. When whites call forth the "model minority" tendency of Asian Americans, that is a ploy to control other racialized minorities, such as blacks and Latinos/as, as well as the Asians themselves. At other times, dominant whites simply relegate Asian Americans to the garbage heap of unassimilable, perpetual aliens, never to be trusted, a status lower even than that of blacks, who are, at least, acknowledged as American.

America, black and white and beyond: are we moving toward a multicultural society, as the liberal campus diversity plans would beguile us to believe, where race is no more than just another kind of difference, and civility is the cure for all social conflict? Or are the postmodern practices of racial discourse and racial construction just as committed as in the past to upholding white supremacy? In this brief discussion, I have tried to argue the latter point.

NOTES

1. *The Nation,* 29 March 1999, 410.
2. Gary Y. Okihiro, *Margins and Mainstreams: Asians in American History and Culture* (Seattle: University of Washington Press, 1994), 31–63.
3. Evelyn Hu-DeHart, "Race, Civil Rights, and the New Immigrants: Nativism and the New World Order," in *Civil Rights and Race Relations in the Post Reagan-Bush Era,* ed. Samuel L. Myers Jr. (Westport, Conn.: Praeger, 1997).
4. Claire Jean Kim, "The Racial Triangulation of Asian Americans," *Politics and Society* 27, no. 1 (1999): 105–38.

PART II

The Social and Cultural Boundaries of Race

~:~

7

Aliens, Misfits, and Interlopers: The Racialized Imagining of the U.S. Latino Communities at the End of the Twentieth Century*

A R T U R O   M A D R I D

IMAGES AND STORIES

"The United States has no history; it has only the movies," or so the eminent novelist Carlos Fuentes is reputed to have said. It is a wonderful "take," to use film discourse. Whatever one's political orientation, most anyone can resonate to that statement. I regret that the quote is not one that can be attributed to me, although my own version would not have been so pithy or so memorable. My statement would be that the United States has no history; rather it has images and stories that have dissembled as history. These images and their accompanying stories predate the movies. Notwithstanding the continuing struggle to eliminate them from U.S. culture, they continue to be present in the consciousness of the citizenry of the United States, and to manifest themselves both in their outrageous forms and in more subtle but no less nefarious ways.

My charge is to address the racial status and experiences of the peoples we label Hispanics and/or Latinos in the United States. The subject is complicated

---

*This was a keynote address given at the "Race in 21st Century America" conference.

and has a complex history. It is deeply intertwined with matters of class, culture, nationality, and religion and is thus not easily deconstructed. The racial status of Latinos (my preferred term) has to do with problematical images and stories that have deep and convoluted roots. Although the issues of race are usually framed and discussed in terms of social science paradigms, my metier as a professor of the humanities is the analysis of discourse, narratives, and images. Thus my remarks will be informed in part by the discussion of images held of Latinos in U.S. society, as well as by the narrative that accompanies those images. To do so I will share with you a number of anecdotes, some of them personal, to illustrate the larger, collective realities and experiences of Latinos. Walter Benjamin is reputed to have said that the only antidote to history is anecdote. If the United States has no history, but rather images and stories that are passed off as history, then it is only appropriate to project different images and tell still other stories, and allow them to form a counterhistory.

ALIENS, MISFITS, AND INTERLOPERS: LATINOS IMAGINED

The U.S. communities labeled as Latino are a diverse set of populations whose roots grow deep in the soil of the United States. Their members, however, have not, either as individuals or as a collectivity, ever been considered part of the "imagined community" of this nation.[1] We have consistently been defined out. We have historically been considered the "other." That is the subtext of the question all Latinos are asked: And where are you from? We are not perceived as being "from here." Rather, we have been considered to be a "foreign other," regardless of our individual or collective histories. Moreover, our imagined "otherness" is shaped by deep-rooted images and stories concerning our ancestors and ancestry. Some are grandiose and exotic, such as those having to do with Spanish conquest and Aztec Empire. Most are disparaging and demeaning, such as those that have to do with religious and cultural practices or racial origins and class status. The experience of the Latino populations has thus been characterized by the exoticization of our history and the denigration of our culture, of our traditions, of our racial and ethnic makeup--that is, of our very being. We have been "imagined" and found wanting. Multiple images or perceptions of Latinos exist, even some that are fully fleshed out and complex. However, the images that principally obtain are reductionist, stereotypical, one-dimensional images and at the most unexpected moments, the most outrageous of these images surface. This latter phenomenon is the social equivalent of the mathematical search for the lowest common denominator, except that it serves no good purpose.

Antonia I. Castañeda, the prize-winning Chicana historian, in her public presentations on the history of Anglo "imagining" of Spanish, Mexican, and indigenous women in eighteenth- and nineteenth-century California, tells of an experience she had as a high school teacher shortly after completing her B.A. She had joined her colleagues for happy hour on a Friday afternoon midway through the school year. As she sat there, enjoying the conviviality of the moment, a male Anglo colleague leaned across the table and said to her: "Isn't it wonderful that you got a college education? Otherwise you would be a prostitute . . . in Mexico." The subject of this imagining had great-grandparents who were U.S. citizens, had been a lifelong resident of the state of Washington, was a native speaker of English, had taken on all the modes and manners of American middle-class society, and moreover was a professional. Her multilayered identity, however, had been reduced to the lowest possible common social denominator almost as fast as most of us can say "God Bless America!"

Ah, yes, you might say, but that was long ago and far away. Allow me to disabuse you of that notion. Shortly after joining the faculty of Trinity University in 1993, I participated in a seminar on diversity with fellow faculty members. One of my colleagues, who was carrying out a study on cross-cultural communication, played for us a videotape of an interview she had filmed with a young Mexican American woman. The subject talked about having had an Anglo boyfriend during high school, and about how, when she had broken off the relationship, he had called her a Mexican whore. She could understand that in his anger he might call her a whore. But why, she wondered, did he feel he had to call her a *Mexican* whore? More recently, at Baylor University a sorority and fraternity joined together for a costume party, the theme of which was "Run for the Border." The sorority members presented themselves in low-cut, off-the-shoulder peasant blouses, barefoot and pregnant.

This is an enduring image in U.S. history, along with that of menacing, dark-skinned men who are either visibly armed or undoubtedly concealing a knife, which is, in part, how the fraternity members at the aforementioned party presented themselves. Renato Rosaldo, the distinguished Stanford University professor of anthropology, tells an anecdote about the academic war over the multicultural curriculum at Stanford University, waged in part in the Letters to the Editor section of the *Stanford Daily*. In one of the many letters on the topic, a letter that prompted Dr. Rosaldo to suspend the exchange in view of a sinister twist in the discourse, an antagonist to the proposed changes in the curriculum warned his fellow academics about the "multi-culturalists," whom, he wrote, ". . . approach you with a smile on their face and a knife behind their teeth."

Still another pervasive image is that of Latinos as interlopers in U.S. society. We are not deemed entitled to be members of the society, much less thought qualified to participate in its institutions. I have, for a good part of my life, found myself in institutional environments and social situations where it was clear to me that I was perceived to be an intruder. My first experiences in this regard were in mainline Protestant churches, the principal places where as a child I came in contact with Anglo children. My Anglo peers knew that they belonged and that they were entitled to be there. They were aware of their privilege, even though they might not have been capable of articulating it. Needless to say, I was keenly aware of my interloper status in U.S. society and its institutions long before I understood what considerations informed it.

Oh well, you might say, that was a lifetime ago; things have changed. Let me tell you a more recent story. Several years ago, but hardly a lifetime ago, I presented myself as a candidate for the presidency of a highly regarded urban institution of higher education and was invited to meet with the selection committee. For reasons that I will not go into today I was not the favorite candidate of the campus representatives on the selection committee. My challenge was thus to confirm the good judgment of the external members of the committee while at the same time convincing the campus members that they had me wrong, that I would make a good president of the institution. I was not, however, quite prepared for the first question of the interview, asked by a member of the board of trustees of the university. "Dr. Madrid," he asked me, "how does a one-dimensional person like you believe he can be the president of a multidimensional institution such as ours?"

In the American social landscape we—, that is, chicana/os, puertorriqueña/os, mexicana/os, hispana/os, and latina/os—have been historically imagined as sluts and villains, aliens, and interlopers, as incompetents and malcontents. We have been historically perceived as corrupt and venal, lazy and lacking in initiative, perverse and criminally inclined, passive, present-time oriented, fatalistic, and the list goes on. That denigration has been the basis for our exclusion and marginalization from the social and institutional life of U.S. society. Sadly, many in our community have come to accept that disparagement as truth. Some of our most gifted and talented members have come to believe that we do not have the right values and beliefs, the proper attitudes and manners, sufficiently elevated goals, even appropriate ancestors, to be good and acceptable members of this society.[2]

What is curious is that the more things have changed, the more they have stayed the same. Thus, what obtained in the past returns to confound us in the present. This society has struggled over the course of the two centuries of its existence to change the ways in which it treats its citizens. Yet U.S. society has had immense difficulty in ridding itself of the narrow way in which it imagines itself and those persons who constitute it. That imagining and its narratives are at the heart of the problem.

We dare not protest too much. "You are too sensitive," we are told. "These are anomalies. And so what? Imagine what it would be like if you were back in Mexico, Puerto Rico, Central America, wherever? Besides, your societies of origin are shaped by racial and class considerations. In fact, you have it pretty good. What are you complaining about? What's your beef? What are you whining about?" I can only say that if those of us whose roots grow deep in what is now the U.S. nation, whose bona fides as American citizens are unimpeachable, whose standing in the society is most elevated and secure are so viewed and dealt with, it is not difficult to imagine the experiences that those Latinos who do not have the protective colorations of complexion, speech, and manners or the armor of political and socioeconomic status undergo.

U.S. Society Imagined

The historical bases for the imagining of communities are multiple. Shared language and culture have historically been the basis for community. Religion has been a powerful force in creating community, and in combination with language, culture, and territory, has historically been the basis of city-states, of empires, and subsequently of nations. Over the course of centuries, however, humans have also imagined themselves in relation to the "other"—the religious other, the racial other, the ethnic other, the cultural other, the gendered other, the sexual other.

The imagining of what became the U.S. community did not initiate with the arrival of peoples of Anglo-Saxon origin on this continent. It had begun in the struggles for political and economic dominance that raged in Europe from the fifteenth through the seventeenth centuries. Those struggles were exacerbated by the ideological tensions that informed the Protestant Reformation, or the Great Schism, depending on one's religious identification. North America was a space removed from the intensity of those struggles. It was a place where the multiple political and religious communities of Northern Europe, having freed themselves from their respective tyrannies, could in greater or lesser measure indulge their interests, practice their beliefs, impose their values on members of their communities, and govern themselves as they saw fit.

Contrary to myth, the communities of the nascent United States were not democratic, inclusive, or tolerant in principle. They became democratic and tolerant out of necessity, in order to unite for purposes of resisting the oppression they had fled but to which they were still subject. Their democratic values and what tolerance for difference existed were moreover not universal, but rather obtained mainly for those who shared maleness, European origins, property, power, and religious beliefs. In the majority of the communities that would subsequently join to form the United States, slaves, servants, and women were, to a greater or lesser degree, chattel. The indigenous populations were wild animals to be controlled, held at bay, or, if necessary and possible, eliminated. The imagined communities of the original thirteen colonies were thus characterized more by exclusion than by inclusion, and the evolving, overarching, imagined collectivity was particularly defined by gender, class, and race, in addition to religious orientation.

For members of the evolving society of the United States, our ancestors were a somewhat removed "other" who lived in the Caribbean, in Mesoamerica, in Central and South America. If in Europe the "otherness" of our ancestors had been marked by differences with respect to religion, to culture, and to political and economic interests, in the Americas that "otherness" also came to be defined by the complexities of their racial and social makeup. The communities of our ancestors included large numbers of Amerindians, blacks, persons of various Asian origins, and peoples of mixed race (*mestizos*), none of whom were included in any of the imagined communities of what would become the United States.

The foundation for what would become the Latino communities of the United States was laid in the nineteenth century as the evolving nation imagined itself first as a continental then as a hemispherical and world power. The emerging U.S. empire, following the dictates of its imagining, termed Manifest Destiny, expanded first into Mexican territory in 1848, then, in 1898, into the remains of the Spanish Empire, including Cuba, Puerto Rico, the Philippines, and the various Pacific island territories. The Latino "other" thus ceased to be abstract and remote, and became concrete and immediate.

In the Southwest, the members of the new American Empire came into contact not only with new groups of indigenous peoples—Apaches, Comanches, Hopis, Navajos, Tewas, Utes, Zunis, and so on—but also with the *mestizo* colonizers of the Spanish borderlands. Although the narratives of the Anglo-American observers were principally characterized by their cultural, religious, and political biases, the predominant preoccupation of the Anglo-Americans was the biological makeup of the *mestizo* peoples they found there. Not only did the *mestizos* coexist with the local indigenous populations, they had also mixed with them. Indigenous ancestry, moreover, did not necessarily correspond to lack of status. Anxiety and concern about this new and complex "otherness" increased as the United States expanded outside its continental boundaries and into the Caribbean and the Pacific. Outside the continent the human mix was even more complex and therefore more problematical for members of U.S. society. The populations of the societies incorporated into the Union in the 1898 war against Spain were not only defined by their indigenous origins, whether American or Asian-Pacific, but also by their African ones. While the peoples of indigenous and African descent did not have the same standing as *mestizos* in these societies, they were not without status, power, or possessions.

The historical literature is replete with expressions of the distaste, of the sense of revulsion felt by Anglo-Americans toward the peoples they conquered.[3] Our ancestors were divided into those who were "Spanish," meaning light complected, European looking, and wealthy, and everyone else, whether indigenous, African, or of mixed origin. By and large, however, our ancestors were seen and dealt with as a class. They were imagined as being a "mongrel" population. The distinctions between those deemed "Spanish" and everyone else were applied only when they served a useful purpose, as to divide in order to overcome.

Our ancestors, by and large, did not choose to become part of the United States. It was imposed on them. This is not to say that there were not those among our ancestors who did identify with the ideals and the ways of the United States. Some of our ancestors participated actively in efforts to have their region become part of the United States. They joined the new society, made theirs the values of the conquering nation, took on its manners and modes, learned its language, adopted its institutions, joined its churches, and, through marriage, sought to incorporate themselves into the new community.

The second half of the nineteenth and the first half of the twentieth centuries are one long series of disillusionments for the peoples of the Southwest, Puerto Rico, and Cuba.[4] Many, perhaps most, of those who sought inclusion were sorely disappointed. Notwithstanding their accommodations (taking on the values, the beliefs, and the ways of the new society and adopting its institutions), the reality was that they did not fit the imagined community of the United States. Their cultural adaptations were not sufficient to make them acceptable to the new society.

The very names they used to refer to themselves—Mexicans, Puerto Ricans, and Cubans—became terms of opprobrium. In an effort to project themselves as part of the new society, of the evolving U.S. imagined community, and to avoid the denigration implicit in their national-origin names, our ancestors took on other names—Hispanic Americans, Latin Americans, Spanish Americans. What they could not do was change the color of their skin, or purge themselves of their racial histories; that is, their social accommodations did not make them acceptable to the new society.

Although some continued to seek space within the new society, others, excluded from it, began to imagine themselves as part of the larger Spanish-speaking world. The *mestizo* populations of the Southwest turned to the evolving Mexican nation and Mexican society for support, nurture, inspiration, and even protection. The peoples of Puerto Rico and Cuba, who had been frustrated in their dreams of national independence, continued to nurture an oppositional nationalist imagining, reaffirmed their language and cultures of origin, and sought nurture and support from their sister societies and nations of the Western Hemisphere.

The Latino Populations Imagine Themselves

During the first half of the twentieth century the population today denominated Hispanic or Latino consisted of three discrete population groups—Mexican Americans, Cuban Americans, and Puerto Ricans—separated from each other by geography, cultural modes, historical experience, civic status, and even language. Each had its own linguistic forms, customs, music, food, and ways of being. As a consequence of their different histories, the different groups interacted with the Anglo-American population and its institutions in different ways. Their numbers were so small, and they were so widely dispersed, that they were, for the most part, invisible. Their presence in American institutions was negligible.

Latinos began to imagine themselves as a pan-ethnic U.S. polity during the social and political fervor of the 1960s. The Hispanic identity was an imagining promoted by groups seeking to benefit from the policies and programs of the Great Society.[5] That imagining was taken up by individuals and organizations that sought to increase their influence in the national electoral and policy processes. It sought to connect communities of persons who thought of themselves in cultural, regional, or national terms, who were separated from each other not only physically but also psychologically, and who had discrete interests. It sought strength in numbers. It sought to skirt cultural difference. It sought to sanitize "otherness," and particularly a racialized "otherness." It sought to evade the heritage of denigration present in the historical designators and the lingering aspects of "foreign otherness" signaled by the alternatives. It was an imagining that was oppositional in nature. Hispanic imagining said: "We are similar if perhaps not identical. We are different but not unlike. Please believe it. Please accept it."

Yet the imagining of a Hispanic polity was also a response to other imaginings taking place within the Mexican American and Puerto Rican communities, and specifically to the challenge posed by the Chicano and Boricua movements to Anglo-American cultural, economic, and political hegemony. If Hispanic advocates emphasized the homogeneous dimensions of our multiple communities, the Chicano and Boricua movements insisted on their diversity. If the proponents of a Hispanic community emphasized definition within and integration into U.S. society, the Chicano and Boricua movements sought identification and connection with the larger hemispheric world. If Hispanic advocates looked for ways of identifying with and accommodating themselves to the institutions of U.S. society, Chicano and Boricua activists challenged those institutions and made common cause with Third World movements. If the term "Hispanic" signaled European origins, the use of "Chicano" and "Boricua" stressed indigenous and African heritage. Chicano and Boricua imagining was oppositional in nature. Chicano and Boricua imagining said: "We are who we are. We affirm it. Believe it. Accept it. Live with it."

Latinos in the 1980s: A Moment in the Sun

At the beginning of the 1980s, we—that is to say, the U.S. populations labeled as Hispanics and/or Latinos—had our moment in the sun, or, to cite Andy Warhol, a more cynical observer of contemporary society, our fifteen minutes of fame. The decade of the 1980s was termed as the "Decade of the Hispanic" by no less than *Time Magazine*. We had developed a national visibility, and, by and large, it was positive. Our struggles had resulted in an assurance that the Latino population was factored, in a limited fashion to be sure, into the policy-making processes of U.S. institutions and was included in the programs growing out of those processes. The market potential of the growing Latino population became evident, and the media, a vital part of the new market forces, promoted the phenomenon. Our culture was seen as having admirable dimensions. We were perceived to be optimistic, dynamic, hardworking, and resourceful. Our modes, manners, and values were praised. Our cultural expression was viewed as rich and fascinating. Needless to say, those views were not universally shared, and the moment did not last.

This positive perception principally obtained before large numbers of Central American refugees and Mexican immigrants became a visible presence not only in Los Angeles and Miami but also in the urban centers, the suburbs, and the rural areas of the rest of the nation; before Spanish-language television became part of the cable television spectrum and we seemed to reside everywhere; before our numbers increased to thirty million; before we became the fourth-largest Latino nation in the hemisphere. Profound changes occurred at the end of the twentieth century with respect not only to the origins, size, and makeup of the Latino populations of the United States, but also in regard to how Latinos perceive themselves and to how they are perceived in U.S. society.[6]

THE NEW LATINO POPULATIONS

If the original U.S. Latino communities had their origins in nineteenth-century U.S. foreign policy, new ones resulted in large measure from the foreign policy of the United States during the second half of the twentieth century. The cold war and its hot episodes displaced Cubans and Dominicans, then Argentines, Chileans, Uruguayans, Guatemalans, Hondurans, Nicaraguans, and Salvadorans, who came to the United States as political refugees. Globalization of the economy displaced additional persons—professionals, entrepreneurs, artisans, functionaries, and peasants—from these societies and other hemispheric nations and brought them as economic refugees to the United States.

The growth and diversity of the new Latino populations brought new imaginings, and complications associated with those imaginings. To the competing imaginings of the original Latino communities were added the diverse imaginings of the immigrants and refugees of the various societies of Latino America. Not previously faced with the necessity to define themselves culturally or racially in their societies of origin, having only to assert their relative class standing within their respective societies, the new Latino populations were shocked and frequently traumatized by the dynamics of identity in the United States. In the United States they became part of a category labeled Hispanic. Their diverse historical experiences and cultural expressions became "conflated," to use Suzanne Oboler's term, with those of the original Latino populations.[7] In the United States they had to define themselves racially and culturally, or risk being lumped with "them." Caste and breeding took on new dimensions and major importance. The denial of indigenous or African ancestry became de rigueur, as did the affirmation of European ancestry and, of course, of *cultura*; that is, of good manners, proper ways, appropriate socialization, propriety of speech—in short, of breeding. These were not so much assertions as protestations. We are not "them"—those people who barely speak Spanish, who betray African or indigenous ancestry, who have no *cultura*, who are so devalued in American society.

Latinos at the End of the Twentieth Century

At the end of the twentieth century there is a powerful sense of the possibilities of a pan-ethnic community. Those who have won the day are the advocates of a Hispanic imagined community. Hispanic is the accepted, public pan-ethnic label, used by the designees and designators alike. Hispanic has become a local, state, and federal designation. Hispanic is the designator of professional associations. Hispanic is the universal situational label we all use, notwithstanding how one might feel about it. For many it is a way of overcoming the stigmatization of historical designators. For others it is a way of coping with, eliding, even dismissing, the irritant of having constantly to explain oneself, to define oneself as being part of, as opposed to being apart from, U.S. society.

While much is made of the public policy dimensions of this imagining, the triumph of the Hispanic imagined community is less a public arena victory than a private sector coup, one driven by a profound appreciation of the purchasing power of thirty million folks and by a sophisticated understanding of their purchasing inclinations. This newly imagined community constitutes not only a large market but a growing one as well. While its diversity might be a critical factor in selling to it, its diversity is not a desideratum in selling it. What is sellable is an artificially homogenized package: the Hispanic market, and its consuming potential. And that has required considerable imagining!

Ultimately, however, the imagined Hispanic community is not one we all fit into, for a variety of reasons.

- First and foremost, the imagined Hispanic community tends to emphasize European origins, and downplays, even dismisses, North African, African, Asian-Pacific, and American origins.
- Second, the imagined Hispanic community, being in no small measure a

function of market forces, is defined by consumerism. One is particularly Hispanic if one is economically and professionally successful and can consume significantly.

+ Third, the imagined Hispanic community downplays, even trivializes, the differences between its own values and beliefs, its various cultural traditions and practices, its ways of being and doing, and those of the dominant culture.

+ Fourth, the traditional modes and manners that the imagined Hispanic community affirms are very much class-defined, and are those that are common to the elites of the various communities.

+ Moreover Latino historical realities and concerns remain the same, as do their inherent contradictions and tensions.

+ Notwithstanding the projection by the mass media of a Europeanized cultural frame and the predominance of European phenotypes both as public and commercial figures, the physical "otherness" of the members of the Latino population inserts itself into the public arena, certainly as supporting cast and audience and not infrequently as central figures. These "others" do not imagine themselves as Hispanic, but instead define themselves culturally, nationally, or politically.

+ Notwithstanding the triumphs of the past three decades—that is, the partial penetration of the major institutions and sectors of U.S. society, in many of those institutions and sectors Latinos are still "onlys," or marginal figures. Moreover, the policies and programs that made Latino gains possible have now been dismantled or are being dismantled.

+ Notwithstanding the progress made in the past three decades to have matters of concern to Latinos conceptualized and dealt with as public issues having a systemic basis, economic and political implications, or policy solutions, Latino needs and concerns are once again being conceptualized as private problems driven by cultural factors. Can't get a job? Learn English! Can't earn a decent wage? Work harder! Feel discriminated against? Go back where you came from!

+ Despite the strength of homogenizing forces in U.S. society, the diverse cultural manifestations of the various Latino communities have become ever more apparent. Given the present-day ease of communication and of travel, as well of as continuing immigration, the differences between and among Latino population groups will not disappear, but instead will be reinforced. Shared culture and cultural expression will not evolve inevitably, but instead will have to be forged.

Moreover, the societal perception of Latinos has changed sharply as the century has drawn to a close. The Latino population is increasingly seen as problematical, and resistance to its presence and interests has grown and spread. Latinos are being reimagined: as "illegal" immigrants; as drug dealers and smugglers; as gangbangers; and so on. That this should happen is not surprising. In fact, these attitudes were present at the beginning of the 1980s. They were, in fact, part and parcel of the ways in which Mexicans and Puerto Ricans (and by extension, the peoples of the Western Hemisphere) historically have been viewed by U.S. society.

While this change in perception is clearly related to economic conditions in the United States, simply attributing the change in perception to economic tensions is not sufficient. There is a marked change in attitude toward the Latino community. Antagonism now informs it profoundly. That antagonism manifests itself in both official and unofficial policy and practice, and is to be found in all U.S. arenas. The most powerful manifestations of this antagonism have been the attacks on what is presented as unfettered immigration. The attitudes are given a reasonable face. They are characterized as having to do with "imagined" immigrants: dark-skinned persons from the Spanish-speaking countries of the Western Hemisphere, who have entered the country illegally. These attitudes supposedly spring from concern about the burden the presence of immigrants—already characterized as "illegal" and as "aliens"—has placed on ordinary American citizens, and particularly on the impact these immigrants have had on black Americans and the working poor. "Those people" are persons who, allegedly, reproduce excessively; take advantage of public welfare; place unwarranted demands on schools, hospitals, and other public institutions; undercut wages and take jobs away from citizens; profit improperly from affirmative action policies and programs; don't pay taxes; don't learn English; don't assimilate; don't become educated; don't become citizens; don't vote (or vote illegally and improperly); don't involve themselves in the society; are separatist, ad infinitum, ad nauseam. In addition, however, "those people" also now include persons who are involved in the drug trade and other illicit activities, who are scofflaws and criminals.

The notorious incidents involving undocumented Mexican workers in the past several years are public knowledge. Less evident or well known are the outrages suffered by the average Latino resident or citizen of the United States, at the hands of the Immigration and Naturalization Service (INS), the Drug Enforcement Administration (DEA), or other of the multitudinous agencies of the United States. I will say that I do not know of any cases involving the interdiction of immigrants of Irish origin, much less interdiction involving physical attacks or pursuit unto death. A startling new development is a proposal to deny citizenship to the native-born children of undocumented immigrants, a status that for more than a hundred years has been part of the bedrock of U.S. society. The issue of immigrants was at the center of a major electoral controversy in 1996, when Loretta Sanchez successfully challenged the notorious Orange County, California, congressman, Bob Dornan, given to reactionary, xenophobic, homophobic, and racist utterances and stances. His unsuccessful but damaging charge was that immigrants had voted illegally. Undocumented immigrants also figure in the tensions over census enumeration, which affects budgetary allocations and congressional representation. All of this is a striking and a rather disproportional reaction, given that less than 10 percent of the Latino population of the United States consists of undocumented immigrants, and a good number of these are refugees created by U.S. foreign policy.

The antagonism against this imagined Latino population is also evident in the harsh and unreasonable attacks on policies and programs designed to promote the welfare of poor children, women, elder citizens, and disabled and otherwise unemployed or unemployable persons. While the dismantling of the U.S. welfare system may not have been aimed specifically at the Latino population, to the extent that it was in response to perceived "undeserving" populations—immigrants, whatever their status—as opposed to the "deserving" poor, and to the extent that the popular perception is that all Latinos are immigrants, reproduce excessively, and do not carry their weight, that dismantling was directed at the Latino population. Latinos have taken the brunt of the social and economic impact, since Latino children, women, families, and elderly constitute a disproportionate part of the impoverished population of the United States.

That antagonism is also evident in the hostility and the challenges to the policies and programs designed to promote equity in contracting, employment, promotions, and admissions to institutions of higher education and particularly to professional programs of study within those institutions. While not directly or exclusively aimed at Latinos, the policies and programs are perceived as improperly benefiting a population that is "foreign," or that is academically and intellectually deficient, and is therefore undeserving.

It is in the area of language and culture that the antagonism to Latinos manifests itself most acutely. Antipathy to the use of Spanish in the public arena has long been the norm. Antagonism to the official use of a language other than English, and. in particular, Spanish became widespread during the 1980s. More recently that antagonism has manifested itself in very different institutional spaces, namely in the workplace and in the family, and it has specifically manifested itself in terms of language. One of the most provocative incidents took place in Texas in 1997, when two employees of a small insurance firm who had been hired to attend to a Spanish-speaking clientele were proscribed from speaking Spanish when not directly engaged with a client. The most outrageous incident in this regard involved an intervention by the judicial system in the most hallowed of private sector areas: the family. In 1995 a Texas judge reprimanded a mother for speaking Spanish to her female child, stating that not speaking English to her constituted abusive behavior and would consign that child to a life as a maid.

Yet the most serious area of the proscription of language is once again in the public arena, in the educational system. In 1998, voters in the state of California overwhelmingly approved an electoral initiative eliminating the use of bilingual education in K-12 educational systems. The initiative was clearly and specifically targeted against the use of Spanish as a language of instruction. Once again the arguments were given a reasonable face. Bilingual education, it was argued, impedes the learning of English, retards development, hinders assimilation, privileges ethnicity, creates divisiveness, promotes reverse racism, fosters separatism, and so on..

The focus of the critics on language is tactical, for the hostility is culturally driven. The discourse of the critics betrays economic, political, ideological, and cultural resentment. What the advocates of bilingual education are defending, its antagonists say, are jobs and political interests. What is being promulgated, they furthermore charge, is anti-Americanism. What is lacking, according to that discourse, is individual, familial, and cultural commitment to and support for learning. This is an old canard outfitted in new clothes. It says that Latino problems are private failings and not subject to public policy solution. It says once again that Latinos do not belong; that the concerns of the Latino populations are illegitimate.

What accounts for this loathing, given the vitality of U.S. culture and the unquestioned global economic, political, and technological hegemony of the United States? I believe that it has to do with fear: fear that the traditional values and historical modes of American society are at risk; fear that control over the society's institutions is being lost; and, in particular, fear of an imagined other that has been historically racialized. Since overt racism and xenophobia are no longer acceptable in American society, there has developed a complicated but very effective politics for dealing with this new situation. These politics promote the cult of economic success, and success in this mind-set is a function of will and hard work. From there it is but a small step to thinking, saying, and believing that the socioeconomic problems U.S. society is experiencing have a cultural foundation. That is to say, xenophobia and racism are not the problem. "They" are the problem, because "they" don't want to speak English, "they" don't get educated, "they" don't integrate, "they" are culturally deficient, "they" don't know their place, "they" are using up our resources, "they" are destroying the quality of our lives, and, even worse, "they" are slowly but surely taking over our society and our institutions. Thus, what "real" Americans must do is reimpose themselves on U.S. society and its institutions, suppressing or at least ameliorating these nefarious tendencies.

We are told, as the century comes to a close, that class has trumped race in these United States. An erstwhile W. E. B. DuBois might even be heard to say that the problem in the United States in the twenty-first century will be the class line. The evidence brought to bear on this matter is weighty and considerable. Among the multitude of voices that declare this to be the case are many we deem authoritative and trustworthy.[8] We would like to believe, and yet suspicions die hard. The memories of racial exclusion, exploitation, and violence linger on. The image of the racialized Latino "other" surfaces all too often, not only for those persons who are poor and lack protections, and not only in the form of chases unto death or in the form of physical and psychological brutalization. Racialization occurs also for Latinos who have taken on the protective colorations of dress, speech, and manners or girded themselves in the supposedly invincible armor of wealth, status, influence, and power. We are reminded of our imagined and undesired "otherness" by patronizing introductions; by not-so-subtle questions about our origins; by eyes that glaze over when we speak; by our absence from social and institutional spaces; by looks that ask: what is she/he doing here? More often than we care to admit, we are reminded of our racialized otherness in more aggressive forms: when, in stores, on interstate highways, and in airports, we realize that the attention we have drawn has to do with the fact that we fit a profile; when we are verbally demeaned, whether in slips of the tongue or in overheard remarks; when through jokes and witticisms we are made parties to the disparagement of the "other"; when we experience rejection, exclusion, or ostracism, especially if we dare not know our place.

We remember, then, that in matters of the heart and the head there exists an awful synchronicity. Bigotry does not disappear, but frequently takes on other forms. It lives side by side with tolerance, and chronically recurs, recharged, revitalized, and reimagined but no less virulent or destructive. When it does, as we know from the experience of Germany's Jewish population, neither manners nor status offer protection against the nefarious and powerful imagining of racism. Thus, while we must attend to the voices that proclaim the declining significance of race in these United States, let us remember that racism is a cancer present at all times in the body politic. Let us not be lulled by its supposed remission, but rather let us be mindful of its regenerative powers. Let us be aware of its capacity to transform itself, and therefore be alert to its multiple disguises. Above all, let us remain constantly on watch for its symptoms and on guard against its manifestations.

I end as I began, quoting and paraphrasing Carlos Fuentes. "Our world," he said in a recent speech, "is moving in two directions. One group is headed towards the global village; the other towards the local village. The global village wears a cold, uncaring, technocratic mask as though macro-economic wisdom did not affect people, only numbers. . . . The local village all too often spills over into religious fundamentalism, ethnic cleansing, hatred of the other, xenophobia and racism. Our sense of belonging to the same human species is being severely challenged." Fuentes goes on to say that what will be needed in the future are new ways for people to remain connected. "The lesson of our unfinished history," he concludes, "is that when we exclude we are poor, and when we include we are rich. We have yet to discover how to reach out, to name and embrace the number of our brothers and sisters. Our arms are capable of holding them."[9]

I wish I had said that. Unlike my position with respect to Carlos Fuentes' previous statement, my "take" on this one would be identical to his, word for word, phrase for phrase, image for image. I would add, however, that we who experience local village life at the center of the global village must be particularly vigilant and exceptionally active against the ravages of both.

NOTES

1. The concept is from Benedict Anderson, *Imagined Communities: Reflections on the Origin and Spread of Nationalism* (New York: Verso, 1983). See also Renato Rosaldo, *Re-Imagining National*

Communities, Stanford Chicano Research Center Working Paper no. 36, Stanford University, 1991. Rosaldo's working paper is a commentary on Benedict Anderson's study.

2. While this is a long-term historical phenomenon, its current-day manifestations are to be found in the writings and statements of such "Hispanic" notables as Richard Rodriguez and Linda Chavez, among others. A rather transparent and recent addition to this corpus is Lionel Sosa's *The American Dream: How Latinos Can Achieve Success in Business and in Life* (New York: Dutton, 1998).

3. See, among others, Ramón A. Gutiérrez, "Unraveling America's Hispanic Past: Internal Stratification and Class Boundaries," *Aztlán, An International Journal for Chicano Research* 17, no. 1 (1987): 79–101; Rodolfo Acuña, *Occupied America: A History of Chicanos* (New York: Harper and Row, 1981); Arnoldo de Leon, *They Called Them Greasers: Anglo Attitudes towards Mexicans in Texas: 1821–1900* (Austin: University of Texas Press, 1983); Abraham Hoffman, *Unwanted Mexican Americans in the Great Depression; Repatriation Pressures: 1929–1939* (Tucson: University of Arizona Press, 1974); Carey McWilliams, *North from Mexico* (New York: Greenwood Press, 1968); and David Montejano, *Anglos and Mexicans in the Making of Texas, 1836–1986* (Austin: University of Texas Press, 1987).

4. See, among others, Acuña, *Occupied America*; Mario A. Barrera, *Race and Class in the Southwest. A Theory of Racial Inequality* (Notre Dame-London: University of Notre Dame Press, 1979); Manuel Maldonado-Denis, *Puerto Rico y Estados Unidos: emigración y colonialismo: un análisis sociohistórico de la emigración puertorriqueña* (México: Siglo XXI Editores, 1978); and Gerald E. Poyo, *With All, and for the Good of All: The Emergence of Popular Nationalism in the Cuban Communities of the United States, 1848–1898* (Durham, N.C.: Duke University Press, 1989).

5. See, among others, Jack D. Forbes, "The Hispanic Spin: Party Politics and governmental Manipulation of Ethnic Identity," *Latin American Perspectives* 19, no. 4 (1992): 59–78; and Laura Gómez, "The Birth of the 'Hispanic' Generation: Attitudes of Mexican-American Political Elites toward the Hispanic Label," *Latin American Perspectives* 19, no. 4 (1992): 45–58.

6. See, among others, Martha E. Giménez, "Latino/'Hispanic'—Who Needs a Name? The Case against a Standardized Terminology," *International Journal of Health Services* 19, no. 3, (1989): 557–71; David Hayes-Bautista and Jorge Chapa, "Latino Terminology: Conceptual Bases for Standardized Terminology," *American Journal of Public Health* 77, no. 1 (1987): 61–71; Harold L. Hodgkinson, *Hispanic Americans: A Look Back, A Look Ahead* (Washington, D.C.: Center for Demographic Policy, 1996); J. Jorge Klor de Alva, "Telling Hispanics Apart: Latino Sociocultural Diversity," in *The Hispanic Experience in the United States: Contemporary Issues and Perspectives,* edited by Edna Acosta-Belen and Barbara R. Sjostrom (New York: Praeger, 1988), 107–36; and Lionel A. Maldonado, "Latino Ethnicity: Increasing Diversity," *Latino Studies Journal* 2, no. 3 (1991): 49–57.

7. Suzanne Oboler, *Ethnic Labels, Latino Lives: Identity and the Politics of (Re)Presentation in the United States* (Minneapolis: University of Minnesota Press, 1995).

8. See, among others, José Calderón, "'Hispanic' and 'Latino': The Viability of Categories for Panethnic Unity," *Latin American Perspectives* 19, no. 4 (1992): 37–44; Edward Murguía, "On Latino/Hispanic Ethnic Identity," *Latino Studies Journal* 2, no. 3 (1991): 9–18; Félix M. Padilla, *Latino Ethnic Consciousness: The Case of Mexican Americans and Puerto Ricans in Chicago* (South Bend, Ind.: University of Notre Dame Press, 1995); Clara E. Rodríguez, "Race, Culture, and Latino 'Otherness' in the 1980 Census," *Social Science Quarterly* 73, no. 4 (1992): 930–38; Rogelio Sáenz and Benigno E. Aguirre, "A Futuristic Assessment of Latino Ethnic Identity," *Latino Studies Journal* 2, no. 3 (1991): 19–32; Laurie Kay Sommers, "Inventing Latinismo: The Creating of 'Hispanic' Panethnicity in the United States," *Journal of American Folklore* 104, no. 411 (1991): 32–54; and María Eva Valle, "The Quest for Ethnic Solidarity and a New Public Identity among Chicanos and Latinos," *Latino Studies Journal* 2, no. 3 (1991).

9. Keynote Address delivered at Weber State University, Ogden, Utah, March 1999.

8

"They are Absolutely Obsessed with Us": Anti-Arab Bias in American Discourse and Policy

HUSSEIN IBISH

The persistent negative stereotyping of Arabs in American popular culture has been so often lamented that when discussing this subject one becomes, ironically, hostage to the oxymoron of a cliché which has had no cultural impact. The key industries of American mass culture, Hollywood and television, for decades have been bastions of anti-Arab stereotyping, and have consistently resisted positive or realistic representations of Arabs and Arab Americans. Negative representations in popular culture reinforce, and are reinforced by, biased and at times hostile journalism in the mainstream news media, academic polemics that urge a confrontational and aggressive approach to the U.S. role in the Middle East, and government programs and policies that are informed by anti-Arab bias and at times even involve the acting out of stereotypes received from popular culture. The result is a self-perpetuating vicious cycle of negativity about Arabs, Arab Americans, and Muslims, who have been all-too-successfully represented and accepted as "the enemy" in contemporary American culture. Thus, even as these stereotypes are increasingly critiqued and demystified by cultural observers, they retain their ubiquity and resulting negative impact on American relations with the Arab peoples and the circumstances for Arab Americans and Arabs living in the United States.

The positioning of the Arab as the "other" of contemporary American society ought, at the outset, to be viewed as an example, albeit a particularly egregious one, of what can be regarded as the universal political function of distinguishing self from other. Politically, the process of "othering" creates the boundaries that define group identity and allow for collective action. Definition of the self in terms of the other is a fundamental prerequisite of ideology, without which rationalization for collective social action is virtually impossible. Whether identified in class terms (i.e., the bourgeoisie), in religious terms (i.e., Jews or Muslims), or in ethnic terms, the other against which the collectivity is defined is a ubiquitous feature of political thought and action. As Ali A. Mazrui puts it, "The 'us' versus 'them' tendency is, in the political arena, almost universal."[1] This process is not arbitrary, and when we see it at work it is answering a specific sociopolitical demand. In American national ideology the other has variously consisted of savage Indians, tyrannical English, corrupt Mexicans, treacherous Confederates, decadent Spaniards, baby-killing Germans, fiendish Japanese, the Evil Empire of World Communism, and now the Green Menace of radical Islam. The need for a demonic common enemy has been most strikingly satisfied when "national interest" has required an ideological and emotional rationale, as in the examples cited previously. The ideological demand, and concomitant public appetite, for a vilified national enemy makes the task of the propagandist under such circumstances one of the simplest social functions—one can hardly fail to engender the requisite loathing to satisfy the ideological demand, no matter how crude, preposterous, or incompetent the defamatory representation of the enemy is. Hence, stereotyping is also strongly linked to "bad art," since it provides a most convenient shortcut for the lazy and unimaginative cultural worker in search of villains.

Of course, the subject of the "othering" process is, ironically, the self rather than the other. From a psychoanalytic perspective, we could say that this demand for a coherent, hostile other, an anti-ego ideal, is a function of the need for an illusion of the unity of the collective self. It not only creates an illusion of superiority, it provides a defense against the reality of internal fragmentation and division, and the ambivalence and complexity of identities within a given group or society. Hence the jouissance of ethnic hatred is affected by an illusion of mastery—a game in which we, by virtue of our collective negative definition of the other, create and define ourselves as masters of reality, as integral, coherent, and superior. So powerful is the emotional demand to which this process responds that even an acute awareness of its function and destructiveness provides a defense against only the most egregious expressions of collective antipathy. Even the most tolerant, generous political movements, Gandhian satyagraha, for example, or Martin Luther King's anti-racist campaigns which emphasized the virtue of loving one's enemy, still depend entirely on a distinction between the self and the other and a supreme conviction of superiority of the self, or at least the cause with which the movement is identified. No political faction, in other words, can be immune to this process. None of this ought to be taken to suggest that defamation, vilification, and scapegoating are acceptable political or rhetorical practices. Yet it is necessary to acknowledge the ubiquity, and even the inescapability, of this tendency in order to clearly confront the degree to which it poses a serious and sometimes subtle and insidious danger.

More often than not, however, the othering process is anything but subtle, and, under conditions of antagonism, it can be frighteningly automatic. In a recent exchange on the CNN television program *Larry King Live*, King, Scott O'Grady (the U.S. pilot who was shot down by Serbs over Bosnia), and Senator John McCain, in the midst of an extraordinary series of historical inaccuracies, had no trouble identifying the new Serbian enemy in general as "barbaric."

> O'GRADY: They have formidable defense systems. You have to look at this—this is the former country of Yugoslavia, front-line defense of the Soviet Union. They're also seasoned soldiers out there. Not only do they have the highly sophisticated equipment, but they're also highly trained.
> KING: Tenacious.
> O'GRADY: Very—barbaric.
> KING: Barbaric—in other words you don't want to get into a hand to hand tussle?
> O'GRADY: Oh, just look at the history of the region with the Nazis when they tried to come into that area—they didn't succeed.
> KING: Senator, can you describe yourself any way in the area of optimistic or pessimistic in a situation like this?
> McCAIN: We are the superior force. Serbia is the size of the state of Ohio. They have old Russian equipment. We have far superior equipment. We have the best trained and professional soldiers in the world. I believe we would prevail and we would prevail quickly and we must do so. These people are barbaric, but they're not professionals and they—they were beaten by the Croatian army, Larry."[2]

There was no debate on this characterization. The Serbs, enemy de jour, had become obviously barbaric, not to mention the "inferior force."

The phenomenon of anti-Arab representation in American culture, the othering of the ArabAmerican and the Arab world, especially popular culture, is undoubtedly overdetermined: it would be virtually impossible to single out a discrete locus for these negative representations, and any attempt to do so is bound to be an exercise in oversimplification. There are, however, a number of important factors in the equation that demand investigation and acknowledgment. As has been demonstrated at length by Edward Said and Michael Suleiman, among others, contemporary bias against Arabs in the United States draws heavily on a long-standing Western antipathy for its Islamic rival.[3] Orientalism and its antecedents laid the groundwork and set in place most of the basic stereotypes that inform our current anti-Arab prejudices. As Michael Suleiman has pointed out, this generalized inheritance from Western culture has combined with several more specifically American ideas to create especially favorable conditions for the positive reception of anti-Arab stereotypes in the American psyche. These particular American tendencies, as Suleiman demonstrates, include "a greater emphasis on the Bible as a literal representation of what happened in the Middle East" in ancient times, the identification of the contemporary Arab people with those peoples of the biblical Middle East who are cast as villains or the enemies of God and the Hebrews, and an identification of many of the Puritan founders of early American society with the ancient Israelites.[4] In this century, Zionists have astutely reversed this identification, casting themselves in the role of the pioneers battling a hostile natural environment and hostile indigenous savages to bring bounty and civilization to a barren land. Thus the Arab in general, and the Palestinian in particular, becomes identified with the Native American. For example, during the 1991 Gulf War, Iraqi-held territory was routinely referred to as "Indian country" by American military personnel.[5] Interestingly, the celebrated Palestinian poet Mahmoud Darwish has also embraced this identification between Arabs, especially Palestinians, and Native Americans, but from the perspective of colonial victim rather than colonial hero. Such specifically American orientations have promoted the development of a particularly negative image of the Arab in the United States during the twentieth century.

As our model of the othering process anticipates, the emergence of this exceptionally negative image has been clearly linked to political developments during the past fifty years, in particular the tension between competing American ambitions for dominance in the Middle East and Arab ambitions for greater independence from Western influence, as well as the problem of Zionism and colonialism in Palestine. As the power of Britain and France waned in the years following the Second World War, the colonial baton in the Middle East was gradually passed from these old imperial powers to the United States. American interest in controlling the oil resources of the Persian Gulf has never been a secret or the subject of any sustained denial. This interest has repeatedly placed United States foreign policy at odds with political movements that express the aspirations of millions of Arabs, such as Arab nationalism or, more recently, revolutionary Islamism. Since the early part of this century, Arab nationalism has emphasized a break with Western powers and influence, a greater Arab unity and independence, and, of course, control of the natural resources of the Middle East, above all, oil. This anticolonial orientation of Arab nationalism was, both in general and at specific moments of crisis, incompatible with the neocolonial role the United States aspired to play in the Arab world, especially the Persian Gulf region and Iran. Thus the United States repeatedly found itself at odds with Arab nationalist movements and regimes, and some of the leading "villains" in the American worldview of past decades include prominent secular Arab nationalist leaders such as Gamal Abdel Nasser, Yassir Arafat, Muammar Qaddafi, and Saddam Hussein. More recently, the rise of revolutionary Islamist movements, as secular Arab nationalism is increasingly regarded as both a proven failure and an inauthentic mimicry of Western political movements, has created a new set of enemies in the American worldview. Islamism in the Arab world received a significant boost from the Iranian revolution and the successful "jihad" against the Soviet Union in Afghanistan, which suggested that both neocolonial superpowers could be successfully ousted from Muslim lands. The status and influence of Islamist movements continue to develop in many parts of the Arab world and, much as Arab nationalism had before it, sets itself against Western influence, both cultural and political, in the Middle East. Islamists, including Ayatollah Khomeini, the leaders of Hamas and Hizbullah, and Osama Bin Laden, have emerged in recent years as the quintessential international villains in the American perspective.

A second major factor in the development of the heightened form of anti-Arab prejudice in contemporary American thought is the Zionist movement and its highly successful propaganda campaign to cast Arabs in general and Palestinians in particular as the villains in the Arab-Israeli conflict. Against the cultural and political background described previously, and operating for decades without significant challenge or critique, the Zionist movement portrayed Arab resistance to the establishment of an ethnically cleansed colonial settler-state in Palestine as a function of Arab fanaticism, intolerance, and anti-Semitism (a theme I shall investigate further). Pro-Israeli propaganda ("hasbara"), particularly emanating from Hollywood and certain forms of extremely biased journalism, has played a major role in casting the Arab in his or her most insidious stereotype— that of the terrorist. This is without question the dominant and most damaging, not to mention unwarranted, image of the Arab in contemporary American culture. It is so pervasive that Arabs are easily and arbitrarily blamed by irresponsible journalists and politicians for events that they have had nothing to do with, such as the bombing of the Federal Building in Oklahoma City or the crash of TWA Flight 800. Ironically, although it has been clearly established that Arabs were not involved in these events, the effect has not been to expose the fallacy at the heart of the stereotypes that gave rise to the error, but rather to reinforce an irrational and semiconscious identification between Arabs and terrorism. The two remain as firmly linked in the cultural landscape as ever and expressions of surprise that Arabs were not responsible for such acts in effect reiterated the stereotypes that produced the rushes to judgment. Thus the Arab remains the quintessential "terrorist" and, in cultural terms, continues to bear a measure of guilt for these events, since these tragedies look like the kind of things for which Arabs are believed to be typically responsible. So insidious are the processes reinforcing these associations that papers such as this one, which attempt to debunk the stereotypes, may ironically have the subtle effect of further solidifying the association between Arabs and terrorism. The "I am not a terrorist" discourse so prevalent among Arab Americans in this sense falls into a trap not unlike that set in the proverbial "candidate's nightmare" question, "when are you going to stop beating your wife?," a question for which there can be no constructive answer. Until we develop an alternative discourse, however, Arab Americans are going to remain in what may well be the self-defeating position I am taking here, of calling attention to the stereotypes by analyzing and objecting to them.

These associations are most damagingly propagated by a widespread but particularly insidious form of "journalism" which makes a fetish out of an alleged connection between Islam, traditional Arab culture, and terrorism, and which is calculated to spread fear and hatred of Arabs and Islam. The worst work of this kind has been done by Steven Emerson, who has argued that almost all major Arab and Muslim organizations in the United States are fronts for or supporters of "terrorist groups." His 1994 television documentary, *Jihad in America*, which was widely broadcast by PBS, advanced the dubious and unsubstantiated thesis that there was an extensive fund-raising network in the United States for "Middle Eastern terrorists." Consisting of little more than innuendo, guilt by association, and unsubstantiated allegations, *Jihad in America* has come to be regarded by many professional journalists as an embarrassing piece of fear-mongering, akin in tone and substance to Red-baiting screeds of the McCarthy era. Yet the atmosphere in the immediate aftermath of the World Trade Center bombing was such that "Jihad in America" won the prestigious Polk Award for Excellence in Journalism. In retrospect, respected journalists like Robert Freidman have accused Emerson of attempting to "create mass hysteria against American Arabs."[6] Emerson has been quick to point the finger at Arabs for any number of tragedies and disasters, publicly blaming Arabs for the bombing of the Federal Building in Oklahoma City and for the crash of TWA Flight 800. Emerson, then a CBS News consultant, told the nation that the 1995 Oklahoma City bombing exhibited "a Middle Eastern trait," insofar as it "was done with the intent to inflict as many casualties as possible."[7] In spite of his penchant for false accusation and wild statements, such as his 1994 claim that the aim of pro-Palestinian Muslims in the United States was the "mass murder of all Jews, Christians, and moderate Muslims," and his well-documented links with Israeli intelligence operatives and right-wing ideologues, Emerson is still called upon as a "terrorism expert" by some of the major American media.[8] Emerson's work is merely the most egregious example of this kind of Arab-bashing, which is by no means unusual in contemporary American journalism.

As Emerson's work has become increasingly discredited, much of the anti-Arab tone and substance of his work has been taken up by one of his former employers, Daniel Pipes, director of the Philadelphia-based pro-Israel Middle East Forum. Like Emerson, Pipes was quick to blame Arabs and Muslims for the bombing of the Oklahoma City Federal Building. Pipes told USA Today on the day after the bombing that "the West is under attack. . . . People need to understand that this is just the beginning. The fundamentalists are on the upsurge, and they make it very clear that they are targeting us. They are absolutely obsessed with us."[9] In the New York Post, Pipes dismissed the very identity of the Palestinian people by arguing that three of the most prominent Palestinians, Yassir Arafat, Edward Said, and George Antonius, were never Palestinians at all, and that they had "decided at various points in the 20th century—the 1920s, 1950s, 1970s—to become Palestinians." Far from a national identity, Pipes concludes, "Being Palestinian, in other words, is a good career move."[10] In the Los Angeles Times, Pipes claimed that most American Muslim organizations "aspire to make the United States a Muslim country, perhaps along the Iranian or Sudanese models." Echoing Emerson's dark conspiracy theories from Jihad in America, Pipes warns that "Some of this ilk even talk about overthrowing the U.S. government and replacing it with an Islamic one. Although it sounds bizarre, this attitude attracts serious and wide-spread support among Muslims, some of whom debate whether peaceful means are sufficient or whether violence is a necessary option."[11] Pipes also claims that the overwhelming majority of Muslims harbor intense anti-Jewish beliefs. In the right-wing magazine *Commentary*, for example, Pipes alleged that "At huge con-ventions closed to the press and public, in speeches and publications that tend to be couched in the historic Muslim languages rather than in English, nearly every Muslim organization in the United States—emphatically including those that carefully maintain a proper demeanor for public, English-language consump-tion—spews forth a blatant and vicious anti-Semitism, a barrage of bias, calumny, and conspiracy mongering of a sort that has otherwise all but disappeared from American discourse."[12] Ironically, Pipes, whose stock in trade is conspiracy theo-ries about fabricated Palestinian identities and Islamic plots to overthrow the U.S. government, is the author of a book on the political functioning of conspiracy the-ories: *Conspiracy: How the Paranoid Style Flourishes, and Where It Comes From*.

Such shoddy journalism has its academic corollaries, too numerous to list, but certainly the most influential of these is Samuel Huntington's *The Clash of Civilizations and the Remaking of World Order*. Huntington, who is widely regarded as one of the most distinguished and influential political scientists in the United States, argues that an unavoidable conflict is emerging between the West and the Islamic world, among other foes. Huntington's arguments about the uniquely vio-lent and conflict-oriented nature of Muslims and Islamic societies are "demon-strated" by social pseudoscience, including charts purporting to quantify the "Militarism of Muslim and Christian Countries" and "Ethnopolitical" and "Ethnic" conflicts. From this he concludes that "Muslims have problems living peaceably with their neighbors."[13] Huntington states simply that "Muslim bellicosity and vio-lence are late–twentieth century facts which neither Muslims nor non-Muslims can deny," and that "quantitative evidence from every disinterested source conclu-sively demonstrates its validity."[14] Huntington's thesis of a "clash of civilizations" has proved highly influential in academic, journalistic, and governmental circles, and, although it has been widely criticized, it has clearly left its mark on contem-porary American worldviews about Arabs, Arab Americans, and the Middle East.

The United States government itself has actively adopted and promoted anti-Arab sentiments through foreign policies that are biased and hostile to the inter-ests of millions of Arab people, through domestic repression of organized Arab American political activity, and by enacting stereotypical representations in gov-ernment activities. The double standards that inform the U.S. government's approach to the question of Palestine, which can be best characterized as a total and unwavering commitment to the interests of the Israeli state and a systematic rejection of Palestinian human and national rights, play a major role in the vicious cycle of self-reinforcing negative representations of Arabs in American culture and American policies that reflect an anti-Arab bias. These double standards are expressed through the massive financial, diplomatic, and military support for Israel from the United States, which appear to be entirely unrelated to Israeli compliance with international norms of conduct. Perhaps most galling to Arabs are the double standards revealed in the steadfast American diplomatic support for Israeli human rights violations. One particularly shocking example of this was the role of the Clinton administration in blocking criticism of Israel at the United Nations over the 1996 Qana massacre, in which the Israeli military bombed a U.N. observer camp in southern Lebanon, killing more than one hundred Lebanese civilians. Another astonishing instance was the 9 February 1999 U.N. General Assembly vote convening a conference on the enforcement of the Geneva Convention in the Israeli-occupied territories, which was opposed by only the United States and Israel. Such actions reflect and promote a prejudice that devalues the rights, including the most basic human rights, and interests of Arabs, and champions the rights, interests, and ambitions of others, most notably Israelis. The news media, guided to a great degree by the government on foreign policy matters and informed by the same cultural background as policy-making officials, repeat these prejudices and communicate them to the public. Double standards wherein some peoples' rights are important while others' are less so, some peoples' suffering is interesting while others' is not, and some people are properly the subjects of history while others are its objects, typify Western journalism on the Middle East. One of the most striking features of U.S. news reporting on events in Palestine, for example, is that it is almost always the Israeli actors who are subjectified, whatever their role. So, for example, when Israelis are victims of Palestinian violence, emphasis is on the suffering of the victims and their families, but when an Israeli such as Baruch Goldstein massacres Palestinians in a mosque, the focus is on the Israeli subject, on what type of twisted thinking could have driven an Israeli army reservist, an American doctor from Crown Heights no less, to do such a thing. In almost all incidents of violence in Palestine, to Western news reports the Palestinians, whether victims or perpetrators, remain a nameless, faceless mass. The bias is even more stark in reporting on Arab-Israeli violence in Lebanon, where the death of each Israeli soldier is accorded great significance, while the deaths of Lebanese civilians are noted in passing, if at all.[15] One of the most respected and accomplished

Western correspondents in the Middle East, Robert Fisk of the British newspaper the *Independent*, explained to a recent gathering at the Center for Policy Analysis on Palestine in Washington, D.C., that he declines to use the term "terrorism" or "terrorist" in covering violence in Palestine and Lebanon because he believes that in this context the term has lost its meaning and is now simply an ethnic pejorative against Arabs, to whom it is exclusively attached. Discriminatory policies, slanted official rhetoric, and biased reportage thus become mutually reinforcing.

Certainly double standards that indicate a disregard for the rights of Arabs are apparent in the attitude both the government and the media of the United States have taken toward Iraq in the 1990s. Journalists have enthusiastically joined with government officials in demonizing Iraq, the Iraqi people, and above all President Saddam Hussein, in the buildup to the 1991 Gulf War and since. To recall only one small example of this disturbing phenomenon, the well-known news magazine *The New Republic* featured a cover in September 1990 sporting a photograph of Saddam Hussein that had been altered to make the Iraqi leader's moustache look more like Adolph Hitler's and that, in a bad pun, was prominently titled "Furor in the Gulf."[16] The Iraqi invasion of Kuwait (which was disapproved of by a great many Arabs and Arab Americans) notwithstanding, the implacable hostility of the United States toward Iraq has been extraordinary. In particular, the genocidal effects of the U.S.-enforced sanctions against Iraq, which have killed well over a million Iraqis, mostly children, have reinforced the impression among both Arabs and Americans that Arab people in general are seen by the U.S. government to be the enemies of this country. The chillingly bland observation by Secretary of State Madeleine Albright that the deaths of over 500,000 Iraqi children have been "worth it" for U.S. foreign policy aims clearly suggests to Americans and Middle Easterners alike that the lives of Arabs, including Arab children, are not particularly valued in the eyes of the United States government.[17] The news media has generally either ignored or downplayed the fact that, according to the United Nations., more than a million individuals have died needlessly over the past seven years in Iraq, and coverage of what many people regard as a humanitarian catastrophe at least, if not an outright genocide, has been amazingly thin. Arabs, in both the United States and the Middle East, are convinced that there are few other ethnic groups whose needless suffering on such a massive scale would be tolerated and ignored, let alone deliberately inflicted. Again one is hard pressed not to see a connection between the dehumanizing representations of Arabs in American popular culture and the casual manner in which American policy dispenses with Arab rights and Arab lives.

Moreover, President Clinton's protestations that his 1998 bombing attacks against Iraq, Afghanistan, and Sudan were not reflective of an anti-Islamic or anti-Arab animus or a generalized conflict between the United States and the Arab World in fact served only to reinforce this very impression. After all, why would one feel the need to specifically deny that these attacks were aimed at targets whose principle characteristics are that they are Arab or Muslim, if this were not a reasonable conclusion, likely to be widespread? Attacks on a manifestly innocent pharmaceutical factory in Sudan and on training camps in Afghanistan for guerrillas who fight Indian rule in Kashmir would appear to have had no logical relevance to the as-yet-unsolved embassy bombings in Kenya and Tanzania, for which the attacks were supposed to be retaliation. Yet, as symbolic targets, they make sense in the context of such recurring themes of the "green menace" as global cabals of Islamist radicals, regionwide terrorist networks that cut across all ideological lines, and the fear of chemical, biological, and nuclear terrorism, which invokes the specter of Saddam Hussein. These themes, familiar to anyone who has been to the movies lately, draw together all Middle Easterners and Muslims who would oppose U.S. policies in the Middle East into one undifferentiated terrorist mass, so that any target in the Muslim world potentially becomes a "legitimate" focus of aggression or vengeance. Indeed, the destabilizing, militarily meaningless, and politically counterproductive cruise missile attacks against Sudan and Afghanistan in 1998 make sense only in terms of a hysterical discourse that in effect brands all Arabs and Muslims as terrorists and therefore function precisely as attacks on Arabs and Islam in general. Official American denials only serve to reinforce this effect, both in the United States and in the Middle East. A similar effect generated by the news media can be seen in the recent spate of implausible news stories suggesting that Abu Nidal, who had been reportedly on his deathbed in Egypt, and Osama Bin Laden, who has been living in caves in Afghanistan for years, had been brought to Baghdad by Saddam Hussein in order to form a new "terrorism international."[18] This silly tale was based on effacing all ideological and other obvious differences between these individuals, whose only connection is that they have been branded Arab arch-terrorists by the government and media, again creating the impression of an undifferentiated terrorist mass.

Arab Americans, particularly those engaged in organized political activity, have encountered official political repression and discrimination that is often informed by anti-Arab bias or stereotypes and that, in turn, reinforce those stereotypes. Arabs, Muslims, and those traveling to and from the Middle East are routinely singled out for often abusive special security measures by airline security and customs officials, based on mandatory government profiling systems. While the specific content of these profiles is secret, the discriminatory nature and disparate impact of such profiling has been well documented by Arab American civil rights organizations such as the American-Arab Anti-Discrimination Committee (ADC).[19] Though the discriminatory nature of the profiling system strongly indicates that it is based in large measure on racist stereotypes of Arabs and Muslims, the Federal Aviation Administration (FAA) has been unable to document a single instance where an individual who posed a danger to airport or airplane security has been apprehended or identified through the profiling system. Such pointless but abusive and discriminatory profiling is a clear example of a government policy that has a mutually reinforcing relationship with popular stereotypes and negative representations of Arab people. The CEO of Northwest Airlines forcefully made this point when he addressed the National Convention of the American-Arab Anti-Discrimination Committee in June of 1996. In response to complaints that airport profiling had led to discrimination against Arab and Arab American travelers, he candidly stated that even if airline agents were given directives not to discriminate on the basis of ethnicity, their behavior would still be affected by what they saw about Arabs in films and on television.

Since the passage of the 1996 Anti-Terrorism and Immigration Acts, the Immigration and Naturalization Service (INS) has begun using secret evidence in politically charged deportation cases. As a result at least twenty-five individuals, all politically active Arabs and Muslims, are currently incarcerated without charge on the basis of secret evidence, which they are unable to challenge or even evaluate. Most of these individuals have resided peacefully in the United States for a number of years, and many have spouses and children who are U.S. citizens. Some have satisfied an immigration judge that they would face certain persecution if returned to their home country. Yet almost all of them remain detained because an INS prosecutor has presented a judge with secret, and therefore unchallenged and untested, evidence alleging that the individual is a "terrorist" or has some "terrorist" affiliation. James Woolsey, former director of the CIA, told a senate judiciary subcommittee on 8 October 1998 that "The INS' procedure in these sorts of cases—uncannily reminiscent of Franz Kafka's *The Trial*—is to collect rumors and unfounded allegations, not investigate them, submit them in camera [i.e., secretly] to the immigration judge, and then demand that the individual in question be held a threat to national security if he does not succeed in refuting the charges of which he is unaware." Woolsey, who is defending six Iraqi men being held on the basis of secret evidence, added that a clear anti-Arab racist bias was present in some of the secret evidence the government had submitted against his clients which was later released, stating that "In ex parte testimony, belatedly declassified, more than one interrogator explicitly expressed bias (e.g., Arabs 'lie an awful lot,' 'there is no guilt in the Arab world') to the immigration court."[20] In an August 1998 letter to Attorney General Janet Reno and INS Commissioner Doris Meissner, Senators Spencer Abraham (R-Mich.) and Edward Kennedy (D-Mass.), the chair and ranking member of the senate subcommittee on immigration, expressed "grave concerns" about the use of secret evidence. "Some believe that recent actions create the appearance that the INS may be using secret evidence only in cases against Arab immigrants," wrote the senators. "This is especially disturbing since many of these cases appear to be based not on any actions of the immigrants, but rather on their purported associations," they added.[21]

Perhaps the most notorious case of the use of secret evidence and indefinite detention without charges or trial is that of Dr. Mazen Al-Najjar of Tampa, Florida, a Palestinian and former professor at the University of South Florida (USF). Dr. Al-Najjar was arrested in May 1997, following unsubstantiated allegations in Steven Emerson's documentary, "Jihad in America," and in articles in the *Tampa Tribune*, which drew on Emerson's accusations, that a think tank associated with USF, the World and Islam Studies Enterprise (WISE), was a front for the Islamic Jihad Organization. Al-Najjar and his brother-in-law, Professor Sami Al-Arian, were active in WISE. The FBI adopted the claim that WISE was a front for Palestinian "terrorists," and accused Dr. Al-Najjar of being a "mid-level operative" in a scheme to fund the Islamic Jihad. An immigration judge ordered him to be held indefinitely on the basis of secret evidence.

Al-Najjar and his wife are both stateless Palestinians, not holding citizenship of any country. The judge ordered Dr. Al-Najjar's family to be separated, with him deported to the United Arab Emirates, and his wife to Saudi Arabia, even though neither country has agreed to accept them. No consideration was given to the fate of their American-born children. A report on the accusations against WISE, Al-Arian, and Al-Najjar by former USF president William Reece Smith Jr., a prominent Tampa attorney, found no indication of a link between Al-Arian, Al-Najjar, or their associates and terrorism. No evidence of any involvement with any terrorist group or activities has been brought forward by the FBI against Al-Najjar or Al-Arian, no criminal charges related to the case have ever been filed, and Al-Arian has been reinstated as an active professor at USF. Al-Najjar, on the other hand, remains in jail.

Al-Najjar's case has won sympathy from unusual quarters. On 20 March 1998, the *Miami Herald* reported that "Al-Najjar has been here since 19 May, so long that even the guy who runs the place [the INS detention center in Manatee, Florida] feels sorry for him. 'C'mon, counselor, get this thing moving,' prison director S. Kent Dodd tells Al-Najjar's lawyer, Luis Coton of Tampa. 'He's been here too long.'"[22] House Minority Whip David E. Bonior (D-Mich), an outspoken opponent of secret evidence, visited Al-Najjar in his jail cell in February 1999. After meeting Al-Najjar, Bonior observed that "Our Bill of Rights specifically grants the right to a public trial and the right to be informed of the nature and cause of the accusation. 'Secret Evidence' makes a mockery of our Constitution, but it is increasingly being used by the INS and the FBI to harass and incarcerate Muslim and Arab American activists."[23] On the other hand, Steven Emerson, whose unsupported allegations led to Al-Najjar's arrest, has been quoted as saying that "I feel much more comfortable knowing that Mazen Al-Najjar is in jail and that Sami Al-Arian cannot speak and propagate his message to young students, because it is militant doctrine under a false veneer."[24]

The discriminatory treatment to which Dr. Al-Najjar and the other twenty-some Arabs indefinitely jailed on the basis of secret evidence have been subject is yet another example of an official government policy that is informed by and in turn reinforces stereotypes against Arabs in the United States. Fortunately, this clear violation of constitutional and human rights has generated considerable opposition, including in the U.S. Congress. Representatives David Bonior (D-Mich.) and Tom Campbell (R-Calif.) have introduced legislation, currently known as H.R. 2121 ("The Secret Evidence Repeal Act"), that would abolish all use of secret evidence in American courts, including immigration courts.

The U.S. government has also employed stereotypical negative representations of Arabs in its law enforcement and military operations. Among the most notorious of these incidents was the 1980 "Abscam" scandal, in which the FBI had an Italian-American agent posing as a stereotypical Arab "oil-sheikh" bribe several members of Congress, whose corruption was captured on videotape. As former U.S. Senator James Abourezk recalls in his memoirs, "After the scandal broke in the press, FBI Director William Webster was asked why the agent had been dressed as an Arab. He responded that it was necessary to choose some ethnic group that the public would believe was capable of bribing congressmen. And yet, no Arab or Arab American had ever been accused of bribing an American politician. There had been, of course, lots of publicity about Koreans, Wasps, Jews, and members of other ethnic groups convicted of bribery, but not about Arabs. Why Webster, ordinarily a respected public servant, felt it was necessary to use any ethnic group is a mystery, but his choice was solid evidence of the bottoming out of the image of Arabs in the United States." Abourezk goes on to state flatly that the "use of a phony Arab figure in Abscam was the direct result of the seven-year escalation, following the oil embargo, of anti-Arab racism that was projected by the media and cheered on by the Israeli lobby."[25] Dismay over "Abscam" and the unabashed endorsement by the FBI of some of the most malicious anti-Arab stereotypes in the operation led directly to the founding of the American-Arab Anti-Discrimination Committee (ADC), the largest Arab American political and civil rights organization in the United States.

Almost twenty years after "Abscam," the government continues to enact, and thereby reinforce, negative stereotypes of Arabs. In the middle of March 1999, The Marine Warfighting Lab conducted another in its ongoing series of "Urban Warrior" exercises at Monterey and Oakland, California. The exercise involved simulations of urban warfare, with several mock foreign locations created for different scenarios. Among the most troubling aspects of the exercise was the simulation of "ethnic groups" by trainees from the Defense Language Institute in the mock urban settings. These actors portrayed stereotypical "Arabs" and "Koreans" in urban crowd situations, taunting the Marines, serving as distractions in the hunts for the "terrorists" in their midst, and begging for help in staged disasters. In this case, the U.S. military apparently found it useful to promote stereotypes and anticipate the ethnicity of enemies and bystanders in future missions for its training exercises. Such exercises are likely to reinforce negative impressions of the ethnic groups and notions of who are "the enemy," while adding nothing essential to training for urban conflict. Just as in "Abscam," the stereotypes used in the Urban Warrior exercises are not only offensive but utterly gratuitous.

The government and news media are, if anything, outdone in defamation of Arabs by the entertainment industry. The shameful history of Hollywood and U.S. television programs in projecting negative stereotypes of Arabs and Muslims (which are often wrongly treated as identical sets by the entertainment industry and, consequently, the public) has been more than adequately catalogued in the work of scholars such as Jack Shaheen, Edward Said, Michael Suleiman, and Yahya Kamalipour. These critics have charted the development of dominant entertainment industry stereotypes of Arabs from the romantic image of the barbaric and hyper-sexualized desert bedouin of the silent film era to the more unambiguous corrupt oil sheikhs and anti-Western, anti-Semitic fanatics of more recent decades. The ubiquity of negative images and the consistency of the anti-Arab stereotypes that are deployed has often been noted. As Jay Stone asked, "When was the last time you saw an Arab character in a movie who was anything but one of the three B's (billionaire, bomber, belly dancer)?"[26] Yet at present the dominant and most damaging stereotype is that of the crazed Arab/Muslim terrorist, which has become a staple of the action film genre, among others. Most observers agree that the 1960 film, *Exodus,* a shamelessly distorted account of the founding of the State of Israel, was a turning point in Hollywood's treatment of Arabs as a demonic and thoroughly evil people who typically commit unspeakable acts against the innocent. The image of the Arab as quintessential terrorist competed with the more dominant image of the corrupt and boorish oil sheikh in Hollywood movies during the 1970s.

By the 1980s, the image of the terrorist, increasingly cast as a hysterical Islamic militant, superceded all other stereotypes as the dominant Hollywood characterization of the Arab. This was the villain of choice in countless low-budget action films of the 1980s, many produced by Canon Films of the Israeli Golan and Globus production company. Films such as *Wanted Dead or Alive* (1987), *Iron Eagle* (1986), *Delta Force* (1986), and many others did their best to promote the ugliest stereotypes of the cruel but cowardly Arab terrorist as the essential and fundamental enemy of the West and Israel specifically, and decency and humanity in general. In the main these films were, however, characterized also by a distinctly low-budget, low-brow quality that partially helped to offset their defamatory content. The 1990s saw a mainstreaming of these images into higher budget, higher profile films, a process that culminated in the 20th Century Fox blockbuster *True Lies* (1994), a high-budget, high-profile vehicle for Arnold Schwarzenegger. While *True Lies* clearly indicates the arrival of the Arab-demonizing action flick at the top of the Hollywood pyramid, the film retains the cartoonish and preposterous qualities of its low-budget precursors.

The same cannot be said of 20th Century Fox's latest Arab-bashing film, *The Siege* (1998). Compared to most of the earlier action films featuring crazed Arab terrorists, including *True Lies,* which never asked to be taken seriously, *The Siege* is a complicated and relatively sophisticated film. It presents itself as a serious intervention in a major public policy and political debate about how the United States should respond to a potential "terrorist threat." Indeed, and in yet another instance of the symbiotic and self-reinforcing relationship between discriminatory policies and defamatory representations, the inspiration for *The Siege* was one of the most troubling government documents to be uncovered in recent years—a Justice Department contingency plan for the mass arrest of thousands of Arabs in the United States, their detention in concentration camps in Florida and Louisiana, and their possible deportation.[27] *The Siege* depicts a savage terrorist campaign by

Arab Americans in New York City, and the government's response of rounding up all young Arab males in detention camps.

Given that it is presented as a socially responsible film with a serious and important message, *The Siege* attempts to promote old stereotypes in a new and potentially more damaging way. In contrast to the cartoonish style of the earlier action films, *The Siege* does its best to seamlessly weave its own fictional world with that of television news. The film begins with footage of the Khobar Tower bombing in Saudi Arabia and actualities of President Clinton denouncing it, and then ascribes the inspiration for the bombing to a fictional character in the film. From these realities the plot emerges, as if nothing more than a logical extension of real events. Through these and other techniques, including the use of the images and voices of well-known journalists and commentators, such as Daniel Schorr of National Public Radio and Arianna Huffington, opining on the fictional events depicted, playing themselves, so to speak, the filmmakers have done their best to blur the boundaries between the evening news and the fictional reality of their movie. Clearly, the intention is to give *The Siege* a heightened verisimilitude, an unusual degree of "ripped-from-the-headlines" believability which no one could have ascribed to *True Lies*, for example.

Although 20th Century Fox and director Edward Zwick insist that it is a socially responsible and antiracist film that warns of the dangers of stereotyping, the representation of Arabs in *The Siege* could hardly be worse. As we have noted, the film investigates how American society would deal with a mortal, even existential, threat posed by terrorism emanating from the Arab American community in Brooklyn. In this sense, *The Siege* belongs as much to the genre of the "disaster movie" as it does to the "action movie," with Arab communities in American cities representing "the disaster." *The Siege* is explicit, especially in its cinematic language, in portraying the presence of Arabs and Muslims in American cities as inherently threatening, a homogeneous mass among whom lurk, indistinguishably, the mad bombers. Images of Arab culture in *The Siege* are almost always accompanied by ominous and "Middle Eastern–sounding" music, and are often shot with unsteady cameras at oblique angles and vertiginously edited to heighten the effects of alienation, disorientation, and danger. The danger of this alien presence is established before the credits roll, in an image that begins with a close-up of the face of a muazzin calling the faithful to prayer. As the camera pulls back and upward, revealing first a minaret, then the whole mosque, and finally its presence in the middle of New York City, ominous music rises to a chilling crescendo. We are clearly meant to be shocked and unnerved by the Arab and Muslim presence in

New York from the outset, and this impression of danger is consistently reinforced throughout the film. Furthermore, in *The Siege* a clear and direct symbolic link is made between Islamic religious practices and terrorism. Images of a Muslim washing his hands before prayer, as hundreds of millions of Muslims do every day, precede the worst acts of terror in the film. The use of repeated images to evoke certain emotions in the audience is a standard and legitimate narrative device for filmmakers. Yet the choice of such a basic act of Islamic faith to serve as the announcement of the presence of evil and the imminence of horrible violence betrays a determination to firmly reinforce fear of Muslims in the viewer's mind.

Defenders of *The Siege* point to the film's harsh critique of martial law and militarism and its support of constitutional freedoms. These elements are clearly present in the film. Yet these socially constructive points are made at the expense of Arab Americans, who are depicted as posing the threat in the face of which civil liberties are upheld. Moreover, the pro–civil liberties elements of the film are muddled, confusing, and confused. What is more likely to stick in the minds of the viewers are the images of Arab and Islamic terrorism that dominate most of the movie, which repeat the ugliest stereotypes of Arabs ad nauseam.

The Siege also features a "good Arab" character, "Frank Haddad," which, it is claimed, offsets the negative images of the other Arab characters. The character is an Arab American working for a fancifully "multicultural" FBI. It must be observed, however, that Haddad is "good" only insofar as he is distanced from traditional Arab culture and Islamic religious practice, which are almost always ominous and threatening in the film. Not only does he demonstrate his loyalty by working for the FBI (the implication being that he would not be as convincingly "American" if he were a grocer, for example), the audience is reassured of his decency by a brief yet all-American and otherwise totally meaningless scene of him playing touch football with his multicultural FBI colleagues. Haddad also establishes his bona fides by displaying the appropriate anti-Palestinian animus in a film which is anti-Arab in general and anti-Palestinian in particular (Palestinians, the audience is warned, "seduce you with their suffering"). In fact, *The Siege* is packed with stereotypes of Arabs and Muslims as violent, unscrupulous, and barbarous. The presence of a token and problematic "good Arab" character does little to offset this.

The Siege went too far, and was offensive to many observers outside the Arab American community, as Arab American and Muslim critiques of *The Siege* resonated with thoughtful segments of American society. Numerous sympathetic articles appeared in many major newspapers, both in the form of reviews of the film and as political stories about the controversy it generated. In a front-page story, the *Washington Post* asked its readers to imagine films in which "A nefarious rabbi exhorts his extremist, ultra-Orthodox followers to plant bombs against Arab sympathizers in America. Innocents are killed and maimed. The FBI starts rounding up Orthodox Jews and putting them in camps. Or how about this: A Catholic priest has molested an altar boy. The Church refuses to hand him and other offenders over to police. The FBI starts rounding up clerics in an attempt to ferret them out."[28] In his widely syndicated column, Roger Ebert, perhaps the most influential newspaper film critic in the country, wrote that "the prejudicial attitudes embodied in the film are insidious, like the anti-Semitism that infected fiction and journalism in the 1930s—not just in Germany, but in Britain and America."[29] Ebert repeated his attacks on the film's anti-Arab content in his popular TV show "At the Movies." Many other critics objected to the disturbing representation in *The Siege* of the Arab American community and had no trouble identifying it as racist and intolerant.

In fact, *The Siege* is only the latest in a series of films that focus on Arab American communities as sources of danger and hotbeds of terrorism. Among the first of these was the 1986 made-for-TV movie *Under Siege*, co-authored by noted journalist Bob Woodward. *Under Siege* depicts a gang of Arab terrorists working out of Dearborn, Michigan, which is home to the largest Arab American community in the country. Like *The Siege*, which depicted a terrorist network based in Brooklyn, another city with a major Arab American community, *Under Siege* is based on the premise that Arab communities in major western urban centers pose a particular danger because of the supposed association between Arab culture and Islam and terrorism. As in *The Siege*, the implication in *Under Siege* is that Arab communities nurture and offer safe haven to terrorists, and that the job of law enforcement in such circumstances is all but impossible because of the difficulty in distinguishing between the terrorists and other Arabs. The Arabic-language signs, graffiti, and other images of traditional Arabic culture and Islamic religiosity are used in these films not only as exotica but as menacing and ominous indications of a dangerous alien presence. The effect, of course, is to smear Arab American communities and engender fear and hatred of them. A similar effect is created by the HBO film *Path to Paradise* (1996), which purports to tell the "true story" of the only major terrorist incident in the United States to have been perpetrated by Arabs, the bombing of the World Trade Center. Every Arab and Muslim figured in *Path to Paradise* is an ugly caricature, and once again the emphasis is on the supposed connection between Arab culture and Islam and terrorism.

Of course, there have been exceptions, where Hollywood films have featured positive Arab characters, although these have been few and far between indeed. *Party Girl* (1995) and *A Perfect Murder* (1998) both featured characters clearly identified as Arabs whose roles were positive and who were not stereotyped in any offensive manner. Disney's 1999 release, *The 13th Warrior*, may prove to have been a real breakthrough, however. *The 13th Warrior* features one of the first Arab heroes in a Hollywood film, the character of Ahmed Ibn Fahdlan, portrayed by Antonio Banderas. It is important to note that this character is not only a hero and a positive figure, but that he is an Arab Muslim character who is not defined purely by his ethnic or religious identity and who has a strong individual personality. It remains to be seen whether *The 13th Warrior* will prove to be an aberration or the signal of a real change in Hollywood whereby American films will consistently include Arab heroes and positive characters and not just terrorists and other negative stereotypes.

Of all the stereotypes propagated through films such as these and other forms of entertainment, as well as through biased journalism and discriminatory policies, none could be more unfair, distressing, or damaging than that of the Arab as anti-Jewish anti-Semite. This stereotype places on the Arab a double burden of anti-Semitism, whereby the Arab is perceived as a Semite through the lens of traditional European anti-Semitic stereotypes, and at the same time is identified as the arch-Jewish anti-Semite. Arabs are bearing the burden, therefore, not only of being the target of stereotypical Western anti-Semitic images, but also of the historical responsibility for a culture of ethnic and religious anti-Semitism which belongs, in fact, to European, not Arab, civilization. Thus the Arab becomes both the target and the supposed source of the worst forms of Western anti-Semitism.

Many of the images used to defame Arabs, especially in the past fifty years, draw on stock images of the Western anti-Semitic cannon. As Jack Shaheen has pointed out, "Resembling the hook-nosed screen Arab wearing burnooses and thobes, screen Jews [in Nazi-inspired German films] also dress differently than the films' protagonists, wearing yarmulkes and black robes. They too appear as unkempt money-grubbing caricatures who seek world domination, who worship a different God, who kill innocents, and who lust after blond virgins."[30] The caricature of Semitic racial characteristics that typifies traditional Western anti-Jewish imagery has been largely transferred to the Arab as overt anti-Jewish anti-Semitism has fallen out of fashion. The similarities between the image of the wealthy, filthy, greedy, vulgar oil sheikh and anti-Jewish imagery are obvious. Yet the parallel also applies to most of the other negative images of Arabs in Western culture today, including the crazed religious fanatic who worships a cruel and alien God. The rise of anti-Arab stereotypes in the United States in recent decades in many ways represents the continued thriving of traditional Western anti-Semitism, in a new guise.

All the more ironic then that one of the most pervasive stereotypes of Arabs is that of the Arab racist, particularly the anti–Jewish anti–Semite. This theme is a standard feature of the defamatory films, television programs, and journalism misrepresenting the Arab-Israeli conflict. The main idea is that opposition to Israel is driven not by concern for Palestinian human and national rights or the injustices of colonialism, but by a hatred toward or dislike of Jews that is supposedly characteristic of Arabic culture and/or Islam. This is often accompanied with rubbish about three thousand years of warfare or an age-old conflict in Palestine, when, of course, the Zionist movement itself is barely one hundred years old. In this way, the passionate Arab opposition to the Zionist movement can be neatly explained without allowing that the establishment of the Israeli state came at another people's expense. Some of the most extreme apologists for Israel in the press and in Congress have taken to insisting that the anger and resentment Palestinians living under Israeli occupation feel toward their oppressors comes not from the experience of having been ethnically cleansed or living under colonial rule and foreign military occupation, without rights or citizenship, but is produced instead by a calculated campaign of indoctrination of hatred in Palestinian schools and media. Resistance to colonialism, resentment of oppression, and struggling for one's human rights thereby become the product of miseducation, indoctrination, and a deep-seated cultural and religious antipathy toward Jews.

While it is true that some elements of Western anti-Semitic discourse have begun to creep into the rhetoric of those living under Israeli occupation, such ideas are still clearly marginal and alien to Arab cultural precepts. There is no foundation for these intolerant attitudes in Arab culture or Islam, and their influence is likely to remain marginal at best, even though they might correspond to the ideological needs of those resisting Israeli occupation.

The characterization of the Arab-Israeli conflict as being driven by traditions of Arab intolerance and anti-Jewish hatred is an attempt to rob Arabs of the right to object to colonialism and oppression, lest they be labeled "anti-Semitic." It is an attempt to shift the primary burden for centuries of religious and ideological anti-Semitism in the West, which has no corollary in Arab tradition, and which culminated in the Holocaust, onto the Arab peoples. The historical record, however, is clear. Even more disturbingly, this discourse threatens to rob Arabs of the heritage of an extraordinary tradition of tolerance and coexistence. The only appropriate response is to reject this stereotype more vigorously than any other, and reclaim and extend this legacy of tolerance and coexistence as robustly as we can. Certainly this is a response that is suggested by the model of identification with which we began. Perhaps the seeds of an alternative discourse on Arab Americans lie in such a gesture, which dispenses with the self-defeating "I am not a terrorist" motif and allows for a far more constructive dialogue. Let the next discussion begin with this.

NOTES

1. Ali A. Mazrui, *Cultural Forces in World Politics* (London: James Curry, 1990), 13.

2. *Larry King Live*, CNN transcripts, 1 April 1999.

3. See, for example, Edward Said, *Orientalism* (New York: Vintage Books, 1978).

4. Michael Suleiman, *The Arabs in the Mind of America* (Brattleboro, Vt.: Amana Books, 1988), 7–12.

5. "Apocalypse Near," *Newsweek*, 1 April 1991, p. 14.

6. John Sugg, "Steven Emerson's Crusade," *Extra*, January/February 1999, pp. 17–20.

7. *CBS News*, 19 April 1995.

8. Sugg, "Crusade," 17–20.

9. "Bomb an 'act of evil,'" *USA Today*, 20 April 1995, p. A1.

10. Daniel Pipes, "Perjurious Palestinians," *New York Post*, 8 September 1999, p. 31.

11. Daniel Pipes, "It Matters What Kind of Islam Prevails," *Los Angeles Times*, 22 July 1999, p. B9.

12. Daniel Pipes, "America's Muslims against America's Jews," *Commentary* 107, no. 5 (1999): 31.

13. Samuel Huntington, *The Clash of Civilizations and the Remaking of World Order* (New York: Simon and Schuster, 1996), 256–58.

14. Ibid., 258.

15. Hussein Ibish, "Retaliating in Advance," *Extra* 12, no. 5 (1999): 24–25.

16. "Aw, shucks," *New Republic* 204, no. 20 (1991): 11.

17. Denis H. Halliday and Jennifer E. Horan, "A New Policy Need for Iraq," *Boston Globe*, 22 March 1999, p. 19.

18. See, for example, "Officials: Bin Laden 'Missing'; Muslim Militant Could be in Iraq," *Arizona Republic*, 14 February 1999, p. A8; "Saddam's New Weapon: Terror; Courting Bin Laden and Nidal," *New York Post*, 1 February 1999, p. 2.

19. *Hate Crimes and Discrimination against Arab-Americans, 1996–97* (Washington, D.C.: American-Arab Anti-Discrimination Committee, 1997).

20. "Prepared Statement of R. James Woolsey before the Senate Judiciary Committee Technology Terrorism and Government Information Subcommittee," Federal News Service Transcript, 8 October 1998.

21. "U.S. Bars or Expels Suspect Immigrants on Secret Evidence," *New York Times*, 15 August 1998, p. A1.

22. Martin Merzer, "The Secret War," *Miami Herald, Tropic Magazine*, 22 March 1998, pp. 12–29.

23. "Bonior Raises Secret Evidence Problem with President Clinton," Press Release, Office of Congressman Bonior, 4 March 1999.

24. Merzer, "Secret War," 12–29.

25. James G. Abourezk, *Advise and Dissent* (Chicago: Lawrence Hill Books, 1989), 253.

26. Jack Shaheen, *Arab and Muslim Stereotyping in American Popular Culture* (Washington, D.C.: Center for Muslim-Christian Understanding, 1997), 12.

27. *Hate Crimes and Discrimination Against Arab-Americans, 1990–91* (Washington, D.C.: American-Arab Anti-Discrimination Committee, 1991).

28. "Hollywood's 'The Siege' Besieged; Film's Portrayal of Arab Americans Protested as I Iarmful," *Washington Post*, 6 November 1998, p. A1.

29. Roger Ebert, "'The Siege' Gets Mired in Muck of Prejudice," *Chicago Sun-Times*, 6 November 1998, p. 27.

30. Shaheen, *Arab and Muslim Stereotyping*, 15.

9

Lupe's Song: On the Origins of Mexican/ Woman-Hating in the United States

DEENA J. GONZÁLEZ

I was motivated to begin tracing the origins of hatred against Mexican women in this society when, repelled and curious in the summer of 1992, I learned of a controversy brewing at UCLA. A fraternity manual had been sent to *The Daily Bruin*, the student newspaper, citing a fraternity initiation ceremony where the invited had sung "Lupe." It was not the first instance of racially derived or misogynistic speech at a fraternity, nor would it be the last. I knew that at U.C. Davis in 1976 a song also entitled "Lupe" had surfaced among the Alpha Gamma Rhos, who today have a lounge in the Alumni Center dedicated to them and who back in the 1970s amplified their initiation ceremonies with the following recitation:

> *Lupe*
> 'Twas down in Cunt Valley, where Red Rivers flow
> Where cocksuckers flourish, and maiden heads grow.
> Twas there I met Lupe, the girl I adore
> My hot fucking, cocksucking Mexican whore.
> Now Lupe popped her cherry, when she was but eight
> Swinging upon the old garden gate,

The cross member broke and the upright slipped in,
And she finished her life in a welter of sin
She'll fuck you, she'll suck you, she'll tickle your nuts,
And if you're not careful, she'll suck out your guts.
She'll wrap her legs round you, till you think you'll die
I'd rather eat Lupe than sweet cherry pie
Now Lupe's dead and buried, and lies in her tomb,
While maggots crawl out of her decomposed womb,
The smile on her face, is a sure cry for more,
My hot fucking, cocksucking Mexican whore.[1]

Able to pick up this project at the end of the millennium, and based on these two related memories, one based in the 1970s and the other in the 1990s, I began research on a topic that I predict will sustain my interest into the next century: I seek to understand the origins of Mexican/woman-hating in this country, its roots and its travels, in much the same way that Gerda Lerner has sought, in her multivolume work, to trace the origins of patriarchy. Why and how can the degradation of Latinas/Chicanas in the instance of "Lupe's Song" continue, unabated it seems? More importantly, what are its suggestions and implications for Southern California specifically, but also for the nation at large, as Latinos become the largest "minority" ethnic population in the United States? What is "known" or "unknown" about Latinas and Mexicanas in general that makes the attitudes of these fraternity singers so commonplace or so ordinary that UCLA's *La Gente*, a local newsletter, ran in 1992 a chronology detailing the trail of the fraternity dirge?[2]

Several reference points act in this essay as guideposts: acts of racial hatred are almost always referred to in the media as innocent but isolated events—at UCLA until the 1990s, fraternities regularly sponsored Viva Zapata parties, or "Tequila Sunrise" parties, but few members of Mexican origin actually enrolled or pledged into these fraternities. Those who did believed that they were breaking the color barriers, and almost to a fault when interviewed by newspapers, each said, "I've never been subjected to prejudice or harassed for being Mexican." Such issues are not my concern in this work. Rather, the toleration, our own, of misogynistic, anti-woman-driven lyrics, the notion of Mexican women dead in graves, consumed by maggots, is my concern. The historical evolution, if you will, of this sort of attitude, seemingly widely shared across campuses, motivated my interest in Lupe.

A second, compelling, point of reference marked the last decade of the millennium: anyone watching the Anita Hill hearings (rarely referred to, interestingly, as the Clarence Thomas hearings) would consider the same concepts of racial hatred and misogyny as foreground to the matter of sexual harassment or abuse. Anyone raped who pursues justice through the legal apparatus, anyone harassed (90 percent of professional women report having experienced harassment in mild to grave degrees at least twice in their careers) and seeking redress or a hearing, knows that the act itself occurs twice. Once when it originally happens, and a second time when charges are filed or pursued, by a legal system set out to protect the "innocent." The courage of an unwavering Anita Hill, recounting time after time the incident of the pubic hair on the can, with the men interested in hearing it not once but fourteen times in one hour by my count in just one segment of the videotape, says it all. Let only the bravest tread here. More, for a conservative, Republican, Baptist woman of her values and background, the agonies endured as revelations about Thomas surfaced and through the act of repetition which became the congressmen's refrain, suggest the subtle shift that allows courts and institutions to mock women, in this case an African American woman who believed in what she was doing. Heroine to some, ill-bred to others, mad or damaged to certain congresspeople, Anita Hill, in those days of interrogation and then in the weeks that followed, took up a torch that she has not laid to rest, and most of the money that she garners serves to support other harassment cases in the courts.[3]

Who are we to believe is at the heart of so much of our own harassments, as experience begins to gain some foothold in the academy and the personal voice is no longer to be held at bay?[4] For historians, who or what to believe is also layered with "how to believe," that is, which document do we choose, how do we use it, how are we to explain its context? The following is an exploration of these crucial historiographic debates as well.

In December of 1992, in the same year as the UCLA controversy over "Lupe's Song," a San Diego State University fraternity, the *San Diego Union-Tribune* states, was cleared of charges that it sang the lewd song during initiation. The fraternity "under attack," in the words of the *Union-Tribune*, was absolved, although the Interfraternity Council found that the song did indeed exist among a sector of the campus community. An initiate had first called attention to the practice, saying he had heard the song across four nights of initiation, but he later retracted his story, saying that he had really heard it only once.[5]

In November of that year, a similar explosion about the same song occurred at California State University, Northridge, when I was giving a talk there at a Chicana-Student Conference. After an incident involving this song, students began protesting the funding of the Zeta Beta Tau fraternity. Chicanas were angry about the way the incident was being handled, one reason for the protests, but they also reflected a concern with a growing number of racist incidents that had occurred on campus: gay-bashing flyers had recently appeared on campus, without outcry or investigation; a swastika had been painted on the Jewish student center; and black stick figures had been painted on buildings across campus. Jeffery Berns, an attorney and ZBT alumnus told the *Los Angeles Times*, in regard to the song, "it was a joke, a poor joke, but a joke."[6] Most were unhappy with the fourteen-month suspension given the fraternity (later lifted by the new vice chancellor). Speech codes and codes of conduct were both voted down by the CSUN faculty. In the same week, a multicultural forum took place to stimulate discussion, but one student told the *Times*, "we need less talk and more action." The Inter Fraternity Council (IFC) president said he wished the ZBT matter had not been made public, for it came during a period of fund-raising for the poor and homeless. He had hoped to have "kept it in our community." "Greeks do a lot for this campus."[7]

Keeping It in the Community

The problem for the IFC president is, of course, that racial speech, racial hatred, and racism are not simply internal matters, any more than harassment is, but they derive and spread from a particular historical location, or, as some told Anita Hill, a "hysterical" location. What do we mean? Until the root of the problem is investigated, all solutions and resolutions will lead down the same road. Al Martínez reported in the *Times* on 12 November 1992 that Zeta Beta Tau fraternity followed all of this by giving itself, as we might have guessed, a Mexican "theme" party in honor of Lupe. ZBT was established by Jewish men who were frequently denied admission into other fraternities, and at CSUN the fraternity is still predominately Jewish. Flyers emblazoned with "in honor of Lupe" and addressed to "chicas and hombres" appeared all over campus, and the fraternity refused to cancel the party when school officials urged them to, as they felt they had a "right to be in solidarity with Theta Xi at UCLA," the fraternity they felt was "under attack" for its usage of "Lupe." Martínez argues rightly in his editorial that Jews and blacks were once targets of fraternity degradation. Ronald Kopita, CSUN vice president for student affairs, suspended the Zeta Betas for their flyer, saying it was an act of insensitivity and impaired vision, "caused by Republicanism in the White House" and an insensitivity toward other people. He said that he did not know "whether their action was one of malice, ignorance or a procedural error," but that he was embarrassed and ashamed that a fraternity of this origin would "put itself in this position," and he "found it particularly insulting, as I am Jewish." Al Martínez, editorializing at the *Los Angeles Times* in the same issue, concluded: "I'm not looking for doxologies at a beer bust, but tunes free of hatred might be nice." What might we imagine of such a doxology?[8]

DOXOLOGY OF LUPE

I offer next, then, not history free of hatred or fearful of examining its consequences, but history layered with a sensibility about racial hatred and the privileges that ignorance of the same bestows. The same point was made in several hundred letters appearing in campus newspapers at the time of the "Lupe" craze, and students on those campuses most affected by the controversy wrote passionately about the need to engage in a discussion and leave behind the fear of conflict that such discussion might engender. This was a useful reminder, given the Colombus Quincentennary madness that also gripped the country in the fall of 1992.

To view fraternity leaders or supporters as depraved or as persons guilty of "error in judgment," as one ZBT alumnus put it, is to miss a key point; to argue that discussion of origins or education campaigns or multicultural fora are an answer is to close in on the particulars. Focusing on Juanita of Downeville (Josefa Segovia), the first woman hung in newly conquered California, is a particular; and to include it as historical example instructs us primarily in the example, which is as important as casting a critical eye on Colombus' deeds, but if left uncontextualized in space, time, and contemporary knowledge, simply retains those aspects of glorification with little meaning in terms of consequences, results, and different interpretations.

To use another example from Chicana history, Chipita Rodríguez, a Mexican woman hung in 1863 in Texas, received renewed media attention during the recent furor over the execution of the very repentant, reborn (as a Christian) murderer Karla Fay Tucker, but she remained "unnamed," without a face or a body. Chipita Rodríguez was identified only as the first woman to be executed in Texas history, with no mention that she was a Mexican woman hung for the murder of a white cowboy who was attempting to harass her and her husband.[9]

Misknowledge, or lack of knowledge, legal scholars, psychologists, and others working in critical race studies agree, is the first step toward complicity in enacted racism. Let us look at the "theme" party. Ostensibly, a celebration—usually of another culture, but rarely of the "native" one—the theme is chosen to allow members of a group to dress differently, and to indulge in behaviors usually or normally considered inappropriate. Mexican theme parties are nothing new at large public universities, or in society generally. Some years ago, a toy convention at Griswold's Hotel in Claremont, California, where I live and work, featured a sleeping Mexican, leaning against a cactus, to promote a particular session among its large gathering.

Since the early 1800s, European, white, nonimmigrant Americans have practiced a dehumanization campaign against people of Mexican origin and especially women. Mexican women in Texas in the 1830s, in New Mexico in the 1830s and 1840s, and in California in the 1840s, were labeled witches or whores. Euro-Americans moving into this area of the country, which belonged to Mexico and was inhabited by Native and Mexican people, practiced terror and rage against the inhabitants of the land. In one small Texas Mexican town alone, 25 percent of the women, according to a Mexican newsletter or flyer, reported that they had been raped by the groups of men camped outside their town when Stephen Austin illegally settled across the Louisiana/Texas border. In New Mexico in the 1820s, 1830s, and 1840s, over 250 travelogues, diaries, and printed collections described Mexican women as subservient to their husbands, and as treacherous, flirtatious, and seductive. In the two hundred sources of this type that I have examined, "swarthy thief and liar" appears 467 times, "brown-skinned" or "dark" appears 943 times, and, of course, other terms have been highlighted by numerous Chicano/a historians this past decade, including "a poor apology of European extraction," "to whom the honorable title of white is poorly applied," and so on. Commonly, Euro-Americans referred to Mexican women as licentious, irrepressible, fond of gambling and dancing, and "priest-ridden," their homes "low, squat, and brown," "testaments to the power of mud," their dress "a study in negligence."[10] The purpose of the comments, of their repetition—like a Whitman refrain—was to converse with the nation and indeed with the world in a specific race dialogue and an anti-Catholic discourse, to create the "raced" dialogue in which we would all imbibe. And so we do, fraternities and historians. In this one-sided "dialogue," women of Mexican origin, Chicanas, are both raced and erased in a proposition that silences our responses not only contemporarily but also historically. Which is more insidious or odious has yet to be determined, but many scholars are documenting the instances of erasure systematically.[11]

Underneath the speculations of the Euro-American traveler (I singularize him) was indeed motive, to create fear, to solicit conquest and takeover, to dispel guilt. "The arrival of the caravan in Santa Fe changes immediately the look of the place," said the writer/speculator James Josiah Webb.[12] We know from the work the "New Western" historians have undertaken that the ideology of control sustained itself happily, especially when lawyers, bankers, and politicians exercised their hand in the management of this takeover, gamble or no.[13] Along with their testimony on land swindles, which they protested vigorously, New Mexican women would testify in court to mistreatment by Euro-Americans, and would file charges of rape, battery, and abuse. In California, Native women had been captured, beaten, and raped by the Spanish since the 1770s, and their small number by the 1840s made them especially alert to Anglo-American abuses; Indian Mexican women were similarly detained and arrested by the forty-niners and other immigrants to California.

In the newer litany, however, we historians face some growing difficulties: while we wish to see the victims of nineteenth-century racial hatred and its accompanying anguish respond in some constructive or understandable ways, by creating for ourselves a refrain of not forgetting, we become victims as well of the dialogue now traversing and uniting these two centuries. The regenerative nature of violence in the American West, copiously and methodically compiled in irrefutable detail by scholars, should make us wonder if we, too, are not carrying forward what Frederick Jackson Turner and Patricia Limerick (to name just two) captured so eloquently as regenerative refrain, the divide between the then and the now hardly different, except that I suppose we might argue that at the end of the twentieth century squeaky voices from the margins are acknowledged here and there in more systematized fashion. Where we who are supremely concerned with such race discourse once never made it into print, much less footnote, today we ask with what ferociousness does Lupe come to be resurrected, or murdered symbolically and in fact? It is the historian's lament, of course, that of recovery and omission, but cognizance hardly makes it easier to regurgitate—how far have we indeed come?

Why do Euro-Americans do what they do, would be another way to ask the question. Impertinent or suicidal though this question might seem—especially in the academy or among academic audiences—it is, essentially, being asked at every turn in the disciplines where faculty and scholars of color exist. Why did Euro-Americans practice violent physical and verbal abuses 150 years ago, and why did they license succeeding generations to continue doing so in this century? Clearly, the rule of law, the laws of social and economic structures in governance and finance mattered, but these alone cannot explain reappearance, reemergence, repetition.

We may find ourselves asking, "do these fraternities today not know better?" The National Institute against Prejudice and Violence reports in a survey of thirty campuses that one of four African American, Latino, Asian, or Native American students is harassed, assaulted, or subjected to slurs each year.[14] In the same period as the CSUN and UCLA controversies, *USA Today* reported that at George Washington University students met to discuss race relations after a student leader called a black student a "nigger." In another incident, Spike Lee attended a rally at University of North Carolina in 1992 to support a black cultural center, and when whites were called "blue-eyed devils," all "hell broke loose." The Center for Democratic Renewal says the battle over space and race has shifted from the streets to the campuses. Sensitivity seminars and apologies were one result of the unleashing of all this pent-up racial anger. Yet, I would question, if in these past two centuries we have seen such clear examples of insensitivity, of a power dynamic so overwhelming that it literally reduces entire groups to the status of outcast—that is, as colonized persons of the former Mexican north, as slaves and former slaves of the South, as people allowed to exist only on reservations or in concentration camps—is it really at all surprising that Lupe comes to us only as whore and in song or verse?

Speculum of the Other

A richer appreciation of the terror and rage this song and its title engenders must take into account the following as well: Lupe, short for Guadalupe, is a popular Mexican and Chicana name. It is no accident that the patron saint of Mexico is vilified in this manner, for in the game of win or lose, Mexico lost. In the nineteenth century, the United States went to war with Hispanic and Latin American powers four times, and won in each round. The United States–Mexican War of 1846-48 witnessed the invasion, and takeover of Mexican lands, nearly one half of them, to be exact.

To the winners belongs history, and this is one way of understanding a doxology of Lupe. Yet, I wish to interject in a different vein. Guadalupe is also the name of the treaty that is said to have resolved the crisis between the United States and Mexico; it is the left-hand side of the hyphenenated term, Treaty of Guadalupe-Hidalgo. Not the virgin then, but Guadalupe the treaty maker, is meant, married in this instance to Father Hidalgo, the right-hand side and acceptably masculine in that he had "voice," being the attacker you will recall, with his "Grito de Dolores," the cry of pain or anguish, *el gritón*. Hidalgo has speech. The virginal, female, patron saint (voiceless, other than ordering the Indian, Juan Diego, to help build her a shrine and spread the word) and the manly priest of independence fame thus attached. A lesbian-gay reading would also ponder the meanings of this union between the virgin, appearing on the back of the sacred and indigenous site on the hill of Tepeyac, and that of the more verbal, articulate Father Hidalgo (not coincidentally, Spanish for gentleman, very Spanish, very gentlemanly, and very much the warrior).[15] To resolve conflict and order the society, Mexicans in 1821 at independence (from Spain) and in 1848 at liberation (from the conquering U.S. army) argued at the treaty table for restoration, reimposing the virginal condition by calling forward a patroness for their republic and refusing to sever church and state issues as brutally as the United States—they considered—would have done. We are left to ponder the image and to ask the underlying questions, would dear Father Hidalgo molest his virginal wife, or would he respect some sort of symbolic boundary and leave her be, unlike the fraternities on this side of the border?

Between Guadalupe, the virgin, the high priestess, and Hidalgo, the Father of the Mexican nation, lie children of all colors and types, including, I would venture to guess, Lupe, "our" mestiza whore of fraternity fame, a fantasy genie, to "Orientalize" her and carry this point a bit further. In the matter of a Chicana-derived doxology of female heroines and not-so-feminine ones (I think of Catalina de Erauso or the very "butch" writings of Sor Juana Inés de la Cruz),[16] the specific self-sexualizations we have created are illustrative. Sandra Cisneros writes in a short story of peering under the Virgen de Guadalupe's skirt or dress.[17] What will she find? One of my students writes in a paper, "What if she's a cross-dresser, or a third gender?" The majority of my students, mostly Latinas, in a recent seminar said they considered the gesture not radical but sacrilegious; "I'd rather not know," they say. "How can we dare look at the virgin's genitals?" wrote another. They are far less conflicted when I remind them that men have done the same to us over the ages, investigating, for example, Catalina de Erauso by medical exam to determine if after she had served her country as a male soldier "the lieutenant nun," and donned male uniforms, she had "become male."[18] Yolanda López, Chicana artist from San Diego and now of San Francisco, painted the Virgen as runner, as seamstress, as old woman, but what really angered Mexican critics, as a doxology gone too far, was her 1980s rendition on the cover of *Fem* magazine in Mexico City showing the Virgen with a hiked up skirt and toeless heels. *Fem's* offices were threatened as targets, its editors denounced in the press and on television, and Yolanda was escorted around Mexico City by armed guard until she left that place.[19]

Under such a rereading, or to stick with my notion of a doxology, as liturgical expression, this one not to a god but rather to newly rendered pantheons of goddesses or historical heroines, we learn from artist's renditions, as well as from the sixteenth-century Catalina de Erauso, the "manly woman," and others one key lesson: gender strategy is accomplished. In the modern moment, where technologized bodies or transgendered identity is an achievement, the accomplishment of gender has come to mean many more interesting things, the art of doubling (two women dressed in bridal gowns, each androgynous but an enactor of "marriage"). This method of doubling, or of mirrors and of severe, consequent misrecognitions (the fraternity boys misrecognize *our* Lupes), underscores new symbolic registers and creates a fiction that in addition to racial discourse we must also analyze because it analyzes us and informs our memories. As historian Susan Striker, a transgendered lesbian historian from Berkeley/San Francisco, puts it, identity as specular fiction.[20]

What does the term "speculum," as used in this context, signify or suggest? That in the mirror or the speculum we find not ourselves—I have suggested in an article on Chicana identity that we know too much about who we are, have too much identity by virtue of our status in this society as the butt and bottom of white male fantasy—but reflections of what we ought to be. Perhaps this is more crucial to historicizing identity than anything fraternities might teach.[21] Another way to read this is to say that the virgin is the virgin is the virgin—do not put her in high heels, for to picture her teetering around for men in objects whose sole intention (as we discovered in the 1970s) was to make us objects and thrust forward our vaginas and boobs, is to suggest that the male intention is unworthy of us. The emphasis lies in the declaration, "unworthy of us," which so many feminists in the 1970s and 1980s grappled with, but usually not as lesbian separatists: rather, most chose the thought and not the action.

Playing boy, as Catalina did, or as Sor Juana wanted to do when she asked her mother to trim her hair and send her to the university to study as boys did—in other words, the transgendering or transsexual paradigm—breaks this entire doxology on Lupe into its constituent parts—what fraternities would have us be, and now in dispute, for it un-does gender fixity (something we Chicana feminists have argued for in articles and books and manifestos and poems) because the malestream or patriarchal tradition so seeks to stabilize a traditional, nonorganic identity, one created from without, but hanging critically if only by its historical strand. Is Lupe to be understood not merely as a "frat" lament, as a Western-conquest/colonized, history refrain, but also as a contemporary white man's suicide, the rope upon which "they" hang themselves? This question is one that Chicana undergraduates, in particular, are asking at the large, public universities in California where many have begun to enroll, despite the demise of affirmative action programs and federal law.

It would be foolish to be sanguine about the role "boys' clubs" play in society today. Fraternities have higher enrollment today than they did twenty years ago. And we have seen that harassers and rapists are just as likely to escape charges and be seated in illustrious positions as they did twenty years ago.[22]

More recently, by quibbling among ourselves over essentializing images—virgin, martyr, witch, or whore—the mother as exemplar of what we might term facetiously "Chicano Central," to use just the one example from our academic debates (that is, the locus of the authenticating voice deeming one type of Chicanismo/ma more Chicano than any other), offers us a recommendation that we suspend all belief in the Chicana mother as much more than a survivor, still hoping, as Lorena Bobbitt told her audience, to "stop the rape": "That's why I took the knife to him, and I can't remember if it was his ear or his penis, but I decided that if he wasn't going to let me get no sleep, he would never again sleep well either. So, I cut if off and then drove away like a crazy one." The notion of sheriff's deputies tromping in the grass looking for another man's penis is quite the graphic representation of our unequal positions. Bobbitt (the man) is newly remarried, with penis reattached ("I can do everything I could an' better," he told Geraldo Rivera on television), while Lorena served one prison sentence because she had no money to make probation and recently has faced new charges, of battering her mother.[23]

Lorena's ironies and miscalculations are not lost on us. Racial fixity is further marginalized in the view of the fraternities because, some decades ago (when the donor for the Alumni Center at Davis was an Alpha Gamma Rho), there was so little Chicana or Chicano presence on campus, and stereotypes reigned. Today the observant ensure—some might bemoan "legislate"—less blatant forms of racism.

In 1989, Irene Auerbach-Smith observed in the UCLA student newspaper that the line-up of Winnebagos on fraternity row the night before the Cal-UCLA game made her shudder.[24] Drawings of splayed women and slogans of "We love fish tacos," "Cheap chicks for sale," and "Don't laugh, your daughter's inside," recall how at crime scenes the spread-eagled body of a woman is common and signifies defeat, degradation, and death.[25] The original spread eagle is the emblem of the Great Seal of the United States, and used as a verb, to be spread-eagled means complete defeat.

The ferocious appearance and repetition of this image is what we must question, but from a critical awareness that repetition serves the interests of the state. From the Anita Hill/Clarence Thomas hearings: "you saw these pubic hairs on the soda can?" "yes" "where?" "on the lid of the can." "What kind of can was it, or soda?" "A coke, I think. I couldn't focus on the make of the coke." "Was there just one hair?" "I recall just one." "How do you know it was a pubic hair?" And so went the deposition: repeat, restate, repeat.[26] In this instance, and in the case of fraternity songs, repetition does not produce the desired result, the material body of Lupe, or in the case of Hill, the breakdown of her testimony (derived from the word testes, which she does not have and so is already negligent, or her testimony negligible).

In 1992 another set of fraternity lyrics surfaced, this time from a Sigma Pi songbook: "Knock, knock! Who's there? Lena. Lena who? Leaner up against the wall, we'll have a gangbang." Or, "Tiajuana, Tiajuana, bring your mother to the gangbang, Yes, you do, So we can fill her full of vodka." A song to Chi O also finds her lying in a pinewood box: "Chi O, Chi O, and now she lies in a pinewood box, For she'd sucked too many Sigma Pi cocks. Get it in, get it out. And now we dig her up again. She did it once, she'll do it again."[27]

The rape refrain serves as message and metaphor. In real life, these boys will become men better distanced and able to distance themselves from Mexican women and some 22 million people of Mexican origin generally. The conquest metaphors of recent centuries, of course, remind one that the conquest of women is still viewed as the conquest of a people. We are likely to enter a period made worse by women's resistances to, and verbal articulations of, crimes against their/our bodies. Moreover, we live in times of sexual discontent, sexual misconduct, and fears based on these which motivate more hate crimes than many other factors, including poverty, neighborhood demise, and all the rest.[28]

Ferociously regurgitive and intended to dehumanize, caricaturize, make less real and yet more available (women's bodies for/to men) all get bound up in "Lupe's Song," and I can think of few other refrains that better specify the operation of Mexican woman-hating in U.S. society. That this story or analysis picks up the song itself in 1992, at the moment of America's extreme fanaticism about the European conquest of 1492, is hardly accidental (Quincentennary fever reached an all-time high pitch in the fall, around 12 October, the same month that UCLA's *Daily Bruin News* and *La Gente* began publishing the accounts of Lupe's reappearance).

MURDER AT THE GATE

A student at U.C. Davis suggested that because her dorm room was across the street from fraternity row, and she got little sleep on the weekends because of the debauchery and bacchanals of the housemates, perhaps students should practice the same routine: no sleep until they give Lupe a burial. Instead, we usually resort to teaching about a cycle of unending prejudice and fear, needing first to understand how racism operates in society, and examining closely the components of this song. First, there is virginity and menstruation, neither of which is a topic for ordinary conversation but the silencing of these is necessary to perpetuate the notion of women as different and unequal. Lupe likes to suck on men's penises, so says the song, and because at eight years of age she was no longer a virgin, she is a logical recipient of any man's penis.

The violence begun in the European conquest of the Americas, Lupe's recitation or refrain seems to suggest, remains unleashed on the cultural and emotional landscape. She'll do anything, and any lover of hers would just as soon "eat Lupe," a rather odd activity, as most misogynists approve of oral sex in only one direction. Finally, Lupe ages, old, decomposing, yet smiling, so happy is she to render even in the grave her services. Happy for the attention, for the act itself, for more, the fraternities sing, happy, in other words, to exist as sex worker and for the pleasures of men. This deformation of Mexican womanhood and the construction of it as such mimics the real, live actions of many men, in the last century and in this one as well; murder was at the gate. The question Chicanas ask, then, is if they cannot have us now exactly as they did then, if we are unavailable or as fierce as Lorena was on that one evening, will they kill us anyway, symbolically? The matter of access, as I have suggested earlier in my discussion of the Anita Hill/ Clarence Thomas hearings, is one issue at stake in these proceedings, historical and contemporary. If more access is possible, as in interracial couplings, then do cross–racial hatreds seethe below the surface in response? The question of subsequent configurations of social and racial relations is equally significant in the hands of a historian, who details the record with a longer view in hand and a particular set of data in the present; this dialogue or refrain, present with past, accepts certain re-readings and misreadings as well.

The question invites our curiosity. Shall we give Lupe a proper burial and then leave her grave undisturbed? In the name of the suicidal Chicana academic and English professor Lora Romero of Stanford University, who ended her life about the time I began to unravel Lupe's Song in this format,[29] and in the name of those who remain depressed because they have endured abuse and violence, as well as the survivors of all manner of inhumane gestures and treatment, I suggest so because to do less is to forget the purpose of much of our work—to rearrange a bit the historical record and make it "less silent," to offer via a counterexample newer readings, and to win over through logical re-readings and the precision of our words oppositions grounded solely on fear (of us, women of Mexican origin) or loathing.

NOTES

1. From *La Gente*, October/November 1992, p. 9; on the history of the "song" and Alpha Gamma Rho fraternity at Davis, see Maricela Corbin, "A Study of the History of Alpha Gamma Rho Fraternity and the UC Davis Chicano/Latino Community, 1975–1993," pamphlet, University of California–Davis. Her sources include: *The California Aggie*, November 1975–February 1976; *The Chronicle for Higher Education*, March 1993; *The Feminist Majority Report*, March 1993; *The Third World Forum*, November 1992.

2. See "'Lupe' Sixteen Years Later: Why Fraternities Continue to Degrade Women," *La Gente*, October/November 1992, p. 9. Also see the letters of students, undergraduate and graduate, in the *Daily Bruin's* Viewpoint section, 9 October 1992, pp. 8, 10, 14. For one Theta Xi response, see Marc Buckhantz, then-president of Theta Xi Fraternity, classified ad. section, *Daily Bruin*, 1 October 1992, p. 36, including his statement, "We harbor no prejudices and embrace a diverse, *yet united campus and society* [italics mine]." . . . "No longer are these songs sung by the members that do know them, nor are they taught to our new members. The time had come for change and we acted accordingly."

3. See Anita Hill's memoir, *Speaking Truth to Power* (New York: Doubleday, 1997), as well as the videotaped hearings available from C-SPAN, 1992.

4. See, on experience as evidence, the rich literature beginning with Joan Scott, *Gender and the Politics of History* (New York: Columbia University Press, 1988).

5. See Jeff Ristine's article in the *San Diego Union-Tribune*, 11 December 1992, ed. 2, 4, 5, 1; B-2

and Sam Enriquez's article in the *Los Angeles Times*, 15 November 1992, p. B-3.

6. Jeffrey Berns, quoted in the *Los Angeles Times*, 12 November 1992.

7. Ibid.

8. See Al Martínez, "'Lupe and the Guys,'" *Los Angeles Times*, 12 November 1992, p. B-2.

9. See Matt Mier, *Mexican American Biographies* (New York: Greenwood Press, 1988) on Chipita Rodríguez; on Karla Fay Tucker, see the newspaper reports emanating from Texas, California, or New York.

10. See Deena J. González, *Refusing the Favor: The Spanish-Mexican Women of Santa Fe, 1820–1880* (New York: Oxford University Press, 1999), esp. chap. 2.

11. See, for example, Emma Pérez, *The Decolonial Imaginary: Writing Chicanas into History* (Bloomington and Indianapolis: Indiana University Press, 1999). Also see Antonia Castañeda, "Women of Color and the Rewriting of Western Women's History: The Discourse, Politics, and Decolonization of History," *Pacific Historical Review* 61 (November 1992): 501–33.

12. See James Josiah Webb, *Memoirs, 1844–1889*, Museum of New Mexico History Library, Santa Fe.

13. Begin with Patricia Nelson Limerick, *Legacy of Conquest: The Unbroken Past of the American West* (New York: Norton, 1987). Also see Richard White, *'It's Your Misfortune and None of My Own': A New History of the American West* (Norman: University of Oklahoma Press, 1991).

14. See the National Institute Against Prejudice and Violence reports, 1993, 1995.

15. For the argument, traced as Chicana-derived or grounded, see Pérez, *Decolonial Imaginary*, 22–27. For a different reading, see Carlos Fuentes, *The Buried Mirror: Reflections on Spain and the New World* (Boston: Houghton Mifflin, 1992), 145–46, on the brilliance of replacing the goddess Tonantzin with the Virgen de Guadalupe, and on the ways a nation of "bastards" (the Indians and *mestizos*) became, in effect, a nation of legitimated Spanish-Mexicans (hyphenated peoples).

16. For the best rendition of what I mean by a "butch," lesbian reading, see Alicia Gaspar de Alba, *Sor Juana's Second Dream* (Albuquerque: University of New Mexico Press, 1999).

17. Sandra Cisneros, *Woman Hollering Creek* (New York: Random House, 1991).

18. Students, Latina Feminist Traditions class, spring 1992.

19. See Yolanda López series of the Virgin, with herself, her mother, and her grandmother as the models in Alicia Gaspar de Alba, *Chicano Art: Inside/Outside the Master's House* (Austin: University of Texas Press, 1998), The Color Gallery, between 88–91. See also *Fem*, 1982.

20. Susan Stryker, paper delivered at Pomona College, California, 1994, and *Gay by the Bay* (Berkeley: University of California Press, 1998). On Catalina de Erauso, see Michelle Stepto and Gabriel Stepto, *Memoir of a Basque Lieutenant Transvestite in the New World* (Boston: Beacon Press, 1996).

21. See Deena J. González, "Chicana Identity Matters," in *Culture and Difference: Critical Perspectives on the Bicultural Experience,* ed. Antonia Darder (New York: Bergin and Garvey, 1995), reprinted in *Aztlan: A Journal of Chicano Studies* 22, no. 2 (1997).

22. Clarence Thomas is one figure, but the universities are full of the same. A good research design would begin with the Hermassie case at U.C. Berkeley in the 1970s and work its way through the Thomas hearings, attesting to the vindictive attitude and protective shield that university settings regularly provide harassers.

23. See *People* magazine, Special Anniversary Issue, 15–22 March 1999, p. 255, which quote Lorena [Bobbitt] Gallo as saying that today she loves shopping, "especially Nordstrom's when they have sales," and who works as a manicurist. To follow her story, see *Time* 142, no. 7 (1993): 67; 142, no. 22 (1993): 45; 143, no. 5 (1994): 99; on the Internet, see *The San Francisco Chronicle,* 27 October 1993, at Lexis-Nexis, Academic Universe: http://web.lexis-nexis.com

24. Irene Auerbach Smith, quoted in the *Daily Bruin,* 7 October 1992.

25. See Jane Caputi, *The Age of Sex Crime* (Bowling Green, Ohio: Bowling Green University Popular Press, 1987).

26. See the videotape of the hearings, eighth hour, C-SPAN.

27. *Daily Bruin News,* 7 October 1992, p. 9.

28. This was the argument that even the mainstream media gathered in following the tragic murder of Matthew Shepard, the gay student killed in Wyoming. See *Newsweek,* 8 November 1999.

29. See the obituaries following her death, Stanford University, faculty notes, Academic Senate, 1997.

10

The Diversity Machine: Moving Multiculturalism to the Workplace

FREDERICK R. LYNCH

Few liberal arts academics seem aware that campus-nurtured multiculturalism has been exported to and transformed by other social institutions, especially within the American workplace. Beginning in the late 1980s, multiculturalism moved to business and government settings as "diversity management," a business-friendly trend crafted by a relatively small number of author-consultants with backgrounds in academe, consulting, and human resources departments. This fledgling social policy movement became a more formidable "diversity machine" as it acquired allies and "diversity champions" among institutional elites.

The diversity machine moved multiculturalism and affirmative action debates beyond black–white racial history by focusing on more complex, multiethnic realities generated by Third World immigration and globalizing markets. These changes allegedly made multiculturalism and ethnic diversity a market-driven "must," rather than mere public relations and "social work." Savvy employers, it was said, would see the competitive advantage in hiring a workforce that mirrored the new ethnic mix. In turn, multicultural management theory has come home to academe in the form of ambitious "mission statements" for organizational change—such as the University of Michigan's "Michigan Mandate."

Indeed, "diversity" has become a high-level mantra ritually chanted in most corporations, universities, government agencies, foundations, and civic and cultural groups, and echoed by leaders in both major political parties. President William Clinton's early proclamation that he would appoint a "White House that looked like America" signaled early acceptance of the new diversity rhetoric at the highest levels of power. Shortly thereafter, former House Speaker Newt Gingrich and other Republicans began invoking the phrase "diversity is our strength," and journalists immediately noted "diversity management" efforts at the 1996 Republication National Convention. The emphasis on diversity, outreach, and "inclusion," was even more pronounced at the 2000 Republican and Democratic national conventions—themes that also echoed throughout the presidential campaigns. Diversity management's assumptions of continuing immigration and globalization were more quietly supported by the major political parties, but both Al Gore and George W. Bush were aggressive in minority outreach efforts. (Yet the GOP's continuing inability to broaden its electoral base produced one of the closest presidential elections in history when more than 90 percent of African Americans and approximately 65 percent of Hispanics voted for Al Gore rather than George Bush. Such results will likely accelerate, rather than dampen, the GOP's diversity drive.)

As the new millenium dawns, then, the diversity machine's theories of "valuing diversity" or "managing diversity" have achieved, at least rhetorically, the primary goal of most social movements: institutionalization.

How did this happen? Has diversity management become more than mere rhetoric in organizational life? Are there "diversity downsides," unintended consequences or conflicts set in motion by this top-down diversity push? I shall address these questions initially by outlining the core diversity management perspectives, then I will show how reinforcing realities, internal divisions, and societal events shaped the policy machine that marketed and publicized these theories. The first half of the chapter relies heavily upon data and analysis drawn from my book, *The Diversity Machine*.[1] The second half of the chapter revisits and updates these findings with new interviews of key policy architects, as well as analyses of new diversity developments in American organizational life.

THE DIVERSITY MACHINE TAKES SHAPE

In the late 1980s, several author-consultants began producing books, articles, and videotapes that re-evaluated both the concept and practice of affirmative action.

R. Roosevelt Thomas, Lewis Griggs, Sondra Thiederman, and others argued that affirmative action was increasingly viewed as backward-looking social work by corporate executives and a growing segment of the public.[2] This "do-the-right-thing" moralism, consultants claimed, increasingly fell on deaf ears. Mandated hiring goals were resented and affirmative action was tainted by suspicions that it forced the hiring of less qualified or unqualified minorities and women. Valuing or managing diversity visions offered new, future-oriented, business-friendly rationales for workforce changes.

Thomas and Griggs argued that the coming demographic transformation of the American workforce and consumer markets, at home and abroad, made "valuing diversity" (Griggs) or "managing diversity" (Thomas) a bottom-line *business necessity*. According to Thomas, rapidly rising numbers of women and minorities, coupled with declining numbers of white males, made a diverse workforce inevitable; legally driven "forced" affirmative action recruitment would fade. More problematic would be management of culturally different employees who wished to "be themselves," and who would resist assimilation into a workplace culture made by and for white males.

The architects of the diversity machine maintained that employers could harness the creativity and full potential of women and minority employees through carefully engineered cultural transformations of white male workplace culture. Culture change would ensure a more productive and tension-free workplace. Retaining a workplace that mirrored changing customer demographics would allegedly provide greater cross-cultural sensitivity and a "competitive edge." Talented prospective minority employees would gravitate to employers where there were others who "looked like them"—an attraction that would also allegedly lure burgeoning blocs of minority and Third World customers.

The new theories of valuing and managing workforce diversity were generated and reinforced by four major events in the wider social environment.

First, there was the publication of the government-sponsored 1987 report by the Hudson Institute, *Workforce 2000*.[3] The report forecast major demographic changes regarding the ethnic mix of the domestic workforce—mainly a rising number of women and minorities and a declining number of white men. These changes wound up being considerably exaggerated by a typographical error in the document's executive summary. Though the full report estimated that 15 percent of net new hires during the 1990s would be white men (that is, the percentage above and beyond white men who were replacing other white men—a substantial number), the executive summary omitted the word "net." One of the most famous typos in social policy history, this mistake produced a widespread, attention-grab-bing myth—congenial to the cause of diversity management—that *only* 15 percent of all new hires in the 1990s would be white men. That the vast majority (more than 75 percent) of the nation's labor force at the dawn of the new century would still be white men and women was usually ignored. Though some leaders in the emerging diversity management movement took care to debunk the myth, others did not. The 15 percent typo often went unchallenged in the popular press and in policy-making circles. Thus, combined with predictions of coming labor short-ages, the realities and the myths of *Workforce 2000* provided diversity management's seductive "demography is destiny" rationale.

A second, more legally compelling impetus for diversity management was the 1991 publication of the U.S. Department of Labor's *Report on the Glass Ceiling*.[4] The report highlighted "glass ceilings," barriers of institutional sexism and racism which allegedly blocked the promotion of women and minorities in large corporations. More significantly, the glass ceiling study symbolized the Labor Department's use of "glass ceiling audits." Government contractors were put on notice that not only would their efforts to hire underrepresented groups be scrutinized but also, pos-sibly, their records of retaining and promoting minorities and women. Diversity management was specifically attuned to employers' anxieties about bureaucratic hassles, fines, or lawsuits on these matters.

The third and fourth factors propelling diversity management were somewhat intertwined: acceleration of Third World immigration into the United States and U.S. corporations' movement overseas in search of new labor and consumer mar-kets. (The fall of communism in 1989, of course, quickened and enriched the lure of overseas markets.) The need to manage and market to burgeoning Third World populations at home and abroad made multiculturalism the peculiar "silent part-ner" of global capitalism—as David Rieff wryly observed.[5]

Internal developments also shaped the diversity machine. As in other expand-ing social movements, a division between leaders and followers appeared. A pro-fessional literature arose. Varying "schools" or approaches to diversity management developed. The diversity machine developed its own differences.

The deepest divisions within the diversity machine could be mapped along two dimensions. First, in the literature and at diversity conferences there were sharp disagreements over whether to separate new diversity management theory and practice from established affirmative action and the latter's exclusive empha-sis on race and gender. (For example, R. Roosevelt Thomas's seminal book *Beyond Race and Gender* was clearly a call to expand the range of "differences" into age, sexual orientation, and work-family conflicts.) Explicitly or implicitly, this expansion into other sociological realms seemed to diminish the campaign against racism and sexism via affirmative action. Any hint of abandoning affirmative action was fiercely resented by consultants who were generally older, African American, and often had backgrounds in affirmative action administration, human resources, and/or the civil rights movement. Those favoring an expanded diversity focus and greater distance from affirmative action were usually younger and more business-oriented.

A second argument among diversity consultants concerned the degree of cultural and organizational change required to accommodate the new diversity. "Cross-cultural educators," such as Sondra Thiederman and Thomas Kochman, were mainly interested in educating and sensitizing employers and employees through lectures and workshops. "Change masters," such as Roosevelt Thomas and Elsie Cross, on the other hand, offered more expensive and extensive prescriptions for cultural transformation of organizations. Through repeated use of surveys, focus groups, and training over a multiyear period, they offered to root out hidden racism, sexism, and other glass ceilings reinforced by taken-for-granted values, norms, and practices.

The broader visions for organizational change often incorporated three major ideological principles drawn from affirmative action and the wider multicultural movement:

1. "Disparate Impact:" Lack of ethnic-gender proportional representation is an indicator of institutional racism or sexism.
2. "Identity Politics": Individual consciousness is heavily determined by group membership, especially race and gender. An individual's viewpoint is assumed to reflect those of his/her ethnic or gender group. (Hence, an Asian on the board of directors would add the "Asian point of view," while a Hispanic manager would be more culturally attuned to Hispanic employees or customers.)
3. "Cultural Relativism": Dominant values and rules are those made by and for white males. In multicultural society, the old color-blind battle cry— "without regard to race, color, or creed"—was considered a sham and a mask for forced assimilation to white male values. Without workplace culture change, "equal treatment is not fair treatment." In a world where "differences are assets," mutual cultural accommodation would replace one-way assimilation.

Both the literature review and the case studies that I conducted in the mid-1990s demonstrated that evaluating the effects of workforce diversity programs has been difficult. Some organizations fell back into affirmative action's "bean counting" metrics—which risked confirming suspicions that the new programs were, indeed, warmed-over affirmative action. In addition, other organizational processes and events, especially downsizing, often clouded progress of diversity programs.

A primary goal of diversity management programs—greater retention and promotion of underrepresented groups—was considerably complicated by the deep, relatively long recession of the early 1990s. The recession and layoffs created a climate of fear and anxiety among employees that was hardly conducive to culture change programs. (With so many millions losing jobs, directives aimed at retention and promotion of specific groups was a delicate issue.) In addition, mergers and efforts to boost stock prices led corporations to persist in layoffs well beyond the end of the recession. Though a few consultants insisted that efforts to increase minority and female promotion rates could be fully initiated in such an environment, most consultants were frustrated. Insofar as there was any money for diversity efforts at all, employers tended to favor half-day or one-day workshops as a "quick fix."

Thus, at conventions, and in newsletters, articles, and books, consultants grumbled that diversity was "stuck in the training mode." The programs often appeared to be "diversity penance," group punishment for high-level organizational transgressions such as a lawsuit or an individual CEO's conversational gaffe. In a similar manner, a workshop was seen as a talisman against discrimination complaints by demonstrating "good faith efforts" in race relations.

Besides the tight training budgets of the recession, extracting greater levels of funding for diversity efforts was made especially difficult by lack of systematic proof that diversity programs delivered promised "bottom-line" results. These results were: greater productivity, sales, and intergroup harmony—partly measured by reduced numbers of lawsuits and discrimination complaints. Another obstacle to moving beyond the training phase was that consultants could not offer examples of specific organizations that "modeled" the successful cultural changes allegedly wrought by diversity management.

On the contrary, beneath the ascendant "diversity-is-our-strength" rhetoric from the White House and corporate boardrooms, there were warnings that the programs could backfire, increasing intergroup frictions instead of reducing them. Rumors circulated of diversity training "blow-ups." A few consultants quietly billed themselves as "mop-up" experts—skilled at cleaning up botched efforts by lesser lights. Some consultants—such as Lewis Griggs—openly admitted that diversity initiatives might initially spur more complaints and problems, as heretofore-oppressed groups felt increasingly empowered.

As the late social historian Robert Nisbet cogently observed, social change usually occurs in response to a series of unanticipated, significant events.[6] The diversity machine had to deal with several such incidents. First, there was the videotaped beating of Rodney King by Los Angeles police and the subsequent trial, which resulted in the 1992 "civil disturbance"—televised throughout the nation. The violence and discord in Los Angeles dashed the early diversity management slogan that "the future is now in L.A!"—an upbeat phrase suggesting that the ethnic mix in Los Angeles modeled coming changes for the rest of the nation.

A second cluster of related events that much disturbed those in the diversity management movement might be contained under the label "the 1994 Republican Revolution." The 1994 election of a Republican majority in Congress was the most obvious signal of this, but consultants viewed this as the capstone of a wider "counterrevolution" against pro-diversity forces in society. "White backlash" against diversity initiatives topped consultants' concerns in forums and newsletter surveys. "Angry white males" were seen as the source of the rebellion against diversity and "political correctness." Prior to the 1994 elections, the counterrevolution was seen as confined to talk radio. However, the mainstream media had picked up the debate over "PC"—a term considered by those in the diversity machine as pejorative labeling of affirmative action and diversity initiatives. The 1994 elections were also viewed as the outcome of a rising number of articles and books critical of diversity and change. Among these, the work that generated the most hostility was Richard Herrnstein and Charles Murray's *The Bell Curve*.[7]

More disconcerting still was the course of the Republican Revolution in bellwether California. In 1994, the state's electorate passed Proposition 187, limiting provision of public services to illegal immigrants. Many in the diversity management movement interpreted this as an outburst of nativism against an inevitably changing ethnic mosaic—and another refutation of "the future is now in L.A!" Finally, out of the 1994 election results arose the most menacing manifestation of the angry white male: the nascent California Civil Rights Initiative (CCRI), aimed at ending ethnic gender preferences in the public sector. The major news media, surprised by the events of 1994, immediately rushed to cover this so-called Son of 187. Though the CCRI nearly failed in its early days for lack of funds, the requisite number of signatures was gathered, and the CCRI became ballot Proposition 209. It passed in November 1996.

Just weeks before the passage of Proposition 209, however, an event occurred that augured well for diversity training in corporate America. In October 1996, tape recordings of high-level Texaco executives discussing a discrimination lawsuit became a hot news item. The tapes, made by a disgruntled employee, initially were thought to contain ethnic slurs, including a reference to "black jelly beans" sticking to the "bottom of the bag." Subsequent analysis of the tapes found that the most incendiary ethnic slur had not been used. Yet the "jelly beans" remark was left to stand as an insult to blacks. (In fact, journalists and social scientists at all familiar with diversity management recognized that the sarcastic reference to jelly beans was in reference to a lecture at Texaco by R. Roosevelt Thomas Jr. He often likened diversity in an organization to a mix of different colored jellybeans in a jar.) Nevertheless, Texaco and its CEO, Peter Bijur, were publicly humiliated and embarked upon a well-publicized diversity makeover program.

Finally, while I have seen little evidence that the criminal trial of O. J. Simpson directly impacted the course of the diversity machine, the polarized reaction to the trial and its verdict undoubtedly affected the national climate of race relations. Polls registered racially divided views of the criminal justice system. Diversity movement alliances between feminists and minority civil rights activists were undoubtedly strained: the trial pitted the feminist cause of justice for battered women against African Americans' anger at a racially biased justice system.

RECENT DEVELOPMENTS IN DIVERSITY MANAGEMENT: KEY CONSULTANTS RECONSIDER

Since the mid-1990s, the drive for diversity management has been affected by four developments: (1) the long-forecast tightening of the labor market and the improved profit picture for most major corporations; (2) continued discrimination lawsuits and resultant public relations campaigns by corporations such as Texaco and Denny's; (3) attempts to publish systematic proof that "diversity works"—arising primarily from increased debate over the use of ethnic and gender preferences in higher education; and (4) increased high-level corporate and political awareness of demographic change.

Though corporate layoffs continued apace during 1998, millions of jobs were also created. Debates continue about the quality and compensation of the new jobs, compared to those eliminated in downsizing. Yet, official unemployment levels have dropped and remain low. The need for skilled workers in urban areas is now quite strong, as indicated by press reports that "Builders and Unions Court New Workers."[8] More than half the chief financial officers at U.S. companies in a quarterly survey by Duke University reported problems finding qualified employees.[9] In some regions of the nation, McDonalds has been forced to offer signing bonuses and pay above the minimum wage. Demand for technically skilled and computer-savvy workers is very strong. In other words, the labor shortages forecast a decade ago in *Workforce 2000* have appeared at last. Furthermore, according to a front-page report in the *Wall Street Journal*, these labor shortages are likely to persist.[10] These developments strengthen the bargaining position of employees who wish to promote workplace changes—on cultural diversity and other matters.

Corporate difficulties with discrimination complaints continue to focus corporate and public awareness on diversity controversies. Resolution of several cases has produced expanded diversity efforts. For example, the settlement of the Texaco lawsuit mandated diversity training for all employees. In addition, a task force was assembled to revise personnel procedures. The former head of the U.S. Justice Department's Civil Rights Division, Deval Patrick, has been made a Texaco vice president. Both Texaco and Mobil Oil have run full-page advertisements extolling workforce diversity in business-oriented publications such as the *Wall Street Journal*, as well as in some major newspapers and news magazines. And, in November 2000, Coca-Cola agreed to pay a record $156 million to settle a discrimination lawsuit filed by black employees. Following the Texaco precedent, the company agreed to have its diversity and human resource practices monitored by a 7-member task force partly comprised of attorneys and other outside experts.

Discrimination complaints at Denny's forced major management changes, extensive diversity training, and more minority members on the board of directors and spurred efforts to expand minority ownership of franchises. Denny's has also sponsored a series of television messages on antidiscrimination and diversity. In July 1998, the giant financial services firm Salomon Smith Barney agreed to settle a class-action bias case brought by female employees. The company promised to spend more than $15 million over four years on programs to recruit and promote women and minorities. In 1999 aircraft manufacturer Boeing Company paid $15 million to settle class-action lawsuits by African American employees alleging workplace discrimination. The company promised programs to enhance retention and promotion of minorities.

Sagging sales or shrinking market share led other corporations to expand minority outreach. In 1998, Nissan Motor Company set a goal of expanding its minority dealerships by 25 percent, and tied compensation of high-level executives to achieving that goal. (General Motors also announced plans to expand the number of minority-owned dealerships.) International Business Machines and Mobil have published full-page advertisements testifying that "diversity works."

How "diversity works" *within* corporations was suggested in a 1998 Korn Ferry/Columbia Business School study of 280 minority executives earning at least $100,000 annually. The findings reinforced diversity management emphases on mentoring, communication, and feedback in fostering upward mobility for women and minorities.[11] (Sixty percent of mentors in the Korn Ferry study were of the same ethnicity or gender as those they helped. With regard to the other forty percent, who take an interest in female or minority career development, a recent *Wall Street Journal* front-page report suggests that Jewish executives, sensitized by their own minority backgrounds, are likely mentors.[12])

Recent attitude surveys of business executives reinforce results cited in *The Diversity Machine*. Among executives, there is general, theoretical support for "workplace diversity"; affirmative action is viewed less favorably. In a December 1997 survey for the television program "Nightly Business Report," 85 percent of business executives (for large and medium-sized firms) thought "workplace diversity" was extremely or very important. Between 75 and 80 percent felt that diversity was "essential to their on-going success." Yet, though a majority of executives reported existence of company-wide policies against discrimination, less than half indicated their organizations actively recruited women or minorities; less than 25 percent provided diversity training. Only 30 percent had affirmative action programs in place. Yet, larger firms were more proactive. Active recruitment of minorities and women was more likely (above 70 percent) and diversity training was offered more often (in 50 percent of larger firms).[13]

On the other hand, affirmative action garnered mixed or negative support. Only half of large company executives (39 percent of all executives) deeply believed in affirmative action, and nearly 60 percent would favor its abolition. Nearly 40 percent felt that affirmative action was not necessary to produce diversity, and nearly double that percentage indicated that business had been forced to hire and promote less than qualified individuals. These findings reinforced those of a Time/CNN poll in which only 33 percent of executives favored set–aside university scholarships for women and minorities and only 12 percent favored hiring goals for African Americans. (Somewhat paradoxically, nearly 90 percent of respondents to the "Nightly Business Report" survey thought that discrimination was not a problem in the workplace, yet 63 percent of business executives in the Time/CNN poll thought racism was a problem for the wider society.)[14]

The most intense pressure to justify diversity programs arose in the wake of popular referenda and court decisions limiting the use of ethnic-gender preferences in higher education admissions. As a result of the 1996 Fifth Circuit Court of Appeals decision in *Hopwood v. University of Texas*, public higher education institutions within that jurisdiction were enjoined from using ethnic preferences in student admissions. (Two of the three justices pointedly observed that skin color was a poor proxy for the desired goal of diversity.) In California, the University of California Regents in 1995 voted to discontinue use of ethnic-gender preferences in admissions, hiring, and contracting, even before this was prohibited for all state agencies by the 1996 passage of Proposition 209. A pending discrimination lawsuit by whites denied admission to the University of Michigan and the spread of Proposition 209–style initiatives to other states has added urgency to the need for systematic proof that "diversity works."

As an answer, William Bowen and Derek Bok, former presidents of Princeton and Harvard, respectively, published *The Shape of the River: Long-Term Consequences of Considering Race in College and University Admissions.*[15] A testament to the power of the diversity machine and its high-level allies was the extensive professional and mass media attention and acclaim accorded this book.

The Shape of the River is largely based on the study of two cohorts of students who graduated from highly selective colleges and universities in 1976 and 1989. The book's main conclusion is that academically selective colleges have been highly successful in using race-sensitive admissions policies to advance educational goals important to everyone. Using race as a factor in admissions helped erode segregation in universities and in students' lives after graduation. Black students at selective schools did have somewhat higher dropout rates than their white peers but also graduated at higher rates than did blacks with similar SAT scores at nonselective schools. Black students did not feel stigmatized by affirmative action, and as many blacks as whites majored in sciences and engineering. (One somewhat contradictory finding, however: "at almost every college in our sample, black students are not only performing less well academically than whites, but also performing below the levels predicted by their SAT scores."[16])

Bok and Bowen discovered that graduates of all races have favorable views of the emphasis placed on diversity by their alma maters—even among whites with lower SATs and those who did not get to attend the school of their choice. Interracial relations in education, claimed graduates, helped them deal with race relations at work and in the wider world. Black graduates were more likely than white peers to attend graduate or professional schools, and were more likely to participate in civic and community activities.

Bok and Bowen were invited by the editors of the *Harvard Business Review* to present "Lessons for Business from Higher Education" in the January/February 1990 issue.[17] With coauthor Glenda Burkhart, they repeated justifications for using racial criteria in admissions: (1) to enhance the quality of the educational experience; and (2) to foster upward mobility of minority students into the mainstream and leadership of American life. Educating people to be the best and to work across the lines of race, class, religion, and background were totally compatible goals highly relevant to business. More darkly, they maintained that societal and corporate stability and order were at stake. Absent "race-sensitive" selection criteria in education and workplaces, American society would be racially polarized, and "corporations will not be healthy unless the society is healthy."[18]

Bowen, Bok, and Burkhart countered arguments that merit and diversity were incompatible by arguing that selection of individuals must be based not only on individual merit but also according to the organization's goals and societal responsibilities. Diversity is a worthwhile goal—for universities and for businesses. (The University of Michigan has just released a study with data and arguments similar to Bok and Bowen's.[19])

Yet, the Bok and Bowen book and spin-off articles have somewhat confused efforts to separate "old" affirmative action from "new" diversity management. The book's exclusive focus on race and its defense of affirmative action "representation" are setbacks to Thomas and authors trying to expand the definition of diversity and promote deeper institutional change. Bok and Bowen's attempt to redefine merit in terms of organizational mission and goals is a limited effort at cultural change. The authors clearly favor the goals of diversity consultants who foster cross-cultural communication. Still, the thrust of the book is assimilationist.

In contrast to the fanfare accorded Bok and Bowen's works was the relative silence toward *Workforce 2020*, a substantial revision of *Workforce 2000*, diversity management's powerful demography-is-destiny rationale. The authors of the new *Workforce 2020* pointedly disowned the "diversity craze" that the original report was credited with launching.[20] They corrected exaggerated predictions about the decline in the percentage of white male workers, and countered claims that minority and female workers must be regarded as "differently qualified." Instead, they insisted that " what the new workers principally need—whether they are white and male or female and minority—are the skills that education must provide, not managers trained in diversity and sensitivity."[21] The chief problems for the twenty-first century workforce will be the maturation of the Baby Boomers (the "graying" of America, not its "browning"[22]) and the threat of a society polarized by age, class, education, and ethnicity.

Key Consultants' Reconsider

Four author-consultants were profiled in depth in The Diversity Machine: Lewis Griggs, R. Roosevelt Thomas Jr., Thomas Kochman, and Sondra Thiederman. Thomas exemplified the comprehensive "change master" approach to organizational change. Griggs and Kochman were also change-oriented but focused exclusively on intensive cross-cultural training, which they hoped would plant seeds for deeper changes in organizational routines and individual consciousness. Thiederman exemplified the ideologically neutral cross-cultural trainer who was content to merely educate and raise awareness—though she, too, hoped that greater knowledge would reinforce equal opportunity ideals and practices.

In mid-March of 1999, I reinterviewed each of them by telephone. By and large, the consultants did not perceive the impact of wider societal events upon the course of the diversity management movement. Their views did echo polling results of business executives rhetorically supporting "workforce diversity" but opposed to mandated hiring or promotion goals.

Kochman, Thomas, and Thiederman viewed progress as slow and incremental. Kochman and Thomas both felt there was somewhat more interest by CEOs in long-term change and increased recognition of the benefits of understanding cultural differences. However, this was primarily driven by concerns of customer sales and service. (In response to increased variations in domestic ethnic markets, Kochman's consulting firm had added new instructional modules on East Asian, Middle Eastern, Russian-Jewish, and Native American cultures.) The characteristically ebullient Griggs saw "great progress" being made.

All four consultants agreed that flush economic times and, especially, tightened labor markets had furthered employer concerns over worker retention and satisfaction—and, hence, "diversity friendly" workplaces. Thiederman felt there was more money available for training (except in health services, where managed care pressures had taken a toll on training budgets). Kochman suggested that training budgets were the same, but that diversity had higher priority.

On the other hand, consultants admitted that the temptation for the one-day workshop and quick fix was still strong. (The wish to "take a pill," said Kochman;

the "silver bullet," sighed Thomas.) All four consultants grumbled about lack of top-level corporate patience and long-term commitment required to achieve full understanding and management of cultural differences. Instead, said Thiederman, organizations often took shortcuts via quotas and stereotypical attempts to "match" employees ethnicity with that of customers.

The author of *Beyond Race and Gender*, R. Roosevelt Thomas Jr., was especially dissatisfied that broader and more complex diversity frameworks were acknowledged only theoretically. In practice, most programs were affirmative-action throwbacks to numbers-driven "representation" within an assimilationist framework. Race was still the primary focus, followed by gender. Thiederman, Kochman, and Griggs concurred, though they added "ethnicity" or immigrant cultures. Griggs emphasized growing awareness and interest in diversity overseas; the other three consultants said little about this.

Age and generational conflict, a growing concern in social policy circles and the mass media, had not registered as yet as a major diversity issue. (Thiederman and Griggs cited some concerns over the work habits of Generation X and Thomas mentioned that generational issues sometimes arose in largely white male workplaces.)

Thiederman, Thomas, and Kochman reluctantly admitted that the "business case" for managing diversity in the workforce was still not deeply accepted among corporate leaders. Thiederman stated that there was "perpetual talk about the business case," but little else. Lack of systematic proof of diversity management's effectiveness was still a roadblock. Thomas admitted that diversity management's case rested, to some extent, on logic and faith, while Kochman admitted as a fact of life that varying economic conditions might limit organizations' abilities to fund diversity initiatives. (Little mention was made of either Bowen and Bok's *The Shape of the River* or the media celebration of it. No one cited the new and unheralded sequel to *Workforce 2000: Workforce 2020*. Nor did any of the four consultants reference President Clinton's *One America* racial initiative.)

Yet, the consultants detected signs that there was a growing awareness of the business case for effectively managing workforce diversity. Taking care to speak for no one but his own consulting firm, Kochman felt that some employers, initially interested only in addressing customer diversity, subsequently developed an interest in "workforce equity." (That course inevitably raised touchy issues of sharing power and arguments over smaller shares of the pie.) Thomas observed that more clients were coming to him in the wake of legal problems—indicating that employers might be thinking more in terms of long-term, fundamental change rather than quick, one-day fixes. Those corporations that had been working toward fuller diversity management for several years, said Thomas, were now taking pause, reevaluating progress and directions. He could think of no corporation that had made the transition to full diversity management: "They're at the river and wondering how to cross it." Thomas compared the ambivalence in transiting from numbers-driven formulae to full diversity to the wider societal dilemma over segregation-integration. Much work had been done on dismantling segregation, but successful integration was another matter.

Griggs and Thiederman saw glimmerings of one of the fondest hopes of diversity consultants: that diversity issues were being woven into general management. Griggs went further than the others in maintaining that an increasing number of CEOs "get it": They differentiate between affirmative action and valuing diversity, and they are more willing to see diversity issues as systemic and requiring long-term nurturing. (Griggs was hesitant to offer examples. He was enthusiastic about the vigorous presentation offered at a recent convention by the new CEO of the embattled Denny's restaurant chain. Beyond that, Griggs could name no exemplar.)

All consultants felt that white male backlash remained a problem to be dealt with through greater "inclusion" of white men in the diversity management dialogue. Griggs suggested that the strength of reaction to diversity by white men was an indicator of real change and progress. Kochman admitted that previous diversity efforts had often targeted white males, increasing polarization. The impact of the Clinton sex scandals, offered Kochman, could be seen within the context of national polarization over diversity issues. Women and minorities who doggedly defended Clinton appreciated his pro-diversity record and saw attempts to "get" Clinton as part of a white-male-led effort to terminate not only Clinton's presidency, but his pro-diversity policies as well. (Griggs was pleased that he had anticipated the Clinton scandal with an instructional videotape, "Sexual Dynamics.")

Only Griggs felt that the notorious Texaco controversy had had much impact. Thomas dismissed the episode as, perhaps, a lesson in short-term crisis management. None were familiar with Texaco's current efforts. Few other societal or political events were cited as shaping the diversity machine or its environments. Thomas felt that the passage of Proposition 209 had, perhaps, caused debate to regress into race-and-gender representation, "the door we came through" but should have moved beyond.

MARKET-DRIVEN MULTICULTURALISM: POSITIVE
PROSPECTS—AND DIVERSITY DOWNSIDES

Favorable factors promoting some forms of diversity management include: (1) rising real and rhetorical recognition of ethnic diversity in workplaces and markets, (2) tight labor markets and spot shortages, (3) increased incidence of workplace harassment lawsuits, and (4) continued affirmative action audits of employers by state and federal regulatory agencies. Whether overseas or within the United States, employers must inevitably pay greater heed to the cultural habits of Third World workers and customers. On the other hand, business executives remain opposed to numerical forms of affirmative action and assign low priority to long-term efforts to transform "white male" workplace culture.

The ambivalent embrace of diversity management by business and political elites must be seen in the context of their assimilationist and economics-oriented worldview, shared with much of the general population. In this perspective, markets and individuals are paramount, while sociological and cultural factors are deemed relatively unimportant. Hence, business and political leaders economically favor Third World immigration and increased offshore manufacturing; but they ignore or only dimly grasp the political and cultural implications of these policies.

Some of these consequences suggest "diversity downsides." Class and demographic polarization—augmented by "diversity flight" of working- and middle-class whites (and blacks) from high-immigration areas—appear to be one such outcome.[23] Another is the rising number of successful reverse discrimination lawsuits by white males. (One of the latest and most remarkable reverse discrimination verdicts occurred on 31 March 1999, when a San Francisco jury awarded $2.7 million to a white male who had applied for a tenure-track job at San Francisco State University after teaching there for years on a part-time basis. One week later, a Sacramento jury found in favor of white plaintiffs in a discrimination lawsuit against the sheriff's department. In addition, there have been several other recent successful verdicts.) [24] Meanwhile, corporations with substantial diversity programs in place—such as American Airlines and Boeing Corporation—are nonetheless being sued on grounds of racial harassment or discrimination, respectively.

Rather than promote "look like America" workplace inclusion, increased ethnic diversity in markets can instead promote balkanization and exclusion. This became apparent during the entertainment media uproar when nearly "all white" casts for the major networks' new, prime-time television programs were scheduled for the fall 1999 season. Amid the subsequent spirals of outrage and apologies—and last-minute additions of some minority actors—it was quietly admitted that markets, not racism, produced the "whitest" programming in more than a decade. Demographic data indicated distinctly different racial television viewing habits and preferences. Programs with largely black casts and themes attracted smaller "niche" audiences, which the major networks (and market dynamics) were tacitly relegating to the smaller networks, such as FOX, or to cable channels, such as Black Entertainment Television. Hence, network producers had all crafted themes and casting to appeal to the single largest consumer group, most favored by sponsors: younger, middle- and upper—middle-class whites, aged eighteen to thirty-four.[25]

Similar marketing in other sectors—not yet revealed and denounced—may partly reflect the reality that multiethnic populations are still surprisingly concentrated in a few urban areas within the United States. Multicultural trends have been greatest in high-immigration states like California, Florida, New York, and Texas—yet, even there, sweeping demographic changes appear to have largely occurred within only a few specific counties.[26]

Nevertheless, the growth of these strategic concentrations of minority and immigrant populations has triggered the most obvious and enthusiastic embrace to date of inclusive, "valuing diversity" rhetoric and strategy by white political elites. In the Republican Party, especially, Spanish language and music is in; open discussions of affirmative action or immigration reforms are out.

The 1994 "conservative revolution" that rocked the diversity machine has been turned on its head by the 1998 elections, especially in states with large immigrant populations, such as California. There, Democrats won the governor's office and a U.S. Senate seat by capturing nearly 70 percent of the burgeoning Latino vote. Consultants warned Republican leaders that appeals to their shrinking white and male base—by criticizing affirmative action programs and immigration—would alienate the swelling ranks of Latino voters.[27]

The early and impressive top-down bandwagon promoting the presidency of Texas governor George W. Bush Jr. owed considerable impetus to the fact that Bush was able to win substantial numbers of Texas' minority voters, especially Hispanics.[28] In the U.S. Congress, the Republican leadership's fear of losing further shares of black, women, and Hispanic voters sidelined attempts by some Republican representatives to end ethnic and gender preferences in government contracting. In Florida, Republican leaders have been openly hostile toward California businessman Ward Connerly's attempts to launch a Proposition 209–style campaign there.[29]

Whatever forms of diversity management prevail in the American workplace and the rest of society, a key conclusion of *The Diversity Machine* is worth restating. The ability to understand cultural differences in increasingly diverse workplaces and markets would seem an obvious advantage. Yet those skills are not necessarily related to skin color. Anyone can be trained in matters of cultural sensitivity. A successful workforce need *not* look like its customer base.

A model of this preference-free, relatively color-blind diversity management was described in a 1998 *Los Angeles Times* case study of the giant Longo Toyota dealership. Reporter Peter Hong found that an individual's ability to sell cars to a highly diverse customer base was largely unrelated to race, color, or gender. Successful sales personnel developed cultural sensitivities to deal with the increasingly multiethnic customer base; those who could not adapt, departed. The only "matching" of salesperson and customer was in those cases where the customer did not speak English. (Evidently, this was not an insurmountable problem for whites: Longo's top salesman was Jewish.)[30]

This more performance-based, color-blind, yet culturally sensitive form of market-driven diversity is likely to be more promising—and legally defensible.[31]

NOTES

1. Frederick R. Lynch, *The Diversity Machine: The Drive to Change the "White Male Workplace"* (New York: Free Press, 1997).

2. R. Roosevelt Thomas Jr., "From Affirmative Action to Affirming Diversity," *Harvard Business Review* 68 (March-April 1990): 107–17; R. Roosevelt Thomas Jr., *Beyond Race and Gender* (New York: AMACON Press, 1992); Lennie Copeland and Lewis Griggs, "Valuing Diversity," videotape series (San Francisco: Griggs Productions, 1987). See also Lennie Copeland, "Ten Steps to Making the Most of Cultural Differences at the Workplace," *Personnel* (July 1988): 58–60; Sondra Thiederman, *Bridging Cultural Barriers for Corporate Success* (New York: Lexington Books, 1991); and Sondra Thiederman, *Profiting in America's Multicultural Marketplace* (New York: Lexington Books, 1991).

3. William B. Johnston and Arnold H. Packer. *Workforce 2000: Work and Workers for the 21st Century.* Prepared for the U.S. Department of Labor (Indianapolis: Hudson Institute, 1987).

4. U.S. Department of Labor, *A Report on the Glass Ceiling Initiative* (Washington, D.C.: Government Printing Office, 1991).

5. David Rieff, "Multiculturalism's Silent Partner," *Harper's*, August 1993, pp. 62–68.

6. Robert Nisbet, *Social Change and History* (New York: Oxford University Press, 1967).

7. Charles Murray and Richard Herrnstein, *The Bell Curve* (New York: Free Press, 1994).

8. "Builders and Unions Court New Workers," *New York Times*, 12 March 1999.

9. *Los Angeles Times*, 7 July 1998.

10. *Wall Street Journal*, 22 March 1999.

11. Korn Ferry International and Columbia Business School, "Diversity in the Executive Suite: Creating Successful Career Paths and Strategies" (New York: Korn Ferry, 1998).

12. *Wall Street Journal*, 28 April 1998.

13. "Nightly Business Report Diversity Survey," 1997, *http://www.nightlybusiness.org/divtext.htm.*

14. Ibid.

15. William G. Bowen and Derek Bok, *The Shape of the River: Long-Term Consequences of Considering Race in College and University Admissions* (Princeton, N.J.: Princeton University Press, 1998).

16. Ibid., 88.

17. Howard Bowen, Derek Bok, and Glenda Burkhart, "A Report Card on Diversity: Lessons for Business from Higher Education," *Harvard Business Review* 77 (January/February 1990): 139–49.

18. Ibid., 141.

19. Patricia Gurin, "Expert Report of Patricia Gurin," *http://www.umich.edu/newsinfo?Admission/Expert/gurintoc.html*

20. Richard W. Judy and Carol D'Amico, *Workforce 2020: Work and Workers in the 21st Century* (Indianapolis: Hudson Institute, 1997).

21. Ibid., xiv–xv.

22. Ibid.

23. See Robert Kaplan, *An Empire Wilderness* (New York: Random House, 1998); Laurent Belsie, "A Melting Pot without Much Melting," *Christian Science Monitor*, 8 March 1999; Deborah Reed, *California's Rising Income Inequality: Causes and Concerns.* San Francisco: Public Policy Institute of California, 1999.

24. See Jonathan Curiel, "White Lecturer Wins Bias Suit against SFSU: Jury Awards $2.75 Million," *San Francisco Chronicle*, 31 March 1999; the Sacramento case was reported on KNBC News, 6 April 1999. Some other cases: "Jury Awards White Woman $2.6 Million for Reverse Bias in PepsiCo Case, " *http://www.nando.com/noframes/story/0,0,2107,46490–75013–538717–0,00html*; white Dallas Police Department officers were successful in overturning a city affirmative action program when the U.S. Supreme Court let stand an appellate court ruling in their favor—see Amy Goldstein, "Court Spurns Affirmative Action Case," *Washington Post*, 30 March 1999. U.S. Air Force officers were successful in a reverse discrimination suit which charged they had been forcibly retired to make way for more minority officers—see Paul Craig Roberts. A white male San Diego firefighter won a reverse discrim-

ination lawsuit against that city's fire department's affirmative action promotion system—see Anne Krueger and Ray Huard, "Firefighter Wins Jury Award in Bias Case," *San Diego Union Tribune*, 29 June 1999. East Orange, New Jersey, settled a reverse discrimination suit in favor of a white applicant for the chief of police position—see "City Settles Police Bias Case by Naming White Chief," http://www.foxnews.com /js_index.sml?content=news /wires2/1007/n-ap-1007–69.sml; White students have been increasingly successful in challenging minorities-only scholarships. In the summer of 1998, a white student at Clemson University received $95,400 court fees and damages in a reverse discrimination challenge to the National Science Foundation's Minority Graduate Research Fellowship Program—see Colleen Cordes, *Chronicle of Higher Education*, 22 June 1998; state regents in Oklahoma suspended new admissions into a minority set-aside grant program for graduate and professional students after a white male filed a class action lawsuit on reverse discrimination grounds—see *http://www.msnbc.com/local/KJRH/35926.asp*; and white contractors have been highly successful in winning reverse discrimination suits against minority contracting set-aside programs

25. Most of the major news media covered the controversy over the network-programming schedule for fall 1999. The initial surge of interest was launched by a *Los Angeles Times* article by Greg Braxton, "A White White World on TV's Fall Schedule," 28 May 1999, and amplified considerably by a similar *Washington Post* front-page article by Paul Farhi, "It's a White, White World of Network TV" (13 July 1999). The *Los Angeles Times* subsequently launched a four-part investigative series on "TV's Diversity Dilemma," in which the demographic and marketing factors behind the programming decisions were explained in the lead article by Brian Lowry, Elizabeth Jensen and Greg Braxton, "Networks Decide Diversity Doesn't Pay" (20 July 1999). Moral denunciations rained from most editorial pages, including those of the *Los Angeles Times*: "Vast Diversity Wasteland" (25 July 1999). The resulting moral panic among media executives and programmers was described by the *Los Angeles Times'* Greg Braxton in "A Mad Dash for Diversity" (9 August 1999).

26. William Frey, "The Diversity Myth," *American Demographics*, June; see also William Frey and Liaw Kao-Lee, "The Out-Migration of Older Non-Native Californians: Will the 'Revolving Door' Continue?" Unpublished monograph. Public Policy Research Institute of California/Milken Institute.

27. See: Scott Lindlaw, "Influential GOP Report Outlines Decline of Party's Fortunes," *Inland Valley Daily Bulletin* (Associated Press), 20 March 1999; George Skelton, Election Shows GOP Needs Some 'New Republicans,'" *Los Angeles Times*, 19 November 1998; Jackie Calmes and Carmen Alicia Fernandez, "Hispanic Vote Shapes up as Key Issue for 2000 Election," *Wall Street Journal*, 18 March 1999.

28. See, for example: John Harwood, "Clinton's 'Third Way' Inspires Republicans to Forge Their Own: Texas Gov. Bush Embodies GOP Efforts to Retake Political Middle Ground," *Wall*

Street Journal, 14 October 1998; Nick Anderson, "California GOP Likes Bush's 'Inclusion,'" *Los Angeles Times*, 20 March 1999; and James W. Robinson, "Kinder, Gentler Bush Helps GOP," *Los Angeles Times*, 20 June 1999.

29. See Terry M. Nel and David S. Broder, "Just Say No to a Vote on Affirmative Action," *Washington Post*, 24 May 1999.

30. Peter Y. Hong, "Diversity Driven by the Dollar," *Los Angeles Times*, 26 May 1998.

31. Using race as a job criterion—hiring blacks to sell to blacks, for example—is facing increased legal scrutiny. See the long analysis "Race-Based Jobs Stir New Debate in Workplace," *Wall Street Journal*, 10 September 1999.

Other Mothers: Public Policy, Popular Culture, and Recent Hollywood Films

A L L I S O N   B E R G

In her pathbreaking book *Black Feminist Thought: Knowledge, Consciousness, and the Politics of Empowerment*, Patricia Hill Collins employs the term "othermother" to describe the "fluid and changing boundaries" between "biological mothers [and] other women who care for children in African and African American communities" (1990, 119). Collins's definition of mothering as a communal responsibility, rather than an individual and essential function of women, is central to her project of re-centering feminist theory from an Afrocentric perspective. In the following discussion of two recent Hollywood films' representations of black and white mothers, I want to retain Collins's expanded definition of the maternal function, but I also want to explore how the notion of an "other" mother functions in popular culture—as it has in public policy—to uphold racially specific categories of mothers by positioning white women and women of color as foils for each other. Thus, while my focus will be on literary and filmic representations, I will situate these representations within a larger framework of maternal ideologies produced, in part, through public policy debates.

Recent feminist scholarship has examined the ways U.S. welfare policy has mediated the two contradictory functions women perform under patriarchal capitalism: reproducing and maintaining the labor force through unpaid labor, and filling low-wage positions in the paid labor force. As Mimi Abramovitz, Gwendolyn Mink, and many others have demonstrated, the policies and practices that encourage some women to remain at home while forcing others into low-wage work have historically been

> predicated on racist assumptions that some women (that is, white women) are fit to be mothers and homemakers and thus "deserve" subsidies allowing them to remain in the home [while] other women (that is, women of color and immigrant women) are deemed "unfit" nurturers . . . and thus are viewed as better suited to fulfill the demands for certain kinds of market labor. (Chang 1994, 271)[1]

For those of us who live in Michigan, the contradictions of such policies were made particularly vivid in 1994 when, just as Governor John Engler proposed making work or school mandatory for all mothers on welfare, a middle-class, Ann Arbor college student lost custody of her young son precisely *because* she was enrolled in college. In the Ann Arbor case, custody was granted to the child's father because the father's *mother* was willing to stay home to care for her grandchild, while the child's mother—because she was in school—could not. Equating "good" mothering with the absence of daycare, this ruling suggested that the best place for middle-class mothers was in the home. Yet, for "other" mothers (in this case, welfare mothers), Governor Engler's plan implied that full-time, stay-at-home mothering was a sign of pathological dependency. Given the persistent racism of welfare mythology, the inadequately maternal middle-class mother (the mother who should stay home, but won't) is most often coded white, while the so-called welfare queen (the alleged drain on national prosperity) is usually coded black. Indeed, as Rhonda M. Williams and Carla L. Peterson argue,

> it is the blackening of gender deviancy that marks "welfare mothers" as threatening cultural aberrations and compels draconian shifts in social policy. The "welfare queens" that haunt popular landscapes are African Americans. We are told that their unwillingness to marry leads to fatherless homes, criminally inclined sons and daughters trapped in and ensnared by intergenerationally transmitted welfare dependency. (1998, 13)

Such images obviously militate against a recognition of black mothers' legitimate claims upon the state.

Juxtaposing public policy and popular culture, we might ask how, on the eve of the twenty-first century, these diametrically opposed visions of motherhood circulate in popular culture. How do they rehabilitate and reconfigure nineteenth- and mid–twentieth-century racial ideologies? And to what extent do they function as mutually dependent and mutually reinforcing cultural myths? Specifically, how might nostalgia for the "good" white mother depend upon and sustain fear of the "bad" black mother, and vice versa? If, as E. Ann Kaplan argues in *Motherhood and Representation* (1992), the "maternal sacrifice paradigm" governing nineteenth-century melodrama has persisted in twentieth-century films—so that, depending on a viewer's identification, the "ideal, self-sacrificing mother threatens to collapse into the evil phallic one"(77)—how is this dichotomy enacted across films marketed for highly segregated film audiences?

Two films released in the fall of 1998—Jonathan Demme's *Beloved* and Carl Franklin's *One True Thing*—make an intriguing study in contrasts. Based on novels by Toni Morrison and Anna Quindlen, these movies presented even more sharply dichotomized images of motherhood than the novels themselves, though the novels were unquestionably worlds apart. While I am not suggesting that images from popular culture reflect public policy in any direct or unmediated way, juxtaposing these two films allows us to consider how cultural anxieties surrounding motherhood are refracted through the lens of race, in both black and white literature and film.[2] I will argue that, while the novel *Beloved* effectively confronts the maternal legacies of slavery, in ways the movie unfortunately attenuates, the novel *One True Thing* upholds a nostalgic and racially exclusive construction of motherhood, in ways the movie unfortunately replicates.

Despite the well-intentioned efforts of everyone involved in the movie *Beloved*, the film failed to reproduce two of the novel's most stunning achievements: its ability to convey the invisible, as well as the visible, wounds of slavery, and its insistence that the brutality of slavery affected both genders equally. Certainly, the marketing strategy for the film *Beloved* relied upon a distortion of the novel's themes. Titling their respective reviews "The Haunting," "Haunted by the Past," and "Bewitching Beloved," the *Village Voice*, the *New Yorker*, and *Time* magazine walked a fine line between acknowledging the novel's central metaphor and sensationalizing the film as one more tale of the supernatural (Hoberman 1998, 155; Denby 1998, 248; Corliss 1998, 75). Full-page ads in the *New York Times* trumpeted the film's cultural significance by proclaiming *Beloved* "One of the Best Films of the Decade," and predicting that "'Beloved' will swim in your bloodstream and echo through your bones," like a "spooky beauty and a natural wonder." At the same time, the movie was pitched as a bitter-but-necessary spoonful of medicine—a sort of antidote to the disease of racism—in ads instructing potential moviegoers that "America . . . needs to remember its past."

Of course, the novel *Beloved* does not provide an easily digestible history lesson. Rather, it gradually reveals not so much the fact of Sethe's infanticide but the horrors of its causes and consequences. Morrison's heroine endures such unspeakable crimes against her maternal body (when a schoolteacher's nephews steal her milk) and her spirit (when she hears her "human" and "animal" characteristics enumerated) that her decision to murder her children rather than subject them to slavery becomes comprehensible, if not heroic. So central are both the experience and the memory of slavery to Sethe's conception of maternity that few readers could fail to understand the serious import, as well as the grim humor, of her offhand remark that "unless carefree, mother love was a killer" (Morrison 1987, 132). Yet, while *Beloved* redefines mother love as contextual and contingent, rather than timeless or essential, the novel suggests that the always-informing presence of slavery need not remain incapacitating. Indeed, Sethe recovers from her long illness only when she renounces a "too-thick" bond with the ghost of her infant daughter and comes to recognize herself as her own "best thing" (274).

Yet, in spite of the novel's ultimately empowering ending, and in spite of white director Jonathan Demme's apparently unself-conscious comment that he was "slavish" in translating the novel to the screen (Corliss 1998, 76), the movie *Beloved* failed to garner the almost unanimous praise accorded the novel. While it received generally positive reviews, just three weeks after the movie's opening, a *New York Times* headline announced that "Despite Hope, 'Beloved' Generates Little Heat Among Moviegoers." Not surprisingly, the film performed especially poorly at suburban malls; yet it also failed to attract young black viewers, drawing its audience most heavily from black women over thirty (Weinraub 1998, B4). In *Black Women as Cultural Readers*, Jacqueline Bobo argues that black women have always been critical consumers of mainstream Hollywood depictions of black women as "dominating matriarchal figures," "ill-tempered wenches," and "wretched victims" (1995, 33). Accustomed to resisting the "ideological domination" of such filmic stereotypes, black, female viewers of *Beloved* had ample reason to welcome Demme's more complex depiction of Sethe.

Yet I would suggest that, however well-intentioned, the movie *Beloved* seriously undermines both the power and the meaning of Morrison's novel by depicting Sethe's and Paul D's experiences during slavery in a few fragmentary and disconnected images. Such images—unframed by a larger narrative of the daily and systematic degradations of life at "Sweet Home" plantation—reduce slavery's impact to the sum of discrete, physically brutal acts, so that Sethe's own murder of her child appears less heroically resistant than mindlessly reflexive. Moreover, the movie's almost total exclusion of the male protagonist Paul D's story turns the novel's focus on re-membering the black family into a psychodrama of mother-daughter relationships, a drama that, for a nonresistant viewer, might easily confirm the "pathological" aspects of the "black matriarchy" criticized by Daniel Patrick Moynihan in his infamous 1965 report. For contemporary viewers still inclined to view black women as dangerously powerful, the movie's final image of a weakened and bedridden Sethe would be almost as comforting as the earlier scene in which the ghost Beloved is successfully exorcised. Since the movie avoids the past of slavery almost as scrupulously as Morrison insists upon it, white viewers could easily conclude that the "damage" that must be set right is caused by Sethe's too-powerful assertion of mother love, not by the history that conditioned her actions.

Nonetheless, Paul D's reminder that Sethe is her "own best thing" affirms an identity for black women outside of (or in this case, subsequent to) motherhood. Anna Quindlen's novel *One True Thing*, on the other hand, resuscitates the nineteenth-century sentimental ideal that motherhood is (literally) an all-consuming activity; thus its motherly heroine, Kate Gulden (played by Meryl Streep), is elevated to the status of sainthood in proportion to her progressive physical decline. Told from the perspective of Kate's daughter, Ellen, Quindlen's 1994 novel depicts the final months of Kate's fatal struggle with cancer, a struggle that prompts her childless, career-driven daughter to discover her softer, more maternal side. Its plot thus extends the concerns of such late 1980s films as *Baby Boom* (1987) and *Fatal Attraction* (1987), which demonstrate the rewards of encouraging, and the dangers of repressing, a career woman's "natural" maternal instincts.

The novel *One True Thing* initially channels readers' sympathies toward the thoroughly modern Ellen, who accuses her father, a philandering literature professor, of causing her mother's death through his self-absorbed dependency on his wife's domestic services. Indeed, Ellen begins the novel insisting on an "essential difference" between her mother's role as the "ideal faculty wife" (Quindlen 1994, 50) and her own high-powered career in journalism. Yet her father's accusation that she "has no heart" (23) so wounds Ellen that she leaves her job in Manhattan and returns to her provincial hometown to care for her dying mother.

Over the course of her reluctant maternal service, Ellen discovers that she has seriously underestimated her mother's intelligence and courage, manifested most dramatically in her mother's decision to end her own life. Though the question of whether Ellen has "assisted" in her mother's suicide brings a contemporary twist to Hollywood's time-honored dying mother plot, Kate's death serves the same symbolic function as the death of any "good" woman in a sentimental novel: it enforces a belated appreciation of the (white) female virtues of self-sacrifice and self-denial. Accordingly, when her mother dies, Ellen abandons the stressful world of journalism to pursue a kinder, gentler career as a therapist specializing in adolescent girls, a job that conveniently weds her intellectual interests to her newfound "heart," by casting her as a surrogate mother to innumerable young women.

Thus, while *One True Thing* appears to offer a feminist tale of mother-daughter bonding, and its ending suggests a happy resolution to the dilemma of career versus family, it actually supports the age-old conception of women's essentially maternal nature. It thus reassures readers that white women, defined historically as the "fittest" mothers, have not completely jettisoned this identity. Indeed, the novel's most significant intertext is *Anna Karenina*, one of several books that Ellen and Kate, desperate to find an interest in common, read together. After her mother's death, Ellen signals her own belated appreciation of selfless maternity by fondly recalling her mother's criticism of the novel:

> I will never be able to think that Anna did the right thing when she closed the door and ran after Vronsky; I will always think of little Seryohza shivering in the hallway, waiting for Maman to return, as I sometimes wait for mine, pausing with the telephone receiver in my hand to make a call and then remembering that the woman I need to speak with has been dead for nearly a decade. (281)

Ellen's nostalgia for the maternal presence she spent her adult life rejecting is an understandable expression of her grief. Unfortunately, the novel as a whole appears nostalgic not only for the one good mother at its center, but for the social fabric of which she was a part. That this social fabric depends on clearly demarcated racial boundaries becomes clear when Ellen returns to her formerly beloved New York City after her mother's funeral, a return Quindlen represents through a seemingly inexplicable reference to *The Wizard of Oz*. Upon entering Greenwich Village, Ellen muses, ambiguously, "There's no place like home . . . There's no place like home," to which her friend obligingly replies, "We're not in Kansas anymore" (270).

That Greenwich Village is not, and can never be, the quintessential white, rural, and safe space immortalized in *The Wizard of Oz* is suggested by the novel's lone reference to an African American figure who appears precisely at this moment. Less a character than a nameless, menacing embodiment of urban life, he is described generically as a "young black man with a squeegee, the skin tight on his facial bones" (269), and his only action is to look up from his hotdog cart to curse the car full of white passengers from the suburbs. This otherwise inexplicable detail seems to be Quindlen's way of demonstrating that Ellen's return to the life of a single, career woman is not only disappointing, but dangerous.

If we take seriously Toni Morrison's assertion in her volume of literary criticism *Playing in the Dark* that "[t]he fabrication of an Africanist persona is reflexive; an extraordinary meditation on the self; a powerful exploration of the fears and desires that reside in the writerly conscious" (1992, 17), what does it mean that a strangely hostile African American man stands, metonymically, for the amaternal landscape of urban life? How does the white fear of black presence that this scene unconsciously reveals reinforce a longing for the racially pure white mother, a mother whose purity is figured through her remove from the touch of the city, the supposed profanity of blackness?

The novel's racist subtext is not directly reproduced in the movie. Instead, the movie version of *One True Thing* adds color to the novel's all-white suburban setting by supplying an African American extra who plays a member of Kate's philanthropic organization, "The Minnies." Yet Meryl Streep's costuming as Kate Gulden works against such calculated diversity by invoking the sanitized white mother from the "Father Knows Best" era. Although the movie, like the novel, is set in the 1990s, Kate appears repeatedly in 1950s-style aprons; indeed, in a none-too-subtle echoing of the novel's *Wizard of Oz* motif, she first appears dressed up as Dorothy for a costume party. As part of its nostalgia for midcentury domestic bliss, the film indirectly associates the comforts of home with the supposed absence of racial discord in the pre–Civil Rights era. Thus, the movie's black "Minnie" not only lacks the hostility of the novel's one African American character, but is virtually indistinguishable from her white peers, since she shares with them the perquisites of upper-middle-class domesticity, namely the leisure to spend endless hours decorating the town square for Christmas.

The movie audience is encouraged to laugh along with Ellen at her mother's anachronistic apron-wearing, but only to heighten their eventual realization of the heroic strength that undergirds the good *white* mother's domesticity. Thus, if the marketing of *Beloved* reduced its plot to the "spooky" story of a murderous black mother and her troublemaking progeny, *One True Thing* produces narrative pleasure by demonstrating that the 1950s (white) mother really did know best. Indeed, the movie intensifies the novel's privileging of maternal over "selfish" female behavior by suggesting that Ellen will reproduce her mother's selfless nurturing. While the novel devotes considerable space to Ellen's return to New York City after her mother's funeral, the movie closes on an image of Ellen kneeling at her mother's grave, patiently teaching her father how to plant flower bulbs.

One True Thing's nostalgic reinscription of the white, middle-class, nuclear family stands in stark contrast to the ending of *Beloved*, in which Sethe's daughter Denver establishes herself as an independent, self-supporting member of Cincinnati's black community. Significantly, Denver's journey away from the "haunted" house on Bluestone Road is facilitated by the communal mothering, or "othermothering," Collins describes, for she derives both physical and spiritual nourishment from a community of black women who provide food for her destitute family and exorcise the ghost of Beloved.

The "other" mother appears in quite a different context in *One True Thing*, which updates the role of the black mammy by transferring it to another woman of color. Besides the African American squeegee-wielder, the only other person of color in Quindlen's novel is an Ecuadoran American home healthcare worker named Teresa, who steps in to care for Kate when the job becomes overwhelming to Ellen. Because Quindlen makes much of Teresa's racial difference—"she had a slight accent and her teeth were very white against her dark face" (117)—it is difficult to disassociate Teresa's superior maternal instincts from her ethnic identity. When Ellen asks her, "Why do you do this kind of work? You could be working in the hospital nursery, bathing babies," Teresa replies: "Anyone can bathe a baby ... not everyone can do this" (123). Of course, not everyone *has* to do this particular form of maternal labor; much as a woman of color might be expected to provide care if Ellen had children, Teresa cheerfully steps in to care for Ellen's mother's infantlike needs. Depicting Teresa as somehow "naturally" better than Ellen at performing this function, Quindlen upholds the notion, convenient to middle-class, two-income households, that women of color are endowed with extraordinary caregiving qualities.[3]

Thus, even as it celebrates white maternal sacrifice, *One True Thing* replicates and extends the myth of the all-nurturing (yet inadequately maternal) black woman, who has been prized as a nurturer of white children, yet not recognized as a worthy mother to her own. Analyzing a spate of recent films employing the "cheerful caregiver-of-color" theme—including *Clara's Heart* (1988), *Passion Fish* (1992), and *Corrina, Corrina* (1994)—Sau-ling C. Wong argues that "in a society undergoing radical demographic and economic changes, the figure of the person of color patiently mothering white folks serves to allay racial anxieties." Wong further suggests that "by conceding a certain amount of spiritual or even physical dependence on people of color—as helpers, healers, guardians, mediators, educators, or advisors—without ceding actual structural privilege, the care-receiver preserves the illusion of equality and reciprocity with the caregiver" (1994, 69).

While I agree with Wong's analysis, it is important to recall that even such falsely comforting images exist alongside images of "bad" black mothers, images certain to produce further racial anxieties—for instance, 1994's *Losing Isaiah* (featuring Halle Berry as a belatedly recovered crack-addicted mother) or 1991's *Boyz N the Hood*. Michele Wallace has characterized the latter film's maternal figures as falling into one of two camps: those who are "white-identified and drink espresso (the Buppie version), or [those] who call their sons 'fat fucks' and allow their children to run in the streets while they offer blow jobs in exchange for drugs (the underclass version)" (1992, 124). Wallace finds these specific images all the more damaging given the film's failure to more fully characterize these women: "We never find out what Tre's mother does for a living, whether or not Doughboy's mother works, is on welfare, or has ever been married, or anything whatsoever about the single black mother whose babies run into the street" (1992, 123).

Certainly white mothers are not exempt from negative portrayal in recent movies, but it is interesting to note that "evil" white mother figures, such as those in *Serial Mom* (1994) or *Hush* (1998), are frequently represented in the genres of horror or satire, not "realism." Such generic distancing makes them unlikely to displace the sentimental white mother—as invoked in such dramas as *Steel Magnolias* (1989), *Little Women* (1994), or *Stepmom* (1999)—in the popular imagination.

My point in analyzing current representations of black and white mothers is not merely to argue that Hollywood reproduces cultural ideologies, or to imply that depictions of motherhood are uniquely susceptible to racist subtexts. Rather, I want to suggest that *One True Thing*, no less than *Beloved*, is "about" race, and that motherhood remains one key arena in which national racial anxieties are worked out. To the extent that race remains a predictable subtext in fictional and filmic images of maternity, helping to define what it means to be an authentic American mother, and to the extent that the "good" mother remains both a cherished national myth and an intensely racialized ideal, motherhood may indeed be America's one true thing.

NOTES

1. See Evelyn Nakano Glenn's model of the racial division of reproductive labor in "From Servitude to Service Work" (1992).
2. While these films are not necessarily representative, their origins in critically acclaimed novels by Morrison, recipient of the 1993 Nobel Prize for literature, and Quindlen, a popular and respected cultural commentator, give them a certain cultural cachet, regardless of their box-office earnings.
3. See Chang 1994.

REFERENCES

Abramovitz, Mimi. 1989. *Regulating the lives of women: The social functions of public welfare from colonial times to the present.* Boston: South End Press.

Bobo, Jacqueline. 1995. *Black women as cultural readers.* New York: Columbia University Press.

Chang, Grace. 1994. Undocumented Latinas: The new "employable mothers." In *Mothering: Ideology, experience, agency,* edited by Evelyn Nakano Glenn, Grace Chang, and Linda Rennin Force. New York: Routledge.

Collins, Patricia Hill. 1990. *Black feminist thought: Knowledge, consciousness, and the politics of empowerment.* New York: Routledge.

Corliss, Richard. 1998. Bewitching *Beloved. Time,* 5 October, pp. 75–77.

Denby, David. 1998. Haunted by the past. *New Yorker,* 26 October, pp. 248–53.

Glenn, Evelyn Nakano. 1992. From servitude to service work: Historical continuities in the racial division of paid reproductive labor. *Signs* 18:1–43.

Hoberman, J. 1998. The haunting. *Village Voice,* 20 October, p. 155.

Kaplan, E. Ann. 1992. *Motherhood and representation: The mother in popular culture and melodrama.* New York: Routledge.

Mink, Gwendolyn. 1990. The lady and the tramp. In *Women, the state, and welfare,* edited by Linda Gordon. Madison: University of Wisconsin Press.

———.1998. The lady and the tramp (II): Feminist welfare politics, poor single mothers, and the challenge of welfare justice. *Feminist Studies* 24(1):55–64.

Morrison, Toni. 1987. *Beloved.* New York: Knopf.

———. 1992. *Playing in the dark: Whiteness and the literary imagination.* Cambridge: Harvard University Press.

Moynihan, Daniel Patrick. 1965. The Negro family: The case for national action. Washington, D.C.: U.S. Government Printing Office.

Quindlen, Anna. 1994. *One true thing.* New York: Random House.

Wallace, Michele. 1992. *Boyz n the hood* and *Jungle fever.* In *Black popular culture,* edited by Gina Dent. Seattle: Bay Press.

Weinraub, Bernard. 1998. Despite hope, *Beloved* generates little heat among moviegoers. *New York Times,* 9 November, p. B4+.

Williams, Rhonda M., and Carla L. Peterson. 1998. The color of memory: Interpreting twentieth-century U.S. social policy from a nineteenth-century perspective. *Feminist Studies* 24(1):7–25.

Wong, Sau-ling C. 1994. Diverted mothering: Representations of caregivers of color in the age of "multiculturalism." In *Mothering: Ideology, experience, agency,* edited by Evelyn Nakano Glenn, Grace Chang, and Linda Rennin Force. New York: Routledge.

12

Cosmic People, Out of Eden

JACK D. FORBES

In California, during the past year, some of us from the Native American and Asian American communities in particular have been struggling against the adoption of a set of social studies–history curriculum standards for the state's schools that totally ignore ethnically or racially mixed peoples as well as Asian Americans and many other groups. Clearly the Republican-controlled State Board of Education considers people of color, whether mixed or not, to be insignificant or perhaps embarrassing appendages to the pageant of European triumph in North America.[1]

In spite of such reactionary attitudes, however, I wish to suggest that we might begin thinking in terms of the "Opportunity of Mixed Race or Cosmic People," for what such people can and often do offer to the world and to the societies in which they live—provided, of course, that colonialism, classism, and other forms of oppression are done away with or diminished.

My research, over a period of four decades, has convinced me that interethnic sexual relationships have been extremely common and, in fact, most major nationalities, including Spaniards, Portuguese, Italians, Turks, Hungarians, Germans, Scots, Irish, English, and French, to name but a few, are extremely mixed peoples, much more mixed (on the whole) than are Mexicans and other Latin

Americans who are often permanently categorized as mestizos, cholos, or other terms denoting mixture, primarily because of an enduring colonialized mentality.

In discussing interrelationships, we must, of course, keep in mind the often assumed difference between inter-"racial" and inter-national or inter-ethnic mixture. Let us pause for a moment and think about the recent and current struggles in Europe between Croats and Serbs, various kinds of Bosnians, Albanians (Shipetars), Serbs, and Romany in Kosovo, and the tensions in Macedonia and other neighboring states.

The photographs of the early refugees pouring into Macedonia and Albania, published in color in our newspapers, revealed many so-called ethnic Albanians with blonde hair, light brown hair, and other northern European features. Normally we think of the ancient peoples of the southern Balkans, such as Greeks and Shipetars, as being overwhelmingly dark-haired. So what do we have here?

It would seem that our media have not told us the truth about Kosovo. Clearly, many of the refugees were highly mixed peoples, possessing genes for blondeness brought into the Balkans largely by the southward migration of the Serbo-Croat peoples from the Carpathians more than a thousand years ago, as well as by occasional visits of Teutonic Goths and wandering Celts at an earlier date. It seems highly likely that the "ethnic Albanians" and the Serbs are, in fact, linked in their ancestries, thanks to centuries of mutual kidnapping, enslavement, rape, and assimilation under various circumstances.

Intermarriage as well as warfare has been extremely common throughout the region, but our media does not like to deal in "subtleties," nor does our government. We were never told that the so-called Muslims of Bosnia speak Serbo-Croat, write with the Greek alphabet, like the Christian Serbs, and were earlier considered to be Muslim Serbs, not simply Muslims. They were denied an ethnic identity by our media, while the Roman Catholic character of most Croats and the Eastern Orthodox character of most of their so-called Serb enemies was ignored. According to my ancient British encyclopedia (1875), Albanians tended to be about half-Muslim, with the rest being Eastern Orthodox or Roman Catholic. In the nineteenth century under Turkish rule, it was common for husbands to be Muslim outwardly while wives were Christian, perhaps because of the pro-Muslim character of Turkish colonialism.

In any event, the animosities in the Balkans, for the most part, cannot be said to be "racial" in the modern sense of the term, and yet they involve the greatest possible animosity (cultivated by politicians and thugs, plus occasional others), with large numbers of people of mixed ancestry caught in a vicious crossfire.

In any case, we must not minimize the crucial importance of inter-ethnic and interreligious relationships or assume that so-called racial differences lead toward a completely unique type of challenge, or opportunity.

We must remember that, historically, interracial contacts also involved international and often interreligious contacts, at least initially. Africans and Americans all possessed nations of their own, national identities, languages, and religions when they initially faced Europeans (or Arabs, in the case of Africans), and that the Africans were always ethnic and religion-specific.

My own involvement with this subject goes back a long way. In 1962-63 several colleagues and I established the Foundation for Race Mixture Research. We hoped that objective information about the history and then-contemporary conditions of racially mixed persons would help in the racial strife of the period. Unfortunately, we soon discovered that the United States Congress had made it clear that race mixture and intermarriage were forbidden topics, for which federal research funding was not available. We, for example, had invited Howard F. Cline, director of the Hispanic Foundation of the Library of Congress, to be a member of our Advisory Council, but he had to decline, with these words: "I hope you understand that this is a rather ticklish matter for someone working under the eye of Congress. . . ." Dr. Cline did, however, offer to help us informally, especially in relation to Latin America.[2]

I personally applied to the National Science Foundation in 1963 for a research grant on "Caucasian-Indian-Negro Race Mixture in the Southwest, 1543-1848: A Study of the Dynamics and Effects of Miscegenation." Albert C. Spaulding, program director for anthropology, responded that

> The topic of your proposed research . . . is not eligible for consideration by the National Science foundation owing to policy restrictions. The restrictions reflect the position of the Foundation as an agency of the Federal Government and do not imply any lack of merit in the proposed study.[3]

My own interest in race mixture had started earlier, perhaps as far back as when, as a young boy, I learned that I was of mixed ancestry, including several Native American nations, many European nationalities, and at least one Euro-Asiatic nation, that of the Hungarians, with their tradition of migration from Lake Baikal. I also grew up in El Monte del Sur, a place that I have written about in a poem as follows:

In my El Monte I saw the meeting of Mexicans
and Okies, half-breed Indians and full-bloods
from south of the border, with Arkies and Texans,
and Middle-Westerners, all thrown together,
and I gave water from our faucet to thirsty
Mexicano farmworkers from the neighboring field,
and my mother's first present from me was a
hand-painted pot made by an artista Mexicano who
lived down at the corner
and my first fights were with a Mexican Indian boy
who had it in for me
and my first loves, that I can remember, were for
brown girls of El Monte and Baldwin Park,
so I know, I saw, I lived the coming together
and I heard Spanish sounds in Aztec throats
sounds still with me now.[4]

As a young man I dated women of Mexican, Irish, East Indian, Chinese, Japanese, and other ancestries, and I became very much interested in marriages across both religious and ethnic boundaries, since I found that some interreligious relationships were as fraught with difficulty as interethnic ones. During 1955 and 1956 I began to do research in the Spanish Archives of California, collecting data on racial characteristics and interracial marriages within the population. I first published on this in 1960 and hoped to produce a book, but, as noted, I could not get the research support. I did, however, produce articles relating to race mixture, in 1966, and later books with a section on the subject, in 1964 and 1967.[5]

I was very much encouraged in my interest by an article written by Milton Mayer, "The Issue Is Miscegenation" (1959) and another titled "Europe Looks at the Cosmic Race" by Magnus Mörner (1961).[6] Mayer argued that race mixture was a key issue in the struggle for black liberation even though many persons were then trying to ignore it. Mörner provided a Latin American perspective, especially in relation to a Stockhom colloquium on "mestizaje in America." He made it seem that my research on interracial relationships was both timely and legitimate. In any case, my work continued even though I ran into hostility from funding sources and publishers. In the mid-1960s I had book projects on race mixture in the United States and on Mexican Americans turned down repeatedly. The latter book finally appeared in 1973, but my race mixture book has appeared only as a reader for a course on "Race and Sex" which I introduced at the University of California, Davis, in 1969-70.[7]

I developed very early, as an outgrowth of my growing up in El Monte del Sur, a keen interest in Chicanos, Mexican Americans, and other Spanish-speaking populations of America, being especially interested in their American or American and African ancestries. Many Latin Americans identified themselves, or were identified, as Native Americans ("indios," "indígenas," or "campesinos"), while others were classified as *mestizos* (mixed-bloods). I was especially intrigued by the permanent status of *mestizo* being assigned to entire populations, a practice that I critiqued in my article on "The Mestizo-Metis Concept" (published in 1973 in *Aztecas del Norte*).[8] I argued that Spaniards were far more *mestizo* than Mexicano and yet they were never treated as a mixed people. The *mestizo* status of Mexicans was related, in my judgment, to their condition as a recently colonialized people.

Subsequently, one of my major interests has been to relate the process of colonialism to both the rise of color/biological racism and to the ouster of Cosmic People from the "eden" of normal acceptance.

In 1981-82, while in Britain, I began active research for my book *Africans and Native Americans*, building upon my earlier work in the Southwest and Mexico. This project also involved me in the production of a series of articles, all of which relate to interethnic interactions, but which explore issues that could not be included in the book. These articles focused upon how designations of race, caste, and ethnicity were manipulated in North and South America by colonial regimes including modern American republics, how envelopment, proletarianization, and inferiorization had affected Native Americans and other people of color in eastern North America under colonialism, and how the U.S. Bureau of the Census for many years continued the practice of manipulating ethnic designations and hiding the numbers of multiethnic persons, probably because of the same opposition to intermarriage in Congress that I encountered in the early 1960s.[9]

Of course, my formal research has been greatly informed by my frequent interaction with my own people of the Powhatan-Renápe tribes of Virginia, Maryland, and New Jersey, virtually all of whom show varying degrees of American, African, and European ancestry, with many other tribes of the East Coast and Oklahoma, with similar kinds of ancestry, and with my own immediate family and in-laws of diverse backgrounds and identities. In addition, we have a dynamic Native community in California whose members range in appearance from so-called full-bloods to blonde, Caucasian-looking types to individuals of African and Filipino mixture, with all kinds of "in-betweens."

In order to understand what goes on in the indigenous world, I think we must discard some assumptions common in euroscience, beginning with ideas of what constitutes a person's identity. *The question of identity* is a difficult one, given the efforts of domineering states and churches, self-serving politicians, and ambitious elites to manipulate how one describes oneself. Unfortunately, eurocentric disciplines have often been submerged beneath a cultural tendency to want everything to be expressed in childlike dichotomies, simple oppositions and dualisms, arbitrary classificatory schemes, and "it must be either this or that" epistemologies. In this, euroscience has often followed the lead of hegemonic states and exclusivist sects, which, in an apparently euro-west Asiatic tradition, demand exclusive loyalties and self-definitions.

In contrast, American traditional societies have tended to employ pluralistic and inclusive epistemologies, as in, for example, tending to regard all things as sacred or worthy of deep respect if they are treated as sacred or holy by some group of people. Thus Indigenous Americans can "worship" with Catholics, Protestants, Jews, in all of their infinite variety while yet retaining their own sacred traditions. In modern times one can be both Catholic and Zuni, Catholic and Quiché, and so on. Religions are, from this perspective, not innately incompatible (closed) systems but rather are different patterns in the human search for closeness to the sacred. Religions and ceremonies are much like rocks, which come in all different colors and shapes and sizes, but which are all equally part of Mother Earth. None are to be disdained. All have value.

Now, this ancient American tradition of "encompassing" is sharply distinct from the modern euro-west Asiatic mind, with its exclusivist and often viciously sectarian viewpoint. Mormons, Pentecostals, and many Catholics, Muslims, and so on, cannot conceive that the Creator has given us as humans many varieties of worship which can be embraced without betraying one's primary religious tradition. Thus, native peoples have often found themselves locked in deadly struggles with missionaries who have demanded total submission, total disassociation from their "pagan" relatives, total denial of their spiritual heritage. In time, however, Native people may yet succeed in "civilizing" even Mormons and evangelicals!

Like religion, identity is not to be found in euroscience's dualistic conception of the world. Rather, it is comparable to a river of relationships in which many streams enter and mix unevenly, with some becoming stronger and others weaker as the river of life flows onward. First, however, we must watch out for this Englatino language of ours, since the very words we use may contain eurocentric biases. "Identity," for example, is a dangerous term because it comes from *idem*, the same, and has to do with being the same person from birth to death, something very useful to empires and authoritarian churches, but perhaps not too useful to us as we might want to change or grow. Self-definition is not a good alternative because "to define" means basically "to set limits" or to draw borders around something, and the trick, of course, is who is to do the defining! A better term might be the Greek expression "autonomia," meaning "self-rule" or "self-law." Thus perhaps we can speak about a person's autonomia, meaning that each person's identity and self-definition are worked out by that person under his or her own rules.[10]

In my article on "The Manipulation of Race, Caste, and Identity" I go into considerable length to discuss alternative ways of looking at ourselves. I point out, for example, that each of us possesses over 32,000 statistical ancestors by about 1600 C.E., born of 64,000 parents and presumably 128,000 grandparents. Thus, genetically speaking, we have been provided with a tremendous range of ancestries, which, in almost all cases, has to embrace many different ethnicities.[11] Here, however, I think it is more important to emphasize a qualitative approach by describing the way that the autonomia of most Native Americans seems to be formed. It is best, I think, to see it as *a series of concentric circles of belongings and relationships*, a concept about which I have been teaching since the early 1970s, when I introduced the course on "Race and Sex: Race Mixture and Mixed Populations" at the University of California, Davis.

At the core of the series of circles would be the extended family, a kinship unit of overriding importance and, in fact, a key element in all Native social, economic, and political life. This unit might not be localized, since it extends outward geographically as well as through other circles by means of either clan membership or the importance of bilateral cousinship.

> The family in the larger sense may often embrace within its folds persons who belong to different "tribes," or, after 1500, belong to different races.

Native people also belong to many groups of close friends, incorporated in formal societies or informal groupings.

> Moreover . . . Native People belong to local communities . . . and nations or confederations of bands and/or communities. Each of these levels provides a type of identity, and all are important.

Yet, beyond the nation were alliances, deepened by real or affirmed kinship, which brought together large numbers of people over broad areas. These alliances were often bonded together by mythic traditions, by longtime sharing of ceremonies, or by specific bonding rituals.

> Identity, then, is really a series of concentric circles, with many layers of importance. No single level can adequately describe or encompass identity. Moreover, in the case of native clans, they run outward through all of the concentric circles and even extend into "alien" [or enemy] groups.

This means that in recent times one could have a mixed Native American-African family with a complex set of relationships:

> Thus, one could have a Nanticoke person in New Jersey married to a Mohegan from Connecticut, both of whom actually possess variable proportions of different tribal and racial backgrounds (e.g., Nanticoke, Pocomoke, Wicomico, black African, and white on the Nanticoke side and Mohegan, Pequot, Narragansett, black African, and white on the Mohegan side). Still further, the two families can include relatives who are living in Philadelphia, Camden, Boston, Providence, et cetera, who have intermarried with other "Indians" or with "blacks."[12]

The eurocentric tendency to divide everything into opposites, so common in discussions of race, nationality, and identity, as well as in "dialectical materialism" and other thought games, must be abandoned when we actually look at the way in which most human beings have related to each other when free from domineering state bureaucracies or exclusivist religious organizations. The boundary lines of states and churches are usually very artificial, and human differences are often purposely manufactured in order to further the interests of those in control (or of those who wish to be in control).

The concept of "race" in the modern sense is, in my judgment, the creation of eurocentric scholars working to intellectually support European imperialism and specifically to provide a rationale of justification for the sacking of Africa, the Americas, Asia, and the Pacific by means of the captive trade, economic rip-off, and seizure of territory and resources. Prior to this period, as I show in my book *Africans and Native Americans*, many peoples were aware of different human colors and physical types, but these variations were not essentialized or organized in classificatory systems. For example, in 1460 a Valencian poet, Jaime Roig, described the people to be seen there as:

> totes de qualque stat
> color, etat,
> ley, nació . . .
> les cristianes, juhies, mores
> negres e lores
> roges e blanques
> dretes y manques . . .
> franques, catives.[13]

This list of Valencians enumerates all persons of whatever status, state, law, and nation, including Christians, Jews, Muslims, blacks and browns, reds and whites, sound and lame, free people and captives.

In 1552 Francisco López de Gómara, in his *Historia*, remarked upon the progression of human colors, from many shades of white, reddish people of different degrees, and colors between black and white such as *leonado* (lionish), *membrillo chochos* (stewed quince), *loro* (intermediate brown), *moreno* (dark brown), and *cenizos* (ash-colored). His conception of the near-infinite variety of colors created by God did not lead to any theory of separate "races," but rather to a continuity of humanity, each color blending into the next.[14]

In any case, European colonialism soon began to alter the above sense of continuity, as the Spanish Empire adopted terms such as *mestizo* and *mulato* to refer to mixed persons, identified as such by legislation. The evolution of the term "hybrid" will also illustrate this process of "racialization." The term *hibrida* originated in Roman times to refer to the progeny of a tame sow and a wild boar. This meaning continued in English until the seventeenth-century, and even later in Portuguese and Spanish. *Hibrida* also eventually came to refer to "one born of a Roman father and a foreign mother, or of a freeman and a slave." In Romance languages, such as Portuguese, *hybrida* continued as late as 1802 to refer to the progeny of mothers and fathers of different countries or diverse conditions. By the seventeenth and eighteenth centuries, Spanish and Portuguese dictionaries included *mestizo* and *mulato* as examples of *hybridae*.

Gradually the meaning of *hybrida* and of *mestizo/mulato* were "racialized," in that cultural and national differences among parents were dropped in favor of "different races" or "species."[15] This change corresponds to the invention of the idea of distinct "species" or "races" among humans by north European thinkers, beginning with Carl Linnaeus (1735). This process continued with David Hume and others. Hume argued not only that all nonwhites (four or five different "species") were inferior to whites, but that they had a separate origin ("an original distinction").[16] I argue that this invention of distinct "species" or "races" was part and parcel of the west European interest in the oppression and captivity of nonwhites, and corresponded to a period in which the captivity of whites was in decline.

The concepts of "race" mixture and of "interracial" marriage are totally dependent upon the invention of race/species as a classificatory concept marking off distinct kinds of human beings (as opposed to different lineages or nationalities). All of the false information circulated about "race" mixture is born in the brew of false science with active imperialism.

In America the Spaniards and other imperialists began gradually to employ "race" as a fundamental concept applied to non-European populations, replacing gradually the idea of nations or nationality. The "regime of castes" arose because "castes" replaced nations, and conquered people were shorn of their ethnicity (as such), often being assigned a caste status instead. This condition continues to distort social reality in much of Latin America even today. [17]

In 1705 the colony of Virginia adopted this language:

> And for clearing all manner of doubts . . . who shall be accounted a mulatto. Be it . . . , that the child of an Indian, and the child grandchild, or great grandchild of a negro shall be deemed, accounted, held, and taken to be a mulatto.[18]

By this act Virginia also began to create castes instead of allowing American and African persons to have their own nations, their own autonomias. Now, after five hundred years of colonialism and several centuries of biased euroscience, we must seriously undertake the task of allowing human beings to recover their own authentic histories, family stories, mythic narratives, and concepts of nation-ness. "Race" should not be one of the tools that we use, except as a means of deconstructing its meaning.

A recent Oprah Winfrey show, wherein several young women of mixed backgrounds presented their negative experiences as "in-betweens," highlighted how much we still have to do. In spite of all that we as scholars know about the rich history of interethnic relationships, these young women were at a loss to relate their own lives to those of the millions of others just like them. What struck my wife and I especially was the complete loss of indigenous connection on the part of one of the young women who was part Native American, but equally striking was the general confusion of genetics with culture and class on the part of all of the participants. Clearly, mixed people suffer from the exclusion of materials about people like themselves in the curricula of most schools and universities, and, of course, in the texts used in those institutions.[19]

Cosmic People are still being kept out of Eden, not only by ethnically prejudiced persons of European ancestry, but also by the fears, sometimes paranoid neuroses, jealousies, pent-up resentments, self-hatreds, and class prejudices of large numbers of non-European and nonwhite persons. Oppressors and victims, lacking accurate information, feeding upon myths and negative scripts, suffering from deprivations and frustrations, and encouraged by an indifferent social order, seem to be locked in an unlovely dance of mutual love/hate, a dance which continues to bar Cosmic People from Eden or which seeks to force the latter to suppress parts of themselves in a form of dreadful self-amputation and abnegation.

NOTES

1. See Jack D. Forbes, "Ethnocide by Exclusion," at Shields Library (Melvyl online system), University of California, Davis. Also condensed in *Because People Matter* (Sacramento periodical), Sept.–Oct. 1998, pp. 1, 8 and in *Currents* (Sacramento area Asian American periodical), 11, no. 4 (1998): 1, 10.

2. Howard F. Cline to Jack D. Forbes, 29 January 1963.

3. Albert C. Spaulding to Jack D. Forbes, 26 April 1963.

4. Jack D. Forbes, "The Thirties," unpublished poem, 1999.

5. Jack D. Forbes, "The Eurindian and the Eurafrican," *Current Anthropology* 1, no. 4 (1960): 335–36; "The Founders of Los Angeles," *Conejo News, Simi Valley News-Advertiser, The Northridger,* and other newspapers, 1960–62; also in *The Flatlands* 2, no. 9 (1967): 3. See also "Race and Sex," in *The Indian in America's Past* (Englewood Cliffs: Prentice-Hall, 1964); "Black Pioneers: the Spanish-speaking Afro-Americans of the Southwest," *Phylon: The Atlanta University Review of Race and Culture* 27, no. 3 (1966): 233–46; "Mexican-Americans and the Problem of Race and Color," *Journal of Human Relations* 16, no. 1 (1968): 55–68 (also in *Aztecas del Norte: The Chicanos of Aztlan* (initially prepared in 1965 but not published until 1973); "California's Black Pioneers," *Liberator* 8, no. 4 (1968): 6–9; and *Afro-Americans in the Far West* (Oakland: Far West Laboratory, 1967, or Washington, D.C.: GPO, 1968).

6. Milton Mayer, "The Issue is Miscegenation," *The Progressive* 23, no. 9 (1959): 8–18; and Magnus Mörner, "Europe Looks at the Cosmic Race," *Americas*, January 1961, pp. 15–18.

7. Jack D. Forbes, *Aztecas del Norte: The Chicanos of Aztlan* (New York: Fawcett, 1973).

8. Ibid., 178–205; also published separately in Spanish in *Plural* XIII-I, no. 145(1983): 21–32; and in *Novedades de Baja California* Año I, vol. I, no. 29, p. 8, and on to issue no. 41.

9. See Jack Forbes, "The Manipulation of Race, Caste, and Identity: Classifying Afroamericans, Native Americans and Red-Black People," *Journal of Ethnic Studies* 17, no. 4 (1990): 1–51; Jack Forbes, "Envelopment, Proletarianization and Inferiorization: Aspects of Colonialism's Impact upon Native Americans and Other People of Color in Eastern North America," *Journal of Ethnic Studies* 18, no. 4 (1991): 95–122; Jack Forbes, "The Use of Racial and Ethnic Terms in America," *Wicazo Sa Review* 11, no. 2 (1995): 53–65; Jack Forbes, "Undercounting Native Americans," *Wicazo Sa Review* 6, no. 1 (1990): 2–26.

10. See my article on using the term "Englatino" for the Creole language that we speak today in North America and the Caribbean: "English Only," *News From Indian Country* 10, no. 1 (1996): 15A.

11. See Forbes, "Manipulation of Race," 37ff.

12. Ibid., 41–42.

13. From Jack D. Forbes, *Africans and Native Americans: The Language of Race and the Evolution of Red-Black Peoples* (Champaign: University of Illinois Press, 1992), 107.

14. Forbes, "Manipulation of Race," 1–2.

15. Ibid., 3–4; Forbes, *Africans and Native Americans*, 100–30.

16. Forbes, *Africans and Native Americans*, 103; Forbes, "Manipulation of Race," 6–8.

17. Forbes, "Racial and Ethnic Terms in America," 60.

18. Quoted in Forbes, "Envelopment," 106.

19. See, for example, my discussion of the curriculum in social science–history adopted by the State of California in 1998 in Forbes, "Ethnocide by Exclusion."

PART III

Race and Public Policy

~:~

13

The Idea of "Race" as a Political Strategy in the Workplace: Historical Perspectives on Affirmative Action

JACQUELINE JONES

In 1834, a group of white workingmen in New Haven petitioned their state legislators to take legal action in order to prevent the migration of African Americans into the state of Connecticut. The petitioners charged that whenever blacks came into job competition with whites, "the white man is deprived of employment, or is forced to labor for less than he requires." Thus these white men claimed that their own "self-preservation" depended upon restrictions on black geographical mobility, for black intruders would, they claimed, inevitably lead to the immiseration of white families. Whites so aggrieved would become "the tenants of an almshouse, or . . . driven from state to state to seek a better lot in Western wilds . . . banished from home and kindred for the accommodation of the most debased race that the civilized world has ever seen. . . ." In sum, then, white labor would maintain its respectability to the extent that "black porters, black truckmen, black sawyers, and black mechanics" could be chased from the streets and wharves of New Haven.[1]

The fact that blacks accounted for only 5 percent of the New Haven population, and only 3 percent of the countywide population, suggests that the petitioners' fears were both misguided and misplaced; African American men lacked the numbers to displace more than a few (if any) white men from their jobs. Yet,

members of this particular group of whites were not acting out some sort of pri-
mal prejudice that rendered all black people threatening to the well-being of all
whites. In fact, the white workingmen of New Haven were reacting to a specific,
perceived threat in the form of two recent initiatives in the area of black education. In 1831, delegates to the first Annual Convention of the People of Color (held
in Philadelphia) had proposed the creation of a black college in New Haven, one
that would combine a classical curriculum with instruction in the skilled trades.
Two years later, Prudence Crandall, a white woman, had opened a school for black
children in the nearby town of Canterbury. The white residents of Canterbury
threw Crandall in jail and attempted to torch her school.[2] Nevertheless, this modest and ultimately failed enterprise loomed large in the minds of the New Haven
petitioners, for in 1834 they declared of all black people, "Not satisfied with depriv-
ing us of our labor, they are determined to become our Lawyers, Physicians,
Divines and Statesmen."[3] Apparently, then, the small number of black people in
New Haven would not rest until they had deprived every white man of his gainful employment, and until they had surpassed all white workingmen in status and
power.

Though a tiny percentage of the total population, blacks in New Haven spoke
in a collective voice—against arbitrary arrests of their own people, in favor of the
rights of citizenship for all people—that left anxious whites with the impression
that blacks constituted a significant political force. The petitioners of 1834 noted
with alarm a recent public spectacle in New Haven, when "a band of negroes
paraded the streets . . . armed with clubs, pistols, and dirks, with the avowed purpose of preventing the law of the land from being enforced against one of the
species."[4] Indeed, Connecticut abolitionists, both black and white, were persistent
targets of pro-slavery white mobs throughout the decade of the 1830s.[5]

The beleaguered black population of New Haven inspired a great deal of contradictory rhetoric on the part of whites. The petitioners of 1834 assumed that any
black jobholder would work for starvation-level wages compared to any "civilized"
white man. Yet this image of the black man as a rapacious job seeker was simultaneously juxtaposed with the image of the black man as a poor person, dependent
on the largesse of the state, a person helping himself "from the public storehouse,
as a legal pauper."[6] In Canterbury, one white politician combined these two
images—the black man as both predatory job-seeker and pathetic public charge—
in a single sentence, maintaining that "The colored people can never rise from their
menial condition in our country" (implying that blacks as a group would remain
inferior in intelligence and ambition compared to whites), while vowing in the next

breath, "they ought not to be permitted to rise here" (implying that it was only a matter of time before blacks took advantage of schools and began to surpass whites in the realms of employment and politics).[7]

Removed from our own time by more than a century and a half, the New Haven case nevertheless helps us to link both the antebellum workplace and public sphere with comparable sites in postindustrial America. During the thirty years or so before the Civil War, the Northeastern and Midwestern regions were undergoing a number of demographic and economic changes that we today would find familiar, at least in their broad outlines: a wave of "new" immigration composed of peoples without much in the way of formal education, people seemingly eager to accept the least desirable jobs the economy had to offer; and dramatic technological transformations that were in the process of reordering and de-skilling the lower echelons of the paid labor force. The rapid improvement in transportation and communication networks placed added pressures on enterprises of all kinds— from large companies to skilled craftsmen—to become ever more efficient, and, if possible, consolidate and streamline their operations. The result was the dislocation of regional populations and the displacement of specific groups of workers.

Then, as now, black Americans demanded that economic rights be linked with citizenship rights. In the process they highlighted stubborn patterns of injustice—the legacy of slavery and discrimination—and at the same time sought to claim their fair share of jobs and educational opportunities. Then, as now, African Americans' public and private struggles inspired seemingly mutually contradictory stereotypes deployed by white politicians—the idea that blacks were both poor and dependent (i.e., overrepresented as "welfare recipients") on the one hand, and tireless in their ambition (and their apparent determination that whites forfeit their livelihoods) on the other. In the antebellum North, as in the postindustrial United States as a whole, the fact that black people represented such a small percentage of the electorate gave white political leaders a license to ignore their claims (and in fact, in most northern states before the Civil War blacks were not even franchised). In turn, black leaders sought to emphasize a kind of racial solidarity that (at least in the long run) obscured the larger issue of class inequality in American society.

As a set of public policies, "affirmative action" is a term that is difficult to define with much precision today simply because it is used as shorthand to describe a whole matrix of initiatives, from college outreach programs to business hiring quotas. In general, though, proponents of affirmative action in the late twentieth century focus on (in much the same way that black people of New

Haven did in 1834) two major issues—first, securing their fair share of jobs within the paid labor force, and second, gaining access to the kinds of schooling and formal training that will prepare them for better jobs.

A brief overview of work patterns among African Americans from the colonial period to the present suggests that historic patterns of discrimination have yielded a bitter legacy, one destined to remain with us into the twenty-first century.[8] During the initial years of colonial settlement, much of the heavy labor associated with staple-crop agriculture in the Chesapeake region and the diversified commercial economy of New England and the Mid-Atlantic was performed by whites—as indentured servants in the South and as the children of landowners in the North. In both regions, the few bound workers who were African, or descendants of Africans, represented not a unique group so much as a subset of bound workers whom masters considered recalcitrant, resistant, and ultimately even subversive to the imperial designs of the British Crown. Other groups in this subset included young men and women servants working off their transportation costs (that is, indentured servants)—not just English folk, but also the resentful Irish and a whole host of persons from rival countries—Portugal, Spain, France, Italy. White colonists regarded Indian laborers, too, with a great deal of apprehension, for indigenous groups seemed particularly threatening to the physical safety of the tiny English military outposts in the New World. During these first years (and, in fact, throughout much of the seventeenth century), then, whites tended to conflate different kinds of workers and consider all of them to be promiscuous, blasphemous, wretched (and possibly dangerous) ingrates. Within a roiling Atlantic World, black people did not appear to be so distinctive as emerging racial ideologies would later make them out to be. Their darker skin color placed them on a broad spectrum of phenotypes (with various Mediterranean peoples just as swarthy). Moreover, those who were non-English-speaking and non-Christian hardly seemed more threatening to the ethnocentric English than did a whole host of other groups (all termed "strangers" by their reluctant hosts).

According to historian Lorenzo Johnston Greene, "There was no color line in colonial industry." Although Greene was referring specifically to New England, the same generalization can be applied to the southern colonies, for after the institution of bondage was codified and systematized in the early eighteenth century, enslaved Africans and their descendants performed a variety of tasks; newly imported blacks might not serve as gentleman's barbers or wig makers, but Creole men (born in this country) did, and members of this latter group worked as sail makers and coopers, cabinetmakers and seamen, as well as field hands and domestic servants. Enslaved women were likewise exploited in opportunistic ways, forced to labor as dairymaids and seamstresses as well as cooks and field hands.

The fact that blacks (qua slaves) were integrated so fully into the colonial labor force is all the more striking considering how quickly matters shifted after emancipation—in the North, beginning in the 1790s or so, and in the South, after 1865. Whereas the institution of slavery had allowed whites to use black workers in almost any way they saw fit—whether as textile mill operatives in the South or as bookkeepers in the North—freedom rendered black men and women direct competitors with white workers (or so the theory went) and necessitated formal mechanisms to keep them "in their place." In the antebellum North, free men of color, former slaves who had worked as skilled craftsmen, now found themselves the targets of discriminatory legislation, and vulnerable to the vicissitudes of the marketplace. In New York City, the proportion of black men who worked as artisans fell to 10 percent in 1860, from 38 percent seventy years earlier.[9] A similar dynamic pertained in the South after the passage of the Thirteenth Amendment; by the end of the nineteenth century, 90 percent of black people in that region were field hands, manual laborers, or domestic servants.

In the postemancipation period in both the North and the South, wary whites (in their roles as employers and members of the laboring classes) began to concoct a myth of black inferiority in the workplace; by 1900 conventional (white) wisdom held that black people were unable to work machines. The palpable absurdity of this claim was lost upon the post–Civil War generation. Though enslaved men and women had worked as textile machine operatives in antebellum Columbus, Georgia, by the 1870s the manager of the Eagle and Phenix Mill in that city could claim, "We do not think the negroes [sic] adapted to the labor of cotton-mills. Their lack of quickness, sensitiveness of touch, and general sleepy characteristics disqualify them for work which needs the requisites they lack. Being far better outfitted for outdoor labor, they will no doubt always be kept so employed." This pronouncement had the quality of a self-fulfilling prophecy; the Eagle and Phenix mill employed eight hundred white operatives and ten black "yardmen."[10] In the northern states, the lack of black machine workers was equally striking; Philadelphia, renowned for its machine jobs related to a host of industrial enterprises, had virtually no black factory employees above the level of janitor until well into the twentieth century.[11]

For black men and women, barriers to machine work yielded devastating short-term and long-term consequences. Traditional forms of labor like domestic service and fieldwork paid less than factory employment and offered little in the way of upward social mobility. Moreover, as machine operatives came to be associated with "modern America," black folks in general came to be associated with a rural past; hence within ever-changing racial ideologies they played no obvious role—as either sellers of goods or as the consumers of those goods—in the new, early twentieth-century consumer economy.

During the Great Depression, the liabilities of this racial division of labor became abundantly clear. Federal entitlements for workers, including Social Security, unemployment compensation, and minimum wage and hour laws, were in reality limited to a particular group of workers—those employed in the industrial sector. Therefore, the vast majority of African Americans derived little or no benefit from these programs; in the process these workers were relegated to the status of second-class citizens within the emerging welfare state. Moreover, the New Deal in general revealed a bias toward wage earners employed full-time by large corporations. By the end of the 1930s, it was clear that the most generous benefits packages—including medical insurance and paid vacations, for example—would go to the employees of large companies, and that, among members of the laboring classes, those workers affiliated with the largest, most powerful unions (like the United Auto Workers) would benefit most of all.

Black workers gained a foothold in industry for the first time during World War II, and twenty years later the federal government ended its long-standing support for discriminatory hiring policies in the private sector. Yet the period from 1940 to 1975 was marked by bitter ironies. After the war, certain industries, like shipbuilding, began to decline, and other industries, like auto making, began to automate their operations, eliminating the need for whole categories of workers-- categories with disproportionate numbers of blacks.[12]

Title VII of the Civil Rights Act of 1964 wrought a genuine revolution in the American workplace. This legislation opened up jobs in clerical and retail sales sectors for black women, and outlawed explicit racial divisions of labor within government and business workplaces. Yet, here again the triumph was bittersweet, for the American economy was in the process of adjusting to a new global marketplace, and various levels of government, in addition to private companies, began to downsize and consolidate their operations. In industries like textiles, black workers were initially welcomed by employers who were seeking to keep wages low and stave off the threat of foreign competition. Yet by the 1980s cheap foreign imports, combined with more sophisticated forms of technology, had rendered many United States textile workers superfluous.[13] Likewise, the entrance of black workers into the positions of bank teller and secretary (for example) coincided with the reorganization of the workplace as a result of the introduction of the computer and other forms of electronic technology. By this time a sizable percentage of the black population remained immobilized in the nation's poorest communities, and their children, doomed to attend the worst public schools, had little hope of competing for places in elite colleges or, later, for good jobs at good wages within an increasingly credentials-conscious economy.[14]

A more detailed examination of the antebellum period may help us to better understand the debate over affirmative action in the late twentieth century. Here we should highlight three issues in particular. First, between 1820 and 1860, the political and economic turmoil in the Northeastern and Midwestern states suggests a dynamic by which white men's fears about their own livelihoods found expression in explicit antiblack sentiments and actions. Second, though a relatively small proportion of the population, black people spoke in a loud, collective voice, demanding justice and linking their economic rights to their political rights. Their presence in the public sphere was countered by white politicians, who easily manipulated the anxieties of their white constituents, claiming that black people as a group posed a dire threat to traditional all-white workplaces. Finally, whites employed contradictory stereotypes of blacks—as either poor and dependent or as cunning and ambitious—in order to fend off blacks' calls for meaningful social change. This discussion, as we shall see, can help us to understand the current debate over affirmative action, a debate that illuminates the complex relationships among politics, demography, and technological change.

In the last few decades before the Civil War, several groups of northern workers suffered from dislocations caused by dramatic changes in their respective regional economies. In New England, family farmers were forced to make a difficult choice between, on the one hand, persevering in wringing a living from the rocky soil, and, on the other, migrating to rural New York State or the Upper Midwest and starting over. In the Midwest, the emerging commercial-agricultural economy mandated large numbers of unskilled, seasonal laborers, creating a class of tenants and hired hands that mocked the notion of the West as the land of unlimited opportunity.

Some craftsmen in the North managed to parlay their small shops into larger commercial operations, but others found themselves without a livelihood, now that the textile and shoe industries were undergoing a process of mechanization (a process that would be substantially complete by the Civil War). The new factories that dotted the New England landscape attracted a diverse lot of workers— children and adults, native-born and foreign-born, women and men.[15] In the cities, an influx of Irish immigrants transformed local job structures; between 1830 and 1860, almost two million Irish—most of them refugees from famine and poverty—entered the United States. In some East Coast cities, these newcomers soon dominated whole categories of labor; for example, in 1855, Irish workers constituted nearly 90 percent of the New York City unskilled labor force.[16]

By their sheer numerical strength, Irish workers managed to overwhelm black dockworkers, waiters, teamsters, and ditch diggers. It was during this period that Frederick Douglass noted the massive displacement of blacks from their jobs by whites: "It is evident, painfully evident to every reflecting mind," he wrote in 1853, "that the means of living, for colored men, are becoming more and more precarious and limited." Referring specifically to the plight of black men in northern cities, he charged, "White men are becoming house-servants, cooks and stewards on vessels—at hotels.—They are becoming porters, stevedores, wood-sawyers, hod-carriers, brickmakers, white-washers and barbers, so that blacks can scarcely find the means of subsistence." In the United States, where men were valued not "for what they are," but rather, "for what they can *do*," the rapid loss of even menial job possibilities for African Americans signaled the group's larger liabilities within the body politic.[17]

During the antebellum period, more and more Americans were beginning to labor in new places, under new conditions, forced to wield, or master, new kinds of tools. In contrast, African Americans stayed clustered in jobs that were static in terms of both organization and technology. A few skilled men and entrepreneurs continued to ply their trades; black barbers shaved white customers in New York and Boston, and black caterers served a Philadelphia elite. Yet, for most black workers, intergenerational continuity in their work revealed their persistent poverty within a world otherwise notable for its expansiveness. Black teamsters and stevedores continued to load and unload ships on the docks of Cincinnati, and black laundresses continued to wash the clothes of white people throughout the Northeast, Mid-Atlantic, and Midwest. These men and women toiled not under one roof with many coworkers, but out in the streets, on the wharves, in small workplaces, or at home. And they worked with relatively primitive forms of technology, or in the absence of technology altogether: The drayman callused his hands by dragging his cart through congested alleyways, and the washerwoman rubbed her knuckles raw on the fluted washboard. Together with waiters and carriage-drivers, these workers remained at the mercy of men and women who expected deference from them. Their jobs tended to be irregular and ill-paid, and offered little in the way of opportunities for advancement, cash accumulation, or home ownership.

The strong arm of the state helped to enforce a racially discriminatory division of labor throughout the North. At the local level, municipal licensing practices and public works hiring policies had an immediate and drastic impact on the chances of black men to find gainful employment. Responding to the demands of whites as voters and purveyors of "mob rule," public officials protected the interests of various groups of white workers. In the early 1820s, the mayor of New York City refused to license a black carman (i.e., teamster) who, he acknowledged, possessed the requisite qualifications. Declaring that he would grant permits only to white men, the mayor explained his decision by "expressing his fears that a compliance would endanger not only the man's safety but his own. He said the populace would be likely to pelt him as he walked along the streets, when it became known that he had licensed a black carman."[18] In Philadelphia, politicians bowed to the wishes of their white constituents when they hired only whites to shovel and clean gutters during winter snowstorms; among all of these emergency municipal employees in 1831, for example, "there was not one man of color to be seen, when hundreds of them were going about the streets with shovels in their hands, looking for work and finding none."[19]

Many states imposed legal restrictions on free people of color as citizens and as workers. For example, the new constitution of the state of Indiana, ratified in 1851, prohibited black migrants from entering the state, decreed that all contracts between blacks and whites were null and void, and imposed fines on the employers of black men and women. Indiana blacks could not vote, and they could not serve as witnesses in trials that involved whites. Though taxpayers, black parents had to contend with the whims of local school boards, which might or might not allow black children to attend the public schools.[20]

Several states that had granted blacks the right to vote in the late eighteenth or early nineteenth century rescinded that right in the antebellum period. New Jersey (1807), Connecticut (1818), New York (1821), and Pennsylvania (1838) all revoked in absolute terms, or for all practical purposes, the legislation that had enabled black men to vote in previous years.[21]

White workingmen feared that black workingmen would necessarily deprive them of their ability to make a living; similarly, white voters feared that black voters would necessarily deprive them of their rights as citizens. In Bucks County, Pennsylvania, in 1837, a group of Democrats, who resented the part played by black voters in swinging a recent election, petitioned delegates to the state's Constitutional Convention with the admonition that "Negroes, whether slaves or free, from the first settlement of our country, have always been considered and treated by our laws, as an inferior race, and never until quite recently, thought or even dared to take any part in the management of our government." The petitioners concluded with a now-familiar theme, that they believed their "rights as white citizens and freemen have thus been violated and trampled upon by negroes [*sic*]." Once again, then, whites charged that the assertion of black rights—in the streets, in the voting booth, or at the courthouse—served to degrade and humiliate all white people.[22] A Democratic Party toast made explicit the resentments of whites over the fact of black emancipation (in the North): "To the light of other days when liberty wore a white face and America wasn't a Negro."[23]

Considering the extreme restrictions on black people's freedom to attend the public schools, move around in search of work, and compete for specific kinds of jobs, it is no wonder that whites of the laboring classes saw them as a group apart. More to the point, white men, who harkened back to the Revolution for their inspiration, could define themselves according to who they were not: Not women, not children, not blacks, not slaves or the sons or grandsons of slaves. The ideology of black inferiority and unworthiness thus helped to shape the consciousness of emerging classes of white workers. The Irish embraced these prejudices readily, for if they could only distance themselves from blacks, they, too, could become "white," now that "whiteness" had more to do with skin color than with poverty or a legacy of collective oppression.[24]

In the antebellum period, northern employers did not need to invoke a specific "racial" ideology in order to justify the exclusion of black workers from factories and other workplaces that relied on machines. Mill owners, for example, targeted certain demographic populations as they pieced together workforces from the available labor pool; hence, some enterprises utilized children exclusively, while others drew upon the availability of unmarried women in rural New England and still others employed eclectic workforces of immigrants and the native born, young and old. The fact that 3.5 million immigrants (Irish and German) entered the United States between 1830 and 1860 alleviated labor shortages in many areas of the North. Under these conditions, employers had no incentive to offer jobs to black men, women, or children, for their entrance into the workplace would have probably created more problems than they as workers were worth—washrooms and departments segregated by race, and the possibility of walkouts and strikes by resentful whites.

At the same time, we can assume that blacks aspired to factory work. Restricted to irregular, manual labor, they inhabited a segment of the workforce from which mill owners regularly drew their employees. The fact that blacks represented such a tiny percentage of the population in any one area was in and of itself no barrier to their use as machine operatives; for, given the opportunity to hold such jobs, blacks would have encouraged others of their group to migrate to those sites. Despite the focus of historians on the anguish suffered by de-skilled artisans, the fact of the matter was that many men and women considered factory work appealing; these included farm boys and girls who chafed under the authority of their fathers and yearned to earn cash wages, as well as canal diggers ready to escape their own brutal world of work out of doors in favor of labor under a roof.[25]

Although employers felt no need to offer a rationale for excluding blacks from machine work, that exclusion eventually gave rise to an unstated workplace policy that held that blacks were incapable of operating sophisticated kinds of machinery. As we have seen, this view held sway in the North until well into the twentieth century.

Barred from "modern" workplaces and deprived of basic rights, blacks lobbied, agitated, and spoke out for an inclusive definition of American citizenship. Repression followed, and racism intensified. The form of prejudice followed the function it served—to reserve the best jobs for whites. As one New York City abolitionist noted, "We dislike them [blacks] because we are unjust to them."[26]

Indeed, black protest assumed many forms within a variety of public venues in the antebellum North, and the black collective voice seemed out of all proportion to the relatively small numbers of people of color who inhabited that area of the country. Beginning in the 1790s, and especially after the 1820s, free blacks intruded upon the white public consciousness with their newspapers, temperance associations, literary societies, suffrage conventions, schools, mutual aid societies, and religious meetings. These gatherings and institutions constituted a form of civic engagement that was not necessarily dependent on the franchise. Moreover, the involvement of African American women in the antebellum political sphere constituted a dual challenge to hierarchical structures based on both race and class. The pronouncements and activities of teachers and preachers like Maria Stewart and abolitionists like Sarah Parker Remond and Sojourner Truth provoked white men and heightened their anxieties. Even ordinary women, like the founders of the Afri-American Female Intelligence Society, a Boston group founded in 1832, declared their intention to become "useful to society"; in other words, they would not content themselves with the subordinate place that emerging racial ideologies sought to establish for them.[27]

Complementing these efforts were frequent and dramatic public displays of distinctive styles of music and dance, styles that insistently proclaimed a proud

African heritage. Black public "performances" could also have overt political significance; beginning in 1801, and several times thereafter, crowds of New York blacks massed to liberate by force slaves who had been brought into the city by their owners. Philadelphia blacks paraded to celebrate the First of August (British Emancipation Day) each year after 1838. Beginning in 1854, Cincinnati black men donned their "Attuck Blues" militia uniforms for drills in public places.[28]

The Cincinnati case reveals a larger principle of antebellum northern life: That public displays of pride and protest among African Americans would in several dramatic instances be met with violence by whites. In 1841, black Cincinnatians staged a celebration commemorating British Emancipation Day with a public meeting at one of the large black churches, followed by an outdoor dinner that featured orators who "admonished all oppressors in every nation that the day is at hand when the hand of Almighty God will sunder the chains of the oppressed in every land." Just a few days later, and as prelude to the attack a white mob launched upon the city's black population, a white workingman expressed his outrage: "White men . . . are naturally indignant when they see a set of idle blacks dressed up like ladies and gentlemen, strutting about our streets and flinging the 'rights of petition' and 'discussion' in our faces."[29] In 1842, a similar black political demonstration in Philadelphia precipitated a devastating race riot against the black community. In both of these instances the attacks led to black out-migration, as workers and leaders came to understand that white authorities would afford them little, if any, protection in the present or the future.

Indeed, more often than not, white officials provided the rioters with moral, if not actual physical, support. A commission established to investigate the 1834 riot against blacks in Philadelphia confirmed popular racial prejudices when it concluded that "many whites, who are able and willing to work, are left without employment, while colored people are provided with work, and enabled comfortably to maintain their families; and thus many white laborers, anxious for employment, are kept idle and indigent."[30]

Clearly, then, several factors shaped the antebellum northern racial division of labor. The individual and collective prejudices of employers played a role, but so too did the fears of members of the white working classes, and the institutionalized racism revealed by political parties and the governmental structures they created. Patterns of migration and immigration, combined with a changing job structure and new forms of workplace technology, all contributed to the scapegoating and marginalizing of a particularly vulnerable group of people. The more black people protested—in the streets, in the courtroom, from the pulpit, on the editorial page—the more white people retreated into an aggressive form of defensiveness.

With the benefit of a century and a half worth of hindsight, we can highlight and analyze this race-workplace dynamic—perhaps with more clarity than we can examine our own situation today. Before drawing explicit parallels between the antebellum period and the late twentieth century, however, I would like to stress that these parallels are hardly exact. Today, in large northern cities especially, groups of poor people are more concentrated, and less integrated into the general population, than was the case in similar places before the Civil War. Today advances in communications technology serve to further certain racial, class, and gender stereotypes—through popular music, the movies, mass advertising, and the nightly news on TV. (In the first half of the nineteenth century, the blending of racist imagery and popular music took place in minstrel halls and vaudeville shows, performances that did not reach large segments of the population). Of course the high-tech global economy—the nexus between international trade and the consumer society—did not exist at all then. Today, in a break with labor-organization traditions, the fastest growing unions consist of multiracial and mul-tiethnic constituents, and minority men and women are playing major leadership roles in some of the largest ones, like the Service Employees International Union, UNITE (a union of needleworkers), and the American Federation of State, County, and Municipal Employees. Finally, during the antebellum period, the state (in the form of federal or state governments) accepted virtually no responsibility for the welfare of poor people, and neither did it seek or play an active role—or indeed, any kind of role—in enforcing what we today would call civil rights. These con-trasts between then and now caution us when we seek to draw lessons from an earlier time in order to understand our own.

Having made that disclaimer, I shall offer some comparisons between affirma-tive action in the northern states before the Civil War and in the United States today. To reiterate a point made above, I am using the term affirmative action loosely, to refer to policies and other efforts that would enable African American men and women to first, acquire jobs commensurate with their talents and train-ing, and second, acquire the kinds of formal education that would enable them and their children to compete for better jobs in the future. In the nineteenth century, government sponsored no formal legislation or programs to achieve this end, and, in fact, the thrust of governmental action—whether through laws, taxes, or licens-ing practices—solidified discriminatory patterns of employment for blacks in gen-eral. Proponents of affirmative action in education and employment were lone voices crying in the wilderness, as it were—individuals like Frederick Douglass and Prudence Crandall, and periodic political and religious conventions sponsored by free people of color. The major white-led abolitionist societies directed their focus toward the evil of slaveholding in the South, paying little or no attention to the plight of black job seekers in their midst, an oversight that rightly infuriated Douglass and other African American leaders.

Now, as then, debates over affirmative action are often cast in the terms of a zero-sum game; in other words, whites assume that for every job won by a black person, a white person must lose a job.[31] In 1995, a nationwide poll conducted by the *Washington Post*, the Kaiser Family Foundation, and Harvard University revealed that many whites perceived blacks as a group to be threatening to their (the whites') way of life. Despite the fact that in the 1990s disproportionate numbers of African Americans were clustered in the ill-paid service sector, about half of all whites believed that blacks had reached parity with—that is, held jobs equal qualitatively to those of—whites, and another 12 percent believed that blacks as a group were better off than white people. (In 1995, the Bureau of the Census categorized about one-third of blacks as poor, compared to about 11 percent of whites.) White people tended to downplay past discrimination as a cause of problems affecting the black community. Furthermore, like whites in the antebellum period, whites in 1995 tended to overestimate the economic threat posed by blacks by exaggerating the size of the black population, now assuming they made up 25 percent of the total (instead of the more accurate 11 percent). In the words of one journalist, whites as a group had "become more hostile to minorities, fearful that more minorities would further erode their diminishing quality of life."[32]

In an era of corporate and governmental downsizing, the growing gap between rich and poor fuels the prejudices of white workers who lack much in the way of formal skills or education. Yet, one would be hard pressed to argue that black people, who constitute only about one-tenth of the total United States population, are the agents of certain whites' increasingly precarious position in the job market. Despite some highly publicized cases of individual white workers losing their jobs to black job candidates or coworkers, in fact, of course, policies related to corporate restructuring, governmental downsizing, and technological innovation, combined with the tendency of businesses to seek out cheap labor overseas, constitute the key factors affecting the shape of the American labor force today.

Larger economic structural issues should not obscure the obvious fact that racial prejudice—on the part of employers and potential coworkers—still plays a part in restricting the job opportunities of black people. A study of hiring practices conducted in 1989-90 in Chicago suggested that employers of entry-level workers conflated the categories of race, ethnicity, and space (that is, residential neighborhood) and as a result shunned young black job seekers as too poor, une-ducated, and temperamentally ill-suited for the rigors of modern office work. In the view of these employers, racial integration of the workforce was a recipe for heightening tensions among workers who did not attend the same schools, belong to the same churches, or live in the same neighborhood. "I wanted a person who was going to fit into this area. . . . You're looking for skills, but you are [also] look-ing for someone who will fit in. . . ."[33] Poor blacks as a group also suffered from the widespread misperception that they are unwilling to accept low-paying jobs, a charge belied by cases of multiple inner-city job applicants for single fast-food restaurant jobs. In fact, black male workers, with fewer opportunities, continued to show a willingness to accept jobs at lower wages than whites—on average, half the 'white rate.'[34]

Complicating the labor-market scene today, but evoking that scene in the antebellum period, is the issue of foreign immigration to the United States. For the last quarter of the twentieth century, desperately poor people fleeing poverty and civil war have been eager to take jobs on the lowest rungs of the employment ladder—Mexicans and Mixtec Indians in California strawberry fields; Chinese men and women in East Coast and West Coast garment-factory sweatshops; Honduran immigrants on poultry farms in the hinterlands of Maine; Cambodian refugees in the service sector of decaying New England mill towns. The fact that these workers at times accept jobs under the most exploitative conditions suggests to some whites that black people are not willing to work at all. At the same time that Southeast Asians and South and Central American refugees struggle to build a new life for themselves in this country, they also serve to depress wages—espe-cially within labor-intensive industries like clothing and agriculture—and elimi-nate whole categories of job possibilities for native-born workers, black and white. The relevant point here, though, is that native-born whites seek to make invidious distinctions between poor black people and the newcomers, providing the new-comers with an incentive to appropriate the racial ideologies that give rise to those distinctions. At the same time, some whites will continue to try to distinguish themselves from all people of color, in a desperate effort to preserve their class and caste privileges in a new kind of economy that abides by no color line.

Local political economies still hold sway over large numbers of American workers. Certain municipalities, like Atlanta, with a black mayor and sizable num-bers of African Americans, can implement affirmative-action policies (similar to those in force in that city during the preparations for the 1996 Summer Olympics).[35] As a counterexample we might cite New York City, where, in the late

1990s, "workfare" recipients toiled at below-minimum-wage pay, displacing large numbers of the working poor—janitors, street cleaners, and office workers—and weakening unions of public employees in the process. At the same time, Mayor Rudolph Guiliani began to crack down on a whole host of workers—taxi drivers, food peddlers on the city streets—enforcing tough new licensing codes and making life even more difficult for the least fortunate residents of the city.[36]

Finally, just as the institution of slavery provided a context for the experiences of free people of color in northern cities during the antebellum period, so does the plight of black men in prisons today provide a subtext for the issue of racial discrimination. State officials all over the country are aggressively tapping into a pool of prison labor for cheap workers, and half of that pool is black. With as many as one-third of all young black men under some kind of court supervision (either in jail or on probation or parole), it is clear that President Ronald Reagan's war on drugs, initiated in the 1980s, is still taking a devastating toll on the integrity of black families and communities. In the early 1990s, almost 2 percent of all potential workers in the United States were in jail, 47.3 percent of them black. By this time, more than half of all states had legalized the practice of prison labor contracting to private employers, covering an impressive array of jobs, including raising hogs, taking hotel reservations by phone, making parts for Hondas, building and fixing circuit boards, and packing golf balls.[37]

Today discussions of affirmative action, both pro and con, usually mask deeper issues—patterns of segregated housing and schooling—that go to the heart of the problem of economic inequality. As we enter the twenty-first century, we are reluctant to confront the fact that we live in an aristocracy of sorts, a society in which the richest and most powerful members pass their status on to their children. These are people who live in wealthy communities and send their children to the best schools, whether public or private. Even household-income parity between blacks and whites of the middle class cannot hide the fact that whites will still enjoy more access to privilege simply because they can count on bequests and legacies from well-to-do parents (in the form of houses, stocks, and cash) in a way that the new black middle class cannot.[38]

Just as responsible white political leadership was lacking in the antebellum North, so are strong, clear voices missing from the partisan-political scene today. During the political campaigns in the year 2000, the budget surplus inspired only two proposals—a tax cut or "fixing" Social Security. Presidential candidates lamented not the lack of medical insurance among large numbers of people, but rather suburban sprawl and lost luggage at airports. We heard little or nothing about the persistent inequality between rich and poor school districts, or about the crumbling housing stock of many inner-city neighborhoods. Furthermore, politicians who persist in painting the social landscape in only black and white miss the larger point—that global transformations are affecting a wide variety of groups in the United States today, and that white people are not necessarily immune to those transformations.

Whither affirmative action in the twenty-first century? Because of historic and persistent structural inequalities in housing and education, equal access to jobs and schools will continue to elude poor black people, as well as poor people in general. Under such conditions, we will be condemned to repeat the mistakes of the past, for in the absence of effective leadership, white Americans will continue to hold black people—as individuals and as a group—responsible for their own liabilities in the workplace. In the antebellum period, this resentment took the form of civil strife and discriminatory patterns of legislation and hiring. Although most privileged Americans are no longer willing to accept a form of racial prejudice that is codified in law, most are more than willing to tolerate extremes between rich and poor.

Leaders in the antebellum period—the so-called Age of the Common Man, the Age of Egalitarianism—at least gave lip service to the ideal of equality of opportunity. Yet that ideal has receded from our civic discourse today, a change illustrated most dramatically by the disparity between the computer-rich high schools in upper-middle-class suburbs, and their woefully underfinanced and understaffed counterparts in poor neighborhoods. These forms of inequality provide fertile ground for demagogues and their mirror images—indifferent leaders who shun the hard questions of justice and equality because their pollsters tell them the answers to those questions will have to be bold and hence unpopular to large numbers of people. So we might well pause and ask ourselves how far we have progressed from the time when a group of white workingmen could claim that only by ridding their workplace of blacks could labor be rendered respectable, that is, by "making the [white] labor respected."[39] Though we emerge into a new century ripe with possibilities, we shall continue to hear many such claims in the future, the angry echoes of voices from our country's past.

NOTES

1. The petition was reprinted in *The Liberator,* 15 February 1834, and in Edward S. Abdy, *Journal of a Residence and Tour in the United States of North America, from April, 1833, to October, 1834,* vol. 3 (London: John Murray, 1835), 246–47.

2. G. Smith Wormley, "Prudence Crandall," *Journal of Negro History* 8 (January 1923): 72–78.

3. Abdy, *Journal of a Residence and Tour,* 246–47.

4. Ibid.

5. Leonard Richards, *"Gentlemen of Property and Standing": Anti-Abolition Mobs in Jacksonian America* (New York: Oxford University Press, 1970), 40.

6. Abdy, *Journal of a Residence and Tour,* 246–47.

7. Andrew T. Judson, quoted in Wormley, "Prudence Crandall," 74.

8. The following discussion is taken from Jacqueline Jones, *American Work: Four Centuries of Black and White Labor* (New York: W. W. Norton, 1998).

9. Shane White, "'We Dwell in Safety and Pursue Our Honest Callings': Free Blacks in New York City, 1783–1810," *Journal of American History* 75 (September 1988): 445–70.

10. Mill supervisor quoted in Edwin DeLeon, "The New South," *Harper's New Monthly Magazine* 48 (February 1874): 411.

11. Walter Licht, *Getting Work: Philadelphia, 1840–1950* (Cambridge: Harvard University Press, 1992).

12. Thomas J. Sugrue, *The Origins of the Urban Crisis: A History of Inequality in Detroit, 1940–1967* (Princeton, N.J.: Princeton University Press, 1996).

13. John J. Donahue III and James Heckman, "Continuous versus Episodic Change: The Impact of Civil Rights Policy on the Economic Status of Blacks," *Journal of Economic Literature* 29 (December 1991): 1603–43; James Heckman and Brook S. Payner, "Determining the Impact of Federal Antidiscrimination Policy on the Economic Status of Blacks: A Study of South Carolina," *American Economic Review* 79 (March 1989): 137–77.

14. Douglas S. Massey and Nancy A. Denton, *American Apartheid: Segregation and the Making of the Underclass* (Cambridge: Harvard University Press, 1993).

15. Thomas Dublin, *Women at Work: The Transformation of Work and Community in Lowell, Massachusetts, 1826–1860* (New York: Columbia University Press, 1979); Jonathan Prude, "The Social System of Early New England Textile Mills: A Case Study, 1812–1840," in *The New England Working Class and the New Labor History,* ed. Herbert Gutman and Donald H. Bell (Urbana: University of Illinois Press, 1987), 90–127; Barbara M. Tucker, *Samuel Slater and the Origins of the American Textile Industry, 1790–1860* (Ithaca, N.Y.: Cornell University Press, 1984).

16. Robert Ernst, *Immigrant Life in New York City, 1825–1863* (Syracuse, N.Y.: Syracuse University Press, 1994), 69.

17. Frederick Douglass, "[Free Blacks Must Learn Trades]," in *Frederick Douglass: The Narrative and Selected Writings*, ed. Michael Meyer (New York: Modern Library, 1984), 349–50.

18. Isaac Candler, *A Summary View of America, Comprising a Description of the Face of the Country* (London: T. Cadell, 1824), 291–92.

19. Leonard P. Curry, *The Free Black in Urban America, 1800–1850: The Shadow of the Dream* (Chicago: University of Chicago Press, 1981), 20.

20. Helen T. Catterall, ed., *Judicial Cases Concerning American Slavery and the Negro* (Washington, D.C.: Carnegie Institution, 1937), 5:31–43. See also Nicole Etcheson, *The Emerging Midwest: Upland Southerners and the Political Culture of the Old Northwest, 1787–1861* (Bloomington: Indiana University Press, 1996).

21. Leon Litwak, *North of Slavery: The Negro in the Free States, 1790–1860* (Chicago: University of Chicago Press, 1961), 64–112; James Oliver Horton and Lois Horton, *In Hope of Liberty: Culture, Community, and Protest among Northern Free Blacks, 1700–1860* (New York: Oxford University Press, 1997), 167–69.

22. Quoted in *The Liberator*, 17 November 1837, p. 185.

23. Quoted in Jean H. Baker, *Affairs of Party: The Political Culture of Northern Democrats in the Mid-Nineteenth Century* (Ithaca, N.Y.: Cornell University Press, 1983), 257.

24. David R. Roediger, *The Wages of Whiteness: Race and the Making of the American Working Class* (London: Verso, 1991); Eric Lott, *Love and Theft: Blackface Minstrelsy and the American Working Class* (New York: Oxford University Press, 1993); Noel Ignatiev, *How the Irish Became White* (New York: Routledge, 1995).

25. See, for example, Peter Way, *Common Labour: Workers and the Digging of North American Canals, 1780–1860* (Cambridge: Cambridge University Press, 1993).

26. James Freeman Clarke, *Present Condition of the Free Colored People of the United States* (New York: New York Anti-Slavery Society, 1859), 5.

27. "The Afri-American Female Intelligence Society of Boston," in *Black Women in White America: A Documentary History*, ed. Gerda Lerner (New York: Vintage Books, 1972), 438.

28. Gary Nash, *Forging Freedom: The Formation of Philadelphia's Black Community, 1720–1840* (Cambridge, Mass.: Harvard University Press, 1988), 177; Paul A. Gilje, *The Road to Mobocracy: Popular Disorder in New York City, 1763–1830* (Chapel Hill: University of North Carolina Press, 1987), 159.

29. William Cheek and Aimee Lee Cheek, *John Mercer Langston and the Fight for Black Freedom, 1829–1865* (Urbana: University of Illinois Press, 1989), 61.

30. Abdy, *Journal of a Residence and Tour*, 330.

31. Thomas B. Edsall and Mary D. Edsall, *Chain Reaction: The Impact of Race, Rights, and Taxes on*

American Politics (New York: W. W. Norton, 1991), 124.

32. Richard Morin, "A Distorted Image of Minorities," *Washington Post*, 8 October 1995, p. A1; Elaine Tyler May, "The Radical Roots of American Studies," *American Quarterly* 48 (June 1996): 191–92.

33. Joleen Kirschenman and Kathryn M. Neckerman, "'We'd Love to Hire Them, but . . .': The Meaning of Race for Employers," and Marta Tienda and Haya Stier, "Joblessness and Shiftlessness: Labor Force Activity in Chicago's Inner City," both in *The Urban Underclass*, ed. Christopher Jencks and Paul E. Peterson (Washington, D.C.: Brookings Institution Press, 1991), 207, 211, 143.

34. Katherine S. Newman, "Working Poor: Low Wage Employment in the Lives of Harlem Youth," in *Transitions through Adolescence: Interpersonal Domains and Context*, ed. Julia A. Graber, Jeanne Brooks-Gunn, and Anne C. Petersen (Mahwah, N.J.: Erlbaum Associates, 1996), 323–44.

35. Kevin Sack, "Atlanta Leaders See Racial Goals as Olympic Ideal," *New York Times*, 10 June 1996, pp. A1, B12.

36. See, for example, Jason DeParle, "What Welfare-to-Work Really Means," *New York Times Magazine*, 20 December 1998, pp. 52–53.

37. Michael Tonry, *Malign Neglect-Race, Crime, and Punishment in America* (New York: Oxford University Press, 1995); Christian Parenti, "Making Prisons Pay," *The Nation*, 29 January 1996, pp. 11–12.

38. David L. Kirp, John P. Dwyer, and Larry A. Rosenthal, *Our Town: Race, Housing, and the Soul of Suburbia* (New Brunswick, N.J.: Rutgers University Press, 1995); Gary Orfield and Susan E. Eaton, and the Harvard Project on School Desegregation, *Dismantling Desegregation: The Quiet Reversal of Brown versus the Board of Education* (New York: New Press, 1996); Melvin L. Oliver and Thomas M. Shapiro, *Black Wealth/White Wealth: A New Perspective on Racial Inequality* (New York: Routledge, 1996).

39. Abdy, *Journal of a Residence and Tour*, 246–47.

14

'Not All Borders are the Same': Immigration and the 'Mexican Menace' in the Midwest

DIONICIO NODÍN VALDÉS

On 8 January 1927, thirty-four white men who identified themselves as "Learned Americans" submitted a prepared statement with recommendations to the U.S. House of Representatives during hearings on Immigration from Countries of the Western Hemisphere, published in the *Congressional Record*. The authors included C. C. Little, then president of the University of Michigan; Professors Edward A. Ross, William H. Kiekhofter, J. E. Irelin, John R. Commons, and Henry R. Trumbower of the University of Wisconsin; and professors from other institutions, mostly Ivy League. Comprising leaders of the professorate from the most prestigious bulwarks of the Knowledge Factory of their day, they were joined by Madison Grant, president of the New York Zoological Society, and Roosevelt H. Johnson and Leon F. Whitney, then president and field secretary, respectively, of the American Eugenics Society. They sought further restriction of immigration to the United States based on national origins to augment legislation passed in 1882, 1917, 1921, and 1924 that severely limited immigration from Asian and European countries. They were interested in curtailing immigration from nations in the Western Hemisphere, which historically had a special relationship with the United States. The "Learned Americans" made two particular recommendations.

First, "We urge the extension of the quota system to all countries of North and South America from which we have substantial immigration and in which the population is not predominantly of the white race who, because of their lower standards of living, are able to compete at an advantage with American workers engaged in various forms of agriculture and unskilled labor." Only two nations in the Western Hemisphere had substantial immigration flows to the United States in the 1920s: Canada and Mexico. Since the Learned Ones considered Canadians people "predominantly of the white race," the flowery language masked the intent of the authors to direct the change in the law at only one nation—Mexico.

The Learned white men of the north made a second point: "We believe that . . . the racial status quo of the country should be maintained [f]or a reasonable degree of homogeneity. . . . Without such homogeneity, we firmly believe, no civilization can have its best development." These public intellectuals created and sought acceptance for notions passing as knowledge that Mexican immigration was a menace to the racial purity and civilization of the United States.

At the end of the twentieth century, it would have been easy to find more than thirty-four white men who shared the sentiments of these "Learned Americans." Perhaps the best known case was radio personality, author, and politician Pat Buchanan, candidate for president in the elections of 1992, 1996, and 2000. While campaigning he advocated a number of changes in U.S. policy regarding Mexico and Mexicans in the United States.

On the stump in 1996, in reference to immigrants from Mexico, he stated: "they've got no right to break our laws and break into our country and go on welfare and some of them commit crimes. . . . [They've] got no right because they've got a lousy government down there [in Mexico], to walk across the borders of the United States with impunity, because this is my country" (Croft 1996). He concurred with the Learned Americans of 1927 that the issue transcended economics, welfare, and cheap labor. Ultimately, his concern was a defense of his race: "There is nothing wrong with sitting down and arguing that we are a European country" (Buchanan 1995b). Along with the Learned Americans, he considered the only knowledge of merit that encompassed in the European tradition, and viewed others as threatening. In a campaign speech he referred to multiculturalism as: "an across-the-board assault on our Anglo-American heritage" (Gunter 1996). Candidate Buchanan, University of Michigan president Little, and the American Eugenics Society could not have been in fuller agreement about the dangers of a Mexican menace to their understanding of the American way of life.

Buchanan is equally frightened by the prospect of hordes swarming across the border: "When you have one, two, three million people walking across your border every year, breaking your laws, you have an invasion" (Kenyon 1996). He offers a more direct solution than the quota system the Learned Americans proposed seventy years earlier: "I will stop this immigration cold. Period. Paragraph. . . . I'll build that security fence, and we'll close it, and we'll say, 'Listen José, you're not coming in'" (Verhovek 1996). Buchanan's proposed security fence was not intended for traffic across the Ambassador Bridge. His rhetoric reflects a constant in perceptions about national borders from the late 1920s through the end of the twentieth century. Buchanan asserts that a fence is necessary to separate white civilization and a nonwhite Mexican menace, to distinguish even more clearly the political border that has gained increasing significance in United States popular culture in the past century and a half. He and the Learned Americans did not attach similar significance to the Canadian border. It is not a racial divide, so no massive security fence is necessary.

The rhetoric of Buchanan and the Learned Americans reflects a common thread in hegemonic popular and political culture and its scholarly circles, namely that Mexico and Mexicans are a racial menace to the white people of the United States. Yet this vision is not uncontested. There have been countervailing, often contradictory, representations created by other purveyors of hegemonic popular culture, politicians, and their academic lackeys. A contrary thread has portrayed Mexican immigrants who cross the border into Texas, New Mexico, Arizona, and California as capable of assimilation into the American way of life and meritorious of citizenship. Even the countervailing representations typically retain a Eurocentric assumption that Mexicans should and must understand the world through a white prism. In addition to the limitations of a Eurocentric bias in dominant popular thought, I wish to address two of its related geographic constrictions, namely the overwhelming association of Mexicans residing in the United States with the Southwest and the United States–Mexico border. The overwhelming focus on a corner of the nation is similarly evident in Chicana and Chicano counternarratives.

Association of Mexicans with the United States Southwest dates from the United States conquest and subsequent acquisition of Mexico's far northern territories. In the Treaty of Guadalupe Hidalgo of 1848, the United States relocated the international border between the two countries and acquired half the territory of its neighboring republic. At the time of the treaty, Mexicans in the United

States were concentrated overwhelmingly in the former Mexican territories, not far from the international border. In subsequent years, and particularly during the course of the twentieth century, people of Mexican birth and descent have moved in substantial numbers to every state in the Union. Unfortunately, most scholarship and popular thought, including that of Chicanos and Chicanas, accepts as common knowledge the geography delineated in the treaty with Mexicans in the United States. At the end of the twentieth century, when millions of people of Mexican birth and their descendants resided outside the Southwest, hundreds of miles from the border between the two countries, the geographic tropes of the Mexican border and the Southwest continued largely unchallenged.

In this essay I will focus on Michigan and the Midwest, and the border with Canada, areas which are also critical to understanding Chicana and Chicano experiences and Mexican-United States relations. First I will examine moments in the history of the region prior to the arrival of Europeans, to demonstrate the fallacy of popular assumptions that Mexicans are solely recent arrivals in the Midwest. I will then examine the region in eras following contact between Europeans and Native Americans, to expose continued Mexican influence and its impact on ideas passing as knowledge in dominant popular culture.

Long before the United States established political control over the present-day Midwest, people from Mexico came to the region on many occasions. Unfortunately, the record they left has not been deciphered very well. In distant times, native peoples brought foods they and their ancestors domesticated in Mexico, including maize, beans, squash, and peppers, to lands in the north. At a later time, when the Toltecs reigned supreme in central Mexico, their influence spread to the present-day United States Southwest. Mesoamerican archeologists refer to the era as the late-classic period (600-900 A.D.), likely extending into the early post-classic (900-1519 A.D.) (Hedrick et al. 1974). At the time a number of ceremonial sites and cities appeared in present-day New Mexico and Arizona with undeniable markings of the civilization associated with Tula in the present-day state of Hidalgo. In locations farther north, including the current Midwest, such massive ceremonial sites appeared less frequently and their stylistic forms show less immediate influence from Mexico. Yet there was a recurring link, the copper trade between the Upper Peninsula of Michigan and Mexican cultures farther to the South. The easy accessibility and purity of Michigan copper made it an item of trade into the present-day Southwest and Mexican interior (Smith 1915).

Linguistic contributions from Mexico to locations in the northern United States have been more difficult to document. The problem stems in part from the less precise nature of language. It is also the result of a bias in dominant paradigms of knowledge that influence current anthropological models of linguistic exchange. Yet dominant visions were not always as narrow as they became in the twentieth century. Academic and popular opinions regarding Mexico's influence on the native people of the Midwest have ebbed and flowed since the rediscovery by archeologists of ceremonial sites and dwellings that long preceded the arrival of Europeans. One important phase occurred during the middle years of the nineteenth century, when the formal discipline of archaeology was young and much important work was performed by amateurs. Many of these investigators had just discovered the writings on ancient Mexico by scholars like William Hinkling Prescott and were dazzled. They attributed a great Aztec influence on ancient peoples of the region, a case in point being the Aztalán ceremonial site in Wisconsin. In later decades, as investigative work became more sophisticated and archeologists uncovered more details, they realized that Aztec contributions were less than previously imagined. Unfortunately, they often denied or downplayed Mexican influence apart from the Aztecs, as the new models they created discounted the likelihood of earlier or later exchanges.

The diminution of Mexican influence on knowledge created by United States scholars in the late nineteenth and early twentieth centuries was the result of several additional factors. One occurred in the aftermath of the United States conquest of Mexico, as the conquering politicians increasingly emphasized the importance of a clearly delineated border between the two countries. The international border limited the geographic imagination in hegemonic United States popular culture, as writers and scholars increasingly emphasized differences that separated Mexican and United States American, rather than finding commonality. Furthermore, the conquest of Mexico, along with conquests of other non-European people in subsequent generations, enhanced a sense of superiority among the purveyors of United States popular culture. Similar notions were articulated through increasingly sophisticated forms of scientific racism, including Social Darwinism and Eugenics, that gained great influence in academic and popular thought. Theoretical possibilities for great achievements by Mexicans diminished proportionately with the degree that European and European American hegemony remained unchallenged.

I will now examine Mexican influences in Michigan and the Midwest during a number of less distant historical moments, using some simple rules of logic. One is that in the absence of formal political borders, there were fewer impediments to imagining the likelihood of interaction and exchange of material goods, ideas, and cultural ways. A second is that European–based scientific models dominated by positivist, culturally narrow viewpoints have low expectations for Mexicans and are of little value (Acuña 1996).

I will first address Mexican linguistic influence by examining the search for roots of the well-known term *Michigan*. Extant theories on its origins most often focus on place-names, presumably originating in the Ojibwa language. James L. Lanman claims that it was taken from "Indian words" [of unspecified origin] "Mitchisawgyegan," meaning, "A Great Lake." Author Hulda Hollands claims that the roots are from "Mish-mai-kin-nac," identified as the northernmost point of the Lower Peninsula and surrounding islands (*Michigan Gazetteer* 1991, viii). Meanwhile, Walter Romig, in *Michigan Place Names*, suggests the name was derived from "two Indian words [unspecified origin], Michi (great or large) and Gama (lake)" (Romig 1973, 366).

The interpretations offered by Lanman, Hollands, and Romig, in comparison with some other possibilities, appear to take long stretches that do not readily conform with another rule of logic common in seeking linguistic derivations, the notion of elegance, or simplicity and closeness of fit. I find two much more elegant roots for the term *Michigan* suggesting Mexican origins. The first is that it was a derivation of the word *Michoacán*, an ancient Mexican kingdom and currently the name of a Mexican state. The term came from resident Tarascos, who associate it with water, as there are many lakes in Michoacán. Similarly, English-speakers seeking derivations associate the name Michigan with water. The Tarascos had a reputation as warriors, who, unlike the Aztecs, had perfected the use of copper weapons, the metal arms permitting them to withstand invasions by their better-known central Mexican counterparts, who never conquered them. This suggests another link involving the ancient people of central Mexico and the copper mines of the Upper Peninsula. More recent Mexican immigrants to Michigan and their children have called themselves *Michicanos* (*Michoacanos*), and still claim that they are in *Michoacán del norte*.

A second and even more elegant possibility linguistically has later chronological roots, deriving from shortly before the moment when English-speaking people officially adopted the term Michigan in its current form. It stems from a later phase of Mexican immigration to Michigan and the Midwest, when Mexico was still a colony of Spain. Instead of coming as indigenous people from Michoacán, this time Mexicans were called Spaniards, especially in English-speaking documents. They were part of the Spanish imperial drive to extend its hold and claims to the *Luisiana* (Louisiana) territory, which Spain acquired in 1763 and controlled until the end of the eighteenth century. Luisiana did not have a clearly delineated border in the north, but the Spanish Crown established several military and civilian settlements in current-day Missouri and Illinois. In an expansive phase of their northward thrust, while at war with England and during the time the United States was fighting for its own independence, the Spanish established a Fort at San José, which the English called St. Joseph, Michigan, in 1781 (Kinnard 1932). The fort at San José appeared in the same year that Mexicans under Spanish rule founded the Pueblo de Nuestra Señora de Los Angeles de Porciúncula in Alta California.

In contrast with later waves of northward migration, these Mexicans were not portrayed as a menace by future United States Americans, because of their common enemy, the English. In England, however, they were represented differently. Like other Spanish-speaking people, they were depicted negatively in many ways, particularly through the English-based Black Legend. The hostile language of the Black Legend was not simply an isolated language of religious scholars and court historians, but was part of a propaganda campaign by England that accompanied its military ventures against Spain and other European nations to achieve imperial domination over the world.

Although the Spanish Crown decided to abandon Fort San José, the fates and the influence of the Mexican soldiers in the Lower Peninsula of Michigan and other parts of neighboring Spanish Luisiana territory merit further examination. Without much risk of speculation, it is not difficult to surmise that Mexican soldiers, dissatisfied with conditions and brutal treatment by their superiors, deserted in large numbers from Fort San José and nearby places, as they did elsewhere. Many former soldiers remained in the region and intermingled and intermarried with native people and with English- and French-speaking people of European origin. Through that interaction, their representations might have influenced the creation and adoption of the term "Michigan" by English-speakers entering the region in the late eighteenth century. The United States Congress decided to accept the term in 1804, during deliberations that resulted in the formation of the Michigan territory in 1805. This decision occurred only four years after the Spanish Crown ceded the Louisiana territory to France. The United States acquired the Louisiana Territory from France by purchase in 1803, and its inhabitants were allowed to maintain their language, customs, and lands, a model for the future Treaty of Guadalupe Hidalgo. The presence of Mexicans in Michigan at this time might also have influenced Nicolas Perrot, who made a claim in an 1864 study that the term Michigan could be traced to French documents. He asserted that in 1653, a group of Huron, fleeing Iroquois pursuers from the Green Bay, "retreated to Méchingan, where they constructed a fort" that successfully withstood a two-year siege (Perrot 1911, 1:151). Although he claims the term has Ojibwa origins, it is perfectly consistent with another possibility in Mexican Spanish. This is the most elegant of all the possibilities as the spelling is identical except for syllabic emphasis. The interpretation that Mexican soldiers from Spanish Luisiana are responsible for the name also has an advantage of being close in time to its official adoption in English. English-speakers might have heard Mexican soldiers or former soldiers settled in the area, reflecting negatively on the experience of being conscripted into the army and brought to the distant shores of a Great Lake, and on their treatment by superiors. According to this interpretation, English-speaking Michiganians adopted the term for their state verbatim from Mexicans, but added an accent mark in an inappropriate place, as often happens in translation. Like Perrot, they thought they heard Méchingan when the Mexicans were saying me chingan.

Relations between English- and Spanish-speaking peoples in North America shifted again in the second quarter of the nineteenth century. Anglo-Americans had been invited to take up residence in far northern Mexican territories and accept Mexican citizenship, but soon overextended their welcome by invading, declaring war, and conquering Mexico. Through the war of conquest in 1846-48, the United States acquired a vast territory and sought to maintain permanent control, which necessitated efforts to demarcate the international border. The conquering nation also incorporated its first large Mexican population, an estimated 100,000-120,000 former citizens of Mexico, residing primarily in the vast region between Texas and Alta California, which became the Southwest of national popular culture.

The conquerors faced a dilemma regarding how to deal with and represent the conquered former Mexican citizens residing north of the newly established border, a quandary that has perplexed them and their descendants to the present. They might encourage Mexicanos to assimilate and be incorporated into the political and popular culture of the nation, in the manner of immigrants from Europe. At the other extreme, they might subordinate them like conquered Native Americans and enslaved Africans and their descendants, in which case representing them as a race apart would serve a purpose. In fact, the conquerors responded with trepidation and ambiguity. On the one hand, in the peace agreement of 1848, the Treaty of Guadalupe Hidalgo, they permitted Mexicans who remained in the United States to become citizens automatically, to retain their land and enjoy all the rights of white citizens. On the other, they wrote laws, created a legal mechanism enforced by police and other elements of the state, and behaved in other ways to dispossess Mexicans of the overwhelming majority of their former landholdings. The conquerors simultaneously denigrated Mexican culture while they failed to enforce their own laws mandating the establishment of public schools for all children, in a manner similar to their treatment of a majority of African Americans and Native Americans. As a consequence, few but the tiny Mexican upper class attended schools regularly until the twentieth century.

English-speaking European Americans expressed similar inconsistencies in ways they represented Mexicans, a profound aspect of identity formation for the conquered people. Some of the early Anglo soldiers and politicos, lusting after the wealth of the Mexican upper class (the *ricos*), used flattery and called them Spaniards while they married their daughters, which enabled them to take possession of the lands. Most conquerors, and their successors who followed them from the east, however, were more contemptuous of Mexicans. Disparaging their appearances, they referred to Mexicans as greasers, half-breeds, and Indians. They also represented Mexicanos as *bandidos*, criminals and lawbreakers. Joaquín Murrieta, Tiburcio Vásquez, Juan Cortina, Three-Fingered Jack García, and Padre Jurata were a few of the long list of Mexicans portrayed in newspapers, novels, and state and territorial legislatures as a menace to the safety and security of European Americans and white civilization. Such representations helped those who lusted after fortune in the Southwest and California to apply different standards in their treatment of Mexicans in the application of laws and customs, thereby excluding them from effective United States citizenship. Thus Mexicans were incorporated as citizens with substantially fewer rights and privileges than individuals and groups recognized as white.

The early twentieth century marks the beginning of another phase of Mexican history in the United States, highlighted by the incorporation of a massive wave of Mexicans who crossed the border between the two countries initially to work. This migration occurred in conjunction with the flowering of the Industrial Revolution in the United States, an essential feature of which involved empire. Despite their reluctance to admit the reality, creators of hegemonic popular thought in the United States could not deny that their nation had become the leading empire in the world. The empire was partly formal and political, as in the conquest and acquisition of Puerto Rico and the Philippine Islands, incorporated as territories. Cuba under the Platt Amendment (1902-33) became a protectorate—protected by the United States, the only country from which it needed protection. In some countries the imperial relationship was less formal, maintained by political manipulation, economic coercion, and occasional invasion, in particular for Mexico and other nations of the Caribbean and Central America. The territories and subordinated nations provided the United States with raw materials for industry; as well as sugar, coffee, tobacco, and other drugs to keep workers in its factories alert; and food to sustain them. The formal and informal colonies also offered the captains of industry markets in which to sell and distribute their surplus production—including mining equipment, utilities, and railroad lines. Another feature of imperialism involved the supply of labor by these nations for industrialized agriculture, railroads, and factories controlled by entrepreneurs from the United States. Mexicans formed the largest group in this unequal relationship, and they worked for United States capitalists in Mexico and the Southwest, as well as in Michigan and other Midwestern states.

They first came to Michigan in large numbers when the United States entered World War I, precisely when the flow of cheap labor from Europe was being cut off. The single most important employer was the sugar beet industry, and in the 1920s Mexican workers spread out in rural locations, concentrated most heavily in the Saginaw Valley and the Thumb, and extending into Isabella County. Mexicans also worked on several railroads, living in boxcars and slums popularly called "jungles" along the tracks throughout the region. In cities they found employment in steel mills, in meatpacking plants, and, in Michigan, in the automobile industry, especially for Henry Ford. They formed barrios in major cities of the region—the Kansas Cities, Chicago, Detroit, Milwaukee, St. Paul, Toledo, Saginaw, Flint, Gary, East Chicago, Indiana, and scores of smaller settlements close to work.

Mexican immigration to the Midwest originated mostly in the central and west-central states of Guanajuato, Michoacán, Jalisco, Zacatecas, and Mexico City, typically via Texas. Preceding the migration, hegemonic representations of Mexicans adopted from the nineteenth and early twentieth centuries appeared in novels, short stories, and the youthful silent picture industry of Hollywood. The most popular images were of *bandidos* and related criminal types, and wild-eyed *revolucionarios* who had participated in the Mexican Revolution. As a U.S. government report noted in 1927, even in the smallest Midwestern towns, where few Mexicanos dared to tread alone, "pictures of Mexican bandits made people's hair stand on end" (Edson 1927). The government report did not assume that Mexicans or African Americans merited inclusion as "people," a term it assumed to be interchangeable with popular representations of "white people." Another hegemonic representation at this time associated Mexicans with drugs, particularly a native

Mexican plant, cannabis sativa, which reportedly spread throughout the region, planted in lowlands along river valleys by railroad maintenance workers and farm workers. In the largest urban districts, including Chicago, Mexican crime was also represented as a threat to serenity and the American way of life, while the heart of the barrio in Indiana Harbor (East Chicago) was portrayed as "the bucket of blood," because of the supposed frequency of knifings (Edson 1927).

The "Learned Americans" in 1927 agreed with many reporters and politicians who referred to this wave of immigration as "the Mexican Invasion," rather than seeing it for what it was: workers following the demands of an international labor market dominated by United States capital. The antiforeign sentiment of the Learned Americans had been whetted during World War I by one strand of the intensified "Americanization Movement," popularly referred to as "100 percent Americanism," a campaign by government bureaucrats, educators, and many employers to assimilate foreigners to unquestioning adoption of American ways. Yet the Learned Americans and other proponents of Eugenics and related strands of dominant popular thought considered Mexicans, Native Americans, Asians, and African Americans incapable of such assimilation. They considered what they called the "Mexican Problem" to be best resolved by an immediate halt to immigration.

Two groups of English-speaking people opposed such restrictionist efforts and challenged the harshest representations of Mexicans. One was composed of a segment of capital, identified by their opponents as "cheap labor advocates." They invested in industrial agriculture, railroads, and some urban industries. They were happy with the workers they employed and portrayed them as contented and docile, while they contested critics who claimed that Mexicans lowered the standards of living for all. A second group, dominated by educators and social workers, espoused a somewhat looser view of assimilation that accepted Mexicans. This second group included educator John Dewey and his student, Horace Kallen, who coined the term "cultural pluralism," and whose ideas are still popular among academics, educators, social workers, and some politicians. Proponents of this view claimed that Mexicans could make good citizens if only given a chance. They suggested a few semiautonomous spaces for Mexicans to speak Spanish, practice their folk arts, take a few classes in practical subjects and Mexican culture, and celebrate the 5 de mayo and 16 de septiembre. While the theories supported by the cultural pluralists gained popularity among academics and educators in subsequent generations, the practices espoused by the "Learned Americans" of 1927 and Pat Buchanan continued to reign supreme in most public school and university curricula three generations later.

Struggles over representations of Mexicans within the dominant political and popular culture took a critical turn with the outbreak of the Great Depression. One group, led by the Republican Party and President Herbert Hoover, the United States Department of Labor (which was responsible for federal immigration policy at the time), and the media they controlled, including the *Chicago Tribune* and the *Detroit News*, blamed Mexicans for the Great Depression. It portrayed Mexicans as a threat to the livelihood of U.S. Americans, not only in the Southwest, but even in the Midwest. Had there been no Midwestern Mexicans, politicians would have been hard-pressed to portray Mexicans as a national problem. Campaigns to remove Mexicans took place in local communities throughout the country, including the Midwest. The repatriation and deportation from the Midwest and the Southwest afforded the Mexican border still greater meaning, for the individuals and agencies involved were satisfied that their task was complete once they dumped the repatriates across the line in Mexico. There was no similar effort on the United States' northern border, and not a single campaign directed at any European immigrant group. The repatriation and deportation campaign suggests a further step in hegemonic representations of Mexicans as a race apart. They were singled out among all racial and ethnic groups as incapable of assimilation and transferred across an international border in order to prevent contact with white people, who were represented as the bearers of U.S. American civilization.

The perception of the Mexican Menace was further intensified at this time, when politicians enacted laws and policies restricting employment to noncitizens and nonresidents of local communities. Bureaucrats often selectively applied these acts to Mexicans to make establishment of residency more difficult. The campaign achieved its success politically in large part because conservative restrictionists, including supporters of Eugenics, gained support from ostensibly liberal social workers and welfare agents, who had formerly considered Mexicans to be assimilable. The bureaucrats were concerned about rising taxes as a result of increasing numbers of Mexicans applying for relief, and about these Mexicans taking jobs and welfare from more deserving "Americans." Thus conservative restrictionists and liberal bureaucrats joined to reduce the clout of conservative "cheap labor advocates." According to many observers in the dominant culture, the early-twentieth-century Mexican presence in the northern United States was thus merely a "a passing phase" in the history of the nation, and they expected Mexicans as a distinct group to soon disappear from the Midwest. This again confirmed that in the hegemonic popular imagination Mexicans in the United States belonged only in the Southwest and close to the Mexican border.

The politicians and bureaucrats failed to consider the possibility of independent agency by Mexicans, particularly children, most of whom were adamantly opposed to and frightened by the prospect of returning to a Mexico they had never seen, as the vast majority were born and grew up in the United States. Nor did these politicians account for the influence of adult Mexicanas (Mexican women), attentive both to their children and to the individual freedoms and material comforts of life in the Midwest. If we believe hegemonic representations, children and mothers had to contend with fathers and husbands who, having lost their jobs and being unable to support their families, were inclined to return to the homeland. If dominant representations of an omnipotent macho Mexican culture were accurate, children and mothers would be no match for fathers in this major decision in the life cycle of the entire family. Yet children and their mothers overwhelmingly had the upper hand, as a majority of Mexicans remained, especially those whose immediate family members resided in the United States.

By the late 1930s, Mexicans had established a permanent presence in cities and towns throughout the region. They quickly joined industrial unions, when permitted, and formed new social and cultural clubs and organizations that served important functions beyond helping to create a sense of community. They used their organizations to demand enforcement of laws protecting their rights and requiring that their children attend school, and they protested against discrimination in public places and at work. Because they were organized as residents and citizens, they also were able to more effectively challenge hegemonic representations of themselves as a menace.

With the World War II economic boom, Mexicans entered factories producing machinery, motor vehicles, and weapons at Willow Run, Detroit, Ypsilanti, Pontiac, Saginaw, and elsewhere in the Midwest. Those just reaching adulthood joined the Armed Forces in greater numbers than did any other ethnic group in the United States. They were not necessarily more loyal citizens, but few had sufficient political influence to obtain draft deferments or employment in those industries considered vital to the national defense, or the class standing to qualify as farmers. Proletarian farmworkers were not eligible for deferments. A well-known case is Hero Street, a Mexican neighborhood located on the edge of a former railroad camp in Silvis, Illinois, surrounded by the Quad Cities of Bettendorf, Davenport, Moline, and Rock Island. The dingy little colonia had the highest proportion of recipients of Medals of Honor, and of deaths, of any street in the United States, not only in World War II, but also in Korea and Vietnam. The actions of Mexican soldiers contradict the representations of Pat Buchanan that

"Hispanics" were not "victims of one hundred years of racial discrimination. There were few Hispanics even in the United States forty years ago. How, then, can the feds [*sic*] justify favoring Hispanics over sons of white Americans who fought in WWII or Vietnam?" (Buchanan 1995b). As in so many cases, Buchanan's language and his representations of knowledge are not consistent with readily accessible facts.

During World War II and the following decades, an economic boom again convinced employers to encourage accelerated Mexican immigration to the United States. Some workers came as *braceros* (contract laborers) employed in agriculture, and in lesser numbers on the railroads and in factories, in Michigan and other parts of the country, initially for the duration of the war. Many settled permanently, while others returned to Mexico briefly but then joined hundreds of thousands of workers from Mexico who came to the United States to fill employers' demands for labor. Immigrants from Mexico were joined by Tejanos to work in the fields and factories of the Midwest. They settled not only in the larger cities, but formed colonias and barrios in medium-sized and smaller towns.

Mexicanos' Midwestern roots sank even deeper during this generation, contradicting the increasingly widespread representations in popular culture and among politicians that depicted them as undocumented "wetbacks" breaking laws to enter the country, or nonresident migrant farm workers. The images, which often passed as "common" knowledge, by focusing on these people's weak legal standing and lack of roots, served again to weaken the political presence and legal standing of Mexicans. Yet the rapid growth of the resident population, in conjunction with events in the national and international arenas, set the stage for the Chicano Movement in the 1960s and 1970s. The organized youth made many impressive material achievements, established a deeper cultural presence, and challenged long-established hegemonic negative portrayals of Mexicans.

A final cycle in the history of the Mexican Midwest began in the late 1960s and 1970s, with an economic restructuring highlighted by the dismantling of the "modern" large-scale factory system. Perhaps the classic case involves the massive steel industry, previously the largest employer of urban Mexicans in the Midwest. At this time, many employers transferred their plants away from the large industrial cities, where workers were organized, sending hundreds of thousands of jobs south to Mexico, Central America, the Caribbean, and elsewhere in the Third World. They simultaneously moved some operations to smaller towns and rural locations in the South, the Southwest, and the Midwest.

The restructuring had contradictory effects on the residents of the region. On the one hand, it permitted a small number of investors and capitalists to acquire vast fortunes. On the other, it resulted in stagnating incomes for European American workers, and sharp declines in earnings for African Americans, Mexicans, and Native Americans. There was more work at lower wages, contributing to the increasing popularity of two-income families and a sharp increase in the length of the individual workweek. Employers intensified their efforts to lure workers directly from Texas and the Mexican border for the new low-wage, nonunionized jobs available throughout the Midwest. Migration from several Latin American countries, overwhelmingly Mexico, reached record levels. By the end of the century, Chicago's population approached 25 percent Mexican. Elsewhere in the Midwest, many new urban barrios, small-town colonias, and trailer park pueblos appeared. The migration has resuscitated several dying neighborhoods and even cities in decline. In the ten states the U.S. Census Bureau refers to as the Midwest, in the twenty years since 1980, Mexicans were responsible for the majority of population growth, indicating that the rapid increase of Mexicans in the nation was not confined to the Southwest.

Assimilationist predictions of narrowing gaps between whites and people of color simply have not occurred in the past generation. According to the 1990 census, of the population over age 25, 81 percent of European Americans graduated from high school, compared with 67 percent of African Americans and only 52 percent of Latinos. Income data is similarly bleak. The per capita income for European Americans in the United States in 1991 was $15,510, while for blacks it was $9,710; and for Latinos it was $8,662.

Politics during the most recent generation was profoundly influenced by the Southern strategy initiated during the Nixon administration, which involved, in part, selective use of data as a basis for increasingly strident and crudely racialized representations of economic, social, and political trends. Politicians seeking electoral power overlooked the material improvements and political empowerment achieved by nonwhite people during the period of social movement activism of the era. and tried to reduce or contain their influence. The strategy recalled that of the Learned Americans of the late 1920s and early 1930s, representing non-white people in the United States, as well the Mexican nation, as responsible for the stagnating conditions of the white working class as a whole. It also involved an overt attack on "affirmative action" and supportive social services, particularly for undocumented and noncitizens, again on the grounds that they were causing damage to more deserving "Americans." The creation of new negative racial representations in popular culture included a refashioned Mexican Menace.

In addition to Pat Buchanan's portrayals, we recall Ross Perot's claim that Mexico was unfairly taking jobs from U.S. workers, which he identified as the "Great Sucking Sound," perhaps the catchiest sound bite from the 1992 election. Other political pundits hopped on the bandwagon to alert the English-speaking public of a new danger of immigration from Mexico, which Representative Lamar Smith (R-Texas) asserted was "the emergent issue of the '90s, not just the influx of illegal aliens, but their cost to American taxpayers and workers" (Puente 1993). The strategy aimed at an exponential increase in the size of the border patrol and raids on undocumented individuals in the workplace. Politicians justified the expanded border patrol by focusing on negative features of life in Mexico and conceived operations that drew attention to the border between the two countries, with names such as, "Gatekeeper," and "Hold the Line" (Herrick 1996). The international borders and the United States' neighbors were not treated equally, as politicians did not seek to fashion negative images of their northern neighbor or the line that separated the United States and Canada. The border patrol engaged in a surge of activity in the second half of the 1990s, and the apprehension rate of undocumented workers by the INS in January 1996 more than quadrupled that of a year earlier (more than 42,000 in 1996, compared with 9,500 in 1995) (Seid 1996). Politicians and border agents consciously racialized the foreign menace, and focused almost exclusively on Mexicans, even in the Midwest, where they form a minority of the undocumented. In slightly more than a decade, beginning in the mid-1980s, more Mexicans were hauled away from Midwestern factories and shops, and the raids more frequently reported, than in the preceding eighty years combined.

Popular representations to the contrary, Mexicans have recent and ancient histories in both the Southwest and the Midwest. Their histories belie the theoretical assumptions on which a great deal of "common knowledge" about Mexicans has been based. For several generations scholars and politicians have sustained an essentialist geography associating Mexicans in the United States with the Southwest and the United States–Mexican border. Chicana and Chicano scholarship and literature tends to accept and buttress the dominant themes, commonly overlooking the explicit and implicit political implications of dominant geographical notions. Mexicans in Michigan, the Midwest, and many regions outside the Southwest had links with Mexico long before the war between the United States and Mexico, when current notions of region and the border between the two countries approached their present forms. Hostile portrayals have set the stage for dominant acceptance of many anti-Mexican political acts for more than a century. Recent arguments by conservative politicians for tightening or closing the border, by implication the United States–Mexican border, has created in the imaginary line separating the two nations another variation of the Mexican Menace. Yet not all borders are the same, as politicians of various persuasions along the boundary between Michigan and Ontario realize. They do not see many Mexicans participating in international traffic, although the Ambassador Bridge, the Detroit-Windsor Tunnel, and the Bluewater Bridge are the fourth, fifth, and fourteenth most important crossing points between the United States and a neighboring country. Nor do the politicos of the Water Wonderland fear an invasion of boat people crossing Lake St. Clair or *mojados* wading across the Detroit River.

Many politicians find racial polarization strategies against Mexicans increasingly difficult to sustain. Many are also concerned about offending a growing sector of the electorate, aware that Governor Pete Wilson of California and other Mexican bashers were badly defeated in recent elections, in part because their efforts unwittingly helped mobilize a Latino, primarily Mexican, population to vote in record numbers. Even Michigan Senator Spencer Abraham, who some consider a voice of reason and moderation on immigration issues, belongs to the ultra-conservative Federalist Society, which seeks all precedent for action in the original U.S. Constitution. If Federalist Society members were to follow ideas prevalent when their Founding Fathers first came to power, they would adopt a relaxed attitude toward borders and immigration. In the 1780s, immigration to the United States was fairly open, and neither its northern nor its southern borders had much meaning in political, social, or cultural terms. Furthermore, many of those Founding Fathers relied on immigrants, including slaves from Africa, to perform onerous tasks. The Federalists of the 1780s and Senator Abraham, like the capitalists of the 1920s, might more accurately be considered "cheap labor advocates." Although conservative on many issues, they were unwilling to accept the hypocrisy of the restrictionists of their day, simultaneously aware that they would be hard pressed to find replacements for their immigrant housekeepers, cooks, nannies, and dishwashers, or lawn keepers to care for their sprawling estates. Furthermore, like the early Federalists, they would not be inclined to accept notions that Mexicans, even represented as Spaniards, were a dangerous race when they shared with Spain a common enemy in England.

Failure of academics to recognize a distant Mexican past and current Mexican presence outside the Southwest has been the result not simply of neglect, but also of the racial biases that inform the paradigms of dominant knowledge. Notions like region and border exist in historically specific and often highly political contexts, as the Learned Americans of the 1920s were well aware. One dangerous trend that has crept into some Chicana and Chicano literary works has been to accept an essentialist notion that "nada existe fuera del lenguage" (nothing exists outside of language). Struggles against racist and anti-Mexican notions in the 1920s by academics opposed to Eugenics were not resolved in texts alone, but simultaneously took place in a much broader arena. There will be more scholars to fabricate the knowledge of the Learned Americans, and new politicians to perform the role of Pat Buchanan. They can be created at the drop of a hat, or purchased for dollars. It is dangerous not to challenge any language that appears under the guise of knowledge that permits characterization of a race, nation, or people as a menace.

REFERENCES

Acuña, Rodolfo F. 1996. *Sometimes there is no other side: Chicanos and the myth of equality.* Notre Dame: University of Notre Dame Press.

Buchanan, Patrick J. 1995a. The racism of affirmative action: Decisions by the U.S. Supreme Court and voters in California will go a long way toward making American law color-blind. *Pittsburgh Post-Gazette*, 23 January.

_____. 1995b. Transcript from ABC News program, "This week with David Brinkley," 2 July.

Croft, Adrian. 1996. Buchanan, Hispanic students clash on immigration. Reuters News Service, 23 February.

Edson, George T. 1927. "Mexicans in Our Northcentral States." Unpublished manuscript, Bancroft Library, University of California, Berkeley.

Gunter, Booth. 1996. Buchanan conservatism burns hot and bright. *Tampa Tribune*, 4 March.

Hedrick, Basil C. et al., eds. 1974. *The Mesoamerican southwest: Readings in archeology, ethnohistory, and ethnology.* Carbondale: Southern Illinois University Press.

Herrick, Thaddeus. 1996. Buchanan shoots from hip at OK corral. *Houston Chronicle*, 27 February.

Kenyon, Peter. 1996. Senate judiciary committee to vote on immigration bill. *NPR Morning Edition.* Transcript no. 1814–2, 29 February.

Kinnard. L. 1932. The Spanish expedition against Fort St. Joseph. *Mississippi Valley Historical Review* 19:173–91.

Lupo, Alan. 1996. The bully who would be president. *Boston Globe*, 10 March.

Michigan Gazetteer. 1991. Wilmington, Del.: American Historical Publications.

Perrot, Nicolas. 1911. *The Indian tribes of the Upper Mississippi Valley and region of the Great Lakes.* 2 Vols. Cleveland: Arthur H. Clark Company.

Puente, María. 1993. Immigration issue of the '90s. *USA Today*, 30 September.

Romig, Walter. 1973. *Michigan place names.* Grosse Pointe: Walter Romig.

Seid, Richard. 1996. Mexico as the U.S.'s political whipping boy. *Christian Science Monitor*, 4 March.

Smith, Samuel. 1915. Pre-historic and modern copper mines of Lake Superior. *Michigan Historical Collections* 39:137–51.

Verhovek, Sam Howe. 1996. Home improvement: A 2,000-mile fence? First, Get estimates. *New York Times*, 3 March.

15

A World without Racial Preference*

DINESH D'SOUZA

"If color-blind admissions policies are put into effect," I was warned at a recent debate on the topic, "the number of black students at the most selective colleges and universities would plummet to around 2 percent. Should we as a society be willing to live with such an outcome?"

I hesitated, and in that moment of hesitation, my interlocutor saw his opportunity. "Well, should we?" he pressed.

The answer, it turns out, is yes. Yet it is an answer that supporters of the current system consider outrageous. They take for granted that the only possible response is "Of course not." So, for example, two pillars of the education establishment, former Princeton president William Bowen and former Harvard president Derek Bok, recently published a widely reviewed defense of affirmative action, *The Shape of the River: Long-Term Consequences of Considering Race in College and University Admissions.* They insist that some form of preferential recruitment is inevitable to avoid the unthinkable outcome of very few African Americans at top-ranked universities. "The adoption of a strict race-neutral standard would reduce

---

*This is a slightly revised review essay previously published in *The Weekly Standard*: All citations can be found in the For Further Reading section of this volume.

black enrollment at . . . academically selective colleges and universities by between 50 and 70 percent," Bowen and Bok observe. "The most selective colleges would experience the largest drops in black enrollment."

These numbers are more or less correct. Yet what they actually illustrate is not the unacceptable future but the unconscionable present: the magnitude of racial preferences currently in effect.

Affirmative action in practice does not mean—as its supporters claim—considering two equally qualified applicants and giving the minority candidate the nod. It has instead come to mean admitting Hispanic and African American students with grade point averages (GPAs) of 3.2 and SAT scores of 1100, while turning away white and Asian American applicants with GPAs of 4.0 and SAT scores of 1300. Far from waging a war against discrimination, advocates such as Bowen and Bok find themselves waging a war against merit. Far from vindicating idealism and promoting social justice, they find themselves cynically subverting the principle of equal rights under the law to the detriment of society as a whole.

Before we can decide whether it is simply too embarrassing to permit elite institutions to enroll a very small percentage of blacks or other minorities, we must first ask the question of what produces the racial disparities that so unsettle us and that seem to require affirmative action to counteract. Consider the example of the National Basketball Association (NBA). It is no secret that the NBA does not "look like America": African Americans, who are 12 percent of the population, make up 79 percent of the players, while Jews and Asian Americans are conspicuously scarce.

Of course, one never hears demands that the NBA establish a preferential recruitment program for Jews or Asians. Yet before the notion is dismissed as simply silly, it is instructive to ask why. The answer is presumably that it is merit and not discrimination that produces the racial imbalance on the basketball court. If the coaches hire the best passers and shooters, we tend to think, it should not matter if some ethnic groups dominate while others are hardly represented.

The lesson to be drawn from this example is that inequalities in racial outcomes that are produced by merit are far more defensible than inequalities produced by favoritism or discrimination. When we turn from the NBA to America's elite colleges and universities, we discover a similar result: Ethnic inequalities are the result not of biased selection procedures but of unequal performance on the part of different groups. Affirmative action has traditionally been defended as necessary to fight discrimination, but has anyone demonstrated that the blacks and Hispanics preferentially admitted to the best universities were, in fact, victims of discrimination? Has anyone uncovered at Berkeley or Princeton bigoted admissions officers seeking to exclude minorities? Is there any evidence that the white and Asian American students refused admission at these institutions were discriminating against anyone? The answer to these questions is no, no, and no. No one has even alleged unfairness of this sort.

There was, at one time, an attempt by advocates of affirmative action to argue for racial and cultural bias in the SAT and other standardized tests that most elite universities require their applicants to take. This argument, however, has collapsed in recent years, and even Bowen and Bok admit that it is no longer possible to claim that the SAT discriminates against blacks or other minorities. In *The Shape of the River*, they try to confuse the issue by insisting on the obvious point that standardized test scores "do not predict who will be a civic leader or how satisfied individuals will be with their college experience or with life." However, they are at last forced to the chagrined confession: "Almost all colleges have found that when they compare black and white undergraduates who enter with the same SAT scores, blacks earn lower grades than whites, not just in their first year but throughout their college careers. . . . Tests like the SAT do not suffer from prediction bias."

This is not to say that the test describes genetic or biological ability. It merely measures differences in academic preparation, and Bowen and Bok acknowledge that the low black enrollments at elite universities that affirmative-action policies seek to remedy are primarily produced by "continuing disparities in pre-collegiate academic achievements of black and white students." On those measures of merit that selective colleges use to decide who gets in, not all groups perform equally.

For the civil-rights leadership, these results have come as a nasty surprise. The movement led by Martin Luther King Jr. originally placed itself on the side of merit in opposition to racial nepotism. If laws and public policies were allowed to judge solely on the basis of individual merit, King repeatedly promised, we would see social rewards in America widely dispersed among groups.

In the generation since King's death, it is this premise—that equality of rights for individuals will invariably produce equality of results for groups—that has proved false. The dismaying truth is that even merit sometimes produces ethnic inequality. Consequently, it is hardly surprising that some who manned the barricades alongside King now insist that merit is the new guise in which the old racism manifests itself. It is now fashionable for advocates of affirmative action to place the term "merit" in quotation marks or to speak sarcastically of "so-called merit." Their main objection is that merit selection is not producing the outcomes they desire, and their enthusiasm for affirmative action can be attributed to their rediscovery of the blessing of nepotism.

Meanwhile, behind the scenes, there has been under way a fascinating debate about why merit produces such ethnic inequality. Two views have dominated the debate. The first is the "bell-curve" position, put forward most publicly in recent years by Charles Murray and Richard Herrnstein, that implies that there may be natural or biological differences between groups that would account for their unequal performance on indices of merit. The second is the traditional liberal position, which insists that when group differences in academic achievement and economic performance exist, they have been artificially created by social depriva-tion and racism.

These two views have functioned like a seesaw: When one goes up, the other goes down. In the early part of this century, most people took for granted that there were natural differences between the races and that these accounted for why some groups were advanced and others relatively backward. This view was fiercely attacked in the middle of this century by liberals, who argued that it was unrea-sonable and unconscionable to contend that natural deficiencies were the cause of blacks' doing poorly when blacks were subjected to so much legal and systematic discrimination, especially in the South.

The liberal view was entirely plausible, which is why the biological explana-tion was largely discarded. However, the liberal view has begun to collapse in recent years, precisely as it has proved unable to explain the world that resulted from its triumph. Consider a single statistic: Data from the college board show that, year after year, whites and Asian Americans who come from families earning less than $15,000 a year score higher on both the verbal and math sections of the SAT than African Americans from families earning more than $60,000 a year.

This stunning statistic, whose accuracy is unquestioned by anyone in this debate, is sufficient by itself to destroy the argument of those who have repeated for years that the SAT is a mere calibration of socioeconomic privilege. Yet it is equally devastating to the liberal attribution of black disadvantage to racial dis-crimination. Even if discrimination were widespread, how could it operate in such a way as to make poor whites and Asians perform better on math tests than upper-middle-class blacks?

On this question, most advocates of affirmative action do not know how to react. Some simply refuse to discuss the implications of the evidence. Others, like Nathan Glazer, seem to adopt a private conviction of the veracity of the bell-curve explanation. A few years ago, in a review of Murray and Herrnstein in the *New*

Republic, Glazer seemed to accept the existence of intrinsic differences in intelligence between the races—while objecting to any mention of the fact in public.

In more recent articles, Glazer has reversed his longtime criticism of affirmative action and said he is now willing to bend admissions standards to avoid the distressing outcome of very few blacks in the best universities. Glazer's second thoughts about affirmative action point to something often missed in such debates—for if the bell-curve thesis is correct, then it in fact constitutes the strongest possible argument in favor of affirmative action.

If there are natural differences in ability between ethnic groups that cannot easily be eradicated, then it makes sense for those of us who do not want America to be a racial caste society to support preferential programs that would prevent the consolidation of enduring group hierarchies. Forced, by the collapse of the liberal view, to accept natural inequality, Glazer unsurprisingly now treats blacks as a handicapped population that cannot be expected to compete against other groups.

There is, however, a third possible view of racial inequality—a view advanced by Thomas Sowell and me and others who find profoundly condescending and degrading the notion that blacks require a "special Olympics" of their own. Basically, we contend that there are cultural or behavioral differences between groups. These differences can be observed in everyday life, measured by the techniques of social science, and directly correlated with academic achievement and economic performance. Even "The Black-White Test Score Gap," a recent study by two noted liberal scholars, Christopher Jencks and Meredith Phillips, proves upon careful reading to implicitly endorse this cultural view. Jencks and Phillips make all the appropriate genuflections to racial pieties, but they are courageously seeking to make the cultural argument more palatable to liberals.

A few years ago, a Stanford sociologist named Sanford Dornbusch was puzzled at claims that Asian Americans do especially well in math because of some presumed genetic advantage in visual and spatial ability. Dornbusch did a comparative study of white, Hispanic, and Asian American students in San Francisco and concluded that there was a far more obvious reason for the superior performance of Asian Americans: they study harder. Asian Americans simply spend a lot more time doing homework than do their peers.

Of course, this sort of finding leaves unanswered the question of why they study harder. The causes are no doubt complex, but one important factor seems to be family structure. It is obvious that a two-parent family has more time and resources to invest in disciplining children and supervising their study than does a single-parent family. For Asian Americans, the illegitimacy rate in this country is approximately 2 percent. For African Americans, it is nearly 70 percent.

Such a huge difference cannot easily be corrected. Indeed, in a free society, public policy is limited in its ability to transform behavior in the private sphere. Still, while not reverting to the discredited liberal position, the cultural view of racial inequality is at least more hopeful than the bell-curve acceptance of ineradicable difference: We cannot change our genes, but we can change our behavior.

One thing is clear: Racism is no longer the main problem facing blacks or any other group in America. Even if racism were to disappear overnight, this would do nothing to improve black test scores, increase black entrepreneurship, strengthen black families, or reduce black-on-black crime. These problems have taken on a cultural existence of their own and need to be confronted on their own terms.

The difficult task of rebuilding the cultural capital of the black community, and the role of black scholars, black teachers, black parents, and black entrepreneurs is crucial. The rest of us cannot be leaders, but we can be cheerleaders. Rather than trying to rig the numbers to make everyone feel better, we are better off focusing our collective attention on developing the skills of young African Americans at an early age so that they can compete effectively with others in later life.

So why doesn't this obvious solution win broad support? In his recent book, *A Dream Deferred: The Second Betrayal of Black Freedom in America*, Shelby Steele argues that affirmative action is popular with black and white elites because it serves the purposes of both groups. White elites get to feel morally superior, thus recovering the ethical high ground lost by the sins of the past, and black elites enjoy unearned privileges that they understandably convince themselves they fully deserve. (In *The Shape of the River*, Bowen and Bok devote several chapters to proving the obvious point that blacks who go to Ivy League schools derive financial benefits in later life as a result and are generally satisfied with attending Yale instead of a community college.)

Steele's book bristles with the psychological insights that are his distinctive contribution to the race debate. White liberals, Steele argues (and he might as well be speaking directly to Bowen and Bok), are quite willing to assume general blame for a racist society causing black failures—so long as it is the careers of other people, all the qualified Asian American and white students rejected from Harvard and Princeton, that are sacrificed in order to confer benefits on blacks and win for liberals recognition as the white saviors of the black race.

What Steele is doing—and it has drawn considerable criticism from reviewers—is something that advocates of affirmative action have always done:

questioning the motives of the other side. For years, conservatives have treated liberals as well meaning in their goals though mistaken in their means. During that same period, liberals have treated conservatives as greedy, uncaring racists. By asking advocates of preferences what's in it for them, Steele unmasks the self-interest that frequently hides behind the banners of equality, diversity, and social uplift.

Steele's main objective is to show that neither the black nor the white elites have an interest in asking fundamental questions: Isn't color-blindness the only principle that is consistent with the fundamental principles of American society? Isn't equality of rights under the law the only workable basis for a multiracial society? Is the black community well served in the long term by a public policy that treats them as an inferior people, incapable of competing with others?

Advocates of racial preferences, "offer whites moral absolution for their sins and blacks concrete benefits that are hard to turn down," Steele observed to me a few weeks before the recent electoral victory of a referendum abolishing affirmative action in Washington state. "I think we are going to lose because our side has only one thing to offer, and that is moral principle." I ruefully agreed that the scales were tipped in precisely that way. Yet the astonishing triumph of the referendum in Washington by a comfortable majority—like the triumph of a similar measure two years ago in California—shows that we should not underestimate the power of moral principle in American politics.

When the issue is posed in the basic vocabulary of right and wrong—a lexicon that is utterly incomprehensible to Bowen and Bok—the tortured rationalizations of affirmative action advocates collapse and the commonsense moral instinct of the American people tends to prevail. There is no cause for conservatives to lose their nerve. The election in 2000 could be the moment when color-blindness is at last the issue on the ballot in many states and at the center of the Republican party's agenda.

16

On Race and History[*]

MANNING MARABLE

How do we cross the boundaries of race and ethnicity, class and gender, religion and language, to create an environment for pluralism, mutual respect, and civility? How can we go about deconstructing racism and other forms of bigotry, while empowering the oppressed? I will examine three interrelated themes: First, the continuing paradox and tension between diversity and democracy. In 1997, President Clinton created a national initiative to encourage a "conversation on race." What should that conversation have included? It should have talked about the process of "racialization," how the liabilities and barriers of race were imposed upon not only African Americans, but also other people of color. It should have examined the institutional processes of how people of color continue to be pushed to the periphery of society's resources and power. Second, I will highlight the contemporary social and economic consequences of racism. The statistical evidence I will present will help illustrate the destructive impact of race and inequality today. Third, I will explore the meaning of resistance—the cultural, political, and social strengths of the African American

---

[*]This was a keynote address given at the "Race in 21st Century America" conference. All citations can be found in the For Further Reading section of this volume.

community. Despite the odds against us, black people and other oppressed people of color have always been the makers of our own history. Finally, I will seed to discover which values and visions are required in order for us to transcend and transform the racial divide.

Let's note first that prejudice is never an accidental element within the makeup of a society. Hatred does not emerge in a social vacuum. Bigotry is not natural or inevitable within human beings. All white people, simply because they are born white, do not have to be racist. All males, just because they are born male, do not have to tolerate sexism, or sexual harassment of women on the job. Intolerance is a social consequence of how society is organized, and we cannot uproot bigotry unless we are also willing to examine seriously the economic and social environment that fosters and perpetuates social inequality and unfairness.

Fear is reproduced when people are taught that the "Other"—the Latino or black or undocumented immigrant—threatens to take their job. Fear hardens into hatred when politicians deliberately create racial scapegoats and homophobic stereotypes in order to win elections. When politicians deliberately play the so-called race card, or now the lesbian/gay card, they create the environment for hate groups and vigilante violence.

If the presidential initiative on race truly wanted to understand the contemporary dynamics of institutional racism, it should have gone first to the prisons and jails across this country, conversing with black, brown, and poor inmates. The criminal justice system today has become our chief means of regulating and controlling millions of unemployed and undereducated black and Latino young men. What lynching was in the South in the 1920s, the death penalty and life sentences without parole have become in the 1990s.

There are currently 1.8 million inmates in U.S. prisons and jails. In California alone, the number of prisoners, which stood at 19,000 two decades ago, now exceeds 150,000. Prison construction has become a multibillion-dollar business, as small towns compete for new prison sites. Since 1990, the number of prisons and jail guards nationwide has grown by 30 percent, to more than six hundred thousand. We are constructing more than one hundred new prison cells every single day in the United States.

The social and racial consequences of regulating the poor and minorities throughout the criminal justice apparatus are, to say the least, devastating. One recent study in Washington, D.C., found that one-half of all African American males between the ages of eighteen and thirty-five are, on any given day, under the control or direct supervision of the criminal justice system—either in prison or jail, on probation, on parole, or awaiting trial. Instead of investing in quality schools and vocational training, we construct new prisons. Instead of providing real jobs at living wages, we pass a crime bill that undermines civil liberties and greatly expands the possible use of the death penalty. A conversation about race must discuss the connections between poverty, joblessness, and crime. By stigmatizing nearly all young Latino and black men as a criminal class, we justify racist stereotypes and reinforce society's racial divide.

The central social dilemma in American history has been the effort to reconcile a vast spectrum of cultures, classes, and communities, groups classified or identified by gender, sexual orientation, and race, into a common political project called democracy. That uneven and often interrupted dialogue and debate has taken many forms: the abolitionist movement of the nineteenth century; the suffragist movement; the struggles for an eight-hour day and the right to organize collectively; the Second Reconstruction, the massive movement of nonviolence and civil disobedience led by Martin Luther King Jr.; the renaissance of the feminist movement in the 1960s and 1970s; the stonewall riot and the emergence of a gay and lesbian rights movement. These are only a few examples of movements that have begun with the category of "difference," as defined both by ourselves and by others, and from that site of identity and culture, have articulated a vision of what political society can and should be. At times, this dialogue has been civil and cordial, at other times, violent and unpredictable, when an exchange of perspectives and attitudes has completely broken down. The Los Angeles civil unrest in 1992, with the arrests of more than twenty-thousand people and the deconstruction of more than one billion dollars in property, represents the collapse of the democratic dialogue: instead of bridges of opportunity and mutual understanding across the boundaries of class and color, we witnessed a fault line cutting a deep chasm within the fabric of society, representing the alienation and anger among the oppressed.

What is our responsibility for creating frameworks for understanding the tensions and possibilities between diversity and democracy? Perhaps the place to begin is with Langston Hughes, the poet laureate of Harlem and black America, who constantly explored the love/hate relationship our people have felt toward American democracy:

> I, too, sing America.
> I am the darker brother.
> They send me to eat in the kitchen

When company comes.
But I laugh, and eat well
and grow strong.
Tomorrow
I'll be at the table
When company comes.
Nobody will dare say to me
'Eat in the kitchen' then.
Besides, they'll see how
beautiful I am, and be ashamed.
I, too, am America.

Hughes presents a powerful perspective on what the democratic project should be about.

It is not expressed in Jefferson's eloquent yet incomplete democratic arguments in the Declaration of Independence, or in Lincoln's Gettysburg Address. "Difference" in society is coded in any number of ways: by race and ethnicity, by gender and sexual orientation, by social class and income, by physical disability. The concept of difference seems to imply that some people are defined as the "norm" and that others occupy a space somewhere in the periphery. From this perspective, "overcoming difference" means forgetting about the real variations among human beings, trying to make those who are on the outside more acceptable, more "normal," like those of us on the inside. So, a generation ago, liberal educators praised their black students when they exhibited the same behaviors or spoke the same language as their white students. Dwelling upon differences between people or groups was certainly divisive. Race was something to be overcome, or at least ignored. If blacks, Latinos, and other people of color could only manage to blend themselves into the normal habits and customs of the mainstream within society and stop acting "differently," racial distinctions could disappear. Liberal educators viewed racism as a product of ignorance, rather than a logical social consequence of patterns of inequality and institutional discrimination.

The category of difference in itself, however, does not tell us much about why American society works the way it does. All Americans are, in certain respects, "different" from everyone else. Yet not all Americans have been routinely denied bank loans, or been refused accommodations in hotels, or had their houses of worship burned to the ground, just because they were "different." Difference has social significance only when it tells us how and why certain groups, for example, have been denied basic economic opportunities and political rights, while others have not. If we approach the study of diversity simply as an uncritical celebration of all cultures, we will not answer any of the questions that are at the heart of American democracy today.

The Institute for Research in African-American Studies at Columbia University, which I direct, is only six blocks away from the heart of Harlem, 125th Street. Every day, in our immediate neighborhood, I can see the destruction of an entire generation of our young people. In New York City, 45 percent of all African American youth dwell in poverty. In central Harlem, one out of eight households has no plumbing or toilet facilities. Every day in New York, an average of seventy thousand children, mostly Latino and black, use illegal drugs. Black and Hispanic youth unemployment exceeds 40 percent. The life expectancy of a black male in Central Harlem is forty-nine years of age.

There are many ways to measure the powerful reality of contemporary racism. For example, discrimination is rampant in capital markets. Banks continue policies of "red lining," denying loans in neighborhoods that are largely black and Hispanic. In New York City in 1992, according to a Federal Reserve Board study, for instance, blacks were turned down for mortgage applications by banks, savings and loans, and other financial institutions about twice as often as whites. Furthermore, even after years of affirmative action programs, blacks and Latinos remain grossly underrepresented in a wide number of professions. For example, African Americans and Hispanics represent 12.4 percent and 9.5 percent, respectively, of the U.S. adult population. Yet, of all American physicians, blacks account for barely 4.2 percent, and Latinos 5.2 percent. Among engineers, blacks represent 3.7 percent and Latinos 3.3 percent; among lawyers, blacks account for 3.3 percent and Latinos 3.1 percent; and for all university and college professors, blacks make up 5 percent and Latinos 2.9 percent. As Jesse Jackson observed in a speech before the National Press Club, while native-born white males comprise only 41 percent of the U.S. population, they are 80 percent of all tenured professors, 92 percent of the Forbes 400 chief executive officers, and 97 percent of all school superintendents.

If affirmative action should be criticized, it might be on the grounds that it did not go far enough in transforming the actual power relations between blacks and whites within U.S. society. More evidence for this is addressed in the 1995 book by sociologists Melvin Oliver and Thomas Shapiro, *Black Wealth/White Wealth*. Oliver and Shapiro point out that "the typical black family has eleven cents of wealth for every dollar owned by the typical white family." Even middle-class

African Americans, people who often have benefited from affirmative action, are significantly poorer than whites who earn identical incomes. If housing and vehicles owned are included in the definition of "net wealth," the median middle-class African American family has only $8,300 in total assets, to $56,000 for the comparable white family. Why are blacks at all income levels much poorer than whites in terms of wealth? African American families not only inherit much less wealth, they are impacted daily by institutional inequality and discrimination. They are still denied home mortgages at twice the rate of similarly qualified white applicants. African Americans also have been less likely to receive government-backed home loans.

Institutional racism is a daily fact of life for African Americans in the United States. Yet you'd never know it by reading Dinesh D'Souza's book, *The End of Racism*. He masquerades as an intellectual, and his book is nothing short of a diatribe of racial intolerance.

Take nearly any random quotation from D'Souza's *The End of Racism*, and you can find an incredible list of racist assertions. For example:

> D'Souza attacks African Americans for pushing for job training programs and employment for the poor: "It seems unrealistic, bordering on the surreal, to imagine underclass blacks, with their gold chains, limping walk, obscene language and arsenal of weapons doing 9-to-5 jobs at Procter and Gamble or the State Department."
>
> D'Souza calls for the repeal of the 1964 Civil Rights Act, and declares that it is "rational" for whites to discriminate against African Americans: "Perhaps discrimination exists because it is rational. It is efficient. It makes economic sense."
>
> D'Souza at one point writes: "The first dysfunctional aspect of black culture is racial paranoia—a reflexive tendency to blame racism for every failure. . . ." Other dysfunctions, he says, include black middle class "rage that threatens to erupt in an orgy of destruction or self-destruction . . . (and the) repudiation of standard English as an academic achievement."

It is no wonder that many intellectuals and public policy experts who espouse conservative, not just liberal, viewpoints have distanced themselves from this pseudoscholarship. When *The End of Racism* was published in 1995, two prominent black conservatives resigned from their positions at the American Enterprise Institute, to protest the center's connections with D'Souza. Mr. Robert L. Woodson, president of the National Center for Neighborhood Enterprise and a winner of the MacArthur Award, and Dr. Glen Loury, a professor at Boston University, held a press conference to denounce D'Souza. Woodson declared, "D'Souza is the Mark Fuhrman of public policy. He denigrates and paints with a single brush the culture of low-income black communities. He describes the culture of low-income black Americans as barbaric." Professor Loury stated that the book "violated the canons of civility." A year later, when D'Souza debated Professor Loury at Boston University, Loury described him as "a thirty-something journalist with no formal research training and a well-deserved reputation as a polemicist. Loury referred to D'Souza's book as "a worthless piece of trash" that was written with "reckless abandon."

For decades, conservative foundations and think tanks have funded researchers in order to influence national debates in public policy. The Adolph Coors Foundation, the Koch Family Foundations, the Lynde and Harry Bradley Foundation, and many others, have invested millions of dollars into an elaborate network of publishing houses, television and radio programs, think tanks, and university-based institutes. This was the group that financed the 1994 racist polemic *The Bell Curve*, by Richard Hernstein and Charles Murray, arguing that blacks were intellectually inferior. Right-wing foundations regularly finance a series of publications that reach millions of readers, including *The American Spectator*, *Commentary*, *The Public Interest*, and *The New Criterion*. According to a study published by People for the American Way, the radical right foundations have "bought themselves the infrastructure of a grassroots movement" whose first order of business has been "to produce materials that foster a climate of hostility to affirmative action, and even to racial minorities."

The Far Right has historically manipulated race as an ideological and cultural weapon to fragment democratic and popular movements in our society. White factory workers are fearful that they may lose their jobs to unemployed African American workers, as bosses use racism to drive down wages and bust unions. When white women encounter gender discrimination on the job, the so-called glass ceiling limiting their salaries and upward mobility, racism becomes a means to divide them on the issue of affirmative action. Race is used to mystify and obscure social reality, to preserve the underlying hierarchy of class power and privilege. Racism keeps millions of white Americans from recognizing and fighting for policies that are in their own material interests.

The vast majority of Americans who receive food stamps and other federal food subsidies are not black, Latino, or Asian American—they are white. The majority of Americans who have directly and personally benefited from affirmative action programs have not been Latino or black—they are white women. The majority of Americans who lack health insurance are white. The struggles for social justice—such as full employment, universal healthcare, and decent housing—are consciously and deliberately undermined by appeals to racial division.

Most Americans will tell you that practical, pragmatic politics is always defined by the "center." How many times have we been told that the effective battleground for determining the future of society is the great American mainstream? That to be a serious factor in politics, we need to work inside the corridors of power, not on the outside. That we need to tailor our political message to be acceptable to contented, complacent suburbanites, who drive RVs and watch cable TV. That by becoming a centrist, or even conservative, we avoid being marginalized, excluded, locked out, and isolated on the political periphery.

I passionately disagree. Fundamental political change in a democracy almost always comes from the boundaries of society, not from the center. Conscious, dedicated minorities, not the numerical majority, become catalysts for change. If you build a political movement to stand firmly on the middle ground, you may find that ground collapsing from under your feet.

How do we achieve democratic change within a society? We must, first, understand how that society actually works. Who gets ahead, and who doesn't? Who is rewarded, and who is punished? Usually, the people we should learn from are those not at the top of society, but at the bottom. Two centuries ago, if we had listened to Thomas Jefferson, we would have gained some important insights in understanding the contradictory relationship between democracy and slavery. Yet we would have had to listen to the slaves themselves, those who had felt the sting of the lash, and those who had been bartered and sold on the auction block, to really know the reality of slavery. We would have had to learn from black abolitionists such as Frederick Douglass, Sojourner Truth, Harriet Tubman, and Martin R. Delany. And yes, we would also have had to talk with Sally Hemmings.

Less than a century ago, women were denied the right to vote in this country. Generations of white male politicians justified and rationalized the exclusion of women. We would have had to listen to the early feminists and suffragists, such as Susan B. Anthony, Frances Ellen Watkins Harper, Ida B. Wells-Barnett, and Mary Church Terrell, to comprehend how sexism compromised the promise of democracy.

How do you achieve change in a democratic society? By recognizing that in a democracy, the majority can be wrong. Only a generation ago, racial segregation was legal in the United States. There were separate and unequal water fountains, public toilets, hotels, restaurants, and churches. Birmingham, Alabama's city council even passed a law making it illegal for blacks and whites to play checkers together! The overwhelming majority of good, middle-class whites in Birmingham supported their racist chief of police, Bull Connor, and their pro-segregationist governor, George C. Wallace. Yet they were wrong. Martin Luther King Jr. did not tell us to wait until the majority of Southern whites changed their minds about segregation. He did not counsel patience, or try to moderate his message of "Freedom Now" to read "Freedom Someday." Several years ago, Proposition 187, which proposed discriminatory policies against undocumented immigrants, mostly Latino people, was being debated in California. A majority of California's registered voters supported this initiative. We must not be afraid to say that the initiative was wrong. Amendment Two passed in Colorado several years ago. This amendment attempted to outlaw local measures protecting the civil rights of lesbians and gays--the same rights that other Americans take for granted. We should affirm our belief in equal justice for all by saying that the homophobic politics behind that measure were mean-spirited, discriminatory, and wrong. We should never be afraid to lose an electoral campaign when we are fighting to affirm democratic rights and equal justice for all.

In a curious way, the conservatives understand this far better than most liberals. You have to be true to your values, because your principles are at the heart of what politics should be. The ideologues of the Far Right, such as Bill Bennett and William Kristol, ground their politics in a set of values. Their only problem is that they've got the wrong set of values.

How do we achieve progressive change on issues of race, gender, sexuality, and class? By celebrating our passionate discontent with the way things are. Contented, satisfied people rarely want things to change too much. If you want to find out what new directions history is taking our society, don't wallow in the mainstream—stand at the edge, at the boundaries. Listen to the poets and the non-conventional music of young people. Learn from those who have little or nothing to lose. Understand the anxiety of the forty million Americans today who lack any medical insurance. Spend time working in a homeless shelter, or walking a picket line with trade unionists. To be passionately discontent is to want our democratic ideals and our egalitarian hopes to be realized in the world around us. It is to challenge conformity, to push the boundaries of "the way things are" to the "way things should be."

In 1854, my great-grandfather, Morris Marable, was sold at the age of nine on an auction block in West Point, Georgia. He was sold for the sum of $500 by the man who was both his owner and his biological father. His mother, who had been a household slave, stood at the side of the auction block, tears streaming down her face, as she witnessed her son being sold to a white man named Marable. The legend in my family is that my great-grandfather never saw his mother again.

It is not sufficient to tell the descendants of former slaves that we should simply forget the nightmare of the past. The national nightmare of slavery, the rape and sale of human beings, is a stain on the conscience of all Americans and cannot be easily obliterated. Dinesh D'Souza's polemics represent the road toward intellectual and moral bankruptcy. We must find the courage to come to terms with that history and with that racial legacy. In doing so, we begin the long journey toward healing and redeeming ourselves.

There is an urgent need for all of us to historicize the dynamics of oppression in the United States. We are all witnesses to each other's history. We cannot in good conscience say that historical responsibility ends when each successive generation disappears from the scene. When evil is generated, it has a life of its own, and it cannot be destroyed by forgetting or not learning the lessons of the past.

In the United States today, there is a direct connection between culture, representation, and power. Our society generally worships the symbols of authority and celebrates hierarchies. We applaud those who are wealthy and despise the poor. Individuals are all too often judged by their market value, rather than by their character as human beings. Our economy glorifies the production of commodities above the development of our young people. Our government deals with poverty by imprisoning the black, the brown, and the poor. The structures of power and privilege deny real opportunity to millions of people.

The great strength and power of the Black Freedom Movement in the United States has been its capacity to link politics with morality. In the "Letter from Birmingham Jail," Dr. Martin Luther King Jr. sharply confronted the hypocrisy and the contradictions of white liberals who professed their dedication to the principles of universal brotherhood and sisterhood, yet were unwilling to commit themselves publicly to the struggles against Jim Crow segregation. King argued that "shallow understanding from people of good will is more frustrating than absolute misunderstanding from the people of ill will. Lukewarm acceptance is much more bewildering than outright rejection." Martin was saying that morality is not separated from politics, that how we run the society should in some way conform with our notions of ethics for how we should treat others and be treated in return. Sometimes it is essential for people of conscience who truly believe in a just and humane society to take a public stand, challenging the institutional evils that we see all around us every day. As Dr. King declared, "I submit that an individual who breaks the law that conscience tells him is unjust and willingly accepts the penalty by staying in jail to arouse the conscience of the community over its injustice, is in reality expressing the very highest respect for the law."

The "Letter from the Birmingham Jail" envisions an America freed from bigotry and hunger, freed from the oppressive institutions of race hatred and social injustice. What we have fought for is a world without stereotypes and without the oppressive symbols that divide and destroy people. The fundamental challenge before us in the construction of a real democracy in America is in learning to listen to our mutual voices and histories, and finding the courage to take personal risks on behalf of those who are not at the centers of power or privilege.

In 1790, the U.S. Congress declared that only whites of European descent would be permitted to become U.S. citizens. African Americans did not legally become citizens of the United States until the passage of the Thirteenth, Fourteenth, and Fifteenth Amendments in the 1860s. Asians born outside the United States were not permitted to become citizens until 1952. People born in Bombay, India, coming to the United States in the early twentieth century were usually defined as "nonwhites" or "colored," not white. If Dinesh D'Souza had emigrated to the United States in 1948 instead of 1978, and had spent his first year here with a black family in Montgomery, Alabama, rather than with a host family in Arizona, he would have an entirely different perspective on the reality of racial oppression in America. I personally would have loved to have been there, to watch Dinesh D'Souza being forced to go to the back of the bus.

17

The FBI's Secret War against the Black Panther Party: A Case Study in State Repression

WARD CHURCHILL

The record of the FBI speaks for itself.
—J. Edgar Hoover, Introduction to *The FBI Story*, 1965

Beginning in August 1967, the Black Panther Party was savaged by a campaign of political repression that in terms of its sheer viciousness has few parallels in American history. Coordinated by the Federal Bureau of Investigation as part of its then-ongoing domestic *counterintelligence program* (COINTELPRO) and enlisting dozens of local police departments around the country, the assault left at least twenty-eight Panthers dead,[1] scores of others imprisoned after dubious convictions,[2] and hundreds more suffering permanent physical or psychological damage.[3] Simultaneously, the party was infiltrated at every level by agents provocateurs, all of them harnessed to the task of disrupting its internal functioning.[4] Completing the package was a torrent of "disinformation" planted in the media to discredit the Panthers before the public, both personally and organizationally, thus isolating them from potential support.[5]

Although an entity bearing its name would continue to exist in Oakland, California, for another decade, as would several offshoots situated elsewhere, the Black Panther Party in the sense that it was originally conceived was effectively destroyed by the end of 1971.[6] In this, it was hardly alone. During the 1960s, similar if usually less lethal campaigns were mounted against an array of dissident groups ranging from the Socialist Workers Party to the Student Nonviolent Coordinating Committee, from the Revolutionary Action Movement to Students for a Democratic Society, from the Republic of New Africa to the Southern Christian Leadership Conference. The list goes on and on, and the results were always more or less the same.[7]

The FBI's politically repressive activities did not commence during the 1960s, nor did they end with the formal termination of COINTELPRO on 28 April 1971.[8] On the contrary, such operations have been sustained for nearly a century, becoming ever more refined, comprehensive, and efficient. This in itself implies a marked degradation of whatever genuinely democratic possibilities once imbued "the American experiment," an effect amplified significantly by the fact that the bureau has consistently selected as targets those groups that, whatever their imperfections, have been most clearly committed to the realization of egalitarian ideals.[9] All things considered, to describe the resulting sociopolitical dynamic as "undemocratic" would be to fundamentally understate the case. The FBI is and has always been a frankly *anti*-democratic institution, as are the social, political, and economic elements it was created and maintained to protect.[10]

Predictably, the consequences of this protracted and systematic suppression of the democratic impulse in American life, and the equally methodical reinforcement of its opposite, have by now engulfed us. These will be apprehended not only in the ever greater concentration of wealth among increasingly narrow and corporatized sectors of society, but in the explosive growth of police and penal "services" over the past thirty years, the erosion of constitutional safeguards supposedly guaranteeing the basic rights of average citizens, and a veritable avalanche of regulatory encroachments reaching ever more deeply into the most intimate spheres of existence.[11] Again, the list of indicators could be extended to great length.

Such trends do not hearken the danger that, if they continue, the United States "may become" a police state. The United States has *been* a police state for some time now. Questions of how to prevent this from happening are at best irrelevant. The only real issue is what to do about it now that it's occurred. The answer, of course, is entirely dependent upon our ability to perceive the precise nature of the problem confronting us. Only thus can we hope to achieve the clarity of vision necessary to devise an adequate response and, from there, chart a truly alternative course into the future. Attainment of the necessary exactitude in assessing our current circumstances and options is itself contingent upon our achieving an accurate understanding of the historical processes that have led us to this pass. History, therefore, is in many ways paramount. Without it we can neither fix our present position nor hope to move forward.

There are, to be sure, a multiplicity of lenses through which we might fruit-fully examine the phenomena at hand. Few of them, however, offer the explana-tory power embodied in the experience of the Black Panther Party. It follows that this essay is intended to both summarize and contextualize the repression of the Panthers, probing the ugly history of their destruction in hopes of gleaning les-sons valuable to those who now strive to take up their mantle. Indeed, it should be viewed in that light, as a conscious effort to make some small contribution to continuing the Panthers' exemplary struggle for liberation.

A HISTORY OF REPRESSION

Despite its carefully contrived image as the country's premier crime-fighting agency, the FBI has always functioned primarily as a political police force.[12] Tracing its origins to the Pinkerton Detective Agency, a government-contracted private firm notorious during the late nineteenth century for its anti-labor brutalities and other service to Big Business, the Justice Department's newly formed Bureau of Investigation (BoI), as it was initially called, could hardly have been expected to conduct itself as anything else. Hence, although its original charter tasked the bureau merely with gathering evidence necessary to support a range of federal prosecutions, it was understood all-around that its real job would be something else again.[13]

The BoI's underlying agenda began to surface on 30 July 1916, when saboteurs blew up a munitions dump on Black Tom Island, in New York Harbor, contain-ing approximately two million pounds of high explosives earmarked to support the British war effort against Germany.[14] Congress reacted by passing the Sedition Act of 1917 and both the Alien and Espionage acts a year later.[15] The last of these statutes facilitated the bureau's formation of what eventually became its Counterintelligence Branch, a component within its overall Intelligence Division explicitly authorized to employ all manner of extralegal techniques in "neutraliz-ing" spies and other such agents of foreign powers.[16]

The Sedition and Alien acts, designed to constrain "subversion" by U.S. citizens and resident aliens, brought about other developments. In fact, an office had already been created within the bureau in 1917 to address the matter in a systematic fashion. Initially unnamed, it was designated the Anti-Radical Division in 1919, redesignated the General Intelligence Division (GID) in 1920, redesignated again during the 1940s as the Internal Security Section, in 1954 as the Internal Security Division, and finally during the 1960s as the Internal Security Branch.[17] Agents assigned to the GID were charged first and foremost with monitoring the activities of those professing the radical ideals of anarchism, socialism, communism, and syndicalism.[18]

Appointed to head up this new effort was a young former law clerk named J[ohn] Edgar Hoover. He was an astute choice. As efficient as he was reactionary, Hoover had by the fall of 1919 compiled dossiers on some 150,000 people. By mid-1921, the number had reached 450,000. Of these, extensive files had been created on approximately 60,000 persons considered to be "Key Agitators." The entire filing system was cross-indexed by locality and political affinity. As of 1920, about one-third of the bureau's headquarters support staff had been allotted to the GID, as well as half of all field agents.[19] Still dissatisfied with the resources available to him, Hoover enlisted local police Red Squads, private security firms like the Pinkertons, and "patriotic" organizations like the American Protective League (APL) and the American Legion to expand the flow of political intelligence.[20] Additionally, he began to develop an extensive network of informants within the radical groups themselves.[21]

Meanwhile, the GID was involved in much more than information gathering. In September 1917, it coordinated nationwide raids by local police and APL members on offices of the Industrial Workers of the World (IWW), an anarchosyndicalist union that stood at the time on the cutting edge of the American labor movement.[22] Although more than two hundred IWW leaders were convicted of "flagrant sedition"—mostly, they'd refused to register for the military draft and had tried to convince others to do the same—the real reason they were targeted was revealed in a Justice Department memo describing them as being involved in a "plot against industrial interests."[23] Virtually the entire leadership of the Socialist Party of America (SPA), which had polled nearly a million votes in the 1914 presidential race, were subjected to similar prosecutions at about the same time.[24]

The capstone of the GID's campaign against radicalism came when, having first whipped up a genuine "Red Scare" on the basis of an alleged anarchist bombing campaign carried out over preceding months, Hoover coordinated what are known as the "Palmer Raids."[25] The first of these, a twelve-city sweep carried out in November 1919, was aimed at alien anarchists. More than four thousand people were arrested, many badly beaten and their often meager possessions destroyed, all of them herded into temporary holding pens lacking adequate sanitation facilities, medical support, and in some cases even food and water. In December, although most of them had immigrated from other countries, an initial batch of 249 selected activists were summarily deported to the newly constituted Soviet Union.[26]

On 2 and 6 January 1920, it was the turn of the Communist and Communist Labor Parties, as "dragnet inquiries" were conducted against them in thirty-three cities.[27] Although neither organization had existed for more than four months, and they had therefore enjoyed little time in which to assemble a substantial membership, more than ten thousand people were arrested and held under conditions essentially the same as those evident after the November roundup. Before the process had run its course, another seven hundred people had been deported for no other reason than that they held political views deemed objectionable by the head of the GID.[28]

The Palmer Raids were a blow from which the anarchist movement in the United States has never recovered. For their part, the residues of the incipient communist parties were driven underground for years.[29] Coupled to the earlier onslaughts against the IWW and the SPA, the wave of deportations in 1919-20 served to thwart the possibility of a viable left-wing alternative in American politics for an entire generation. While much has been made by FBI apologists about the bureau's subsequent decade-long withdrawal from repressive operations, the fact is that under such circumstances it really needed to do no more than it did during those years.[30] For J. Edgar Hoover himself, the "Time of the Raids" also paid significant personal dividends. On 13 May 1924, the virtuosity of his service to the status quo resulted in his appointment as director of the entire BoI.[31] It was a job he would hold for the rest of his life.

On the Matter of Race

The depth of his antipathy toward political leftists was by no means Hoover's only ideological qualification for his new position. A middle-class Virginian born and raised, the intensity of his belief in white supremacism dovetailed quite well with the need of U.S. elites to maintain African Americans in a perpetually subordinate economic position.[32] From this perspective, *any* sort of activity that might disturb the rigid race/class hierarchy of American life constituted a "threat" and was subject to targeting by the bureau. There are a number of examples that could be used to illustrate this point, beginning with the BoI's criminalization of world heavyweight boxing champion Jack Johnson in 1910,[33] but the best is probably that of Marcus Garvey, head of the United Negro Improvement Association (UNIA).

Although the Jamaica-born Garvey might at one time have qualified as a "radical"—Hoover described him as such, and as "the most prominent Negro agitator in the world"—the sorts of programs he advocated during the 1920s were not especially different from those currently espoused by the right wing of the Republican Party.[34] Under his leadership, UNIA, which to this day remains the largest organization of African Americans ever assembled, devoted itself mainly to the realization of various "bootstrapping" strategies (i.e., undertaking business ventures as a means of attaining its twin goals of black pride and self-sufficiency). Nonetheless, despite UNIA's explicitly capitalist orientation, or maybe because of it, Hoover launched a GID inquiry into Garvey's activities in August 1919.[35]

When this initial probe revealed no illegalities, Hoover, describing any such outcome as "unfortunate" and railing against Garvey's "pro-Negroism," ordered that the investigation not only be continued but intensified.[36] UNIA was quickly infiltrated by operatives recruited specifically for the purpose, and a number of informants developed within it.[37] Still, it was another two years before the GID was able to find a pretext—Garvey's technical violation of the laws governing offerings of corporate stock—upon which to bring charges of "mail fraud." Convicted in July 1923 by an all-white jury, the UNIA leader was first incarcerated in the federal maximum-security prison at Atlanta, then deported as an undesirable alien in 1927. By then, the organization he'd founded had disintegrated.[38]

Hoover, in the interim, had vowed to prevent anyone from ever again assuming the standing of what he called a "Negro Moses."[39] More than forty years later, he was repeating the same refrain, secretly instructing his COINTELPRO operatives to "prevent the rise of a 'messiah' who could unify and electrify . . . a well-concerted movement" of African Americans to improve their socioeconomic and political situations. In 1968, his concern was expressed with regard to Martin Luther King Jr., Elija Muhammed, and Stokely Carmichael, but along the way an untold number of others—Chandler Owen, for example, and A. Philip Randolph—had been subjected to the attentions of the FBI simply because they were deemed "defiantly assertive [about] the Negro's fitness for self-governance."[40]

Bureau agents investigated all black-owned newspapers, recruited paid black informants, and tapped the telephones and bugged the offices of racial advancement groups ranging from the procommunist National Negro Congress to the anticommunist NAACP. Investigative fallout included a mail cover on Rev. Archibald J. Carey Jr.'s, Woodlawn African Methodist Episcopal Church in

Chicago, where the Congress of Racial Equality had an office; a file check on Olympic track and field champion Jesse Owens (an agent compared the date of Owens's marriage with the birthday of his first child); and the transmittal of derogatory information on the NAACP and the National Urban League to prospective financial contributors.[41]

In effect, Hoover was committed to "the repression of any black dissident who challenged second-class citizenship," irrespective of that person's ideological posture or the mode by which his or her politics were manifested.[42] In this he sometimes displayed a surprising if unintended degree of public candor, at one point actually going so far as to insist that investigation of black activists was justified insofar as their collective threats of "retaliatory measures in connection with lynching" represented a challenge to "the established rule of law and order."[43] In private, he was often even more forthright, employing crude racial epithets such as "burrhead" when referring to Martin Luther King and others.[44]

It is almost impossible to overpersonalize the FBI's focus and conduct from 1924 to 1972 in terms of Hoover's own outlooks and attitudes. Absolutely dictatorial in managerial style, he involved himself directly in the hiring of new agents until well into the 1960s, mainly to ensure that they shared his biases. Those inclined to disagree either never made it into the bureau, were transferred to dead-end positions in remote backwaters, or found themselves abruptly fired. Hence, as he built his monolith from 441 agents at the outset to 4,886 in 1944, and to nearly 8,000 at the time of his death, Hoover was able to wield it ever more efficiently as an instrument with which to work his will.[45]

The more important point, however, is that Hoover enjoyed such power because he was allowed to by those who exercised powers far greater than his own. He could, in other words, have been removed at any moment during his long and sordid career, had the workings of his will not ultimately reflected the desires of America's elites. Moreover, it is important to recall that, notwithstanding the litany of "excesses, improprieties and outright illegalities" for which he would be posthumously condemned,[46] J. Edgar Hoover was until the very end, among "respectable" whites at least, one of the most popular public officials in American history.[47]

COINTELPRO

The initial COINTELPRO, aimed at the Communist Party, U.S.A., was ordered on 28 August 1956. Although this was the first instance in which the Internal Security

Branch was instructed to employ the full range of extralegal techniques developed by the bureau's counterintelligence specialists against a domestic target in a centrally coordinated and programmatic way, the FBI had resumed such operations against the Communist Party (CP) and to a lesser extent the Socialist Workers Party (SWP) on a more ad hoc basis at least as early as 1941.[48] Instructively, Hoover began at the same time to include a section on "Negro Organizations" in reports otherwise dedicated to "Communist Organizations" and "Axis Fifth Columnists."[49]

Both surveillance of and counterintelligence directed against "subversives" had become standard FBI procedure by the end of World War II, and were increasingly regularized and refined during the ensuing spy cases and show trials attending the "Second Red Scare" of 1946-54.[50] In this, the bureau was helped along immensely by passage of the Smith Act, a statute making "sedition" a peacetime as well as a wartime offense, in 1940. This was followed, in 1950, by the McCarran Internal Security Act, requiring all members of the CP and other designated groups to register with a federal "Subversive Activities Control Board" and authorizing their roundup and mass internment in the event of an insurrection or war with the Soviet Union. In 1954, there was also the Communist Control Act, a statute outlawing the CP and prohibiting its members from holding certain types of employment.[51]

Viewed against this backdrop, it has become a commonplace that, however misguided, COINTELPRO-CPUSA, as the 1956 initiative was captioned, was in some ways well intended, undertaken out of a genuine concern that the CP was engaged in spying for the Soviet Union. Declassified FBI documents, however, reveal quite the opposite. While espionage and sabotage "potentials" are mentioned almost as afterthoughts in the predicating memoranda, unabashedly political motives take center stage. The objective of the COINTELPRO was, as Internal Security Branch chief Alan Belmont put it at the time, to block the CP's "penetration of specific channels of American life where public opinion is molded," and to prevent thereby its attaining "influence over the masses."[52]

Expanded in March 1960, and again in October 1963 to include non–party members considered sympathetic to the CP, the COINTELPRO served as a sort of laboratory in which the bureau's communications, logistics, and internal procedures were worked out and agents perfected the skills necessary to conducting a quietly comprehensive program of domestic repression.[53] From the outset, considerable emphasis was placed on intensifying the bureau's longstanding campaign to promote factional disputes within the party. To this end, the CP was infiltrated more heavily than ever before—it has been estimated that by 1965 approximately one-third of the CP's nominal membership consisted of FBI infiltrators and paid informants—while bona fide activists were systematically "bad-jacketed" (that is, set up by infiltrators to make it appear that they themselves were government operatives).[54] A formal "Mass Media Program" was also created, "wherein derogatory information on prominent radicals was leaked to the news media."[55]

Still more ominously, beginning in 1966, an effort dubbed "Operation Hoodwink" was begun in which undercover agents were used to convince the leadership of New York's five Mafia families that CP organizing activities on the city's waterfront constituted a threat to the profits deriving from their union racketeering, smuggling, and related enterprises. Although it never materialized, the intended result was the murder of key organizers by the mob's contract killers.[56] Thus, under COINTELPRO, not only the methods but the objectives of operations directed against U.S. citizens were rendered indistinguishable from those involving foreign agents. All pretense that those targeted possessed constitutional or even human rights was simply abandoned. As one anonymous but veteran COINTELPRO operative reflected in 1974, "You don't measure success in this area by apprehensions, but in terms of neutralization."[57]

Meanwhile, on 4 August 1960, a second COINTELPRO was unleashed to "disrupt the activities of organizations . . . seeking independence for Puerto Rico."[58] On 12 October 1961, a third "disruption program" was launched against the SWP.[59] This was followed, on 2 September 1964, by "a hard-hitting, closely supervised, coordinated counterintelligence program to expose, disrupt and otherwise neutralize the Ku Klux Klan (KKK) and specified other [white] hate groups."[60] On 23 April 1965, Hoover ordered the beginnings of what would become, in May 1968, COINTELPRO–New Left, an operation intended to destroy the effectiveness of predominately white leftist organizations like Students for a Democratic Society and the Student Mobilization to End the War in Vietnam.[61]

Then, on 25 August 1967, twenty-three field offices were instructed to commence another "hard-hitting and imaginative program," this one "to expose, disrupt, misdirect, discredit, or otherwise neutralize the activities of [civil rights and black liberation organizations], their leadership, spokesmen, membership, and supporters."[62] On 4 March 1968, " COINTELPRO-Black Nationalist Hate Groups," was expanded to include all forty-one FBI field offices.[63] Specifically targeted were the Southern Christian Leadership Conference (SCLC), the Student Nonviolent Coordinating Committee (SNCC), the Philadelphia-based Revolutionary Action Movement (RAM) and the Nation of Islam (NoI).[65] As has been noted, SCLC's Martin Luther King Jr., SNCC's Stokely Carmichael, and NoI head Elija

Muhammed were targeted by name. Scores, perhaps hundreds, of individuals were shortly added to the various lists of those selected for personal "neutralization," as were organizations like the Republic of New Africa (RNA) and Los Angeles–centered United Slaves (US).[66]

During the spate of post-Watergate congressional hearings on domestic intelligence operations, the FBI eventually acknowledged having conducted 2,218 separate COINTELPRO actions from mid-1956 through mid-1971.[67] These, the bureau conceded, were undertaken in conjunction with other significant illegalities: 2,305 warrantless telephone taps, 697 buggings, and the opening of 57,846 pieces of mail.[68] This itemization, although an indicator of the magnitude and extent of FBI criminality, was far from complete. The counterintelligence campaign against the Puerto Rican independence movement was not mentioned at all, while whole categories of operational techniques—assassinations, for example, and obtaining false convictions against key activists—were not divulged with respect to the rest. There is solid evidence that other sorts of illegality were downplayed as well.[69]

All of this, supposedly, occurred without the knowledge of anyone outside the FBI. The fact is, however, that high government officials were repeatedly informed, beginning with identical letters written by Hoover on 8 May 1958 to Attorney General William Rogers and Robert Cutler, Special Assistant to President Dwight D. Eisenhower, advising them that the bureau had initiated a program "designed to promote disruption within the ranks of the Communist Party." This was followed on 8 November with Hoover's personal briefing of Eisenhower's entire cabinet on the nature of COINTELPRO-CPSUA.[70] On 10 January 1961, another set of identical letters was dispatched, this time notifying Attorney General-designate Robert F. Kennedy, Deputy Attorney General–designate Byron White, and Secretary of State–designate Dean Rusk of what he called "our counterattack on the CPUSA."[71] The FBI director also conducted personal briefings on "special projects" for Attorneys General Nicholas Katzenbach (1965), Ramsey Clark (1967), and John Mitchell (1969), as well as for Marvin Johnson, an aide to President Lyndon Johnson (1965).[72]

It is true that Hoover was less than detailed in these and other reports. It is equally true, however, that he was never asked to provide further information. His superiors were told enough to know that there was much more to be learned about the FBI's domestic counterintelligence program. Indeed, they were sufficiently apprised to know that it smacked of political policing in its most illegitimate form. That none of them ever inquired further is indicative only of their mutual desire to retain a veneer of "plausible deniability" against their own potential incrimination if the program were ever to be exposed.[73] Furthermore, since none of them elected to avoid jeopardy by simply ordering a halt to such operations, we can assume only that they viewed COINTELPRO as a useful and acceptable expedient to maintaining the status quo.

COINTELPRO-BPP

The late 1960s were a period of unparalleled flux in the twentieth-century United States. In the process of losing a major neocolonial war in Southeast Asia, and faced with a rising tide of guerrilla insurgencies throughout the Third World, U.S. elites were beset by a substantial lack of consensus about how best to restore global order. Simultaneously, they were confronted with the emergence of a highly dynamic "New Left" opposition, not only on the home front but also in western Europe.[74] By May of 1968, they had witnessed the near overthrow of the Gaullist government in France, and a huge student movement was offering something of the same prospect in West Germany. Even within the Soviet Bloc, a massive anti-authoritarian revolt had challenged prevailing structures in Czechoslovakia, further threatening the balance of cold war business as usual.[75]

Within the United States itself, the liberal, equalitarian civil rights movement of the early 1960s had been transcended in mid-decade by a far more demanding movement for the attainment of "Black Power."[76] By 1967, this had evolved into an effort to secure the outright liberation of African Americans from what was quite accurately described as "the system of internal colonial oppression." These shifts were marked by an increasing willingness on the part of black activists to engage in armed self-defense against the various forms of state repression and to develop a capacity to pursue the liberatory struggle by force, if necessary. Shortly, groups emerging within other communities of color—the Puerto Rican Young Lords Organization (YLO), for example, as well as the Chicano Brown Berets and the American Indian Movement (AIM)—had entered into more or less the same trajectory.[77]

A fresh generation of white radicals had simultaneously developed their own movement and, for a while, their own agenda. Students for a Democratic Society (SDS), probably the preeminent organization of Euroamerican new leftists in the United States during the 1960s, had been founded early in the decade to pursue visions of "participatory democracy" among the poor and disenfranchised.[78] With the 1965 buildup of U.S. troop strength in Vietnam, however, it adopted an increasingly pronounced anti-imperialist outlook. By mid-1968, SDS could claim eighty thousand members and was in the process of birthing an armed compo-nent of its own.[79] A year later, in combination with a broad array of other activist groups, it was able to bring approximately one million people to the streets of Washington, D.C., to protest the war in Southeast Asia. Even combat veterans showed up in force.[80]

Added to this potentially volatile stew was a burgeoning "counterculture" com-posed primarily of white youth, including a not insignificant segment drawn from the country's more privileged circles. Not especially politicized in a conventional sense, they nonetheless manifested a marked disinclination to participate in the functioning of American society as they encountered it, and were to some extent seriously engaged in attempting to fashion an "alternative lifestyle" predicated in the professed values of peace, love, and cooperation.[81] All told, from elite and dis-sident perspectives alike, the appearance was that America was on the verge of "coming apart at the seams."[82]

For a number of reasons, in 1967 it began to appear as if the Black Panther Party, a smallish but rapidly growing organization founded by Huey P. Newton and Bobby Seale in Oakland a year earlier,[83] might hold the key to forging a relatively unified movement from the New Left's many disparate elements. In part, this was because of the centrality the black liberation struggle already occupied in the radi-cal American consciousness.[84] In part, it was likely because the Panthers, almost alone among organizations of color, had from the outset advanced a concrete pro-gram and were pursuing it with considerable discipline.[85] It was also undoubtedly due in no small measure to the obvious courage with which they'd faced off against the armed forces of the state, a matter personified by Party Defense Minister Newton's dubious conviction in the killing of a white cop, and the skill with which Minister of Information Eldridge Cleaver was able to publicize it.[86]

In any event, "by 1968-69 the Panthers were considered by many to be the exemplary revolutionary organization in the country and the one most explicitly identified with anti-imperialism and internationalism."[87] As such, the party had become far and away "the most influential" such group in the United States, an assessment confirmed by J. Edgar Hoover, when, in September 1969, he publicly declared the Panthers to be "the greatest threat to the internal security of the coun-try."[88] Meanwhile, on 25 November 1968, he had ordered the initiation of "imagi-native and hard-hitting [counter]intelligence measures designed to cripple the BPP," and, on 30 January 1969, a considerable expansion and intensification of the effort to "destroy what the BPP stands for."[89]

Hoover's agents obliged. Although every dissident group in the United States was targeted by COINTELPRO during the late 1960s, the Black Panther Party was sledgehammered. Of the 295 counterintelligence operations the bureau has admitted conducting against black activists and organizations during the period, a staggering 233, the majority of them in 1969, were aimed at the Panthers.[90] And this was by no means all. "Counterintelligence was far more pervasive than the readily available record indicates," one researcher has observed. "It is impossible to say how many COINTELPRO actions the FBI implemented against the Panthers and other targets simply by counting the incidents listed in the COINTELPRO-Black Hate Group file. The bureau recorded COINTELPRO-type actions in thousands of other files."[91]

Several of the operations targeting other African American organizations—SNCC, for example—were explicitly designed to impair the Panthers' ability to develop coalitions.[92] The same can be said with respect to approximately half the 290 COINTELPRO actions recorded as having been carried out against SDS and other white New Left organizations from May 1968 through May 1971, and at least some of those conducted against Latino groups like the Young Lords and the Brown Berets served the same purpose.[93] There were also myriad operations to neutralize specific individuals, and another host that have never been admitted at all.[94] What party founder Huey P. Newton aptly described as the "war against the Panthers" entailed every known variant of counterintelligence activity on the part of the FBI and collaborating police departments, and thus constitutes a sort of textbook model of political repression.[95]

[Using a variety of sources, including governmental staff reports and hearings, in 400 footnotes, Churchill delineates in chilling detail the actions of the FBI in misrepresenting and curtailing the activities of the Black Panther Party. These concerted efforts consisted of two fronts: one aimed at the party itself and the other at its supporters and allies. The techniques used against its supporters were various: a media offensive designed to block the black community's support, the silencing of the BPP's own newspaper, and the disruption of their social programs in the community. To prevent BPP alliances, the FBI infiltrated and disrupted other radical organizations, such as SNCC, and smeared those who would speak in favor of the Panthers, including 'Friends of the Panthers.' The techniques used against the party itself were more sinister. By infiltrating the BPP and spreading false information, FBI operatives were able to exacerbate intergroup tensions. The most serious actions by far were the many raids and pretext arrests directed against BPP members and chapters, and the malicious prosecutions of key activists nationwide, culminating in outright assassinations of its leaders. Although these activities were clustered for the most part between 1967 and 1973, the aftershocks continued into the next decades. —*Eds.*]

The War at Home Continues

In retrospect, it seems both fair and accurate to observe that the Black Panther Party never had a chance. Both the relative inexperience of its leadership and the obvious youthfulness of the great majority of its members served to prevent the party from offering anything resembling a mature response to the situation it confronted. The scale and intensity of the repression to which it was subjected, moreover, especially when taken in combination with the sheer speed with which the onslaught materialized and the manner in which it was not only sustained but intensified from 1968 to 1971, make it quite doubtful that even the most seasoned group of activists would have done better.

"Given the level of sophistication, unlimited man-power and resources available" to the FBI and its local police collaborators, it should come as no surprise that the Panthers were destroyed. Instead, as imprisoned party member Herman Bell has observed, we should find it "remarkable . . . that the Party lasted as long as it did."[96] Furthermore, as former New York Panther leader Dhoruba Bin Wahad has pointed out, "What's most amazing is how much was accomplished in so short a time. The growth of the Party, its programs and resiliency, the support it was able to command from the community, all that was put together in just two years, really. Had it not been for COINTELPRO, one can readily imagine what might have been achieved."[97]

Both Bell and Bin Wahad believe there are important lessons to be learned from the experience of the BPP. One of the most important of these must be that, despite the highly publicized conclusions of the Church Committee and other official bodies during the mid-1970s that COINTELPRO was an inherently criminal enterprise,[98] and despite a raft of more localized findings over the years that the criminality at issue extended even to murder, not one cop or agent has spent so much as a minute of time in prison as a result. The fact is that although two of the only four FBI men ever charged with COINTELPRO-related offenses were convicted in 1980, they were pardoned by President Ronald Reagan before setting foot inside a cell.[99]

With all due sanctimony, Reagan intoned that the pardons were necessary and appropriate because the early 1980s were "a time to put all this behind us" and begin a "long overdue process of national healing and reconciliation."[100] Such remarkably forgiving views toward official perpetrators of COINTELPRO-era offenses did not, of course, extend to their victims. Former Panthers like Bin Wahad and Geronimo ji Jaga (Pratt), continued to languish in prison without so much as a sidelong glance from the president, no matter *how* blatantly fraudulent the charges that landed them there.

Nor does the fact that the convictions of Bin Wahad and ji Jaga were eventually overturned prove the old saw that "in the end, whatever its deficiencies, the system works." To quote ji Jaga,

> If the system worked the way they'd have you believe, I'd never have gone to prison in the first place, much less spent 27 years there. Dhoruba wouldn't have gone to prison for nineteen years. [David] Rice and [Ed] Poindexter would not still be sitting in prison out in Nebraska, and Mumia [Abu Jamal] wouldn't be on death row. If the system worked the way they say it does, the agents and the cops and the prosecutors who perjured themselves and fabricated evidence when they framed us would themselves be in prison, right alongside those who murdered Fred Hampton, Mark Clark, and Bunchy Carter. And those things didn't happen, did they?[101]

To the contrary, many of those involved in making COINTELPRO a "success" tangibly benefited by their activities. A prime example is that of Richard Wallace Held, arguably the agent most responsible for fabricating the case against ji Jaga himself.[102] So valuable to the FBI were his peculiar skills that, in 1975, he was detached from his slot in Los Angeles and sent to South Dakota, where he assisted in assembling an equally fraudulent case against American Indian Movement leader Leonard Peltier.[103] Then, in 1981, while still relatively junior, he was promoted to the position of Special Agent in Charge (SAC), San Juan. In this role, he presided over a plethora of legally dubious operations against the Puerto Rican independence movement, including a series of island-wide raids conducted on 30 August 1985.[104] For this coup he was rewarded again, this time by being promoted to the more prestigious position of SAC, San Francisco. There, his major achievement appears to have been the attempted neutralization by car bombing of Earth First! activists Judi Bari and Darryl Cherney on 24 May 1990.[105]

Still more to the point is the fact that the Reagan administration's response to the idea that FBI officials might be held to some extent accountable for their more egregious violations of civil and human rights was simply to legalize much of what had been deemed criminal about COINTELPRO only a few years earlier.[106] This was undertaken through a series of congressional hearings designed to demonstrate the need for the bureau to "combat terrorism," including the "flexibility" to neutralize "organizations and individuals that cannot be shown to be controlled by a foreign power, and have not yet committed a terrorist act but which nonetheless may represent a substantial threat . . . to the security of our country."[107]

Although legislation affording specific statutory authorization for the bureau to engage in COINTELPRO-style activities has accrued piecemeal during the years since 1985, and is still in some respects being formulated, Reagan cut to the chase on 4 December 1981 by signing Executive Order 12333, for the first time openly authorizing the CIA to conduct domestic counterintelligence operations.[108] On 7 May 1983, Attorney General William French Smith confirmed the obvious by announcing a new set of FBI guidelines allowing agents to resume full-scale "investigative activity" vis-à-vis any individual or organization they wished to designate, on whatever basis, as "advocat[ing] criminal activity or indicat[ing] an apparent intent to engage in crime."[109]

One clear indication of what this meant will be found in the so-called CISPES terrorism investigation of the late 1980s, during which the FBI used the pretext that the Committee in Solidarity with the People of El Salvador maintained relationships with several Latin American guerrilla organizations to surveille, infiltrate, and disrupt not only the CISPES itself, but hundreds of other dissident groups in the United States.[110] Determining the true extent of this sustained and altogether COINTELPRO-like operation has proven impossible, given Reagan's Executive Order 12356 of 9 April 1983, greatly expanding the authority of U.S. intelligence agencies to withhold on grounds of "National Security" documents they would otherwise have been legally required to divulge under the Freedom of Information Act.[111]

At the local level, the proportionate deployment of police, both in terms of personnel and as measured by the budget allocations necessary to acquire more sophisticated weaponry, computerization, and the like, has swelled by approximately 500 percent since 1970.[112] Simultaneously, there has been a distinct militarization of law enforcement, a matter evidenced most readily in the proliferation of SWAT units across the country. First created by the LAPD for purposes of assaulting Panther offices in 1969, by 1990 "every police department worth its salary had a SWAT team, a special weapons and tactics squad. Every one."[113]

Since 1980, the entire apparatus has been increasingly tied together under a national command structure.[114] In large part, this was accomplished by the Federal Emergency Management Agency (FEMA), headed during the early Reagan years by California-based counterinsurgency specialist Louis O. Giuffrida. This corresponded with consolidation of the FBI database, inaugurated by J. Edgar Hoover during World War I and expanded steadily thereafter, in a form including files on virtually *every* American citizen. During Giuffrida's tenure, FEMA ran a series of exercises—dubbed "Proud Saber/Rex 82," "Rex 84/Nighttrain," and so on—testing the procedures through which rapid deployments of federal, state, and local police could be integrated with those of the national guard, military, and selected civilian organizations in times of civil unrest.[115] All told, such "scenarios" resemble nothing so much as a refined and expanded version of the BoI/police/APL amalgam evident from 1917 through 1920.

Although there have been several major exceptions—the Philadelphia police bombing of MOVE headquarters in 1985, for example, as well as the CISPES investigation and operations against several right-wing organizations—the still-evolving U.S. police/intelligence/military complex does not appear to have been devoted extensively to the business of direct political repression.[116] Rather, its purpose to date seems primarily to have been to intensify the condition of pacification to which oppressed communities, especially communities of color, had been reduced by COINTELPRO by the early 1970s.

Most prominently, this has taken the form of a so-called War on Drugs, declared by the Reagan administration during the mid-1980s and continued by both Republican and Democratic successors through the present date.[117] Leaving aside the facts that U.S. intelligence agencies have been heavily involved in the importation of heroin and cocaine since at least as far back as the late 1960s—and that if the government were really averse to narcotics distribution in the inner cities, the FBI would have assisted rather than destroyed the BPP's antidrug programs and attempts to politicize street gangs like the Black P. Stone Nation in Chicago—the "war" has been used as a pretext by which to criminalize virtually the entire male population of young African Americans and Latinos.[118]

The United States had by 1990 imprisoned a greater proportion of its population than any country on the planet. One in three men of color between the ages of eighteen and twenty-five is, has been, or will shortly be incarcerated, a rate making an American black four times as likely to do prison time as was his South African counterpart during the height of apartheid.[119] Physically, the U.S. penal system has expanded by more than 300 percent since 1969 to absorb this vast influx of "fresh meat," an expense that, like spiraling police appropriations, has been underwritten with tax dollars once allocated to education and social services. Even at that, the construction of private prisons has become one of the fastest growing sectors of the U.S. economy, while the approximately two million prisoners have themselves been increasingly integrated into the system as a ready source of veritable slave labor fueling transnational corporate profits. In states like Alabama and Arizona, the 1990s have even witnessed the reappearance of 1930s-style chain gangs.[120]

While the "crime of black imprisonment" has reached epidemic proportions, the situation of the Afroamerican community has, according to every statistical indicator, steadily deteriorated.[121] By the early 1980s, the repression of the black liberation movement could already be correlated to a decline in living standards to a level below that evident in 1959, a trend that has since been continued without interruption.[122] In many ways, such circumstances can be tied not only to resurgent racism but to the increasing marginalization of the American workforce as a whole, a matter associated more with the station of genuine world dominance presently enjoyed by the United States, and the consequent policies of economic globalization pursued by its corporate elites, than with domestic policies per se.[123]

A Legacy of Lessons

In sum, the conditions of poor and racially oppressed people in the United States today are objectively worse than those that gave rise to the Black Panther Party and affiliated groups a third of a century ago. It requires no great leap of intellect or understanding to appreciate that it was the destruction of the BPP and its allies that allowed this degenerative process of socioeconomic decay to set in, or that the best and perhaps only antidote resides in a reconstitution of something very Panther-like in its essence. By this, I mean an organization or movement that is truly multinational/multiracial in both orientation and composition, committed to the attainment of practical self-determination on the part of the subjugated, and willing to defend its achievements by *every* necessary means.

For much too long, the history of the party has been the preserve of poseurs and opportunists, deployed mainly as a "moral lesson" on why the ideals of liberation are inherently "unrealistic," the consequences of serious struggle toward such goals much too severe to be undertaken by "reasonable" people. The latter, such purveyors of "political pragmatism" habitually insist, are devoted exclusively to modes of activism centering in a "nonviolent" and an at best incrementally "progressive" vision, rather than one of revolutionary transformation, their strategies devoted exclusively to situational "renegotiations of the social contract" through such state-sanctioned tactical expedients as voting, lobbying, and litigation, boycotts and more symbolic protest.[124]

Nowhere in such "alternative" prescriptions is there a place for development of the popular capacity to physically confront, much less defeat, the increasingly vast repressive apparatus with which the status quo has elected to defend itself against precisely the sorts of meaningful socioeconomic and political change progressivism purports to pursue. Indeed, anyone suggesting that such concepts as armed self-defense are both useful and appropriate tools within the present context is automatically, and usually vituperatively, consigned ipso facto to the realm of "counterproductivity."[125]

It is high time such postulations were interrogated, challenged, and discarded. The legacy of the Panthers must be mined not for its supposed negative lessons but for the positive values, ideals, and analyses which propelled the BPP so rapidly to a position of prominence, and which lent its members their astonishing valor and tenacity. To excavate the understandings embodied in the party's programmatic successes, no matter how abbreviated the interval in which these were evident, is to reclaim the potentials that attended them. Such a project is worthy if for no other reason than that nobody, of *any* oppositional orientation, has been able to equal the party's record and appeal in the post-Panther context.

Only in this way, moreover, can we arrive at a proper apprehension of the party's theoretical/organizational defects, to appreciate and correct them in their own terms, and thus avoid replication of the emic contradictions that beset the BPP in its original form. For instance, such investigations should offer insights as to how groups might best retain internal discipline without being afflicted with the sort of despotism and stratification exemplified by Huey Newton's "personality cult."[126] Other questions demanding clarification concern the proportionate blend of lumpen and nonlumpen members best suited to organizational functioning under particular circumstances;[127] the most appropriate balance to be drawn between overt service/survival programs and often covert armed components; the manner and extent to which these should be rendered interactive; and the relative degree of emphasis and pace of development most productively accorded to each under given conditions or phases of struggle.[128]

In many ways the most important lesson to be gleaned from the Panther experience has to do with the nature of the enemy with which all domestic oppositionists, regardless of the ideological and other distinctions that divide us, are mutually faced. No elite willing to assemble an apparatus of repression comparable to that evident in the United States, or to wield it with the savagery evident in the Panther example, displays the least likelihood of being susceptible to the powers of logic, moral suasion, or other such nonviolent manifestations of popular will. On the contrary, to the extent that these approaches might at some point demonstrate a capacity to compel fundamental alterations in the bedrock of social order, they will be suppressed with essentially the same systematic and sustained resort to lethal force that was once visited upon the BPP.[129]

Those committed to achieving fundamental change rather than cosmetic tweakings of the existing system are thus left with no viable alternative but to include the realities of state violence as an integral part of our political calculus[130] We are in a war, whether we wish to be or not, the only question before us being how to go about winning it. Here too, the legacy bequeathed by the Black Panther Party provides invaluable lessons. By studying the techniques with which the counterinsurgency war against the party was waged, we can, collectively, begin to devise the ways and means by which to counter them, offsetting and eventually neutralizing their effectiveness.[131]

The current prospects for liberatory struggle in the United States are exceedingly harsh, even more than was the case a generation ago. Far harsher, however, is the prospect that the presently ascendant system of elite predation might be allowed to perpetuate itself indefinitely into the future, exploiting and oppressing the preponderance of the population in the midst of every moment along the way. We owe it to ourselves to abolish the predators, here and now, or as rapidly as possible, enduring whatever short-run sacrifice is required to get the job done, reaping the longer term rewards of our success. We owe it to those who sacrificed before us to fulfill the destiny they embraced. Most of all, we owe it to our coming generations to free them from that against which we must struggle. Thankfully, the fallen warriors of the Black Panther Party have left us many tools with which we may at last complete their task.

NOTES

1. "Evidence and Intimidation of Fascist Crimes by U.S.A.," *The Black Panther*, 21 February 1970.

2. See, generally, Akinyele Omowale Umoja, "Set Our Warriors Free: The Legacy of the Black Panther Party and Political Prisoners," in *The Black Panther Party Reconsidered*, ed. Charles E. Jones (Baltimore: Black Classics Press, 1998), 417–42.

3. Safiya Bukhari-Alston, "We Too Are Veterans: Post-Traumatic Stress Disorders and the Black Panther Party," *The Black Panther*, February 1991.

4. Citizens Research and Investigation Committee and Louis Tackwood, *The Glass House Tapes: The Story of an Agent Provocateur and the New Police-Intelligence Complex* (New York: Avon Books, 1973); Jo Durden-Smith, *Who Killed George Jackson? Fantasies, Paranoia and the Revolution* (New York: Alfred A. Knopf, 1976).

5. William Kunstler, "Writers of the Purple Rage," *The Nation*, no. 227, 30 December 1978.

6. Ollie A. Johnson, "Explaining the Demise of the Black Panther Party: The Role of Internal Factors," in *The Black Panther Party Reconsidered*, ed. Jones, 391–414.

7. See generally, Ward Churchill and Jim Vander Wall, *The COINTELPRO Papers: Documents from the FBI's Secret Wars against Dissent in the United States* (Boston: South End Press, 1990).

8. U.S. Senate, Select Committee to Study Government Operations with Respect to Intelligence Activities, *Hearings on Intelligence Activities, Vol. 6: The Federal Bureau of Investigation*, 94th Cong., 1st Sess. (Washington, D.C.: GPO, 1995), 30, 605.

9. Robert Justin Goldstein, *Political Repression in Modern America, 1870 to the Present* (Cambridge/New York: Two Continents/Schenkman, 1978).

10. Isaac Balbus, *The Dialectic of Legal Repression* (New York: Russell Sage Foundation, 1973).

11. Diane Gordon, *The Justice Juggernaut: Fighting Street Crime, Controlling Citizens* (New Brunswick, N.J.: Rutgers University Press, 1990); Elihu Rosenblatt, ed., *Criminal Injustice: Confronting the Prison Crisis* (Boston: South End Press, 1996).

12. On creation of the bureau's "gang-busters" mythology, see Richard Gid Powers, *G-Men: Hoover's FBI in Popular Culture* (Carbondale: Southern Illinois University Press, 1983).

13. Attorney General George Wickersham, 1910 Report to Congress; quoted in Sanford J. Ungar, *FBI: An Uncensored Look Behind the Walls* (Boston: Little, Brown, 1975), 40.

14. Jules Witcover, *Sabotage at Black Tom: Imperial Germany's Secret War in America, 1914–1917* (Chapel Hill, N.C.: Algonquin Books, 1989).

15. Thomas I. Emerson, *The System of Free Expression* (New York: Random House, 1970), 101–10.

16. Ungar, *FBI*, 96–118.

17. Curt Gentry, *J. Edgar Hoover: The Man and the Secrets* (New York: W.W. Norton, 1991), 79, 212–13; Athan Theoharis, *Spying on Americans: Political Surveillance from Hoover to the Huston Plan* (Philadelphia: Temple University Head, 1978), 55.

18. William Preston Jr., *Aliens and Dissenters: Federal Suppression of Radicals, 1903–1933* (New York: Harper & Row, 1963), 63–87.

19. Gentry, *Hoover*, 79.

20. Ungar, *FBI*, 42. On the Red Squads during this era, see Frank Donner, *Protectors of Privilege: Red Squads and Police Repression in Urban America* (Berkeley: University of California Press, 1990), 7–43.

21. American Civil Liberties Union, *The Nation-Wide Spy System Centering in the Department of Justice* (New York: ACLU, 1924).

22. Melvin Dubkosky, *We Shall Be All: A History of the IWW* (Chicago: Quadrangle, 1969), 398–422; Gentry, *Hoover*, 71–72.

23. Quoted in William R. Corson, *The Armies of Ignorance: The Rise of the American Intelligence Empire* (New York: HarperColophon, 1980), 363.

24. Robert K. Murray, *Red Scare: A Study in National Hysteria, 1919–1920* (New York: McGraw-Hill, 1964), 18–26.

25. Fred J. Cook, *The FBI Nobody Knows* (New York: Macmillan, 1964), 89–90.

26. Richard Gid Powers, *Secrecy and Power: The Life of J. Edgar Hoover* (New York: Macmillan, 1987), 78, 86–88.

27. Preston, *Aliens and Dissenters*, 220–21.

28. Gentry, *Hoover*, 93–94; Murray, *Red Scare*, 218.

29. Theodore Draper, *The Roots of American Communism* (New York: Viking Press, 1957), 197.

30. "When the rabble was quiet, the violence abated"; Robert Wiebe, *The Search for Order* (New York: Hill & Wang, 1967), 290.

31. Cook, *FBI Nobody Knows*, 127–37.

32. Powers, *Secrecy and Power*, 5–35.

33. Cook, *FBI Nobody Knows*, 57.

34. Robert A. Hill, "The Foremost Radical of his Race: Marcus Garvey and the Red Scare, 1918–1920," *Prologue* 16 (winter 1984); Robert A. Hill and Barbara Blair, eds., *Marcus Garvey: Life and Lessons* (Berkeley: University of California Press, 1987).

35. Emory J. Tolbert, "Federal Surveillance of Marcus Garvey and the UNIA," *Journal of Ethnic Studies* 14, no. 4 (1987): 27.

36. Hoover's 11 October 1919 memo summarizing the results of the first investigation, and recommending that it be continued, is reproduced in Churchill and Vander Wall, *COINTELPRO Papers*, 12.

37. Tolbert, "Federal Surveillance," 27–31; informant report is reproduced in Churchill and Vander Wall, *COINTELPRO Papers*, 13. Also see Theodore Kornweibel Jr., *Seeing Red: Federal Campaigns against Black Militancy, 1919–1925* (Bloomington: Indiana University Press, 1998), 19–35.

38. Ted Vincent, *Black Power and the Garvey Movement* (Oakland, Calif.: Nizga, 1987), 203.

39. Quoted in Hill, "Foremost Radical," 229.

40. The first quote is taken from an Airtel dated 4 March 1968 and addressed from Hoover to

all Field Offices; reproduced in Churchill and Vander Wall, *COINTELPRO Papers*, 108–11 (quote at p. 110). The rest will be found in U.S. Department of Justice, *Investigation Activities of the Department of Justice*, S. Doc. 153, 66th Cong., 1st Sess. (Washington, D.C.: GPO, 1919), 162–63, 187.

41. Kenneth O'Reilly, *"Racial Matters": The FBI's Secret Files on Black America, 1960–1972* (New York: Free Press, 1989), 19.

42. Ibid., 14.

43. The statement, which appears in U.S. Department of Justice, *Investigative Activities*, 163, was made in 1919, a year in which seventy-six documented lynchings of African Americans occurred.

44. Quoted in David Garrow, *The FBI and Martin Luther King, Jr.: From "Solo" to Memphis* (New York: Penguin, 1981), 160.

45. Powers, *Secrecy and Power*, 150, 255; Ungar, *FBI*, 325.

46. Gentry, *Hoover*, 725–46.

47. Powers, *G-Men*,, 284–85.

48. Theoharis, *Spying*, 136; U.S. Senate, Select Committee to Study Government Operations with Respect to Intelligence Activities, *Final Report: Intelligence Activities and the Rights of Americans, Book II*, 94th Cong., 2d Sess. (Washington, D.C.: GPO, 1975), 66.

49. O'Reilly, *"Racial Matters,"* 18.

50. David Caute, *The Great Fear: The Anti-Communist Purge under Truman and Eisenhower* (New York: Simon and Schuster, 1978).

51. Michael Belknap, *Cold War Political Justice: The Smith Act, the Communist Party, and American Civil Liberties* (Westport, Conn.: Greenwood Press, 1977); William Tanner and Robert Griffith, "Legislative Politics and 'McCarthyism': The Internal Security Act of 1950," in *The Specter: Original Essays on the Cold War and the Origins of McCarthyism*, ed. Robert Griffith and Athan Theoharis (New York: New Viewpoints, 1974), 174–89.

52. Quoted in Theoharis, *Spying*, 136.

53. Ibid. I say COINTELPRO-CPUSA served as a "laboratory" because the party was known by the bureau to be essentially moribund before the program was initiated; see William C. Sullivan with Bill Brown, *The Bureau: My Thirty Years in Hoover's FBI* (New York: W.W. Norton, 1975), 266.

54. U.S. Senate, *Hearings on Intelligence Activities*,, 821–26.

55. Ibid., 88–89, 170–72, 186–88, 486–94, 535–38, 766–84.

56. Memos concerning Operation Hoodwink are reproduced in Churchill and Vander Wall, *COINTELPRO Papers*, 42, 44–45.

57. Quoted in Ungar, *FBI*, 120.

58. Memo, Hoover to San Juan and New York field offices, 4 August 1960; reproduced in

Churchill and Vander Wall, *COINTELPRO Papers*, 68. Also see "COINTELPRO en Puerto Rico," *Pensamiento Critico*, summer 1979.

59. Hoover's memo initiating the operation is reproduced in Cathy Perkus, ed., *COINTELPRO: The FBI's Secret War on Political Freedom* (New York: Monad Press, 1975), 19.

60. The appearance is that while the bureau was genuinely committed to destroying the Klan's autonomy, this was done mainly for purposes of using it more efficiently as an asset in simultaneous counterintelligence operations against the civil rights movement; Sullivan with Brown, *The Bureau*, 126–33; Theoharis, *Spying*, 141–45.

61. U.S. Senate, Select Committee to Study Government Operations with Respect to Intelligence Operations, *Supplementary Detailed Staff Reports on Intelligence Operations and the Rights of Americans*, Book III, 94th Cong., 2d. Sess. (Washington, D.C.: GPO, 1976), 23–27, 475–83.

62. As with other COINTELPROs, this one was lodged under William C. Sullivan's Domestic Intelligence Division (Division Five). More specifically, it was administered by Sullivan's head of Racial Intelligence, George C. Moore. Moore placed Theron D. Rushing in charge of coordinating the counterintelligence initiative itself; U.S. Senate, *Hearings on Intelligence Activities*, 383–85; U.S. Senate, *Staff Reports*, 20–21.

63. U.S. Senate, *Hearings on Intelligence Activities*, 386–92.

64. Ward Churchill and Jim Vander Wall, *Agents of Repression: The FBI's Secret Wars against the Black Panther Party and the American Indian Movement* (Boston: South End Press, 1988), 45–47.

65. A 22 January 1969 memo in which Hoover appears to credit the bureau with the assassination of Malcolm X is reproduced in Churchill and Vander Wall, *COINTELPRO Papers*, 102. Also see Clayborne Carson, *Malcolm X: The FBI File* (New York: Carroll and Graf, 1991); George Breitman, Herman Porter, and Baxter Smith, *The Assassination of Malcolm X*, 2d ed. (New York: Pathfinder, 1991).

66. Garrow, *FBI and Martin Luther King*; Sullivan with Brown, *The Bureau*, 133; O'Reilly, *"Racial Matters,"* 366; Imari Abubakari Obadele, *Free the Land! The True Story of the RNA in Mississippi* (Washington, D.C.: House of Songhay, 1984); Maulana Karenga, *Roots of the US/Panther Conflict* (San Diego: Kawaida, 1976).

67. U.S. Senate, *Hearings on Intelligence Activities*, 601.

68. U.S. Senate, *Intelligence Activities and the Rights of Americans*,, 301, 632.

69. The FBI admitted, for example, that it engaged in a total of 238 "surreptitious entries"—i.e., burglaries—against fourteen targets between 1942 and 1966 for purposes of gathering political intelligence. In truth, restricting the time frame to just the years 1952 through 1957, there had been more than five hundred such "black bag jobs" conducted in Chicago alone; M. Wesley Swearingen, *FBI Secrets: An Agent's Exposé* (Boston: South End Press, 1995), 165.

70. U.S. Senate, *Intelligence Activities and the Rights of Americans*, 281–82; U.S. Senate, *Hearings on*

Intelligence Activities, 819–20; U.S. Senate, Staff Reports, 62–64.

71. U.S. Senate, Hearings on Intelligence Activities, 821–26.

72. Theoharis, Spying, 142.

73. Former Attorneys General Katzenbach and Clark, for example, testified before the Senate Select Committee on 3 December 1975, that they had either never seen or not understood Hoover's memoranda briefing them on "COINTELPRO–White Hate Groups"; U.S. Senate, Hearings on Intelligence Activities, 202, 206–7, 213–18, 221, 224, 231–35, 240–47, 513–27.

74. John Gerassi, ed., The Coming of the New International: A Revolutionary Anthology (New York: World, 1971); Paul Joseph, Cracks in the Empire: State Politics in the Vietnam War (Boston: South End Press, 1981); Carl Oglesby, ed., The New Left Reader (New York: Grove Press, 1969).

75. George Katsiaficas, The Imagination of the New Left: A Global Analysis of 1968 (Boston: South End Press, 1987).

76. Stokely Carmichael and Charles V. Hamilton, Black Power: The Politics of Liberation in America (New York: Vintage, 1967).

77. Barbara Joye, "Young Lords," in The Movement Toward a New America: The Beginnings of a Long Revolution, ed. Marshall Goodman (Philadelphia/New York: Pilgrim Press/Alfred A. Knopf, 1970), 238–41; Carlos Muñoz Jr., Youth, Identity, Power: The Chicano Movement (New York: Verso, 1989); Paul Chaat Smith and Robert Allen Warrior, Like a Hurricane: The American Indian Movement from Alcatraz to Wounded Knee (New York: New Press, 1996).

78. James Miller, "Democracy Is in the Streets": From Port Huron to the Siege of Chicago (New York: Simon & Schuster, 1987).

79. Ron Jacobs, The Way the Wind Blew: A History of the Weather Underground (London: Verso, 1997).

80. Nancy Zaroulis and Gerald Sullivan, Who Spoke Up? American Protest against the War in Vietnam, 1963–1975 (Garden City, N.Y.: Doubleday, 1984), 263–73.

81. Theodore Roszak, The Making of a Counterculture: Reflections on the Technological Society and Its Youthful Opposition (New York: Doubleday, 1969). On efforts to politicize this disenchanted mass, see Abbie Hoffman, Revolution for the Hell of It (New York: Dial, 1968); Abbie Hoffman, Woodstock Nation: A Talk Rock Album (New York: Vintage, 1969).

82. William L. O'Neill, Coming Apart: An Informal History of America in the 1960s (Chicago: Quadrangle, 1971).

83. On the founding of the Black Panther Party for Self-Defense, as it was originally called, see Huey P. Newton, Revolutionary Suicide (1972; reprint, New York: Readers and Writers, 1995), 110–13.

84. Nikhil Pal Singh, "The Black Panthers and the 'Undeveloped Country' of the Left," in The Black Panthers Reconsidered, ed. Jones, 57–108.

85. Bobby Seale, "The Panther Program," in Seize the Time: The Story of the Black Panther Party and Huey P. Newton (New York: Random House, 1970), 59–68. For emulations by other groups

see, e.g., "Young Lords Party 13 Point Program and Platform," in *The Black Panthers Speak*, ed. Philip S. Foner (Philadelphia: J.B. Lippencott, 1970), 235–37.

86. Gene Marine, *The Black Panthers* (New York: New American Library, 1969); Edward M. Keating, *Free Huey! The True Story of the Trial of Huey P. Newton for Murder* (Berkeley, Calif.: Ramparts Press, 1971).

87. Singh, "Undeveloped Country," 64.

88. U.S. Senate, *Intelligence Activities and the Rights of Americans*, 187.

89. U.S. Senate, *Staff Reports*, 528–31.

90. Ibid., 188.

91. O'Reilly, "Racial Matters," 291.

92. Clayborne Carson, *In Struggle: SNCC and the Black Awakening of the 1960s* (Cambridge, Mass.: Harvard University Press, 1981), 284.

93. Goldstein, *Political Repression*, 451–52; U.S. Senate, *Staff Reports*, 214–15.

94. According to retired FBI agent Arthur Murtagh, many of the worst COINTELPRO actions were never recorded in writing; U.S. Senate, *Hearings on Intelligence Activities*, 1044.

95. Huey P. Newton, *War against the Panthers: A Study of Repression in America* (New York: Harlem River Press, 1996).

96. Herman Bell, "The BPP and Political Prisoners," *The Black Panther*, February 1991, p. 11.

97. Quoted from Chris Bratton's and Annie Goldson's excellent documentary film, *Framing the Panthers in Black and White: Dhoruba Bin Wahad, the Black Panther Party and the FBI's Counterintelligence Program* (New York: Pressa, 1990).

98. For the best overview of these findings, see Morton Halperin, Jerry Berman, Robert Borosage and Christine Marwick, *The Lawless State: The Crimes of U.S. Intelligence Agencies* (New York: Penguin, 1976).

99. Nicholas Horrock, "Gray and Two Ex-FBI Aides Indicted in Conspiracy in Search for Radicals," *New York Times*, 11 April 1978; Tony Poveda, *Lawlessness and Reform: The FBI in Transition* (Pacific Grove, Calif.: Brooks/Cole, 1990), 83.

100. Eve Pell, *The Big Chill* (Boston: Beacon Press), 193–94.

101. Interview with Geronimo ji Jaga, People's International Tribunal for Justice for Mumia Abu-Jamal, Philadelphia, 6 December 1997 (tape on file).

102. This assessment of the weight carried by Held in the Pratt case is based on interviews with appeals attorney Stuart Hanlon (San Francisco, April 1987) and former agent M. Wesley Swearingen, who worked in the Los Angeles COINTELPRO Section during the crucial period (Santa Fe, N.M., October 1994).

103. Documents demonstrating Held's involvement in the Peltier case are reproduced in Churchill and Vander Wall, *Agents of Repression*, 268, 269.

104. Augusto Delgado, "La invasión del viernes 30," *Claridad*, 12 September 1985; Candida Cotto,

"Madrugada del 30 augusto," *Claridad*, 12 September 1985; Juan Mari Bras, "El escirro Richard Held," *Claridad*, 13 September 1985; Manuelo Coss, "Delicuente al servicio del FBI," *Claridad*, 20 September 1985.

105. In 1993, Held retired from the FBI. He now serves as head of security for the Visa Corp.; Ward Churchill, "The FBI Targets Judi Bari: A Case Study in Domestic Counterinsurgency," *Covert Action Quarterly*, no. 47 (winter 1993–94); also see Ward Churchill, "COINTELPRO as a Family Business: The Strange Case of the FBI's Two Richard Helds," *Z Magazine*, March 1989.

106. In the wake of the Felt/Miller convictions, the FBI Agents Association, an exceedingly potent lobby, went to work to ensure that none of its members would again be subject to prosecution for comparable criminal activity; Donald Kessler, *The FBI* (New York: Pocket Books, 1993), 344.

107. Senator Jeremiah Denton, 25 March 1983; quoted in Pell, *Big Chill*, 194.

108. Pell, *Big Chill*, 200. Also see "The Executive Order," *Covert ActionInformation Bulletin* 16 (March 1982). The CIA had, of course, been involved in such activities for a considerable period; "CIA Reportedly Recruited Blacks for Surveillance of Panthers," *New York Times*, 17 March 1978; Newton, *War against the Panthers*, 90–92, 106–7; Winston A. Grady-Willis, "The Black Panther Party: State Repression and Political Prisoners," in *Black Panther Party Reconsidered*, 369.

109. Quoted in Pell, *Big Chill*, 201.

110. See, generally, Ross Gelbspan, *Break-ins, Death Threats and the FBI: The Covert War against the Central America Movement* (Boston: South End Press, 1991).

111. Pell, *Big Chill*, 60, 204.

112. See, generally, Craig Uchida and David Weisburg, eds., *Police Innovation and Control of the Police* (New York: Springer-Verlag, 1993).

113. Dhoruba bin Wahad, "War Within," in *Still Black, Still Strong: Survivors of the U.S. War against Black Revolutionaries*, ed. Jim Fletcher, Tanaquil Jones, and Sylvère Lotringer (New York: Semiotext(e), 1993), 49–50. Also see Michael Dewar, *Weapons and Equipment of Counter-Terrorism* (London: Arms and Armour Press, London, 1988); Ward Churchill, "To Serve and Protect? The Social Context of Michael Dewar's *Weapons and Equipment of Counter-Terrorism*," *New Studies on th Left* 14, nos. 1–2 (1989).

114. The decision to create a fully national counterintelligence/counterinsurgency apparatus, and to coordinate it with comparable establishments in several other countries (notably West Germany and Great Britain), can be dated from an international "counterterrorism" conference hosted by the FBI in San Juan, Puerto Rico, from 28 August–1 September 1978; "Secret Counter-Insurgency Conference Held in Puerto Rico," *SI: Research Papers*, October 1982, on file with author.

115. Diana Reynolds, "FEMA and the NSC: The Rise of the National Security State," *Covert ActionInformation Bulletin* 33 (1990).

116. On right-wing organizations, see, e.g., James Corcoran, *Bitter Harvest: Gordon Kahl and the Posse Comitatus Murder in the Heartland* (New York: Viking, 1990); Jess Walter, *Every Knee Shall Bow: The Truth and Tragedy of Ruby Ridge and the Randy Weaver Family* (New York: ReganBooks, 1995); Daniel P. Stern, *A Force upon the Plain: The American Militia Movement and the Politics of Hate* (New York: Simon and Schuster, 1996).

117. The dating is a bit nebulous, but is most commonly dated from Reagan's 1986 signing of a National Security Directive expanding the role of U.S. military forces ostensibly combating drug suppliers in Latin America. Actually, the preliminaries had commenced as early as 1982; Elaine Shannon, *Desperadoes: Latin Drug Lords, U.S. Lawmen, and the War America Can't Win* (New York: Viking, 1988), 85, 362.

118. See, e.g., Alfred W. McCoy, *The Politics of Heroin: CIA Complicity in the Global Drug Trade* (Chicago: Lawrence Hill, 1991); Peter Dale Scott and Jonathan Marshall, *Cocaine Politics: Drugs, Armies, and the CIA in Central America* (Berkeley: University of California Press, 1991); Clarence Lusane, *Pipe Dreams: Racism and the War on Drugs* (Boston: South End Press, 1991). Also see Sam Meddis, "Drug arrest rate is higher for blacks," *USA Today*, 20 December 1989.

119. Marc Mauer, "Americans behind Bars: Comparative Rates of Incarceration," in *Cages of Steel: The Politics of Imprisonment in the United States*, ed. Ward Churchill and J. J. Vander Wall (Washington, D.C.: Maisonneuve Press, 1992), 25–26. Also see James Austin and Aaron M. Davis, *The Impact of the War on Drugs* (San Francisco: National Council on Crime and Delinquency, 1989).

120. See Daniel Burton-Rose, Dan Pens, and Paul Wright, eds., *The Celling of America: An Inside Look at the Prison Industry* (Monroe, Maine: Common Courage Press, 1998).

121. The phrase is not a new one. See Steve Whitman, "The Crime of Black Imprisonment," *Chicago Tribune*, 28 May 1967.

122. Martin Carnoy, *Faded Dreams: The Politics and Economics of Race in America* (Cambridge, U.K.: Cambridge University Press, 1994).

123. See, e.g., Catherine Caufield, *Masters of Illusion: The World Bank and the Poverty of Nations* (New York: Henry Holt, 1996); William Greider, *One World, Ready or Not: The Manic Logic of Global Capitalism* (New York: Simon and Schuster, 1997).

124. Contributions to this "discourse" over the past thirty years have been legion. The linchpin of contemporary articulation will probably be found, however, in Gene Sharp's *Social Power and Political Freedom* (Boston: Porter Sargent, 1980). Also see Sharp's three-volume *Politics of Nonviolent Action* (Boston: Porter Sargent, 1973).

125. For critique, see Ward Churchill with Mike Ryan, *Pacifism as Pathology: Observations on the Role of Armed Struggle in North America* (Winnipeg: Arbiter Ring, 1998).

126. Ollie Johnson discusses this and related issues in "Demise." Probably most constructively, he brings perspectives offered by the late C. W. Cassinelli to bear on the BPP's "Newton cult" phenomenon; C. W. Cassinelli, "The Law of Oligarchy," *American Political Science Review* 47 (1953). Of related interest is the "elite theory" expounded by Robert Michels in his *Political Parties: A Sociological Study of the Oligarchical Tendencies of Modern Democracy* (New York: Free Press, 1962).

127. Based in part upon his interpretation of and effort to adapt the work of Frantz Fanon to the U.S. context, Huey Newton had from the outset taken recruitment of the criminalized black inner city underclass as a high priority for the Party; see, e.g., the chapter entitled "The Brothers on the Block," in Newton's *Revolutionary Suicide*, pp. 75–78. Eldridge Cleaver then subjected the idea to a considerable honing and development, most explicitly in his essay, "On Lumpen Ideology," *Black Scholar* 3 (1972). Other especially useful readings in this connection include David G. Epstein's "A Revolutionary Lumpen Proletariat?" *Monthly Review*, December 1969; Clarence J. Mumford's "The Fallacy of Lumpen Ideology, *Black Scholar* 4 (1973); Kathleen Cleaver's *On the Vanguard Role of the Black Urban Lumpen Proletariat* (London: Grass/Roots, 1975), and Chris Booker's "Lumpenization: A Critical Error of the Black Panther Party," in Black Panther Party Reconsidered, 337–62. .

128. A superb recent analysis of these matters is offered by Dhoruba Bin Wahad in his "Toward Rethinking Self-Defense in a Racist Culture: Black Survival in a United States in Transition," in *Still Black/Still Strong*, ed. Fletcher, Jones and Lotringer, 57–76. Also see Clarence Lusane, "To Fight for the People: The Black Panther Party and Black Politics in the 1990s," in *The Black Panther Party Reconsidered*, ed. Jones, 443–63.

129. As is readily evident in Robert Justin Goldstein's monumental study, *Political Repression in Modern America*, the same sorts of violently repressive techniques have been employed to a greater or lesser extent against every potentially effective movement in the United States for more than a century, irrespective of the targets' adherence to nonviolent principles.

130. See, e.g., the argument developed by Joy James in *Resisting State Violence: Radicalism, Gender and Race in U.S. Culture* (Minneapolis: University of Minnesota Press, 1996).

131. The segment entitled "Prospects for the Future" in Brian Glick's *War at Home: Covert Action Against U.S. Activists and What We Can Do About It* (Boston: South End Press, 1989), while grossly inadequate, represents a start in this regard.

18

The Treaty of Guadalupe Hidalgo and *Dred Scott v. Sandford:* "Aren't They All Illegal Anyway?"

GUADALUPE T. LUNA

"Go Back to Mexico!"
—Former Congressman Dornan, *Las Vegas Review-Journal*, 1996, B11.

INTRODUCTION

This essay considers the impact of immigration law and policy on domestic race relations, with a specific focus on case law impacting Chicanas/os and African Americans. Immigration law speaks volumes about race relations and presents a "deeply complicated, often volatile, relationship . . . between racism directed toward citizens and that aimed at noncitizens."[1] Chicanas/os, since the conquest of the former Mexican territories in 1848, and African Americans, since their forced arrival to the United States, continue to confront challenges calling into question their citizenship status. Charismatic politicians, for example, have ordered Chicanas/os to go back to Mexico, and in a number of instances, moreover, both groups have been discouraged from entering public spaces without proof of citizenship. The effect of restrictive immigration law thus demonstrates that people of color undergo disparate treatment. The fact of disallowing the use and enjoyment of citizenship status given to the dominant population provides a tool with which to advance studies of race for the twenty-first century. Within this construct two points surface.

The first considers the Treaty of Guadalupe Hidalgo, an international peace agreement negotiated between the United States and Mexico in 1848, following the conquest of the former Mexican territories.[2] The treaty created a legal relationship with those of Mexican descent.[3] Both before and after the conquest of the former Mexican Republic, United States officials declared that even without the treaty, the "blessings of American law" would protect Mexicanas/os and their property interests.[4] The evidence, however, shows that the United States violated this legal relationship—with consequences leading into the contemporary period.

The second focus considers the *Dred Scott v. Sandford* decision where Mr. Scott sought his freedom from slavery and recognition as a citizen before the U.S. Supreme Court. The Court, however, rejected Mr. Scott's petition, and through the Court's interpretation of the United States Constitution and of the purported purpose of its founding framers, denied him citizenship status. The decision is considered one of the "most important . . . in the history of the Supreme Court of the United States,"[5] and for this reason, becomes a valuable and essential tool for examining the status of people of color within the hegemony of mainstream law.

Part I presents an alternative theoretical construct identified as Latina/o Critical Race (LatCrit) theory and demonstrates the exclusion of Chicanas/os within the culture of Anglo-American law.[6] This section further addresses challenges to Chicana/o citizenship status. Part II examines the *Dred Scott* decision. Both strands of law present an alternative lens with which to examine the intersection of race and law.

Given the nature of unequal treatment, collaborations for transforming marginalized communities facing the arbitrary whims of charismatic politicians, are long overdue.[7] Thus, the goal of this essay is to offer an alternative means by which to study domestic race relations. The commonalities between race and immigration law and challenges to citizenship status provide excellent opportunities for such collaborations, if we wish to thwart immigration and legal structures disallowing the full membership of both communities.

I. A Theoretical Construct: LatCrit Theory and Linkages

The intent here is not to collapse the social, racial, and historical legal experience of Chicanas/os and African Americans into one false norm.[8] Left to the realm of traditional law, both of these groups are rendered invisible in the interplay between legal structures and subordinated communities. Because the linkages connecting the consequences of unequal treatment under Anglo-American law are obscured, it remains difficult to clearly exhibit the similarity in impact of the law on these two groups. Yet, a painful legacy of lynchings, segregation, poverty, and generations of unequal treatment, extending into the contemporary period, is shared by Chicanas/os and African Americans. We require newer theoretical models in studying race, class, gender, and other identities if we wish to promote the enjoyment of "nothing less than the right to have rights" equal to those of the dominant population. LatCrit theory is one such form of study in law.

This theory presents an alternative method that can increase efforts toward joining marginalized communities and promote coalition building. As we progress toward a more sophisticated examination of race, LatCrit theory advocates placing our communities at the center of academic investigations and linking theory with praxis. As a relatively new enterprise, LatCrit promotes anti-subordination by unpacking the particularities advanced by institutional and legal structures. This process not only creates a tool to reject the racial politics of the present, but also opens a window to expose the complexities of race within the construct of traditional Anglo-American law. Ultimately, it engages new configurations that can promote coalitions to both thwart and confront the legacy of manipulated hegemonic law.[9]

Accordingly, by placing both the Chicana/o and African American communities at the center of our study, this essay hopes to demonstrate that historical amnesia prevents our understanding the nature and the significance of the linkages between these communities. Invisibility in dominant legal analysis falls under its own weight when subjected to this new theoretical lens.

II. CHICANAS/OS AND AFRICAN AMERICANS: COMMON LINKAGES

At first blush it would seem Mr. Scott's bid for freedom would have no connection to the legal struggles of Chicanas/os.[10] That one group is legally characterized as white, the other black, presents certain analytical differences. Yet, in comparing the two forms of jurisprudence, several commonalities come into view.[11]

First, both bodies of law encompassed property as a primary issue. In the Chicana/o case law, the property at issue involved land and access to long-held natural resources. Mr. Scott's former status as a slave encompassed human beings as the property at issue,[12] and as the Court reasoned, in its interpretation of the original meaning and intent of the founding framers, the "right of property in a slave is distinctly and expressly affirmed in the Constitution."[13] Second, both areas of law generated from federal courts. Third, the study of these cases makes evident how property law intersects with race.

The linkages between the Chicana/o land grant adjudication and *Dred Scott* have borne little study, even though the federal court rulings demonstrate the similarity of challenges confronting outsiders within the hegemony of mainstream law.[14] The consequence thereby obstructing progressive alliances between the two groups.

Chicanas/os: A Historical Framework

If "citizenship is understood to mean full members of the state, entitled to the basic rights and opportunities afforded by the state,"[15] the exclusion of Chicanas/os from legal investigations obscures three points directly restricting the full attributes of citizenship allowed the dominant population.[16] They include (a) the extent to which federal law breached the Treaty of Guadalupe Hidalgo; and (b) the extent to which federal law yielded to the dictates of state law; and, while beyond the scope of this study, (c) the extent to which state actions encroached on federal authority to control public lands.[17] In sum, the law disallowed legal remedies that thereafter placed Chicanas/os as outsiders within traditional law and ultimately denying them the full economic and political integration allowed the mainstream population.

1. Chicanas/os and Citizenship.

> On the question of citizenship it must be admitted that we have not been very fastidious. Under the late treaty with Mexico, we have made citizens of all grades, combinations, and colors. The same was done in the admission of Louisiana and Florida. No one ever doubted, and no court ever held, that the people of these territories did not become citizens under the treaty. They have exercised all the rights of citizens under the treaty. They have exercised all the rights of citizens, without being naturalized under the acts of congress.[18]

Several historians assert that the Treaty of Guadalupe Hidalgo and its aftermath left many questions unanswered about the actual legal status of Mexicans remaining in the United States. Fundamental questions, they say, arose over the meaning of citizenship and the property rights granted by the treaty to Mexicanos.[19] Yet, before and after the conquest of the former Mexican provinces, the United States promised Chicanos citizenship status. Outside of Article VIII, protecting their property interests, Article IX provided that

> The Mexicans ... shall be incorporated into the Union of the United States and be admitted, at the proper time ... to the enjoyment of all the rights of citizens of the United States according to the principles of the Constitution; and in the mean time shall be maintained and protected in the free enjoyment of their liberty and property, and secured in the free exercise of their religion without restriction.[20]

The provision clearly guaranteed constitutional and other legal protections, permitting the "enjoyment of all the rights of citizens." Nonetheless, those of Mexican descent witnessed challenges as to their citizenship status.

2. Dominguez and People v. De La Guerra The earliest challenges to the racial standing and citizenship of Chicanos surfaced in two key cases. The first involved Constitutional Delegate Dominguez, a wealthy Mexican rancher who served as a member of the delegation at the first California Constitutional Convention. At this convention, proposed legislation attempted to limit the franchise to white males, causing a Mexican delegate to "argue that many Californios were dark-skinned, and that to disenfranchise them would be tantamount to denying them a part of their citizenship as granted by the Treaty of Guadalupe Hidalgo."[21] The Mexican census identified Dominguez as a *mestizo*, a label that would have barred his participation in the state's convention. After rigorous debate an exception, however, was eventually made, and Dominguez ultimately permitted to sign the relevant legal document.

The second example of challenges to their "citizenship status" case involved Pablo De La Guerra.[22] Born in 1819 in Santa Barbara, California, De La Guerra came from a well-established Mexicano family residing in the former Mexican territories. Although elected to a judicial position, De La Guerra confronted litigation in *People v. De La Guerra* seeking to disallow him from the judicial position. The grounds for the proposed overthrow of his electoral victory relied on state legislation requiring that "no person shall be eligible to the office of District Judge, who shall not have been a citizen of the United States, and a resident of this State for two years." De La Guerra argued in his defense that because the Treaty of

Guadalupe Hidalgo granted him citizenship status, he should be permitted the judicial position.

De La Guerra's challengers in arguing that the Treaty of Guadalupe Hidalgo did not permit citizenship asserted that citizenship required an Act of Congress. Because Congress had yet to establish appropriate procedures permitting citizenship, they argued, disqualifies De La Guerra as noncitizen. The Court, nonetheless, applied the Treaty of Guadalupe Hidalgo and ruled that the "treaty was intended to operate directly, and of itself to fix the status of those inhabitants. . . ." It ultimately recognizing De La Guerra a citizen of the United States.[23]

3. *The California Land Act of 1851 (CLA)*. The next realm of legal challenges to the right of Chicanas/os to enjoy their citizenship surfaces in the land grant context. This venue, placing Chicanas/os at risk, includes the defense of their property interests following the conquest of the former Mexican provinces. Notwithstanding the Treaty of Guadalupe Hidalgo and the purported "protection of other laws," Congress required anyone claiming a land grant to present their claims to a Board of Land Commissioners with subsequent appeals in the federal court system. The California Land Act of 1851 shifted the burden of proof to the landholders, requiring that they demonstrate that they were in fact landholders. This directly contradicted Article VIII of the treaty, which had promised to protect their property interests. Notwithstanding Constitutional considerations, this new legislation consequently disregarded treaty law as the supreme law of the land.

While it directly conflicted with the treaty and with Constitutional provisions, the CLA nonetheless required that "in deciding on the validity of any claim . . . ," they were to be ". . . governed by the Treaty of Guadalupe Hidalgo, the law of nations, the laws, usages, and customs of the government from which the claim is derived, the principles of equity, and the decisions of the Supreme Court of the United States, in so far as they are applicable.[24] United States law regarding property rights furthermore also applied.

The first case analyzing the Treaty of Guadalupe Hidalgo and the CLA before the U.S. Supreme Court encompassed litigation involving a non-Chicana/o in *Fremont v. United States*. The claimant involved John Fremont, a known instigator of the war conflict who sought confirmation of a purported land grant transferred to him by former Alta California governor Alvarado. In an opinion authored by Chief Justice Taney of the U.S. Supreme Court,[25] the Fremont decision encompassed "the most important and the leading case on this branch of the law, and . . . exercised a controlling influence on all subsequent decisions. . . ."[26]

Determining the validity of Fremont's claim required the Court to apply the CLA. Specifically, to look to "the law of nations, the laws, usages and customs of the Government from which the claim is derived, the principles of equity and the (prior) decisions." For example, Mexican Colonization law obligated grantees to settle and cultivate the land within a one-year period. The conditions attached to the original grantee's land grant petition to the Mexican government further disallowed transferring land without the permission of Mexican officials.

The facts of the case reveal that Fremont violated Mexican law by his purported purchase of the grant and thus rendered his claim unlawful and illegal. The evidence shows this illegality through (a) the transfer of the tract without the permission of Mexican officials, (b) the failure to settle or cultivate the tract within the one-year period, and (c) the absence of documentation. None of these violations, however, kept the Court from reaching outside the rules in force to rule on Fremont's behalf.[27]

The Court reasoned, moreover, that nothing barred an American citizen from purchasing property. This rationale shows the Court skirting constitutional provisions as to the nature of treaty law, its status as the supreme law of the land, and the California Land Act. The court reached beyond the intent and design of the law, furthermore, in its determination of law governing proof of land ownership.[28] And while this holding privileged Fremont with invaluable gold mine property of inestimable worth, the consequences of this case thereafter produced a number of arbitrary rulings impacting Chicanas/os when presenting their claims for confirmation.

Several examples emphasize the legal experiences of Chinacas/os in defense of their property interests. The standard and type of proof required by courts in presenting a claim of ownership varied, depending on who presented a claim for confirmation surfaced as a common challenge.[29] In some instances, proof of residing on the grant, in conformance with Mexican colonization law governing land grants, failed to protect grantees. This underscores Fremont's confirmed grant, in which colonization requirements were neither performed nor followed.[30] Chicanas/os with documents and adhering to land grant procedures also "failed" to persuade judicial actors of the validity of their claim of ownership. In several instances, furthermore, they faced challenges as to the authority of Mexican officials granting petitions for land in the annexed territories. Chicanas/os charges that government officials destroyed their land grant documents, disallowed the protection of law and further expedited dispossession. In contrast, the lack of documents, the failure to perform conditions attached to grants, reputations, and other fine-line distinctions that lacked consistencies protected non-Chicanas/os.[31]

In the New Mexico territories, other challenges derived from the attorney general rewriting Mexican law by omitting legal procedural rules that governed the land grant petition process. Land-grant scholar Malcolm Ebright reports that the Supreme Court relied on the revised text in determining whether a grantee had demonstrated the validity of his or her claim.[32] By omitting legal rules and legal presumptions, the U.S. Supreme Court therefore relied on false, legal norms and processes and promoted imprecise analytical reasoning.[33]

Finally, other pressures surfaced from third parties, squatters seeking home-steads, and public agricultural legislation. In sum, the extensive and irretrievable losses sustained as a result of erratic and arbitrary rulings and extra-legal actions placed those of Mexican descent outside of traditional law.[34] Chicanas/os without property, thereafter, deprived very little means to protest their subsequent legal marginalization.

Following the conquest, times were not good for those of Mexican descent. Although the Treaty of Guadalupe Hidalgo granted them citizenship status, Chicanas/os endured challenges to their full membership within the dominant culture. Lynchings, segregation, poll taxes, and other extra-legal methods pre-vented and/or denied them the right to vote and further challenged their ability to sustain a full measure of citizenship status.

Because Chicanas/os have been primarily ignored by formal legal investiga-tions, their outsider status expedites a legal culture in which immigration law directly disallows them the full attributes of citizenship.[35] While Europeans immi-grating to the United States find relatively easy acceptance into the culture,[36] Chicanas/os are forced to defend their physical, cultural, and linguistic attributes, and are at times prevented from opening bank accounts, renting apartments—or simply buying pizzas—without proof of citizenship. In sum, the law's construction of Chicanas/os as outsiders ultimately denied them the full economic and political integration allowed mainstream culture, with consequent effects into the present.

III. Dred Scott v. Sandford and African Americans

Neither the class of persons who had been imported as slaves, nor their descen-dants could be citizens of the United States.[37]

Next, *Dred Scott v. Sandford* bears witness to shifting judicial and legislative "standards" that constructed the outsider status of African Americans. The case before the Court involved several issues, but the focus here is on Mr. Scott's appeal for citizenship.[38] Rejecting Mr. Scott's petition, the Court indicated its reliance on the U.S. Constitution and the Framers' "original intent" with regard to property. In considering whether Mr. Scott was a citizen and deemed to be part of the "constituent members of this sovereignty," the Chief Justice "reasoned" that

> We think they are not, and that they are not included, and were not intended to be included, under the word "citizens" in the Constitution, and can therefore claim none of the rights and privileges which that instrument provides for and secures to citizens of the United States. On the contrary, they were at that time considered as a subordinate and inferior class of beings, who had been subjugated by the dominant race, and, whether emancipated or not, yet remained subject to their authority, and had no rights or privileges but such as those who held the power and the Government might choose to grant them.[39]

This deference to the Constitution conflicts with the constitutional interpretations missing from the Chicana/o land grant cases. The Court's resistance to banning slavery, furthermore, shows its regard of property rights as applied to majority status individuals and "their right of property in a slave." The Court "reasons" that

> The right to traffic in it, like an ordinary article of merchandise and property, was guaranteed to the citizens of the United States, in every State that might desire it, for twenty years. And the Government in express terms is pledged to protect it in all future time, if the slave escapes from his owner. This is done in plain words—too plain to be misunderstood. And no word can be found in the Constitution which gives Congress a greater power over slave property, or which entitles property of that kind to less protection than property of any other description. The only power conferred is the power coupled with the duty of guarding and protecting the owner in his rights.

That the newly annexed territories did not recognize slavery could no doubt have factored in the *Dred Scott* decision. The Court's deference to the Constitution, thereby, exposes an inconsistent position with respect to people of color.

In *Dred Scott*, those of African descent are not regarded as citizens. In the Mexican cases, although treaty law defined a legal relationship between those of Mexican descent and the United States, the court disregarded the Treaty of

Guadalupe Hidalgo as well as the Constitution. Ignoring its reasoning from the Mexican cases, in which it privileged non-Mexican petitions, the Court furthermore did not apply its previous principles from yet other land grant periods of law. This judicial switch heading of case law reasoning and analysis from previous decisions is evident in *Dred Scott*. The decision imposed adverse consequences on Mr. Scott because of the Court's selective interpretation of constitutional principles and corresponding law. Yet not all is as simple as it seems. This inconsistent legal treatment, on its face, exposes a "consistency." By its rulings, the Court defined both groups as second-class "citizens" and outsiders to mainstream law. Because of the Court's actions, its language, and the attendant legal culture, however, it created space for the subaltern to protest the politics of exclusion and legal consequences and policies targeting both communities.

These decisions, and their trajectories, reached long into the future with white supremacy targeting African Americans by way of lynchings, segregation, denial of the right to vote, and other forms of institutional racism, and directly link law to the subordination of these communities. These rulings harshly and directly affected communities of color, and institutionalized insurmountable legal barriers, another example of the selective enforcement of Anglo-American law.

IV. SUMMARY/CONCLUSION

In comparing the case law involving our communities of Mexican and African descent, the purpose of this preliminary investigation is not to essentialize their legal realities. In the war over who is permitted to declare citizenship and who is "permitted" to enjoy its attributes, we must underscore the nature of arbitrary laws that have legally constructed these communities of color as outsiders. That Chicanas/os are legally identified as white must not be seen as a hindrance for progressive coalitions and joint efforts toward eradicating racial injustice for two reasons. First, Chicana/o legal experiences demonstrate that law constructed the nation's newest citizens as outsiders. Second, the legal treatment toward citizens of color in U.S. society demonstrates the outgrowth of hostility derived in large measure from long-ago historical periods. To the present, immigration laws and policies both intentionally and by default target those of Mexican descent on the basis of their race and reflect the colonial experience. Similarly, lynching, lawlessness, segregation, and the denial of the franchise have disallowed African Americans from full membership in mainstream culture.

In the contemporary period, the politics of exclusion and legal hierarchies continue to deny Chicana/o and African American communities the full benefits of citizenship. Chicanas/os cannot stop at rest stops without proof of citizenship; African Americans are discouraged from entering public venues and witness extreme measures that focus on their race. The goal of LatCrit theory on building knowledge and linking theory with practice emphasizes the great need to join in progressive coalitions. With such action an attendant consequence can directly target the racial politics of the present that seeks to limit our citizenship status. By linking these joint histories, Latina/o Critical Race theory shows the attributes of full citizenship for all groups as long missing, reveals a manipulation of mainstream law to privilege the dominant population, and demonstrates how an attendant legal culture facilitates discriminatory practices toward the nation's people of color.

History exposes the contradictions specific to each racial group, their racial identities, and its causation with law and legal institutions. Even more critically, the full measure of judicial decisions, legal institutions, and their connections to our communities obligates us to discontinue our invisibility within legal history by ardently pursuing yet further disclosure.

NOTES

The title phrase "Aren't They All Illegal Anyway" is a response, followed by an inquiry as to what efforts a state agency located in a major metropolitan Midwestern region was making toward reaching rural farmworkers.

A conceptional framework and material of this presentation draws from On the Complexities of Race: The Treaty of Guadalupe Hildalgo and Dred Scott v. Standford, 53 *University of Miami Law Review* 691 (1999). For a more complete analysis of the case law interpreting the Treaty of Guadalupe Hidalgo, see Guadalupe Luna, "Chicana/o Land Tenure in the Agrarian Domain: On the Edge of a Naked Knife," 4 *Michigan Journal of Race & Law* 39 (1998).

1. Kevin R. Johnson, *How Did You Get To Be Mexican? A White/Brown Man's Search for Identity* (Philadelphia: Temple University Press, 1998).
2. "Treaty of Peace, Friendship, Limits and Settlement between the United States of American and The Mexican Republic, Treaty of Guadalupe Hidalgo," 2 February 1848, U.S.-Mex., Stat. 922, 929. Executed in the City of Guadalupe Hidalgo on 2 February 1848, the treaty's

ratification took place in Queretaro, Mexico, on 30 May 1848. Its final proclamation was made on 4 July 1848. Article IX of the Treaty of Guadalupe Hidalgo provided for the citizenship of those choosing to remain in the annexed territories.

3. For an account of the conflict between the United States and Mexico, see Elizabeth Haas, "War in California," in *Contested Eden: California Before the Gold Rush*, ed. Ramón A. Gutiérrez and Richard J. Orsi (University of California Press, 1998).

4. Hunter Miller, "Treaty of Guadalupe Hidalgo," Docs. 122–50: 1846–1852, 5 Treaties and Other International Acts of the United States of America, 256 (1937) citing Secretary of State James Buchanan.

5. Cass R. Sunstein, *The Dred Scott Case with Notes on Affirmative Action, The Right to Die & Same-Sex Marriage*, 1 Green Bag 2d 39 (1997). The competing constitutional theories arising from Dred Scott are beyond the purposes of this preliminary essay. As to how the decision is characterized, see Paul Finkelman, "The Dred Scott Case, Slavery and the Politics of Law," 20 *Hamline L. Rev.* 1 (1996). As to its controversy Mark A. Graber, "Desperately Ducking Slavery; Dred Scott and Contemporary Constitutional Theory," 14 *Const. Comment* 271 (1997) provides: "Commentators across the political spectrum describe Dred Scott as "the worst constitutional decision of the nineteenth century," "the worst atrocity in the Supreme Court's history," "the most disastrous opinion the Supreme Court has ever issued," a "ghastly error," a "tragic failure to follow the terms of the Constitution," "a gross abuse of trust," "a lie before God," and "judicial review at its worst." Id.

6. Moving toward a more sophisticated examination of race in law, LatCrit theory promotes placing our communities at the center of academic investigations and linking theory with praxis. As a relatively new endeavor, LatCrit theory promotes anti-subordination in requiring unpacking of the particularities advanced by institutional structures. LatCrit theory further calls for progressive coalitions between subordinated groups. This path is taken because race-based investigations that are exposing the disparate treatment of people of color are under assault. Daniel A. Farber and Suzanne Sherry, "The 200,000 Cards of Dimitri Yurasov: Further Reflections on Scholarship and Truth," 46 *Stan. L. Rev.* 647, 652 n.38 (1994). In contrast LatCrit theory as applied here seeks to demonstrate how law from one historical period established the subordinate status of both communities. It rejects, moreover, concepts of essentialism. "The concept of essentialism refers to the issues raised by false universalisms, identity splitting, the assumption of natural principles, and a form of reductionism. False universalisms refer to "overgeneralizations or unstated reference points [that] implicitly attribute to all members of a group the characteristics of individuals who are dominant in that group." Theresa Raffaele Jefferson, "Toward A Black Lesbian Jurisprudence," 18 *Boston College Third World L. J.* 263 (1998).

7. Citizenship is "generally understood to mean full members of the state, entitled to the basic

rights and opportunities afforded by the state." Thomas Alexander Alienkoff, David A. Martin, and Hiroshi Motomura, "Immigration," *Process and Policy* 1 (West Publishing, 1998). The authors define citizenship as "a term generally understood to mean full members of the state, entitled to the basic rights and opportunities afforded by the state. But reality, of course, is more interesting and complicated. . . . ."

8. Professor Berta Esperanza Hernández-Truyol asserts, "Normativity, in all its forms—be it maleness, whiteness, or straightness—creates a false sense of universality of what is right, desired, and desirable. At one time, this idea was used to support racial subordination." See Berta Esperanza Hernández-Truyol, "Indivisible Identities: Culture Clashes, Confused Constructs and Reality Checks," 2 *Harv. Latino Law Rev.* 199, 214 (1998).

9. See, e.g., Francisco Valdes, "Latina/o Ethnicities, Critical Race Theory, and Post-Identity Politics in Postmodern Legal Culture: From Practices to Possibilities," 9 *La Raza Law J.* 1 (1996). Environmental racism in our communities of color serves as an example of denied linkages. See, e.g., David L. Hanna, "Third World Texas: NAFTA, State Law, and Environmental Problems Facing Texas Colonias," 27 *St. Mary's L. J.* 871 (1996).

10. Several authors are seeking to exclude Latinas/os from race-based investigations or seeking to eliminate their racial status. See, for example, Robert L. Turner, "Is Race Obsolete?" *Boston Globe Magazine,* 22 September 1996, p. 13.

11. Both groups witnessed the invasion and disruption of their communities. Slave traders seeking labor for agricultural and other enterprises forcibly stole Africans from their communities, brought them to this country, and left native communities in chaos. While the horror and violence of slavery cannot be measured, Chicano communities also witnessed chaos and destruction resulting from American forces invading and laying political claim to their land, property, and natural resources.

12. The issues in *Dred Scott* involved whether Mr. Scott could sue in federal court, determining the constitutionality of the Missouri Compromise, and whether the effect of his residing in non-slave states affected his standing in Missouri. On the surface they appear to bear little relevance with Chicana/o property struggles. These issues, nonetheless, are conjoined in many respects with Chicana/o citizenship struggles.

13. *Dred Scott v. Sandford,* 60 U.S. 393 (1857).

14. Another shared point includes federal-state relations. For examinations of this point see Eric T. Dean Jr., "Reassessing Dred Scott: The Possibilities of Federal Power in the Antebellum Context," 60 *U. Cin. L. Rev.* 713 (1992); Alfred L. Brophy, "Let Us Go Back and Stand upon the Constitution: Federal-State Relations in *Scott v. Sandford,*" 90 *Colum. L. Rev.* 192 (1990). In the Chicana/o land grant case law the relevant federal concern includes the effect of the Treaty of Guadalupe Hidalgo on state relations. Finally, other connections come by way of black contributions to the settlement of the Mexican provinces.

15. Johnson, *How Did You Get To Be Mexican?* In referencing immigration law and the neglect of race-based studies, Professor Johnson asserts that "the treatment of 'aliens'," particularly noncitizens of color, under the U.S. immigration laws reveals volumes about domestic race relations in the nation. A deeply complicated, often volatile relationship exists between racism directed toward citizens and that aimed at noncitizens." Id.

16. As to the nature of how immigration impacts Latina/os see, Sylvia R. Lazos Vargas, "Deconstructing Homo[geneous] Americanus: The White Ethnic Immigrant Narrative and Its Exclusionary Effect," 72 *Tulane L. Rev.* 1493 (1998): Kevin R. Johnson, "'Melting Pot' or 'Ring of Fire'?: Assimilation and the Mexican-American Experience," 85 *Cal. L. Rev.* 1259 (1997).

17. While the issue of whether state actions encroached on federal authority to control public lands is beyond the scope of this study, this issue is well developed in the control of Native American land and interpretation of treaty law. See generally Francis Paul Prucha, *American Indian Treaties, The History of a Political Anomaly* (Berkeley: University of California Press, 1994).

18. Mr. Justice McLean, in his dissenting opinion in *Scott v. Sandford,* 19 How. 533, citing *People v. De La Guerra,* 40 Cal. 311 (1870).

19. Martha Menchaca, "Chicano Indianism: A Historical Account of Racial Repression in the United States," 20 *Am. Ethnologest* 583, 584 (1993). Martha Menchaca asserts: "When the United States acquired Mexico's northern frontier, the mestizo ancestry of the conquered Mexicans placed them in an ambiguous social and legal position."

20. Article IX, Treaty of Guadalupe Hidalgo, supra note, art. IX. The Spanish translation provides:

> Los Mexicanos que, en lost territorios antedichos . . . segun lo estipulado en el artículo precedente, serán incorporados en la Union de los Estados Unidos, y se admitiran en tiempo oportuno . . . al goce de todos los derechos de ciudadanos de los Estados Unidos conforme a los principios de la constitucion y entretanto serán mantenidos y protejidos en el goce de su libertad y propiedad, y asegurados en el libre ejercicio de su religion sin restriccion alguna.

Id. The Spanish text is included because of the mistranslation of Spanish documents by legal actors.

21. Leonard Pitt, *The Decline of the Californios, A Social History of the Spanish-Speaking Californians, 1849–1890* (Berkeley: University of California Press, 1971), 43–46.

22. *People v. De La Guerra,* 40 Cal. 311 (1870).

23. See also *De Baca et al. v. The United States and the Navajo Indians* 36, C. Cls. 407 (1901) involving whether a child of Spanish parents born in New Mexico in 1809 was by birth an American citizen.

24. The California Land Act of 1851, Sec. 11.

25. *Fremont v. United States* 58 U.S. (17 How.) 542 (1854). As to the nature of Fremont's spying activities on behalf of the United States, see A. Brooke Caruso, *The Mexican Spy Company, United States Covert Operations in Mexico, 1845–1848* (Jefferson, N.C.: McFarland, 1991).

26. *United States v. Cambuston* 25 F. Cas. 266, 272 (D. Ca. 1857) (No. 14, 713).

27. Fremont, 58 U.S. (17 How.) at 565.

28. See, for example, *Botiller v. Dominguez*, 130 U.S. 238 (1889) (observing courts failing to follow the treaty).

29. Several historians contend that the nation's high regard for property deemed the land grant adjudication process fair. See Paul Gates, *Land and Law in California: Essays on Land Policy* (Ames: Iowa State University Press, 1991).

30. *Peralta v. United States*, 70 U.S. (3 Wall.) 434 (1865). For background on this litigation, reference John S. Hittell, "Mexican Land Claims in California," in *A Documentary History of the Mexican Americans*, 271.

31. See generally *United States v. Pendell*, 185 U.S. 189 (1902) (during American occupation of El Paso del Norte military personnel destroyed documents). Fremont who also gathered granting documents, testified he lost them in the mountains. *United States v. Cambuston*, 25 F. Cas. 266, 267 (D.C.Cal. 1859) (No. 14,714).

32. Malcolm Ebright, *Land Grants and Lawsuits in Northern New Mexico* (University of New Mexico Press, 1994).

33. See Guadalupe T. Luna, "Chicanas, Land Grant Adjudication, and the Treaty of Guadalupe Hidalgo: This Land Belongs To Me," *Harv. Latino Law Rev.* (publication forthcoming 2001) citing Secretary of State James Buchanan in his lobbying against a provision in the Treaty of Guadalupe Hidalgo that would have ensured protection of Mexican-owned property. During his lobbying in voting for the removal of the provision (Article X), Buchanan asserted that the country's laws as "blessings" would otherwise protect grantees. Hunter Miller, "Treaty of Guadalupe Hidalgo," Docs. 122–50: 1846–1852, 5 Treaties and Other International Acts of the United States of America, 256 (1937) reports on the nature of James Buchanan and his lobbying.

34. Philip D. Ortego, "The Chicano Renaissance," in *La Causa Chicana, The Movement for Justice*, edited by Margaret M. Mangold (Family Services Association of America, 1971/1972), 53. ("Mexican Americans themselves were kept at arm's length as outsiders."). As to their invisibility in law, see, e.g., Berta Esperanza Hernández-Truyol, "Indivisible Identities: Culture Clashes, Confused Constructs and Reality Checks," 2 *Harv. Latino Law Rev.* 199 (1998); Kevin R. Johnson, "Los Olvidados: Images of the Immigrant, Political Power of Noncitizens, and Immigration Law and Enforcement," 1993 *BYU. L. Rev.* 1139.

35. As to the nature of how immigration laws impact on Latinas/os see, Sylvia R. Lazos Vargas,

"Deconstructing Homo[geneous] Americanus: The White Ethnic Immigrant Narrative and Its Exclusionary Effect," 72 *Tulane L. Rev.* 1493 (1998); Johnson, "Melting Pot" 85 *Cal. L. Rev.* 1259 (1997).

36. Dennis Nodín Valdés, *Al Norte, Agricultural Workers in the Great Lakes Region 1917–1970* (Austin: University of Texas Press, 1991). Compare with the forced repatriation of Chicana/o communities in Detroit, Michigan, and other regions. Id.

37. *Dred Scott v. Sandford*, 60 U.S. 393 (1857).

38. The three critical issues before the court involved (a) whether Mr. Scott could sue in federal court; (b) whether the Missouri Compromise was constitutional; and (c) whether the effect of his residing in nonslave states affected his standing in Missouri.

39. *Dred Scott v. Sandford*, 60 U.S. 393 (1857).

19

Whither Affirmative Action?
Historical and Political Perspectives

GERALD HORNE

Affirmative action is like a giant oak under assault by a fierce wind. Spectators marvel at how this entity can remain standing in the face of this biting attack. What is lost sight of is precisely what is not seen: the sturdy roots that insure that despite the ferocious manhandling of affirmative action, this program will not be easy to uproot. In fact, the roots of this program extend to some of the more searing events in this nation's history. Profound domestic imperatives and pervasive global pressures have guaranteed that affirmative action will not be eviscerated easily; this remains the case as we embark on a new millennium.

◆　◆　◆

It should not be forgotten that the Civil War, a conflict that remains the bloodiest in this nation's bloody history, was the initial impetus for precursors of affirmative action. The Freedmen's Bureau, which extended aid to the newly freed slaves after the Civil War, could easily be viewed by affirmative action's critics as one of the initial forms of "reverse discrimination."[1] After all, such aid was extended overwhelmingly to those of African descent on the rationale that they were the ones who had been enslaved and, therefore, were in need of assistance—just as the Federal

Emergency Management Administration provides aid to those who have been victims of natural disasters, like hurricanes, not to those who have not been so affected: presumably, FEMA assistance to the victims of Hurricane Mitch in the southern United States in 1998 could be deemed "reverse discrimination" against those in the north who went unscathed. Such reasoning was rejected by the U.S. Congress when it ratified the Thirteenth Amendment to the Constitution, which ruled that not only slavery but the "badges" of slavery would also be unconstitutional.

What are the "badges of slavery? The exact parameters are unclear, but in 1968 the U.S. Supreme Court suggested that failure to sell a home to an African-American on the basis of race could be seen as a "badge" of slavery justifying congressional and legal action.[2] The Thirteenth Amendment, which does not have the impediment of the Fourteenth Amendment, which requires action by the state—as opposed to individuals—in order to be applicable, is potentially one of the more powerful arrows in the quiver of defenders of equality. In other words, the kinds of compensatory measures that affirmative action demands could be justified—particularly for African Americans—on the basis that such measures are seeking to eradicate a "badge" of slavery, racial discrimination that hinders one's opportunities in the marketplace. Similarly, the Thirteenth Amendment does not have the recently imported defect of the Fourteenth Amendment requiring "strict scrutiny" by the courts of measures involving race; such a high standard has made it quite difficult for race-based affirmative action to survive attack.

Unfortunately, in these conservative times the courts have chosen not to heed clear constitutional signals and, instead, have opted to become captive to the right-wing agenda. In fairness, the courts are not solely culpable; those affirmative action proponents who have failed to acknowledge that this program's origins and continuation depend more on obtaining political conditions than on simple legal arguments also should share part of the blame. For, as so often is said, the courts read the newspapers and election returns, and if they have been doing either lately it has become difficult to ignore the message that conservative nostrums are in vogue—and this fashion is a partial result of affirmative action proponent's failure to adopt the appropriate political approaches.

In other words, when affirmative action has taken steps forward, it has been precisely because of a congenial political environment. This was the case in the early 1940s when the winds of war were blowing throughout the world; it was at that moment that the well-known African American labor leader, A. Philip Randolph, threatened to lead a "March on Washington" because of, inter alia, rampant employment discrimination. The administration of Franklin D.

Roosevelt had sought to fend off demands by African Americans by claiming that his party—the Democratic—was dependent on conservative Dixiecrats and could not afford to offend them. This plea had been remarkably effective in blunting black demands. However, as a result of the global pressure represented by the drumbeat of war, the White House acquiesced and the president issued an executive order that even today is being employed to insure nondiscrimination by recipients of government contracts; this remains one of the more powerful edicts emerging from Washington mandating affirmative action.

Unfortunately, proponents of affirmative action did not draw a clear dual lesson from this episode: that mass action or the threat thereof, combined with a close attention to the global pressure on the powers-that-be, is the most reliable guarantee of the continuation and extension of affirmative action generally and antidiscrimination measures specifically.

This lesson was lost almost as soon as World War II—which had prompted the executive order—concluded and the cold war began, with its own unique pressure on the racial order in the United States. On 8 May 1946 Acting Secretary of State Dean Acheson wrote a revealing letter to the Fair Employment Practices Commission—itself a creation of the exigencies of war and the threat of black mass action; in this stunning missive, Acheson provided a veritable map exposing the pressure points which needed to be pushed in order to bring civil rights concessions: ". . . [The] existence of discrimination against minority groups in this country," he said, "has an adverse effect upon our relations with other countries." How did he know this? "We are reminded over and over by some foreign newspapers and spokesmen," he responded sheepishly, "that our treatment of various minorities leaves much to be desired." That was not all. "While sometimes these pronouncements are exaggerated and unjustified, they all too frequently point with accuracy to some form of discrimination because of race, creed, color or national origin."

This was at a time when Washington was seeking to charge Moscow with human rights violations, as the cold war was gathering steam. Yet how could Washington do so credibly when the United States itself kept "minority groups" in thrall to a bestial and atrocious racism? This was the dilemma Dean Acheson was patiently seeking to explain to the FEPC. Seemingly flustered, he added, "frequently we find it next to impossible to formulate satisfactory answers to our critics in other countries; the gap between the things we stand for in principle and the facts of a particular situation may be too wide to be bridged." What were the consequences? "An atmosphere of suspicion and resentment in a country over the way a minority is being treated in the United States is a formidable obstacle to the development of mutual understanding and trust between the two countries." Such a consequence could be fatal in the context of deteriorating relations between Washington and Moscow. So, what to do? "We will have better international relations," he counseled, "when these reasons for suspicion and resentment have been removed."

Acheson found this proposition "quite obvious," and this formed the basis for the postwar assault on Jim Crow, an assault that had affirmative action as a central component. Continually, he stressed that "the existence of discriminations against minority groups in the United States is a handicap in our relations with other countries. The department of state, therefore, has good reasons to hope for the continued and increased effectiveness of public and private efforts to do away with these discriminations."[3]

Some proponents of affirmative action were well aware of the wind in their sails provided by the global correlation of forces. Unfortunately, in the vanguard of these proponents were those soon to be deemed beyond the pale because of their opposition to the gathering cold war policies of the United States, chief among them W. E. B. Du Bois.[4] Du Bois's friends, the black attorney William Patterson and his comrade Paul Robeson, filed a petition with the United Nations charging the United States with genocide against African Americans. This démarche received maximum publicity abroad, containing as it did 150 pages of evidence of racial killings, lynchings, beatings, and other terrors, as well as charges of conspiracy in the federal, state, and local governments. Angered, the U.S. government seized the passports of Patterson, Robeson, and Du Bois, effectively barring them from reaching real and potential allies in the international community.[5] With the erosion of their influence, the idea of taking advantage of global conditions for domestic advantage faded rapidly.

Belatedly the NAACP seems to be arriving at the realization that it is foolhardy for an oppressed minority to ignore potential allies abroad and rely solely on those within the borders of this nation. In the December 1998 edition of their journal, *Crisis,* the well-known international lawyer Gay McDougall writes persuasively,

> As state and federal courts are becoming more hostile to affirmative action programs and to challenges to governmental actions that have a discriminatory impact on communities of color, the civil rights struggle may gain added value and momentum from a return to the court of international public opinion. U.S. civil rights groups should evoke international human rights norms in their advocacy campaigns and court challenges."[6]

This was timely advice—sadly, it was not heeded at the dawning of the cold war.

Still, the other prod for affirmative action—mass action or the threat thereof—remained. In August 1965 a devastating torrent of civil unrest swept through Los Angeles. A simple episode of police brutality directed at African Americans led to the torching of numerous businesses, "looting," and at least thirty-four deaths. A combined force of almost sixteen thousand National Guardsmen, Los Angeles Police Department forces, and related law enforcement personnel had to be enlisted to quell this insurrection. Los Angeles, a city where sources of water are few and far between, was beset by fires that could have led to its total destruction. It was recognized instinctively that ultimately widespread racial discrimination was the cause of this near-holocaust, and that improving the life chances of African Americans in all spheres of life was the only reliable way to insure that such an event would not recur. Appropriately chastened, political elites began to search for methods to avoid the recurrence of such an event. Days after the fires had been extinguished, a high-level aide to then governor Edmund "Pat" Brown told his boss that what needed to be done immediately was a "significant expansion of our highly successful but severely limited affirmative action program." Even the conservative John McCone, a former director of the Central Intelligence Agency, was forced to conclude that "if one segment of society cannot [advance] then the dynamics of our economy will be adversely affected." This was not altogether altruistic thinking. The commission headed by McCone that investigated the events in Los Angeles concluded that if more of an effort had been made to curb economic discrimination against African Americans, "such that today Negro-white salary and employment figures were comparable, the white race [sic] would itself have made extremely significant economic gains from this."[7] That is, if Negroes had more money to spend on housing and consumer items, those that manufactured such—who largely were not Negroes—would have profited.

President Lyndon B. Johnson was thinking along parallel lines. Weeks earlier, at Howard University, he had uttered his now famous remarks, providing the rationale for affirmative action: "You do not take a person who, for years, has been hobbled by chains and liberate him, bring him up to the starting line in a race and then say, 'you are free to compete with all the others,' and still justly believe that you have been completely fair."[8]

Thus, 1965 marked a turning point in the battle for affirmative action. Yet, it is extremely important to understand how this conjuncture was reached. As Johnson was speaking these soothing words at home, a bitter war was being waged abroad against socialist Vietnam, as the cold war became extremely hot: African

American troops were essential to the prosecution of this conflict and it would have been difficult to preserve their already faltering morale if they had thought their sons and daughters back home were not receiving justice. Furthermore, the flames of Watts helped to illuminate the inescapable point that equity for African Americans was a precondition to national unity.

◆ ◆ ◆

Of course, the United States was far from being the only nation suffering from a legacy of bigotry, nor was it the only nation that was seeking to address such. For some years now, India, which will probably be the world's largest nation in the twenty-first century, has reserved some government jobs, not to mention seats in universities, to members of lower castes.[9] Elected village councils have seats reserved for women and members of lower castes, and parliament itself sets aside more than a fifth of its seats to members of "scheduled castes and tribes," the lowest social rung. The Congress Party, which intermittently has ruled India for the past fifty years, is seeking to reserve a third of all party posts for women and a fifth for minorities and lower castes.[10] An equivalent in the United States would be for a percentage of jobs in Washington to be reserved for minorities, or a number of seats in the entering class of the University of North Carolina to be reserved for minorities, or for the Democratic party to reserve leading party posts for minorities. Hence, though a firestorm of protest has erupted in the United States about affirmative action, in global terms, policies here are rather tepid, and lacking in scope and ambition.

The Southeast Asian nation of Malaysia, with a population less than one-tenth that of the United States, also provides examples of affirmative action that far surpasses what this nation has witnessed. Malaysia's leader, Dr. Mahathir Mohammed, has remarked that his nation is a "uniquely multiracial country. Even the Negroes of America are more easily integrated with whites than are the different races in Malaysia integrated among themselves."[11] This statement is not as far-fetched as it sounds. There is an indigenous Malay plurality that constitutes perhaps 55 percent of the population, though a sizable population of Chinese origin of about 35 percent controls a good deal of the commanding heights of the economy, and a population of Indian origin constitutes a significant percentage of the working class. Language, religious, and cultural differences separate these groups. Affirmative action in Malaysia, like its counterpart in the United States, was spurred by 1960s riots—there in May 1969, with over two hundred fatalities and thousands made homeless. The tensions revealed led directly to aggressive measures to assuage the pressing needs of the Malays, particularly in the realms of higher education, rural health care, and set-asides for business. Again, though weaker measures in the United States have elicited howls of outrage, such programs in Malaysia have been described—and not inaccurately—as "the world's most extensive affirmative action programme and one of its most successful."[12]

Europe also has been the scene for affirmative action. British police have been threatened with a cut in their budgets unless they recruit more officers from ethnic minorities, to reflect the growing diversity of the population. Scotland Yard's commissioner, Sir Paul Dondon, has pledged to try to recruit up to 20 percent of his force from such groups to meet the new requirement and to reflect London's racial mix. Sir Paul has said that 20 percent of Londoners are "black, brown or Chinese," and a force that reflects this diversity is in tune with the wishes of people in this important capital; yet only about 3 percent of the police force are members of these minorities. Police management is planning to introduce bursary and fellowship schemes—along with other measures that comprise a form of affirmative action—to encourage these groups to enter the police force. Increasingly in London it is recognized that policing of the city will be more effective if the police force better reflects the region's population.[13]

Not surprisingly, the global pressure that forced the United States to improve its racial situation also has influenced other nations with far less influence. Equally unsurprising is the fact that the push toward affirmative action often has come in the wake of civil unrest—be it in Los Angeles or Kuala Lumpur—or has been motivated by the desire to prevent same, as, for example, in London. In today's United States, there is a widespread perception that with the end of the cold war, global pressure on the United States has been reduced correspondingly, and with the era of urban unrest presumably ending in the 1960s, there is less domestic pressure to rectify racial injustice. This is the difficult dilemma faced by advocates of affirmative action.

◆   ◆   ◆

However, this is not an impossible dilemma, for support for affirmative action remains widespread. A 1996 survey by the National Opinion Research Center found that 79 percent of respondents support affirmative action defined as policies that promote equal opportunity in hiring, promotion, and government contracts without quotas.[14] This should not be deemed overly surprising. After all, affirmative action benefits the overwhelming majority in this nation—minorities and nonminority women—and that they would endorse what is in their own self-interest is not terribly shocking.

Even those who are not direct beneficiaries of affirmative action have endorsed these measures. Some corporate executives recognize that this nation faces a human capital deficit absent affirmative action; that is,. as the class of new entrants to the workforce is disproportionately comprised of minorities and nonminority women, this nation faces the dire prospect of economic gridlock as long as these groups are consigned to the bottom rungs of the socioeconomic ladder, for the bulk of the population will not have the capital to consume what is being produced. Such a prospect faced apartheid South Africa, and this was a major force leading to the first all-race elections of 1994, which culminated in Nelson Mandela's presidency.[15] Thus, affirmative action becomes a means to insure that the United States can continue to produce a necessary complement of engineers, physicians, professors, and the like from the human capital that is available, and, similarly important, can avoid crises of overproduction, where goods are being produced without consumers to purchase them.

In short, affirmative action is just another means by which human resources can be distributed efficiently. There are other ways to do this. For example, I recall a trip I made to Japan some years ago. I rented a car and drove into a filling station. A number of young men came out to wash the window, check the tires and the oil, and so on. Of course, I paid at the pump for this, as the price of gas there is much higher than it is in this nation. However, the government in Tokyo has decided that this is a social price that will be paid to integrate these young men—who, most likely, will not be attending college—into society. In the United States, when one drives into a filling station one winds up pumping one's own gas, checking one's own tires, and so on; there may be three or four young men there, but they are not there to help you—though they may relieve you of your wallet, if not your life. Gas is much cheaper here, but one winds up paying, in any case, for prisons, car alarms, car insurance, and the like. Affirmative action, thus, is a mechanism to deploy human capital; in fact, it is a relatively inexpensive way to deal with the deployment of human capital.

This is not a point that employers can dismiss with insouciance. By the year 2030, approximately 40 percent of all citizens in this nation will be members of minority groups. Even if one excludes the most significant recipient of affirmative action--nonminority women—this is a sizable chunk of the potential labor force.[16] Even today more than $600 billion in purchasing power is generated by minorities. This is a market that no alert corporation can afford to ignore—or alienate. Likewise, it makes sense for corporations in an increasingly competitive global environment to seek to utilize Spanish-speaking Latinos in South America and

African Americans in Africa. Affirmative action facilitates these policies, which are wise for business.

Thus, the National Association of Manufacturers has concluded that "affirmative action makes good business policy." Ninety percent of 120 corporate CEOs surveyed by *Fortune* magazine in 1984 said their companies had implemented affirmative action programs to satisfy "corporate objectives unrelated to government regulations." Indeed, 95 percent said they would continue to use affirmative action regardless of government requirements. In a more recent 1992 survey of CEOs, only 2 percent called affirmative action programs "poor."

Lucio A. Noto, the chairman of Mobil Corporation (subject of a merger with Exxon), echoed these themes, adding, "I have never felt a burden from affirmative action because it is a business imperative for us." He has tied "management compensation to progress in these areas." William McEwen, an executive of Monsanto Corporation, testifying before a House subcommittee in 1985, was dismissive of the attack on affirmative action as mandating quotas: "Business," he said, "sets goals and timetables for every aspect of its operations, [including] profits, capital investment, productivity increases, and promotional potential for individuals. Setting goals and timetables for minority and female participation is a way of measuring progress and focusing on potential discrimination."[17]

No doubt these executives are well aware of the human capital dilemma faced by U.S. business; perhaps they are also aware of the privileges—often seemingly invisible—that benefit those of their race and gender. Even when those privileges are glaringly obvious, the outcry does not appear to be significant. Press reports have revealed, for example, that certain colleges have become so concerned about dropping male enrollments that they have dipped further down in their pool of applicants for men than for women. Hence, they have downplayed the grades and test scores of these males in order to maintain gender balance—that is, they have engaged in a form of affirmative action.[18] This infuriated feminist scholar Cynthia Harrison. "Doesn't that mean," she thundered, "that admission was denied to qualified women in favor of 'less qualified' men? Isn't that affirmative action? Where were the voices of outrage from those who sounded the clarion against race and sex-based 'preferences' in California? Or are preferences all right when the beneficiaries are (white) men?"[19] These were penetrating questions that were difficult to address.

Thus, even in California, where the passage of Proposition 209 was thought to sound the death knell for affirmative action, the domestic imperative for it has been difficult to overcome. In San Francisco the Board of Supervisors voted in

September 1998—two years after the ratification of Proposition 209—that affirmative action would be extended in city contracting. The "rapidly approved ordinance says that 65 percent of all city departments are headed by white men, and that many 'continue to operate under an 'old boys' network dominated by Caucasian males." Such a system, it says, "creates a barrier to the entry of women and minority-owned businesses and puts those firms at a competitive advantage in their efforts to secure contracts."[20]

This action by the traditionally progressive City by the Bay has been matched by the judiciary. In December 1998 Judge Lloyd Connelly upheld a state law that allows community colleges, under certain circumstances to give "preferences" to job candidates who are female, black, or Latino—Proposition 209, which was thought to have invalidated all forms of affirmative action, notwithstanding. In circumstances where the law allows community colleges to use "preferences"—specifically to overcome the effects of past discrimination—state and federal courts have held that such are permissible because they serve a compelling government interest, the judge concluded. California adopted the law in question in 1978 in response to findings that the state's community college system employed disproportionately low numbers of women and members of racial and ethnic minority groups, given their share of the population, in staff, faculty, and administrative positions, and had maintained artificial barriers to their employment in the past. The judge's decision drew a sharp distinction between laws that impose a rigid numerical quota and those that are more flexible; the judge interpreted Proposition 209 as applying to the former, not the latter.[21]

Yet, though there is widespread support for affirmative action, the fact that Cynthia Harrison's passionate pleas were met mostly with deafening silence is suggestive of the fact that affirmative action is far from receiving unanimous endorsement. Though some courts have seemed to indicate that they will smile more on gender-based—as opposed to race-based—affirmative action, the need for both initiatives are clear. As one circuit court opinion put it, "gender conscious affirmative action programs may rest safely on a weaker evidentiary foundation than race or ethnicity conscious programs."[22] It would be simple to conclude that powerful elites are more sensitive to equity for their wives and daughters than for those deemed to be beyond their family—and the pale—that is, peoples of color.

Nonetheless, it is not as if nonminority women are flourishing. Equal Rights Advocates, a public interest law firm specializing in litigation on behalf of women, has noted that less than 5 percent of senior management posts are held by women, along with 6.9 percent of the seats on corporate boards; similar disproportions can be found at various levels of U.S. society ranging from the U.S. Congress to the professoriate.[23] Such stunning figures bespeak the fact that whatever the level of support for it, stiff opposition to affirmative action has been a hallmark of this country.

Indeed, there has been a pounding litany on this front that has demoralized many affirmative action proponents. Proposition 209 in California, the *Hopwood* case in Texas, the affirmative action referendum that passed in the State of Washington in 1998, and similar initiatives across the nation are indicative of the fact that one would have to be naïve to believe that affirmative action will survive absent a campaign to preserve it. Essentially, what has not captured the public eye—unlike Proposition 209, *Hopwood*, and the like—presents ever more daunting challenges. In the 105th Congress, which concluded in 1998, Senator Jesse Helms of North Carolina introduced S. 188, a bill to eliminate all federal affirmative action programs; S. 189, a bill to bar the executive branch of the federal government from establishing any additional class of individuals that is protected against discrimination; and S. 47, a bill to prohibit the executive branch of the federal government from establishing an additional class of individuals that is protected against discrimination in federal employment and for other purposes.[24] Senator Mitchell McConnell of Kentucky and Congressman Charles Canady of Florida have sought to gut Executive Order 11246 and the affirmative action policies of the past seven Republican and Democratic presidents by specifically seeking to bar the use of any numerical objectives such as goals and timetables in all federal programs. They would also eliminate the use of affirmative action to remedy past or present discrimination, forbid consent decrees that utilize race-conscious remedies, and outlaw even those programs that adhere to the "strict scrutiny" standard set by the U.S. Supreme Court.[25]

Such conservative maneuvers are reflective of the fact that affirmative action has attracted powerful foes on the Right. Senator Jesse Helms, for example, used an anti–affirmative action commercial to no small effect in his victorious 1990 campaign against Democratic—and African American—challenger Harvey Gantt; it featured a white hand crumpling a rejection letter from a potential employer as a voice-over narration announced that he had not received this job because a black person had. The anti–affirmative action cry has been quite useful in the effort to build and consolidate the Republican right–wing.[26] In fact, some of the same corporate forces who have announced their support for affirmative action also have been generous in their campaign donations to the Republican Right.[27] This is why it would be foolish to take for granted the widespread backing for affirmative action.

Moreover, the right-wing attack on affirmative action has begun to take ever more curious turns. Former GOP presidential candidate Pat Buchanan has questioned the percentage of Jewish and Asian American students at Harvard, feeling that their numbers there exceed their proportion in the nation's population, while the percentage of "non-Jewish whites" at this Cambridge school is supposedly lagging. According to Buchanan,

> it is clear that Evangelical Christians, Catholics, Mormons . . . are the victims of a bigotry so embedded that Harvard cannot see it right in front of its eyes. As for the ethnic identity of Harvard's rejects it must include many kids of Scots-Irish, Irish, Welsh, German, Italian, Greek, Polish, Czech, Slovak, Slavic, Scandinavian, Russian, Croatian, Serbian, Lithuanian, Latvian and Estonian descent—and dozens of other small ethnic groups.

Buchanan concluded, "now we know who really gets the shaft at Harvard—white Christians."[28] Buchanan's alarmist remarks were echoed by Ron Unz, the California entrepreneur who spearheaded the effort to oust bilingual education from his state.[29] These inflammatory words caught the eye of the Jewish weekly, the *Forward*, which termed these ideas "redolent of either black-shirt appeals to the lumpen or the modest proposals of Jonathan Swift. . . ."[30]

This exchange points up the obvious: though some would think the fallout from the assault on affirmative action would be limited to African Americans, this is an unrealistic wish. Inevitably others will be swept into the line of fire.

◆ ◆ ◆

Affirmative action has attained some of its most significant victories and attracted some of its most implacable foes in the realm of education. The most recent effort to rebut this opposition, the longitudinal study conducted by the former president of Princeton University, William Bowen, and the former president of Harvard University, Derek Bok, seeks to place fact and hard data where too often anecdote has reigned.[31] For example, Shelby Steele has written that "the effect of preferential treatment [*sic*]—the lowering of normal standards to increase black participation—puts blacks at war with an expanding realm of debilitating doubt, so that the doubt itself becomes an unrecognized preoccupation that undermines their ability to perform, especially in integrated situations." There are many unexamined, unsubstantiated presuppositions in this bald assertion—"preferential treatment"? "lowering of normal standards"?—but the larger point is that the underlying premise is inaccurate. After an exhaustive survey, Bowen and Bok find the assumption about "debilitating doubt" to be unproven.[32]

Bowen and Bok also find it striking that it is primarily racial diversity that has attracted scorn, while other kinds of diversity—e.g., the geographic variety—have not. For example, schools like Princeton purport to be national institutions and, therefore, seek to attract students from across the country; as such, it is probably easier for a student from Montana or Idaho to be admitted to this Ivy League institution than for a student from New Jersey or New York with similar credentials; in part this stems from the fact that it is easier to attract students from the latter states than the former, yet this kind of diversity does not attract the kind of scorn heaped on racial diversity.

There are related issues. It has been reported that "special considerations in admissions for the rich and well-connected has been part of the UCLA culture for years. . . . In some cases, [former] UCLA Chancellor and his top aides were instrumental in securing spots for lesser qualified or rejected applicants who were sponsored by donors and other supporters." This list of the well connected included movie producer Jon Peters, former paramour of Barbra Streisand; Lawrence Irell, founder of a major law firm; LA county supervisor Zev Yaroslavsky; and a number of others. In one case the son of Chancellor Young's neighbor was admitted though his 2.95 GAP and his 860 SAT meant that he was—technically—ineligible for admission. This happened in the context of a tense debate within the University of California Board of Regents about affirmative action. Hostile to affirmative action was Regent Leo Kolligian, a Fresno attorney; in voting for draconian measures, he declared, "To me, when you give preferential treatment, you're not exercising equal rights . . . That's not the way I understand the Constitution." Yet, four months before, his record reveals that Kolligian had leaned heavily on UCLA officials to admit the daughter of a Fresno area builder who had been rejected with a 790 SAT score, considered anemic by UCLA standards. This was one of thirty-two such requests since he had become a regent in 1985. Apparently, there are those who feel that "affirmative action" should be limited to the well connected.[33]

The well connected and affluent have other advantages in gaining admissions to college—for example, the ability to hire tutors for the SAT for as much as $400 per hour: Does this not suggest that the SAT measures the size of one's pocketbook more than one's ability to excel in college?[34] The affluent and well connected can also hire private counselors at similar rates who can advise them on tactics and strategies for gaining admission to a college of choice; does not affirmative action help to level this uneven playing field?[35]

Unfortunately, Bowen and Bok do not spend much time debunking the pervasive authority of the SAT administered by the Educational Testing Service of Princeton, New Jersey; however, others have not been so circumspect.[36] Professor Robert Sternberg of Yale University has outlined three kinds of intelligence: practical, creative, and analytical. He maintains stoutly that colleges and universities mostly seek the latter, to the detriment of the other two; this is partially a result of the hegemony of the SAT. However, as he points out, "many people have good ideas that never go anywhere because they lack the practical persuasive skills to convince anyone of their worth." Instead, institutions establish self-perpetuating mechanisms that continually reproduce the status quo. Some societies, for example, make selections on the basis of religion, then create self-fulfilling prophecies by perpetuating institutions based on this principle. There are other analogues to this. Chief executives are, on average, three inches taller than the people they supervise. Army generals are, on average, four inches taller than their troops. Professor Sternberg laments the fact that schools and employers too often neglect students who may be "street wise" and brimming with creative ideas but who never make it to first base.[37]

The question of measuring subjective factors in making decisions in employment or otherwise is no more critical than in the National Football League. There two-thirds of the players are African American. And there, not coincidentally, objective and quantitative measures—speed in the forty-yard dash, how many pounds one can bench-press, weight, height, etc.—are significant in determining who makes the team. Of course, these factors are not exclusively determinative, which is one reason why the position of quarterback—the most "glamorous" position on the field—is disproportionately held down by Euro-Americans.

Worse, the head coaching position—a post that can pay in the seven figures—where subjective and qualitative factors are deemed to be important in making the determination of who is to be hired, is almost exclusively reserved for Euro-Americans. In December 1998 seven of these plum jobs were open—out of a total of about thirty—and the preliminary assessment was that none should be shocked if African Americans, who dominate the game on the field, would not walk away with any of these positions.[38] This begs the question of ownership where African Americans are even scarcer. If African Americans cannot obtain executive posts in a field where they have dominated, then—a fortiori—affirmative action is a must in those spheres where they have been marginalized historically.

◆   ◆   ◆

At the end of the day, affirmative action can be said to have widespread support, the right-wing attacks on it notwithstanding. However, if it is to survive, careful analysis must be made of how it came into existence in the first place: this was through mass struggle—as exemplified by the Civil War, the attempted "March on Washington" of the early 1940s, the urban unrest of 1960s—and close attention to the global environment. Anything less will only insure that affirmative action becomes the equivalent of a policy "dodo bird"—effectively extinct—as the new century dawns.

NOTES

1. Donald G. Nieman, *To Set the Law in Motion: The Freedman's Bureau and the Legal Rights of Blacks* (Milwood, N.Y.: KTO Press, 1979); Howard A. White, *The Freedmen's Bureau in Louisiana* (Baton Rouge: Louisiana State University Press, 1970).

2. *Jones v. Alfred H. Mayer Co.*, 392 U.S. 409, 88 S. Ct. 2186, 20 L.Ed.2d. 1189 (1968).

3. President's Commission on Civil Rights, *To Secure These Rights* (Washington D.C.: Government Printing Office, 1947), 146.

4. Gerald Horne, *Black and Red: W.E.B. Du Bois and the Afro-American Response to the Cold War, 1944–1963* (Albany: State University of New York Press, 1986).

5. Gerald Horne, *Communist Front? The Civil Rights Congress, 1946–1956* (London: Associated University Presses, 1988), passim.

6. Gay McDougall, "From Civil Rights to International Human Rights," *Crisis*, December 1988, p. 7.

7. Gerald Horne, *Fire This Time: The Watts Uprising and the 1960s* (Charlottesville: University Press of Virginia, 1995), 349, 38.

8. Lee Rainwater and William L. Yancey, *The Moynihan Report and the Politics of Controversy* (Cambridge: MIT Press, 1967), 126.

9. Oliver C. Cox, *Caste, Class and Race: A Study in Social Dynamics* (Garden City: Doubleday, 1948).

10. *The Economist* (London), 19 December 1998.

11. Iam Emsley, *The Malaysian Experience of Affirmative Action: Lessons for South Africa* (Cape Town: Human & Rosseau and Tafelberg, 1996), 104.

12. Ibid., 7

13. *South China Morning Post* (Hong Kong), 22 October 1998.

14. See, e.g., http://www.now.org/issues/affirm/affirmre.html

15. Robert Massie, *Loosing the Bonds: The United States and South Africa in the Apartheid Years* (Garden City: Doubleday, 1997).

16. U.S. Bureau of the Census, *Statistical Abstract of the United States* (Washington, D.C.: Government Printing Office, 1997).

17. See, e.g., *http://www.acenet.edu/programs/DGR/AffAction/works/business.html*

18. *New York Times*, 6 December 1998.

19. *New York Times*, 9 December 1998.

20. *Los Angeles Times*, 23 September 1998.

21. *Chronicle of Higher Education*, 11 December 1998; *Los Angeles Times*, 3 December 1998.

22. See, e.g., *Engineering Contractors Association v. Metro Dade District*, 122 F3d 895, 905 (11th Cir 1997).

23. See, e.g., *http://www.equalrights.org/AFFIRM/stats.html*

24. See, e.g., *http://www.affirmativeaction.org/97/leg.html*

25. See, e.g., *http://www.acenet.edu/programs/DGR/AffAction/threats/threats.html*

26. Dan T. Carter, *From George Wallace to Newt Gingrich: Race in the Conservative Counterrevolution, 1963–1994* (Baton Rouge: Louisiana State University Press, 1996).

27. Thomas Ferguson, *Golden Rule: The Investment Theory of Party Competition and the Logic of Money Driven Political Systems* (Chicago: University of Chicago Press, 1995).

28. *New York Post*, 28 November 1998.

29. *Wall Street Journal*, 16 November 1998.

30. *Forward*, 4 December 1998.

31. William G. Bowen and Derek Bok, *The Shape of the River: Long-Term Consequences of Considering Race in College and University Admissions* (Princeton, N.J.: Princeton University Press, 1998).

32. Ibid., 261, 265.

33. *Los Angeles Times*, 21 March 1996.

34. *New York Times*, 10 January 1999.

35. *Los Angeles Times*, 29 December 1998; *http://www.educationalconsulting.org*

36. Robert Hayman, *The Smart Society: Society, Intelligence and Law* (New York: New York University Press, 1998).

37. *Financial Times*, 25 September 1998.

38. *New York Times*, 28 December 1998.

PART IV

Strategies for Racial and Social Justice

~:~

20

A Critique of Race Dialogues and Debates in the United States

JAMES JENNINGS

INTRODUCTION

Many civic leaders and activists have raised calls for dialogues about the continuing or future place of race in U.S. society. Fueling these calls are various demographic and social developments changing the racial and ethnic composition of the nation. In the last several decades, racial and ethnic diversity among the total population, as well as within specific communities of color, has been increasing rapidly. While growing racial and ethnic diversity may be restricted to some parts of the country, it is increasing dramatically in those particular places, especially in larger cities and some states. Many cities are continuing to tip racially and ethnically away from majority-white status. States with relatively large populations, like California, Texas, and Florida, reflect significant growth among people of color, particularly Latinos, blacks, and Asians.

This unfolding demography is influencing the political terrain, as well. Issues such as the place of blacks in the Democratic Party, the relationship between blacks, Latinos, and Asians in national and state politics, the racial or ethnic impact of social welfare policies, or even the future of the national two-party system are molded by the nation's current and future demography. At the precipice of anticipated major demographic and social changes, continuing race and ethnic divisions loom as a key concern. Race divisions are manifested in terms of where people live, where their children attend school, their life expectancy rates, and what they have achieved or have access to, in terms of a range of social, economic, and cultural benefits. In light of this situation, it seems that the Kerner Commission's warning in its report issued in 1968 that the United States was developing into two societies, a black and a white one, has to be amended.[1]

The Kerner Commission explicitly pointed to a fundamental and entrenched racial divide in this nation. Social and economic indications are that various kinds of racial and ethnic divides do exist, but these are not restricted to only blacks and whites. A review of racial and ethnic history shows that this was never an accurate description of race in the United States. Certainly the nation's demography does not justify this limited description any longer. The Kerner Commission's focus on a racial divide, however, coupled with problems in housing, schools, police relations, and economic opportunities, is still a relevant and important public concern.

Some corporate and foundation leaders and representatives of other sectors believe that race remains an unresolved issue in this nation. Reflecting this belief, the call for racial dialogue was highlighted by President William Clinton's appointment of a study commission to plan and implement a series of national forums focusing on this issue.[2] This call was in response to racial problems and divisions manifested in civic and political attitudes, residential and schooling patterns, and continuing racial gaps involving health, poverty, employment, and wealth. This school of thought proposes that continuing racial gaps in employment, housing, wealth, health, and public safety show that race and racism remain significant challenges to U.S. social democracy, and therefore, the role of government should be an activist one in responding to these issues. Many citizens who adhere to this view see the need for political mobilization on behalf of social and economic measures aimed at racial divisions and discrimination.

There are other observers, in contrast to this particular orientation about the state of race relations, who argue that race is no longer problematical in this society. These voices tend to emphasize the racial progress and reconciliation that has taken place in the last several decades. They believe that we now live in a "post–Civil Rights" period, where continuing social and economic problems facing blacks and others usually indicate deficiencies within these groups, rather than with race or racism. There are many differences of opinion within this school of thought. While some here would propose that any racial progress should be celebrated because it indicates that the nation is no longer racist, as was the case during periods of de jure segregation, others in this camp see race or racism as not especially significant in explaining the racial gaps in living conditions. They would instead focus on natural abilities and native intelligence, or on cultural and group attitudes as explanation for continuing racial gaps. Generally speaking, this school has accused the Civil Rights leadership of being anachronistic regarding the need for continuing political mobilization and agitation aimed against racial and sexual discrimination. Proponents of this orientation posit that emphasis should be on the racial progress that has been realized, since this is far more important than presumably of isolated incidents of racial hatred and violence or continuing social and economic problems facing blacks and mentioned above. Furthermore, these people say, continuing racial gaps in living conditions reflect not discrimination but a range of other explanations including human capital, economic restructuring, cultural attitudes, and native intelligence.

After reviewing some of the current debates and dialogues, as well as earlier studies about race, I conclude that there are four themes missing in both of these schools of ideas and discussions. These themes are critical, however, in understanding fully the current racial situation, as well as the possible future of race relations in the United States. The themes include (1) the historical and conceptual linkage between struggles for, prima facie, racial equality and the expansion of social and economic democracy; (2) racial problems as a reflection of social and caste order rather than personal attitudes and prejudice; (3) race as *racially and ethnically multicultural* and international phenomena; and (4) the role of wealth and race divisions in U.S. society. The exploration of these themes is essential for finding ways of reducing or eliminating racial problems reflected in different living conditions for various groups and in reducing the possibility of racial and ethnic tensions in this nation. A politics aimed at moving society toward social justice and racial collaboration, whether at the local community, state, or national level, has to reflect an understanding of these themes in order to mobilize people or voters in support of progressive public agendas. The next section of this essay begins with a critique of the ideas of those suggesting that race or racism is insignificant in explaining the life chances of blacks. The essay then examines in detail the four issues that have to be part of a full and honest dialogue about race in this nation.

POST–CIVIL RIGHTS PERIOD?

Many scholars and observers argue that the nation has turned an important cor-ner in terms of race and the historical problem of racism. One of the latest books reflecting this theme is Stephen and Abigail Thernstrom's *America in Black and White: One Nation, Indivisible.*[3] Generally speaking, the genre of works proposing that racial divisions and racism are no longer significant issues requiring govern-ment or public attention have not satisfactorily dealt with numerous incidents of brutal racism in our nation. Writings, such as that of the Thernstroms, compel us to consider the meaning and implications of many examples of racial hatred in our society. Such thinking forces us to ask if Jasper, Texas, where a black man was lynched due to his race in 1998, was just an isolated incident? Was the Rodney King beating in 1991 another isolated incident? How should we view the killing of Amadou Diallo and the beating of Abmer Louima by white New York City police officers in 1998? Do the eight thousand racial hatred crimes reported by the FBI in 1998 mean anything for our discussions about race? Are these examples of racial crimes committed by wayward people? Or do they reflect a societal layer of racial hatred that periodically emerges? If the latter, what social, economic, or political forces serve as the foundation for this layer of racial animosity in U.S. society?

It is informative to examine the logic of contemporary observers who suggest that race divisions and consequent problems have been overcome, finally, in our society and that therefore policies aimed at rectifying race divisions and dispari-ties, such as affirmative action, are moot. These observers do not approach inci-dents of racial hatred and brutality as reflective of the fundamental policies or practices of institutions or leadership; therefore, these are events that can be ignored in their discussions about race. Some of the arguments presented by pro-ponents of this school of thinking are remarkably similar to the logic utilized by some interests in the 1950s and 1960s in attempts to derail the Civil Rights Movement or convince the public at that time that blacks were indeed moving too fast. According to these arguments, those individuals, representing every race and ethnic group in this society, whocall for more racial equality are dismissed as trou-blemakers and agitators.

The arguments and logic that we hear today against the need for expanding government efforts at racial and economic democracy in this society are shrouded in new statistics, but essentially remain the same as those made in the 1940s, 1950s, and 1960s by those who were opposed to the Civil Rights Movement. One text that illustrates this connection is Martin Luther King Jr.'s eloquent *Letter from a*

Birmingham Jail, written in April 1963.[4] His words show that the rationalizations offered today against agitation for social and economic justice are not new ideas. Additionally, these current arguments do not reflect the missing themes mentioned earlier. There are five components of these arguments that reflect a historical and circular logic that is key to the ideological framework of this school.

One component is the proposal that racial progress realized thus far is proof that racism is no longer a problem. A second claim is that rhetorical support for racial equality by whites, as evidenced in surveys and polls, represents ample and undeniable evidence of operational and substantive support for racial equality. A third component of this framework is the accusation that those who call for social change or are not satisfied with the contemporary extent or state of racial progress are either guilty white liberals or militant blacks, and therefore their claims are not credible. The fourth suggestion is that egregious outbreaks of racial and ethnic hatred, such as the recent lynchings cited earlier, do not reflect systemic racism but rather the isolated actions of deplorable individuals. Interestingly, despite the fact that there are thousands of reported incidents of racial harassment and violence every year in this country, one finds some writers in this school proposing that these incidents perhaps are encouraged by the very calls for racial and social justice. Again, the words of Dr. King. in response to those who made similar arguments during the early sixties seem particularly appropriate: "Isn't this like condemning the robbed man because his possession of money precipitated the evil act of robbery?"[5] Finally, there is the perennial reminder by the fifth component of this school of thinking that blacks in the United States are treated well compared to minorities in other societies, and therefore problems in this nation are not really as bad as they seem. These proposals represent the foundation for concluding that the nation no longer need be concerned about addressing racial divisions or social injustice in this society. This is a framework that discourages public dialogue about racial matters, and closes the door to historical, political, or economic critiques of continuing racial divisions in the United States.

MENDING RACE AND RACISM?

There are many people who believe that problems related to race, including racism, continue to exist and require some degree of attention. This thinking is reflected in the President's Initiative on Race. His race commission has enunciated five goals aimed at resolving the nation's racial problems, including,

(1) to articulate the President's vision of racial reconciliation and a just, unified America; (2) to help educate the nation about the facts surrounding the issue of race; (3) to promote a constructive dialogue, to confront and work through the difficulty and controversial issues surrounding race; (4) to recruit and encourage leadership at all levels to help bridge racial divides; and, (5) to find, develop, and implement solutions in critical areas such as education, economic opportunity, housing, health care, crime and the administration of justice—for individuals, communities, corporations and government all levels.[6]

While these are lofty goals, the dialogues generated by this initiative, as well as the president's own statements and policies, reflect a disconnection from the themes mentioned earlier.

A national dialogue on race as recently enacted by President Clinton is appropriate for problems like prejudice and bigotry. But racial hierarchy, reflected in social and economic inequalities and the cultural domination and alleged superiority of European life, cannot be challenged simply on the basis of dialogue. As pointed out by Dr. William Alberts, who has written extensively on the media's role in perpetuating racial divisions, "'a great and unprecedented conversation of race' . . . describing President Clinton's race commission redefines the problem of the 'racial divide.' The focus automatically shifts from group discrimination . . . to interpersonal relationships. By its very nature, talking implies an equality that does not exist."[7] A dialogue on race that will help to overcome racial divisions requires some focus on the themes cited above. Understandably, this will complicate dialogues, but it is essential that race and race divisions be approached comprehensively, reflecting historical, social, economic, and political patterns and connections.

RACIAL EQUALITY AS SOCIAL AND ECONOMIC JUSTICE

One theme that has not been emphasized in some studies and dialogues about race is the inherent linkage between struggles for racial quality and the pursuit of social justice and economic democracy. Some of the racial debates, for example, are ensconced with the notion that these struggles were aimed merely at attaining a legally color-blind society. A legion of books about the Civil Rights Movement, however, as well as a review of earlier racial struggles, clearly indicate that these episodes were part of a broader vision of social justice. We can turn to W. E. B.

Du Bois's *Black Reconstruction in America 1860-1880*, for example, to note that freed blacks in the Reconstruction governments in the South were aggressive in adopting expansive social welfare policies that served to redistribute wealth among poor and working-class sectors, regardless of color.[8] They defined and operationalized their new freedom within a framework of expanding social and economic justice for all people in the South.

James W. Button's *Blacks and Social Change: Impact of the Civil Rights Movement in Southern Communities* indicates that in many local areas struggles for racial equality were actually aimed at policies and practices that would redistribute wealth and basic economic benefits and services to poor and working-class people.[9] He gives examples of how the Civil Rights movement in several southern cities, for example, was part of local struggles for police and fire protection, clean neighborhood streets, public works, recreation programs, and other public services.

Many individuals involved in struggles to achieve racial equality understood that legal equality was but a step, albeit a key one, in moving toward social and economic equality. The end product of the struggle, therefore, was not legal equality, but rather social and economic policies reflecting justice and fairness. This is suggested in a recent article by historian Linda Gordon, focusing on the history of black women activists involved in welfare issues from the 1890s up to the Second World War.[10] As Gordon shows in her essay, "Black and White Visions of Welfare: Women's Welfare Activism, 1890-1945," for the most part black women activists defined the struggle for racial equality within a framework of an expanding social and economic democracy. Their struggles were never limited to the unitary notion that the adoption of racial equality on the books would respond to social and economic inequalities and injustices in actual practice.

This idea is also reflected in Robin Kelley's examination of busing struggles in some southern cities. This issue did not merely involve breaking down the doors of segregation in the abstract. As he writes, "Sitting with whites, for most black riders, was never a critical issue; rather, African Americans wanted more space for themselves, they wanted to receive equitable treatment, they wanted to be personally treated with respect and dignity, they wanted to be heard and possibly understood, they wanted to get to work on time. . . ."[11] This author shows, in other words, that these local struggles did not only reflect some reference to the Civil Rights Movement, but also focused on who would be able to utilize certain urban spaces in order to pursue economic activities.

The struggle for racial equality in the pursuit of social justice and economic democracy has been overlooked in some reports on race relations, as well as in the recently issued report commissioned by the Clinton administration. Yet, the fundamental purpose of racial equality is the attainment of social and economic democracy. Racial equality is not merely an end, it is the means to a vision and actualization of social justice. Although this was recently pointed out eloquently in Charles V. and Dona Hamilton's *Dual Agenda: The African-American Struggle for Civil and Economic Equality*, it is a fact that has unfortunately generally been overlooked in studies about race.[12] This is a very important fact, however, because if racial equality is to be measured simply on the basis of the legal ending of apartheid in this nation and the endorsement of color-blind language in our laws, then it means that the struggle for social justice and economic democracy is finished, as far as some observers are concerned.

Struggles for racial equality hardly have been confined to the attainment of legal equality. As racial struggles evolved many people have been compelled to move beyond the concept of legal equality because they have realized that a society can be socially and economically unjust, yet with color-blind language profess and show legal equality. Again, the words of Dr. King are appropriate.: "We can never forget that everything Hitler did in Germany was 'legal.'"[13] It is this realization, as pointed out recently by historian Eric Foner, that propelled the Civil Rights Movement to approach the idea of freedom not simply as the legal dismantling of apartheid in this nation, but rather as a movement in the pursuit of social and economic equality.[14]

RACIAL HIERARCHY

A theme that has been left out of many race studies involves the existence of racial hierarchy in this society. The idea of "racial hierarchy," or a racial order, proposed by intellectuals like Robert Blauner, Louis Kushnick, James and Grace Lee Boggs, and William Nelson more than thirty years ago, suggests that the nature of racial problems is not one simply of misunderstandings, or attitudes, or even prejudice and bigotry.[15] Rather, race problems and divisions reflect a social, economic, and cultural order in this society where white life is valued far more than black, or Latino, or Asian, or non-European life, Michael Jordan, Oprah Winfrey, or Colin Powell notwithstanding.

Racial hierarchy is reflected in historical and persistent disparities in education, health, unemployment, housing, arrest rates, and poverty rates. All of these areas show a continuing racial gap that has been unchanged for generations.

In other words, race is defined and operationalized not solely on the basis of attitudes, or prejudice, as is suggested in some parts of the work of Gunnar Myrdal, *An American Dilemma,* but more fundamentally on an entrenched social order.[16] In this sense, Oliver C. Cox's classic work, *Caste, Class, and Race: A Study in Social Dynamics,* may be more relevant for understanding and analyzing race relations in the contemporary period.[17] This social order is supported by institutional and structural relationships linking economic, political, and cultural dynamics. Racial hierarchy has a profound historical context that is still a relevant factor in race relations today. Since history is sometimes treated as the "past" and therefore no longer relevant for race today, it is important to revisit some historical facts.

Contemporary political and economic institutions of this nation were originally built on race, class, and gender inequalities. In particular, race has played a major role in the establishment and practices of political institutions, economic policies, and social relations of the nation since its founding, and these decisions continue to impact our society today. A small group of white slave-owners formulated institutional policies and practices on the basis of white skin privileges. With the utilization of "color-blind" language, coupled with hypocritical appeals to universal equality, a system of white-skin privilege was endorsed and embodied in the U.S. Constitution.

White-skin privileges were continually put into practice, regardless of laws and professed ideals of equality on the part of white leadership, in the form of Jim Crowism, daily lynchings, and sustained campaigns of terror, in the nineteenth century, and certainly throughout the twentieth century as well.

For most of the nation's history, as pointed out by Yale University professor Roger Smith, "the measures government took to promote economic and political opportunities, material prosperity, education, transportation, housing, and other goods were of direct avail primarily to white male citizens or some subset thereof. . . ." [18] Many U.S. presidents and their administrations contributed to the maintenance of racial divisions and racism for political gain. Reflecting white supremacist views, U.S. presidents were often openly hostile to black people and other people of color. Presidents like Warren G. Harding, Calvin Coolidge, and Herbert Hoover, just to name a few, refused to condemn organizations like the Ku Klux Klan in its decades-long campaign of racial terrorism. President Franklin Roosevelt referred to blacks as "semi-beasts" and frequently as "darkies" and "niggers," as did Presidents Truman and Richard Nixon.[19] One historian, Kenneth O'Reilly, author of *Nixon's Piano: Presidents and Racial Politics from Washington to Clinton,* shows convincingly, in my opinion, the complicity of presidents and their administrations in the exploitation of racial divisions, either for political or electoral gain or because they really believed that whites are superior to blacks.[20]

These examples are historical but they point to patterns of political and economic behavior that are still utilized in the contemporary period. For example, in spite of the lofty goals enunciated by President Clinton in appointing the Initiative on Race, he too has capitalized on race divisions for political and electoral gain, and thereby has helped to perpetuate a racialized social and economic order. As observed by journalist Mumia Abu-Jamal, President Clinton has exploited race for political advantage in a number of ways:

> His skillful use of the "black faces in high places" strategy, while ostensibly in support of the black [middle-class], masked an attack on the black working poor, who were central, subliminal targets of a "New Democrat" attack, designed to ease white, suburban anxiety. In this context, the so-called Welfare "Reform" Act, the Anti-Habeas Corpus Bill (so-called Anti-Terrorism Bill), and his administration's opposition to the Racial Justice Act are utterly understandable. The public dissing of strong, outspoken black women like rapper Sister Soulja, Law Professor Lani Guinier, and Dr. Joycelyn Elder was also a calculated effort to appeal to white ethnics, by showing he could put blacks in their place: subordinate.[21]

These historical and contemporary examples suggest that racial hierarchy continues to represent some basis for political or economic gain for whites that are subsidized by blacks.

A pervasive and sometimes invisible system of white skin privilege—for whites as a group—is reflected in this racial hierarchy. An example of how racial hierarchy operates to invisibilize white-skin privileges involves affirmative action in higher education. Affirmative action, as limited as it is in concept and application, benefits many groups. As pointed out by writer Steven J. Rosenthal, affirmative action, rather than being divisive, has actually helped whites, women, and people of color: "By integrating workplaces and schools and by concretely demonstrating to whites that minorities and women can do any job that white men can do, affirmative action has historically reduced the divisive racist attitudes of whites and created more of a basis for multiracial unity."[22] The benefits of affirmative action are confirmed by another observer, Professor Cedric Herring, who writes that

> affirmative action programs in the workplace are associated with higher incomes, better jobs, and more coworker acceptance for those whom they were intended

to help. Indeed, they are correlated with higher incomes for racial minorities, women, and people from low-income backgrounds without appearing to do significant harm to the economic well-being of white males who work in such settings.[23]

In spite of these kinds of benefits that go beyond race, the issue of contention with affirmative action, as we know, is that as soon as some of its benefits are realized by blacks, Latinos, or Asians, some claim that this is, ipso facto, discriminatory against whites.

According to the editors of *The Journal of Blacks in Higher Education*, this resistance to affirmative action is hypocritical in light of the benefits that are realized by whites in higher education, due to no other reason than that they are white. It is observed here:

> The conservative position is that they should be abolished because we live in, and must be faithful to, a meritocratic society. Accordingly, it is said that students should be admitted to educational institutions solely on the basis of individual merit or personal qualifications. But this statement is pure hypocrisy. In fact, the number of academically under-qualified white students admitted each year to college for political, family legacy, or financial influence far exceeds the number of black students admitted under racial preferences.[24]

The editors provide a specific example of this situation. In 1997 Harvard admitted 132 black enrollees, but 264 white enrollees, not as academically qualified, but who had parents who attended Harvard or were on the faculty of Harvard. The Federal Office of Civil Rights reported that these legacy admits on the average had SAT scores 35 points lower, lower grade point averages, and lower class ranks than average black enrollees. In this same year MIT admitted 64 black enrollees, but 325 white students as legacy admits who were not as qualified as the black enrollees.[25] Yet, there is no outcry about lowering standards in terms of underqualified white students at Harvard or MIT.

RACE AS MULTICULTURAL AND INTERNATIONAL

The third theme that is overlooked in many race studies is the fact that race involves multicultural and international dynamics. Racism is not exclusively a problem focusing on the treatment of, and resistance on the part of, blacks in the

United States. Nor are race and racism simply a national problem; this problem is international in scope. Race divisions have been utilized to limit or to deny social and economic benefits to many communities of color. After much protestation, this was acknowledged, in part, in the President's Initiative on Race. Unfortunately, this acknowledgment came only after insistent concern and dismay at the committee's initial ignorance of this matter. The final report does not do justice to this issue, in my opinion.

Political relationships between communities of color have major significance for the development of race relations and public policy. Urban politics and public policy in many cities will be shaped by the particular political posture of, coalitions of, or conflicts between blacks, Latinos, and Asians. This observation is confirmed, in part, by a look at the nation's 'racial' urban eruptions in the last fifteen years or so. This was a key issue evident in the Liberty City rebellions in Miami in the early 1980s, as well as in those in Washington, D.C., in 1990, in Washington Heights in New York City in 1991, and in several cities in 1992 in the aftermath of the infamous Rodney King beating. There were many social and economic factors associated with these urban rebellions, but the state of relations between blacks, Latinos, and Asians was also critical.

RACE AND THE ROLE OF WEALTH

Finally, the fourth theme that is overlooked in some race studies has to do with the relationship between race and the management and distribution of wealth. The management and distribution of wealth, and the concentration of wealth, is a topic that is almost completely overlooked in many of the studies and discussions about racial issues and problems in this nation. It was certainly overlooked in the recent President's Initiative on Race. The status of race, as well as its future role, is inextricably linked to national politics and the economy in ways that maintain divisions and dampen the possibilities for the expansion of social democracy. This is a historical relationship that continues in the contemporary period. Race and ethnic divisions have been functional for interests that could be threatened by class-based challenges. W. E. B. Du Bois's chapter, "Back Toward Slavery" in his *Black Reconstruction in America 1860-1880* is classic in showing this relationship between race and wealth, and how blacks and poor whites were exploited to maintain a system of economic privilege for the bourbon and land gentry in the South immediately after the U.S. Civil War.[26]

The analytical model developed by Du Bois was repeated in yet another classic work in political science, V. O. Key Jr.'s *Politics, Parties, and Pressure Groups*, first published in 1942.[27] In this work, Key showed how racial divisions and fear were utilized to build the political careers of segregationists in the Democratic Party and thereby allow these elected officials to ignore the economic needs of poor and working-class whites, and instead nurture the needs of wealthy and powerful whites. A genre of books, as a matter of fact, beginning with work by Herbert Aptheker, *Afro-American History: A Modern Era*, Meyer Weinberg's *A Chance to Learn: A History of Race and Education in America*, Robert Allen's *Black Awakening in Capitalist America*, Forest G. Woods's study of the Reconstruction period, *Black Scare*, and more recently Michael Goldfield's *The Color of Politics*, and others, examine the relationship between race and the distribution and concentration of wealth in our society.[28] Essentially, political and electoral exploitation of race and ethnic divisions have served to buffer the owners and managers of massive wealth from popular discontent, and to guarantee the elections of political managers who will not threaten the upward concentration of wealth into a few hands.

Professor William J. Wilson offers a glimpse of how this issue is operationalized in politics. He observes that despite the growth in the national economy, poor and working-class people are hurting economically. Wilson posits that even some sectors of the middle class will begin feeling the pain of job turnover, declining real wages, and higher costs for education and health services, generating social insecurities and fears.[29] He argues that it is during these kinds of periods, especially, that race and ethnic divisions are utilized to neutralize class-based tensions and anger. He writes that "during periods of high levels of economic anxiety the frustrations of citizens need to be channeled in positive or constructive directions. . . ." But,

> In the past several years . . . the opposite has frequently been true. In a time of heightened economic insecurities, the poisonous political rhetoric (featuring the demonization of minorities, immigrants, and welfare mothers, as well as the open attacks on affirmative action programs) of certain highly visible political spokespersons has increased racial antagonism and channeled frustrations along paths that divide the racial groups. . . . Instead of focusing on the economic and political forces that have disrupted the economic lives of citizens, these divisive messages encourage them to turn on each other—race against race.[30]

In the last two decades we have experienced significant decline in real wages, massive public disinvestments, and rapid militarization. Through tax breaks and actual subsidies, hundreds of billions of dollars have been given to major corporations by local and state governments.

This situation has grown so egregious that *Time* magazine produced a special report on corporate welfare in order to shed light on this concern. They opened this special report with the following query:

> How would you like to pay only a quarter of the real estate taxes you owe on your home? And buy everything for the next 10 years without spending a single penny in sales tax? Keep a chunk of your paycheck free of income taxes? Have the city in which you live lend you money at rates cheaper than any bank charges? Then have the same city install free water and sewer lines to your house, offer you a perpetual discount on utility bills—and top it all off by landscaping your front yard at no charge?[31]

In essence, this represents the basis of our economic development policies for neighborhoods and cities.

These policies have been virtually insignificant in terms of job creation, neighborhood development, provision of quality schooling or decent health facilities; and affordable and decent housing. Yet continuing race and ethnic divisions, as well as attacks on policies aimed at overcoming these divisions, serve to keep this issue off the table of the public agenda. It is ironic: working-class and middle-class whites who may be intensely against policies that benefit blacks, Latinos, and Asians—policies like affirmative action, universal access to higher education, and targeted investments in places where people of color tend to reside—are actually arguing against their own economic interests when one considers this in the context of the concentration of wealth and its implications for wages, job security, public safety, and basic and affordable health services.

CONCLUSION

By way of conclusion and summary, I offer two brief observations. First, the four themes I have described have been ignored in many reports on race in this nation, and, as I stated earlier, to a certain extent in President Clinton's dialogue on race. Yet, I would propose, these four themes are necessary for a complete and holistic dialogue about race and its future in the United States. This means that the nation's racial problems cannot be confined by defining them as simply a product of a lack of dialogue. Additionally, the matter of social justice cannot be ignored in relation to race and racial divisions. Problems like continuing discrimination and racism, documented in numerous government reports, persistent poverty, racial and ethnic disparities in health, and glaring racial disparities in the criminal justice system, all indicate that there are still significant racial problems and divisions in this society that must be addressed on the basis of the pursuit of social justice. This is exactly why the prominent Bishop Thad Garrett, a member of the conservative group who met with President Clinton in 1998 in response to the race initiative, admonished some of his colleagues not to gloss over these kinds of problems and divisions.[32]

My second observation is that the decade of the 1990s, compared to those of the 1940s and 1950s, is certainly very different in terms of how people of various hues are treated by law. Despite a history defined and built upon race divisions and white-skin privilege, there have been significant victories in challenging the maintenance and utilization of race divisions and racism as a prop for a system of social and economic injustice. Though it has become fashionable in some ideological camps today to disparage the so-called civil rights legislation that followed the Brown decisions, in fact the Civil Rights Act of 1964, the Voting Rights Act of 1965, and the Fair Housing Act of 1968 represented important legislative and constitutional victories in this nation's rejection of apartheid. Yet, these important victories are but one part of the battle to move our society toward social and economic democracy. Aside from the tactical question of the continuing effectiveness or utility of particular Civil Rights organizations and their programs, the "Civil Rights Movement" to move this society closer to social and economic justice is not over.

NOTES

1. Kerner Commision, *Report of the National Advisory Committee on Racial Disorders*, 1 March 1968, in *The Kerner Report: Report of the National Advisory Committee on Civil Disorders* (New York: Bantam, 1968)

2. The President's Initiative on Race, *One America in the 21st Century: Forging a New Future* (Washington, D.C.: U.S. Government Printing Office, 1999).

3. Stephan Thernstrom and Abigail Thernstrom, *America in Black and White: One Nation, Indivisible* (New York: Simon and Schuster, 1997).

4. Martin Luther King Jr., "Letter from a Birmingham Jail," in *A Testament of Hope: The Essential*

Writings of Martin Luther King, Jr., ed. James M. Washington (San Francisco: Harper and Row, 1986), 289–302.

5. Ibid., 295.

6. The President's Initiative on Race, *One America* , 10.

7. William Alberts, correspondence with author, 21 September 1998.

8. W.E.B. Du Bois, *Black Reconstruction in America 1860–1880* (1935; reprint, New York: Atheneum, 1985).

9. James W. Button, *Blacks and Social Change: Impact of the Civil Rights Movement in Southern Communities* (Princeton, N.J.: Princeton University Press, 1989).

10. Linda Gordon, "Black and White Visions of Welfare: Women's Welfare Activism, 1890–1945," in *We Specialize in the Wholly Impossible: A Reader in Black Women's History*, ed. Darlene Clark Hine, Wilma King, and Linda Reed (New York: Carlson Publishing, 1995), 449–85.

11. Robin D. G. Kelley, *Race Rebels: Culture, Politics, and the Black Working Class* (1994; reprint, New York: Free Press, 1996), 75.

12. Charles V. Hamilton and Dona C. Hamilton, *Dual Agenda: The African-American Struggle for Civil and Economic Equality* (New York: Columbia University Press, 1997).

13. King, "Letter," 295.

14. See Eric Foner, "African Americans and the Story of American Freedom," *Souls: A Critical Journal of Black Politics, Culture, and Society* 1, no. 1 (1999): 16–22.

15. See Robert Blauner, *Racial Oppression in America* (New York: Harper and Row, 1972); James and Grace Lee Boggs, *Revolution and Evolution in the Twentieth Century* (New York: Monthly Review Press, 1974); William E. Nelson Jr. and Philip Meranto, *Electing Black Mayors* (Columbus: Ohio University Press, 1977); Louis Kushnick, "Racism and Class Consciousness in Modern Capitalism," in *Impacts of Racism on White Americans*, ed. B. P. Bowser and R. Hunt (Beverly Hills, Calif.: Sage Publications, 1981), 191–216.

16. Gunnar Myrdal, *An American Dilemma: The Negro Problem and Modern Democracy* (1944; reprint, Piscataway, N.J.: Transaction Publishers, 1996).

17. Oliver C. Cox, *Caste, Class, and Race: A Study of Social Dynamics* (1948; reprint, New York: Monthly Review Press, 1959).

18. Roger M. Smith, "Toward a More Perfect Union: Beyond Old Liberalism and Neo-Liberalism," in *Without Justice for All: The New Liberalism and Our Retreat from Racial Equality*, ed. Adolph Reed Jr. (Boulder, Colo.: Westview Press, 1999), 343.

19. See Earl Ofari Hutchinson, *Betrayed: A History of Presidential Failure to Protect Black Lives* (Boulder, Colo.: Westview, 1996).

20. Kenneth O'Reilly, *Nixon's Piano: Presidents and Racial Politics from Washington to Clinton* (New York: Free Press, 1995).

21. Mumia Abu-Jamal, "A Presidency of Betrayal," 10 September 1998. *http://www.iacenter.org/betrayal.htm* (26 July 1999).

22. Steven Rosenthal, "Affirm Equality, Oppose Racist Scapegoating: Myths and Realities of Affirmative Action," in *African Americans and the Public Agenda: The Paradoxes of Public Policy*, ed. Cedric Herring (Thousand Oaks, Calif.: Sage Publications, 1997), 118.

23. Cedric Herring, "African Americans, The Public Agenda, and the Paradoxes of Public Policy," in *African Americans and the Public Agenda: The Paradoxes of Public Policy*, ed. Cedric Herring (Thousand Oaks, Calif.: Sage Publications, 1997), 11.

24. "Naked Hypocrisy: The Nationwide System of Affirmative Action for Whites," *Journal of Blacks in Higher Education* 18 (winter 1997/1998): 40.

25. Ibid., 41.

26. Du Bois, *Black Reconstruction*, 670–710.

27. V. O. Key Jr., *Politics, Parties, and Pressure Groups* (1942; reprint, New York: Thomas Y. Crowell Co., 1964).

28. See Herbert Aptheker, *Afro-American History: The Modern Era* (Secaucus, N.J.: Citadel Press, 1971); Meyer Weinberg, *A Chance to Learn: A History of Race and Education in America* (London: Cambridge University Press, 1977); Robert Allen, *Reluctant Performers: Racism and Social Reform Movements in the United States* (Washington, D.C.: Howard University Press, 1983); Forest G. Woods, *Black Scare* (Berkeley: University of California Press, 1970); and Michael Goldfield, *The Color of Politics: Race and Mainsprings of American Politics* (New York: New Press, 1997).

29. William J. Wilson, preface to *African Americans and the Public Agenda: The Paradoxes of Public Policy*, ed. Cedric Herring (Thousand Oaks, Calif.: Sage Publications, 1997).

30. Ibid., xi.

31. Donald L. Barlett and James B. Steele, "Special Report: What Corporate Welfare Costs You," *Time Magazine* 152 (November 1998).

32. Telephone conversations with Bishop Thad Garrett in 1998 and 1999.

21

Class, Race, and Labor Organization in the United States of America

MICHAEL GOLDFIELD

In the United States of America, the fate of U.S. labor—its ability to win lasting gains, its success in sustaining solid organizations, its episodic periods of class consciousness, as well as its brief flirtations with broader class and independent political organizational forms—has always been closely tied to the issue of race. This is not only true today, but has been the case from the earliest colonial beginnings. A brief review of this history is helpful in gaining some perspective on the present period. (Much of this discussion follows the more detailed analysis in my recent book, *The Color of Politics*, New York: New Press, 1997.)

As a first cut, the history of race relations in the United States may be summarized succinctly: Throughout most of U.S. history, despite a wide range of resistance, non-whites have been discriminated against, excluded, and denied equal access to political, social, and economic opportunities. Although employers and the ruling class in general have been responsible for the racial subordination of non-whites, most majority white labor organizations—with a few important exceptions—have participated in this oppression. In contrast, there have been several brief periods when large numbers of whites, perhaps majorities, have been supportive of, or at least not antagonistic to, equality for non-white minorities.

These periods include the years immediately preceding the American Revolution of 1776-1783, the early part of Reconstruction after the Civil War (1867-74), a stretch of the 1930s and 1940s, and a few years in the middle 1960s at the height of the civil rights movement. At times, however, for more extended periods, certain white majority unions have been committed in practice (as well as rhetorically) to interracialism and, to varying degrees, to racial egalitarianism. While certainly not the dominant tendency in U.S. labor history, solidaristic labor struggles and organizations have often emerged, not merely in hospitable situations, but even in the most unlikely times and places, including the Deep South during the most racially oppressive periods.

Today, as the United States of America increasingly moves from what had previously been largely a biracial society to one where large percentages of the population have ethnic roots that are Hispanic and Asian, as well as African and European, it is especially important to focus on the circumstances of American Indians, Hispanics, and Asians, along with African Americans, when discussing racial minorities (see, for example, the evocative essay by Mike Davis, "Magical Urbanism: Latinos Reinvent the US Big City," 1999). Nevertheless, historically and even today, the circumstances of non-white, non-black minorities cannot be understood without a clear understanding of the oppression of African Americans, historically the most consistently oppressed and economically central of all non-white groups. Thus, in a short essay, my major focus must of necessity be on black-white relations.

I. PRE–TWENTIETH CENTURY

During the seventeenth century on the North American mainland, the domination of non-whites seems to have been quite different than it was later to become. While Native Americans were racially oppressed by the colonists from an early period, there appears to have been some rough equality in the oppressive treatment of bond servants and slaves, whatever their racial or ethnic characteristics. Most were held in conditions of virtual enslavement, with little protection of their rights. All could be mutilated, tortured, or killed with no punishment for the perpetrators. As a consequence, as Edmund Morgan notes, "Black and white serving the same master worked, ate, and slept together, and together shared in escapades, escapes, and punishments" (Morgan 1975, 155). Colonial society between 1660 and 1683 was shaken by a series of lower-class revolts, many taking place in Virginia, the most populous, wealthiest colony. The most significant such revolt was Bacon's Rebellion, where Nathaniel Bacon's interracial followers, fighting for freedom from servitude and demanding a series of democratic measures, temporarily seized control of the colony, burning Jamestown, the capital, to the ground and forcing the governor and his forces to flee to Maryland.

A dramatic change in the nature of race relations in the North American colonies, however, began to take place during the late seventeenth century. With the turn from an integrated labor force of mostly British bond servants to one made up of predominantly African hereditary life-time slaves, colonial elites began more differentiated treatment for whites and blacks, and established a race-based legal system, which stripped blacks of virtually all rights while giving some minimal protections to poor whites. The system of white supremacy was most stark in the main slave states, led by Virginia and South Carolina, but it was eventually to become the norm in all of the original colonies. The system of racial oppression was extended even to free blacks, who were often disenfranchised, refused the right to testify and gain redress in court, and subjected to far more severe punishments than whites who committed similar transgressions. On one point it is important to be absolutely clear: White supremacy and racial slavery were developed, not primarily for cultural or psychological purposes (i.e., because of previously existing prejudice) but because they advanced the most powerful economic interests in the colonies and the colonial homeland. Du Bois, writing in 1940, was quite clear on the causal chain:

> I think it was in Africa that I came more clearly to see the close connection between race and wealth. . . . And then gradually this thought was metamorphosed into a realization that the income-bearing value of race prejudice was the cause and not the result of theories of race inferiority; that particularly in the United States the income of the Cotton Kingdom based on Black slavery caused the passionate belief in Negro inferiority and the determination to enforce it even by arms. (Du Bois 1940, 129; for opposing views see Degler 1971; Jordan 1977).

It is highly tempting to describe an unbroken history of white supremacy and oppression of non-whites throughout the eighteenth, nineteenth, and early twentieth centuries. There is much evidence to support such a position.

The dominance of southern slave interests at the time of the founding of the republic in the late eighteenth century was installed in the U.S. Constitution.

While the Continental Congress rejected the attempt of South Carolina delegates to place the adjective "white" in the constitution, it acceded to the slave owners on virtually every other demand. Black slaves were counted as property, taxable at a rate of $^3/_5$ their market value; yet, slave owners were given added political clout by counting their disenfranchised slaves as $^3/_5$ of a person for representation purposes, thus rewarding slave masters with additional congressional seats. The Continental Congress also acquiesced to a draconian fugitive slave law that allowed southern slave catchers to seize any suspected runaways (even those who might have been free and northern born), with no rights of judicial review until they were returned to the place from whence they supposedly escaped. With the rise of cotton in the 1790s after the invention and widespread employment of the cotton gin, the system of white supremacy in the South and the country as a whole intensified, as cotton fortunes dominated the country, not merely in Virginia and South Carolina, but eventually across the whole South. By 1860, for example, the twelve wealthiest counties in the country were all in the cotton South. The economic importance of the South was reflected in the region's national political dominance. Five of the first seven presidents, for thirty-two out of its first thirty-six years, for fifty of its first sixty-four years, were slave owners, as were a majority of House speakers, cabinet members, and Supreme Court justices.

After the American Revolution, union organization began to develop in the country's urban centers. These, often militant organizations, so revered by many contemporary labor historians (see Wilentz 1984, for example), were white, exclusionary, and racist. One can see them clearly as the forerunners of the racially exclusive railroad and American Federation of Labor craft unions, some of whom did not drop their formal racial qualifications until the 1960s, while some, like certain construction craft unions today, still serve to function as de facto blocks to African Americans desiring to work in their trades.

In a broad sense, the intense racial oppression in the society at large was reflected in labor organizations. In addition, the participation of unions in the racial oppression of blacks was generally extended to other ethnic groups, particularly those that were non-white. Nowhere did unions oppose the slaughter of Native Americans that proceeded throughout the nineteenth century. Anti-Chinese programmatic sentiments pervaded organized labor, resulting in the exclusion of Chinese and other Asians from employment; the barring of further immigrants; discrimination in schools, eating places, and public accommodations; and even at times large-scale murder. Samuel Gompers, the head of the American Federation of Labor, authored a pamphlet against Chinese immigrants, in which he denounced them for bringing "nothing but filth, vice, and disease" (Goldfield 1997, 148). Labor organizations held these stances not merely on the West Coast, where Asian workers were often numerous, but even in those states in the West and Northeast where hardly any were to be found. Attitudes toward Mexicans and Mexican Americans followed along similar paths, becoming even more intense late in the nineteenth century with the rise of imperialism, as the jingoism of Manifest Destiny was accompanied by occupation of one Latin American country after another.

Racist attitudes, however, were not merely the province of narrow, backward, craft unions. They were to pollute even the most class-based and progressive of organizations. The American Railway Union, which in 1894, in a massive national strike, declared war on the capitalist class, overruled the advice of their leader, Eugene Debs, and refused to accept black railroad workers as members (Foner 1955, 255). The Socialist Party had a number of important leaders, including Milwaukee Congressmen Victor Berger, who were openly racist. Yet, even those organizations that were in many ways progressive on equality for blacks were often racist when it came to Chinese. The mineworkers journal supported legislation to exclude Chinese immigration. The Knights of Labor on the West Coast became involved in anti-Chinese activity. Even the National Colored Labor Union had a plank supporting Chinese exclusion. The Socialist Party, which had a similar position, was denounced in 1910 by Debs, who was its nominal leader, calling its position "utterly unsocialistic, reactionary and, in truth, outrageous," having "no place in a proletarian gathering under the auspices of an international movement that is calling on the oppressed and exploited workers of all the world to unite for their emancipation" (Black 1963, 71).

Yet, the preceding story, while a major part of the full account, is by itself incomplete. There were also important periods that involved struggle and organization by black workers, interracialism, and some support for the rights of African Americans and at times Mexicans, if not necessarily American Indians and Asians, by white workers and the organizations that they dominated. This, too, is an important part of the background of the racial dimensions of labor organization in the United States.

During the period leading up to the American Revolution, many in the revolutionary movement began to extend the demand for liberty to black slaves. Calvinist, Baptist, and Quaker leaders urged freedom for the slaves. Strong, although episodic, attacks on slavery were also made by artisan spokesmen including James Otis and Nathaniel Appleton of Boston and Benjamin Rush and

Thomas Paine of Philadelphia (Young 1993). While the demands for abolition were part of the idealistic expansiveness that often accompanies revolutionary struggles, they were based on and pushed forward by a number of substantial social forces.

Starting in the 1730s, revolts by enslaved plantation workers heightened in frequency and intensity around the world. The Virgin Islands, Dutch Guyana, St. Kitts, Antigua, the Bahamas, St. Martin's, St. Bartholomew, Anguilla, and Guadeloupe were all the sites of major rebellions during the 1730s. Tacky's Rebellion in Jamaica in 1760, involving thousands of slaves, led to far-reaching abolitionist pamphlets and agitation on the North American mainland. The period before the Revolution saw perhaps the greatest wave of slave rebellions in North America, including those in New Orleans, New York City, Perth Amboy, New Jersey, Georgia, South Carolina, North Carolina, and numerous other places. These struggles gave urgency and immediacy to the demands of free blacks and their supporters for full equality.

In addition, as many colonial scholars now accept, it was the mobs in seaport towns (including New York, Boston, Philadelphia, and Charleston) that played the dominant role in all the events leading up to the War for Independence. These mobs, unlike the elected bodies based on white male property-holders, were made up primarily of members of the laboring classes, including unskilled laborers and seamen, artisans, indentured servants, black slaves, women, and also children. Samuel Adams was inspired by one such riot against the British in Boston in 1747 to see the mob as embodying "the fundamental rights of man," suggesting that the phrase "All men are created equal" had, at least for some people, a universal quality (Blackburn 1988, 111). Both the extensive slave unrest and the multiracial, male and female, lower-class portside mob actions pushed the demands for freedom for all, including blacks, to the fore. Ultimately, however, the American Revolution was largely led and dominated by the commercial and plantation elites—including John Jay, John Hancock, Alexander Hamilton, Samuel Adams, Patrick Henry, George Washington, Thomas Jefferson, and James Madison—whose interests did not include granting freedom to their highly profitable enslaved black workforce (Young 1976; Nash 1979; Blackburn 1988, 115, chap. 3 generally).

The period after the Civil War led to a renewal of interracial labor activity, particularly in the South. Southern dockworkers were often successful in building strong interracial unions. In New Orleans, city workers sometimes displayed impressive degrees of interracial solidarity, well after disenfranchisement and the hardening of white supremacy in the 1890s (Arnesen 1991). Black and white miners in Alabama likewise organized and struggled together against the prevailing racial tide, while for a brief period in the 1880s and 1890s, the Knights of Labor organized both black and white workers in the most unlikely places across the South (Lewis 1987). From 1910 to 1913, the Brotherhood of Timber Workers, which was eventually to affiliate with the Industrial Workers of the World (IWW), organized black and white workers in the Deep South (see, for example, Green 1973).

During the 1890s virtually all labor struggles, whether in all-white or racially mixed venues were badly defeated. There is one inescapable conclusion, however, that can be drawn. In those racially mixed industries where unions were racially exclusive (as in rail during the 1894 Pullman strike and steel after the defeat of the 1892 Homestead strike), they did not easily rebound. In those where there was a commitment to interracialism and some level of egalitarian practice (as in mining and longshore), interracial unions maintained their existence and remained poised for a rebirth.

At this point it is helpful to make some useful distinctions. Interracial unions, in contrast to racially exclusive ones, are open to members of all racial and ethnic groups. They may or may not be racially egalitarian, however, meaning that racially subordinate groups may or may not get the same treatment, rights, and benefits as members of the dominant white racial group, and that the union as an organization may or may not fight for their full rights at work and in general. While a union is or is not interracial, there is a wide range of degrees of commitment to racial egalitarianism. The problem historically has been with white workers and their leaders, who have in the vast majority of instances been unwilling to unite with their non-white brethren and break with the racial status quo. Non-white workers, especially African Americans, have almost always been willing to unite with and support whites, especially after their initial doubts about the intentions of their white brethren were overcome.

As I have argued for the United States in my recent book *The Color of Politics*, and as Robin Blackburn makes clear about the origins of racial slavery for the whole New World in his magisterial *The Making of New World Slavery*, the whole system of racial domination, the development of white racial identities, and the instantiation of broad patterns of racial discrimination, along with their tacit, if not explicit, support by large numbers of whites, including many workers, are complex phenomena, deeply rooted in the most fundamental socioeconomic structures of capitalist society. Thus, the most current and highly simplistic theories that attempt to analyze today's racist structures and to give prescriptions for the future are often at best incomplete.

In trying to understand the possibilities and conditions for racially egalitarian, class solidaristic labor organizations, there are, in particular, two one-sided and erroneous positions that need to be understood, criticized, and rejected as inadequate. Highly popular today are the arguments that assert that all whites (especially white workers) are irrevocably racist and have no possibilities for change, at least in the short run (Hill 1993). In some versions of this pessimistic thesis the reasons are psychological (having to do with innate group desires for antagonism and dominance) or cultural (having to do with the dead weight of centuries of Eurocentric chauvinism that are central to white identity; see Roediger 1991 for insightful analysis). In more materialist versions of this argument, it is sometimes asserted that it is in the immediate interests of white workers to support the racial subordination of non-white workers, in order to gain more leverage for themselves in the labor market. I have argued extensively elsewhere against these views. Let it suffice to say that the numerous historical examples of interracial solidarity in U.S. history belie the all-encompassing conclusions necessitated by these positions.

There is, on the other hand, an opposing position, historically common on the Left, that there is a certain inevitability to the formation of racially egalitarian industrial unions, at least when African Americans make up a substantial portion of the workforce, and the union is predisposed in this direction. Thus, the logic of successful industrial unionism requires the organization of inclusive, solidaristic unions when the industries are composed of low-skilled, racially and ethnically heterogeneous workforces. This position, however, is belied by the many such situations where interracial unions were not successfully organized, even in seemingly favorable circumstances. The failures of the 1919-20 strike waves in the racially and ethnically diverse meatpacking and steel industries in the proletarian center of Chicago, for example, were largely due to the racial narrow-mindedness of many white workers and their unions. Widespread interracial labor struggles and organization did not fully emerge until the 1930s.

The preceding simplistic formulations fail to link the systems of racial domination and the related attitudes of white workers to the broad structures of modern capitalist development and the important economic interests that benefit from the racial domination of subordinate groups, as well as the intense social pressures—including rewards and punishments—that are put on people to go along with the dominant racial practices, however much they may be evolving.

II. THE 1930S

While only the crudest of economic determinists would attempt to read political organization and development directly from economic development, one ignores such factors at one's peril. Such is a common problem today, especially prominent among many who engage in cultural analysis, including a number who consider themselves to be on the Left. An examination of the tremendous upsurge of inter-racial industrial unionism during the 1930s and 1940s (including the new, broader culture of solidarity) must begin with economic development and demographics. Since the time of the Civil War, U.S. industry had engaged in relatively continu-ous, rapid expansion. The growth in the nineteenth century was virtually unprece-dented. Pig iron shipments, for example, over 50 percent higher in 1866 than in 1860, with a price more than doubled, had more than doubled again by 1872, almost doubling anew by 1885, more than doubling once more by 1890, and con-tinuing a phenomenal growth through 1900, even as they were being in part replaced by the rapid increase in the use of steel. Railroad tracks, 35,000 miles in 1865, had increased to 207,000 miles by the turn of the century. Hog slaughtering rose from 166,000 in 1860 to 4,000,000 in 1878, while bituminous coal mined went from 9 million tons in 1860 to 212 million tons by the turn of the century. Growth in these and other industries continued into the first three decades of the twenti-eth century.

In the North, industrial employment before World War I was overwhelmingly white, in contrast to the South, where African Americans had gained important footholds in many industries during the late nineteenth century. These industries included coal and metal mining, especially in Alabama, iron and steel, longshore, railroads, tobacco, food processing, and wood. Before 1900, 90 percent of African Americans were located in the South, largely employed in rural agriculture. With the expansion of northern industry at the beginning of World War I, and the con-comitant cutoff of European immigration, black workers began to migrate to the industrial cities of the North in large numbers, as well as to southern cities. By 1940, over six million African Americans, almost 48 percent of the total black population, were classified as urban. New York City, with a black population of almost 92,000 in 1910, 1.9 percent of the total population, had 477,494 (or 6.4 percent) in 1940. Chicago had a black population of 282,244 (8.4 percent of its total) in 1940, while Detroit, with only 5,000 blacks in 1910, had 150,000 by 1940, nearly 10 percent of its population. Similar stories can be told for Philadelphia, Baltimore, Washington,

D.C., St. Louis, Kansas City, Newark, Indianapolis, Cincinnati, Pittsburgh, Cleveland, and Los Angeles, among others.

Mexicans and Chicanos were drawn in large numbers into southwestern and West Coast agriculture and food processing during this period, as well as to metal mining throughout the Southwest. Puerto Rican workers increased their employment in New York City, while Asian Americans made inroads in canning and other industries on the West Coast. The militant sugar plantation workforce in Hawaii, numbering tens of thousands by the 1920s, was overwhelmingly non-white, with Japanese and Filipinos making up the largest groups (Daniels 1981; Asher and Stephenson 1990).

While economic development and changes in industrial and occupational structures, as well as the racial, ethnic, and sexual composition of occupations and industries, are never the whole story, they are the indispensable starting point, not only for the 1930s, but for all periods, including the present.

Facing this new industrial configuration, with its multiracial, multiethnic workforce, the Congress of Industrial Organization (CIO) from its beginning in 1935 not only advocated inclusive interracial unions, but espoused egalitarian rhetoric. The question naturally arises of the degree to which these claims represent a real break from AFL racial policies, and the degree to which they were merely a continuation of AFL racial practices in a new industrial setting—a setting in which white workers who could not control the labor market for themselves in unskilled industrial workplaces without enlisting the support of their fellow black and other non-white workers made the necessary opportunistic overtures. The answer to this question is not simple, for the CIO and its various component unions had a wide range of racial practices. Individual unions were at times and in some places quite forthright in their stands in asserting the rights of their non-white members. At other times and places, CIO officials and particular unions hardly seemed any different from the AFL. In addition, there are some unions that began as racially progressive, yet later became quite backward, as well as one or two examples of the opposite.

The range of CIO practice was particularly striking in southern industrial cities like Memphis, Tennessee, the commercial center for inland cotton trade and manufacturing at the top of the Mississippi River delta. There the Communist–led United Cannery, Agricultural, Packing, and Allied Workers of America (UCA-PAWA; after 1944 the Food and Tobacco Workers of America, FTA) began organizing black workers who were previously considered unorganizable. UCAPAWA Local 19 in Memphis had black leadership, including its president, and was quite militant. Its almost unbroken string of organizing successes stimulated the organization of white workers in both integrated workplaces and those that were overwhelmingly white, showing that the fears of racially conservative CIO leaders—that organizing blacks first would alienate the white workers—were, at the very least, exaggerated.

Conservative Memphis CIO director W. A. Copeland, who owed his position largely to national CIO leader and Philip Murray ally John Brophy, opposed integrated meetings of black and white workers and expressed special venom for the FTA's racial polities. Copeland was supported by fellow Memphis Newspaper Guild leader Pete Swim, who fought national CIO policy directives to combat racial discrimination. Copeland criticized FTA Local 19 for hiring a black office secretary, opposed the use of blacks as negotiators, and denounced "racial mixing" of whites and blacks at CIO parties. Racist leaders were supported by "moderates" in the CIO national office, not so much because they completely agreed with the racial attitudes, but because their desire to eliminate Communist influence and to achieve respectability among business leaders and national political elites far outweighed their commitments to building interracial solidarity or even to aiding a dynamic growing labor movement—a legacy for which today's dwindling union organizations are still paying dearly (see Honey 1993).

Left-led unions were generally committed not only to integrated unionism but to varying degrees of racial egalitarianism. Some, like the FTA, the Mine Mill and Smelter Workers (which in addition to its black membership in Alabama had significant Mexican and Chicano membership in the Southwest), and the United Packinghouse Workers were majority white unions with significant numbers of non-white workers. These unions fought aggressively for job rights for their members, engaged in antiracist education, and were highly involved in fighting Jim Crow practices outside their workplaces. There were also certain Left-led unions with only small percentages of black and other non-white workers who engaged in similar activities. These unions included the Farm Equipment Workers (FE), the Fur and Leather Workers, and the National Maritime Union; the latter, with barely 10 percent black membership, had a black man, Ferdinand Smith, as its secretary-treasurer. The Left unions, however, were not always exemplary. The Transport Workers Union, despite its rhetorical commitment to racial egalitarianism and its strong stance in Philadelphia supporting the upgrading of black employees to higher positions in the face of a white racist hate strike, was unwilling for a long time in its home base of New York City to push for more minority hiring against the sentiments of its overwhelmingly white Irish membership. The United Electrical Workers was often guilty of the same lack of commitment. The

West Coast longshoremen leadership, while aggressively championing civil rights in their San Francisco stronghold, with its significant minority of black workers, refused to challenge the racially exclusive policies at San Leandro and other locales. (For a summary of Left-led unions, see Goldfield 1993.)

Yet, as a rule the Left-led unions were far better than the non-Left unions, with the possible exception of the mineworkers, whose long history of interracialism was to a large extent part of the ethos of the union. The differences can be seen clearly between the Communist-led FE and the United Auto Workers (UAW), under the putatively racially liberal social democrat Walter Reuther. The contrast was especially vivid in Louisville during the late 1940s and early 1950s, where the FE and the UAW had representation in the same plant complex. FE Local 236 represented all production and maintenance workers except those in the foundry. In 1949, Local 236 had 6,000 members, 14 percent of whom were African American. The local had extensive black leadership, including numerous black stewards in majority white departments. They were also unusually aggressive around issues of racial equality, both within the plant and in the community at large. The adjoining foundry, with 1,500 workers, represented by the UAW, was half black. There is no evidence, however, that civil rights issues were important to this local. A 1953 study by the hardly radical National Planning Association found that in contrast to the main plant, the foundry still had racially separate locker rooms designated "White" and "Colored," which had as yet received no protest from the UAW local (Gilpin 1992, 545-46).

Left and racially egalitarian unionism was largely defeated during the late 1940s. The CIO right wing, under the guise of anticommunism, destroyed and undermined the most promising bulwarks of interracial unionism. FTA's largest local, Local 22 in Winston-Salem, was attacked so badly by the national CIO in a race-baiting campaign that the local not only was decertified in a National Labor Relations Board campaign, but years later could not be reorganized by the AFL-CIO (Goldfield 1993). The Steelworkers, who had shared some of the racially egalitarian perspective of the United Mine Workers in their initial organizing, soon solidified as an organization whose department seniority system served to protect the better-paying, higher-skilled jobs for white workers. Under their president, Philip Murray, they took the lead in destroying the interracial Mine Mill locals in Alabama by openly appealing to the racism of white workers. Years later, the CIO was still trying to figure out why the black community in Birmingham would have nothing to do with them (Huntley 1977).

III. THE POST-WORLD WAR II PERIOD

The period after World War II is correctly seen by many on the left as a time of bureaucratization and retreat by the CIO, of loss of militancy and grass-roots democracy, of drawing closer to the capitalist class on both domestic and foreign policy. All this is true. What is not sufficiently emphasized in such accounts is the degree to which their retreat on racial issues was at the center of these changes.

With the defeat and expulsion of the left unions, the purging of leftist militants who were committed to civil rights throughout the union movement, and the consequent abandonment by the national CIO of basic commitments to civil rights for minorities at the workplace and in society at large, the possibilities for racially egalitarian unionism diminished greatly. Nevertheless, the CIO, particularly more liberal anticommunist unions like the auto workers, maintained an undeserved reputation on civil rights. The huge postwar housing boom, largely financed by government loans (in particular VHA and FHA), completely excluded non-whites, especially African Americans. Skilled construction jobs for housing and the massive highway construction also excluded minorities. Hardly a peep was heard from the politically sanitized, bureaucratized CIO. Within the individual CIO unions themselves the situation of minorities was hardly more salutary.

In steel, blacks were hired by management into the lowest-paid, most unskilled, hardest, dirtiest, and most unhealthy jobs, in foundries, blast furnaces, and coke plants. The steelworkers union did not oppose this discriminatory hiring process. Worse still, they defended it, enforcing via contracts a system of departmental seniority that locked minority workers into their areas of original hire, with no rights to transfer to better jobs in other departments.

In mining, the UMWA historic commitment to interracial unions had brought many benefits to black miners. Mass mobilizations of black and white miners provided the shock troops for much CIO interracial organizing, especially in the South. In the end, however, the UMWA proved unwilling to defend the jobs of its black members as the industry began to automate rapidly after World War II. When their jobs were eliminated in greater proportion to those of white miners, the union did not demand that black workers have priority in gaining newly created jobs over recently hired, lower-seniority, white employees. From 1930 to 1950, the number of black miners in the country decreased from fifty thousand to thirty-five thousand, while the total number of miners barely declined. When mechanization caused the total number of miners to drop from more than 500,000 in 1950 to 139,000 in 1970, black employment plunged to 3,700, virtually eliminating them from the industry. By the time the mine workers finally won companywide seniority in many districts, during the 1960s, black workers were already gone.

In the auto industry, the UAW leadership was long on rhetoric and short on action. With its largest base of support in the lily-white, racially exclusive skilled trades jobs, the Reuther leadership spent far more time and effort during the late 1940s and early 1950s attacking the racially egalitarian FE than it did aiding in the fight for racial equality. It vehemently opposed the demands for more minority representation in leadership bodies; it rejected the demands for access to semi-skilled and skilled positions in the auto plants; it directed its most aggressive attacks not at racial discrimination but at those locals that wanted to press the attack, especially left-wing ones like the heavily black Ford River Rouge Local 600. The figures and the inaction by the UAW tell the story. In 1960 in Detroit, for example, when 25 percent of Chrysler workers and 23 percent of GM workers were black, African Americans made up only 24 of 7,425 skilled workers at Chrysler and only 67 of 11,125 at General Motors (Sugrue 1996, 105).

What the large CIO unions might have done in fighting against racial dis-crimination is suggested by the struggles of black workers and the remnants of the labor left during the 1950s. The UPWA, the FE, Mine Mill, the less radical sleep-ing car porters, what remained of the United Public Workers during the McCarthy period, as well as the several-hundred-member Local 1199, made up mostly of Jewish druggists, continued successful civil rights activity. The CP-sup-ported National Negro Labor Council (NNLC), subpoenaed, harassed, and red-baited by the government and the national CIO, with support from only a small segment of the labor movement, carried on numerous labor–related civil rights activities in the early 1950s. In Cleveland, Ohio, for example, in December 1952, the NNLC mobilized 1,500 pickets protesting the refusal of American Airlines to hire blacks in any but the most unskilled positions. Twenty percent of the demonstra-tors were white. In Louisville in 1953, the NNLC engaged in a yearlong campaign to get the new General Electric plant to hire and upgrade black workers; in that city they put similar pressure on Ford and General Motors and on the railroads. In all these cases in Louisville they had the support of the large FE International Harvester local union (Goldfield 1997).

While African Americans were generally excluded from more-skilled jobs during the post–World War II period, and even from some less-skilled jobs, as in southern textile, and driven out of certain industries where they had been a large percentage of the labor force (e.g., southern sawmills, tobacco manufacturing, and coal mining), they were hardly marginalized in the economy. In meatpacking, the steel industry, the auto industry, farm and construction equipment, transportation, and hospital work, African American workers, while heavily concentrated in the lower-paying occupations, were disproportionately employed in the industries as a whole.

Despite their greater representation in many of the old CIO unions, black worker influence did not translate into greater militancy by their unions around civil rights. CIO unions had been at the head of the battles for racial equality during the 1930s and 1940s. Yet, as the new civil rights movement emerged during the 1950s and 1960s, unions were at the margins. The sit-in movement which began in February 1960 had as its leadership and foot soldiers African American college and high school students. When working-class people became involved—in Montgomery, Alabama, for example, it was the cooks, housekeepers, and other African American workers who were the vast majority of those who boycotted the buses—it was not generally under union auspices.

With some notable exceptions, labor struggles by blacks for equal rights were not led by unions; rather, they often targeted white-led labor unions as part of the problem. Black workers and civil rights organizations repeatedly picketed publicly financed construction sites around the country that refused to hire non-white workers. In one celebrated instance in 1964 at the city-financed Bronx Terminal Market, New York City officials intervened to force the hiring of one black and three Hispanic plumbers. When the non-white plumbers, who had previously been refused membership in Plumber's Local 2, arrived for work, all the union plumbers, supported by their former business agent, George Meany, then president of the ALF-CIO, walked off the job. Black caucuses existed during the 1960s and 1970s in thousands of workplaces, making demands for equality that should have been made previously by their unions. In the steel industry, both the companies and the unions resisted the demands for equality by black steelworkers. Both were the target of large numbers of suits under Title VII of the 1964 Civil Rights Act.

Certain unions, however, briefly used the impetus of the civil rights movement to aid in the organizing of African American workers. AFSCME (American Federation of State, County, and Municipal Employees) was among the most prominent of these. Their successful campaign to unionize the overwhelmingly black Memphis sanitation workers was made famous by the assassination of Martin Luther King there.

IV. The Present Situation

Over the past several decades women and non-whites have become an increasingly large percentage of the labor force in many countries. These trends are especially dramatic in the United States of America. As recently as 1960, women there participated in the labor force at a rate of less than 38 percent (less than half that of men). By 1998, the figure was 59.8 percent, with increases registered virtually every year and projected to continue into the future. This relatively rapid change, along with the origins and close relation of this change to the civil rights movement in the 1960s, is largely responsible for the breadth and unique characteristics of the U.S. women's movement (*Statistical Abstract* 1995, 400-1; 1998, 168).

Non-whites have increased substantially as a percentage both of the U.S. population as a whole and of the labor force. The proportion of African Americans has increased slightly during recent decades, making up 12.7 percent of the total population of the country and 11.6 percent of the labor force. Even greater increases have taken place among other minorities, especially Latinos and Asians. Since 1980, the number of Hispanics in the population and labor force has more than doubled, constituting in 1997 10 percent of the total population and 9.6 percent of the civilian labor force (*Statistical Abstract* 1995, 400-401; 1998, tables 34 and 648, online). Because of the large numbers of illegal immigrants, as well as notorious problems in counting transient and inner-city populations, these figures are far from exact, although they are certainly suggestive of the dramatic demographic changes that have been reshaping the country. Non-whites at present represent as much as twenty-five percent of the labor force, with much higher concentrations in many places.

Thus, the percentage of non-whites in the labor force is at an all-time high. The previous high percentage of non-whites (not counting the initial colonial period, when Native Americans made up the majority of the population of the continent), however, was overwhelmingly African American (at the time of the American Revolution, over 20 percent of the colonial population was black, mostly southern slaves), making the United States for most of its early history primarily a biracial society.

Today, on the other hand, the percentages of various white and non-white groups make the politics and social life of the country more fully multiracial. California is perhaps the forerunner of this new trend, with its population as of 1997 51.1 percent non-white (*Statistical Abstract* 1998, table 34, online).

Where in the economy are these growing numbers of non-whites located? Some suggest that minorities, African Americans in particular, are becoming increasingly marginal to contemporary U.S. society. There is, to be sure, important evidence to substantiate this argument. For several decades unemployment rates for Latinos (with the exception of Cubans, who stand midway between other Hispanics and whites) and blacks have been double that of whites. Surveys taken among the unemployed and discouraged workers (those who are out of work but are not currently looking for a job and are thus not counted among the officially unemployed) suggest that several times more minorities than whites say they would take a job if they could find one. The prison population of 1.5 million is heavily minority, currently approximately one-half African American. Poverty and unemployment go a long way to explaining why the U.S. military is dispropor-tionately non-white. In 1995 African Americans made up 19.4 percent of all enlisted personnel, although only 11.4 percent of officers. Furthermore, there are, of course, numerous industries, including high-paying ones like steel, auto, and meatpacking, which formerly employed disproportionate numbers of African American and other non-white workers and which have dramatically cut back their labor forces in recent decades (see, e.g., Yates 1996).

Yet, a focus on the preceding information, while an important part of the story, is selective and by itself gives an erroneous picture. On the one hand, there are a number of industries whose workforces are declining (including mining, agri-culture, and petrochemicals) in which minorities are underrepresented. On the other hand, minorities, particularly blacks, are disproportionately represented in a number of sectors that have grown the most, including transportation, communi-cations, utilities, government employment, social services, hospitals and health care, cleaning and building services, protective services, prison personnel, and, as already mentioned, the military. African Americans have also made gains in employment in certain sectors that were previously closed to them, including wholesale and retail sales and certain areas of manufacturing, most notably tex-tiles. Thus, African Americans and other minorities are heavily concentrated not only in sectors that are crucial to the production of surplus value and the mainte-nance of capitalism today, but also in those sectors that will undoubtedly remain vital in the foreseeable future.

In virtually every industry (whether they are overrepresented or underrepre-sented) African Americans and other non-whites are disproportionately located in the lower-pay and lower-status, although still highly essential, occupations. In the growing and important health care industry, for example, African Americans are concentrated in the lowest-ranking occupations. While in 1998 they made up only 4.9 percent of doctors and 2.8 percent of dentists (a decrease from 1994), they made up 9.3 percent of registered nurses, 17.4 percent of licensed practical nurses, and 34 percent of nurses aides, orderlies, and attendants. The story can be told across industries, with blacks in 1998 making up 25.9 percent of telephone operators, 28.2 percent of postal clerks, 20.2 percent of bus drivers, over 30 percent of garbage collectors, and 29.2 percent of correctional officers in the nation's prisons, sadly one of the fastest growing U.S. industries. With the exception of social workers and a few other occupations, minorities are grossly underrepresented in a number of higher-level job classifications. Among airline pilots, tool and die makers, aerospace and petroleum engineers, auto mechanics, electricians, carpenters, construction superintendents, and architects, blacks make up only small percentages (Hirsch and Macpherson 1996; U.S. Department of Labor 1999, 178-83).

There is some measure of debate over the degree to which the present situation of minorities in the labor force is due to present discrimination or whether it is the result of a combination of historic discrimination combined with recent large-scale changes in the domestic economy. There is further debate about whether blacks as a whole are better off or worse off since the civil rights movement of the 1960s. Finally, and related to this, are the questions of whether racial discrimination has lessened or gotten worse, and the associated question of whether whites, particularly white workers, will ever change, with an increasing number of liberals and putative leftists taking a highly pessimistic stance. While I believe that the pessimistic conclusions are unwarranted over the long run, the factual situation is highly contradictory, leaving itself open to a wide variety of interpretations. It is worth taking note of some of these contradictory trends.

First, one would want to note that the civil rights movement ameliorated the harsh system of white supremacy that existed in the country, particularly in the South. Most important is that the repressive and extremely violent system of racial oppression, supported by the state (including the federal government), that existed in the southern rural areas prior to the 1960s has been mostly dismantled. Black elected county sheriffs have replaced the lynch law racists in the Mississippi Delta and other areas in the Deep South, insuring that violence against African Americans is no longer all-embracing. Institutions and activities in many parts of the South appear to be far more interracial than in much of the North. Certain white attitudes in the country as a whole, at least as expressed in public opinion polls, have changed substantially. By the 1980s white Americans overwhelmingly responded favorably to integrated schools and transportation, equal access to jobs, open housing, and even the right of people of different races to intermarry if they so chose. Several decades earlier, most whites rejected these views. It is tempting to argue that much of this attitudinal change is superficial. Yet, the change in attitude toward interracial couples is especially striking. Before the 1960s, racially mixed couples, in virtually every part of the country, with but a few neighborhood exceptions in some parts of the North, were a prescription for violent attack and universal condemnation. Many erroneously argued that sexual feelings were at the root of racist attitudes. Today, interracial intimacy is just another piece of the complex landscape. The civil rights movement successfully exerted enormous pressure to gain access to large areas of U.S. society largely unavailable to middle-class and working-class minorities. Educational opportunities opened up. Public employment opportunities grew. Many formerly all-white occupations that involved face-to-face contact with whites, including bank tellers, store clerks, and bus drivers, have become disproportionately non-white.

Because of these many changes, numerous conservatives argue that there are no more discriminatory barriers, only a debilitating ghetto culture and lack of individual will. Such a position is not new and has been asserted by conservatives and other bigots throughout U.S. history. Many liberals and social democrats, on the other hand, have minimized the existence of current discrimination and attributed the plight of minorities, particularly the most impoverished people in inner city areas, to be a result of structural changes and historic discrimination, problems that could conceivably be overcome by broad social democratic policy initiatives. Both of these views, in my opinion, are equally wrong.

If, as I have argued, the key to understanding the system of racial domination and the racial attitudes of whites is located in the socioeconomic system, then the question that ought to be asked is the following: If the historic system of racial domination and white racist attitudes were rooted in the southern plantation economy—and that economy has largely disappeared—what keeps African Americans suppressed, and what explains the continued virulence of white racism?

The economic interests which benefit from the continuing racial domination of African Americans, and their availability as a lower-priced segment of the labor force, are, of course, still substantial. Yet, their specific availability is neither as absolute nor indispensable, as was the case for southern plantation owners. This role could just as well be filled by other non-whites, as well as by the bottom layers of lower-class whites, and particularly by the large number of legal and illegal immigrants, including those who are white. In part, the system of racial domination continues because of the weight of tradition, habit, and culture, and the attendant vested privileges and interests that reap advantages from the present arrangements. While the interests that benefit from continued racial discrimination are neither as powerful nor as incorrigibly resistant as the earlier planters, at a time of economic dislocation and uncertainty the costs and stakes involved in dismantling white supremacy completely are high. In an economy that is generating few new resources and where the standards of living for the vast majority are not rising, resources used for one area must be diverted from others. It would take enormous resources to train, educate, and elevate the disproportionately minority, unskilled, workforce and the unemployed, who are currently at the bottom of the occupational and earnings structure. It would require a massive redistribution of resources and income, at a time when the trend in terms of both private income and public spending is in the opposite direction. For those whose program is to siphon more of the wealth to the rich, a political agenda that blames the non-white poor for their own plight, pandering to the racism and occasionally legitimate fears of many whites, is highly self-serving. It is clear that the current agendas of both major parties which eschew substantial redistribution of resources and major structural changes in the system of power—and accept the current system of racial domination and white racial attitudes as a given—can provide us with no source of hope.

In this context, the maintenance and continual regeneration of white racist attitudes rests on several bases. The first is the continued existence of segregation in housing, schools, and many other aspects of daily life. Separation, rather than familiarity, tends to breed fear and contempt. Second, for numerous African Americans, segregated life in poor urban areas has many dehumanizing aspects. As Frederick Douglass noted, racist attitudes find fertile soil when whites see the degraded conditions of life under which many African Americans are forced to live. We thus have something of a vicious circle, where the system of racial domination and its historic effects helps reinforce racial prejudice, which in turn makes it more difficult for many whites to envision broader, more structural solutions to the problems of poor black urban areas. As a consequence, blacks at all levels of society, in all circumstances, continue to be stigmatized by many whites. On the other hand, African Americans are more integrated into the occupational structure, many workplaces, and the visible national culture than ever before. This situation generates tendencies to break down traditional patterns of racial prejudice. It is the existence of these differing structural features of society that provide the basis for the many contradictory features of current race relations that I have noted and that appear around us every day in the United States.

Yet, structural features alone can hardly determine social relations directly. In a period when the groups and movements advocating racial egalitarianism are weak, the field remains dominated by politicians appealing to whites on racial issues, and those who would use divide and conquer tactics to keep the people who least benefit from current arrangements from uniting in common cause. Thus, the present period is one of both instability and flux for the system of racial domination and race relations, with the looming possibility of increasing dominance of racial scapegoating.

Under a stagnant and highly dislocating capitalism, racist attitudes find a fertile soil among those who feel most insecure. One sees this phenomenon all around the globe, in Europe as well as in more insecure areas such as the former Soviet Union and its former sphere of influence, parts of Africa, Asia, and the Middle East. Without a solidaristic labor movement that aims at the cause of people's problems—the nature of capitalism itself—many will continue to turn to finding scapegoats. The same public opinion polls that show many whites becoming more liberal on certain racial issues also show them having racist, factually incorrect, and hostile views about welfare, affirmative action, and previously about busing. Overwhelming numbers of whites in Louisiana voted for former Ku Klux Klan leader and protofascist, racist David Duke in two major elections; one feels that others across the nation would have done likewise if they had had the same chance (Goldfield 1997).

Despite the highly contradictory nature of the present period, which includes the enthusiastic, if often strained, acceptance of African Americans and other minorities in music, literature, sports, and other cultural venues, there is much that signals retreat, much of it seemingly orchestrated by those in power. There is a tendency among many liberals to see this retreat as largely the province of the Republicans. While this position is wrong, they are clearly at the cutting edge of racial retreat. The signals are striking. In 1995, when the new Republican majority Congress took over, they brought in sixty-five new pages, high school or college students who perform errands; of the sixty-five, sixty-four were white, the other Asian American. In previous recent sessions, fifteen to twenty were Latino, African American, or other minorities. A conscious attempt was made to diminish the number of black federal judges under Presidents Reagan and Bush. From 1980 to 1992, only 2 of the 115 judges appointed to the U.S. Courts of Appeals were black, one of whom was Clarence Thomas (Higginbotham 1996, viii). Perhaps the signature of the Reagan/Bush years was the hysterical Republican political advertisements during the 1988 presidential campaign, blaming Democratic candidate Michael Dukakis for the crimes of black rapist Willie Horton. The Democrats, too, have made their symbolic, although necessarily more subtle (since they, unlike the Republicans, rely on a substantial black vote), appeals to white racism. Jimmy

Carter first won the Georgia governorship by successfully wooing Wallace supporters there, long before he emphasized his belief in "ethnic purity" during his winning 1976 presidential campaign. Bill Clinton's snubbing of Jesse Jackson and his calculated attack on hiphop singer Sister Souljah at a Rainbow Coalition meeting during the 1992 campaign gave similar assurances to whites. The gutting of welfare and affirmative action; the harsher stances being taken toward immigrants, especially along the Mexican border; the heavy emphasis on policing; the draconian anti-crime bills; and the increased use of the death penalty disproportionately applied to non-whites, are all aimed at letting white citizens know that the Democratic Party has little sympathy for the plight of people of color.

V. The Labor Market and Minorities

The racist rhetoric, actions, and appeals by politicians are even more troubling because they are part of a general tendency to discriminate against and keep subordinate racial minorities generally. Despite the high-profile publicity that has been given to the issue of affirmative action, there is much evidence that women and racial minorities still face an enormous degree of discrimination in the labor market. The evidence for this is extensive and overwhelming. I have already indicated the underrepresentation of minorities in upper-level working-class occupations and their disproportionate numbers at the upper end of the spectrum. In higher-level occupations the picture is even more extreme. The 1995 federal Glass Ceiling Commission report, for example, found that women held only 3 to 5 percent of the senior-level jobs in major corporations. In addition, only 5 percent of the women who held these positions were minorities. Among men the situation is equally skewed. Ninety-seven percent of senior-level male managers are white, 0.6 percent are African American, 0.3 percent are Asian, and 0.4 percent are Hispanic. African American men with professional degrees earn only 79 percent of the amount that their white male counterparts do, while African American women with professional degrees earn only 60 percent of this amount (Glass Ceiling Commission 1995, 12).

The evidence from urban construction labor markets is equally grim. Skilled construction labor was heavily black in the period after the Civil War, in good part because of the large numbers of slave artisans who did skilled work in the antebellum period. By the end of the nineteenth century such labor was almost exclusively done by whites, as African American workers were eliminated by a combination of employer hiring policies and racially exclusive craft unions, and sometimes as a result of violent attacks by white workers. During the 1960s, as I have indicated, construction contractors and unions were subjected to enormous pressures by the civil rights movement, a highly mobilized black community, and ultimately by federal, some state, and some local governments. By the 1970s, a few of these labor markets had opened up to black workers. One of the more successful places was Philadelphia. By 1979, minorities there represented 17.4 percent of the construction labor force. Yet, with the decline of the protest movements and the elimination of government pressure, informal racially discriminatory mechanisms have reasserted themselves. Skilled, qualified, African American construction workers are no longer hired as frequently or as consistently by construction companies and their overwhelmingly white supervisors as are comparable white workers (*New York Times*, 9 July 1995). A recent study by Timothy Bates and David Howell shows that the percentage of minorities employed on construction projects within New York City has declined substantially since the late 1970s (Bates and Howell 1997). This study is particularly illuminating because the jobs are all in the city, where there exists a skilled pool of minority workers for the jobs, and where public transportation is more than adequate to get these workers to job sites. Thus, in this case at least, and perhaps many others, it is not the geographic location of jobs (i.e., so-called spatial mismatch) or a lack of available skilled minority workers that has caused these declines, but out and out racial discrimination.

There exists a broad range of additional data of various sorts that provides further convincing evidence for the continued existence of widespread labor market discrimination by employers. Numerous studies done by the Urban Institute, for example, involved sending testers to apply for the same jobs. Anglo male applicants, most of the time, advance much further along in the hiring process than their identically qualified African American and Hispanic matched counterparts. This research shows that minority applicants are just treated differently than whites. In addition to this type of overt discrimination, there is the de facto discrimination that results from the fact that a large amount of hiring is done through informal networks, networks that are almost always all white. As George Galster summarizes these studies: "Both overt hiring discrimination and seemingly benign hiring techniques, therefore, contribute to the lower earnings, limited employment, and occupational/industrial segregation of minorities." (Galster 1993, 1449; see also Cross et al. 1990).

VI. Unions and Race Today

As we have already seen, African Americans and other non-white minorities are a large and growing part of the labor force. They are heavily concentrated both in those occupations and industries that are already highly unionized and also in those areas where the labor force is expanding most rapidly, including health care, services in general, government, communication, and transportation. Minority workers represent both a tremendous reservoir of support for labor unions and a great potential for new organizing. A look at some statistics is revealing.

In 1998, 13.5 percent of whites in the nonagricultural civilian labor force were members of unions, while 17.9 percent of African Americans were members, both figures representing a significant decrease since 1995 (Hirsch and MacPherson 1996, 19; U.S. Department of Labor 1999, 219). Hispanics and other non-white minorities were slightly more unionized than whites. Surveys taken since the 1970s have also shown that black workers who were unorganized were more than twice as likely to say that they would join a union if one began to organize their workplace. Women, Hispanics, and southerners in nonunion workplaces also responded more favorably than northern white males. Aside from the more complex reasons of political consciousness, there is an economic basis for such greater pro-union attitudes. Economic studies have shown that unions have a dual effect on wages. On the one hand, they tend to raise the average wage significantly, thus raising the pay of all employees. On the other hand, they narrow the wage dispersion between the top and the bottom. Since women and minorities tend to be among the lowest paid, union organization tends to raise their wages by a greater proportion than those of white males. The AFL-CIO has increasingly become more diversified by sex and race, with women and racial minorities making up a greater percentage of the total membership. In addition, the best prospects for current organizing appear in those venues where women and minorities are heavily concentrated. These related factors are among the more important reasons why at least some unions have developed a more diverse leadership group, with increases in women and minorities in top, visible leadership positions.

The response of unions to the continued discrimination in the labor force, its changing demographic makeup, and the changing complexion of union membership, however, has varied greatly. Many unions, of course, have responded by doing nothing at all. They have neither attempted to organize new segments of the labor force nor have they altered the complexion of their leadership, nor have they made any efforts to fight discrimination in the workplaces they represent or the society at large.

Between 1960 and 1975, the public sector at the federal, state, and local level went from barely 5 percent of the workforce organized to almost 40 percent. A disproportionate number of the workers organized in this sector were female and minority. The main public sector unions, including the postal unions, whose organization came much earlier, thus have not only a disproportionately minority and female membership, but an increasingly diverse leadership body at both the national and local levels. These unions include the American Federation of Teachers (AFT), the National Education Association (NEA), the American Federation of Government Employees (AFGE, representing federal workers), and the American Federation of State, County, and Municipal Employees (AFSCME), representing state and local government workers. Each of these unions has substantial representation of women and minorities in national and regional leadership bodies, with the NEA and the AFGE having had African American presidents. AFSCME's executive council of thirty-three members in 1997 included nine female members and approximately a dozen minority members (of whom ten were African American, one an Asian-American, and one a Latino, as far as can be seen from their names and pictures). Other unions, including most of the old CIO unions, as well as almost all of the old AFL unions, have been much slower to change their leadership composition even when their membership base has changed substantially. The 1982 Civil Rights Commission report on equal employment opportunity and unions paints a fairly dismal picture, at both the national and local levels.

Yet, composition of leadership bodies and their degree of diversity, while an important piece of information, hardly tells the whole story. In the battle to gain equal employment opportunities in the wake of the civil rights movement of the 1960s, very few unions—the exceptions being several former left-wing unions—took the lead in fighting for the rights of minority workers. Despite rhetorical stances in favor of civil rights, most unions, including the UAW, the teamsters, and the steelworkers, were the object of both struggles by black worker caucuses and massive antidiscrimination suits. In general, these unions defended existing discriminatory arrangements, rather than playing a role in fighting against them (see, e.g., Hill 1982, 1987, 1993; Rose 1989). The best that unions during this period and at the present time have done is to make their leadership bodies more diverse. Some unions, including the new AFL-CIO leadership, have trumpeted this diversity.

The record, however, in fighting for the rights of women and minorities on the job is rather weak, with the exception of certain campaigns of equal pay for equal work. Little has been done to open up hiring and to integrate white male preserves, except in token amounts. The initial impetus for such change, mandated by the federal government under Title VII of the 1964 and 1972 Civil Rights Acts, has receded, with few unions willing to pick up the baton. One sees little evidence of the type of campaigns that left unions waged during the 1930s and 1940s on behalf of non-white workers, or even the hiring and upgrading campaigns by the labor left in the early 1950s. Today's unions play little role in mass protests against housing and mortgage lending discrimination, neighborhood and school issues, police brutality, and other issues of importance to minority communities. Unions today have done little to combat the racial attacks on welfare and affirmative action, although unions on the West Coast have had important involvement in fighting anti-immigrant hysteria. In general, today's unions, with or without the current change in leadership at the top of the AFL-CIO, seem quite hesitant to confront issues of racial inequality. Even when unions themselves are directly victimized, little publicity is given. An example of the latter is the selective racial hiring by management at the Cannon Mills textile plants in North Carolina. As black workers became increasingly pro-union, employers began hiring more whites and Hispanics. When Hispanics became pro-union, employers began hiring non–English-speaking Asians. Such racial tactics should have been publicly exposed to the maximum.

The assertion of an aggressive, racially egalitarian policy by unions is virtually impossible as long as they stay tied to the Democratic Party. As the Democratic Party has moved more into line with the racial conservatives (the ending of welfare, abandonment of affirmative action, support for more repressive anti-crime legislation including more police and the extension of the death penalty), the AFL-CIO under the Sweeney leadership has deepened its embrace. Independent, aggressive, class-based action against racial subjugation is impossible today without a rejection of the Democratic Party.

A change in policy by unions is essential to achieving not only broader class goals, but also the minimal ones in which mainstream labor leaders claim to be interested. The labor movement will not be invigorated without aggressive appeals to and representation of the interests of female and minority workers. Having a diverse face and stressing merely lowest common denominator issues, without also confronting sexual and racial inequalities, will not lead to a dynamic labor movement. Further, without stressing broad class issues, including the grievances of those most excluded and oppressed, the labor movement will never project the broad, socially progressive image that will enthuse wide layers of the working and middle classes. No radical social change or broad class mobilization in the United

States has ever had even a chance of success without doing this to some degree. Such are the lessons from the periods of the American Revolution, post–Civil War Reconstruction, the 1890s, the 1930s, and, in a negative sense, today. The increasingly multiracial labor force presents exciting new possibilities for those interested in union organizing, in regenerating the labor movement, and in the empowerment of the working class as a whole. Many of the most inspiring labor struggles in recent years have been those of the multiracial, multiethnic labor force, including the organizing of hotel and service workers in Las Vegas, the organizing of janitors in large cities, the successful unionization of Cannon Mills, in Kannapolis, North Carolina, the organization into labor unions of the largely Latino southern California drywall workers, and the recent strike by the largely immigrant workforce at IBP (International Beef Processors).

The demands for full equality for the current more sexually, ethnically, and racially diverse workforce must address the special grievances of women and African Americans, but also those of Hispanics, Asians, Native Americans, a variety of new immigrant groups, and others. These demands of these latter groups include immigration reform, language usage and bilingual education, as well as job access and the elimination of glass ceilings. To put such things in a slogan form, a revitalized labor movement must break with the business-dominated two-party system, take broad aim at the capitalist system, lead struggles around a wide range of class issues in society at large as well as at the workplace, and place the demands for sexual and racial equality at the top of its marching banner.

REFERENCES

Arnesen, Eric. 1991. *Waterfront workers of New Orleans: Race, class, and politics, 1863–1923.* New York: Oxford University Press.

Asher, Robert, and Charles Stephenson, eds. 1990. *Labor divided: Race and ethnicity in the United States labor struggles, 1835–1960.* New York: State University of New York Press.

Bates, Timothy, and David Howell. 1997. The declining status of minorities in the New York City construction industry. *Economic Development Quarterly* (forthcoming).

Black, Isabella. 1963. American labour and Chinese immigration. *Past and Present* 25 (July): 59–76.

Blackburn, Robin. 1988. *The overthrow of colonial slavery, 1776–1848.* London: Verso.

———. 1997. *The making of New World slavery, from the baroque to the modern, 1492–1800.* London: Verso.

Cross, Harry et al. 1990. *Employer hiring practices: Differential treatment of Hispanics and Anglo job seekers.* Washington, D.C.: Urban Institute Press.

Daniels, Cletus E. 1981. *Bitter harvest: A history of the California farmworkers, 1870–1941.* Berkeley: University of California Press.

Davis, Mike. 1999. Magical urbanism: Latinos reinvent the US big city. *New Left Review* 234 (March/April): 3–43.

Degler, Carl. 1971. *Neither black nor white: Slavery and race relations in Brazil and the United States.* New York: Harper.

Du Bois, W. E. B. 1940. *Dusk of dawn.* New York: Harcourt, Brace, and World.

Foner, Philip S. 1955. *History of the labor movement in the United States.* Vol. 2. New York: International Publishers.

Galster, George. 1993. Polarization, race, and place. *North Carolina Law Review* (June): 1421–62.

Gilpin, Toni. 1992. Left by themselves: A history of the United Farm Equipment and Metal Workers Union, 1938–1955. Ph.D. diss.,. Yale University.

Glass Ceiling Commission. 1995. *Good for business: Making full use of the nation's human capital.* Washington, D.C.: U.S. Government Printing Office.

Goldfield, Michael. 1993. Race and the CIO: The possibilities for racial egalitarianism during the 1930s and 1940s. *International Labor and Working-Class History* 44 (fall): 1–32.

———. 1997. *The color of politics: Race, and the mainsprings of American politics from colonial times to the present.* New York: New Press.

Green, James R. 1973. The Brotherhood of Timberworkers, 1910–1913: A radical response to industrial capitalism in the southern U.S.A." *Past and Present* 60:161–200.

Higginbotham, A. Leon. 1996. *Shades of freedom: Racial politics and presumptions of the American legal process.* New York: Oxford University Press.

Hill, Herbert. 1982. The AFL-CIO and the black worker: Twenty-five years after the merger. *Journal of Intergroup Relations* 10(1): 5–78.

———. 1987. Race, ethnicity, and organized labor. *New Politics* 1(2): 31–82.

———.1993. Black workers, organized labor, and Title VII of the 1964 Civil Rights Act: Legislative history and litigation record. In *Race in America: The struggle for equality,* edited by Herbert Hill and James E. Jones Jr., 263–341. Madison: University of Wisconsin Press.

Hirsch, Barry T., and David A. Macpherson. 1996. *Union membership and earnings data book.* Washington, D.C.: Bureau of National Affairs.

Honey, Michael. 1993. *Southern labor and black civil rights: Organizing Memphis workers.* Urbana: University of Illinois Press.

Huntley, Horace. 1977. Iron ore miners and mine mill in Alabama, 1933–1952. Ph.D. Dissertation. University of Pittsburgh.

Jordan, Winthrop D. 1977. *White over black: American attitudes towards the Negro, 1550–1882.* New York: W.W. Norton.

Lewis, Ronald L. 1987. *Black coal miners in America: Race, class, and community conflict, 1780–1980.* Lexington: University of Kentucky Press.

Morgan, Edmund S. 1975. *American slavery, American freedom: The ordeal of colonial Virginia.* New York: Norton.

Nash, Gary B. 1979. *The urban crucible: Social change, political consciousness, and the origins of the American Revolution.* Cambridge: Harvard University Press.

Roediger, David. 1991. *The wages of whiteness: Race and the making of the American working class.* London: Verso.

Rose, David L. 1989. Twenty-five years later: Where do we stand on equal employment opportunity law enforcement? *Vanderbilt Law Review* 42.

Statistical abstract of the United States 1995. Washington, D.C.: U.S. Department of Commerce.

Sugrue, Thomas J. 1995. Crabgrass-roots politics: Race, rights, and reaction against liberalism in the urban north, 1940–1964. *Journal of American History* (September): 551–78.

————. 1996. *The origins of the urban crisis—Race and inequality in postwar Detroit.* Princeton, N.J.: Princeton University Press.

U.S. Commission on Civil Rights. 1982. *Nonreferral unions and equal employment opportunity.* Washington, D.C.: U.S. Government Printing Office.

U.S. Department of Labor. 1999. *Employment and earnings, January.* Washington, D.C.: U.S. Government Printing Office.

Wilentz, Sean. 1984. *Chants democratic: New York City and the rise of the working class, 1788–1850.* New York: Oxford University Press.

Yates, Michael. 1996. Organizing African Americans: Some economic and legal dimensions. Unpublished ms. presented at the conference on African Americans, Labor and Society: Organizing for A New Agenda, Wayne State University.

Young, Alfred, ed. 1976. *The American Revolution: Explorations in the history of American radicalism.* DeKalb: Northern Illinois University Press.

————, ed. 1993. *Beyond the American Revolution: Explorations in the history of American radicalism.* Dekalb: Northern Illinois University Press.

22

The Abolitionist Alternative in the Twenty-First Century

JOHN GARVEY

If the task of the nineteenth century was to overthrow slavery, and the task of the twentieth century was to end legal segregation, the key to solving this country's problems in the twenty-first century is to abolish the white race as a social category—in other words, eradicate white supremacy entirely.

—from the *Call to Renew the Legacy of John Brown*, 1999

The politics of the new abolitionism is intended to provide a direct and explicit challenge to whiteness. Its goals are to promote treason among old "whites" and to struggle against the recruitment of new "whites" in order to develop a powerful constituency for human freedom.

There are three views of the new abolitionists which are relevant to the present discussion: first, (as many others have pointed out) race is a social, not biological, category; second, the boundaries of whiteness have been and can be contested and redrawn, with the result being a more expansive or constricted membership in the white club; third, whiteness should be abolished (such an abolition having nothing to do with the physical existence of any human being) because such abolition is essential to human progress. Let me review these three points.

While there is still some debate among paleontologists, the prevailing view now places the origin of the human species in eastern Africa, just under 200,000 years ago. The species spread out from that point in time and place. Subsequent developments tended to promote a relatively stable inbreeding among folks in the varied regions, and relatively superficial characteristics (skin color, hair texture) became more or less common among stable populations in various places. Yet that variation did not and does not constitute a basis for the differentiation of the human population by race.

Indeed, for biologists, race is "virtually invisible:"

> Eighty-five percent of human genetic variation consists of the differences between one person and another within the same ethnic group, tribe or nation, another eight percent is between ethnic groups, and a mere seven percent is between "races." In other words, the genetic difference between, say, two randomly picked Swedes is about twelve times as large as the difference between the average of Swedes and the average of Apaches or Walpiris. (Pinker 1994, 430)

To argue that something is social means to argue that it is the result of human activity rather than the consequence of some natural process, such as the differentiation of human beings as males and females. Human beings have been at this thing called life a long time, and it is relatively hard for us to understand that what seems natural is not. Our understanding is complicated by the fact that merely claiming that something is social does not address the issue of "how" it is social. Thus, race can be understood by adherents of a social constructionist viewpoint, variously, as something that was imposed by rulers on underlings, as something that was an act of human imagination gone awry, or as something framed by privileges extended to some and denied to others. Our preferred understandings depend a great deal on answers to some fundamental questions, such as where ideas come from. Those who believe that ideas spring forth without reference to material reality will answer differently from those who acknowledge the press of circumstances on ideas. Those of us who advocate a "new abolitionism" subscribe to the notion that circumstances matter a great deal and that it is circumstances that establish the preconditions for race. Put simply, people were not favored socially because they were white; rather they were defined as "white" because they were favored. Race itself is a product of social discrimination. At the same time, as I hope to make clear, we insist that human actions matter a great deal as well.

A profound contribution was made to our understanding of race and whiteness by the political activist and historian Ted Allen. Allen (1994, 32) argues that racial oppression is distinguished in its formative stage by the reduction of "all members of the oppressed group to one undifferentiated social status, a status beneath that of any member of any social class within the colonizing population." The Irish were the first victims. Allen makes the perhaps obvious point that the Irish did not have skin colors especially different from those of the English or the Scots settlers. In a number of articles and in a two-volume book entitled *The Invention of the White Race*, Allen has argued that whiteness was invented by the planters of Virginia to forestall the threat of a unified rebellion of the laboring population—African and English—in the late seventeenth century. He points out that the word "white" had not previously been used to differentiate those of European ancestry. The conditions of servitude for those from Europe and Africa were the same; all were indentured; all could look forward to years of wretched survival or early death. Yet, none were slaves; after the 1670s, however, according to Allen, the planters decided that those of African descent would be slaves, with no right to manumission after a period of time, and their children would be property as well. On the other hand, the servants of European ancestry could be freed after the period of indenture and their children would be free—and poor. The newly christened "whites" bit the bait—they exchanged the dream of freedom for the nightmare of a less degrading servitude.

Although the passing of hundreds of years could easily let us think that the "invention" of whiteness was an instance of the exercise of the rulers' power, it is likely that the process by which those pale-skinned laborers who once knew themselves to be the bedmates and imagined themselves to be the soul mates of their dark-skinned fellows became "whites" took its own roundabout path through numerous acts of principled refusal, cowardice, and resignation (Malik 1996). The details of the making of the "white" working class in those early days are perhaps beyond our ability to research and recover, but we should not imagine that whiteness was imposed any more unilaterally than any other effort by rulers to change the terms of their rule.

In any case, other researchers have charted the ways in which whiteness has been made and remade in the years since. Time and again, new groups arrived from afar, served out a cruel apprenticeship (perhaps their version of indentured servitude), demonstrated their willingness to act white and accept the benefits of membership, petitioned for admission to the club, and then became loyal members. Non-European ancestry is not an insurmountable barrier to membership, nor is the extent of oppression suffered in the native land or upon arrival here. Only those of African ancestry remain permanently barred. And, as perhaps is obvious, all of those who (by appearance) had both African and European forebears were deemed, by the one-drop rule, to be black.

There are many deemed white today whose ancestors were not. At times, the inclusion of one group or another has been much contested. The Irish were the first to be tried. In the middle of the nineteenth century, Irish immigrants were refugees from racial oppression in their native land and were portrayed as brutes in America. Some predicted amalgamation of the Irish and the African. Instead, the Irish became white (Ignatiev 1996). Each subsequent inclusion of potentially non-white immigrants (such as the Italians, the Hungarians, the Jews) into whiteness was a defeat, rather than, as is often imagined, yet another chapter in a glorious history of immigrant triumph.

What difference has whiteness made? A quick accounting yields the following. Whiteness was the foundation stone for the widespread support of slavery on the part of poor whites for almost two hundred years. After slavery was abolished, in spite of the remarkable challenge posed and the example provided by the freed slaves during Reconstruction, race remained the centerpiece of social control in the United States. When the populists rose up at the end of the nineteenth century to challenge the rule of the railroad and bank barons, it was race that destroyed the movement. When the first unions fought to exist, it was race that made them institutions not of the working class but instead of white workers. The list goes on. While American capitalism was establishing the material prerequisites of common wealth, the whites were insuring that the wealth would remain in private hands.

The support of individuals for whiteness is not necessarily motivated by "prejudice." All that is necessary is the willingness of those ensconced within its quarters or those seeking entrance to accept its privileges. Currently, their privileges include protection from arbitrary abuse by the police; better homes and neighborhoods; the availability of adequate, if not necessarily high-quality, public schooling; relatively open access to the labor market and opportunities for advancement; the ability to travel without harassment by automobile on the highways of the country; and the opportunity for the more or less unhindered expression of ethnic aspirations. Thus, the Amish in Pennsylvania and the Hasidic Jews in New York are able to sustain cultural forms dramatically at variance with late-twentieth-century customs without jeopardizing their status as whites in good standing. Lest the benefits accruing to those considered white be underestimated, there is a great deal of statistical evidence from many spheres (life expectancy, unemployment, income and wealth, achievements in school and results from schooling, arrests/bail setting/ sentencing) which confirms the prevalence of a thoroughgoing race differential—a differential significant enough that, as Andrew

Hacker has pointed out, when questioned most whites make clear their preference for being white rather than black and are hard-pressed to put a price tag on the possibility that their racial assignment might be changed (Hacker 1992). (I, of course, recognize that this sentiment coexists ambivalently with a deep-seated attraction for elements of traditional and contemporary black culture and an apparently genuine admiration for black athletes among broad sections of the white population.)

How are these privileges maintained in the post–Jim Crow era, with formal/legal equality the law of the land? Perhaps the key to understanding it is to remember the ways in which an awful lot of white folks, north and south, east and west, resisted real, as opposed to formal, equality in the aftermath of the Civil Rights Movement. To cite just a couple of New York examples from the late 1960s: in Forest Hills, a neighborhood in Queens, white residents adamantly opposed the construction of housing that would have led to the effective desegregation of that all-white neighborhood; in 1966, white voters defeated a proposal to establish a civilian review board for the police; and in 1968, the teachers' union struck to defeat community control of the schools, a goal that had been adopted by black activists frustrated by the failure of efforts to integrate the schools. In other words, the privileges of whiteness have not only been bestowed by rulers; they have been zealously protected by the beneficiaries.

The prevailing arrangements of white privilege, and the negotiation of terms of possible incorporation of new whites, are maintained by an interplay between institutions and popular activity. Those institutions include the various bureaucracies, the police, the courts, the jails and prisons, the schools, the universities, the hospitals, and the unions. They include those agencies acknowledged to have a role of social preservation, those intended to ameliorate the worst consequences of life under the prevailing social and economic circumstances, and even those intended to reform those circumstances (such as funded community organizations and local economic development initiatives).

This hardly works by magic. Elected officials, and those who staff the various apparatuses, respond quite vigorously to popular sentiment and any potential threat to their continuation in office. Yet, many of the key social interactions are obscured. Take schools as an example. Perhaps one of the most remarkable features of present-day schooling—in spite of all but complete local governance—is the virtually constant differential in achievement between black and white students across the country. White students overpopulate the gifted programs and black students overpopulate the lowest tracks (especially the special education one). In a recent study published in *Race Traitor*, Jane Manners traced the ways in which segregation was repackaged in Montclair, New Jersey, a suburban town celebrated for its integrated schools. In that town, nominal integration of buildings has been accompanied by a methodical segregation of educational opportunity and enrichment. White parents are effectively assured that their children will not suffer because of their physical association with black children, and every effort is made to make that assurance real (Manners 1998).

At the same time, other whites insist on more traditional forms of separation. Just recently, *The New York Times* reported on events in two nominally integrated New York City community school districts. In the first, District 28 (covering Forest Hills and Jamaica), the school board has decided to spend five million dollars in federal magnet school funds—intended to promote and support school integration—to improve seven schools in the northern half of the district (Sengupta 1999). One of those schools is PS 144. Its students are said to be 37 percent Asian, 19 percent Hispanic, 4 percent black, and 40 percent white. Yet the school board claims that the magnet funds are needed to increase the white enrollment to 50 percent. According to the local superintendent, Neil Kreinick, the "only way you can succeed in New York City and most big cities" is to attract more white students from the nonpublic schools (B8). Meanwhile, only two schools in Jamaica (the predominantly black half of the district) are to receive magnet school funds. The resourcefulness of the white folks is extraordinary—they have even figured out how to use money intended to promote integration to support the maintenance of white privilege.

The other story is from District 10 in the Bronx (a district including relatively wealthy white Riverdale and relatively poor black Marble Hill). In the Riverdale end of the district, Middle School 141 has an enrollment of about 1,400 students—half from Riverdale and half from Marble Hill. A group of Riverdale parents has proposed the redesign of the school so that it would include a new "rigorous" high school. In order to do so, the zone for the middle school would have to be redrawn, thereby excluding many of the Marble Hill children (Waldman 1999). What's perfect about this solution is that it's well known that the public high schools in the Bronx, with the exception of the Bronx High School for Science (a school that admits students from all over the city on the basis of performance on an exam taken in the eighth grade), constitute an educational dead zone. If the plan for a redesigned school is adopted, then the children of Riverdale who do not do well enough on the exam will have an alternative to the educational misery that is the destiny of their age-mates down the road. What is especially revealing about this episode is that the efforts to redesign the school are being led not by reactionaries, but by certified liberals in the reform wing of the Democratic Party. As is often the case, those who imagine that they know better rest easy in their conviction that social responsibility is dependent only on intent.

Thus, I suggest that this whiteness that we struggle against is not merely the product of rulers' efforts to perpetuate their rule, but is as well, if not more, the result of the efforts of lots of ordinary people to improve the circumstances of their lives within the racial terms set down by the past. This need not involve any self-conscious motivation to do harm. Instead, it is accomplished through what appears to be unobjectionable participation in a wide variety of institutional relationships and practices—in trade unions, schools, political parties, pension funds, real estate transactions, and so forth. In any case, those who have become accustomed to privilege, for the most part and for most of the time, act to preserve that privilege rather than abolish it. Indeed, when they perceive that their relative advantage is being taken away, some resort to popular protest to secure it—even to the point of challenging the rule of those whose existence as rulers they seem all but incapable of recognizing otherwise. Those "new" immigrants who aspire to share in the privilege become quite accustomed to justifying their complicity by citing their own experience of prior hardship and diligent effort. This is not to suggest that they do not encounter discrimination, danger, or degradation. It is, however, to suggest that their yearning for whiteness is politically poisonous.

New abolitionists propose a struggle against many years of sedimented reality—wherein white privilege is passed down through generations and sustained through the normal workings of most of the social and economic institutions of the country. By way of example, abolitionists in New York are attempting to organize and support efforts to disrupt the normal workings of the police department and of those institutions, such as the police union, which protect the police. Specifically, this could involve a challenge to the forty-eight-hour rule, enshrined in the police contract, which allows officers a protected grace period when they face possible charges for misconduct. Yet it will also involve a challenge to those legislators who accept contributions from the union and routinely support legislation favored by that union.

There is no shortage of other possible targets, such as tracking in the schools and, in more than a few cities, segregated elite high schools. Some of our suggested remedies are quite simple—for example, in the case of the segregated high schools in New York (which base admission on performance on an examination), we propose that admission be granted to a proportionally appropriate number of top-performing students in each of the city's community school districts—a variation on the fixed-percentage admissions policies recently adopted by the public university systems in Texas and California.

Just as important, however, abolitionists advocate and applaud the breaking of the "racial contract" in every sphere of human life. Thus, we celebrate those "white" teenagers who insist on their right to wear the clothes they prefer, to listen to the music they like, to choose the friends and lovers they wish. We appreciate those artists, such as Russell Banks, who dare to go deep into the white folks' lives, dreams, and nightmares and imagine that there is a future for them on the other side of their complicity with the miserableness sustained by whiteness.

In all our efforts, we are guided by a simple proposition. Black folks spend their lives fighting to abolish whiteness. We pay close attention to and support their efforts—to stop profiling on the highways, to end the warehousing of their children in special education, to end discriminatory practices in medical research and diagnosis, to expose the pseudoscientists who scheme of new racial biologies, to battle against the exclusionary practices of the construction trade unions, to end the criminalization of black youth and the consequent imprisonment and denial of citizenship rights to millions.

What do the nonabolitionists think and do? First, the dissolutionists. There is some evidence that whiteness is being dissolved—not as the product of principled struggle but instead by the development of capitalism itself. If this path were to be followed, there would be no preferential treatment granted to white workers; they would be eligible to be as badly paid and as badly treated as those considered non-white. Thus, race differentials, such as the effective guarantee of higher wages for white construction workers through the Davis-Bacon Act, would be eliminated.

The outline of this approach can be seen in the recommendations of the Advisory Board to President Clinton's Initiative on Race. Yet that dissolution is proceeding by fits and starts, and it is not at all clear that it will be carried through to a conclusion. Not surprisingly, any dismantlement of whiteness is opposed by many beneficiaries of the previous order and by some who wish to become beneficiaries. Therefore, those, such as Clinton, who desire dissolution with minimal conflict and with minimal electoral losses, prove to be unreliable advocates. Clinton nominates Lani Guinier but does not support her. As an important aside, at least two distinctive contributions by Guinier to the cause of abolition deserve mention—the recommendation of proportional representation as an alternative to redistricting and the recommendation that standardized test scores be used to set minimum thresholds of satisfactory performance as an alternative to strict rank ordering (Sturm and Guinier 1996).

Similarly, Clinton convenes the Advisory Board for his Initiative on Race, accepts its recommendations, and then sends it off to a virtual reality. Today, in March of 1999, if someone calls the number for the President's Initiative on Race, he or she is informed, by a recorded message, that the initiative has become the president's "One America Initiative." The message also advises callers what to do if they have experienced discrimination at the hands of employers, real estate agents, or police officers—press another key. If and when a caller presses that other key, the electronic messenger gives you another number to call. If a caller persists through the messages and leaves his or her own message asking how one might obtain a copy of the Advisory Board's report, chances are that a White House staffer will call back and let you know that there are no copies of the report available for public distribution (there are two copies in the office—one for the director of the initiative and the other for the public relations staff). There is a copy available for downloading from the web, but they've been having some problems lately so people haven't been able to download it. It's virtual reality without the virtual.

Meanwhile, others who desire dissolution, without fundamental alteration of the social landscape, affirm affirmative action within limits. Thus, Bowen and Bok (1998) write a book to demonstrate that "race-sensitive" admissions policies will not dilute the quality of the nation's leadership, but oppose the introduction of a "fixed-percentage" admissions policy to state institutions of higher education since it would diminish "the pool of students who can compete effectively for positions of leadership in business, government, and the professions." Nonetheless, the dissolutionists still affirm their good intentions: "Individuals of every political stripe agree that, ultimately, we must fix the K-12 'pipeline' (or 'river' to adopt the Bowen-Bok metaphor). But this will take years." (Zwick 1999, 35)

It is probably worth noting that there are some, such as Jim Sleeper and the Thernstroms, who believe that the dissolution project has been completed and that the only thing that stands between black folks and the end of whiteness as a social obstacle is their own effort (Sleeper 1997; Thernstrom and Thernstrom 1999). I ask them, simply and straightforwardly, the Andrew Hacker question: Are they willing to become black?

Next, there are the expansionists and the restrictionists. Since the mid-1960s, the popular white viewpoint on race has been framed primarily by the debate between the populist/Klan/Nazi far right and the more traditional conservative/

neoconservative right. In the recent past, this has been incarnated in two variants, the conservative typified by politicians such as Newt Gingrich and Rudolph Giuliani and the quasi fascist or fascist, typified by David Duke and Tom Metzger. While the two frequently share some ideas and language, it is important to differentiate them. Let me suggest that they can be considered respectively as white expansionists or restrictionists.

Although it is often submerged, the political project of the Gingrich/Giuliani sector allows for a significant recomposition of whiteness to allow for the inclusion of Hispanics and "new" immigrants. Yet it demands a more or less consistent opposition to the blacks and a defense of traditional white prerogatives. It is, I think, highly unlikely that the political potential of the Gingrich/Giuliani sector is going to be much diminished by an "unmasking the racist" approach. At the same time, it does seem clear that Giuliani's political ambitions have been interfered with by the continuing protests concerning the murder of Amadou Diallo. There has been no shortage of commentary in New York suggesting that the mayor is to blame for the unrelenting assaults against the black residents of the city. Yet there has been far too little commentary about the fact that he launched those assaults with the advice and consent of the white people who elected him to do just that. They will be unmoved by an unmasking of the mayor.

At the same time, the forces represented electorally by David Duke and those to his right can imagine no expansion of whiteness. They hold out a vision of a purified America, an America purified of blacks, of Jews, and (occasionally) of capitalists. They are hardly a homogeneous group, and they often spill over into the conservative camp. A "virtual" illustration of this can be seen on the web page of the Council of Conservative Citizens (COFCC.org). There you will find those who call for the restriction of immigration, the rehabilitation of those who fought for the Confederacy, the extension of plebiscite rights to the states (as was granted, however symbolically, not long ago to the residents of Puerto Rico), and white proletarian revolutionaries as well as a link to the neo-Nazi National Front in France. I hope it is obvious that the threat represented by those forces cannot be effectively combated by a defense of mainstream institutions. For the young people who see nothing but a bleak future (such as those described by Raphael Ezekiel in *The Racist Mind*), only the promise of a total alternative will suffice (Ezekiel 1996).

We are frequently urged to recognize that there is something new about the situation in the United States today and to expand our conversation and analysis "beyond black and white." Those who urge the recognition of the racialized ways in which those other than the descendants of Africans are oppressed in America risk becoming part of an effort not to abolish whiteness but instead to rehabilitate it through the inclusion of new "non-whites." Unfortunately, I believe that what we are being urged to recognize as new is quite old, and the ground is being laid for a reconsolidation of the oldest. Simply put, I am afraid that a reconceptualization of intermediate categories between black and white will allow for a smoother recomposition and preservation of whiteness and a renewed appreciation for the old whites. Thus, in an essay entitled "White Loss," in a collection entitled *Beyond Black and White*, Michelle Fine, Lois Weis, Judi Addelston and Julia Marusza conclude:

> The time has come to shift the sands so that whiteness and maleness are reinvented. Adult women and men must invite and invent pedagogies that begin to unscramble various forms of masculinities for young boys and men. . . . Carving out safe spaces, white males need to analyze critically the banner of privilege they once carried, and have now lost, and the sites of white masculinity from which productive identities can be spawned. All other "demographic groups" have begun this work of consciousness raising and critical identity reformation. (Fine, Weis, Addelston, Marusza 1997, 300)

The white studies folks, who are almost never abolitionists, are not hostile to the proliferation of other identities. Indeed, they know that such a proliferation makes their own work to rehabilitate whiteness more palatable. This approach is connected to a project of "rearticulation of whiteness." In that vein, the otherwise formidable Howard Winant replaces a whiteness formed by biology with a whiteness formed by culture but insists that culture has, for all practical purposes, the same permanence as biology (Winant 1997). Among other objections to that point of view, I would ask what white culture is. What cultural practices do the steelworker and the corporate financier who executes the billion-dollar deal that results in the liquidation of the steel mill share in common? None. They share only the privileges of the white skin and, as a result, the steelworker imagines that he has something—other than his humanity—in common with the financier.

The politics of those who counsel rearticulation and deconstruction rather than abolition are a politics of despair—rooted in a conviction that ordinary people cannot transform themselves and are incapable of ruling society. Their "politics" is a politics of multicultural education and diversity and sensitivity training. As one radio commentator pointed out, it is a good thing that they did not have diversity consultants available during slavery or we might still be dealing with a "rearticulated" enslavement of human beings.

Outside of the circles of the Far Right and the militia movements, the desirability and possibility of radical change seem very strange these days. In large part, the political stage, which once seemed so full of possibilities, was transformed because of large developments—the liquidation of a large chunk of American industry, the suppression and defeat of the black movement, the end of the war against Vietnam. Yet it was transformed as well by developments internal to the movement—generally, the incorporation of activists within a whole variety of mainstream institutions. Whereas the Left was once the source of many of the most penetrating critiques of the limitations and perversions of governmental and quasi-governmental institutions (such as large medical centers, universities, the public schools, social service agencies, and unions), its adherents are now content to be the most forthright defenders of those institutions against attacks from conservative Republicans and, perhaps worse still, the promoters of the government's police agencies as the front line of defense against the insurgent forces of the Right. The only things that distinguish those who imagine themselves to be on the Left from their liberal counterparts is a willingness to organize occasional public protests and a pronounced tendency to write in impenetrable prose—a style that often suggests a critique far more throughgoing than in fact it is. The notion that a Left might be concerned with the vision of a new world and not a defense of institutionalized accommodations to the existing state of affairs is greeted in most quarters as nostalgic.

As the possibility of social transformation receded, a renewed defense of whiteness became the cornerstone of the Republican strategy to win the South away from the Democrats, and it became the script of choice for conservative mayoral candidates from Los Angeles to New York. As race became an ever more potent weapon for those seeking a reversal of the popular victories of the 1950s and 1960s, the white Left sought out excuse after excuse for why whiteness could not be directly challenged.

Let me give two quite different examples that provide specific illustrations of this excuse making in practice. From 1970 until 1978, I drove a yellow taxi in New York City. For much of that time, the taxi fleet owners and the elected leadership of the taxi workers union engaged in a relentless campaign of vilification against the so-called gypsy cabs. Those were cabs that cruised the predominantly black neighborhoods of the city as a result of the refusal of most yellow cab drivers to take black passengers to those neighborhoods and/or to remain in them once taken there by a fare. Inevitably, the gypsy cabs were taken by their passengers into other neighborhoods, and the fleet owners and union leaders were determined to resist any infringement into what they imagined to be their territory. To be precise, the union leadership had seized upon the gypsy cabs to explain away a disastrous reduction in taxi drivers' wages subsequent to a new contract negotiated in early 1971. In any case, the story I wish to tell is not so much about the venal motives of either taxi fleet owners or incumbent union leaders. Instead, I want to highlight the response of the group of mostly young Left activists of which I was a part.

The work that we did together forced us to deal with lots of complicated issues in ways that were respectful of the mostly older workers we were trying to engage. For example, we spent many hours discussing whether we would publicly support the victory of the National Liberation Front in Vietnam; we spent many more hours discussing whether we would support the right of those gypsy cabs to cruise all the streets of the city. Ultimately, in a show of principled lack of principle, we decided that we would have no position on the issue. We failed the test of solidarity with our fellow workers because we thought that the "white" cab drivers would not be able to rise to the challenge of supporting something that they thought would be detrimental to their own short-term interests—even though it was the right thing to do.

Another version of this same failure was on display some years later when the anti-apartheid movement in the United States organized its campaign to persuade pension funds to divest themselves of investments in companies with holdings in South Africa by convincing those covered by those pension funds that such divestment would not affect the value of their retirement pensions. The argument was that if divestment did result in lower pensions, then no request would be made of the prospective pensioners to support the struggle in South Africa.

At the same time, blacks are being cautioned, even by some who know the history of whiteness and blackness quite well, such as George Lipsitz, the author of the much acclaimed *The Possessive Investment in Whiteness* (Lipsitz 1998). He recounts an old Moms Mabley joke about a black lawyer being denied the right to vote in Mississippi—in spite of the fact that he can explicate the state constitution and a biblical passage—because he is unable to read a Chinese newspaper. When the voting registrars ask the lawyer what the Chinese paper means, the lawyer responds that it means that no matter what he does they are not going to let him vote. Lipsitz argues:

> the operative assumption beyond this assertion is that it is unreasonable to
> expect someone who is "American" to be able to read a Chinese newspaper. This

is in no way to belittle the black claim for inclusion contained in Mabley's story, only to warn that in the current multiracial and international context in which racial identities are made and unmade, a simple black-white binary, or indeed any binary opposition, will not help us address or redress the possessive investment in whiteness. (212)

In an essay in the recently published *The Real Ebonics Debate*, Theresa Perry warned otherwise:

> One of the most serious theoretical flaws embedded in most conversations about multicultural education and changing demographics is the assumption that all people of color in this country are similarly situated politically and that their cultural formations carry similar political salience. The school performance of African Americans in minority/majority school districts should compel us to inject the notion of "a racial caste group" into discussions of multiculturalism in schools, in the workplace, and in the economic order. (Perry 1998, 212n. 1)

The use of race or whiteness as a way to analyze social realities does not directly address the issue of the extent of misery endured by an individual or members of various groups. Although the point has been made before, it is worth repeating that it's difficult to compare suffering. Hunger, pain, fear, terror, anxiety, self-doubt, and derogation are all available in ample supply, and simple rankings of relative misery probably do not help much in allowing us to imagine a way to create a world where the cards are not so terribly stacked against the possibility of human freedom and pleasure. Yet, as I hope I've made clear, there is another way to look at this issue. It involves an examination of the ways in which individuals find themselves placed in different groups, the ways in which they understand their relative good or bad fortune, and the ways in which they imagine overcoming their misfortune.

To place this in perspective, let us take a moment to look at South Africa earlier in this century. As is commonly known, the South African people were divided into four major population groups—the Africans, the Europeans, the Coloureds, and the Asians. While all but the Europeans were victims of systematic state and personal oppression as a result of that classification system, it is also true that oppression was measured out in different dosages and modalities. Not too surprisingly, according to No Sizwe (the pseudonym of Neville Alexander), in *One Azania, One Nation*:

... the educated elite, which had absorbed the capitalist ethos, inevitably formed organizations which catered for disabilities felt to be peculiar to the groups from which they themselves originated. Thus, without exception, all the political organisations of the oppressed which were formed up to approximately 1918 were essentially caste organisations concerned with the betterment of their own particular group and with gaining economic and political concessions for 'their' people. (No Sizwe 1979, 47)

The South Africans put up with white rule for another century.

If we wish to challenge those who rule, those who are fundamentally responsible for the misery we put up with, we will have to challenge the way that they rule—including the ways that their rule is perpetuated by our own deeds. The continued existence of the white race as a social formation allows for the continued oppression of the black population, restricts human freedom, distorts all popular movements that rise up to challenge various injustices, and prevents progress on almost every front.

Some—no, many—will be skeptical of the possibility that the white race can be abolished. Indeed, the loyalty of most whites to their race and the earnest desire of other newcomers to insist upon enrollment seem to confirm its durability. Yet, times change and with them their possibilities. There was a time in many parts of the world where the people thought it obvious that their rulers were either divine or endowed by the divinity with the right to rule. Yet the monarchies fell and the earth still turned.

What would it mean for whites if all differentials were eliminated? Keeping in mind the percentage of black folks in the country, how much would unemployment and/or imprisonment increase for those now considered white if the race differential was eliminated? Not a whole lot. However, there would be an enormous change in their understanding of their predicament. Without whiteness, those who rule would have to resort to other forms of social control. Put simply, ruling groups have two alternatives to secure the orderliness and cooperation of those they rule over—persuasion or coercion. When persuasion fails, coercion is resorted to. If whiteness were abolished, the police would have to become equal opportunity beaters. That would be a victory for us all and would create the possibility of an end to police abuse and even policing itself.

We urge upon so-called whites and those yearning to be white the abolitionist project because we believe that they can be better than they are. We believe that they too have dreams of freedom, but that those dreams are buried. We do so because we remain convinced of the possibility of radical change—where, instead of spending our time debating the extent of the meanness we are prepared to put up with, we would be imagining and creating the possibilities of free human personalities. We should be clear. Our project is not intended to win over a majority of the whites or of the potential whites. Instead, we wish to attract enough of them, either those already discontented with whiteness or those disgusted with the whole social order, so that we can build a movement against whiteness. Neither the nineteenth century's abolitionists nor the twentieth century's civil rights activists ever constituted majorities. Still, they made decisive contributions to human freedom. We hope to do the same.

REFERENCES

Allen, Theodore W. 1994. *The invention of the white race.* New York: Verso.

Bowen, William G., and Derek C. Bok. 1998. *The shape of the river: Long-term consequences of considering race in college and university admissions.* Princeton, N.J.: Princeton University Press.

Ezekiel, Raphael. 1996. *The racist mind: Portraits of American neo-nazis and Klansmen.* New York: William Morrow & Co.

Fine, Michelle, Lois Weis, Judi Addelston, and Julia Marusza. 1997. White loss. In *Beyond Black and White,* edited by M. Seller and L. Weis, 283–301. Albany: SUNY Press.

Hacker, Andrew. 1992. *Two nations: Black and white, separate, hostile and unequal.* New York: Charles Scribner's Sons.

Ignatiev, Noel. 1996. *How the Irish became white.* New York: Routledge.

Lipsitz, George. 1998. *The possessive investment in whiteness.* Philadelphia: Temple University Press.

Malik, Kenan. 1996. *The meaning of race: Race, history and culture.* New York: New York University Press.

Manners, Jane. 1998. Repackaging segregation: A history of the magnet school system in Montclair, New Jersey. *Race Traitor* 8:51–97.

No Sizwe. 1979. *One Azania, one nation: The national question in South Africa.* London: Zed Press.

Perry, Theresa. 1998. I'on know why they be trippin': Reflections on the Ebonics debate. In *The real Ebonics debate: Power, language, and the education of African-American children,* edited by T. Perry and L. Delpit. Boston: Beacon Press.

Pinker, Steven. 1994. *The language instinct: How the mind creates language.* New York: William Morrow & Co.

Sengupta, Somini. 1999. In Queens, integration tool skips racially isolated schools. *New York Times.* February 23: B1–8.

Sleeper, Jim. 1997. *Liberal racism.* New York: Penguin Books.

Sturm, Susan, and Lani Guinier. 1996. The future of affirmative action: Reclaiming the innovative ideal." *California Law Review* 84:953–1036.

Thernstrom, Stephan, and Abigail Thernstrom. 1999. *America in black and white: One nation, indivisible.* New York: Simon & Schuster.

Waldman, Amy. 1999. Bronx neighbors spar over school: Plan for an academy widens racial and economic rifts. *New York Times.* February 25:B1–10.

Winant, Howard. 1997. Beyond blue eyes: Whiteness and contemporary U.S. racial politics. *New Left Review* 225:73–88.

Zwick, Rebecca. 1999. Backdoor affirmative action. *Education Week.* February 10:56–35.

23

Play that Funky Logical Positivism, White Boy; Or, If You Are Going to Be White, Do It White

R OBERT W EISSBERG

Since the early 1970s I have tried to keep abreast of scholarship in "racial politics." Only in the most incidental way, perhaps like a fifteenth-century European hearing tales of exotic lands beyond the ocean, have I encountered "Whiteness Studies." To be frank, my initial reaction to such rumors was to suspect a parody, perhaps a mischievous undergraduate "Center for White Culture" featuring Diet Pepsi and Hostess Twinkies plus an annual showing of Steve Martin's *The Jerk*.

This premonition proved grossly inaccurate as I ventured into "Whiteness Studies." The assembled materials revealed a burgeoning industry far beyond anything anticipated (Johnson 1999 offers an up-to-date extensive bibliography). The respectability of its many academic outlets made my discovery even more noteworthy. The field even possessed its own special journal—*Race Traitor*. What might "White Studies" have to say about "whiteness"? A naïve outsider might guess Whites Studies to extol "whiteness" as Black Studies celebrates blackness. Surely much about "whiteness" inspires pride: prodigious economic and scientific accomplishment, long traditions of personal freedom and resistance to tyranny, a rich artistic heritage, and on and on. Indeed, feting "whiteness" is arguably unnecessary—achievement is patently obvious. Who invented oft-imitated Western civilization? Whites demand no special awareness month or convoluted textbook role models. We crave no contrived feel-good flattering history. If conscious emulation—even among blacks—is the yardstick, whiteness is revered worldwide. How many ill people of color eschew "white medicine"? Many more blacks seek entrance to "white" schools than vice versa.

This celebration of whiteness was not to be encountered. Endlessly, in sundry imaginative styles and formats, I read how whites perpetrate measureless evils, impose horrendous oppression, and inflict untold calamities on modern society. In this enterprise older writings praising "white virtues" become incontestable evidence of genocidal intent. "White pride" is inherently depraved, never commendable. If "white patriots" speak out, they are excoriated as genocidal white supremacists or racial bigots. The search for the evil emanating from whiteness is ingenious; innocent-appearing historical episodes or commonplace cultural artifacts prove it all. Everything seemingly unmasks pathological "white privilege" that ineluctably debilitates blacks. In a nutshell, the study of whiteness is *exclusively* an exercise in condemnation. The ebullience perhaps hearkens back to when the germ theory of disease was discovered. Eureka! Now, after eons of immense human suffering, misdirected scholarship, and dead-end cures, conquering the pox is a finally reachable goal. The phrase "White Plague" might even be appreciated by some.

Yet, as these materials accumulated, I further sensed that this project was less a well-formulated academic field than a desultory impulse, sharing but superficial vocabulary and vague ideological affinities. How, then, can one grasp this nascent creature? Assessment is deceptively complex. On the one hand, to assemble its academic revelations likely imposes a preordained failure. Solid scholarship requires decades of labor, and to say "What have you achieved since 1990?" is grossly unfair. Physics, the Queen of the Sciences, took centuries to secure modest respectability. Still, *something* should emanate from all these efforts, if only some promising clues regarding future inquiry. Further complicating my task is its selectivity. "Whiteness" is a somewhat foreign academic topic for me, and I may have ignored or misinterpreted many worthy contributions.

This assessment poses three broad questions. If this divergent whiteness literature cannot decisively answer them, at least a good-faith effort in their direction is required. Avoidance of the inescapable is a more serious sin than uncertain replies. Our underlying evaluative framework rests on logical positivism: conclusions must be empirically understood and demonstrated according to logical rules across multiple observers. We eschew "truths" by ideological declaration. Agitprop has its place, but not masquerading as academic scholarship. The perceptive reader will naturally sense that "Whiteness Studies" are being tried wholly within the court of science, perhaps the quintessential "white" proclivity. Given that I am white, and descend from innumerable white ancestors, this predilection is inevitable.

Our three guiding questions are:

1. What is distinctive about being "white"? Is this attribute merely skin color or an entire configuration of traits? Additionally, is this "whiteness" inescapably biological, or is it a learned cultural artifact? Regardless of source, can a white-skinned person "be black" and vice versa? Finally, is "whiteness" a dichotomy or are there degrees that, perchance, follow the contours of well-known racial classification systems? Might rednecks even belong to the Nordic race?

2. What is it about whites, ceteris paribus, compelling their adversity toward non-whites? History teaches that whites have long vilified each other (as have non-whites). The names Hitler and Stalin are sufficient on this point. Yet, one of the recurring themes in whiteness explications is that repugnance is especially directed against people of color. Given the ample opportunities for white-on-white carnage, why add fresh victims to the list? Might this be likened to a biological tropism, an urgency that transcends rationality? Is such inter-racial hatefulness explainable *exclusively* by whiteness?

3. If, as it is relentlessly asserted, whites sustain their superior position *unfairly*, how is this done? After all, superiority is not ipso facto egregious, save for doctrinaire egalitarians. That the fastest person wins a footrace does not prove cheating. By the same token, is the overrepresentation of whites among the powerful proof positive of grand usurpation? Conceivably, this privilege rests upon superiority in intelligence, organizational talent, industriousness, and all else promoting mastery. We demand "smoking gun" proof of unfairness.

Our conclusion then takes up two issues. First, what are the prospects for whiteness as an academic field? Group-centered departments—Women's Studies, Gay and Lesbian Studies, plus various ethnic-based university units—now proliferate. Such fashionableness need not, however, certify intellectual worthiness. Does "white studies" portend future disciplinary accomplishment? Second, we explore, albeit speculatively, what sustains this peculiar academic endeavor. We submit that securing this academic beachhead has less to do with scholarly worthiness and everything to do with political management. Radical critics are on target when they accuse oppressive universities of bolstering "the establishment," though this "oppression" may explain their own academic position. Indeed, without this "oppression" the whiteness field would likely vanish as a campus entity.

Before proceeding, an ideological disclaimer might be appropriate. Exposing hidden research "bias" is a time-honored disciplinary exercise, so let me save curious readers needless speculation. I find whiteness studies appalling. It comprises a portion of the larger anti–Western Civilization impulse—this is the same crowd celebrating multiculturalism, cultural relativism, Afrocentrism, eco-feminism, and sundry other dubious fads defining the contemporary "New Left." Such views are ill-advised, romanticized rejections of merit-based, rule-of-law societies progressing via science. Whiteness devotees assuredly have every right to their views, and I wish them no harm. Unfortunately, their triumph can only bestow the Hobbesian misery on us now infecting the Third World. That millions of these wretched souls yearly seek the evil West's rewards while a tiny handful drift backward speaks loudly to relative worthiness. To be plainspoken, those condemning whiteness can surely find a comfortable home in many far-distant paradises.

Defining "Whiteness"

Definitional quarrels over "race" are seemingly endemic. It is "merely a social construct" to some, while others embrace an unforgiving biological determinism. Perchance cultural anthropologists and geneticists reside on different planets. Everybody possesses his or her favorite evidence, and the debate often resembles medieval theological clashes. Yet, having acknowledged these disagreements, race-based analysis demands some position if one seeks to align traits with racial affinities. To speak of "whiteness" as explaining something—good or bad— requires a firm theory of race.

Suppose whiteness were indeed socially constructed, learned, or otherwise environmentally determined. That is, one could become "white" as one might elect nationality or religious affiliation. Though this view may seem odd, anecdotal accounts of this phenomenon abound. Over forty years ago, Norman Mailer, in *The White Negro*, depicted whites mimicking the black "jazz" style. Today stores like The Buckle market "urban" styles to white wannabes in rustic shopping malls light years from urban ghettoes. The rap and hip-hop market is also supposedly dependent on white teenagers. Phil Rubio's "Crossover Dreams" (1996) provides a catalogue of imitation. Conversely, blacks often attempt to "act white," as witnessed by black undergraduates decked out in "Waspy" Ralph Lauren and Tommy Hilfiger. One can only marvel at bumpkins buying FUBU hooded sweatshirts while Hood denizens parade in Perry Ellis J-51 class yacht jackets.

If, on the other hand, race were genetically hard-wired, our discourse on whiteness diverges profoundly. "Crossing over" is a purely superficial charade. Whites are white regardless of style: Vanilla Ice is an imposter. Today's wannabe "cool" FUBU-attired Iowa farm boy will, if biologically inclined whiteness scholars are correct, display his true racial colors when economic choices intervene. Ditto for the young black male proudly sporting multiple polo pony embroidery—he is black notwithstanding protective camouflage. Each acts out scripts despite occasional fraternization with the enemy. More important, requisite social policy will profoundly vary according to this hypothesized nurture/nature mix. If whites are genetically foredoomed toward evil, of what utility is education or similar volitional enticement? Why admonish those incapable of goodness? In plain English, whites may have to be forcibly tamed as one might domesticate dangerous beasts. To reiterate, theories of race-based politics require confronting the origins of these differences: where one goes depends on where the journey begins.

One would predict that whiteness study adherents would cluster at the hard-wired genetic end of the continuum. This position is scientifically sensible, given their insistence that white behavior overwhelmingly issues from whiteness itself. Plainly, white skin—the quintessential "whiteness" ingredient—is 100 percent genetically determined. No social constructionist avers that "white people" are "really" black people if observed under darkness. Imposters—the "Soul Mans" and similar wannabes—are easily detected. This is far less true for religion or nationality. Even the most extreme environmental variations, from diet to schooling, cannot alter skin color, outside momentary sunburn or medical conditions (e.g., jaundice). Moving to the Arctic Circle will not assist insecure blacks to "pass."

More importantly, innumerable other intractable traits are seemingly genetically anchored in whiteness. Though the scientific evidence here lacks the conclusiveness of skin pigment, a substantial role for heredity in multiple traits with unambiguous sociopolitical implications is uncontestable. Yes, white people act "that way" since they are born "that way." J. Philippe Rushton (1995) offers prodigious quantities of pertinent empirical research, and skeptics are advised to consult the original monographs regarding the environmental-heredity balance as well as the precise definitions of these oft-controversial terms. In the meantime, let me offer a brief sampling of "in-born" racial difference. In varying degrees, compared to blacks, whites are genetically more inclined toward law abidingness, marital stability, sexual restraint, intelligence, organizational talent, and cautiousness. Compared to blacks, whites are less compulsive, less sociable, less aggressive, and less inclined toward domination. By contrast, blacks outshine whites in earlier physical development and procreational capacity. *The Bell Curve* extends this list. Via differences in IQ (which is substantially inherited), black-white differences exist in healthiness, poverty, and proneness to accidents, among other traits.

To be sure, an army of black Rushtons might very well fashion scientific findings painting a quite dissimilar picture—African Americans were genetically superior to whites in terms of sensitivity to injustice, love of community, and untold other virtues. This research might also depict whites as inherently disposed toward anti-black oppression and genocide. Indeed, some black researchers, for example Leonard Jefferies, do voice these views. Yet these are unproven assertions, not demonstrated facts. Until contrary data arrives, the picture that Rushton and others similarly inclined paint is the scientific standard. To reiterate, it may be inaccurate, but there exists no empirically demonstrated coherent alternative. Rebuke is not disconfirmation. This unflattering portrayal of blacks also meshes well with plain-Jane reality, namely black-dominated nations being characterized by impending economic collapse, turmoil, lawlessness, epidemics of sexual transmitted disease, and other qualities consistent with established racial genetic differences.

Nothing in present-day genetic research predicts whites being hard-wired to follow the script advanced by whiteness devotees. Again, only unsupported assertions are advanced, not proof. For all the claims of Herrnstein, Murray, and Rushton regarding the impact of genes, none claims that whites are genetically uniquely disposed against non-whites. Whites may exploit people of color, but they also exploit fellow whites, and, most central, this selection is not genetically passed across generations. If some "white Devil" gene exists, it remains undiscovered. The best-case genetic argument is that whites are inclined to avoid blacks (and vice versa), and this is certainly demonstrated in daily life. Avoidance, however, is not oppression.

How, then, do whites come to act "white," according to the Whiteness Studies script? Are nefarious white traits learned as part of a white culture or, perchance, biologically ingrained? These are momentous questions, perhaps requiring decades of careful inquiry, but it is difficult to imagine the claims of whiteness study advancing beyond speculation without thorough investigation. My read of whiteness scholarship comes up empty on these attention-demanding matters. The source of characteristic white behavior, the relationship of ancestry to present-day sociopolitical proclivities, the hereditary gradations among peoples' temperaments, and the role of genetic factors in conditions afflicting non-whites remain beyond discussion, let alone systematic examination. Offered instead is a parade of non sequiturs, specious arguments, and unsubstantiated invectives.

The matter is often "solved" by a selective exegesis of "revealing" novels. Matthew Frye Jacobson's (1998) approach to "race" illustrates this easygoing cosmology (also see, for example, Aanerud 1997). Via various quotations, he "demonstrates" that racial terminology has varied in the United States by user and time period (for example, terms such as 'Hebrew' and 'Celt' were once commonplace racial labels). Fair enough—colloquial vocabulary is seldom precise. He then concludes (in a peculiar logical leap) that racial categories therefore lack any intrinsic meaning (4). This would be as if a historian of science decided that since gravity (or hundreds of other building-block concepts) has proven definitionally troublesome, it is nonexistent and should therefore be banished from scientific discourse. The "logic" is that measurement imperfection certifies a chimera. Nevertheless, he seems unable to escape the "realness" of race, and his concluding remarks (in the epilogue) comically attempt to distinguish, among others, "Nordics" from Italians as subspecies of "whites."

Hartigan (1997), in his ethnographic study of white Detroit neighborhoods, similarly illustrates this pervasive confusion. He gets to the heart of this matter by announcing ". . . I examine whiteness as something akin to a message or transmission in which varying occurrences of errors repeat their irregularities at each increasingly minute level of attention to the content of message/error" (181-82). One can only guess what such jargon means, and subsequent explication piles it on. Lopez (1996) similarly takes this hard-line social construction position but goes one step further when he proclaims that "We live race through class, religion, nationality, gender, sexual identity, and so on" (xiii).[1] In other words, so it would seem, a person might lose his or her "whiteness" if he or she changed religions or sexual preferences. This "fact" will surely be of value for those blacks interested in "passing." No doubt, at least among these White Studies aficionados, the gospel of race's biological "meaninglessness" is so plain, so transparent, that only fools dissent.

Those still unconvinced of this shoddiness in grappling with what makes "whiteness" distinctive are advised to scan the pertinent essays in Delgado and Stefancic's Critical White Studies: Looking Behind the Mirror (1997). Judged by the sheer number of articles between its covers, the varied sources of the contributions, and the institutional standing of most authors, this hefty tome is surely authoritative state-of-the-art regarding Whiteness Studies. Part 9, "Biology and Pseudoscience," with its ten articles, would seem particularly promising to enlighten us on these biological queries. No such luck—the origins of whiteness continue to be mysterious. Instead, the discussion is about only intelligence. A reoccurring theme (save Adrian Wooldridge's superb essay) is that "intelligence" is a meaningless, hopeless, ambiguous, and evil concept. In this banquet of caviling, Herrnstein and Murray's *The Bell Curve* is the predictable pièce de résistance. Jerome Kagan, for example, argues that the abstract idea of "general intelligence" not only is nonexistent, but to speak of it invites mischievous consequences. Even if it does exist, it is situationally determined and infinitely varied. Andy Hacker nicely obfuscates matters by showing substantial variation in college graduation across white ethnic groups. No mention is made of how this happens or its significance for whiteness. For Michael Lind the matter of cognitive talent is entirely political—the various ebbs and flows within the conservative movement now have ushered *The Bell Curve* to the forefront of public consciousness. The book's falsity is axiomatic. Rosen and Lane delve into the *Bell Curve's* footnotes, the background of those cited, and their sources to expose its racist, eugenics-oriented origins. Daniel Kanstroom provides a brief account of Nazi racial policy against Polish Jews. Derrick Bell blithely asserts that *The Bell Curve* has it backward— blacks are really smarter than whites. And so it goes, with each author taking his or her shot at intelligence and the very hint of (white) racial superiority.

In prizefighting language, everything is counterpunching. Nothing, absolutely nothing, explains why whites act distinctively white (or even why they commonly seem more intelligent than blacks). The logic is bewildering: even if intelligence is taken as a surrogate for whiteness, why does bashing research enlighten us on why white people act white? Surely a *Bell Curve* countervision with whites as the pre-ordained "bad guys" is feasible. If whites are inescapably driven to be white, these putative experts on whiteness have no inkling of an explanation. Not a single essay puts any empirical meat on the skeletal bones of the whiteness paradigm. In this "debate" one side (whites) have offered copious scientific evidence explaining, among other things, why whites exceed blacks economically and academically while being less crime-prone. Meanwhile, on the contra side, the White Devil is relentlessly excoriated but nothing is said regarding how this Devil came to be and what drives its evilness. Not a single iota of empirically based countertheory is displayed.

Perhaps various contributors to *Race Traitor* (Ignatiev and Garvey 1996) can illuminate the source of this white devilishness. Unlike the academic-style articles, essays here are avowedly polemical. Given that this is a confessed ideological outlet unhampered by the "scholarly" constraints, frankness on sensitive, arguable topics may emerge. If anybody can "Tell it as it is," we expect it here. Yet, for connoisseurs of theoretical precision and elaboration, even in its incipient state, the essence of "whiteness" remains darkly obscured in these oft-simplistic vitriolic musings.

A genetic account of whiteness was initially anticipated, given the enterprise's announced purpose: ". . . to abolish the white race from within" (Ignatiev and Garvey 1996, 2). This surely suggests whiteness to be hard-wired genetically. Shades of "final solution" are even invoked by the "abolish" terminology and the surrounding revolutionary rhetoric. To abolish means to eliminate, and when applied to groups numbering in the hundreds of millions, this can *only* signify genocide. Kinder, ameliorative terms like "re-educate," "reform" or "re-direct" are absent. Even acknowledging rhetorical excesses necessary to galvanize troops, this is strong language. Nevertheless, the bulk of *Race Traitor* intimates pure social construction. "Whiteness," it is alleged, is historically constructed (9) and not (sans any documentation) recognized by the natural sciences (36). The phrase "so-called white race" (quotation marks insinuating an oxymoronic term) is liberally sprinkled about. Whiteness, say these authors, is a privileged club that one joins at birth (10), perhaps as one is born into a religion. Still, these white authors repeatedly confess that abandoning their whiteness is exceedingly difficult. That this tenaciousness might hint at biological sources is never raised, however.

This cavalier attitude toward scientific distinction is particularly evident in how whiteness scholars treat variation in whiteness. Physical features alone, obviously, make sharply determined racial categories problematic. The key question is how to address these visible trait-behavior links if race-related differences are to be understood scientifically. Are those of mixed ancestry one or the other or some blend? Where do Asians fit in this whiteness cosmology? Invariably, the standard scientific stratagem is exceptionally arduous, highly nuanced, and bewilderingly complex (see, for example, Cavalli-Sforza 1994; Whitney 1998). Still, the overall thrust of this biology-based research is that commonplace categories—for instance, Asian, black—are discernable genetically though researchers do not always share a common terminology. Groups can shade into others, as would be expected given migration and breeding patterns. Jensen (1998, 429), for example, provides data showing that Iranians and North Indians are surprisingly genetically close to Europeans. An understanding of the exceedingly complex meshing of these corporal characteristics with cultural proclivities is slowing emerging (Rushton 1999).

Compare this empirical approach to what transpires in whiteness research. Daniels's stance (1997) is typical (also see Martin et al. 1999). Here the scientific study of genetic differences across groups is, naturally, briskly dismissed as "pseudoscientific." How, then, can distinction be made? Easy—just ask undergraduates for their impressions (and, oddly, these amateur judgments are labeled "scientific"). We find, for example, that several nationalities—Portuguese, Spaniards, Italians, Bulgarians—inspire uncertainty or confusion regarding their whiteness. Daniels's conclusion is that "whiteness" ultimately depends on a nation's world status, matters such as economic development or NATO membership. By contrast, to be a poorer nation consigns a people to blackness. To be sure, racial perceptions are a legitimate topic of inquiry, but this should not be confused with a scientific account of genetic attributes. Inappropriate data are being collected. Given the research design's ease—a simple questionnaire to captive undergraduates—it is no wonder that the whiteness field draws adherents.

To recap, our review cannot settle nature versus nurture debates or what personality traits congeal with what racial group. Our query concerns how the Whiteness Studies project confronts these intimidating questions. Matters are resolved by proclamation, not research. Science is conspicuously absent throughout. Popular culture—films, TV, music—is far more likely to be the source of authoritative "hard data" (Hill's 1997 anthology on whiteness overflows with essays dissecting the essence of whiteness in pop culture). Since intelligent discourse requires adequate proof on the origins question, this neglect is hardly trivial. These arguments' overall direction also seems curious. Though a genetic racial theory seems more compatible with this White Devil cosmology, the socially constructed path is instead chosen. One can only speculate regarding this peculiar election. Perhaps performing real science requires excessive effort. The field's practitioners might well fear that honest scientific inquiry will yield the "wrong" outcomes (i.e., blacks, not whites, are genetically predisposed toward interracial mayhem and oppression). Who knows? We shall not venture opinions on this sensitive issue. What is noteworthy is the embarrassing neglect of systematic empirical inquiry.

AVERSION TO NON-WHITES

Permeating this whiteness literature is the supposition that whites "have it in" for blacks and people of color more generally. This aversion is sacred creed, barely needing expression. To be fair, the historical record of white-on-black imposed misery is immense, from slavery to brutal colonization, and virtually every other horror imaginable. This record might be appended with contemporary data on inequality of income, education, and whatever else comprises rewards in American society. White treatment of blacks in the United States and elsewhere certainly cannot be defended as unending kindness, though matters have undoubtedly improved.

Yet, no account of white-on-black viciousness proves that there is something preordained about whites victimizing blacks simply because they are blacks. Such an argument is illogical, far closer to feel-good therapy or a ploy to extract benefits by imposing guilt. "Paranoia" might also occasionally describe this inclination. For one thing, whites have, since time immemorial, inflicted even greater suffering on fellow whites. Between the various fifteenth- and sixteenth-century religious bloodbaths plus two world wars, whites have doubtlessly slaughtered more fellow race members than blacks (one might plausibly add that blacks may have exceeded whites in the slaying of blacks). A more credible argument is that whites are capable of colossal bloodshed and wickedness, and have been equal-opportunity purveyors of torment. It is bizarre to intimate that whites have turned on each other only when convenient blacks were unavailable. History would show, I believe, that white carnage directed against blacks was largely incidental to other, nonracial goals--for example, acquiring wealth or territory. Save the killing of Tasmanians, massacring people of color is not akin to a primordial sporting urge. Even when scrambling for African colonies, whites were perfectly content to slaughter white rivals. Furthermore, to proclaim the obvious, the attack on black slavery was led by European and American whites—not black Africans—and this contravened narrow economic interests.

Closer to home are inconvenient facts galore evincing no deep-seated white genocidal impulse toward non-whites. Among those whites loathing blacks, the overwhelming response is physical separation, not inflicting harm. As opponents of immigration loudly complain, non-whites of all stripes (including Africans) would *love* to become permanent Americans if only the INS would acquiesce. Many are successful, as the population statistics proclaim yearly. Are black immigrants masochists or fools, incapable of calculating costs versus benefits? Why do Haitians daily seriously risk death to join smothering cultural whiteness? Equally telling, for decades white-controlled governments have lavished untold billions of white taxpayer money on black assistance schemes. What diabolical oppressive plot explains white-controlled officials pushing uncounted civil rights laws, affirmative action plans, and other ameliorative programs on fellow whites? If the United States were Iraq, African Americans might have been exterminated as if they were Kurds.

Those oft-recounted tales of white police officers brutalizing innocent blacks have not reflected official policy for decades, and honestly represent only a miniscule fraction of all interracial police contacts. Do not be mislead by the rare violent hate crime: far more blacks murder whites than vice versa. Listening to white studies devotees, one might surmise that the United States were a grim, Nazi-style police state in which blacks were akin to Jews. To paraphrase the redoubtable George Orwell, only an intellectual could accept such preposterousness.

Finally, much alleged anti-black "oppression" is not the genuine article. This is an awkward subject, but a dose of frankness is essential. Many blacks and their white allies commit what I have labeled "Social Kevorkianism"—self-inflicted misery. Why must white-led anti-crime campaigns in black neighborhoods be "oppression"? Are drug dealers misunderstood freedom fighters? After all, victims are usually blacks, and rampant criminality hardly innervates black communities. Does disrespecting law enforcement assist blacks, particularly when they are a numerical minority, dependent on white-controlled legal institutions? Strict lawfulness is an ally of a minority, not an enemy. Ditto for the imposition of the "standard" (read "white") educational curriculum in schools with large black populations. Flattering student deficiencies via Afrocentric education or instructing in black street slang only exacerbates economic shortcomings, despite the momentary escape from drudgery. Even abolishing the racial spoils system—affirmative action and all the rest—is but a blow against continued dependency on bureaucratic whim. Imagine if a "friend" of blacks advised tolerating black-on-black crime and dumbed-down education, and suggested that blacks could have decent employment only if companies were compelled to hire marginally qualified blacks? With such allies, who needs enemies?

How, then, can the faithful respond to this awkward portrayal? Can anyone explain what makes blacks so enticing as singular targets of white malevolence? Not surprisingly, grand silence serves as the counterargument. One extended treatment—Theodore W. Allen's *The Invention of the White Race*—elaborately compares how the English brutalized the Irish with American treatment of blacks. This is hardly smoking gun proof of inherent anti-black proclivity. More typically are bits and pieces of historical analysis supplemented with slanted accounts of particular incidents. One anthology—*Black on White: Black Writers on What It Means to be White* (Roediger 1998)—offers up seven essays by black writers on "White Terror." None depict anything contemporary and all are fictional, not hard-nosed empirical data. At most, this "white terror" may be best understood as some vague memory. Surely if ample documentation of this "terror" existed it would be depicted in excruciating detail. Consider the multiple historical snippets touching on U.S. race relations presented in *Critical White Studies*, Part 3 (Delgado and Stefanic 1997). Hauled before the bar are the usual suspects, from nineteenth-century white racial superiority advocates to, naturally, Beelzebub Herrnstein and Mephisto Murray. Yes, the record does convincingly show anti-black malice, but the same record displays white hatred toward *everyone*. A more accurate appraisal is that the past was truly Hobbesian; imposing wickedness had more to do with avarice, technological advantage, and numerical superiority than with unabashed racial ideology.

White maliciousness toward blacks is also "demonstrated" by compiling long lists of alleged insults, slights, and affronts in interracial personal relationships. This tactic is a staple in the "find racism everywhere" industry. It is assumed that any white aversion to blacks, even if quite reasonable or the outcome of honest miscommunication, "proves" the deeper pathology of American society in general and whites in particular. Maurice Berger's *White Lies: Race and the Myths of Whiteness* (1999) exemplifies this type of indictment of whites. It consists of an endless parade of telling "incidents': the author's mother (a dark-skinned Jew) being denied stage roles due to her "blackness," white college students' definition of female beauty (light-colored skin), disputes between a black singer and a white conductor over musical interpretation, a summer camp fight in which whites cheered the white combatant and blacks the black combatant, and on and on. Every incident is, predictably, given an anti-white spin. Berger argues (32-36) that anti-black stereotypes are, of course, false, but that their persistence reveals the seriousness of the white pathology. As is typical, no hard data are presented. Clearly, to judge these "offenses" by the usual historical standards of oppression constitutes an enormous reach, even a debasement of the word "oppression." Such "offensiveness" is far better understood as the normal friction inherent in a multiracial society, not an innate white hatred of blacks.

A revealing insight into this putative white anti-black impulse is offered by bell hooks, a widely read author in today's college curriculum. For her, "whiteness" is so powerful and terrifying that as a youngster she instinctively sought to avoid it (hooks 1997, 175). Even when whites were not physically absent, this terrifying power was felt, and, she claims, this dread still endures for all blacks. What explains today's terror? After all, lynch mobs are long gone. Apparently, blacks possess a special ability to detect this fear, even if invisible to whites. A personal tale recounts her attendance at a cultural studies conference. Daily conference events reawakened her fear of white supremacists as she witnessed the conference's "whiteness" reflected in speakers, seating arrangements, and audience participation. Regardless of the ordinariness of proceedings, this exposure was "horrifying" (177). Perhaps whiteness resembles Plutonium—even minute quantities invisibly incapacitate those unlucky exposed blacks.

When it comes time to finger today's overt anti-black devils, who do you call? The tiny white militias and similar malcontents, of course. The section of *Critical White Studies* (Delgado and Stefanic 1997) labeled "White Consciousness, White Power" alarmingly identifies the by now familiar (and miniscule) fringe hate groups—the Klan and the neo-Nazis. Shades of scare tactic direct-mail solicitations foretelling catastrophes unless contributions are immediately forthcoming. Nothing is said about black or Hispanic groups preaching similar racist messages. Mike Hill (1997, 1-2) likens Oklahoma bomber Timothy McVeigh to an "all-American" defendant, while noting that he is both blue-eyed and blond. Hill then recounts various militia-police confrontations (which were almost entirely white-on-white), plus the Unabomber, as symptomatic of an immense outpouring of white terrorism. Muteness surrounds the shocking figures regarding black-on-white crime versus white-on-black criminality. That efforts to rescind racial preference in California and Washington were *opposed* by a "Who's Who" of American commerce goes unmentioned in these diatribes. Ditto for the white establishment voluntarily accepting affirmative action. Nor is much said of the varied legal convolutions executed by white judges to assist blacks, often at considerable economic loss to whites. Scholarship of this sort gives one-sidedness a bad name.

This gross inattention to reality is puzzling. Perhaps old habits die hard—bashing sinful whites has now become ingrained, and since no twelve-step programs exist for this disorder, it continues unabated. Or, to put a more practical spin on this enterprise, heaping blame upon whites is the ticket to "The Man's" generosity. We have a fancy version of urban begging—scruffy blacks badger anxious prosperous whites, who fork over pocket change rather than risk an "incident." Perchance deeper psychological needs are being met by this outpouring, but enough said regarding this divorce from reality.

ACHIEVING WHITE DOMINATION

That whites (especially white males) dominate unfairly is a core element of the White Studies faith. Whiteness is typically likened to a club membership automatically bestowing prosperity, prestige, and immense personal freedom, plus a welcomed relief from criminal code enforcement. This privilege is, critically, unearned: nothing about whiteness *intrinsically* explains white superiority. So-called objectively defined ability is but a sham, a culturally imposed justification for this privilege. One expert (McIntosh 1997) even asserts that white males are trained not to recognize their immense advantage. The awesome power to dominate is entirely unconscious. Whites have achieved their ill-gotten gain *only* by force, deceit, manipulation, and similar nefarious tactics, *never* by talent and hard work.

Both argument components—unfair advantage by whites and their domination—have ample degrees of truth. History overflows with countless examples of past white—usually WASP—manipulation of lines separating the haves from the have-nots. Nobody could possible deny what transpired to Asians, Jews, and blacks in America's universities and businesses. As a child I recall being told of how many giant corporations refused to hire Jews, no matter how gifted, and how Ivy League schools all had "Jewish quotas." Every non-WASP group in American history can undoubtedly recount similar exclusionary tales. No contest here regarding the charge of untold millions being banished from the Waspy establishment.

The white domination element is also plain to see, and not only historically, but also in the present. Regardless of how calculated, whites command nearly everything of significance, though Asians are quickly closing in. A thousand pages could depict this topic without exhausting it. Equally telling, the economic and educational benefits recently gained by blacks are, to be embarrassingly blunt, largely unearned prizes *given* to them by powerful whites. Beyond a few sideshow areas—sports, entertainment—white accomplishment is unchallenged. Moreover, judged by recent trends, this black inadequacy is unlikely to change. Decades may pass before blacks can independently enter the establishment sans benevolent white assistance or state legal compulsion.

Yet, acknowledging these disconcerting facts hardly confirms underhanded white manipulation. History *does* change, thankfully, and allegations of unfair privilege must always be established anew. A burden of proof exists on those claiming departure from uprightness. It is insufficient, as some scholars allege, to show this domination by documenting the "invisibility" of whiteness (Wander, Martin, and Naayama 1999). Nor do we find it credible that white domination is somehow imposed via rhetoric (Nakayama and Krizek 1999). Can an intelligent person really believe that altering vocabulary will bestow wealth on the ill-educated? Likewise, will banning such "racist" movies as *Pulp Fiction* and *Ace Ventura: When Nature Calls* free blacks to achieve economic equality (Giroux 1997)?[22] Facts, not accusations, airy speculations, or close readings of popular culture, are essential.

How, then, is this white unfairness charge to be substantiated? To repeat, the *un*fairness of white domination, not racial disparities, demands explanation. This task requires painstaking inquiry into society's inner workings. Inequality itself cannot be proof positive of evil. The facile (and oft-popular) contention that exact proportionality proves "fairness" makes a historically bizarre argument. To expect income or any other commodity of worth to be equally distributed across untold societal divisions poses an unmeetable standard. If this is our criterion, unfairness is both permanent and ubiquitous. Nothing more needs to be said and we can stop here.

Can Whiteness Studies build a credible case beyond "differences prove unfairness"? Though tedious in execution, this task is exceeding commonplace, given all the energetically enforced discrimination statutes and the huge numbers of lawyers and bureaucrats earning livelihoods here. A would-be accuser would merely need to compile all the incidents of racial (and gender) discrimination to document a pattern of widespread systematic exclusion of non-whites from education, commerce, government, and all else that mattered.[3] Alas, accusations are long on rhetoric and short on facts. Turgid jargon typically substitutes for hard analysis.

Consider, for example, George Lipsitz's *The Possessive Investment in Whiteness* (1998). Its subtitle—*How White People Benefit from Identity Politics*—seemingly offers the promise of showing how white folk "do it." The book begins by announcing that race has no biological meaning ("a scientific fiction") and, most critically, ". . . that white Americans are encouraged to invest in whiteness" (vii). This, then, is the secret—whites possess an instrument that perpetuates their superiority. What is this lucrative investment instrument? Lipsitz suggests the profit from discriminatory housing, unequal education, and the intergenerational transfers of wealth (vii). That any citizen can invest in rental housing (and that racial discrimination has been illegal for decades) or that public education abounds with prodigious programs to assist blacks goes unmentioned.[4] Nor does he notice that the draconian inheritance tax exempts estates of less than $600,000 (or that the civil rights movement was funded by white plutocratic foundations). A magical flavor permeates this "reasoning"—whites enjoy lucrative secret devices denied to blacks that subsidize racial control. When a white enrolls his or her child in a "good school," this "proves" nefarious "investment in whiteness" (perhaps here too whites possess a confidential list of such miraculous institutions and refuse to share them with blacks). Indeed, Lipsitz seems to argue that everything about American society is but a devious ploy to sustain white command (xviii). It is blithely alleged, without documentation, that racial inequality is merely a consequence of white self-serving nonenforcement of anti-discrimination laws (xix). Competing explanations are never considered.

A few details of this twisting of history to suit a convoluted argument deserve special mention. Laws normally construed as pro-ordinary people (e.g., Social Security, the Wagner Act, federally guaranteed home mortgages) become covert devices for repressing blacks (5). Highway construction and similar infrastructure projects such as urban renewal and improved sewage facilities are but means to facilitate white flight (6). Environmental racism, law enforcement, and soaring black drug use are likewise given their conspiratorial due. There is scarcely a contemporary public policy or event—tax reform, campaigns to restore traditional morality, deindustrialization, or just about any other effort to improve peoples' lives--that escapes "proof" of white malfeasance (chap. 2). Even the existence of numerous legal efforts to assist blacks is reinterpreted to show evil intent (e.g., civil rights laws were drafted to be largely ineffective and unenforceable) (25). Nothing is made of the fact that allegedly anti-black actions (e.g., unequal educational funding) also detrimentally affect poor whites. Lipsitz ardently assaults California's anti-immigration Proposition 187 as racist, though it could reasonably be argued that the influx of low-wage immigrants hurts African Americans economically (chap. 3). And so it goes. Let us be clear: We are not saying that Lipsitz is wrong. Rather, his analysis does not follow the strictures of acceptable social science research. Difficult, hardly self-evident positions are made true *only* by assertion, and reasonable counterclaims never even appear.

"Documentation" of this unearned white privilege is little more than an exercise in postmodern, jargon-filled rambling. A seemingly easy opportunity to score points has been passed up. Various essays in *Critical White Studies* (Delgado and Stefanic 1997) offer similar illustrations of peculiar reasoning. Wildman with Davis (1997) contends that language is critical for sustaining white privilege, but this imputes an enormous (and undemonstrated) impact to mere labeling. Did things change all that much when "colored people" became "Negroes," only to become "African Americans" a few decades later? Predictably, caviling about race being entirely socially constructed abounds, but silence covers why this "artificial" trait is so objectively consequential (Mahoney 1997; Wildman 1997). Is everyone driven by a mass delusion? The one article actually utilizing empirical data— Sacks's analysis of the GI Bill (1997) makes a very sparse case regarding events already nearly fifty years old while ignoring black beneficiaries. In short, not only is the evidence on white unfair privilege not convincing, but the material presented is irrelevant.

Yet, as they say in late-night TV commercials, "wait, there is more!" Consider one convoluted argument in a different anthology (Frankenburg 1997). The expert here begins by condemning affirmative action foes as totally uninterested in "facts." What are the facts, then? Now it can be told: the smoking gun proof of contemporary white male advantage is the Roosevelt New Deal and the GI Bill (Wellman 1997, 318). Again, this is dubious truth by shaky proclamation. The familiar self-imposed problems often holding blacks back economically—a disdain for education, crime, substance abuse—are "irrelevant." Wellman even accuses white college students of performing "status degradation ceremonies" to subvert black and Hispanic academic attainment (325).

As the Soviets were fond of exclaiming, this selectivity is "no accident." Even if we give full credit to every race-based discrimination accusation, the larger picture would, I believe, *demonstrate the opposite conclusion*. To wit, under current arrangements, the federal government's heavy bureaucratic hand grants non-whites immense unearned privilege. The reality is that many non-whites, thanks to white-imposed law, possess bogus admission tickets to "the club." As a thousand-page book could document past white abuses, a similar book depicts today's abuses in reverse. That present-day white domination *might* be a consequence of past privilege hardly undermines this statement's accuracy. Just as it was once patently obvious that gifted Jews were not "invited" to Harvard, it is equally plain that academically deficient blacks are given red-carpet treatment at prestige schools. This narrative holds elsewhere—blacks (and to a lesser extent, women) are being *forced* into clubs everywhere. Relentless government pushing of affirmative action, "voluntary" set-asides, and all the rest advanced in the name of "fairness" far outweighs the occasional truly exclusionary episode.

This does not end the "controversial" rejoinder to White Studies claims. If forthright discussions of this matter were permitted, whites would surely insist that their superior positions are fully earned. Impolite facts patently confirm this accusation—trillions of dollars expended to engender equality have come to naught. Exorcising *The Bell Curve* cannot invalidate that today's material success follows IQ contours, and that IQ is unequally distributed racially (Murray 1997 further confirms this point). Indeed, in the court of empirical evidence, *everything overwhelmingly* points in the direction of white (and Asian) *earned* accomplishment vis-à-vis the position of blacks. This generates immense awkwardness, and those few brave souls who admit it face considerable risk, but the facts are inescapable. If one craves success in our society, here's the recipe: manage to be born intelligent and then eschew lawlessness, marry, limit family size, avoid drugs, save money, cultivate "bourgeois values," and defer consumption. In other words, to be painfully forthright, act white.[5] If you desire club admission, accept the club's rules, and this means mimicking whites. This is hardly obligatory, and many daily opt otherwise, but, as they say, membership has its privileges.

CONCLUSIONS

Our brief *tour d'horizon* has not, to be unfashionably candid, uncovered much of scholarly usefulness. The faithful can, assuredly, argue that the jury remains out and, provided ample time and resources, the wasteland will bloom. This is possible, though it seems unlikely. It is not that the measurement predicaments have proven more vexing than anticipated, or that theoretical dead-ends have imposed incapacitating pessimism. More telling is the flight from empirically verified knowledge. Whereas the old Socialist Left worshiped science, the contemporary Left construes it as "the enemy," a bastion of white maleness directed against women and people of color. An aversion exists toward the very techniques of social science—collecting accurate data, fashioning logical arguments, testing competing hypotheses, and all the rest comprising analytical rigor. The entire whiteness enterprise, being part of this new Third World Order, embraces "truth by proclamation." Assertion is heaped upon assertion without much regard for theory or logic, let alone fairness. This is anti-white propaganda, not scholarship.

Given all the alternative analytical frameworks for disentangling society's bewildering complexities, why invest additional resources here? Is there something fundamentally more insightful about whiteness vis-à-vis class, ethnicity, religion, or any of the many other more conventional explanatory factors commonly applied to comparable quandaries? Can "whiteness" be expanded beyond "one more factor" added to an encompassing analytical framework? If I were a betting man (and I am not), I would wager that the chances of whiteness emerging as a powerful intellectual endeavor are two in number: slim and none.

This pessimism partly derives from trying to explain so much with so little. Properly executed, whiteness studies should be integral to a much larger endeavor—perhaps "cultural racialism" might be the apt term. Here whiteness is but one point on a variable scale (cultural ramifications of underlying racial identity), and analysis would necessarily incorporate "Asianness," "blackness," "Pacific Islanderness," and all the rest. This is not, however, what Whiteness Studies practitioners have in mind. The present project explains a litany of constants (oppression, etc.) with a single—if oft-confused—constant (whiteness). This is no easy task within the logical positivist template, with its stress on systematic covariation. Nor are propositions advanced by whiteness devotees ordinarily even testable, let alone disprovable. No matter how whites assist blacks, this is twisted into hurtfulness. Does "genuine assistance" denote only those white behaviors satisfying fluid black demands? And if this agreeableness brings disaster (for example, sanctioning inner-city crime), does this become further proof of duplicitous white evil? Opportunities for escaping logic are endless. This casualness might pass muster in some disciplines, but within universities honoring social science rigor, whiteness studies will forever remain on the low-status fringe.

This dismal methodological assessment is not as calamitous as it might first appear. Not every academic venture worships at the mighty scientific altar. Diplomatic immunity from logical rigor is common in estimable scholarship. If social science correctness were the singular ticket of admission to truth, the doorman would bar ample portions of Western Civilization. Philosophy, ethics, theology, and literature all reveal stunning truths while shunning strict positivism. In that sense, the whiteness studies toilers reside in exemplary company. Nor, for that matter, do sins of the methodological type ipso facto confirm falseness. The etiquette of method cannot guarantee veracity: the "best" social science is often plain wrong, while half-baked hunches have proven brilliantly accurate (witness the dismal predictions regarding the Evil Empire's collapse). Perchance, absolutely everything said in this body of anti-white propaganda is correct, despite copious technical shortcomings.

Alas, even this glimmer of hope misleads. The whiteness enterprise is unlikely to rise beyond a banquet of sour complaint. If a single reason explains my pessimism, it is the field's deep politicization sans any corrective incentive. The wages of propaganda are inescapable: One fashions a cult of the true believers and then ignores reality. Toeing the party lines, monitoring the zigs and zags of intellectual fashion, is unfailing, and with that devotion honest scholarship is unachievable. To confess that *The Bell Curve* contains *some* truths, or that at least *some* black calamities are self-imposed, or that whites have *some* virtue commits heresy. Heretics are excommunicated and denied easy access to the publication necessary for academic career advancement.

It is the unforeseen academic welcome accorded this enterprise that draws our attention. Though White Studies departments are unlikely to rival their Black Studies counterparts, a toehold has been gained and expansion seems imminent. It is as if the city's most exclusive club, one famous for excluding everyone short of the Rockefellers, suddenly admitted a pauper. Or, to be more concrete, why would a prestigious law journal publish something so outlandishly bizarre that the essay resembles a hoax (see Bell 1997)? Surely no commercial or monetary incentive explains this institutional graciousness. Whiteness scholars rarely attract bountiful campus enhancing grants or remember beloved alma mater in their munificent bequests. Intellectually the project is unjustifiable. In an earlier era this material would have been consigned to cheaply printed pamphlets, coffeehouse diatribes, and related "alternative" outlets.

Understanding this "mainstreaming" requires an appreciation of the university's current role in political domestication. American universities have continuously performed as multitask creatures—tutoring the white-collar workforce, polishing elite offspring, enriching local economies, or supplying mass entertainment via sports. Today, "keeping the political peace" is the latest appended job description. For comparative peanuts a university assembles a coterie of promising disrupters and placates them via handsome and prestigious remuneration. Entire departments serve as co-optive antibodies to render dangerous ideas "safe" by quarantine. They provide autonomous homelands for dangerous foolishness, so to speak. Those once hatching Central Cafe Bolshevik schemes are now given offices, titles, and secretaries, and encouraged to channel their rantings into obscure journals created for that unique purpose. That this inflammatory material goes unread, save by other well-kept proselytizers, cements a perfect marriage of convenience. Who ever heard of a revolution galvanized by well-paid tenured faculty? When the University of Jena denied Karl Marx a teaching position, there was hell to pay. This is not about to happen again.

This co-optation is hardly evil or unique to contemporary troubled conditions. Compared to the alternatives—for example, police spies or incarcerating dissenters—it is wonderfully benign, even democratic. History overflows with admirable exemplars. French monarchs brought potential malcontents to Versailles and distracted them by indulging their rapacious venal appetites. Otto Von Bismarck pacified German religious quarrels by incorporating churches into the state and putting local pastors on the government dole. Within a few decades, religious fervor wilted as state-subsidized clerics abandoned their congregations. The Bolsheviks skillfully brought "leading elements" from all of society safely into the fold with a sprinkling of special concessions. Measured against competing historical techniques for insuring domestic tranquility, co-option leavened with flattering corruption is a no-brainer. It works cheaply and painlessly.

Thus fathomed, I can only conclude with hearty accolades for whiteness studies. *Bravissimo!* I look forward to more unconvincing essays, more thick edited collections, more well-appointed conferences, and whatever else promotes tranquility. Better to cater to the malcontents than expel them in boxcars to ferment revolution. Given discontent's inescapability in a meritocracy, soothing failures requires attention. Substituting ersatz accomplishment for the genuine article is especially essential now that the downtrodden, thanks to self-esteem *über alles*, refuse their deserved subordination. The only questions are how, at what cost, and and how to square domestication with practicality. University-sponsored "makework" activity is definitely the "Best Buy" in this outlandish marketplace. Critics of today's society are absolutely correct in pointing the finger. Universities (along with "system" components) *are* repressive in the sense of choking off dissent, but it is a repression that seems especially enjoyable to its well-compensated victims.

NOTES

1. This "imprecision equals nonexistence" argument concerning the reality of race is a virtual signature of the whiteness literature. As we note elsewhere, the underlying logic is preposterous, for it fails to acknowledge the distinction between ordinary and scientific usage while denying the possibility of progress. It also reflects the antiscientific bias commonplace in today's New Left, of which Whiteness Studies is one element. Lopez's Appendix A usefully assembles court cases addressing who is and is not "white." Interestingly, these historical decisions correspond quite closely with modern genetic data on breeding populations (or racial groups, for those who prefer that term).

2. Like others in this field, Giroux is adept at twisting facts to prove manipulation. In his lengthy (and highly negative) explication of the movie *Dangerous Minds* (a tale of a white teacher in the ghetto), Giroux faults the use of rap for the musical score as reinforcing right-wing assumptions about black culture. One can only imagine they outcry if Mozart had provided the musical background.

3. We would exclude those actions involving poor restaurant service and similar acts of "offensiveness," since these did not bear on economic inequality. A good case could also be made to exclude settlements in which neither guilt nor innocence was formally established--e.g., the Texaco settlement. Here the resolution impetus probably had more to do with adverse publicity than with guilt.

4. The "economic reasoning" here does not explain why government must often provide or subsidize low-income housing for blacks. If, as claimed, this "discriminatory housing" were so lucrative, white capitalists should flock to it. Obviously, however, its very unattractiveness

mandates government intervention. Lipsitz is also mute on why blacks behave as whites in the rents they charge to blacks. If black owners charged less, surely this would drive white landlords from the industry.

5. "Manage to be born intelligent" may strike the reader as an impossibility, but ample evidence suggests that parents can shape their children's biologically determined intelligence via practices such as breast-feeding, avoiding drugs, and other health-related measures (see Jensen 1998, 500–516, for a sampling of these factors). The key point is that even in a world where intelligence determines economic position, individual choice remains powerfully relevant.

REFERENCES

Aanerud, Rebecca. 1997. Fictions of whiteness: Speaking the names of whiteness in U.S. literature. In *Displacing whiteness: Essays in social and cultural criticism*, edited by Ruth Frankenberg. Durham, N.C.: Duke University Press.

Allen, Theodore W. 1994. *The invention of the white race. Volume one: Racial oppression and social control.* London: Verso.

Ansley, Frances Lee. 1997. Stirring the ashes: Race, class, and the future of civil rights scholarship. In *Critical white studies: Looking behind the mirror*, edited by Richard Delgado and Jean Stefanic. Philadelphia: Temple University Press.

Bell, Derrick A. 1997. Thank you, Doctors Herrnstein and Murray (or, who's afraid of critical race theory). In *Critical white studies: Looking behind the mirror*, edited by Richard Delgado and Jean Stefancic. Philadelphia: Temple University Press.

Berger, Maurice. 1999. *White lies: Race and the myths of whiteness.* New York: Farrar, Straus and Giroux.

Cavalli-Sforza, Luigi L. 1994. *The history and geography of human genes.* Princeton, N.J.: Princeton University Press.

Daniels, Doug. 1997. The white race is shrinking: Perceptions of race in Canada and some speculations on the political economy of race classification. In *Critical white studies: Looking behind the mirror*, edited by Richard Delgado and Jean Stefancic. Philadelphia: Temple University Press.

Delgado, Richard, and Jean Stefancic, eds. 1997. *Critical white studies: Looking behind the mirror.* Philadelphia: Temple University Press.

Frankenberg, Ruth, ed. 1997. *Displacing whiteness: Essays in social and cultural criticism.* Durham, N.C.: Duke University Press.

Giroux, Henry. 1997. Racial politics and the pedagogy of whiteness. In *Whiteness: A critical reader*, edited by Mike Hill. New York: New York University Press.

Hacker, Andrew. 1997. Caste, crime and precocity. In *Critical white studies: Looking behind the mirror*, edited by Richard Delgado and Jean Stefancic. Philadelphia: Temple University Press.

Hartigan, John Jr. 1997. Locating white Detroit. In *Displacing whiteness: Essays in social and cultural criticism*, edited by Ruth Frankenberg. Durham, N.C.: Duke University Press.

Hill, Mike. 1997. Introduction: Vipers in Shangri-la whiteness, writing, and other terrors. In *Whiteness: A critical reader*, edited by Mike Hill. New York: New York University Press.

———, ed. 1997. *Whiteness: A critical reader.* New York: New York University Press.

hooks, bell. 1997. Representing whiteness in the black imagination. In *Displacing whiteness: essays in social and cultural criticism*, edited by Ruth Frankenberg. Durham, N.C.: Duke University Press.

Ignatiev, Noel, and John Garvey, eds. 1996. *Race traitor.* New York: Routledge.

Jacobson, Matthew Frye. 1998. *Whiteness of a different color: European immigrants and the alchemy of race.* Cambridge: Harvard University Press.

Jensen, Arthur. 1998. *The g factor.* Westport, Conn.: Praeger.

Johnson, Parker C. 1999. Reflections on critical white(ness) studies. In *Whiteness: The communication of social identity*, edited by Thomas K. Nakayama and Judith Martin. Thousand Oaks, Calif.: Sage.

Kagan, Jerome. 1997. The misleading abstractions of social science. In *Critical white studies: Looking behind the mirror*, edited by Richard Delgado and Jean Stefancic. Philadelphia: Temple University Press.

Kanstroom, Daniel. 1997. Dangerous undertones of the new nativism. In *Critical white studies: Looking behind the mirror*, edited by Richard Delgado and Jean Stefancic. Philadelphia: Temple University Press.

Lind, Michael. 1997. Brave new right. In *Critical white studies: Looking behind the mirror*, edited by Richard Delgado and Jean Stefancic. Philadelphia: Temple University Press.

Lipsitz, George. 1998. *The possessive investment in whiteness: How white people benefit from identity politics.* Philadelphia: Temple University Press.

Lopez, Ian F. Haney. 1996. *White by law: The legal construction of race.* New York: New York University Press.

Mahoney, Martha R. 1997. Racial construction and women as differentiated actors. In *Critical white studies: Looking behind the mirror*, edited by Richard Delgado and Jean Stefancic. Philadelphia: Temple University Press.

Martin, Judith N., Robert L. Krizek, Thomas K Nakayama, and Lisa Bradford. 1999. What do white people want to be called? A study of self-labels for white Americans. In *Whiteness: The Communication of Social Identity*, edited by Thomas K. Nakayama and Judith Martin. Thousand Oaks, Calif.: Sage.

McIntosh, Peggy. 1997. White privilege and male privilege: A personal account of coming to see correspondence through work in women's studies. In *Critical white studies: Looking behind the mirror*, edited by Richard Delgado and Jean Stefancic. Philadelphia: Temple University Press.

Murray, Charles. 1997. IQ and economic success. *Public Interest* 128 (summer):21–35.

Nakayama, Thomas K., and Judith Martin, eds. 1999. *Whiteness: The communication of social identity.* Thousand Oaks, Calif.: Sage.

Nakayama, Thomas K., and Robert Krizek. 1999. Whiteness as a strategic rhetoric. In *Whiteness: The communication of social identity.* Thousand Oaks, Calif.: Sage.

Roediger, David R., ed. 1998. *Black on white: Black writers on what it means to be white.* New York: Schocken Books.

Rosen, Jeffrey, and Charles Lane. 1997. The sources of *The Bell Curve.* In *Critical white studies: Looking behind the mirror,* edited by Richard Delgado and Jean Stefancic. Philadelphia: Temple University Press.

Rubio, Phil. 1996. Crossover dreams: The "exceptional white" in popular culture. In *Race Traitor,* edited by Noel Ignatiev and John Garvey. New York: Routledge.

Rushton, J. Philippe.1995. *Race, evolution and behavior.* New Brunswick: Transaction Publishers.

———. 1999. Ethnic differences in temperament. In *Personality and person perception across cultures,* edited by Y-T Lee, C. R. McCauley, and J. Draguns. Mahwah, N.J.: Erlbaum.

Sacks, Karen Brodkin. 1997. The GI Bill: Whites only need apply. In *Critical white studies: Looking behind the mirror,* edited by Richard Delgado and Jean Stefancic. Philadelphia: Temple University Press.

Wander, Philip C., Judith N. Martin, and Thomas K. Nakayama. 1999. Whiteness and beyond: sociohistorical foundations of whiteness and contemporary challenges." In *Whiteness: The communication of social identity,* edited by Thomas K. Nakayama and Judith Martin. Thousand Oaks, Calif.: Sage.

Wellman, David 1997. Minstrel shows, affirmative action talk and angry white men: Making racial otherness in the 1990s. In *Displacing whiteness: Essays in social and cultural criticism,* edited by Ruth Frankenberg. Durham, N.C.: Duke University Press.

Whitney, Glayde. 1998. Diversity in the human genome. In *The real American dilemma: Race immigration and the future of America,* edited by Jared Taylor. Oakton, Va.: New Century Books.

Wildman, Stephanie, with Adrienne D. Davis. 1997. Making systems of privilege visible. In *Critical white studies: Looking behind the mirror,* edited by Richard Delgado and Jean Stefancic. Philadelphia: Temple University Press.

Wooldridge, Adrian. 1997. Bell curve liberals: How the left betrayed IQ. In *Critical white studies: Looking behind the mirror,* edited by Richard Delgado and Jean Stefancic. Philadelphia: Temple University Press.

24

What's Sexuality Got to Do with It?

Urvashi Vaid

The prospect of including a commitment to gay, lesbian, bisexual, and transgender (GLBT) equality as part of a movement for racial and economic justice raises skepticism for some, anxiety for others, and disbelief in most. What's sexuality got to do with it, people of color who are not queer often ask. That's a white issue, we're told. Let's get racism taken care of, it is often said, and then we can get to these "other" problems. These reactions are part of the problem queers of color face, and the underlying reasons for such reactions are varied and complex, as well as historical and cultural. Here, however, I want to examine the structural reasons that underlie the construction of sexuality as "other" to race. Specifically, I want to explore the limits of racial identity-based politics, the impact of the absence of ideology in our movements, and the really tough challenges embedded in "including" sexuality in existing racial identity-based movements. My analysis will be presented in three parts and uses as its principal archive examples from the immigrant Asian experience in America, an experience that is quite bizarrely idealized and distorted by conservatives like Dinesh D'Souza, author of *The End of Racism: Principles for a Multicultural Society*.

First, I believe that we are at a moment when the paradigm of ethnic and race-based organizing needs to be examined and questioned, across the board. Next, I make a parallel argument from the gay and lesbian context about the value and limitations of sexual orientation as a primary basis for a movement. Finally, I question the meaningfulness and even the racial content of concepts like "South Asian" and "Asian Pacific American" identity. Instead of a nationalist or ethnic-based model, we need economic justice-based organizing, because such a framework provides more fruitful opportunities to challenge racism and start connecting issues of gender with sexual orientation and the problem of challenging white supremacy.

Certainly racism is a serious reality and an obstacle for all people of color in America, and for Asian Pacific Americans in particular. Thus the political movements we are building in the United States are rightly focused on exposing and developing strategies to displace white supremacy. However, I also think that immigrant communities and even the broader movement for racial justice in this country can deploy ethnicity as a device to build a false racial solidarity, which conveniently ignores the currents of gender, sexuality, and class differences that run underneath. This deliberate strategic avoidance of anything but race was evident at the "Race in 21st Century America" conference when the capable theorist William Julius Wilson spoke about needing to stay away from issues like homophobia because he believed it would divide the multiracial coalition he posits as essential to combating racism.

The lessons of history teach us that organizing only around identity-based politics does not lead to liberationary outcomes. Yet this conclusion begs the question, what is the goal of an Asian Pacific American politics? Or a black movement politics? Or a Latino politics? What are we trying to achieve by creating people of color movements? Do we agree on our goals, and will we ever agree? To the extent that we agree that racism is reproduced through economic exploitation, wouldn't the goal of ending structural economic inequality be better served by organizing a movement that is not based upon racial identity?

I want to propose that in order to address racism, structural economic inequality, and sexism—as well as to "include" sexuality in a racial justice movement at every level—communities of color must be willing to engage in a drastic reconsideration of heterosexism, patriarchy, and our notions of family and culture. For example, no inclusive, anti-homophobic, Asian movement can emerge without a re-visioning of Asian family and culture. I am not at all confident that we are at a place where such questioning, re-visioning, and redefinition are taking place or even possible.

Overall, my argument is that while racial identity-based organization and identity maintenance have been vital strategies that retain relevance, they are not, on their own, enough to end racism. Thus I believe that the inclusion of sexuality within the context of movements of color must be premised upon the willingness to accept some discomfort; indeed, this approach has encountered stiff resistance. Nevertheless, for those progressive organizations in African American, Asian Pacific American, and Latino communities seeking to deepen the struggle for human rights in the United States, the scary truth is that seeking inclusion and awareness of "sexuality" will probably be easy. Yet, transforming the institutions of family, relationships, and gender and power dynamics in communities of color—which is what sexuality brings to the table—still lies ahead of us.

Dana Takagi rightly notes that the adding-on or adding-in of sexuality into the melange of Asian identities in America is, on its own, not enough. If sexuality is submerged into the preexisting, hierarchical, ethnic-based narrative, we are not redefining very much, and not, in fact, opening up very much space for queer Asians like me, nor are we making real social change.[1]

THE ETHNIC MODEL: ASIAN PACIFIC AMERICAN ORGANIZING

We live in a moment in which the effects of racism on people of color are visible everywhere, yet we are urged to ignore them and reinterpret them through the lens of a libertarian ideology arguing that inequality is not a byproduct of the failure of the economic system, but of the failure of the individual and the collapse of the "traditional" family structure from which that individual comes. In short, racism disguised as "race-neutral" policies is now dominant.

The goal of this resurgent racial bias is to reimpose white supremacy in the workplace, in the award of government contracts, and in the allocation of public resources. Conservatives want Americans to believe that by erasing race and by getting rid of affirmative action programs, people of color will be "freer"; but this nonsense obscures the truth about how institutionalized and embedded racial prejudice is, as well as how closely linked racism is to class. Few of us are "free" to move up the ladder of success, business, and educational hierarchy on our merits alone—opportunity and freedom are conditioned by economic privilege. Few are "free" to go to college without financial assistance, and perhaps fewer of us are "free" to break out of the class-lines assigned us by our race and birth. Merit for people of color in America is a cigarette, not the way the system works for us; the facts do not support the libertarian nonsense of conservative writers like Dinesh D'Souza.

The idea of an Asian Pacific American political movement is rooted in the particular experiences of prejudice faced by Asians and immigrants in the United States, and it borrows heavily from the model of ethnic-based organizing that has characterized the civil rights struggle in the United States. Ethnic or race-based organizing has been an effective strategy in American politics—for asserting political power, for securing public policy solutions that meet the needs of the particular constituencies that are organizing, and perhaps most importantly, for developing a strong sense of self and self-worth in a context that whitens all difference. Organizing as racial or ethnic-based groups has been useful, and it is for this reason that many Asians are adopting the race-based model of organizing today. There are very good reasons why we are organized around our ethnicity or nationality. Yet, I remain skeptical of this strategy as a panacea or even the best model.

My skepticism about ethnicity or nationality as the basis for organizing is best elaborated through the Asian Pacific American political movement that I see emerging around me. The confusion or distrust I feel about organizing as Asian Pacific Americans comes in three forms. First, economics as much as race conditions the experience of racism of Asians in America. Our Asian Pacific American movement thus far has had little to say about economic justice. Second, the irony of the framework of Asian Pacific American is that the term "American" defines and unites us far more than do the terms "Asian" or "Pacific." Third, while the model of race-based, ethnic-based, or even identity-based organizing is very valuable in terms of definition, individual empowerment, and community organizing, it is of limited value as a transformational device.

My parents, like many Asian, South Asian, and Pacific people, came to America for "economic opportunity." Some came by choice, while others came as economic slaves (laborers), building up American railways and infrastructure at the turn of the century and serving the households of immigrant families as indentured slaves today. Asians in this country have, by and large, completely bought into capitalism. This despite the fact that capitalism is now strip-mining the economies of many of our countries of origin, has not provided relief to the millions in the world who are poor and living at subsistence levels, and is simultaneously creating enormous disparities in freedom, opportunity, and power between rich, middle class, working class, and poor.

We are model minorities in our acquiescence to the system staying the same. Thus, in this country, the same immigrants who are suffering from the racist immigration policies of the Republican Right staunchly oppose health care reform

or a social safety net. Indians in the United States—at least of my parents' generation—are quite conservative and more often than not Republican (although
being a Democrat these days offers little solace to those of us who are progressive).

Many people I know believe that if one works hard, he or she can get ahead;
that people who are poor and on welfare are shiftless; that economic security and
property are the ultimate goals in life (all framed in the guise of providing for your
family, but at its core no different from the insatiable greed that motivates all capitalists). Ironically, the condition of Asians and Pacific people in America is more
linked to economic forces and the ups and downs of capitalism than it is to the
deep well of racism that is a part of the American psyche. American labor is
already resentful of immigrant labor. Reform Party activist and conservative
Patrick Buchanan's message resonates well with many people in this country. If
jobs tighten up in the United States, the visas will dry up for immigrants. The
boom in high-tech jobs that has provided tremendous opportunities for Asian
engineers and programmers hinges on the success of speculative and volatile markets which have inflated the value of Internet and computer stocks, creating a
wealth that cannot last for most and will benefit only a very few. I am not aware
of a progressive Asian Pacific American movement dealing with these and other
economic contradictions and tensions.

Furthermore, I am skeptical of the term "Asian Pacific American" because it
means so little. We are more tied together by our shared experiences of marginalization in white America than we are by our Asian American-ness, or our ties
nationally, historically, linguistically, or culturally. Most of us do not know a thing
about each other's countries of origin or histories. For second- and third-genera-
tion Asians in America, it's enough of a challenge to learn about our own ethnic
and cultural heritage. To forge a sense of common solidarity with each other has
thus been difficult. I do not believe that the large numbers of Indians in America
feel a sense of kinship with Japanese Americans, with Chinese Americans, or with
Filipinos. Instead, they feel kinship along the tradition-bound lines we have always
followed: family, caste, nationality, and language—the conventional links. Given
this truth, are we, in fact, trying to force onto our wildly diverse immigrant cultures a commonality that will never be shared? Is the commonality more about
expediency in American politics—the need to be counted as a minority group, to
be able to marshal votes, etc.—than it is about reality? Will we ever be able to
deliver a voting bloc as Asians, given our radical diversity?

This brings me to a final point for us to consider as we think about radical
identity formulation from the perspective of the Asian experience in America

today: does identity politics work? The answer is, it depends upon your goal in using it. For what does it work and for what does it fail? I think it works to create self-esteem, empowerment, and visibility in the American political system, and it works for community building and organizing. Yet identity-based organizing fails as a vehicle to revamp the political, social, and economic system in this country. It needs to be linked to broader goals. If identity-based movements had an ideological basis, they might be more interesting.

LESSONS FROM THE QUEER CONTEXT

The queer movement is facing an analogous crossroads in its reliance on identity as the principal means of organizing. Structural heterosexism, or institutionalized racism, explains why we have single-issue movements dedicated to the eradication of these forms of prejudice. Pervasive prejudice, violence, and discrimination are why we have a gay, lesbian, bisexual, and transgender (GLBT) movement.[2]

Yet the GLBT movement today confronts two dilemmas: the first is its profoundly radical challenge to the most basic and intimate forms of human life—desire and family. How do we make ourselves appealing when we are indeed really unsettling to the order of heterosexism? Second, we confront the same limits of organizing along the ethnic-model of organization as do other groups of color; that is, without ideological unity, without an economic policy agenda, and with only our sexual orientation to connect us to each other, we never seem to really get to the heart of the structural problems we encounter.

The queer movement is one whose full acceptance will require deep changes in society's treatment of sex, desire, gender, human relationship, and family. It is a movement that generates the most extreme kinds of psychological reactions in people, because they can, in some sense, see themselves affected by desire and touched by it (which makes them uncomfortable). It is a movement condemned by some of the most powerful texts and contexts in America—especially religion. In order for GLBT people to be fully accepted in America, it will require what theologian Robert Goss calls the sexual reformation of the church.[3] In short, the GLBT movement is not a safe, easy, or simple movement.

Still, the queer movement, like the emerging Asian Pacific American movement, has reached the same dilemma that confronts every civil rights movement today. We have begun to approach the point of partial fulfillment, where the system has accommodated somewhat to admit us, to change some laws, to open up a little bit, but the underlying prejudice and structural barriers to full equality remain in place. We have created zones of freedom inside a fundamentally intransigent system—family, marriage, state and economic order. In terms of public policy, we have ended up working piecemeal on small solutions that benefit particular communities in the short run, while not making systematic changes that could benefit society in the long run. This is because we do not have an ideological basis for our social justice movements.

We find ourselves at a crossroads as a gay and lesbian movement, and while both roads are legitimate, one leads farther than the other. Down one road lies the method we have been pursuing—of working solely or exclusively within the lesbian, gay, bisexual, and transgender context, on so-called gay rights issues that solely affect "us" as queers. Down the other road lies the project of not just trying to fit in, but trying to change the world and institutions we encounter. If we walk down this second road, we quickly realize that our fight to end discrimination on the basis of sexual orientation intersects with women's effort to overturn our second-class status, with the struggle for racial justice and equality, and with the quest for a fairer economy and a cleaner environment.

What we attempt in walking down the second road is the project of building a kind of political and social change movement that is different from the civil rights movements we have built thus far; we face the challenge of refocusing from equality to justice. To do so, we must build a movement that focuses on economic justice, racial justice, and gender justice.

Let me stress that neither choice—single-issue politics or multi-issue politics—is inherently right or wrong. Each is, however, quite different. Let me also emphasize that I am not arguing that we must abandon all of the single-issue or identity-based work we are doing—just that we must supplement it with new organizing, which we are not doing. I want a movement that is not just focused on identity but that is actively engaged in defining the kind of society we want to live in as we enter the twenty-first century. Is this possible? I do not know.

Is this necessary? Yes. It is necessary to create this common movement because we face a totalizing Right/opposition that cannot be defeated by anything but a systematic countermobilization. Right-wing ideas about public policy and the ordering of cultural life are not merely cyclical swings in the historic pendulum of policy. They represent a serious effort to restore the very values and hierarchies that social justice movements have struggled to transform, and to construct something that has not before existed in America—a theocratic state.[4] In place of gender equality, the ideological Right advocates male supremacy. In place of remedies aimed at addressing centuries of racial discrimination against African Americans, they propose policies blind to the impact race plays on economic opportunity. In place of a social welfare role for the state, the ideological Right proposes either the elimination or the privatization of all government service programs. These ideas are antithetical to the policies and values of social justice movements.

Are we organized enough to deal with these huge and complex changes? If we are to be honest with ourselves, we must answer that we are not well organized, and are not handling these changed circumstances very well. Why? If we look at our work historically, we can see that we have not paid attention to the most basic kinds of lessons: to thrive, every movement must have a strong and motivated base. The organization and motivation of such a base is not something that just happens by osmosis, on its own, or through a media campaign. It happens through systematic and creative grassroots community organizing—something that too few of our civil rights organizations do, even to this day.

The problem that exists lies squarely in the realm of constituency support for these ideas. Because of the way we are structured—issue by issue, or identity by identity—social justice movements cannot boast the kind of ideological or political unity that is found on the conservative Right. Furthermore, because we have invested less time and skill in organizing, social justice movements seem to have less clout to deliver on our goals (such as preventing recent setbacks at the ballot box regarding affirmative action programs, immigration, and gay rights).

This is precisely the gap at which racial justice and civil rights movements of the twenty-first century must take aim. We can and must rebuild a constituency for social justice. Creative work should be done to expand the capacity of social justice movements in various fields to defend their policies and to increase their reach. New ways to forge constituencies among social justice organizations working on discrete issues should be attempted. We can and must develop new structures out of the way we now operate in order to be more successful, both nationally and locally. We can and we must have the courage of our values to take the risk of joint action and new cooperation. We can and must take the leap of faith in order to build the trust that common purpose requires.

Constituency building to oppose the Right requires that we not restrict ourselves to a movement built around racial or ethnic identity, gender, or sexual orientation alone. In short, we simply cannot build a common movement unless we look honestly at both the good things and the bad things we get by organizing issue by issue, color by color, identity by identity.

QUEERING ASIAN PACIFIC AMERICAN ORGANIZING

This conference is to be commended for acknowledging that heterosexuality is not the only kind of sexuality in communities of color. This is a truth denied in many of our racial communities. All too often, Asian activists, for example, still hear the canard that homosexuality is a Western thing or a corruption of truly Asian values. The histories of Asian sexualities in each of our countries of origin remain to be discovered and uncovered by scholars of younger and future generations. The truth that I know is that there is indeed a rich tradition of same-sex love and experience in every culture and continent of the world. Whether it understands itself as "gay" or "lesbian" or "transgender" or "bisexual" is debatable, but the existence of same-sex behavior and same-sex love the world over should not be obscure to anyone. It is not just a Western or white thing, and it never was.

Certainly you all know that queers in America face tremendous barriers to fully living our lives: discrimination, violence, and prejudice are pervasive and the norm. Whether the context is employment discrimination, family recognition, criminal law, immigration, health care, HIV, military issues, or hate violence, GLBT people face a lot of problems and challenges. A tremendous amount of information and documentation exists regarding these realities.[5]

The point I want make is twofold: (1) yes, indeed, a progressive racial justice movement ought to take up the challenge of being an ally to the GLBT movement. We need to recognize that ending prejudice based on sexual orientation is a progressive stand and one that is integral to movements based upon the principle of justice. The unpopularity of homophobia does not justify anyone's silence. For queers like me, a multi-issue movement is essential. This first level of inclusion is where we find ourselves today—still arguing for the most basic kind of recognition from communities of color. The specifics of the fight vary by race and ethnicity; the level of visibility of queer people of color varies in each community of color—for example, South Asian GLBT people have emerged in our communities only in the past nine years, while an organized African American GLBT movement has existed for arguably over twenty years.

(2) The deeper challenge that queerness poses to communities of color and to society at large is similar to the challenge that feminism poses, and this is a challenge I am not so sure our people, even progressives, are willing to take up. That challenge is to the very idea of the family that we have been raised with, and consequently the unyielding patriarchal, heterosexist, and authoritarian premises upon which it is sustained.

In the *New Yorker* in mid-February of 1999 there was a wonderful example of my point within the Asian context. The article concerned a twenty-year-old Indian woman from Queens. Her struggle to define her own life and yet to please her parents and fulfill their expectations is heartbreakingly familiar to each of us who is Asian. She is expected to get married (accepting this without question), to settle on the person her father selects, to produce children, to be the good and obedient daughter, and to be the subject of statements like this one from her father: "When you are married, my life will be complete." This story is typical, and it is contemporary. The Indian family exerts this kind of pressure and control inside itself, and is coded with enormous heterosexist expectations. The Latino, black, and other family structures have their own gender and heterosexist codes and norms.

What does it mean that we are all raised in families where compulsory marriage and compulsory heterosexuality are the unquestioned norm? What does it mean that to stand against this structure means to be ostracized by family and community, and in some instances to be killed by one's own father for disobedience? Why do we tolerate and accept the blatant double standard in Asian families for girls and boys? Why do young Asians in America feel they must go along with this and that they have no recourse, short of radical rebellion and acting out? What does it mean that the dominant critique of the family in the black community is not feminist, but comes out of right-wing or liberal think tanks? How can gay, lesbian, bisexual, or transgender persons be accepted into this old conception of family?

We need to create ways to organize around the so-called private family issue—i.e., publicizing what has been privatized, and questioning and adhering to an expressed willingness to engage in meaningful interrogation and disagreement. This, to me, is the undone work of "internalizing" the meaning of movements for women's liberation and sexual freedom into the Asian Pacific American. There can be no more than token interrogation of these issues unless we are willing to examine the gender biases of the families and communities from which we come.

CONCLUSION

Gandhi wrote that morality consists of doing what we ought to do. He argued that mere observance of custom and usage was not morality. That moral actions are those guided by justice and respect for the Divine Will. That moral acts involve no coercion and are not motivated by self-interest. If I help my neighbor because he is suffering, I commit a moral act. If I help my neighbor because I want credit for helping him through his suffering, my action may still be a good deed, but in Gandhi's argument it is not moral. Merely by pursuing our own liberation and freedom we are not engaged on a moral course.

If we place our liberation movements in the service not just of one identity or one sector of social justice, but rather in the service of building a more just society, then we will be a movement that is unstoppable, because our course will be spiritually and politically just. Consequently, merely adding sexual orientation as a category to the lineup of things racial or ethnic will not actually change a great deal at all.

NOTES

1. Dana Y. Takagi, "Maiden Voyage: Excursion into Sexuality and Identity Politics in Asian America," in *Asian American Sexualities: Dimensions of the Gay and Lesbian Experience,* edited by Russell Leong (New York: Routledge, 1996), 21–35, 28. For other readings in this field, see also Rakesh Ratti, ed., *A Lotus of Another Color: An Unfolding of the South Asian Gay and Lesbian Experience* (Boston: Alyson Press, 1993); Connie Chung, Alison Kim, and A. K. Lemeshewsky, eds., *Between the Lines: An Anthology of Pacific/Asian Lesbians* (Santa Cruz, Calif.: Dancing Bird, 1987); Karen Aguilar-San Juan, ed., *The State of Asian America: Activism and Resistance in the 1990's* (Boston: South End Press, 1994).

2. John D'Emilio, *Sexual Politics, Sexual Communities: The Making of a Homosexual Minority in the United States, 1940–1970* (Chicago: University of Chicago Press, 1983); Barry D. Adam, *The Rise of A Gay and Lesbian Movement* (Boston: G.K. Hall, 1987); Margaret Cruikshank, *The Gay and Lesbian Liberation Movement* (New York: Routledge, 1992); Urvashi Vaid, *Virtual Equality: The Mainstreaming of Gay and Lesbian Liberation* (New York: Anchor Books, 1996); John Manuel Andriote, *Victory Deferred: How AIDS Changed Gay Life in America* (Chicago: University of Chicago Press, 1999); Cathy Cohen, *The Boundaries of Blackness: AIDS and the Breakdown of Black Politics* (Chicago: University of Chicago Press, 1999); Dudley Clendinen and Adam Nagourney, *Out for Good: The Struggle to Build a Gay Rights Movement in America* (New York: Simon & Schuster, 1999).

3. Robert Goss, professor of religion, Webster University, St. Louis, Missouri, in a conversation with the author in March 1999.

4. Sara Diamond, *Roads to Dominion: Right-Wing Movements and Political Power in the United States* (New York: Guilford Press, 1995); Sara Diamond, *Spiritual Warfare: The Politics of the Christian*

Right (Boston: South End Press, 1989); Chip Berlet, ed., *Eyes Right: Challenging the Right-Wing Backlash* (Cambridge, Mass.: Political Research Associates, 1995).

5. Nan Hunter, Tom Stoddard, and Sheryl Michaleson, *The Rights of Lesbians and Gay Men: The Basic ACLU Guide to a Gay Person's Rights* (New York: Bantam, 1992); see also web sites for various gay rights organizations, such as the National Gay and Lesbian Task Force (*www.ngltf.org*); Lambda Legal Defense and Education Fund (*www.lambdalegal.org*); and the Gay and Lesbian Alliance Against Defamation (*www.glaad.org*).

25

Socioeconomic Inequality: Race and/or Class*

WILLIAM JULIUS WILSON

I

I am very pleased to deliver one of the keynote addresses at this important conference on "Race in 21st Century America." As we approach the twenty-first century, I am reminded of the remarks of the brilliant Harvard economist Richard B. Freeman, who recently pointed out that "falling or stagnating incomes for most workers and rising inequality threaten American ideals of political 'classlessness' and shared citizenship. Left unattended, the new inequality threatens us with a two-tiered society . . . in which the successful upper and upper-middle classes live lives fundamentally different from the working classes and the poor."[1]

Whereas Americans experienced broadly and rapidly rising real income from the end of World War II through 1973, after 1973, "average wage growth [adjusted for inflation] slowed dramatically and remained slow even in the buoyant economy of the late 1990s."[2] Moreover, as seen in figure 1, income inequality, which had stabilized through the mid-1970s, began to grow rapidly thereafter. Indeed, whereas each of the bottom four quintiles' share of aggregate income declined from 1975 to

---

*This was a keynote address given at the "Race in 21st Century America" conference. This address was derived from a larger study by the author, *The Bridge over the Racial Divide: Rising Inequality and Coalition Politics* (Berkeley: University of California Press, 1999).

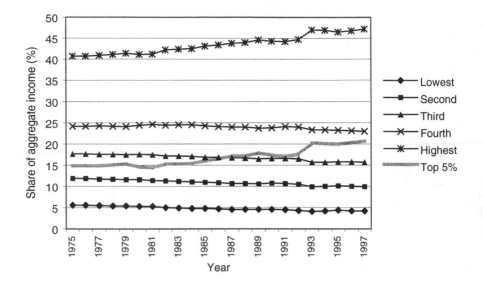

Figure 1. Share of Aggregate Income Received by Each Fifth and Top 5 Percent of All Families: 1975–1997. Source: Current Population Survey, March 1997.

1997, the share of the highest quintile increased significantly, and the top 5 percent's share of aggregate income rose considerably above that of the bottom three-fifths. "It is possible that the current strong economy will help to slow or even reverse some of these trends," states the Harvard economist David Ellwood.

> There are some indications that less skilled workers have faired slightly better in recent years. But there is little evidence to suggest that the basic changes in the economy that must be behind the long-term trends are changing.[3]

These trends are associated with the rate of productivity growth and the level of skill bias in the economy, but they can also be related to the strength of what M.I.T. economist Frank Levy calls "the nation's equalizing institutions," which refers to "the quality of education, the welfare state, unions, international trade regulations, and the other political structures that blunt the most extreme market outcomes and try to insure that most people benefit from economic growth."[4] As Levy points out, "we cannot legislate the rate of productivity growth and we cannot legislate the economy's level of skill bias in technological change and trade. That is why equalizing institutions are important."[5]

I see the need for a national multiracial political coalition with a broad-based agenda to strengthen these equalizing institutions. A large, strong, and organized political constituency is essential for the development and implementation of policies necessary to reverse the trends of the rising inequality and to ease the burdens of ordinary families.

Political power is disproportionately concentrated among the elite, most advantaged segments of society. The monetary, trade, and tax policies of recent years have arisen from and, in turn, have deepened this power imbalance. While elite members of society have benefited, ordinary families have fallen further behind. However, as long as middle- and lower-class groups are fragmented along racial lines, they will fail to see how their combined efforts could change the political imbalance and thus promote policies that reflect their interests. Put another way, a vision of American society that highlights racial differences rather than commonalities makes it difficult for us to see the need for and appreciate the potential of mutual political support across racial lines.

Accordingly, as the new millennium approaches, the movement for racial equality needs a new political strategy. That strategy must appeal to America's broad multiracial population, while addressing the many problems that afflict disadvantaged minorities and redressing the legacy of historic racism in America.

In the last decade the nation seems to have become more divided on issues pertaining to race. Affirmative action programs are under heavy assault. Broad public sympathy for those minority individuals who have suffered the most from racial exclusion has waned. Indeed, as our country confronts jarring new economic conditions, many white Americans have turned against a strategy that emphasizes programs benefiting only racial minorities.

Several decades ago efforts to raise the public's awareness and conscience about the plight of African Americans helped to enact civil rights legislation and, later, affirmative action programs. In the 1980s, African American leaders' assertion that black progress was a "myth"—rhetoric used to reinforce arguments for stronger race-based programs—ironically played into the hands of conservative white critics. Although this strategy may have increased sympathy among some whites for the plight of black Americans, it also created the erroneous impression that federal antidiscrimination efforts had largely failed, and it overlooked the significance of the complex economic changes that have affected the black population since the early 1970s. Perhaps most pernicious of all, arguments for more and more government race-based programs to help African Americans fed growing concerns, aroused by demagogic messages, that any special effort by politicians to deal with black needs and complaints was coming at the expense of the white majority.

Meanwhile, from the early 1970s through the first half of the 1990s, national and international economic transformations placed new stresses on families and communities—stresses that are hardly confined to blacks. Along with African Americans, large segments of the white, Latino, Asian, and Native American populations also experienced growing economic insecurities, family breakups, and community stresses. Such conditions could hardly fail to breed racial and ethnic tensions.

In this social climate, some conservatives attempted to unite white Americans around anger at the government and racial minorities. Their political messages seem plausible to many white taxpayers, who see themselves as being forced to pay for programs perceived as benefiting primarily racial minorities.

Why did such messages resonate with many in the white population during the first half of the 1990s? The answer to this question is complicated. Let me attempt to spell it out for you.

II

When affirmative action programs were first discussed in the 1960s, the economy was expanding and incomes were rising. It was a time of optimism, a time when most Americans believed that their children would have better lives than they had. During such times a generosity of spirit permits consideration of sharing an expanding pie.

In the decades immediately after World War II, all income groups experienced economic advancement, including the poor. A rising tide did indeed lift all boats. In fact, as shown in the top graph of figure 2, between 1947 and 1973 the lowest quintile in family income experienced the highest growth in annual income, which meant that the poor were becoming less poor, not only in relative terms but in absolute terms as well.

However, this pattern began to change in the early 1970s. Growth slowed, and the distribution of inflation adjusted income started to become more unequal. Whereas average family income gains from 1974 to 1997 continued for the higher quintiles, the lowest quintile actually experienced annual declines in income during this period, and the second-lowest, annual stagnating incomes. Data on individual wages based on deciles (see figure 3) show a pattern of growing inequality that is

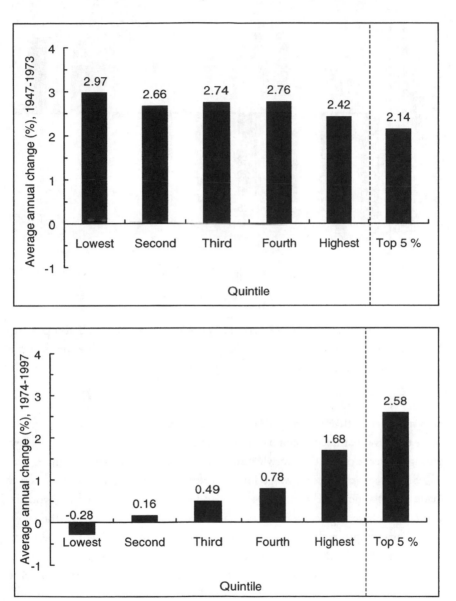

Figure 2. Real Average Family Income Growth by Quintile. Sources: Figures for 1947–1973 are from The Statistical History of the United States, Colonial Times to 1970 *and* Money Income of Households, Families, and Persons in the United States, 1992. *Figures for 1974–1997 are from the* Current Population Survey, March 1997. *Annual change is calculated using 1997 CPI-U adjusted dollars.*

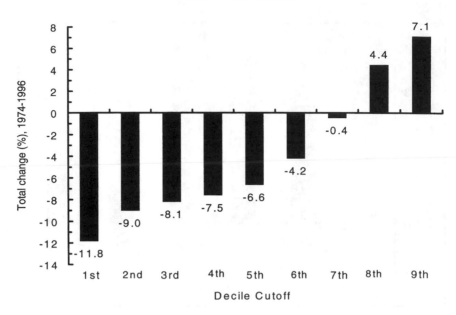

Figure 3. Wage Growth for All Workers, 1974–1996. Source: Monthly Labor Review, December 1997, "Has Wage Inequality Stopped Growing?" Annual data are from the Current Population Survey, Outgoing Rotation Group, in 1996 dollars.

even more severe than the inequality based on family income. The wages of those at the top have continued to climb from 1974 to 1997, while the wages of those below the eighth decile cutoff, the overwhelming majority of workers, fell steadily.

Since 1979, the median wage for Americans overall, after adjustments are made for inflation, has dipped 10 percent, and the hardest hit have been workers without a college degree—a category that represents three-quarters of the labor force. For example, male high school graduates with five years' work experience have lost an average of almost 30 percent in real wages between 1979 and 1997. If the economic trends in place before 1973 had continued, the annual income of a young male high school graduate today would have been $33,000; instead, his current income in 1997 was $13,000.[6] Many families were unwilling to accept the lower living standard that their real income implied. Women therefore flooded the labor market, many out of choice, but a sizable percentage out of necessity.

Thus the downward trend in wages during the past two decades has lowered the incomes of many citizens, especially the least well off. This trend continued uninterrupted during the first half of the 1990s. Working-class Americans felt economically pinched, barely able to maintain current standards of living, even on two incomes. Seven and a half million workers held two or more jobs in 1996, an increase of 65 percent since 1980.[7] Various research studies have indicated that the time on the job for the average worker has increased significantly in recent years. Estimates range from 163 hours a year since 1980, or roughly an extra month a year, to a 66-hour increase in annual work.

Commenting on this situation, Harvard economist Richard Freeman states:

> Falling incomes and rising inequality have occurred despite U.S. success in generating jobs and a huge work effort by Americans. Since 1974, the U.S. employment/population ratio has grown from 65 percent to 71 percent while OECD Europe's has fallen from 65 percent to 60 percent. Americans work considerably more hours and take less vacation than Europeans; according to the newest OECD data, we even work more than the Japanese. The experience of prolonged earnings declines and rising inequality in the context of job growth and economic expansion is unprecedented in U.S. economic history.

Many workers were insecure about keeping their jobs. For example, a 1994 nationwide poll revealed that 40 percent of the workers in America worried that they might be laid off or have their wages reduced. Many feared that they would not be able to afford to send their children to college. Many believed that for all their hard work, their children's lives would be worse than theirs. For example, a 1995 Harris poll, conducted for *Business Week*, revealed that only half of all parents expected their children to have a better life than theirs; nearly seven out of ten believed that the American dream has been more difficult to achieve during the past ten years; and three-quarters felt that the dream would be even harder to achieve during the next ten years.

The economic anxiety evident during the first half of the 1990s lingers on through the more robust economic period in the second half of the 1990s, albeit in a reduced form. Perhaps this explains why there has been so much worker restraint during the mid- to late-1990s in the face of a prolonged economic recovery. Since 1993 the U.S. economy has added more than fifteen million jobs. The unemployment rate declined to 3.9 percent in October 2000, the lowest since 1970. Yet, prices have not increased very much, in part because wages, the main element of costs, have not increased much either.

Despite high levels of employment and labor shortages in some areas, workers have been surprisingly hesitant to demand higher wages. Few would have predicted that kind of behavior in such a favorable job market. As M.I.T. economist Paul Krugman recently pointed out, "Apparently the recession and initially jobless recovery left a deep mark on the national psyche."[8] Workers' confidence has been shaken by downsizing and the specter—real or imagined—that many of their jobs could be done for a fraction of their salaries by workers in Third World countries. Indirect evidence of workers' anxiety can be seen in the rate of voluntary resignations. Usually, when unemployment drops, voluntary resignations increase, because the favorable job market enables those who resign to find new jobs, presumably at higher pay. However, The "quit" rate has fallen during this period of low unemployment.

In a recent survey of a random sample of the American public, 68 percent of the respondents overall and 72 percent of the noncollege graduates surveyed expressed concern about the sending of jobs overseas by American companies. Commenting on this finding, Princeton economist Alan Krueger states, "The fact that the public is so scared of globalization may mean that wage demands have been moderated as a result."[9]

Workers in the United States feel that they cannot rely on weak unions to bargain effectively for higher wages, and if they lose their jobs they feel compelled to take other employment soon, on whatever terms they can get. "With such a nervous and timid workforce," wrote Krugman in 1997, "the economy can gallop along for a while without setting in motion a wage/price spiral. And so we are left with a paradox: we have more or less full employment only because individual workers do not feel secure in their jobs. . . . The secret of our success is not productivity, but anxiety."[10]

Unfortunately, during periods when people are beset with economic anxiety, they become more receptive to simplistic ideological messages that deflect attention away from the real and complex sources of their problems. These messages increase resentment and often result in public support for mean-spirited initiatives. Candidates for public office and elected officials advance arguments that hinge on the apprehensions of families, including arguments that associate the drop in their living standards with programs for minorities, immigrants, and the welfare poor. During periods of economic duress it is vitally important therefore that leaders channel citizens' frustrations in more positive or constructive directions.

During the first half of the 1990s, a period of heightened economic anxiety as the country was staggering from the effects of the 1990-92 recession, just the opposite frequently occurred. The poisonous rhetoric of certain highly visible spokespersons (such as Pat Buchanan, Louis Farrakhan, Al Sharpton, David Duke, Rush Limbaugh, and Governor Pete Wilson, as well as Newt Gingrich and several other congressman who framed the 1994 Personal Responsibility Act in the House Republican's "Contract with America") increased racial tensions and channeled frustrations in ways that divided groups in America. Instead of associating citizens' problems with economic and political changes, these divisive messages encouraged them to turn on each other—race against race, and citizens against immigrants.

III

We must understand that racial antagonisms are products of situations—economic situations, political situations, and social situations. Average citizens do not fully understand the complex forces that have increased their economic woes—the slowing of economic growth and the declines in annual real family income, changes in the global economy and the rise in wage dispersion. They are looking for answers as they cope with their own anxieties.

The answers that have most recently proved to be the most powerful and persuasive to the general public have come not from progressives, who are more likely to associate economic and social problems with the complex changes of the late twentieth century. Rather, they have come from conservative spokespersons, with effective, often mean-spirited sound bites that deflect attention from the real sources of our problems.

Sadly, these include messages directed against minorities and affirmative action, immigrants, and welfare recipients. The effectiveness of these messages was demonstrated in the months leading up to and following the Congressional election of 1994, when conservative Republicans gained control of the U.S. Congress. However, since 1996 the frequency and intensity of these messages have noticeably decreased. I think that we can thank continued improvement in the economy for that. Ordinary Americans are still economically anxious and continue to be worried about their future, but public opinion polls reveal they are more satisfied today than they were in 1994, when the Republicans took over Congress, and in 1995, when conservative political leaders perceived that their pronouncements about the adverse effects of affirmative action, welfare, and immigration would resonate with the general population. I believe that it is now time for proponents of multiracial coalitions to build on this shift in the public's mood.

If we develop a new public dialogue on how our problems should be defined and addressed, we can create a climate in the United States that bridges the divide among groups and lays the foundation for multiracial political cooperation. It is important to appreciate, first of all, that the poor and the working classes of all racial groups struggle to make ends meet, and that even the middle class has experienced a decline in its living standard. Unlike the top 20 percent of the U.S. population, these groups are struggling. Indeed, "virtually all of the past decade's economic growth has gone to the upper 5 percent of families. Since the early 1970s, while the income of the top 1 percent of households had doubled, family and household incomes have stagnated or declined for 80 percent of the population."[11] Thus, despite improvements in the economy, these Americans continue to worry about unemployment and job security, declining real wages, escalating medical and housing costs, the availability of affordable child care programs, the sharp decline in the quality of public education, and crime and drug trafficking in their neighborhoods.

Moreover, inequality in the labor market is growing at the same time that new constraints on the use of federal resources to address social inequities have emerged. The retirement of the baby boomers over the next twenty to thirty years will increase the burden on Medicare and social security, with powerful consequences for overall tax and spending decisions. Programs earmarked for the poor could undergo sharp cuts and even elimination. In addition to new time limits on the receipt of welfare benefits, public housing and food stamp programs have been cut for impoverished Americans. Eroding public-sector support for the poor seems destined to increase pressures for economic survival in the low-wage labor market. Millions of the jobless poor now receiving welfare assistance are slated to enter the labor market, where they will compete with the working poor for available jobs. Furthermore, as stated previously, even substantial segments of the middle class have experienced a decline in their living standards.

Changes in the American family structure have increased the need for social and family support among all racial groups. One-quarter of all families and six of every ten black families today are lone-parent families, and most of these lone parents are never-married mothers.[12] Today, one-half of all marriages end in divorce, and only one-half of divorced fathers make the payments that they owe by law in support of their children. If current trends continue, one-half of the children in the United States will experience at least part of their childhood in a lone-parent family.[13] "Families with multiple earners rise toward the top of the family income distribution, while families with just one earner fall toward the bottom," states economist James K. Galbraith. "As the number of single-headed households rises, so too will inequality. This pattern is compounded in the real world by the grim fact that single-headed households also comprise, to a large extent, those with the most unstable employment experiences at the lowest hourly wages."[14]

Changes in family structure have been accompanied by significant changes in work and family responsibilities. Since the 1940s the proportion of women in the labor force has increased, especially since 1970, when women's rates of labor force participation began to accelerate. In 1950 only one-third of high-school-educated women were employed; today, two-thirds are working. More than half of the women with young children are also working, which is twice as many as two decades ago. Furthermore, most working women do all of their family's housework in spite of their employment outside the home.[15]

Added to these burdens, women have taken on increasing responsibility for the care of older relatives. "In the past decade, such caregiving has increased three-fold," states Stanley Greenberg. "Almost three-quarters of those caring for the elderly are women, two-thirds of whom work outside the home. This is why ordinary Americans are starting to demand a serious debate about social and family support, even as the country's elite are pressing ahead with a long-term bipartisan agenda centered on deficit reduction, entitlement reform, and free trade."[16]

Despite being officially race neutral, programs created in response to these concerns—programs that increase employment opportunities and job skills training, improve public education, promote better child and health care, and reduce neighborhood crime and drug abuse—will profoundly benefit the minority poor, but they will also benefit large segments of the remaining population, including the white majority.

National opinion poll results suggest the possibility of a new alignment in support of a comprehensive social rights initiative that would include such programs. If such an alignment is attempted, it ought to feature a new public rhetoric focused on problems that plague broad segments of the American public—from the jobless poor to the struggling working and middle classes—and to emphasize integrative programs that will promote the social and economic well-being of all groups. Yet these groups will have to be effectively mobilized in order to change the current course taken by policy makers. I believe that the best way to accomplish this is through coalition politics.

Because an effective political coalition in part depends upon how the issues to be addressed are defined, I want to repeat that it is imperative that the political message underscores the need for economic and social reform that benefits all groups, not just America's minority poor. The framers of this message should be cognizant of the fact that changes in the global economy have increased social inequality and enhanced opportunities for antagonisms between different racial groups. They should also be aware that these groups, although often seen as adversaries, are potential allies in a reform coalition because they suffer from a common problem: economic distress caused by forces beyond their own control.

For example, if inner-city blacks are experiencing the most severe problem of joblessness, it is a more extreme form of an economic marginality that has affected most Americans since 1973. Unfortunately, there is a tendency among scholars, policy makers, and black leaders alike to separate the economic problems of the ghetto from the national and international trends affecting American families and neighborhoods. If the economic problems of the ghetto are defined solely in racial terms, they can be isolated and viewed as requiring only race-based solutions, as proposed by those on the Left, or narrow political solutions with subtle racial connotations such as welfare reform, as strongly proposed by those on the Right. To repeat, the growing joblessness among the inner-city poor represents the most extreme form of economic marginality stemming in large measure from changes in the organization of the economy, including the global economy.

For example, changes in the economy have led to a sharp decline in the relative demand for low-skilled labor. This has adversely affected blacks more than whites because a substantially larger proportion of African Americans are unskilled. Although the number of skilled blacks (including managers, professionals, and technicians) has increased sharply in the last several years, the proportion of those who are unskilled remains large. This is because the black population, burdened by cumulative experiences of racial restrictions, was overwhelmingly unskilled just a few decades ago.[17]

The factors involved in the decreased relative demand for low-skilled labor include the computer revolution—that is, the spread of new technologies that have displaced low-skilled workers and rewarded the more highly trained, the rapid growth in college enrollment that has increased the supply and reduced the relative cost of skilled labor, and the growing internationalization of economic activity. Two developments facilitated the growth in global economic activity: (1) advances in information and communications technologies, which significantly reduced transportation and communications costs and thereby encouraged companies to shift work to low-wage areas; and (2) trade liberalization policies, which reduced the price of imports and raised the output of export industries.[18]

The overall impact of trade liberalization policies continues to be debated by economists, but I think that it would be an ideal issue around which to organize an intergroup dialogue that could help facilitate the development of an intergroup political coalition.

It is true that liberalized trade has increased exports in areas such as aerospace industry, with beneficial effects for highly skilled workers. At the same time, increasing imports that compete with labor-intensive industries (for example, apparel, textile, toys, footwear, and some manufacturing industries) have hurt low-skilled labor.[19] This is one of the issues raised by House Democrats, who in 1997 and again in 1998 voted overwhelmingly against President Clinton's "fast tract" proposal on free trade. The legislation that the president introduced was written to attract Republican support. It therefore did not include the labor and environmental protection standards demanded by Democrats and their allies, union leaders and environmentalists.[20]

The Democrats were not persuaded by Clinton's argument that Americans stand to gain from an economy dominated by high technology and an educated workforce. The House Democrats argued instead that blue-collar workers would be forced into a "race to the bottom" through competition with developing countries that do not have the labor laws and environmental protections that have evolved in the United States. As House Minority Leader Richard Gephardt put it, the question is not *whether* to trade, since we all know that trade is important for the overall health and growth of the economy. The question is *how* to trade. Moreover, union leaders, often branded as "protectionist," indicated that they would not have opposed the fast-tract legislation if it had guaranteed workplace and environmental rights. As Frank Borgers, a professor of labor relations at the University of Massachusetts, put it, "If you raise labor standards in low-wage countries, that's good for them and good for us. It would slow the exodus of jobs."[21]

During debates on the fast-tract trade bill in 1997, the vast majority of democrats in the House of Representatives told Clinton that "American trade policy is skewed in the wrong direction. They sought to equalize the terms of competition between workers in the United States and other countries rather than focus on protecting intellectual property rights or other corporate interests."[22]

An intergroup coalition of organized labor, environmental groups, and Hispanic organizations, including the Hispanic caucus in the House of Representatives, fought against the president's bill on free trade. Black leaders such as Maxine Waters, John Lewis, and Jesse Jackson were involved in this debate, but their efforts were not highly visible. If the proposed fast-tract legislation of trade were to increase the displacement of low-skilled labor in this country, it would create enormous problems for the large proportion of African American workers who are unskilled and concentrated in labor-intensive industries. For example, 40 percent of all workers in the apparel industry, one of the industries most vulnerable to the impact of free trade, are African American.

Issues that are defined explicitly in racial terms understandably tend to attract more attention from the black leadership. Yet it is important that black leaders expand their vision and address race-neutral issues that significantly affect the African American community with the same degree of attention they give to race-specific issues.

The displacement problem associated with free trade is a race-neutral issue that ought to bring together the swelling ranks of have-not Americans—that is, the low- to moderate-income groups, including African Americans, whites, Latinos, Asians, and Native Americans—in an important and constructive dialogue on national economic policy. The fast-tract trade bill has once again been defeated in the U.S. House of Representatives, but the pressure to open U.S. markets to goods produced cheaply in countries that lack reasonable safety, wage, and environmental standards for their workers is unlikely to abate.

As we think about other issues of national economic policy that affect low- to moderate-income families and that ought to engage different racial groups in a national dialogue, one immediately comes to mind—the need to generate national support for achieving and maintaining tight labor markets—that is, full employment.

Such a goal by definition challenges the monetary policies supported by Wall Street, policies by which the Federal Reserve, concerned with keeping inflation in check, keeps labor markets from tightening by maintaining or creating high interest rates: as interests rates rise, unemployment rates climb.

In a critical assessment of this approach, University of Texas economist James K. Galbraith points out that the principal causes of the rising inequality in the wage structure

> lie in the hard blows of recession, unemployment, and slow economic growth, combined with the effects of inflation and political resistance to rising real value of the minimum wage. These are blows that, when once delivered, are not erased in any short period of economic recovery. They can be reversed, and in American history have been reversed, only by sustained periods of full employment alongside controlled inflation and a determined drive toward social justice. We last saw such a movement in this country in the 1960s, and before that only during World War II.[23]

However, Galbraith goes on to point out that beginning in 1970 the government's goal of full employment was abandoned in favor of fighting inflation. The only instrument deemed suitable for this purpose was high interest rates produced by the Federal Reserve. Unfortunately for the average worker, high interest rates elevate unemployment.[24]

As economic analyst Jeff Faux pointed out, this is a value issue. The Federal Reserve Board "protects the value of financial assets over the value of jobs by consistently overestimating the level of unemployment necessary to retain price stability."[25] Economists are not sure what constitutes the right level of unemployment to stabilize prices. Yet, in the last few years, when tighter labor markets have failed to trigger inflation, the opinions of the financial punditry have consistently been wrong on this question.[26]

A powerful multiracial coalition that included the swelling ranks of the low- to moderate-income have-nots could, as a part of its national agenda, demand that the president appoint, and Congress approve, members to the Federal Reserve Board who will ensure that it upholds "its mandate to pursue both high employment and price stability by probing much more forcefully the limits of the economy's capacity to produce without inflation."[27] Policies that are effective in promoting full employment and controlling inflation will likely draw the support of the more advantaged—higher-income members of society as well. Currently, the discussion of how to control inflation is a complex one that involves mainly intellectual and financial elites. Yet I think that Jeff Faux is absolutely correct when he argues that "Americans are more likely to participate in a national debate over what it takes to achieve full employment than in the current dispiriting argument over how many people must be denied work in order to make the bond market comfortable."[28]

Such a debate over employment policies would be greatly facilitated if we were able to overcome our racial divisions and to develop and coordinate local grassroots organizations that could join established national leaders or generate new ones in a powerful political coalition.

IV

Given America's tense racial situation, especially in urban areas, the formation of a multiracial reform coalition will not be easy. Our nation's response to racial discord has been disappointing. In discussing these problems we have had a tendency to engage in the kind of rhetoric that exacerbates, rather than alleviates, urban and metropolitan racial tensions. Ever since the 1992 Los Angeles riot, the media has focused heavily on the factors that divide rather than on those that unite ethnic groups.

Emphasis on racial division peaked in 1995, following the jury's verdict in the O. J. Simpson murder trail. Before the verdict was announced, opinion polls revealed that whites overwhelmingly thought that Mr. Simpson was guilty, while a substantial majority of blacks felt that he was innocent. The media clips showing public reaction to the verdict dramatized the racial contrasts—blacks appeared elated and jubilant; whites appeared stunned, angry, and somber. America's racial divide, as depicted in the media, seemed wider than ever. As one observer, on the eve of the first Simpson verdict, put it: "When O. J. gets off, the whites will riot the way we whites do: leave the cities, go to Idaho or Oregon or Arizona, vote for Gingrich . . . and punish the blacks by closing the day-care programs and cutting off their Medicaid."[29]

The country's deep racial divisions certainly should not be underestimated, but the unremitting emphasis on these gaps has obscured the fact that African Americans, whites, Latinos, Asians, and Native Americans share many concerns, are beset by many similar problems, and have important values, aspirations, and hopes in common.

Take the issue of values. An analysis of the responses to questions that were variously asked in the national surveys conducted by National Opinion Research Center's General Social Survey since 1982 reveals only marginal racial differences in core values pertaining to work, education, the family, religion, law enforcement, and civic duty. For example, in a 1982 survey, 90 percent of whites and 89 percent of blacks felt that one's own family and children were very important; in a 1984 survey, 88 percent of whites and 95 percent of blacks felt that the obligation of American citizens to do community service was very or somewhat important; and in a 1993 survey, 95 percent of whites and 92 percent of blacks felt that hard work in life outcomes was either important or very important, and 97 percent of blacks and 88 percent of whites supported the view that being self-sufficient was either very important or one of the most important things in life.[30]

Also consider the perception of problems. As revealed in table 1, questions about whether problems pertaining to public schools, jobs, affordable housing, families, and health care were getting worse or harder for the people with whom the respondents identify ("people like you or families like yours") elicited considerable agreement across racial and ethnic groups.

TABLE 1. ARE THE PROBLEMS OF PEOPLE LIKE YOU (OR FAMILIES LIKE YOURS) GETTING WORSE?

PERCENT SAYING "WORSE" OR "HARDER"

PROBLEM	WHITES	AFRICAN AMERICANS	LATINOS	ASIAN AMERICANS
Public schools	55	57	45	47
To get good jobs	56	60	50	56
To find decent, affordable housing	55	49	55	48
For families like yours to stay together	45	48	40	34
Health care	44	39	30	30
Number of respondents	802	474	252	353

Source: Adapted from Jennifer Hochschild and Reuel Rogers "Race Relations in a Diversifying Nation," in *New Directions: African Americans in a Diversifying Nation* (edited by James Jackson), forthcoming, based on data from the Washington Post/Kaiser Foundation/Harvard Survey Project 1995.

TABLE 2. POLICY PREFERENCES FOR CONGRESSIONAL ACTION

PERCENT SAYING "STRONGLY FEEL CONGRESS SHOULD DO"

POLICY ISSUE	WHITES	AFRICAN AMERICANS	LATINOS	ASIAN AMERICANS
Limit tax breaks for business	39	41	41	30
Balance the budget	82	79	75	75
Cut personal income taxes	52	50	55	46
Reform the welfare system	83	73	81	68
Reform medicare	53	58	59	58
Put more limits on abortion	35	32	50	24
Limit affirmative action	38	25	30	27
Number of respondents	802	474	252	353

Source: Adapted from Jennifer Hochschild and Reuel Rogers "Race Relations in a Diversifying Nation," in *New Directions: African Americans in a Diversifying Nation* (edited by James Jackson), forthcoming, based on data from the Washington Post/Kaiser Foundation/Harvard Survey Project 1995.

Furthermore, consider views on major policy issues. As seen in table 2, except for affirmative action and abortion, there are no notable differences across racial and ethnic groups on reported strong preferences for Congressional action—with overwhelming support for balancing the budget and changing the welfare system, less enthusiasm for cutting personal income taxes and reforming Medicare, and even less for business tax breaks. Finally, as Jennifer Hochschild and Reuel Rogers point out, there is considerable convergence in views across racial and ethnic groups with regard to policy preferences for solving particular problems, including education, crime, gang violence, and drugs.

The development and articulation of an ideological vision that captures and highlights commonalities in basic core values and attitudes is paramount in establishing the case for a progressive multiracial political coalition and defusing the opposition of pessimists who promote the more limited advantages of group-specific political mobilization.

I end with this point. Discussions that emphasize common solutions to commonly shared problems promote a sense of unity, regardless of the different degrees of severity in the problems afflicting different groups. Such messages bring races together, not apart, and are especially important during periods of racial tension.

Because the problems of the new social inequality (the gap between the expanding have-nots and the haves) are growing more severe, a vision that acknowledges racially distinct problems and the need for remedies like affirmative action, but at the same time emphasizes the importance of transracial solutions to shared problems, is more important now than ever. Such a vision should be developed, shared, and promoted by all progressive leaders in this country, but especially by political leaders.

A new democratic vision must reject the commonly held view that race is so divisive that whites, blacks, Latinos, Asians, and Native Americans cannot work together in a common cause. Those articulating the new vision must realize that if a political message is tailored to a white audience, racial minorities draw back, just as whites draw back when a message is tailored to minority audiences. The challenge is to find issues and programs that concern the families of all racial and ethnic groups, so that individuals in these groups can honestly perceive mutual interests and join in a multiracial coalition to move America forward.

Despite legacies of racial domination and obstacles thrown up by recent events, a politics about problems and solutions relevant for people across racial and ethnic groups is very possible in the United States today. Progressive leaders should forcefully articulate such a message and work to fashion the multiracial coalitions that must be at the heart of any progressive new majority in American democracy.

NOTES

1. Richard B. Freeman, *The New Inequality: Creating Solutions for Poor America* (Boston: Beacon Press, 1999), 4.

2. Frank Levy, *The New Dollars and Dreams: American Incomes and Economic Change* (New York: Russell Sage, 1998), 2. Levy points out that from April 1997 to March 1998, hourly wages, adjusted for inflation, grew by a respectable 2 percent. He notes, however, that "this growth occurred in a labor market that most people judge too tight to sustain"(2).

3. David Ellwood, "Winners and Losers in America: Taking the Measure of the New Economic Realities," Papers presented at the Aspen Domestic Strategy Group Meeting, July 1988, Aspen, Colorado.

4. Ibid., 3.

5. Ibid., 4.

6. Jeff Faux, "You Are Not Alone," in *The New Majority: Toward a Popular Progressive Politics*, ed. Stanley B. Greenberg and Theda Skocpol (New Haven, Conn.: Yale University Press, 1997).

7. Sylvia Ann Hewlett and Cornel West, eds., *War Against Parents: What We Can Do for America's Beleaguered Moms and Dads* (New York: Houghton Mifflin, 1998)

8. Paul Krugman, "Superiority Complex," *New Republic*, 3 November 1997, p. 21.

9. Alan B. Krueger, "What's Up with Wages?" Mimeograph from the Industrial Relations Section, Princeton University, 1997.

10. Krugman, "Superiority Complex," p. 22.

11. Freeman, *The New Inequality*.

12. U. S. Bureau of the Census, *Current Population Reports*, series P-20 (Washington, D.C.: GPO, 1997).

13. Kristin Luker, *Dubious Conceptions: The Politics of Teenage Pregnancy* (Cambridge: Harvard University Press, 1996).

14. James K. Galbraith, *Created Unequal: The Crisis in American Pay* (New York: Free Press, 1998), 12.

15. In fact, three-quarters of working women do all or most of the family's housework. Stanley B. Greenberg, "Popularizing Progressive Politics," in *The New Majority*, ed. Greenberg and Skocpol.

16. Ibid., 292

17. David Schwartzman, *Black Unemployment: Part of Unskilled Unemployment* (Westport Conn: Greenwood Press, 1997).

18. Ibid.

19. Ibid.

20. John M. Broder, "Party Spurned, Repays Clinton with Rebellion," *New York Times*, 11 November 1997, pp. A1 and A6.

21. Quoted in Steven Greenhouse, "Business and Labor Struggle with Globalization," *New York Times*, 2 August 1998.

22. David Sanger, "A Handicap for Clinton, but U. S. Still Dominates," *New York Times*, 11 November 1997, p. A6.

23. Galbraith, *Created Unequal*, 8–9.

24. Ibid.

25. Faux, "You Are Not Alone," 32.

26. Ibid.

27. Ibid.

28. Ibid.

29. Quoted in Frank Rich, "The L.A. Shock Treatment," *New York Times*, 4 October 1995.

30. Findings from the General Surveys of the National Opinion Research Center of the University of Chicago. Considering the prevailing stereotypes, the findings on self-sufficiency are counterintuitive. Although there is a 9 percent racial gap, an overwhelming majority of respondents from both races strongly supported the idea of self-sufficiency. The only other finding that should be mentioned pertains to views on the importance of being married. Whereas 43 percent of the black respondents felt that being married was very important or one of the most important things in life, 53 percent of the white respondents felt this way.

For Further Reading

Aguilar-San Juan, Karin, ed. *The State of Asian America: Activism and Resistance in the 1990s*. Boston: South End Press, 1994.

Allen, Paula Gunn. *The Sacred Hoop: Recovering the Feminine in American Indian Traditions*. Boston: Beacon Press, 1992.

Allen, Theodore. *The Invention of the White Race*. New York: Verso, 1994.

Appiah, Kwame Anthony. *In My Father's House: Africa in the Philosophy of Culture*. New York: Oxford University Press, 1992.

Asante, Molefi Kete, and Abu S. Abarry, eds. *African Intellectual Heritage: A Book of Sources*. Philadelphia: Temple University Press, 1996.

Bataille, Gretchen M., and Charles L. P. Silet, eds. *The Pretend Indians: Images of Native Americans in the Movies*. Ames: Iowa State University Press, 1980.

Bean, Frank D., and Marta Tienda. *The Hispanic Population of the United States*. New York: Russell Sage Foundation, 1990.

Berkhofer, Robert Jr. *The White Man's Indian: Images of the American Indian from Columbus to the Present*. New York: Knopf, 1978.

Bieder, Robert E. *Science Encounters the Indian, 1820–1880: The Early Years of American Ethnology*. Norman: University of Oklahoma Press, 1986.

Boas, Franz. *Anthropology and Modern Life*. New York: Norton, 1928.

Bowen, William G., and Derek C. Bok. *The Shape of the River: Long-Term Consequences of Considering Race in College and University Admissions.* Princeton, N.J.: Princeton University Press, 1998.

Brodkin, Karen. *How Jews Became White Folks and What That Says about Race in America.* New Brunswick, N.J.: Rutgers University Press, 2000.

Carby, Hazel. *Race Men.* Cambridge, Mass.: Harvard University Press, 1998.

Carr, Helen. *Inventing the Primitive: Politics, Gender and the Representation of Native American Literary Traditions, 1789–1936.* New York: New York University Press, 1996.

Chavez, Linda. *Out of the Barrio: Toward a New Politics of Hispanic Assimilation.* New York: Basic Books, 1991.

Churchill, Ward. *Fantasies of the Master Race: Literature, Cinema and the Colonization of American Indians.* San Francisco: City Lights Books, 1998.

Cochran, David Carroll. *The Color of Freedom: Race and Contemporary American Liberalism.* Albany: State University of New York Press, 1999.

Cohen, Cathy. *Boundaries of Blackness: AIDS and the Breakdown of Black Politics.* Chicago: University of Chicago Press, 1999.

Cohen, William B. *The French Encounter with Africans: White Response to Blacks, 1530–1880.* Bloomington: Indiana University Press, 1980.

Conley, Dalton. *Being Black, Living in the Red: Race, Wealth, and Social Policy in America.* Los Angeles: University of California Press, 1999.

Council of Economic Advisers for the President's Initiative on Race. *Changing America: Indicators of Social and Economic Well-Being by Race and Hispanic Origin.* Washington, D.C.: U.S. Government Printing Office, September 1998.

Crenshaw, Kimberle et al., eds. *Critical Race Theory: The Key Writings that Formed the Movement.* New York: New Press, 1996.

Davis, F. James. *Who Is Black? One Nation's Definition.* Philadelphia: Pennsylvania State University Press, 1991.

Delgado, Richard, and Jean Stefancic, eds. *Critical White Studies: Looking behind the Mirror.* Philadelphia: Temple University Press, 1997.

———, eds. *The Latino/a Condition: A Critical Reader.* New York: New York University Press, 1998.

———, eds. *Critical Race Theory: The Cutting Edge.* Philadelphia: Temple University Press, 1999.

Del Pinal, Jorge, and Audrey Singer. *Generations of Diversity: Latinos in the United States.* Washington, D.C.: Population Reference Bureau, October 1997.

Donovan, Kathleen M., ed. *Feminist Readings of Native American Literature.* Tucson: University of Arizona Press, 1998.

Drinnon, Richard. *Facing West: The Metaphysics of Indian-Hating and Empire-Building.* New York: Meridian, 1980.

D'Souza, Dinesh. *The End of Racism: Principles for a Multicultural Society.* New York: Free Press, 1995.

Entine, Jon. *Taboo: Why Black Athletes Dominate Sports and Why We Are Afraid to Talk about It.* New York: BBS Public Affairs, 2000.

Eze, Emmanuel Chukwudi. *Race and the Enlightenment: A Reader.* Cambridge, Mass.: Blackwell Publishers, 1997.

Farley, Reynolds, ed. *State of the Union: America in the 1990s.* New York: Russell Sage Foundation, 1995.

Farnya, Stan et al., eds. *Black Right: The Bold New Voice of Black Conservatives in America.* Westport, Conn.: Greenwood Publishing Group, 1997.

Fischer, Claude S. et al. *Inequality by Design: Cracking the Bell Curve Myth.* Princeton, N.J.: Princeton University Press, 1996.

Fong, Timothy P. *The Contemporary Asian American Experience: Beyond the Model Minority.* New York: Prentice Hall, 1998.

Forbes, Jack. D. *Africans and Native American: The Language of Race and the Evolution of Red-Black Peoples.* Urbana: University of Illinois Press, 1993.

Frankenberg, Ruth. *White Women, Race Matters: The Social Construction of Whiteness.* Minneapolis: University of Minnesota Press, 1993.

Garcia, Alma M., and Mario T. Garcia, eds. *Chicana Feminist Thought: The Basic Historical Writings.* New York: Routledge, 1997.

Gates, Henry Louis, Jr., ed. *"Race" Writing and Difference.* Chicago: University of Chicago Press, 1985.

Gilroy, Paul. *The Black Atlantic: Modernity and Double Consciousness.* Cambridge, Mass.: Harvard University Press, 1993.

———. *Against Race: Imagining Political Culture beyond the Color Line.* Cambridge, Mass.: Harvard University Press, 2000.

Goldberg, David. *Racist Culture: Philosophy and the Politics of Meaning.* Oxford: Blackwell Publishers, 1993.

Golden, Marita, and Susan Shreve, eds. *Skin Deep: Black and White Women Write about Race.* New York: Anchor Books, 1996.

Gossett, Thomas F. *Race: The History of an Idea in America.* New York: Oxford University Press, 1997.

Gould, Stephen Jay. *The Mismeasure of Man.* New York: W.W. Norton and Company, 1981.

Griswold Del Castillo, Richard. *The Treaty of Guadalupe Hidalgo: A Legacy of Conflict.* Norman: University of Oklahoma Press, 1991.

Hacker, Andrew. *Two Nations: Blacks and White, Separate, Hostile and Unequal.* New York: Ballantine Books, 1995.

Hannaford, Ivan. *Race: The History of an Idea in the West.* Washington, D.C.: Johns Hopkins University Press, 1996.

Harjo, Joy, and Gloria Bird, eds. *Reinventing the Enemy's Language: Contemporary Native Women's Writings of North America.* New York: W.W. Norton and Company, 1997.

Herrenstein, Richard J., and Charles Murray. *The Bell Curve: Intelligence and Class Structure in American Life*. New York: Free Press, 1994.

Hine, Darlene Clark, and Jacqueline McLeod. *Crossing Boundaries: Comparative History of Black People in Diaspora*. Bloomington: Indiana University Press, 1999.

Hine, Darlene Clark, and Kathleen Thompson. *A Shining Thread of Hope: The History of Black Women in America*. New York: Broadway Books, 1998.

Horsman, Reginald. *Race and Manifest Destiny: The Origins of American Racial Anglo-Saxonism*. Cambridge, Mass.: Harvard University Press, 1981.

Hu-DeHart, Evelyn, ed. *Across the Pacific: Asian Americans and Globalization*. Philadelphia: Temple University Press, 1999.

Hurtado, Aida. *The Color of Privilege: Three Blasphemies on Race and Feminism*. Ann Arbor: University of Michigan Press, 1996.

Ignatiev, Noel. *How the Irish Became White*. New York: Routledge, 1995.

Jencks, Christopher, and Meredith Phillips, eds. *The Black-White Test Score Gap*. Washington, D.C.: Brookings Institution Press, 1998.

Jordan, Winthrop D. *White over Black: American Attitudes toward the Negro, 1550–1812*. Baltimore: Penguin, 1968.

Kawash, Samira. *Dislocating the Color Line: Identity, Hybridity, and Singularity in African-American Literature*. Stanford, Calif.: Stanford University Press, 1997.

The Kerner Report: The 1968 Report of the National Advisory Commission on Civil Disorders. New York: Pantheon Books, 1968.

Kim, Elaine H. et al., eds. *Making More Waves: New Writings by Asian American Women*. Boston: Beacon Press, 1997.

Kuper, Adam. *The Invention of Primitive Society: Transformations of an Illusion*. London: Routledge, 1988.

Lee, Sharon M. *Asian Americans: Diverse and Growing*. Washington, D.C.: Population Reference Bureau, June 1998.

Lipsitz, George. *The Possessive Investment in Whiteness: How White People Profit from Identity Politics*. Philadelphia: Temple University Press, 1998.

Lynch, Frederick R. *Invisible Victims: White Males and the Crisis of Affirmative Action*. New York: Praeger, 1991.

———. *The Diversity Machine: The Drive to Change the "White Male Workplace."* New York: Free Press, 1997.

Marable, Manning. *Beyond Black and White: Transforming African-American Politics*. New York: Verso, 1995.

———. *How Capitalism Underdeveloped Black America*. Updated edition. Cambridge, Mass.: South End Press, 2000.

Marx, Anthony W. *Making Race and Nation: A Comparison of the United States, South Africa, and Brazil.* Cambridge, England: Cambridge University Press, 1998.

Massey, Douglas S., and Nancy A. Denton. *American Apartheid: Segregation and the Making of the Underclass.* Cambridge, Mass.: Harvard University Press, 1993.

Michaelsen, Scott. *The Limits of Multiculturalism: Interrogating the Origins of American Anthropology.* Minneapolis: University of Minnesota Press, 1999.

Mills, Charles W. *The Racial Contract.* Ithaca, N.Y.: Cornell University Press, 1997.

———. *Blackness Visible: Essays on Philosophy and Race.* Ithaca, N.Y.: Cornell University Press, 1998.

Minn, Pyong Gap, ed. *Asian Americans: Contemporary Trends and Issues.* Thousand Oaks, Calif.: Sage Publications, 1995.

Montagu, Ashley. *Man's Most Dangerous Myth: The Fallacy of Race.* New York: World Publishing, 1942.

Moore, Joan, and Harry Pachon. *Hispanics in the United State.* Englewood Cliffs, N.J.: Prentice Hall, 1985.

Okihiro, Gary Y. *Margins and Mainstreams: Asians in American History and Culture.* Seattle: University of Washington Press, 1994.

Oliver, Melvin L., and Thomas M. Shapiro. *Black Wealth/White Wealth: A New Perspective on Racial Inequality.* New York: Routledge, 1996.

Ong, Paul M, ed. *The State of Asian Pacific America: Transforming Race Relations.* Los Angeles: Leap Asian Pacific American Public Policy Institute and UCLA Asian American Studies Center, 2000.

Pedraza, Sylvia, and Ruben G. Rumbaut, eds. *Origins and Destinies: Immigration, Race, and Ethnicity in America.* Belmont, Calif.: Wadsworth Publishing, 1996.

Pollard, Kelvin M., and William P. O'Hare. *America's Racial and Ethnic Minorities.* Washington, D.C.: Population Reference Bureau, September 1999.

The President's Initiative on Race. *One America in the 21st Century: Forging a New Future.* Washington, D.C.: U.S. Government Printing Office, 1997.

Richard, David A. J. *Identity and the Case for Gay Rights: Race, Gender, Religion as Analogies.* Chicago: University of Chicago Press, 1999.

Roediger, David R. *The Wages of Whiteness: Race and the Making of the American Working Class.* London: Verso, 1991.

Ruiz, Vicki, and Ellen Carol DuBois, eds. *Unequal Sisters: A Multicultural Reader in U.S. Women's History.* New York: Routledge, 2000.

Rushton, Philippe. *Race, Evolution, and Behavior: A Life History Perspective.* New Brunswick, N.J.: Transaction Publishers, 1997.

Said, Edward. *Orientalism.* New York: Pantheon, 1978.

Sandefur, Gary D. et al., eds. *Changing Numbers, Changing Needs: American Indian Demography and Public Health.* Washington, D.C.: National Academy Press, 1996.

Shah, Sonia, ed. *Dragon Ladies: Asian American Feminists Breathe Fire.* Boston: South End Press, 1997.

Sheehan, Bernard W. *Seeds of Extinction: Jeffersonian Philanthropy and the American Indian.* Chapel Hill: University of North Carolina Press, 1973.

Sleeper, Jim. *Liberal Racism.* New York: Penguin Books, 1997.

Smedley, Audrey. *Race in North America: Origin and Evolution of a Worldview.* Boulder, Co.: Westview Press, 1993.

Smith, Barbara. *The Truth Never Hurts: Writings on Race, Gender, and Freedom.* New Brunswick, N.J.: Rutgers University Press, 1998.

Smith, Robert C. *Racism in the Post–Civil Rights Era: Now You See It, Now You Don't.* Albany: State University of New York Press, 1995.

Smith, Valerie, ed. *Not Just Race, Not Just Gender.* New York: Routledge, 1998.

Sniderman, Paul M., and Edward G. Carmines. *Reaching beyond Race.* Cambridge, Mass.: Harvard University Press, 1997.

Snipp, Matthew C. *American Indians: The First of this Land.* New York: Russell Sage Foundation, 1989.

Snowden, Frank M., Jr. *Before Color Prejudice: The Ancient View of Blacks.* Cambridge, Mass.: Harvard University Press, 1983.

Somerville, Siobhan. *Queering the Color Line: Race and the Invention of Homosexuality in American Culture.* Durham, N.C.: Duke University Press, 2000.

Stannard, David E. *American Holocaust: Columbus and the Conquest of the New World.* Oxford: Oxford University Press, 1992.

Stanton, William. *The Leopard's Spots: Scientific Attitudes toward Race in America 1815–59.* Chicago: University of Chicago Press, 1960.

Steinberg, Stephen, ed. *Race and Ethnicity in the United States: Issues and Debates.* Oxford: Blackwell Publishers, 2000.

Suro, Roberto. *Strangers among Us: How Latino Immigration Is Transforming America.* New York: Alfred A. Knopf, 1998.

Takaki, Ronald. *Iron Cages: Race and Culture in 19th Century America.* New York: Oxford University Press, 1979.

———. *A Different Mirror: A History of Multicultural America.* Boston: Little, Brown and Company, 1993.

Tamayo Lott, Juanita. *Asian Americans: From Racial Category to Multiple Identities.* Walnut Creek, Calif.: Altimira Press, 1998.

Thernstrom, Stephan, and Abigail Thernstrom. *America in Black and White: One Nation, Indivisible.* New York: Simon and Schuster, 1997.

Thornton, Russell. *American Indian Holocaust and Survival: A Population History since 1492.* Norman: University of Oklahoma Press, 1987.

Tucker, William H. *The Science and Politics of Racial Research*. Chicago: University of Illinois Press, 1994.

Vaid, Urvashi. *Virtual Equality: The Mainstreaming of Gay and Lesbian Liberation*. New York: Anchor Books, 1995.

Wattenberg, Ben J. *The First Universal Nation: Leading Indicators and Ideas about the Surge of America in the 1990s*. New York: Free Press, 1991.

Webster, Yehudi O. *The Racialization of America*. New York: St. Martin's Press, 1992.

Williams, Patricia J. *The Alchemy of Race and Rights*. Cambridge, Mass.: Harvard University Press, 1991.

Wilson, William Julius. *The Bridge over the Racial Divide: Rising Inequality and Coalition Politics*. Berkeley: University of California Press, 1999.

Wing, Adrien Katherine, and Derrick A. Bell, eds. *Critical Race Feminism: A Reader*. New York: New York University Press, 1996.

Young, Robert J. C. *Colonial Desire: Hybridity in Theory, Culture and Race*. New York: Routledge, 1995.

Zia, Helen. *Asian American Dreams: The Emergence of an American People*. New York: Farrar Straus & Giroux, 2000.

About the Editors and Contributors

EDITORS

Curtis Stokes is Associate Professor in James Madison College and Director of Black American and Diasporic Studies, Michigan State University.

Theresa Meléndez is Associate Professor in the Department of English and Director of Chicano/ Latino Studies, Michigan State University.

Genice Rhodes-Reed is Director of the Human Relations and Community Services Department for the City of Lansing, Michigan.

CONTRIBUTORS

Allison Berg is Assistant Professor of American Culture and Writing in James Madison College at Michigan State University.

Ward Churchill is Professor in the Department of Ethnic Studies at the University of Colorado at Boulder.

Dinesh D'Souza is John M. Olin Scholar at the American Enterprise Institute.

Jack D. Forbes is Professor Emeritus in the Department of Native American Studies at the University of California at Davis.

George M. Fredrickson is Edgar E. Robinson Professor of United States History at Stanford University.

John Garvey is one of the founding editors of *Race Traitor*, the journal of the new abolitionism, and a founding member of the New Abolitionist Society. He works in the Office of Academic Affairs at the City University of New York.

Nathan Glazer is Professor Emeritus of Education and Sociology at Harvard University.

Michael Goldfield is Professor in the College of Urban, Labor, and Metropolitan Affairs at Wayne State University.

Deena J. González is Associate Professor in the Department of History and Chicano/a Studies at Pomona College.

Alan H. Goodman is Professor of Biological Anthropology at Hampshire College and Co-director of the U.S. Southwest and Mexico Programs.

Darlene Clark Hine is John A. Hannah Professor of History at Michigan State University and President-elect of the Organization of American Historians.

Gerald Horne is Professor of African and Afro-American Studies and Director, Institute for African-American Research, University of North Carolina at Chapel Hill.

Evelyn Hu-DeHart is Professor of History and Director of the Center for Studies of Ethnicity and Race in America at the University of Colorado at Boulder.

Hussein Ibish is Media Director for the American Arab Anti-Discrimination Committee.

James Jennings is Professor of Political Science and Senior Fellow in the William Monroe Trotter Institute at the University of Massachusetts–Boston.

Jacqueline Jones is Professor and Chair of the Department of History at Brandeis University.

Guadalupe T. Luna is Associate Professor in the College of Law at Northern Illinois University.

Frederick R. Lynch is Associate Professor in the Department of Government at Claremont McKenna College.

Arturo Madrid is Murchison Distinguished Professor of Humanities at Trinity University.

Manning Marable is Professor of History and Director, Institute for Research in African-American Studies, Columbia University.

Audrey Smedley is Professor in the Department of Anthropology at Virginia Commonwealth University.

Urvashi Vaid is Director of the Policy Institute of the National Gay and Lesbian Task Force.

Dionicio Nodín Valdés is Professor in the Department of History and Chicano Studies at the University of Minnesota.

Robert Weissberg is Professor in the Department of Political Science at the University of Illinois at Urbana-Champaign.

William Julius Wilson is Malcolm Wiener Professor of Social Policy in the John F. Kennedy School of Government at Harvard University.

Naomi Zack is Professor in the Department of Philosophy at the University of Albany, SUNY.